The Right to Dress

CW01500198

This is the first global history of dress regulation and its place in broader debates around how human life and societies should be visualised and materialised. Leading scholars on Asian, Latin American, Ottoman and European history shed new light on how and why items of dress became key aspirational goods across society, how they were lobbied for and marketed, and whether or not sumptuary laws were implemented by cities, states and empires to restrict or channel trade and consumption. Their findings reveal the significance of sumptuary laws in medieval and early modern societies as a site of contestation between individuals and states and how dress as an expression of identity developed as a modern 'right'.

GIORGIO RIELLO is Professor of Global History at the University of Warwick and Chair of the Pasold Research Fund. He is the author of several books, including *Cotton: The Fabric that Made the Modern World* (Cambridge, 2013), which won the World History Association Book Prize 2014, and *Luxury: A Rich History* (2016).

ULINKA RUBLACK, FBA is Professor of Early Modern European History at the University of Cambridge, and is a Fellow of St John's College. Her previous books include *Dressing Up: Cultural Identity in Early Modern Europe* (2011), which won the Bainton Prize. She is co-editor, with Maria Hayward, of *The First Book of Fashion* (2015).

The Right to Dress

*Sumptuary Laws in a Global Perspective,
c. 1200–1800*

Edited by

Giorgio Riello
University of Warwick

Ulinka Rublack
University of Cambridge

CAMBRIDGE
UNIVERSITY PRESS

CAMBRIDGE
UNIVERSITY PRESS

University Printing House, Cambridge CB2 8BS, United Kingdom

One Liberty Plaza, 20th Floor, New York, NY 10006, USA

477 Williamstown Road, Port Melbourne, VIC 3207, Australia

314-321, 3rd Floor, Plot 3, Splendor Forum, Jasola District Centre, New Delhi - 110025, India

79 Anson Road, #06-04/06, Singapore 079906

Cambridge University Press is part of the University of Cambridge.

It furthers the University's mission by disseminating knowledge in the pursuit of education, learning and research at the highest international levels of excellence.

www.cambridge.org
Information on this title: www.cambridge.org/9781108469272
DOI: 10.1017/9781108567541

First published 2019
First paperback edition 2020

A catalogue record for this publication is available from the British Library

Library of Congress Cataloging in Publication data
Names: Riello, Giorgio, editor. | Rublack, Ulinka, editor.
Title: The right to dress : sumptuary laws in a global perspective,
c. 1200–1800 / edited by Giorgio Riello, University of Warwick,
Ulinka Rublack, University of Cambridge.
Description: New York, NY, USA : Cambridge University Press, 2019. |
Includes bibliographical references and index.
Identifiers: LCCN 2018039105| ISBN 9781108475914 (hbk) |
ISBN 9781108469272 (pbk)
Subjects: LCSH: Luxury–History. | Sumptuary laws–History.
Classification: LCC HB841 .R54 2019 | DDC 344/.09–dc23
LC record available at https://lccn.loc.gov/2018039105

ISBN 978-1-108-47591-4 Hardback
ISBN 978-1-108-46927-2 Paperback

Contents

Figures

Figures

Map

Table

Contributors

EVA I. ANDERSSON works at the Department of Historical Studies, Gothenburg University, Sweden. She completed her PhD in 2006 with a dissertation entitled 'Clothes and the individual in medieval Europe'. Between 2009 and 2012 her research project 'Clothes, gender and status 1500–1830' was funded by the Swedish Research Council. Her publications cover subjects such as manners of dress, sumptuary laws, and the relationship between clothing and perceptions of gender, status and national identity in medieval and early modern Sweden.

FRANCISCO BETHENCOURT is Charles Boxer Professor of History at King's College London. He is the author of *Racisms: From the Crusades to the Twentieth Century* (2013) and *The Inquisition: A Global History, 1478–1834* (2009). He organised an exhibition on *Racism and Citizenship* at the Padrão dos Descobrimentos, Lisbon in 2017. He holds a Major Leverhulme Fellowship to work on 'The New Christian Trading Elite (1497–1773)'.

BRUNO BLONDÉ teaches early modern social and economic history at the University of Antwerp, where he is affiliated with the Centre for Urban History and the Urban Studies Institute. He publishes on the history of urban networks in the Low Countries, pre-industrial transport, the history of material culture, retail trade and consumption, urban growth and social inequality.

BUYUN CHEN is Assistant Professor in the Department of History at Swarthmore College, US. She is a cultural historian who specialises in the material culture of pre-modern China. Her research seeks to understand how the circulation of objects shaped the formation of knowledge and practice, both local and mobile.

ADAM CLULOW is Associate Professor at Monash University in Melbourne. His first monograph, *The Company and the Shogun: The Dutch Encounter with Tokugawa Japan* (2014), won multiple awards including the Jerry Bentley Prize in World History from the American Historical Association. He is most recently the editor with Lauren Benton and Bain Attwood of *Protection and Empire: A Global History* (2017).

ROBERT S. DUPLESSIS is Isaac H. Clothier Professor of History Emeritus at Swarthmore College (USA). He has published widely on early modern economic, material culture and textile history. His most recent book is *The Material Atlantic: Clothing, Commerce, and Colonization in the Atlantic World, 1650–1800* (2015). He is currently completing a revised edition of *Transitions to Capitalism in Early Modern Europe*.

REBECCA EARLE is Professor of History at the University of Warwick. Her most recent book *The Body of the Conquistador* (2012) explored the centrality of food to the construction of colonial space, and the 'racial' categories that underpinned it. She is currently writing a history of the potato, which uses the emergence of the potato as an Enlightenment super-food to explore the connections between everyday life and new ideas of individualism, political economy and the state.

TOBY GREEN teaches in the departments of History and Spanish, Portuguese and Latin American Studies at King's College London. He is the author of *The Rise of the Trans-Atlantic Slave Trade in Western Africa, 1300–1589* (2012) and *A Fistful of Shells: West Africa from the Rise of the Slave Trade to the Age of Revolution* (2019). He was a recipient of a 2017 Philip Leverhulme Prize in History.

MARIA HAYWARD is Professor of Early Modern History at the University of Southampton. Her research interests include textiles and dress in late medieval and early modern Europe. Her publications include *Dress at the Court of King Henry VIII* (2007), *Rich Apparel: Clothing and the Law in Henry VIII's England* (2009), *The Great Wardrobe Accounts of Henry VII and VIII* (2012) and *The First Book of Fashion,* edited with Ulinka Rublack (2015).

KATSUYA HIRANO teaches history at Universty of California–Los Angeles. He is the author of *The Politics of Dialogic Imagination: Power and Popular Culture in Early Modern Japan* (2014). He has published numerous articles and book chapters on settler colonialism, critical theory and cultural and intellectual history of early modern and modern Japan, including 'Politics and Poetics of the Body in Early Modern Japan', published in *Modern Intellectual History*.

ANDRÉ HOLENSTEIN is Professor of Swiss History and Comparative Regional History at the University of Berne, Switzerland. He is a member of the Swiss Academy of Humanities and Social Sciences (SHAS) and vice-president of the Swiss Association for the History of the Eighteenth Century. He is the author of *Mitten in Europa. Verflechtung und Abgrenzung in der Schweizer Geschichte* (2014) and, with Patrick Kury and Kristina Schulz, of *Schweizer Migrationsgeschichte von den Anfängen bis zur Gegenwart* (2018).

CATHERINE KOVESI is a historian at the University of Melbourne. Her research centres on discourses surrounding luxury consumption in early modern Italy; clothing, textiles and gender; Florentine and Venetian family history; and the history of women religious in Australia. She is the author of *Sumptuary Legislation in Italy, 1200–1500* (2001) and has published several articles on sumptuary laws.

LUCA MOLÀ is Professor of Early Modern Europe: History of the Renaissance and the Mediterranean in a World Perspective at the European University Institute in Florence, Italy. He is also a member of staff of the Department of History, University of Warwick. He has written on the history of the silk industry and on the history of innovation and patents in Renaissance Italy.

MARIA GIUSEPPINA MUZZARELLI is Professor of Medieval History at the University of Bologna, Italy. She has worked extensively on the history of mentality, the history of women and the history of dress and fashion. Among her works are *Disciplinare il lusso* (edited with A. Campanini, 2003), *Guardaroba medievale. Vesti e società dal XIII al XVI secolo* (2nd ed. 2008) and *Breve storia della moda in Italia* (2011).

GIORGIO RIELLO is Professor of Global History and Culture at the University of Warwick and the current Chair of the Pasold Research Fund. He is the author of four books, among them *Cotton: The Fabric that Made the Modern World* (2013), which won the World History Association Prize, and *Luxury: A Rich History* (with P. McNeil, 2016). He has published extensively on the history of textiles, trade and material exchange between Europe and Asia in the early modern period and has co-edited a dozen books, among which are *The Spinning World* (2009), *How India Clothed the World* (2009), *Writing Material Culture* (2015; 2nd ed. 2019), *Global Gifts* (2018) and *Threads of Global Desire: Silk in the Pre-Modern World* (2018).

MATTHEW P. ROMANIELLO is Assistant Professor of History at Weber State University and editor of *Sibirica: Interdisciplinary Journal of Siberian Studies*. He is the author of *The Elusive Empire: Kazan and the Creation of Russia, 1552–1671* (2012) and the forthcoming *Enterprising*

Empires: Russia and Britain in Eighteenth-Century Eurasia. He was previously Professor of History at the University of Hawai'i at Mānoa and an editor of *The Journal of World History.*

ULINKA RUBLACK, FBA, is Professor of Early Modern European History at the University of Cambridge and a Fellow of St John's College. She is the author of *The Crimes of Women in Early Modern Germany* (1999), short-listed for the Longman Prize; *Reformation Europe* (2005, 2nd rev. ed. 2017), *Dressing Up: Cultural Identity in Renaissance Europe* (2010), which won the Bainton Prize and *The Astronomer & the Witch: Johannes Kepler's Fight for his Mother* (2015), a finalist for the Digby Prize. She has edited *Gender in Early Modern German History* (2010), the *Concise Companion to History* for Oxford University Press (2011), the *Oxford History of the Protestant Reformations* (2016), *Hans Holbein: The Dance of Death* (2016) – a *Spectator* Art Book of the Year – and, together with Maria Hayward, *The First Book of Fashion* (2015).

ISIS STURTEWAGEN has worked as a post-doctoral researcher at Leiden University and the University of Antwerp (Centre for Urban History). In 2016 she defended her PhD dissertation on the consumption of fashion and clothing in the Low Countries during the fifteenth and sixteenth centuries. She holds an MA in archaeology from Ghent University, with a thesis on headscarves in the late Middle Ages.

AMANDA WUNDER is Associate Professor of History at Lehman College and a faculty member in Art History, History and Renaissance Studies at the Graduate Center of the City University of New York. She works on the cultural history of early modern Spain. Her publications include *Baroque Seville: Sacred Art in a Century of Crisis* (2017).

MADELINE C. ZILFI is Professor of Middle East and Islamic History at the University of Maryland, College Park. Her research and teaching focus on Ottoman social and cultural history in the seventeenth and eighteenth centuries, particularly with regard to slavery and dependency and popular religious movements. She is the author of *Women and Slavery in the Late Ottoman Empire* (2010) and author and guest editor for a collection of papers on Middle Eastern televised social and historical fiction, forthcoming in *Review of Middle East Studies* in 2018.

Acknowledgements

The project that led to this book started as a conversation between the editors concerning the importance of dress in pre-modern societies and the relationship between individual behaviour and collective social, economic and cultural forces as experienced in sumptuary regimes. We soon realised that any in-depth analysis had to rely on the expertise of scholars working in specific world areas, who bring to this volume new research and interpretations. We are grateful to the Leverhulme Trust for supporting a workshop, held at Warwick in May 2014 as part of the activities of 'The Luxury Network', at which initial drafts of several of the papers in this volume were presented. The editors organised a panel on 'The Right to Dress' at the 17th World Economic History Congress, held in Kyoto in August 2015, where several further papers were presented and discussed.

This volume has benefitted from the insightful comments provided by the anonymous readers and by Michael Watson at Cambridge University Press. Contributors to this volume have not just participated in events in Britain and Japan but have also read and commented on each other's papers. They joined a group of other colleagues who have assisted us by commenting on draft chapters. We wish to thank in particular Francisco Bethencourt, Susanna Burghartz, Trevor Burnard, Robert DuPlessis, Rebecca Earle, Suraiya Faroqhi, Kate Fleet, Anne Gerritsen, Maria Hayward, Martha Howell, Catherine Kovesi, Dana Leibsohn, Lesley Miller, Luca Molà, Beverly Lemire, Janine Maegraith, Maria Giuseppina Muzzarelli, Christine Ruane, Dagmar Schäfer, Timon Screech, Karin Sennefelt, Kim Siebenhüner, John Styles, Sophie White, Marieke de Winkel and Amanda Wunder. Special thanks to Helen Clifford, who has patiently read the entire manuscript, and to the team at Cambridge University Press who have helped us with this publication.

Introduction

Ulinka Rublack and Giorgio Riello

In the late sixteenth century, Michel de Montaigne sat down in his library to write about the vexing theme of sumptuary laws. 'To declare that only princes may eat turbot and wear velvet and gold braid', the French essayist mused, was 'but enhancing such things and making everyone want to have them'.[1] Montaigne agreed with Plato: young people should never change from 'fashion to fashion in their dress, comportment, dances, sports and songs'.[2]

Today anyone fashion-minded is more likely to associate the name Montaigne with luxury shopping in Paris rather than with a humanist writer who looked back to the ancients. The French capital's Avenue Montaigne is named after the essayist but epitomises couture fashion consumption with global appeal. Constant change and continued spending now underpin market economies. The expression of different identities through dress is associated with creativity and is regarded as integral to the aesthetics of dynamic societies. Men's fashion shows mark the annual calendar alongside those for women. Dress regulations of course continue to operate in the Western world – in relation to work, leisure, particular forms of sociability, institutional codes, and ethnic and religious expression. Yet no one's expenditure on clothing is regulated by the state. By contrast, up to the end of the eighteenth century, sumptuary laws (from the Latin word *sumptus* meaning expense) sought to regulate social difference in many parts of the world and imposed policies about who could spend how much on what types of dress and accessories, feasts and funerals, horses or carriages.

This collection of essays is the first to investigate the global history of sumptuary regulation and primarily focuses on dress. It is dedicated to the memory of Sir Christopher Bayly, whose influential account *The Birth of*

---

[1] Michel de Montaigne, *The Complete Essays*, ed. and trans. M. A. Screech (Harmondsworth: Penguin, 1987), No. 43. 'On Sumptuary Law', 300.

[2] Ibid., 302. Montaigne opposed 'running after novelties and honouring those who invent them' as such seemingly trivial attitudes corrupted 'all morals'.

1

the Modern World (2004) showed why a history of dress and comportment lie at the heart of our understanding of cultural change. Bayly argued that bodily practices on the one hand became more interconnected and uniform in the modern world, but on the other they could also enforce a sense of difference and nationalist antagonism as well as hybridity.[3] Bayly's interest in the body as a 'site on which anthropologists and social historians chart the influence of the state and methods of social discipline' has guided our project.[4] Although Bayly's realm of analysis was the nineteenth century, his work has encouraged us to reflect on the ways in which relative sartorial freedom in many societies – a 'right to dress' that most of us consider fundamental to our human condition and liberties – is a recent phenomenon and the outcome of political processes which affect populations in intimate ways and are shaped by them in turn. This means that we need to enlarge our notion of political rights to include social, economic and cultural dimensions of consumption and expression. Bayly's work prompted us to investigate historical change across the world by looking at differing and contrasting experiences and to explore why, for most of the period between 1200 and 1800, legislators, religious and political leaders as well as moral thinkers such as Montaigne believed regulation to be much more important than freedom of expression. At the same time, opposing voices ranged across a broad spectrum from merchants to consumers, intellectuals to members of some religious elites. The right to dress as one liked and regardless of status – let alone gender and ethnic markers – needs to be made visible as a key site of historical contestation in which many actors took part, staking out their claims to how human life and societies should be visualised and materialised.

An examination of the history of dress regulation therefore opens up key central processes of social, political, economic, legal, religious and cultural change in new ways. What needs to be explored for modern as much as for pre-modern societies is Bayly's 'complex parallelogram of forces constituted by economic changes, ideological constructions, and mechanisms of the state'.[5] This parallelogram of forces can be mapped out for specific events, such as the famous 8 Brumaire, year II (29 October 1793) of the French Revolution, which decreed that everyone was free to 'wear whatever clothing and accessories of his sex that he finds pleasing', only to mandate in articles 2 and 3 that previous articles

---

[3] C. A. Bayly, *The Birth of the Modern World 1780–1914: Global Connections and Comparisons* (Oxford: Blackwell, 2004), 1, 12–15.
[4] Ibid., 17.
[5] Ibid., 7.

on dress remained in force and wearing the red, white and blue cockade was obligatory.[6] Yet our book demonstrates that we need to focus, above all, on long-term change to chart how and why items of dress became key aspirational goods across society in the Middle Ages, how they were lobbied for and marketed, and whether or not sumptuary laws were implemented by towns, states and empires to restrict or channel trade and consumption. This results in a dynamic and nuanced account of the importance of dress in pre-modern societies and into the eighteenth century, which comprehensively revises the notion that clothing remained static and was considered to 'make' people by according them a clear place in a social hierarchy.

The volume is divided into four parts which will hopefully make it easier to navigate the eighteen contributions by specialists in very different periods, societies and cultures. Each part introduces different geographical areas and political structures. We begin, in Parts I and II, with Northern Europe and Italy simply because archival material and the historiographical discussion to date are especially rich in relation to them. Since the early twentieth century studies on sumptuary laws in medieval and early modern Europe have provided many of the categories and indicated the key issues that are still at the centre of attention today. Research on Italy is particularly abundant and as the essays in Part II show, offer evidence not just on the laws themselves but also on their application and negotiation. Part III turns to the European maritime empires where in settler societies sumptuary laws came to be structured by criteria of race and the relationship between mother country and colony. Finally Part IV considers world empires, such as the Ottoman Empire and China, as well as the case of pre-colonial West Africa, and shows the importance of sumptuary laws in the government of both society and the court. The aim of this volume is not to be exhaustive, as many areas of the world have not been included and some of them are still to be investigated. We wish instead to address the phenomenon of sumptuary laws in a comparative and global framework. This introduction sets out the close thematic connections between contributions in different parts of this book, which ideally will be read together. It provides an overview of the historiography on sumptuary legislation and broader assessment of new avenues of research which reshape our understanding of these past societies and the phenomenon of sumptuary laws as a whole.

---

[6] For a detailed discussion see Cissie Fairchilds, 'Fashion and Freedom in Revolutionary France', *Continuity & Change* 15/3 (2000): 419–433.

What are Sumptuary Laws?

The past decades have seen an increased interest in the study of sumptuary legislation, especially for the period of transition towards modernity. In Europe and elsewhere sumptuary laws could become a tool used by states to regulate manufacturing systems and moral economies via the medium of expenditure and consumption of not only clothing but also banquets, festivities and funerals. Traditionally considered within the history of dress, sumptuary laws had instead a much broader significance in medieval and early modern societies as they mediated between individuals and states to regulate consumer behaviour and values. Today, as in the early modern period, a great deal of discussion surrounds the legal standing, implementation and moral value of such laws.[7]

Historical interpretations of these regulatory efforts differ markedly. As Daniel Roche asks for the period up to the eighteenth century, were sumptuary laws able to impose 'conformity to custom' on European populations who inhabited a 'sartorial old regime' with clear hierarchies? Or did they instead – as Alan Hunt posits – underpin the notion that states were to morally and economically regulate their citizenry and thus form a marked tool of governmentality? Or, as Martha Howell has recently argued, did sumptuary legislation even help to 'give birth to the discourse of the modern self' by forcing people to distinguish between exterior display and interiority?[8] Studies of sumptuary laws are mostly limited to European regions and states, with a focus on how they were adapted to local conditions. This book by contrast considers sumptuary regulations as a global phenomenon and wishes to evaluate their differing

---

[7] We should distinguish a 'sumptuary law' from a 'clothing law'. Whilst the former were mostly intended to forbid – for instance the wearing of specific items of apparel – the latter were mostly aimed at forcing people to wear or use specific garments, as for instance in the case of Western clothing imposed on the civil administration by Peter the Great of Russia at the end of the seventeenth century or by the Emperor of Japan in the nineteenth century. On the definition of a 'clothing law', see: Donald Quataert, 'Clothing Laws, State, and Society in the Ottoman Empire, 1720–1829', *International Journal of Middle East Studies* 29/3 (1997): 403–425. For clothing laws in Japan and Russia, see: H. Ken'ichiro, 'The Westernization of Clothes and the State in Mejii Japan', in Giorgio Riello and Peter McNeil (eds.), *The Fashion History Reader: Global Perspectives* (London: Routledge, 2010), 405–415; Christine Ruane, 'Clothes Shopping in Imperial Russia', *Journal of Social History* 28/4 (1995): 765–782.
[8] Daniel Roche, *The Culture of Clothing: Dress and Fashion in the Ancien Régime*, trans. Jean Birrell (Cambridge: Cambridge University Press, 1994); Alan Hunt, *Governance of the Consuming Passions. A History of Sumptuary Law* (New York: Palgrave Macmillan, 1996); Martha Howell, *Commerce before Capitalism in Europe, 1300–1600* (Cambridge: Cambridge University Press, 2010), 208–260.

nature, functioning and socio-economic consequences across the early modern world.[9]

In this introduction, we explain why dress is an important prism through which we can investigate the roles of states and some key interpretations of early modernity. We do so by focusing on five topics. First, our analysis considers the nature of sumptuary laws *vis-à-vis* the existence of other legal and economic measures to increase commerce and support craft, their relationship to innovation and trade and the eventual decline of regulation. In order to do so, we secondly need to understand how sumptuary laws were created, how they were implemented and what allowances they made in the attempt to bring together consumers, legislators, local authorities and economic actors. Sumptuary laws did not simply regulate people's behaviour but provided precise instructions on which goods were allowed and, in doing so, enshrined markers of how to achieve social ascent. So, our third aim relates to identifying which items of dress and adornment sumptuary laws actually referred to, in order to understand how they interlinked with patterns of consumption, luxury, fashion and product diversification. Like any regulations, sumptuary laws acted selectively on communities and across social hierarchies. Our aim is therefore to question the extent to which men and women experienced constraints to their choices in order to explore how sumptuary laws shaped, for instance, understandings of masculinity and femininity and gendered practices of adornment. Finally, we discuss when and why the 'right to dress' – the individual and collective assertion of freedom in consumption – entered the political discourse of different societies and became embedded within ideas about the individual in societal relations, consumption and the economy.

As many of the essays in this book make clear, we rely on a long tradition of archival study and historical interpretation of these regulations both in Europe and in other parts of the world. Sumptuary laws were first considered by late nineteenth-century French, Italian and Spanish historians, including amateur, local and legal historians, as documents offering the means to reconstruct regional and even urban consumption, especially for the later Middle Ages.[10] Dress was singled out as the most important category covered by sumptuary laws, though the latter often

---

[9] In a similar vein, see the recent book by Beverly Lemire, *Global Trade and the Transformation of Consumer Cultures: The Material World Remade, c. 1500–1820* (Cambridge: Cambridge University Press, 2018), ch. 3.

[10] See Maria Giuseppina Muzzarelli, 'Le leggi suntuarie nello specchio della storiografia', in Laura Righi and Giulia Vettori (eds.), *Il lusso e la sua disciplina: aspetti economici e sociali della legislazione suntuaria dall'antichità all'età moderna*, Atti del seminario, Trento, 17–18 March 2016 (Trento: Università degli studi di Trento, forthcoming 2018).

included a variety of types of expenditure and most especially banquets, festivities (baptisms, marriages, funerals, etc.) and means of transport (horses and trappings, coaches, palanquins, etc.). Over the twentieth century dress historians studied sumptuary laws in order to glimpse at the clothing of medieval patricians or to unlock royal wardrobes. The history of costume made use of sumptuary laws, along with other documents such as inventories and extant garments, and interpreted them mostly in terms of the social hierarchies they reveal within specific civic or national societies.[11]

The study of specific localities, towns and cities remained central to these studies. Meanwhile, economic and social historians slowly entered the field in the 1960s and fostered a broader and more comparative framework of investigation. Donald Shively's important 1964 analysis of sumptuary regulations in Tokugawa Japan embedded sumptuary laws within a socio-cultural agenda of change thus providing a model for later studies, especially in Europe.[12] In the 1990s, research by Neithard Bulst on Germany and France, as well as Maria Giuseppina Muzzarelli's and Maria Grazia Nico Ottaviani's transcription and interpretation of the sumptuary laws of two key Italian regions, allowed historians to delve into complete sets of records for the first time.[13] Catherine Kovesi's work was equally important in providing the first comparative analysis of sumptuary laws across the Italian peninsula, while the sociologist Alan Hunt's 1996 overview was the first attempt at conceptualising sumptuary laws at a transnational and comparative level.[14]

Nearly a quarter of a century after Hunt's influential publication, with its emphasis on the laws' function to enshrine governmentality,

[11] See, for instance, Kent Roberts Greenfield, *Sumptuary Law in Nürnberg: A Study in Paternal Government* (Baltimore: Johns Hopkins University Press, 1918); Frances Elizabeth Baldwin, *Sumptuary Legislation and Personal Regulation in England* (Baltimore: Johns Hopkins University Press, 1926).

[12] Donald H. Shively, 'Regulation and Status in Early Tokugawa Japan', *Harvard Journal of Asiatic Studies* 25 (1964–65): 123–164.

[13] Bulst's research is extensively discussed in Rublack's contribution; Maria Giuseppina Muzzarelli (ed.), *La legislazione suntuaria. Secoli XIII–XVI. Emilia-Romagna* (Rome: Ministero per i beni e le attività culturali. Direzione generale degli archivi, 2002); Maria Grazia Nico Ottaviani (ed.), *La legislazione suntuaria. Secoli XIII–XVI. Umbria* (Rome: Ministero per i beni e le attività culturali. Direzione generale degli archivi, 2005).

[14] Catherine Kovesi Killerby, *Sumptuary Legislation in Italy, 1200–1500* (Oxford: The Clarendon Press, 2001); Hunt, *Governance of the Consuming Passions*. Sumptuary laws have attracted also the interest of other scholars, especially those interested in material culture and material life. See Arjun Appadurai, 'Introduction: Commodities and the Politics of Value', in Arjun Appadurai (ed.), *The Social Life of Things: Commodities in Cultural Perspective* (Cambridge: Cambridge University Press, 1986), 25–26.

sumptuary laws can be understood in relation to new themes that are at the cutting edge of recent historiographies. First, this book acknowledges the importance of a booming literature on consumption, product innovation and material culture that has given new theoretical vigour to the study of dress. Sumptuary laws are now interpreted by giving attention to the highly diversified materials they attempted to regulate and the idea of consumption in medieval and early modern societies. They do not only tell us about a normative system, but also index a dynamic world of consumer goods and bodily practises that provided a map for social ascent and expression. They could include generously measured allowances rather than conservative restrictions. Second, fashion and luxury are therefore concepts central to this book. Several of the contributions query the meaning of sumptuary intervention as well as its application and reach in relation to what we might call the political economy of consumption, fashion and luxury in societies as different as Ming China, Tudor England and Colonial Latin America. Third, the global perspective challenges us to avoid thinking of different realities as separate instances drawing on specific social contexts and dealing with precise sources. This book attempts instead to present a global picture of synchronic manifestations that – although they are not necessarily directly connected – allow us to think of the nature of the pre-modern world beyond the usual divisions that set Europe apart from other states and empires in Asia, the Americas and Africa. In order to do so, we rely on the linguistic and archival expertise of colleagues working in different area studies to provide fresh research in a field that is often dominated by outdated bibliographies. This equips scholars to further explore the questions Bayly posed: whether and when dress and bodily practices might increasingly have served to express values and aspirations in similar ways across the globe, and how the interests of merchants intersected with state policies, empire building and ideological, religious and social change.

Sumptuary Laws in Time and Space

Reading sumptuary regulations across countries and continents reveals a shared concern on the part of many medieval and early modern legislators, rulers, moralists and religious authorities. Dress, once a material manifestation of permanence, hierarchy and stability in society, was now seen as changing in its material forms, fleeting in its meaning and increasingly luxurious. To make things worse, regulations pointed out that people attributed a great deal of importance to what they wore, investing considerable sums of money in garments and accessories that could seem all but superfluous. Only moral restraint coupled with legal intervention could guide subjects and citizens in their consumer choices.[15]

Sumptuary laws were already present in the ancient world, especially in republican and imperial Rome, although their regulation of conspicuous consumption rarely included clothing.[16] They reappeared in Europe in 1157 when the Italian city of Genoa – a prosperous trading port and one of the peninsula's main maritime republics – enacted its first sumptuary law. Over the course of the next two centuries several more Italian city states issued similar laws, sometimes enacting them repeatedly and updating them on a regular basis. In Italy alone more than three hundred sumptuary laws were enacted in the period from 1200 to 1500.[17] Other countries were soon to follow: early modern France produced about a hundred sumptuary laws and the German principalities an estimated three to five thousand (including mostly acts and regulations). Sumptuary laws were also abundant in sixteenth-century England.[18]

Sumptuary regulations were also to be found outside Europe. They were enacted in China in the seventh century BCE. By the Tang dynasty (618–907 CE), eight primary groups had been identified among the privileged elites and subjected to detailed legislation. However well before this, in the Han period (206 BCE–8 CE), contemporaries lamented that *su-feng* (untitled nobility) such as merchants, artisans and money-lenders did not follow sumptuary laws.[19] Sumptuary regulations existed in the early Islamic Middle East.[20] In the early fourteenth century, the Sultan of Delhi Muhammad bin Tughluq forbade the use of cloth imported from Russia and Egypt and dictated that 'nobody can dress and ride with saddles covered or embroidered with gold except he upon whom the Sultan bestowed them'.[21] Sumptuary laws reiterated the importance of hierarchy, though in Asia as in Africa such hierarchy

[15] See Hans Medick, 'Une Culture de la considération. Les vêtements et leur couleur à Laichingen entre 1750 et 1820', *Annales Histoire, Sciences Sociales* 50 (1995): 754–755.

[16] Giuseppe Dari-Mattiacci and Anna E. Plisecka, 'Luxury in Ancient Rome: Scope, Timing and Enforcement of Sumptuary Laws', *Legal Roots* 1 (2012): 189–216; Emanuela Zanda, *Fighting Hydra-like Luxury: Sumptuary Regulation in the Roman Republic* (London: Bloomsbury, 2013).

[17] See the table of Italian sumptuary laws in Catherine Kovesi Killerby, *Sumptuary Law in Italy* (Oxford: Clarendon Press, 2002), 28–29.

[18] Susan Vincent, *Dressing the Elite: Clothes in Early Modern England* (Oxford: Berg, 2003), 117–51, esp. 118–121.

[19] Ping-Ti Ho, 'Aspects of Social Mobility in China, 1368–1911', *Comparative Studies in Society and History* 1/4 (1959): 333.

[20] Yedida Kalfon Stillman, *Arab Dress: A Short History from the Dawn of Islam to Modern Times*, ed. Norman A. Stillman (Leiden: Brill, 2000), 39, 77, 110–112.

[21] Cit. in Joginder K. Chawla, *India's Overland Trade with Central Asia and Persia* (New Delhi: Munshiram Manoharlal Publishers, 2006), 87.

was imposed by and aimed to confirm the rule of emperors and their courts.[22]

From the late seventeenth century onwards, while in most of Europe sumptuary laws were either being repealed or ignored, they were issued in several areas of the expanding European maritime empires in Asia and the Americas, such as in Spanish Colonial America and the territories controlled by the European East India companies. In seventeenth-century Lima sumptuary laws thus banned 'negroes, mulattos and zambos' from carrying swords and other weapons, and black and mulatto women from wearing woollen cloth, silks or lace.[23] In Portuguese India, the viceroy requested sumptuary laws as a measure to curb the pervasive 'luxury that exists', predominantly in relation to litters and fabrics with which they were furnished. This was in 1715, almost twenty years after a sumptuary law had been passed in Portugal.[24] Perhaps most surprisingly, sumptuary laws were used to regulate the consuming habits of Europeans and non-Europeans in the Dutch possessions of Batavia and the Cape. Notwithstanding the fact that no sumptuary provisions existed in the mother country, the Governors-General of Batavia issued ordinances in 1647 banning the use of parasols for slaves and later the use of conspicuous chaises and carriages, and also limiting the number of slaves accompanying their masters and mistresses.[25] Such sumptuary acts

---

[22] Craig Clunas makes an argument for a similarity between the Chinese and the European sumptuary laws in the period 1550–1650, including their interest in materials rather than cut and their lack of success in guiding consumption. Craig Clunas, *Superfluous Things: Material Culture and Social Status in Early Modern China* (Cambridge: Polity, 1991), 147–152. See also Timothy Brook, *Confusions of Pleasure: Commerce and Culture in Ming China* (Berkeley: University of California Press, 1999), 228–237.

[23] Tamara J. Walker, *Exquisite Slave: Race, Clothes, and Status in Colonial Lima* (Cambridge: Cambridge University Press, 2017); Rebecca Earle, 'Luxury, Clothing and Race in Colonial Spanish America', in Maxine Berg and Elizabeth Eger (eds.), *Luxury in the Eighteenth Century: Debates, Desires and Delectable Goods* (London: Palgrave, 2003), 223. For Mexico see: Osvaldo F. Pardo, 'How to Punish Indians: Law and Cultural Change in Early Colonial Mexico', *Comparative Studies in Society and History* 48/1 (2006): 102–103; Abby Sue Fisher, 'Trade Textiles: Asia and New Spain', in Donna Pierce and Ronald Otsuka (eds.), *Asia & Spanish America: Trans-Pacific Artistic and Cultural Exchange, 1500–1850* (Denver, CO: Denver Art Museum, 2009), 185–187.

[24] A sumptuary law had been enacted in 1698 and a final sumptuary act was passed in 1749. Nandini Chaturvedula, 'On the Precipice of Ruin: Consumption, Sumptuary Laws, and Decadence in Early Modern Portuguese India', *Journal of World History* 26/2 (2015): 355–356.

[25] Robert Ross, 'Sumptuary Laws in Europe, the Netherlands and the Dutch Colonies', in Nigel Worden (ed.), *Contingent Lives: Social Identity and Material Culture in the VOC World* (Rondebosch: University of Cape Town, 2007), 385–388. Similar laws were applied to the Cape with small changes. Stan Du Plessis, 'Pearls Worth Rds4000 or Less: Reinterpreting Eighteenth Century Sumptuary Laws at the Cape', *Working Papers* 336, Economic Research Southern Africa: https://ideas.repec.org/p/rza/wpaper/336 .html [last accessed 1 January 2018]. See also Adam Clulow's chapter in this volume.

Figure i.1 *Teatime in a European house in Batavia*, by Jan Brandes, 1779–1785. Pencil on paper, 15.5 x 19.5 cm. Rijksmuseum, Amsterdam NG-1985-7-2-15.

manifested concern about the high levels of consumption by Europeans in Asia and the Americas, not just in relation to dress but also to the number of servants and slaves and to visible manifestations of wealth such as the means of transport used (Figure i.1). In India, which did not have any tradition of sumptuary laws, the new laws focused on ostentatious means of transport.

Why did sumptuary laws become more numerous in Europe in the thirteenth century, increase in number up to the early seventeenth century but all but disappear by the nineteenth century? Alan Hunt has connected the enactment of sumptuary laws with high economic development thus supporting the hypothesis of a direct relationship between economic growth, the appearance of fashion and attempts at curbing conspicuous spending.[26] Similarly, Neithard Bulst and Martha Howell have suggested an evolution of sumptuary legislation from 'unspecific' regulations enacted by individual European cities before the mid-fourteenth century

---

[26] Hunt, *Governance of the Consuming Passions*, 22–41.

to rules based on a more precise reading of hierarchical difference in the period up to the early sixteenth century. These were followed by a third phase in which territorial states replaced urban legislation, especially in the sixteenth and seventeenth centuries.[27] Yet these explanations do not always fit such a precise chronological pattern: in most areas, sumptuary laws continued to be issued even in periods of economic involution, as in the case of the Southern Netherlands; city-based, national and imperial laws coexisted across time, as in the case of the German states.

If sumptuary laws are considered beyond the borders of Europe, there is a risk of taking the omnipresence of sumptuary laws across time and space as a sign of a coherent phenomenon. In reality, we need to differentiate pathways, in contrast to a literature that sometimes presents a rather indiscriminate jumble of reference, hopping across centuries in relation to different societies in Europe and beyond. The fact that sumptuary laws were present in not only most of the emerging European states but also in China, Japan, the Ottoman Empire and in colonial settings provides us with a challenge as well as an opportunity. Cross-references between different sumptuary laws – even those of neighbouring cities – are extremely rare. With the exception of colonial legislation, informed as it were by concerns and regulations imposed by mother countries, all other sumptuary laws considered in this book were generated within specific cities, states and empires.

We are therefore left with specific instances of regulation and resistance that have first to be understood within the context that produced them. Yet, this limitation should not prevent us from thinking comparatively. For instance, one has to observe that, with major exceptions for Russia and North America, clothing regulations seem to have been devised by societies that were urbanised. In 1500, more than 150 European cities had at least 10,000 inhabitants; by 1600 their number had risen to 220.[28] Edo in Japan was by the early eighteenth century probably the first city in the world with one million inhabitants. Cities like Suzhou or Shanghai in China were also dynamic centres of commerce, consumption and fashion.[29] Urban dwellers created concentrated markets for goods, and

---

[27] Neithard Bulst, 'Zum Problem städtischer und territorialer Kleider-, Aufwands- und Luxusgesetzgebung in Deutschland (13. bis Mitte des 16. Jahrhundert)', in André Gouron and Albert Rigaudière (eds.), *Renaissance du pouvoir législatif et genèse de l'Etat* (Montpellier: Publications de la Société d'Histoire du Droit et des Institutions des Anciens Pays de Droit Ecrit, 1988), 29–57; Howell, *Commerce before Capitalism*, especially 236.

[28] Heinz Schilling, *Die Stadt in der Frühen Neuzeit* (Munich: Oldenbourg, 1993), 6–9, drawing on Jan de Vries's research.

[29] Mark Elvin, 'Blood and Statistics: Reconstructing the Population Dynamics of Late Imperial China from the Biographies of Virtuous Women in Local Gazetteers', in Harriet

towns obviously held markets and fairs, which were attractive for whole regions that demanded increasingly productive economic hinterlands. Towns housed diversifying groups of occupations and professions. These groups provided much of the social context within which market consumption unfolded, often with greater intensity. In Japan as in parts of Europe, a rooted elite of governing families could seek to restrict the political influence of such groups through sumptuary laws. In turn, they used status-conferring goods to demonstrate their sense of social worth and to express emotions, values and aesthetic pleasure.[30]

The Function of Sumptuary Laws

Hierarchy was key to pre-modern societies. Yet, the context so far described alerts us to the fact that by the later Middle Ages commerce and social dynamism had made clothing an unreliable signifier of social status which threatened increasingly complex hierarchies. This characteristic lament, in an English proclamation issued in 1588 by the extremely fashion-conscious Elizabeth I, can be found in preambles accompanying sumptuary laws:

The Queens Majestie hath considered into what extremities a great number of her Subjects are fallen by the inordinate excesse in apparell, contrary both to the good lawes of the Realme, and to her Majesties former admonitions by her Proclamations, and to the confusion of all estates, among whom diversitie of apparell hath bene alwayes a speciall and laudable marke, and finally to the impoverishing of the Realme, by dayly bringing into the same of superfluitie of forreine and unnecessarie commodities, not able to be anwered with the naturall marchandise of the Realme.[31]

The (unrealised) aim of sumptuary laws was therefore to create social distinction by reinforcing established ideas of hierarchy, making it visible and recognisable. This was a utopic project that relied on ideas of past times when hierarchies had existed untouched and unchallenged. Yet the reality is that in many medieval and early modern societies such hierarchies remained poorly defined. Italian city states – both republics and *signorie* – distinguished between the nobility, the burghers and the lower levels of society, though as in the case of Venice the laws applied to

---

T. Zurndorfer (ed.), *Chinese Women in the Imperial Past: New Perspectives* (Leiden: Brill, 1999), 152; Brook, *Confusions of Pleasure*, 218–237.

[30] Martha Howell, 'Fixing Movables: Gifts by Testament in Late Medieval Douai', *Past & Present* 150 (1996): 41–42.

[31] Paul L. Hughes and James F. Larkin (eds.), *Tudor Royal Proclamations. Vol. 3. The Later Tudors, 1588–1603* (New Haven: Yale University Press, 1969), 3 (13 February 1588).

all social ranks.[32] As late as the seventeenth century, Swedish sumptuary laws identified four estates: the nobility, clergy, burghers and farmers. Yet the complexity and articulation of social hierarchy alone cannot explain the contours of sumptuary legislation. France, more than any other nation state, had a complex hierarchical system that had developed over time. As early as 1292, European sumptuary laws included at least thirty-two different positions of status in society, while French sumptuary laws focused only on the aristocracy.[33] By contrast, in the Low Countries the majority of dress regulations targeted citizens who wore noble dress in an attempt to express political alliance and power.[34] A Strasbourg ordinance in 1660 distinguished 256 professions and linked them to six divisions of rank – a sign of how this centre of cross-cultural consumption grappled with increased status differentiation.[35]

This book underlines the importance of the observation that across time and space sumptuary laws might have fulfilled different functions: in Europe, for instance, they addressed the needs of the courtly and ruling elites to reinforce hierarchy, or they could be a tool of social competition between the nobility and the rising bourgeoisie later in the sixteenth and seventeenth centuries, as Amanda Wunder suggests in Chapter 9 on Spain. A second function performed by sumptuary laws was connected with ritual and power. In China, for instance, they served to articulate the political power of emperors through ritual knowledge, establishing a notion of supremacy according to which dress was an imperial concession and privilege accorded to specific ranks of the civil administration

---

[32] Carlo Marco Belfanti and Fabio Giusberti, 'Clothing and Social Inequality in Early Modern Europe: Introductory Remarks', *Continuity and Change* 15/3 (2000): 360; Maria Giuseppina Muzzarelli, 'Reconciling the Privilege of a Few with the Common Good: Sumptuary Laws in Medieval and Early Modern Europe', *Journal of Medieval and Early Modern Studies* 39/3 (2009): 597–617; Daniel Roche, *La culture des apparences. Une histoire du vêtement XVIIe-XVIIIe siècle* (Paris: Fayard, 1989), 54–56.

[33] Neithard Bulst, 'La legislazione suntuaria in Francia (secoli XIII-XVIII)', in Maria Giuseppina Muzzarelli and Antonella Campanini (eds.), *Disciplinare il Lusso. La legislazione suntuaria in Italia e in Europa tra Medioevo ed età moderna* (Rome: Carocci, 2003), 121–136. On the French sumptuary laws see: Sarah-Grace Heller, 'Anxiety, Hierarchy, and Appearance in Thirteenth-Century Sumptuary Laws and the Romance of the Rose', *French Historical Studies* 27/2 (2004): 311–348; and Pascal Bastien, '"Aux tresors dissipez l'on cognoist le malfaict": Social Hierarchy and Transgressions of French Sumptuary Laws, 1543–1606', *Renaissance & Reformation/Renaissance et Reforme* 23/4 (1999): 23–43.

[34] The idea of 'livery' as a form of dress to express affiliation was based on the expression of institutional rather than personal identity. See Ann Rosalind Jones and Peter Stallybrass, *Renaissance Clothing and the Material of Memory* (Cambridge: Cambridge University Press, 2000), 5; and for the late medieval period: Joan Crawford, 'Clothing Distribution and Social Relation. c. 1350–1500', in Catherine Richardson (ed.), *Clothing Cultures, 1350–1650* (Aldershot: Ashgate, 2004), 153–164.

[35] See the discussion in Rublack's Chapter 1 in this volume.

and court. In the less autocratic context of Tudor England, royal apparel was used as a benchmark for magnificence, allowing for instance only Henry VIII to wear purple cloth and cloth of gold and silk. In other parts of Europe, however, it was aspiring men in new professions – from artists to clock-workers, mercenary soldiers to perfumers and inventors – who were clearly intrigued by the possibilities of experimenting with social roles as much as with aesthetic experiences through visual practices.[36] Sumptuary legislation could even have the unintended effect of stimulating the production of different cuts, colours, luxury ornaments and avoidance language in order to circumvent legislation. In fifteenth-century Florence, it clearly provided a motor for fashion innovation, for instance in relation to gown neckline ornaments.[37]

Governmentality was central to some legislators. Sumptuary law was only one tool among many that they had at their disposal to secure the prosperity of a city, kingdom or empire by encouraging fiscal restraint and the productive use of scarce resources.[38] To many, dress appeared a wasteful investment. Forty per cent of a patrician family's income in renaissance Florence was devoted to clothing, with particularly extravagant spending on feasts like weddings, which asserted a family's status. Legislators attempted to curb this spending, though they had to make many exceptions that acknowledged the need for splendour especially on the part of the families representing the state and government.[39] Sumptuary laws were supported by local economic interests as they often banned the purchase and wearing of foreign luxuries. The English laws of 1337, for example, prohibited all men and women – with the exception of the King and Queen and their children – from wearing cloth imported from outside England, Ireland, Wales or Scotland.[40] Sumptuary laws could therefore also be designed to protect local industries against competition, thus revealing an economic rather than solely social concern.

---

[36] Maria Hayward, *Rich Apparel: Clothing and the Law in Henry VIII's England* (Aldershot: Ashgate, 2009).

[37] Collier Frick, *Dressing Renaissance Florence*, 188–191.

[38] N. B. Harte, 'State Control of Dress and Social Change in Pre-Industrial England', in D. C. Coleman and A. H. John (eds.), *Trade, Government and Economy in Pre-Industrial England* (London: Weidenfeld and Nicolson, 1976), 137.

[39] This was the case in Venice during important state visits, so as to display the maximum wealth to diplomatic visitors. The same happened when Charles Stuart, Prince of Wales, arrived unexpectedly in Madrid in the spring of 1623 with the intention of finding a royal bride. For the occasion, the sumptuary laws that Philip IV had passed just a month earlier had to be suspended to impress the British prince. Amanda Wunder, 'Innovation and Tradition at the Court of Philip IV of Spain (1621–1665): The Invention of the Golilla and the Guardainfante', in Evelyn Welch (ed.), *Fashioning the Early Modern: Dress, Textiles and Innovation in Europe, 1500–1800* (Oxford: Oxford University Press, 2017), 117.

[40] Harte, 'State Control of Dress', 134.

Sumptuary laws did not just curb expenditure but could act as a 'luxury tax', as the chapters in this volume on Russia and Italy show. In admitting their own ineffectiveness, such laws attempted to raise revenue for the coffers of the state by imposing fines or by allowing individual people to pay to have forbidden items exempted. The revenue created was used for projects that benefitted the community, for civic buildings and in aid of charities. Pragmatism prevailed as the revenue generated by the laws contributed to the 'commonwealth' by granting dispensations to those who could afford it.[41] This fiscal nature of sumptuary laws assumed a fiscal-military character in the case of Portugal. In the Iberian kingdom, sumptuary regulations were conceived to retain the spending power of the most powerful aristocratic families in order to ensure that the nobility would be ready in case of war.

All the same, legislators and moral leaders routinely insisted on the moral values of sumptuary laws. Many preachers supported their implementation as they perceived a direct relationship to exist between conspicuous consumption, expensive clothing and moral and sexual depravity.[42] The Italian preacher Bernardino da Siena (1380–1444), for instance, publicly admonished women: 'You are not as you used to be. I see a widow today ... with her forehead bare and her cloak drawn back to show her cheek. And how she shapes it over her brow! That is a prostitute's gesture!'[43] According to Bernardino, the type of clothing worn and its use made the difference between honest women and whores. Sumptuary laws upheld and supported religious norms in terms of the regulation of shame, gender and respect for established social rules, as we will see later in this chapter. In Catholic areas such as Italy or Iberia this role was played by preachers and prelates, while in Protestant parts of Switzerland the idea of anti-aristocratic frugality justified the republican rightness of sartorial self-restraint, as André Holenstein demonstrates in this volume. This moral rhetoric could be adopted by merchants in order to pose in a specific political framework. At the same time, new European ideologies of the market from 1600 onwards stressed religious justifications of wealth and sensual, tasteful enjoyment of fashionable accessories and goods and could see their value as the glue of civil societies.[44]

[41] Elizabeth Currie, *Fashion and Masculinity in Renaissance Florence* (London: Bloomsbury, 2016), 19–20.

[42] Aileen Ribeiro, *Dress and Morality*, 2nd ed. (Oxford: Berg, 2003), esp. 59–73.

[43] Cit. in Carole Collier Frick, *Dressing Renaissance Florence: Families, Fortunes and Fine Clothing* (Baltimore: Johns Hopkins University Press, 2004), 186.

[44] See Vera Keller, *Knowledge and the Public Interest, 1575–1725* (Cambridge: Cambridge University Press, 2015).

These ideologies were a significant new driving force long before the eighteenth century.

The Enactment and Enforcement of Sumptuary Laws

While the law underlined an urgent need for reforms, short periods of legislative action and legal enforcement in reality were typically followed by years and sometime decades of inaction, although Swiss cities such as Berne, Basel and Zurich were an important exception well into the eighteenth century. The Holy Roman Empire, by contrast, did not issue any new imperial ordinance between 1577 and 1806. In some cases, legislation was prompted by major political change. In 1368 Zhu Yuanyhang as new Ming emperor of China abolished the custom of wearing barbarian dress. The new laws forced a return to Tang (618–907 CE) style. As BuYun Chen explains in this volume, these laws were incorporated into the 1397 Great Ming Code (*Da ming lu*), but no further sumptuary laws were enacted until 1528.

Were most sumptuary laws too sporadic to be effective? Their wording tells us little about whether sumptuary laws had real impact on people's lives or if they were instead nominal affirmations of power among cultural and political elites. Historians can draw on cases in which sumptuary laws were openly challenged. Nicolosa Castellani, wife of Nicolò Sanuti, earl of Porretta near Bologna in Italy, rejected the law as damaging to the position of women. In an 1453 oration written in Latin she addressed Cardinal Bessarione, who had penned the Bolognese laws, and underlined how sumptuary laws did not allow women to sartorially represent their social rank and that of their husbands. She explained that the recent laws deprived noble women of one of the few social markers available to them in a world in which they were otherwise excluded from public life.[45] This documentation has been unearthed by Catherine Kovesi, and this volume is complemented by her analysis of a later and similarly remarkable petition, presented in 1566 to the authorities of the city of Milan on the part of the merchants, gold and silk workers and embroiders of the city. While previous grievances emphasised the rights of individuals, the Milanese petition argued in defence of the economy as a whole to contend that the luxury trades of the city would suffer because of the laws enacted the previous year.

A further way to assess the impact of sumptuary laws is to consider what Giulia Calvi calls their 'microhistories': how common citizens

---

[45] Catherine Kovesi Killerby, '"Heralds of a Well-Instructed Mind": Nicolosa Sanuti's Defence of Women and their Clothes', *Renaissance Studies* 13/3 (1999): 255–282.

faced sumptuary prosecution. Calvi analyses 255 trials held against 215 Florentine women and 40 men in the two years following the issuing of a new sumptuary law in Florence in 1638.[46] Clearly motivated by renewed sumptuary zeal, the city's authorities appointed 'birri' (policemen) to patrol the streets of Florence and apprehend anyone wearing forbidden garments, accessories and jewellery. Those found in breach of the law had to pay fines. Calvi's findings show that the Florentine trials included a cross-section of burghers who were active consumers – not only notaries and wealthy citizens, but also simple weavers, hawkers, hat- and shoemakers, butchers and barbers.[47] The same cannot be said of the trials in Padova, analysed by Molà and Riello: here prosecutions across centuries targeted the city's elites, mostly in response to new iterations of the law.

The cases of Florence and Padova allow us also to consider the formal system of sumptuary policing put in place. Florence, for instance, appointed as early as 1330 so-called 'Ufficiali delle Donne' (Clerks of Women) who had the power to stop and search anyone who might be considered in breach of the law. Similar figures were present in Padova, where 'Provveditori sopra le Pompe' (sumptuary officials) were charged with patrolling the streets, often apprehending culprits outside churches.[48] In Japan, as Katsuya Hirano shows, a 1682 ordinance banned luxurious garments and established that officers should inspect the clothing of passers-by and instantly arrest all those who were too expensively dressed. A decade later, the *Reformationskammern* (Reformation Chamber) of Bern in Switzerland obliged the city's fire wardens, clerks and messengers to act as sumptuary officials and promised them one-third of the fine as a reward.

Punishment varied widely. The letter of the law could once more be different from its application. China and Japan meted out the harshest of punishments, including death, banishment and imprisonment. In the West Indies, free people of colour wearing clothing deemed only for white people were threatened with severe punishment, including enslavement. Punishment was at times collective, affecting the families of individuals targetted. In the Ottoman Empire a decree of 1734 ordered that husbands of women circumventing the laws were to be expelled from the city, or else face imprisonment. Perhaps most

[46] Giulia Calvi, 'Leggi suntuarie e la storia sociale', in Muzzarelli and Campanini (eds.), *Disciplinare il lusso*, 213–230.

[47] Ibid., 222–223.

[48] Officials were not allowed into churches, sacred spaces were considered to be outside the jurisdiction of the law. However they could stand just outside their perimeter. For Florence, see: Collier Frick, *Dressing Renaissance*, 183.

remarkable is the case of Spain, where prosecutors could impose penalties on descendants: the descendants of heretics, for instance, were forbidden to wear velvet and other precious fabrics, as it was believed that heterodox religious beliefs were inherited via blood. Yet by contrast to the zealous enforcement elsewhere, in the Swiss city of Bern in 1694–1696 only 10 per cent of the 261 citizens indicted for transgressing sumptuary laws were imprisoned.

Laws could be applied selectively by imposing amnesties and allowing the use of some forbidden items. Maria Giuseppina Muzzarelli explains how in 1401 the Bolognese authorities allowed men and women to register items of prohibited clothing and termed them 'sealed garments' (*vesti bollate*). This registration produced revenue for the city's coffers and avoided the wastage that would have been caused by not allowing their use.[49]

These examples emphasise how difficult it is to paint a detailed overall picture of how effective sumptuary laws might have been in shaping individual behaviour and societies at large. Archival records of prosecutions remain rare, which has led many historians to think that sumptuary laws were often disregarded. As early as 1330 the Florentine Giovanni Villani observed that:

in spite of all these strong ordinances, outrages remained; and though one could not have cut and figured cloth, they wanted striped cloth and foreign cloth, the most that they could have, sending as far as Flanders and Brabant for it, not worrying about the cost.[50]

More than two centuries later Philip Stubbes, commenting on England, reiterated the point that infractions were common:

those who are neither of the nobility, gentility nor yeomanry, no, nor yet any magistrate, or officer in the commonwealth, go daily in silks, velvets, satins, damasks, taffetas and such like, notwithstanding that they be both base by birth, mean by estate and servile by calling.[51]

By the end of the ancient regime, at least in Europe, such laws had no longer sufficient legal force to be re-enacted. They simply faded out of the legal measures adopted by states and empires. With the exception of revolutionary France, there was no single law establishing the 'right to dress' as such. The freedom to choose what to wear became instead an 'implicit right'.

---

[49] For the complete list see: Maria Giuseppina Muzzarelli (ed.), *Belle vesti, dure leggi: 'In hoc libro continentur et descripte sunt omnes eet singules vestes'* (Bologna: Costa editore, 2003).
[50] Giovanni Villani, *Cronica* (Venice, [1330] 1537), book 9, ch. 150.
[51] Philip Stubbes, *The Anatomie of Abuses* (London: Richard Jones, 1583), 10r.

We finally need to draw attention to areas of the world where sumptuary laws were never or rarely enacted. If sumptuary intervention was a widespread tool of political and social intervention, why are there states and even empires where they were mostly absent? These include polities as different as Mughal India and Safavid Iran, the Dutch Republic, and British, Dutch and French Colonial America. In all of these places, the legal tool of the sumptuary law was well known, but it was rarely applied. An explanation might be found in the difference and relationship between convention and the law. It is clearly true that what we might call the rhetoric of sumptuary legislation depended strongly on the political, economic and religious context in which such laws were produced. Yet there were places where the law played a relatively minor role in the building of social conventions that might have been dominated instead by tacit forms of social control. This was the case in autocratic regimes, such as the central Asian empires, in closely-knit communities as in North America and in republics with egalitarian aspirations, as in the case of the Netherlands. Unlike all other European polities, the Netherlands passed only a single sumptuary law, issued by Archduke Philip the Fair in 1497 for all Burgundian territories, including those that later became the Dutch Republic. No further laws were enacted in the following centuries, though so-called *plakkaats* were issued admonishing citizens against the wearing of expensive dress. These however were not legally binding.[52]

Material Culture and Sumptuary Laws

Three key changes meanwhile marked the diversification of dress in the early modern period and made it more accessible in many parts of the globe. First, sumptuous fabrics were ingeniously produced in lesser qualities and imitations. Second, the reach of global products dramatically increased. Third, merchants increased their lobbying to gain access to broader markets, and distribution mechanisms for goods improved.

The production of silk and silk imitations greatly diversified in sixteenth-century Europe, so much so that Swedish legislators around 1600 faced an affluent burgher class in Stockholm with access to fifteen different types of silks and half-silks. In England, such goods 'established gradations of status' to dictate the very 'tenor of social relations'.[53] Yet some communities were more equal than others in providing access to

---

[52] Simon Schama, *The Embarrassment of Riches: An Interpretation of Dutch Culture in the Golden Age* (London: Collins, 1987), 186–187; Ross, 'Sumptuary Laws in Europe', 385.
[53] Alexandra Shepard, *Accounting for Oneself: Worth, Status, and the Social Order in Early Modern England* (Oxford: Oxford University Press, 2015), 303.

the finest of fabrics. Evidence from inventories in Antwerp demonstrates that almost every household across all social classes possessed at least one item of silk or half-silk as early as the mid-sixteenth century. Forty per cent of those who lived in just one room and thus belonged to the poorer classes owned some velvet. Less expensive silk and half-silk items were abundantly produced in the Netherlands and left almost entirely unregulated.[54]

The lower classes would have owned merely accessories in such fabrics, such as detachable sleeves or hoods. Yet these had the power to change a person's entire appearance. Hans Holbein's large portrait of Georg Gisze is a case in point. It moreover shows why members of the upper as much as lower classes might prefer an expensive accessory rather than the sumptuousness created through the use of silk for a major item of dress. Gisze was a Hanseatic merchant who traded and lived in London. He would have attached his splendid red satin sleeves to the red upper garment – the doublet – which would have been woven from less costly as well as warmer woollen or woollen and linen threads (Figure i.2). Merchants had to continuously consolidate their reputation through their comportment, dress and behaviour, in order to demonstrate self-control, trustworthiness, discretion and the ability to follow rules. They promoted measured pleasure in fine possessions, while it remained important to endorse modesty rather than an interest in limitless profit and gain. Gisze and his community would therefore wish to be represented in fine but not ostentatious clothing, which provided a model for a broader section of society of how to appropriately consume attractive dress.

Ingenious crafting turned some luxurious appearances and sensations into affordable novelties and often responded to prohibitions in sumptuary legislation. Restrictive legislation, in other words, could turn out to be productive and stimulate the invention of new types of craft techniques, processes and products. Spanish makers thus invented new types of wool trimmings when silk decorations were prohibited. German felt hats meanwhile could imitate smooth, precious velvet, by intricately looping silk or woollen yarn all across their surface. In England, glazed linen was achieved through 'ironing' fabric with heavy glass in a finishing process that made it as shiny as silk – a process that had to be repeated after washing such fabrics or wearing them for a period of time (Figure i.3). As Maria Hayward argues in this volume, the range of

---

[54] See Adam Clulow's contribution on the Netherlands in Chapter 11 of this volume; for a recent exploration of this theme see Evelyn Welch (ed.), *Fashioning the Early Modern*.

Figure i.2 *The Merchant Georg Gisze*, by Hans Holbein the Younger, 1532. 85.7 x 97.5 cm. Gemäldegalerie, Staatliche Museen zu Berlin.

decorative techniques available in England increased greatly during the sixteenth century. Ottoman rulers sharply distinguished between what was worn outside or inside the home, regulating the former but not the latter, surely fuelling a market for indoor leisurewear. As Zilfi reveals, headgear probably remained the most important and varied item on Ottoman streets, as in so many societies.

These changes in the availability of lower grade silks, accessories or imitation fabrics intersected with the growth of global trade and the greater dissemination of global goods in particular areas. In Portugal, as early as the sixteenth century, overseas expansion changed patterns of consumption in the south as much as in the north of the country.[55] As Francisco Bethencourt shows, textiles from China as well as Indian calicoes and chintzes were widely consumed in the northern city of Porto by 1600. Both Portugal and Spain began to export textiles to their Empires.

---

[55] Annemarie Jordan Gschwend and K.J.P. Lowe (eds.), *The Global City: On the Streets of Renaissance Lisbon* (London: Paul Holberton, 2015).

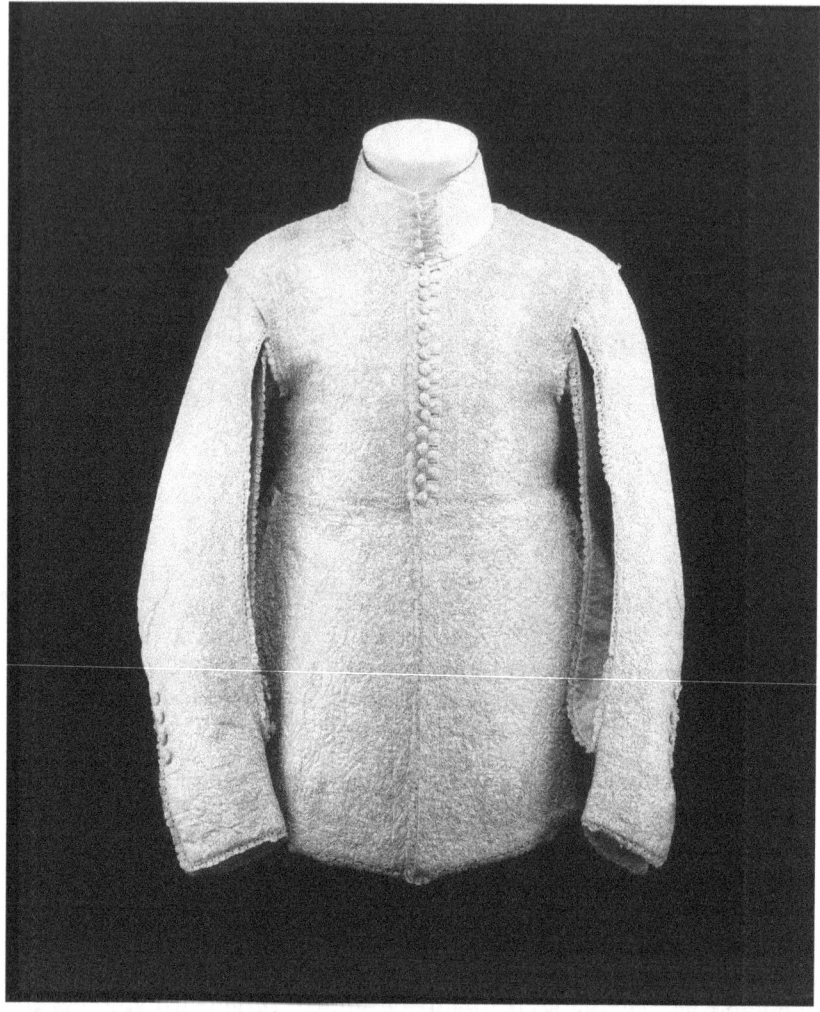

Figure i.3 Doublet. Glazed linen, embroidered with linen thread. Made in England, c. 1635–1640. Victoria and Albert Museum 177–1900.

By the eighteenth century, Portuguese merchants successfully lobbied for the abolition of sumptuary legislation that imposed restrictions on blacks and mulattos in order to maintain benefits for the national economy and women in particular. The eighteenth century obviously marks an extra-ordinary shift in the availability of luxury goods from Asia across Europe, as well as a marked increase in intra-European luxury production.[56] In Switzerland, annual fairs, weekly markets and peddlers now distributed such goods and their imitations into the mountainous countryside. The production of Swiss-made 'Indiennes' was booming, so much so that Switzerland's national economy ranked second after England in producing cotton textiles for European markets. But there was no moral outcry, as with the English 'calico craze', precisely because these were not imports. Instead, towns protected the industry.[57] Meanwhile a city such as Antwerp listed 2,291 retailers (excluding peddlers) in 1700 for about 70,000 inhabitants, which means that each retailer supplied thirty-one local customers with their wares. These retailers functioned as middlemen and arbiters of well-judged taste, selling also affordable novelties such as buttons and buckles.[58]

Such improved distribution and retailing was not just a European phenomenon, as global trade became more interconnected in and between Europe, Asia, the Americas and Africa during the early modern period. In Japan, Dutch imports such as felted wool no longer remained the privilege of rural daimyos, as they had in the early seventeenth century, but – in the view of moralists – began to mark out the extravagance of the urban population.[59] As Rebecca Earle demonstrates for the Spanish Americas, historians therefore have to train themselves to understand what particular fabrics would have looked like and where they would have come from in order to detect syncretic dress habits in early modern artistic depictions. It is not sufficient for historians, in other words, to simply read regulations. They need to develop material literacy through handling a broad range of textiles in collections, understand how they were made, talk to curators and equip themselves with the skills to read and interpret visual representations.[60]

---

[56] Maxine Berg, 'In Pursuit of Luxury: Global History and British Consumer Goods in the Eighteenth Century', *Past & Present* 182 (2004): 85–142; and Maxine Berg., *Luxury and Pleasure in Eighteenth-Century Britain* (Oxford: Oxford University Press, 2005).

[57] Kim Siebenhüner, 'Calico Craze? Zum geschlechtsspezifischen Konsum bedruckter Baumwollstoffe im 18. Jahrhundert. Ein Blick von England zur alten Eidgenossenschaft', *L'Homme* 27/1 (2016): 33–54.

[58] Ilja van Damme, 'Middlemen and the Creation of a "Fashion Revolution": The Experience of Antwerp in the Late Seventeenth and Eighteenth Centuries', in Beverly Lemire (ed.), *The Force of Fashion in Politics and Society: Global Perspectives from Early Modern to Contemporary Times* (Aldershot: Ashgate, 2010), 30.

[59] On the use of wool in Japan, see: Joyce Denney, 'Japan and the Textile Trade in Context', in Amelia Peck (ed.), *Interwoven Globe: The Worldwide Textile Trade, 1500–1800* (London: Thames & Hudson, 2013), 63–64.

[60] Anne Gerritsen and Giorgio Riello, 'Introduction: Writing Material Culture History', in Anne Gerritsen and Giorgio Riello (eds.), *Writing Material Culture History* (London: Bloomsbury, 2015), 1–13.

Sumptuary laws in the very act of freezing material life and detailing the admissible and the forbidden, found it difficult to cope with change, with fashion, technological invention and new products. As noted before, a constantly changing vocabulary for garments and colours made it easy for people to circumvent legislation, as sources such as inventories suggest.[61] In sixteenth-century Florence, for instance, tailors continued to direct their skills towards continuously inventing new styles of clothing and decoration.[62] Fashion was not restricted to aristocratic elites; it moved in 'multiple directions'.[63] The re-issuance of laws can be read as an attempt to keep up with times by extending the remit of the law to new goods, cloths and garments. Yet, in reading iterations of the law, one is struck by how such a task was all but impossible.

Sumptuary Laws and Gender Differences

Dress played a constitutive role in constructing gender difference in Europe from the thirteenth century onwards, as the shape of clothing changed increasingly from tunic-shaped garments for both men and women to dresses for women and tight hose and upper garments for men. Thus the gendered body was 'invented' and the visualisation of sexual difference through dress made normative.[64] Some laws began explicitly to act against cross-dressing. These policies seem peculiar to Europe, as other parts of the world allowed some unisex types of garment. Female dress at the Mughal court, for instance, consisted of loose leg garments worn below a diaphanous robe which therefore made them visible. Trousers therefore did not serve as a universal marker of gender difference.[65]

Expressions of masculine power were, of course, often significantly enhanced through distinctive dress practices. In Benin, for instance, the king enjoyed exclusive access to luxury fabrics and jewellery, while the

[61] See for instance the clothing registers cited for the city of Siena for the year 1562 by Paula Houti. They show how taffeta was an extremely popular if prohibited material. Paula Houti, 'Dress, Dissemination, and Innovation: Artisan Fashions in Sixteenth- and Early Seventeenth-Century Italy', in Evelyn Welch (ed.), *Fashioning the Early Modern*, 155–156.

[62] Elizabeth Currie, 'Diversity and Design in the Florentine Tailoring Trade, 1550–1620', in Michelle O'Malley and Evelyn Welch (eds.), *The Material Renaissance* (Manchester: Manchester University Press, 2006), 167–169.

[63] Evelyn Welch, 'Art on the Edge: Hair and Hands in Renaissance Italy', *Renaissance Studies* 23 (2008): 268.

[64] Odile Blanc, *Parades et Parures. L'invention du corps de mode à la fin du Moyen Age* (Paris: Éditions Gallimard, 1997).

[65] Rosemary Crill, *The Fabric of India* (London: V&A Publishing, 2015), 106.

cut of garments remained irrelevant. Meanwhile nudity among boys represented their subordination to elder males, and only when their initiation was complete were they allowed to become consumers of dress, jewellery or umbrellas as high-status accessories. German and English sumptuary laws typically rewarded male political participation with the privilege of greater sumptuousness. This identified male honour above all with political influence and wealth, and female honour with sexual restraint and belonging to a status-dominant male-headed household.

Male expressions of power through dress could be restricted at specific conjunctures if they seemed overly excessive. The enormous ruffs that made their wearers more imposing and signalled wealth and leisure in the late sixteenth and early seventeenth centuries were criticised as signs of excess and effeminacy when worn by men. In Spain, the size and adornment of men's ruffs were restricted at numerous times between the 1580s and 1620s. They were first restricted to a maximum width of seven centimetres. Yet by 1600 a considerable width of eleven centimetres was deemed legitimate, no doubt in response to countless petitions by enraged men. Spaniards nonetheless had to keep adapting, and let go of their ruffs twenty years later when Philip IV ruled that only plain collars could be worn, decorated with a stiff neckband.

Regulations could relate to gendered bodily practices, which included hair fashions. The famous Petrine reforms in Russia thus mandated 'modernisation' by prohibiting beards. Fines were so substantial that even elites were unable to pay – barbers must have been extremely happy to cater for this new clean-shaven look among the urban population. Russian priests were particularly enraged, as facial hair signalled male authority and wisdom and was therefore constitutive for the way they inhabited their office.

Sumptuary laws were more typically used to enforce gendered religious ideals among women, as when seventeenth-century Swiss magistrates imposed the wearing of traditional veils in church. Quakers and other religious groups meanwhile opposed 'gay stomachers' or excessive nudity among women in order to endorse notions of moral virtue.

Married women across societies were generally granted greater consumptive privileges than single women, although young unmarried women sometimes enjoyed particular privileges to make themselves more attractive. Swedish sumptuary laws focused their efforts on 'common women' – prostitutes – to enforce sexual morality. Philip IV of Spain cleverly allowed no one *but* prostitutes to wear the outsized, wide-hipped farthingales and low-cut bodices that had become so fashionable. The king might have followed the ancient lawgiver Zaleucus (seventh century BCE), whose reform code for the Locrian tribe in central

Greece stipulated that only courtesans should wear gold jewellery and garments with precious purple borders, so as to inspire contempt for such items. Michel de Montaigne greatly advocated this idea.[66] Yet, as Wunder remarks, the effect of such measures in Spain remains doubtful. Velasquez continued portraying courtly ladies in these farthingales, and critics claimed that travellers would mistake honourable women for prostitutes.

Much the most difficult question to answer in any generalised way is to what extent laws in fact constrained men and women, irrespective of their social and marital status, in different ways. A crucial result of the research presented in this volume is that no clear-cut geographical pattern can be identified. Martha Howell's notion that legislators 'in northern lands did not typically concentrate ... on women in writing their sumptuary laws' turns out to be too general.[67] Instead, we can identify three patterns: most legislation in specific countries tended to focus either predominantly on women, predominantly on men or jointly on men and women. Switzerland is the most notorious case in point: its extensive regulation focused mostly on women. These laws were tightly linked to a defence of Swiss Republicanism which equated self-control with an anti-sensual, hard and military masculinity and frugality. Well into the eighteenth century, hundreds of women in Basel, Berne, Geneva and Zurich had to pay fines for appearing overly sumptuous. Fathers had to appear in court to justify their daughters' clothing, and this in turn meant that households would have discussed decisions about spending on headdresses or fabrics with care. Dress was treated as a highly political issue in order to defend equality in the confederation.

This means that Switzerland had more in common with Italy and the Ottoman world, where sumptuary legislation had always been primarily directed against women, than with England, which for its part had much in common with Sweden, Spain and Portugal. Ottoman social controls remained centred on women well into the nineteenth century and remained dependent on male members of the family to defend them in court, as women remained legal minors for most of their lives. In the eighteenth century fashionable items such as wide collars or light-coloured coats were legislated against as symbols of the moral disfiguration of Ottoman society, signalling social impropriety and irreligion as well as economic profligacy. Fashionable women in Italy, by contrast, were allowed to declare their goods and, as Muzzarelli suggests,

---

[66] de Montaigne, *The Complete Essays*, No. 43. 'On Sumptuary Law', 300.
[67] Howell, *Commerce before Capitalism*, 211.

husbands presumably paid fines as a type of luxury tax, drawing on their wives' dowries.

English women, by contrast, were not mentioned in Henry VIII's three acts of apparel after 1510, although it was expected that they would wear the same fabrics as their fathers or husbands.[68] As in Portugal, the behaviour of women was regarded as a domestic matter and was left largely unregulated by the law, although more evidence has recently emerged to show that English dress was regulated sporadically after sumptuary legislation fell out of use in 1604. In 1611, for instance, London's Common Council concerned itself with appropriate clothing for apprentices and maid-servants in order to prohibit heels, silk-gowns, ruffs and other luxurious items. Laura Gowing has found that young women could be reported to the Lord Mayor for extravagance in their use of dress, as when the seamstress Apolonia Maddox reported her apprentice Frances for wearing her best clothes every day. Fine clothing was used as a tool within social hierarchies in the microcosm of daily life, and hence an apprentice cloth-worker in London in 1662 was reprimanded for wearing his hat at work.[69]

Scottish and German legal codes typically addressed both men and women. However a proclamation in April 1684 was nonetheless directed at several women in Edinburgh who had gone abroad in forbidden fabrics 'upon pretext that they are only Night-Gowns, Undress or Mantois'.[70] Maria Hayward's article in this volume therefore underlines the wider world of luxuries that had become available through the increased manufacture of fine cottons. A late seventeenth-century poem entitled 'The Ladies Petition to the Parliament against the passing of the Sumptuary Act' even demanded that 'poor born maids' in Scotland should enjoy the pleasures of light and alluring fabrics.[71] This, in other words, imagined certain luxuries and the sensations associated with them as social right.

Merchants, as we have seen, kept pushing for the extension of trade and thus the idea that masculinity and femininity were enhanced through dress. The Japanese merchant classes even cultivated a distinctive ideal of stylishness during the seventeenth century which prized richly embroidered kimonos with complicated tie-dye patterns. This linked to new spaces and venues where female fashionability was performed and valued. A 1670 fashion contest in Kyoto lauded the most fashionable

---

[68] Hayward, *Rich Apparel*, 21.
[69] Laura Gowing, 'The Manner of Submission': Gender and Demeanour in Seventeenth-Century London', *Cultural & Social History* 10/1 (2013): 36.
[70] See note 139 in Maria Hayward's Chapter 3 in this volume.
[71] Printed in full in F. J. Shaw, 'Sumptuary Legislation in Scotland', *The Juridical Review* 24 (1979): 113–115. See the contribution by Maria Hayward, p. 120.

Figure i.4 *Courtesan and Attendant in Early Spring*, by Kakondō (Japanese, active 1716–1736). Hanging scroll: ink, colour and gold on paper. 130 × 54 cm. Metropolitan Museum of Art, New York: Mary Griggs Burke Collection, Gift of the Mary and Jackson Burke Foundation, 2015. Accession Number: 2015.300.125.

lady in the realm – perhaps the earliest record for a beauty and fashion contest for women on a national scale (Figure i.4).[72]

Ethnic Difference and the Crafting of National and Global Identities

Sumptuary laws, finally, reflected and shaped understandings of ethnic difference. This volume shows that they did so in four distinct ways. First, regulations could serve to mark religious or ethnic difference. Second, they could be part of racialised policies. Third, sumptuary laws could restrict the types of dress foreigners were permitted to wear by demanding conformity to either local standards or to the regulations of their home territories. Fourth, we can chart processes that were working towards greater uniformity across the globe as a result of commercial expansion: Indian cotton clothes dressed slaves in the Caribbean and the Americas, while 'West-African chiefs prized printed cloths from the same continent', which means that 'Indian weavers and African entrepreneurs became active agents' in commerce created by the European expansion.[73]

Clothing laws were widely used across the globe to mark ethnic or religious belonging, rather than to punish sumptuousness. Jews and Muslims in Spain were required to wear special clothing to distinguish them from Christians up to 1492. Moriscos likewise had to endure such regulations during the sixteenth century, as did Jews elsewhere.[74] Ottomans expected only Muslims to wear green. Zilfi's Chapter 15 however emphasises that in practise ethnic variety expressed in local customs remained characteristic and led to a constant mixing of styles. Such laws need to be distinguished from clothing traditions. Islamic Mughals, for example, distinguished themselves from the draped Hindu style through a tailored look that fitted the upper part of tunics to the chest. They introduced tightly fitted breeches up to the ankles below the wide, lower parts of a tunic, which reached down to the knees and were tied around the waist with a belt.[75]

---

[72] Eiko Ikegami, *Bonds of Civility: Aesthetic Networks and Political Origins of Japanese Culture* (Cambridge: Cambridge University Press, 2005).

[73] Bayly, *Birth*, 19; Giorgio Riello, *Cotton: The Fabric That made the Modern World* (Cambridge: Cambridge University Press, 2013).

[74] For an outstanding recent study of Italy see Flora Cassen, *Marking the Jews: Politics, Religion and the Power of Symbols* (Cambridge: Cambridge University Press, 2017), on Moriscos see Javier Irigoyen Gracia, *Moors Dressed as Moors: Clothing, Social Distinction and Ethnicity in Early Modern Iberia* (Toronto: Toronto University Press, 2017).

[75] Carlo Marco Belfanti, 'Was fashion a European invention?', *Journal of Global History* 3/3 (2008): 423.

Racialised clothing laws can be identified in China, where the new Emperor Zhu Yuanyhang abolished 'barbarian' Mongol Yuan dress in 1368, restoring that worn by the Han Chinese. This was part of his campaign to establish his rule, and through which he shaped the hierarchies of his loyal subjects through uniformity in dress according to their status as subjects, whether official, commoner, merchant or gentry, and male or female. Still, as BuYun Chen notes, tombs show that Mongol styles persisted. In England, Henry VIII repeatedly prohibited traditional Irish dress and hairstyles.[76] He also emphasised the importance of the use of English cloth and furs for those below the rank of knights.[77] Slave women in Brazil were forbidden to wear silk and embroidery from around 1700 onwards, but no records about the implementation of these laws survive. By 1749, as we have seen, Portuguese merchants protested against any restrictions imposed on black and mulatto people in the Portuguese colonies. They pointed to the many young Portuguese women employed in the textiles trade, which sent its goods overseas to an expanding consumer market of respectable citizens. Economic interests thus facilitated politically progressive views.

In the colonial Caribbean and North America, slaves were dressed by their owners and laws sought to regulate basic attire. As in Europe, men who wore liveries and instantiated their owner's prestige were permitted to wear fine clothes, but did not own them. Slaves in Dutch Surinam by the 1760s still faced new prohibitions against the wearing of hats, shoes or stockings. As DuPlessis suggests, appropriate dress was meant to morally shape free people of colour, who were prohibited to use the same dress or jewellery as white colonisers in order to demonstrate their modesty and respect for superiors. Merchants were criticised for subverting such moral codes and hierarchies through selfish gain. Whites retained all the defining power to determine what constituted excessive apparel – and therefore allowed regulations to be created at a whim. Subtle differences served to classify people racially through accessories, as when white cuffs remained reserved for whites, and yellow cuffs and white feathers for free people. This meant that free people became racialised by appropriating white sartorial behaviour.

Colonists living in Latin America were at odds with Spanish policies that sought to foster the inclusion of Amerindians by extending Spanish customs and civilisation to them. The concern of colonisers in these societies, by contrast, was to uphold differences and construct caste and related claims through clothing. This is visible in *casta* paintings (paintings

[76] Hayward, *Rich Apparel*, 27.
[77] Ibid., 63.

Figure i.5 *From Spaniard and Morisca, Albino Girl* [6. De español y morisca, albina], casta painting by Miguel Cabrera (Mexico, c. 1715–1768), 1763. Oil on canvas, 131.13 × 105.09 cm. Los Angeles County Museum of Art. Purchased with funds provided by Kelvin Davis in honour of the museum's 50th anniversary and partial gift of Christina Jones Janssen in honour of the Gregory and Harriet Jones Family: M.2014.223.

that imagine the mixing of people of different racial backgrounds) like the one in Figure i.5, which shows a Spaniard and a Morisca (a Muslim converted to Christianity) and their offspring. A clear sense of sartorial conspicuousness is conveyed in the lavish calico skirt with floral motifs, the embroidered cuffs, the pearl earrings and the Mexican shawl (*rebozo*) worn by the lady. The Spanish man is depicted wearing a sleeveless leather coat with attached red sleeves and next to him is an expensive silver-inlay Spanish gun. Sumptuary laws became more restrictive in the seventeenth century than they had been during Philip II's reign, while the colonised continued to fight for their right to dress as they liked and proudly wore syncretic fashions which served to express aspirations globally in more uniform ways.

Although foreign travel was often seen to be particularly corrupting by European commentators, the liberties of foreign citizens were usually treated with care. For example Swedish authorities generously made exemptions for resident foreigners, many of whom were German and Dutch, but ordered them to dress according to their estate in their home country, which would have been unclear to many of them. Swedes, in turn, sometimes pretended to be foreign. French fashion was frequently identified as licentious in cut, as when a Dutch moralist worried about women who wore little crosses between their partially uncovered breasts, 'as Christ hanging between two murderers'.[78] Russia promulgated prohibitions against the dress of foreigners in terms of its cut rather than its incorporation of foreign fabrics, which were extensively imported during the seventeenth century. In 1701, the Petrine government promulgated a new law requiring urban citizens to wear German, Saxon or French dress, a unique case in which the foreign was no longer feared as corrupting, but rendered normative.

Conclusion: Modernity and the 'Right to Dress'

Sumptuary laws gradually disappeared towards the end of the early modern period, although, as this volume has stressed, in some places they had never been adopted or implemented at all. England and the Low Countries had abandoned the enforcement of sumptuary legislation by the early seventeenth century. Across the rest of Europe, sumptuary legislation acts became less frequent and more limited in their scope. The last European sumptuary laws were passed in Poland in 1776 and in Bavaria in 1818.[79] Consumption nonetheless continued to be regulated through fiscal measures, the regulation of production, as well as the quality of manufacture and present-day competition law. This framework differs significantly from medieval and early modern state regulation. Modern states might intervene in regulating products – for instance the salt and sugar content in our food – but have left the consumption of food or dress to the private realm. Schools, clubs, religious orders, some university colleges and companies in turn impose rules about how to dress 'appropriately' on their employees and members, yet they possess limited legal authority to govern collective choices.

---

[78] See Adam Clulow's Chapter 11 in this volume, on the Netherlands.
[79] Harte, 'State Control', 133; Ross, 'Sumptuary Laws in Europe', 383.

The essays in this volume chart a long history of debate and negotiation on, and contestation of, how much people should be allowed to spend. Unlike previous research which has stressed the formal limitations imposed by sumptuary laws, we treat them as fluid and responsive to societal concerns. Today, we witness the ongoing contestation of formal and informal clothing norms to demarcate social, gender and ethnic identities. Sumptuary laws might no longer be endorsed by states – at least in the West – but a 'right to dress' in the broader terms of the 8th Brumaire, allowing a person, regardless of their sex, to wear what they find 'pleasing', has still not been fully attained.

Rather than locate a turning point, we might wish to understand the gradual shaping of the idea of an inalienable 'right to dress' during early modernity instead. Toby Green's Chapter 18 on sumptuary laws in West Africa offers an important counterpoint in this respect, as it calls attention to the practices allowing rulers to monopolise luxury and use sumptuary laws as a form of authority and control over subjects. This contrasts with the trajectory followed not just by Europe but also by China, Japan and North and Latin America, where luxury, fashion and conspicuous consumption – all areas that sumptuary rules attempted to regulate – created great social dynamism in the medieval and early modern period. Dress, as sixteenth-century Milanese merchants reminded the magistrate, created industries, industrious subjects and urban wealth as a resource in times of war. Eighteenth-century Portuguese merchants told the king that his 1749 law, which excluded black and mulatto people from wearing sumptuous dress in Brazil, would damage trade and undermine political support. By the nineteenth century, Japanese villagers as much as townspeople ridiculed sumptuary legislation as the 'three days laws'. In all these ways, the aspirational consumption of dress across the globe became a vital motor of social, cultural, economic and political change which the following contributions discuss in detail.

Part I

Sumptuary Laws in Medieval and Early Modern Europe

1   The Right to Dress: Sartorial Politics in Germany, c. 1300–1750

Ulinka Rublack

Introduction

In the first book of his famous *Essays*, Michel de Montaigne reflected on how humans should be valued. Not through their 'finery', the sixteenth-century French writer opined, but by the beauty of their soul and hence their moral conduct. Clothing and its accessories deceived: 'As one of the old writers amusingly put it: "Do you know why you think he is so tall? You are including his high heels!"'[1] Montaigne saw fashion as a driver of inequality. Yet his contemporaries were fascinated by fashionable goods. Urbanisation brought with it more concentrated markets and greater social differentiation. It led to the proliferation of marketing strategies, as well as the production of dress items across a broad spectrum of value which encouraged the purchase of small luxury items or imitations of precious fabrics across society. Fashion innovation thus was not restricted to aristocratic elites – as early as the thirteenth century, German moralists could satirise that peasants dressed like knights and wore Venetian gloves when ploughing the fields.[2] This was obviously exaggerated, but there is no doubt that tailors and mercers invented new styles affordable for their diverse clientele, and Italian merchants in Germany made profitable business by trading semi-luxuries.[3] In the early 1500s even Erasmus wondered how fellow humanists could 'be dogmatic about the correct language for ancient garments' since in his own lifetime he had 'witnessed so many changes of fashion'.[4]

[1] Michel de Montaigne, *The Complete Essays*, ed. and trans. M. A. Screech (Harmondsworth: Penguin, 1987), 289, No. 42, 'On the inequality there is between us'.
[2] Jan Keupp, *Die Wahl des Gewandes: Mode, Macht und Möglichkeitssinn in Gesellschaft und Politik des Mittelalters* (Sigmaringen: Jan Thorbecke Verlag, 2010), 50.
[3] Fernand Braudel, *The Mediterranean and the Mediterranean World in the Age of Philip II*, vol.1, trans. S. Reynolds (New York: William Collins, 1972), 213; G. Aubin, 'Bartolomäus Viatis. Ein Nürnberger Großkaufmann vor dem Dreißigjährigen Krieg', Vierteljahreszeitschrift für Sozial-und Wirtschaftsgeschichte, 33 (1940), 145–157.
[4] Desiderius Erasmus, *The Collected Works: Correspondence* (Toronto: University of Toronto Press, 1974), x: 340, No. 1479.

We therefore need to restore colour and detail to our image of dress in the early modern period. Criminal records can open a window onto the clothing of common artisans. In 1527, for instance, a baker arrested as an 'Anabaptist' – a loose religious grouping of men and women with radical ideas – testified that he had purchased a red leg garment with a blue gown and a small yellow cap at a second-hand market in the east German town of Erfurt. Their leader wore a similarly colourful ensemble: a long-tailed hooded cloak with multicoloured buttons, a blue doublet, red hose and yellow garters.[5] None of this was unusual. A radical political pamphlet published during that very same year set out that cities should be reduced to ruins to transform Christian life. Everyone was to live in villages. Property was to be held in common and people would only wear garments they could produce 'in the village – white, grey, black, blue'.[6] This vision of communal clothing in restrained colours remained marginal. It clearly would have transformed the religious radicals' own look.

Fashionable clothing and colours thus continued to be signal media of symbolic communication across German society as it divided into Protestant and Catholic lands after the Peace of Augsburg in 1555.[7] In 1500, the German lands of the Holy Roman Empire numbered around 10 million people, and this figure continued to grow steadily to 16–17 million until the Thirty Years' War (1618–1648). The pressure on resources was intense. By 1538 one chronicler remarked that there was such a surplus of people that 'villages and towns run together'. Germany's economy was highly commercialised.[8] It was also increasingly interconnected with European and overseas trade. The Augsburg accountant Matthäus Schwarz and his son Veit Konrad, alongside their colleagues at the Fugger merchant company, provide a powerful example of innovative communities of taste among young professional men from the 1520s to the 1560s, who sourced clothing for each other from Italy

---

[5] Kat Hill, *Baptism, Brotherhood, and Belief in Reformation Germany: Anabaptism and Lutheranism, 1525–1585* (Oxford: Oxford University Press, 2015), 60–61.

[6] Michael G. Baylor ed., *The Radical Reformation* (Cambridge: Cambridge University Press, 1991), 213.

[7] See the findings of Kirsten O. Frieling, *Sehen und gesehen werden: Kleidung an Fürstenhöfen an der Schwelle vom Mittelalter zur Neuzeit (ca. 1450–1530)* (Sigmaringen: Jan Thorbecke Verlag, 2013), 293; Andreas Krass, *Geschriebene Kleidung: Höfische Identität als literarisches Spiel* (Tübingen: Niemeyer, 2006); Jan Keupp, *Die Wahl*; Ulinka Rublack, *Dressing Up: Cultural Identity in Early Modern Germany* (Oxford: Oxford University Press, 2010); Jutta Zander-Seidel (ed.), *In Mode: Kleider und Bilder aus Renaissance und Frühbarock* (Nürnberg: Germanisches Nationalmuseum, 2015); Jutta Zander-Seidel, *Textiler Hausrat: Kleidung und Haustextilien in Nürnberg von 1500–1650* (Munich: Deutscher Kunstverlag, 1990).

[8] Thomas A. Brady, *German Histories in the Age of Reformations, 1400–1650* (Cambridge: Cambridge University Press, 2009), 22–24.

Figure 1.1 Veit Konrad Schwarz, aged 18, dressed for Hans Zäch's wedding; *Book of Clothes*, II 34, 1560. Schwarz notes the substantial sums of money he has paid his tailor. 23.5 x 16 cm. Herzog Anton Ulrich-Museum Braunschweig, Kunstmuseum des Landes Niedersachsen.

to Antwerp and thought carefully about collective outfits to be worn at public events such as weddings (Figure 1.1).[9]

Lower down the social scale, the licence to dress boldly lured young journeymen into soldiering, which exempted them from sumptuary laws. Broadsheets depicting them, and manuscript and printed books of costume gained particular popularity in the German lands and disseminated information about a broad range of clothing styles. Print created new imaginative communities for the early modern age. To be fashionable meant to be 'up with the times', to aspire to honour, rank and

[9] Ulinka Rublack and Maria Hayward eds., *The First Book of Fashion: The Book of Clothes of Matthäus and Veit Konrad Schwarz* (London: Bloomsbury, 2015).

civility, as well as to express emotions. By 1568, the ingenious Frankfurt publishing magnate Sigmund Feyerabend printed the famous *Book of Trades*, which described many of the trades connected to dress and the range of fashionable goods they offered in some detail. In 1577, Hans Weigel's *Trachtenbuch*, the most comprehensive book of costume of men and women across the world published so far appeared in Nuremberg. It was followed in 1586 by another of Feyerabend's successful ventures – Jost Amman's *Frauentrachtenbuch*, which focused on women's dress and followed his previous work for Weigel in depicting the appearances of common people, such as Nuremberg maidservants, who braided cheap woollen hairpieces from Italy in green, purple and red into their blonde hair (Figure 1.2).[10]

As the verse and many of the images in the Book of Trades indicate, ingenious German crafting made luxurious appearances and sensations increasingly affordable. Not much of the clothing from this period survives, but some extant artefacts reveal what craftspeople and seamstresses achieved. A German felt hat from the second half of the sixteenth century, for instance, demonstrates that its elaborate technique imitated smooth, precious velvet, which was strictly regulated by sumptuary laws. Cheap felt was covered with intricate looped stitches made of black silk or woollen yarn. These tiny loops were then cut open to create a regular, soft crepe texture.[11]

None of this would have been seen as just a minor fashion trend. Around 1600, early cameralism endorsed German experiments in textile production as much as in the use of new dyes or the production of decorative ribbons. By 1622, Jakob Bornitz penned his influential treatise *On the Sufficiency of Things*, which built on Giovanni Botero's views that economic wealth underpinned a reason of state. Bornitz recommended that the textile arts should not be unduly curtailed by sumptuary laws – they produced great profits and strengthened the commonwealth. Cotton-textiles, he reported, were now manufactured by craftsmen throughout Saxony, Meissen and Prussia. Breslau craftspeople had invented a new mix of wool and linen which imitated silk. Common fabrics appeared in new forms in Silesia, Bohemia and elsewhere. Their export would generate further wealth for artisans and royal treasuries through taxation. At fairs the sale of multi-coloured and artfully woven ribbons displayed

---

[10] Both the Frauentrachtenbuch and the Book of Trades were published in Latin and German editions; for an edition and translation of the latter see Theodore K. Rabb, *A Sixteenth-Century Book of Trades: Das Ständebuch* (Palo Alto: Sposs, 2009). For a discussion of Weigel see Rublack, *Dressing Up*, 146–163 and 248–252.

[11] Zander-Seidel, *In Mode*, No.66, p.128, the reference to the Saxon hat in the text is from Veit Konrad, not Matthäus Schwarz.

Figure 1.2 Hans Weigel, *Trachtenbuch* (1577). Nuremberg woman attending an invitation to a meal. The Master and Fellows of Trinity College, Cambridge.

human inventiveness. For Bornitz and his followers, changing 'fashions and luxury goods demonstrated the potential of human ingenuity and innovation'.[12]

Such recent findings question Daniel Roche's and Jan de Vries's contention that the period before 1700 needs to be characterised as an old rule of dress. Roche argued that dress during this 'sartorial ancien régime' was inert and immobile, 'especially among the lower classes and in the countryside'. As clothes clearly marked a person's social position, sumptuary laws imposed 'conformity to custom on everyone' and there was an 'extreme desire for control'. Roche regarded these characteristics as diluted 'to some extent' by the 'growth of the urban economy and of fashion and the subsequent confusion of ranks' during the seventeenth

---

[12] Vera Keller, *Knowledge and the Public Interest, 1575–1725* (Cambridge: Cambridge University Press, 2015), 116–117, and the quote on 117.

century. Yet he followed Fernand Braudel's assertion that these changes only accelerated from 1700 onwards.[13]

Jan de Vries's influential 2008 account of the 'industrious revolution' still followed this historiography. He regarded the period prior to 1700 as a 'drab sartorial world', in which white linen colours and expensively dyed woollens in red or bright blue 'formed rare exceptions' to demonstrate their wearers' exceptional status. This explains why dress plays such an insignificant role in this landmark history of what people 'aspired to acquire' during the sixteenth and seventeenth centuries.[14] Research on Germany has sometimes adopted this perspective. Michael North's study of consumption in the Enlightenment affirms that 'the discourse on fashion was new for the eighteenth century'.[15] Other researchers agree with Roche's claim that legislation 'obsessively' targeted dress. 'When safely controlled', Martha Howell argues, sumptuary legislation 'seemed to guarantee the good society: not only to signal rank and thus secure social hierarchy but also to stabilize gender roles, assure appropriate sexuality, encourage fiscal restraint, and repress pride'.[16] In addition, Howell holds that such laws forced people to differentiate between their outer, material, and inner immaterial selves and thus produced subjectivities. Alan Hunt argues that sumptuary laws enshrined a new mode of 'governmentality' which marked a step towards modernity as they underpinned the notion that the state was to morally regulate its citizenry.[17]

---

[13] Daniel Roche, *The Culture of Clothing. Dress and Fashion in the Ancien Regime*, trans. Jean Birrell (Cambridge: Cambridge University Press, 1994), 56. Braudel had posited in 1979 that rural dress was virtually immobile for centuries. He briefly commented on 'curious' Dutch paintings with market scenes which revealed that bourgeois clothing changed a great deal, but principally regarded only court and aristocratic dress as subject to fashion prior to the eighteenth century. Fernand Braudel, *Civilisation and Capitalism 15th–18th Centuries, Vol. 2: The Wheels of Commerce*, trans. Sian Reynolds (London: Harper Collins, 1982), 352.

[14] Jan de Vries, *The Industrious Revolution. Consumer Behavior and the Household Economy, 1650 to the Present* (Cambridge: Cambridge University Press, 2008), 135. The French sociologist Pierre Bourdieu meanwhile argued that common people continued to actively resist the aestheticisation of clothing and a capitalist grind which constantly produces new needs through fashion. Their clothing style is positively marked by 'realism' and a functional rather than symbolic use of dress; see the apt criticism by Hans Medick, *Weben und Überleben in Laichingen 1650–1900. Lokalgeschichte als Allgemeine Geschichte* (Göttingen: Vandenhoeck, 1996), 381.

[15] Michael North, *Material Delight and the Joy of Living': Cultural Consumption in the Age of Enlightenment in Germany*, trans. Pamela Selwyn (Aldershot: Ashgate, 2008), 46.

[16] Martha Howell, *Commerce before Capitalism in Europe, 1300–1600* (Cambridge: Cambridge University Press, 2010), 236.

[17] Alan Hunt, *Governance of the Consuming Passions: A History of Sumptuary Law* (Houndsmill: Macmillan, 1996).

This raises the crucial question of whether sumptuary laws were ever prominent enough to shape people's awareness as a determining factor and whether they were 'safely controlled' for any extended period. How can we think about the role of the state in relation to economic, social and ideological factors as motors of change? It is currently difficult to suggest a clear answer, as the literature on German sumptuary legislation, the economic policies and practices in relation to clothing trades, is far more limited than might be assumed and no recent study of these sumptuary law exists. Key arguments in the literature can be traced back to outdated studies which have been misinterpreted. Hunt's interest in the rise of governmentality thus was inspired by Marc Raeff's 1983 monograph *The Well Ordered Police-State*, which surveyed ordinances regulating religion, health, education, building, material progress and administration across several of the German states. Raeff briefly discussed sumptuary laws to point out that eighteenth-century ordinances became less detailed and severe in order to allow for greater consumption, social mobility and individual expression.[18] Hunt, by contrast, argued that sumptuary legislation helped to pave the way for modernity through *regulation*. Yet to capture German sumptuary legislation Hunt relied on Kent Greenfield's 1918 study of Nuremberg. Greenfield's slim volume was based on two printed compilations of ordinances, which mostly focused on laws against sumptuousness at weddings and the period up to 1500.[19] His actual conclusions contradicted Hunt's later argument. Nuremberg laws after 1500 became more liberal. They displayed, as Greenfield notes 'a tendency to be less exacting in their denials, and more liberal in their concessions ... The intervals between the surviving laws are too long and the dates of the laws too uncertain to make it possible to trace with great accuracy the changing views reflected in them'.[20]

Clearly, more research is needed to assess the nature and impact of local as much as state legislation. This article first maps out evidence for shifts in the intentions of regulation during the Middle Ages and six-teenth century. It then focuses on the *Imperial* regulation for the German lands, as they signalled political concerns which were to be taken up in territorial and urban legislation. I next turn to evidence for legisla-tion and its enforcement in individual territories and in cities. My argu-ment is that German legislation often made very generous allowances,

---

[18] Marc Raeff, *The Well-Ordered Police State: Social and Institutional Change through Law in the Germanies and Russia, 1600–1800* (New Haven: Yale University Press, 1983), 252; 80–81.

[19] Kent Roberts Greenfield, *Sumptuary Laws of Nürnberg: a study in paternal government* (Unpublished PhD thesis, Johns Hopkins University, 1915).

[20] Greenfield, *Sumptuary law*, 133–135.

was hardly ever 'safely controlled' for any length of time and in many areas did not exist or was not enforced at all. This makes it problematic to argue that restrictions became a major historical force which shaped people's perceptions of themselves, enshrined rational economic policies, a modernising regime of social regulation, or hindered modernisation by making the economy more static. Rather, sumptuary legislation points to possibilities for people to dress in relation to their status as well as aesthetic aspirations, which made dress such an important aspect of contemporary visual culture and the 'micro-management' of social standing through the acquisition of aspirational goods.[21]

The Late Medieval Background

Medieval sumptuary laws initially aimed to curtail expenses people lavished on baptisms, weddings and funerals. During the early thirteenth century, magistrates in a number of German towns in addition began to issue ordinances against overly sumptuous dress. Lament about immorality, luxurious dress and the fear of divine punishment grew after the Black Death, in the second half of the fourteenth century. Military defeat as much as epidemics were blamed on new excesses in dress. Sumptuary legislation reflected a growing concern for social regulation from the fourteenth century in response to plague, famine, extended warfare and greater mobility. It equally admonished all citizens of whatever rank or simply contrasted nobles and peasants to save people from divine punishment for the sin of *superbia*.[22] Ninety-five urban ordinances can be identified for the period 1400–1449, and the first territorial sumptuary regulation also dates to this period. In total 140 ordinances were issued during the second half of the fifteenth century, and these were followed by 120 ordinances in the period 1500–1549.[23]

During the late fifteenth century, regulations for the first time began to differentiate between people of different social ranks and set out restrictions and allowances for each group. Frankfurt was the first city to adopt this new format in 1488, to counteract impoverishment. Higher-ranking local women involved in trade, who felt degraded in relation to patrician women, immediately re-negotiated them, so that a new

---

[21] For the term 'micro-management' in this context see Giora Sternberg, *Status Interaction during the Reign of Louis XIV* (Oxford: Oxford University Press, 2014).

[22] On the moral character of legislation before 1500 see Keupp, *Wahl des Gewandes*, 51–75.

[23] Neithard Bulst, 'Zum Problem städtischer und territorialer Kleider-, Aufwands- und Luxusgesetzgebung in Deutschland (13. bis Mitte des 16. Jahrhundert)', in André Gouron and Albert Rigaudière (eds.), *Renaissance du pouvoir législatif et genèse de l'Etat*, (Montpellier: Socapress, 1988), 29–57, here 44; 29; 35.

ordinance followed in 1489.[24] Neithard Bulst, the leading specialist on sumptuary legislation in this period, regards this new character of legislation as a mark of imperial regulation and advanced state building, as the first imperial sumptuary laws in 1495 likewise distinguished different social ranks.[25] Sumptuary laws were now designed to 'fix clear social boundaries' as well as secure social privilege. Some ordinances in addition regulated that dress had to be gender specific, and thus rigidly separated feminine from masculine dress. Sumptuary laws need to be seen in relation to the immense growth of regulation during this time, which affected common people and marginal groups such as Jews, beggars and prostitutes.[26] The fact that legislation increasingly reiterated previous laws indicates the authorities' commitment, although there is little indication that fines (as the most common form of punishment for sumptuousness) were actually collected. It is therefore unlikely that magistrates were motivated by fiscal concerns and generated a luxury tax, in which case they would have been keen to collect these fines.[27] Ordinances were legitimised as acts designed to protect the future of communities and thus 'the common good'. They were underpinned by the perception that church legislation was ineffective, although some clerics were extremely active in preaching against luxurious dress.

Bulst convincingly argues that sumptuary legislation was nonetheless counterproductive in attempting to ensure social order by fixing rank. Rather, these regulations unintentionally set out rules to identify how social boundaries could be challenged and offered a sartorial map toward social ascent.[28] The question for Bulst remains whether people's growing desire for luxuries fuelled the authorities' desire to discipline the population, or whether the authorities' growing pressure motivated people's desire for greater freedom to express their specific rank by sartorial means.[29] What needs to be underlined is that Bulst's as well as Jan Keupp's more recent work on the German Middle Ages clearly support the argument that fashion across social ranks had already become a marked feature of this society. Moreover, laws were potentially not just restrictive but *productive* in providing a 'map towards social ascent' that impacted upon individual strategies of social identification.

---

[24] I am very grateful to Julia Schmidt-Funke, of Jena University, for letting me read her Habilitation which analyses the regulation of consumption in Frankfurt, and will be published in 2018.

[25] Bulst, 'Zum Problem', 45–47.

[26] Bulst, 'Zum Problem', 31–33.

[27] Bulst, 'Zum Problem', 55.

[28] Bulst, 'Zum Problem', 58.

[29] Bulst, 'Zum Problem', 57.

Dress and Imperial Politics

The emergence of the Holy Roman Empire as a body which issued regulations for the German lands and addressed itself to territories and towns means that the Empire (rather than individual cities) needs to be considered for a discussion of German sumptuary law from 1500 onwards. This is important to bear in mind in comparison to Italy, where legislation remained entirely civic and territorial.

Discussions at the imperial level must have been influenced by the fact that dress had been increasingly used as tool of symbolic politics at major and minor courts throughout the Holy Roman Empire since the late fifteenth century.[30] Barbara Stollberg-Rilinger has influentially demonstrated how participants at imperial and territorial courtly gatherings mobilised symbols to uphold and challenge reciprocal expectations about the functioning of the Holy Roman Empire as institutional order. Her work follows cultural historians and sociologists by highlighting that institutions present themselves above all through rituals of investiture and honour, and through the use of titles, images or architecture. Symbolic means imbued past institutions with an aura of necessity. Yet these symbols did not necessarily have the same and intended effects. This made the public political sphere of this period highly dynamic. It was constituted by competing claims and symbolic registers, so that by closely examining symbolic communication we can understand politics.[31]

Dress and its colours formed a central part of these symbolic languages. It constituted evolving understandings of the political order through the visualisation of hierarchies and offered identifications which changed through time.[32] The politics of dress therefore was not peripheral for those involved in law-making on an imperial level – it was integral to their own existence. As Kirsten Frieling has recently underlined, the precise ranking of German territorial rulers was not fixed, apart from the privileged position of those who elected the emperor. Hierarchies had to be constituted, negotiated and defended face-to-face. Written accounts of these encounters dwelt at length on appearances to provide a particular memory of a person with his or her claim to magnificence and

---

[30] Frieling, *Sehen und gesehen werden*.

[31] Stollberg-Rilinger, *Des Kaisers alten Kleider: Verfassungsgeschichte und Symbolsprache des Alten Reichs* (Munich: Beck, 2008); see also her textbook *Rituale*, (Frankfurt-am-Main: Campus, 2013), 100–114. This approach has led to many fruitful explorations in related areas; see, for instance, Peter Burschel and Christine Vogel (eds.), *Die Audienz: Ritualisierte Kulturkontakte in der Frühen Neuzeit* (Vienna: Böhlau, 2014).

[32] Keupp, *Wahl des Gewandes*, 149, 227, 284–287.

distinction. At weddings, sumptuous clothes were changed several times each mark-graves day and those who wanted to show off their alliances coordinated particular ensembles in advance. This in turn meant that rulers were driven to stipulate increasingly what was to be worn by those attending significant events. Emperor Maximilian in 1495 clearly advised on what types of robes and furs archbishops, dukes and mark-graves should wear at the Imperial Diet. Particular cuts, materials and colours continued to be used as marks of distinction, and this in turn meant that everyone's eyes were trained to pick up on these refined differences to decode specific claims.

The electors and dukes were increasingly elevated as a visually homogeneous group of superior rank. More formalised rules for this group were intended to prevent further rivalries – at least at imperial gatherings – but could also lead to further conflicts about precedence and an individual's disregard of these rules. Meanwhile international marriage alliances continued to play a crucial role in introducing new and diverse fashions to German courts, and Frieling argues that this diversity coexisted with new trends for the homogenisation of appearances among the ruling elites. Liveries greatly gained in importance as rulers attempted to link their claims over subjects and the nobility to these vestimentary codes. Around 1500, therefore, dress had become a vital tool of governance.[33]

German imperial ordinances relating to sumptuary legislation date from 1495, 1497, 1498, 1500, 1518 and 1521. They culminated in two imperial 'police ordinances' which included paragraphs on the regulation of dress in 1530 and 1548. A final, almost identical version was issued in 1577. These imperial ordinances in turn manifestly influenced some urban and territorial laws. Yet it is crucial to underline from the outset that the renewed 1577 Imperial Police Ordinance remained unchanged until the end of the Holy Roman Empire in 1806, although declarations of 1648 and 1792 announced the intention to rework it.[34] The period 1495–1548 marks the high point of concerns about the expression of rank through dress. Afterwards, the Empire's regulation on sumptuary law would remain static for 231 years. It can therefore be concluded that the regulation of dress after 1577 was certainly no longer presented as an integral part of policy making and that there was no pressure from the Imperial Estates to update laws. Contrary to Hunt's and Howell's

---

[33] Frieling, *Sehen und Gesehen werden*. For the following period see Claudia Schnitzer, *Höfische Maskeraden: Funktion und Ausstattung von Verkleidungsdivertissements an deutschen Höfen der Frühen Neuzeit* (Tübingen: Niemeyer, 1999).

[34] Matthias Weber, *Die Reichspolizeiordnungen von 1530, 1548 und 1577. Historische Einführung und Edition* (Frankfurt-am-Main: Klostermann, 2002), 13.

claims, sumptuary legislation was not a marked feature of imperial governmentality and was far from obsessive. The Empire's top elites had effectively created protective laws to reproduce their privileges.[35] Moreover, craft innovation, merchant lobbying and mercantilist interests in innovative textile production co-existed uneasily with moral fears about declining hierarchies of rank.

1530: The Empire's Sumptuary Moment

The 1530 Imperial Police Ordinance (IPO) therefore needs to be considered in detail, as it documents an exceptional moment when sumptuary legislation really was made to matter in imperial politics, to ensure social order. Its preparation had been begun in 1521, and a committee further refined drafts for discussions, which led to the ratification of the ordinance in November 1530. The ordinance was printed in 1531, in the form of a pamphlet numbering thirty-one pages. These comprised thirty-nine *unnumbered* paragraphs, which therefore would have been difficult to reference and refer to. This materiality of print needs to be taken into consideration if we wish to assess the effectiveness of legislation. If we number them retrospectively, we find that articles one to seven focused on blasphemy, while articles nine to twenty-two concerned sumptuary legislation.[36] This means that twenty-three of the thirty-nine articles focused on dress.

Emperor Charles V's preamble for the 1530 ordinance stated fiscal and social reasons for the importance of sumptuary legislation: growing luxury among 'knights, the nobility, burghers and peasants' had extracted money from Germany to pay for the importing of 'gold cloth, velvet, damask, silk satin, foreign cloth, precious bonnets, pearls and gold' used in dress. Nobody was able to distinguish princes and peasants, or anyone else. This judgement was reiterated in 1548 and 1577.[37] Article nine specified that everyone was to be dressed according to his or her 'rank, honour', but, significantly, also in relation to 'wealth', in order to clearly signal different ranks.

Peasants

Common peasants and day-labourers stood at the bottom of this hierarchy, and only the 1530 ordinance provided instructions on restrictions

---

[35] See also the chapter by Sturtewagen and Blondé in this volume.
[36] Weber, *Reichspolizeiordnungen*, 27.
[37] Weber, *Reichspolizeiordnungen*, 132.

and allowances. Yet even here the rules were surprisingly generous, and underline the central aim of preventing excessive expense in relation to income. Men in this group were first told to wear fabric made in the German lands, but immediately granted that second-hand (*außgescheyden*) velvets or Netherlandish lighter fabrics could be worn. Hose, for the legs, could be made from fabric imported from Mechelen and Lier in Flanders. Doublets were not to have voluminous sleeves – this left scope for interpretation – and not to be slashed. The cut and quality of linen shirts was not mentioned, with the exception of prohibitions against any precious embroidery on the collar which used gold- or silver-thread, pearls or silks. Gowns were generously allowed to have six folds and reach down to half of the lower calf. Placards (a stomacher or covering to infill the front of a low-cut doublet, called *Brusttuch*, for which precious materials were often used), were prohibited, and so were ostrich feathers, silk points to lace the hose, or wide bonnets and 'openly cut' shoes, which refers to the shape of horn-shoes fashionable at the time. Dyes were left unregulated.

Women and children from these low social groups had to keep to the same regulations, and were particularly reminded that this ruled out wearing collars or veils with gold borders, gold, silver or silken girdles, coral paternoster as well as any decorative items of gold, silver or pearl. Unmarried women, however, were allowed to wear one silken hair-band. The wearing of fur was regulated only for peasant wives, who were prohibited from wearing anything other than low-quality furs from lambs and goats, without any borders or trims.[38] There was no differentiation between peasant and day labourer, and nothing was said about those who did not fit the notion of common peasant. The regulation for peasants, in sum, left much scope for colourful dress and for fine linens as well as fabrics produced in Germany, and were characterised by allowances as much as restrictions.

Burghers

The 1530 ordinance next discussed burghers and urban inhabitants in general, who were sub-divided into three groups. Common burghers, artisans and mercers stood at the bottom. None of them were permitted to wear gold- or silver-thread, pearls, velvet or silk, any slashed or trimmed clothes, bonnets, marten fur or any other precious fur, but instead allowed fox, polecat or lamb. Journeymen and servants in the

---

[38] Weber, *Reichspolizeiordnungen*, 142.

crafts were told not to use metal-thread, silk or ostrich feathers, slashed clothing, and otherwise told to keep to the rules for male craftsmen. Political participation equated social promotion. Craftsmen elected to the magistracy were allowed to dress as merchants.[39]

Burgher wives and children were to observe these same rules. However, wives were permitted to wear one golden ring worth the considerable sum of five or six florins, though without any precious stone. One collar could even be sewn with silk, and one veil worn with a golden trim up to two fingers' width. These women were also very generously allowed a damask or silk-satin partlet as well as a girdle up to the value of ten florins which could display silver metalwork. Unmarried women in this group were additionally permitted to wear a velvet band with silver decoration. The ordinance thus served to heighten the prestige of marriage for women of this lowest rank in the urban community and generally honoured as much as announced women's decorative presence in the city. To be well dressed in this period meant to demonstrate civility (Figure 1.3).

As in the case of peasants, gowns were singled out as the most representative garment for merchants and tradespeople. They were prohibited to wear any velvet, damask, silk-satin or silk gowns, or hair nets made with gold, silver, pearls, or silk.[40] Yet they were allowed an expensive woollen gown (*schamlott*), a material which at first had been made from camel hair, but then used high quality woollens, sometimes mixed with silk or watered wool for a moisée effect. Merchants and traders were further allowed to wear golden rings and silk doublets, but not velvet or scarlet-red silk satin.

The upper limit of expenses on cloth was fixed at two florins per ell. In Augsburg the ell traditionally equated to c. 60 cm.[41] Top quality furs, such as marten and lynx, were likewise forbidden, although fur from the throat of martens (*Kelmader*) was permissible for men and fur from Siberian squirrels (*Veh*) for married women. Wives were otherwise told to keep to these same rules and not to use more than two ells of velvet, silk, silk-satin or damask (120 cm) for trimmings on their dresses. Their girdles were not to be worth more than twenty florins, which was a very substantial sum. A border on their velvets was to measure no more than four fingers in width. Velvet and silk partlets with gild closures likewise could not be worth more than twenty florins. Daughters and other unmarried women were allowed hair-bands worth ten florins.[42]

[39] Weber, *Reichspolizeiordnungen*, 143.
[40] Rublack and Hayward (eds.), *The First Book of Fashion*.
[41] *Augsburger Stadtlexikon*, online source.
[42] Weber, *Reichspolizeiordnungen*, 144.

Figure 1.3 Herman Tom Ring? *Portrait of a Lady Aged 29.* Oil painting, 1582. Note the rich jewellery typical of wealthy citizens. Victoria and Albert Museum.

A key feature of this regulation therefore was to regulate excessive expense on dress, in the traditional spirit of sumptuary legislation, and with a particular focus on the most expensive imported fabrics, furs, costly metals and pearls, as well as cochineal dye. Yet, despite their expense, damask, silk and velvet could be used for smaller dress items as well as for borders on dresses. As a consequence, trade in these precious textiles remained considerable.

Magistrates and Patricians

Finally, the law identified a top group of magistrates and patricians, who did not earn a living through their own labour but lived off rents and interest. They were to keep to the same rules as merchants, but in addition permitted to have their *schamlott* woollen gowns trimmed with the substantial length of up to three ells (c. 180 cm) of velvet and marten-fur lining. They were allowed velvet and silk doublets, second-hand scarlet hairnets (worn below bonnets) as well as silk hairnets, and rings up to a maximum value of fifty florins. Their wives were allowed fours ells (c. 240 cm) of silk or velvet for their dresses, but no scarlet trims, a gold chain worth up to fifty florins and a girdle for up to thirty florins.[43]

The Nobility

Noblemen were allowed damask and silk as fabric for their outfits, as well as six ells (c. 360 cm) of velvet for trimmings. Golden rings and hairnets as well as golden chains threaded through with a traditional *schnürlein* – band – could be worn up to the enormous value of two hundred florins – the cost of a sizeable house at the time. Knights were allowed to wear a necklace for up to four hundred florins as well as marten lining. Married noblewomen could own four silken gowns to wear in public, one made of velvet, and the others made of damask. These could be trimmed with up to a quarter of an ell (c. 10 cm) of pearls and silver. Those married to a knight could use gold for trimmings. Every wife was permitted to own more dresses to pass on to her children, but not to wear them in public. Wives were also allowed bonnets and gold caps with up to forty florins' worth of decoration, as well as borders of gold-thread on all their apparel for up to forty florins, and jewellery in addition to rings worth up to two hundred florins.[44]

Doctors and their wives were permitted to dress freely according to their 'rank and liberty'. A final article concerned earls and lords, who were classed lower than knights, although their wives were allowed jewellery valued up to six hundred florins.[45]

Imperial Legislation after 1530

The Empire gave up on any notion of comprehensive guidance on dress in the 1548 IPO. It contained only seven articles on dress, which were most specific in relation to the upper orders, and essentially removed the bulk of sumptuary legislation. 'Citizens, peasants and other subjects' were grouped together in one article. Every local territorial ruler and urban magistrate was told to issue an ordinance within one year which would define honourable dress as well as punishments for offenders. Non-obliging authorities would be punished with a fine by

---

[43] Weber, *Reichspolizeiordnungen*, 144–145.
[44] Weber, *Reichspolizeiordnungen*, 147.
[45] Weber, *Reichspolizeiordnungen*, 147.

the Emperor.[46] An identical article was reissued in 1577, yet no initiative to punish authorities is known.[47] This final IPO comprised 38 articles, and these were numbered for the first time. The 1530 regulations for the nobility, knights, doctors, earls and lords (*Graven und Herrn*) were essentially copied, even with the same figures for the money which could be spent on fabric or jewellery – it was thus likely to have been instantly disregarded as outdated.[48]

This suggests, in sum, that considerable attention was given to sumptuary legislation in 1530, but that it quickly became clear that local ordinances with regulations specific to the population in the towns and countryside were needed to implement changes. Imperial legislation from 1548 onwards limited itself to specifying regulations for the nobility, knights and earls. They remained unadjusted, and thus were not given any further attention. These top elites effectively had created protective laws to reproduce their privilege and did not enforce any new regulation for themselves between 1530 and 1806.

Assessing Imperial Legislation

There is hence no evidence in the imperial legislation to suggest, as Howell does, that 'to judge from the quantity and the intensity of the surviving legislation, in that age a good governor had no more urgent task than to ensure that the population was appropriately attired'.[49] While the 1530 and 1548 ordinances signalled urgency, the following ordinance did much less so. 1530 stands out as the Empire's sumptuary 'moment' instead of the beginning of a movement. The significance of these imperial police ordinances nonetheless lies in the fact that they first constituted a programme of central norms which needed to be legally reinforced to ensure the 'common good' and order in a Christian polity. They were primarily directed at the imperial estates rather than the populace as such, and in turn some territorial rulers legitimised their own legislation with reference to the IPO. In Austria, Ferdinand I's 1542 first police ordinance to incorporate a regulation of dress by rank likewise copied the 1530 regulations.[50] To call these laws successful appears unjustified, given that they were already hopelessly outdated in 1577 and then remained unchanged. Austrian regulations in relation to

---

[46] Weber, *Reichspolizeiordnungen*, 181.

[47] Weber, *Reichspolizeiordnungen*, 229.

[48] Weber, *Reichspolizeiordnungen*, 181–186; 230–232.

[49] Howell, *Commerce*, 214.

[50] Gertraud Hampl-Kallbrunner, *Beiträge zur Geschichte der Kleiderordnungen mit besonderer Berücksichtigung Österreichs* (Wien: H. Geyer, 1962), 23–24 and 44.

common people were not changed until 1659 and then abandoned after 1687.[51] As in relation to the *Carolina*, Charles V's Imperial Law Code in 1530 which remained intact until 1806, the Empire's legislation simply fossilised. This is significant for any account of state-building in the period. German imperial sumptuary legislation should be regarded as neither an engine of social disciplining nor a marker of a well-governed police state. Hence it opened the way for territorial diversification and innovative mercantile policies in relation to textile products that were marketed in the German lands (Figure 1.4).

Territorial Laws

This leaves us with the question whether German territories consistently and effectively regulated expenses on appearances in order to ensure and enshrine a symbolic, material politics of social inequality in the public sphere. I shall first examine evidence for two large territories in the south of Germany and then turn to one of Germany's Catholic archbishoprics in the north of the country.

Lutheran Württemberg

Württemberg was the largest duchy in south-west Germany and joined the Lutheran Reformation in 1534. Its first police ordinance in 1549 exactly reiterated the 1530 imperial articles on clothing for common peasants and added slight variations to legislation for urban citizens and tradespeople.[52] The dukes of Württemberg frequently renewed legislation, but continued to keep regulations for the rural population close to the 1530 law while updating regulations for the urban population. Yet they mostly seem not to have enforced their local implementation through officials. Ducal officials were principally tasked with criminal offences, while lower courts were staffed by local men.[53] In the town of Leonberg, close to Württemberg's capital of Stuttgart, local court records survive dating to the late sixteenth century. Samples show that almost no cases of sumptuary excess were tried by the lower or church court.[54] Achim Landwehr has therefore argued that implementation was

---

[51] Hampl-Kallbrunner, *Kleiderordnungen*, 43, 49.
[52] Lioba Keller-Dressler, *Die Ordnung der Kleider: Ländliche Mode in Württemberg 1750–1850* (Tübingen: tvv–Verlag, 2003).
[53] For a discussion of the Württemberg legal system see Ulinka Rublack, *The Crimes of Women in Early Modern Germany* (Oxford: Oxford University Press, 1999).
[54] Achim Landwehr, *Policey im Alltag: Die Implementierung frühneuzeitlicher Policeyordnungen in Leonberg* (Frankfurt-am-Main: Klostermann, 2000), 343–345.

Figure 1.4 Hans Weigel, *Trachtenbuch* (1577). Frontispiece, L.11.33. The Master and fellows of Trinity College, Cambridge.

never at stake, but rather an insistence on the 'state's defining power of the common good'.[55]

After 1549, Württemberg's police ordinances principally repeated the same text well into the seventeenth century, and this, as we have

---

[55] Landwehr, *Policey im Alltag*, 43.

seen, was in line with stagnant imperial legislation. As Duke Frederick I took over rule in 1593, he wished the duchy's economy to grow through improvements in infrastructure, milling, water-supply, silk and linen production. His son John Frederick followed these early cameralist principles.[56] The 1621 ordinance thus repeated the 1549 police ordinance.[57] A final, new and much sharper police ordinance incorporating sumptuary laws only followed in 1712. It prohibited burghers from wearing cotton and *Indienne* garments.[58] Yet it only mentioned the economic and fiscal rationale of these regulations: not to uselessly impoverish families and deprive the state of taxation. This fifth Württemberg police ordinance was also the first to separate the people in the countryside into two groups and to distinguish nine groups altogether, including court personnel.[59] Sheilagh Ogilvie points to one campaign to implement these laws in the Black Forest town of Wildberg in 1713, which listed 110 people who had to pay fines within one year – most of them women aged between 25 and 29 who wore caps, placards or trims which were deemed too sumptuous, as they used velvet fabrics. Six offenders wore cotton fabrics. Those who found themselves in court mainly came from socially mobile bourgeois classes, whose overly sumptuous spending before marriage was seen as a threat to the social order. Ogilvie also demonstrates that women and men in some localities were occasionally disciplined for their overly sumptuous dress in church convents or local courts, and in relation to items of dress not regulated by state legislation.[60]

The duchy did not renew its sumptuary legislation after 1712, but issued a number of edicts relating to the prohibition of costly mourning dress, church dress and official dress. These could insist that proper dress needed to be worn, rather than prohibiting sumptuousness.[61] Inventories in eighteenth-century Laichingen, a small proto-industrial town, bear out that the population bought darker colours for their Sunday dress in order to comply with these regulations.[62] Light cottons with their bright

---

[56] Walter Grube, *Der Stuttgarter Landtag 1457–1957: Von den Landständen zum demokratischen Parlament* (Stuttgart: Ernst Klett, 1957), 263.
[57] See also Werner Fleischhauer, *Die Renaissance im Herzogtum Württemberg* (Stuttgart: Kohlhammer, n.d.), 339.
[58] Medick, *Weben*, 385–387.
[59] Medick, *Weben*, 43–44.
[60] Sheilagh Ogilvie, Markus Küpker, Janine Maegraith, 'Die lokale Regulierung des Konsums im frühneuzeitlichen Württemberg', in Sigrid Hirbodian, Sheilagh Ogilvie, R. Joanna Regnath (eds.), *Revolution des Fleißes, Revolution des Konsums? Leben und Wirtschaften im ländlichen Württemberg von 1650–1800* (Ostfildern: Thorbecke, 2015), 55–74.
[61] Medick, *Weben*, 387.
[62] Medick, *Weben*, 391. Correct appearances in the town-hall remained a contentious issue well into the nineteenth century.

prints became increasingly common, especially as neckerchiefs. Between 1768 and 1793, duke Carl Eugen of Württemberg even attracted traders from Germany and beyond to sell a wide variety of luxury and affordable popu-luxe items in the Lutheran territories' capital of Stuttgart during an annual fair. Female and male tradespeople vied for the best stalls and sold a mixture of cheerfully coloured fabrics alongside fans, stockings, clocks, hats, coffee pots and small items of jewellery as items of 'gallantry'. Ceramics depicting the popular fair replicated the allure of choice and spread an emotional culture which cultivated the pleasures of shopping.[63]

Catholic Bavaria

Bavaria was another sizeable as well as influential territory in the empire, and it was Catholic. In 1526, Duke Wilhelm and Duke Ludwig of Bavaria issued an extensive dress ordinance to fight the impoverishment caused by excessive sumptuousness. The ordinance distinguished eight broad status groups in seventeen articles.[64] Regulations concerning the urban and rural populations nonetheless reveal that master craftsmen in towns were generously permitted satin, silk-satin and high-quality woollen fabric for their gowns, as well as taffeta and other types of silk-taffeta (*Zendl*) for their doublets. Gold thread was not permitted on shirts, partlets, or headwear. Low-quality furs, such as fox-fur, were permitted. Wives of master craftsmen were allowed these same fabrics and trimmings from velvet and silk to up to a quarter of an ell. Silver jewellery was allowed for decorating the paternoster, and for a wedding ring, as well as two lots of silver for the girdle or dress decorations. Bonnets could not be lined with costly marten fur, but otherwise could be worn in any shape and form. Veils could be decorated with some gold, and daughters were permitted pearl hair-bands.[65]

Journeymen and mercenaries were not allowed any gold, silver, velvet, marten-fur or any other fur lining for their bonnet. Day-labourers in towns were grouped together with the rural population and priests' maidservants, and were permitted to wear dress only from fabric worth half a florin per ell. Men in these status groups, and even rich peasants, were told not to wear slashed clothing, bonnets, or any fur

---

[63] Sabine Hesse, *Herzog Carl Eugens Venezianische Messe in Ludwigsburg und Stuttgart* (Stuttgart: Württembergisches Landesmuseum, 2008).

[64] Veronika Baur, *Kleiderordnungen in Bayern vom 14. bis zum 19. Jahrhundert* (Munich: Wölfle, 1975), 25–26.

[65] Baur, *Kleiderordnungen in Bayern*, 48.

other than from goats or lambs. Women were allowed one velvet and silken hair-band.[66]

Yet this ordinance was never printed. Nor was there a Bavarian response to the 1530 and 1548 Imperial Police Ordinances. The 1577 IPO was followed by a territorial ordinance in 1578 which included sumptuary legislation. It differentiated seven groups: peasants and other professions in the countryside, such as inn-keepers; members of the urban population (citizens, artisans and tradespeople); merchants, magistrates and judges; patricians in the four main towns; knights and nobility; earls and *Freiherrn*; and, finally, maidservants.[67] A quarter of any fine was to be paid to the authorities and to the person who had denounced the culprit, while the other half would be donated to the poor. This remained the pattern.[68] This ordinance newly regulated the size of collars for peasants, which were to be low cut and simple in style. Gowns were now permitted to show trimmings of up to three fingers'-width of satin or silk-woollen union cloths. Common citizens in towns were allowed trimmings of up to two fingers of velvet, rings and jewellery for up to ten florins, hair-bands for up to six florins and girdles with silver for up to eight florins, as well as fox fur.[69]

The Bavarian 1626 Ordinance

While no further Bavarian police ordinances were issued during the seventeenth century, Maximilian I (1597–1651) issued detailed printed sumptuary laws in 1626. These likewise distinguished seven groups: peasants, and other professions in villages; the urban population as separated into three groups: a lower group, merchants and patricians; and doctors. Unusually, this ordinance mandated that children up to the age of thirteen were to be dressed according to the rank below their parents.[70] The entire rural population was told to wear German fabrics, and no costly linens, no gold, no silken garters, while silver was allowed only for the wedding ring. Common rural folk were told to wear lamb or calf fur, while rich peasants were allowed goat or ram fur. Women and children, however, could have their gowns modestly trimmed with satin and velvet imitate. Scarlet was prohibited as a colour.

[66] Baur, *Kleiderordnungen in Bayern*, 49.
[67] Baur, *Kleiderordnungen in Bayern*, 27.
[68] Baur, *Kleiderordnungen in Bayern*, 89.
[69] Baur, *Kleiderordnungen in Bayern*, 49.
[70] Baur, *Kleiderordnungen in Bayern*, 31.

Common urban citizens were permitted two fingers'-width of velvet imitate trimmings for women's dresses, as well as two silk borders. Garters could be made only of lower-quality taffeta, and silk stockings were to be changed for woollen or linen stockings. Expensive cordovan shoes made from fine suede leather were outlawed, and there were the usual prohibitions on the qualities of fur. Intricate cordwain purses with eight silver buttons and four closures were permitted – the ordinance thus responded to the attractiveness of such fashionable accessories. Wreaths worn for weddings were not to cost more than six florins, and the value of false braids was likewise limited. Girdles could be worn up to the value of twelve florins.[71]

Maximilian's 1626 ordinance was the first and last printed and properly issued sumptuary legislation in Bavaria. Delinquents were asked to pay a third of the value of each overly sumptuous item of dress as a fine, and half of it if they were caught again. The item could be confiscated if a person is offended again or there could be public forms of punishment.[72] The 1626 ordinance was followed by several reform attempts, which never passed into legislation.

An ordinance in 1737 announced a new era of regulation. It issued a catalogue of licencing fees which were to be paid for exemptions. Those who were caught with overly sumptuous clothes for which they had not bought a licence on paper were to be fined, while those offending more than twice could be publicly punished. This marks the beginning of a new regime of luxury fines, from which the nobility at court with their families as well as livery-wearing employees were exempt.[73]

The eighteenth century thus emerges as a period in which fiscal concerns became dominant in territories. The duchies of Bavaria and Württemberg otherwise differed in the thoroughness of reforms. Lutheran Württemberg followed imperial legislation in its initial impetus as well as in its stagnation, and focused on the urban population, although the legislation seems to have only occasionally been implemented.[74] Bavarian concerns about excessive consumption preceded the 1530 imperial legislation, and may have been a motor for it. Legislation initially was nonetheless rather generous; yet major, printed legal ordinances in 1578 and

---

[71] Baur, *Kleiderordnungen in Bayern*, 55.
[72] Baur, *Kleiderordnungen in Bayern*, 83.
[73] Baur, *Kleiderordnungen in Bayern*, 37, 84. Further research needs to establish how these fines were implemented.
[74] Medick, *Weben und Überleben*, offers a detailed discussion of the extent to which inventories reveal that social distinction in dress was broadly observed in a small weaving town marked by Pietist beliefs during the eighteenth century, and the scope for individual choices by men and women ranging from surgeons and bakers to day-labourers.

1626 kept sumptuary laws relevant to territorial governance in a Catholic state. The 1626 laws were noticeably stricter for urban inhabitants than those in Lutheran Württemberg at the same time, which still repeated the 1549 legislation.[75]

Catholic Münster

This poses the question of whether or not confessional differences shaped sumptuary politics. Münster was a powerful Catholic archbishopric in Northern Germany, and can serve as a final example of territorial responses to imperial legislation. In 1571, archbishop Johann von Hoya sought to regulate excessive expenses at festivities and articles incorporated in a new police ordinance that made distinctions solely between inhabitants in towns and the countryside.[76] The latter were prohibited from wearing any gold as well as collars and sleeves made from velvet and silk fabrics. They were asked to wear 'common' linen and woollen fabrics, but allowed to have one 'honorable dress of English cloth'. Women were allowed to wear a specific long dress which had become fashionable in the town of Münster (a *Fuecken*) if they felt it appropriate to their rank, yet only lined with common fabric.

This ordinance hence was less restrictive than the 1530 IPO because it allowed peasants to wear jewellery and accessories from metals and materials other than gold and also allowed one outfit to be made from foreign fabric. It left urban citizens entirely unregulated, and was repeated in exactly the same form several times up to 1628. It was not renewed in a further ordinance in 1652.

The first edict which specifically targeted sumptuous dress dates from 1764, and this was by far the most comprehensive regulation the territory had ever witnessed. This was a period which furthered the consumption of locally produced fabrics, and it appears that the edict was enforced and thus further developed and renewed in 1765. Import taxes for foreign cloth were specified. By 1768, the ordinance solely addressed taxable peasants.[77] Yet these sumptuary laws were lifted in 1791 in response to petitions and in view of the fact that they had not been successfully implemented.[78] Max Franz of Austria, Münster's new archbishop, saw no economic benefit in such regulations and made

---

[75] See also Fleischhauer, *Renaissance*, 339.
[76] Benno König, *Luxusverbote im Fürstbistum Münster* (Frankfurt-am-Main: Klostermann, 1999), 58, 91.
[77] König, *Luxusverbote*, 171–177.
[78] König, *Luxusverbote*, 211.

explicit that he did not wish to curtail the pleasures of his subjects in consumption.[79]

Assessing Territorial Legislation

This indicates, in sum, that there was no confessionally specific and uniform response in the German lands, and this is borne out by evidence from Catholic and Lutheran towns. While Bavarian politics continued to see sumptuary laws as relevant, the archbishopric of Münster did not issue any new legislation between 1571 and 1765. Its initial laws only regulated rural populations, but were more generous than imperial laws. Little evidence survives for any of the three territories on how these laws were implemented, and Württemberg records document that courts staffed by local citizens did not employ informers or receive any denunciations of other locals which they followed up. Very rarely can we trace lower-class women who bought more luxurious items, were reported by neighbours or officials and punished for wearing them.[80] Fiscal concerns became important with mercantilist politics during the eighteenth century, but by the end of the century Münster's enlightened Catholic archbishop could argue for the pleasures of sartorial consumption and abolish all legislation. More research is needed on other German territories, but the evidence presented so far casts further doubt on the notion that sumptuary legislation was 'safely controlled' in this period or that it was a central tool of social disciplining. The lists of police regulations in the German lands bear this out: many regulations of dress and luxury continued to focus on weddings and baptisms, and sumptuary laws made up a small percentage of the regulation involving social order (Figure 1.5).[81]

Urban Legislation

This finally leads us to a discussion of urban legislation in the early modern period. Lieselotte Eisenbart was the first to highlight the new importance of divisions by rank in early modern legislation and established that these most frequently distinguished only between three

---

[79] König, *Luxusverbote*, 226.
[80] Ogilvie, *Die lokale Regulierung*, 73–74.
[81] Karl Härter and Michael Stolleis have led a research project at the Max Planck Institute for Legal History that has made available lists and short summaries of police ordinances for most German territories and towns in a multi-volume set; see their *Repertorium der Policeyordnungen der Frühen Neuzeit*, 10 vols. (Frankfurt-am-Main: Victorio Klostermann, 2000–).

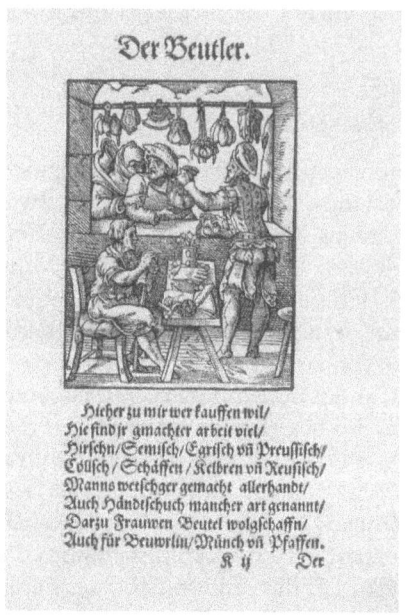

Figure 1.5 Jost Amman, *Ständebuch* (Book of Trades), purse- and glove-maker. British Museum.

ranks.[82] A Strasbourg ordinance from 1660 stood out: it named 256 professions and linked them precisely to six divisions of rank.[83] It is testimony to how aware magistrates had become of social differentiation. Maidservants, seamstresses and other wage-earning women stood at the bottom of the hierarchy. The second lowest rank encompassed thirty-five badly paid professions, such as male day-labourers and basket weavers. Next followed a group of 104 professions of the lower middling classes: simple scribes, lower officials or low-ranking shopkeepers, for instance. The upper middle class was linked to forty-nine professions, such as silk embroiderers, goldsmiths, clock-makers and respected officials. The next rank further distinguished between those who descended from an honourable family and those who had accrued wealth and honour through personal success. The highest rank was preserved for those of the magistracy and similarly high-ranking

---

[82] Lieselotte Constanze Eisenbart, *Kleiderordnungen der deutschen Städte zwischen 1350 und 1700: Ein Beitrag zur Kulturgeschichte des deutschen Bürgertums* (Göttingen: Musterschmidt, 1962), 60.

[83] Eisenbart, *Kleiderordnungen*, 33.

civic offices. This legislation particularly emphasised that foreign dress corrupted a 'German, chaste and Christian' spirit in response to the influence of French fashions in Strasbourg.[84]

German urban legislation was issued by magistrates, and typically used as a tool to enshrine their own privileges. This contrasts with the case of Cologne, the Rhenish, Catholic metropolis of trade, in which magistrates used an absence of legislation to champion a culture of equality. Cologne never issued any sumptuary legislation relating to everyday dress; the magistracy occasionally sought to restrain sumptuousness at funerals. By 1623, the mayor mentioned the IPO in a speech generally admonishing against 'excessive sumptuousness' and 'foreign inappropriate dress'. It was not until 1697 that the magistrate drafted a first proper dress ordinance for discussion, which does not seem to have been passed as a law. Its purpose was to finally distinguish different classes and their sumptuary privileges among the population. The document only survives as a fragment, and lists the first class, which predictably consisted of members of the old families, whose influence had been reinstated, as well as doctors and key urban diplomats. Gerd Schwerhoff argues that this absence of any proper sumptuary legislation corresponds to the 'political philosophy of the Cologne bourgeoisie', according to which everyone, rich and poor, high and low, were meant to live together in 'equity and equality' (*Billigkeit und Gleichheit*).[85] Extant early seventeenth-century clothes from the upper bourgeoisie certainly document a love of style, fine fabric and colour, influenced by strong trade links with the Netherlands.[86]

Most sumptuary or dress laws were incorporated in general police ordinances and formed a small part of these long-winded regulations. They typically targeted sumptuousness at weddings, funerals and festivities rather than everyday dress, and thus continued the medieval focus of regulations. Although more research still needs to be done, we know that separate sumptuary ordinances were issued in Augsburg (1582), Brunswick (1623, 1650), Lübeck (1642, 1639) and Nuremberg (1657, 1693). Even in cities with some governmental activity in relation

---

[84] Eisenbart, *Kleiderordnungen*, 62–63, 86; see also Léone Prigent, *La perception du vêtement féminin des élites et des classes populaires à Strasbourg, Mulhouse et Colmar (XVIIe–XVIIIe siècles) image de soi, image de l'autre*, unpublished manuscript, 2008. My thanks to Sonia Calvi for making this available.

[85] Gerd Schwerhoff, '"Die Groisse Oeverswenckliche Costlicheyt Zo Messigen": Bürgerliche Einheit und ständische Differenzierung in Kölner Aufwandsordnungen (14.-17. Jahrhundert)', in *Rheinische Vierteljahresblätter* 54 (1990): 95–122.

[86] Karen Stolleis and Johannes Pietsch (eds.), *Kölner Patrizier– und Bürgerkleidung des 17. Jahrhunderts: Die Kostümsammlung Hüpsch im Hessischen Landesmuseum Darmstadt* (Riggisberg: Abegg Stiftung, 2008).

to sumptuousness we find many gaps and inconsistencies over time.[87] In Augsburg, the brief 1582 laws were implemented only up to 1585, and with a particular focus on women's fur-hats. In Schwäbisch-Hall, efforts to implement sumptuary legislation collapsed in 1688, after a twelve-month effort during which the constable and his wife tried to spot wrongdoers on the street and these in turn found many excuses to justify why their dress appropriately expressed their rank.[88] Some towns discussed draft regulations with particular interest groups, as in the case of Nuremberg, where 'honourable women' were consulted to discuss an ordinance in 1599.[89] In relation to the effect of these ordinances Eisenbart concludes: 'That sumptuary ordinances despite all efforts on the whole remained without effect is well known.'[90] The force of fashion meant that these laws, as Eisenbart put it, were 'outdated the moment they were enacted'; hence the endless lament that they were never observed. Even the extreme 1660 Strasbourg ordinance was unrealistic in its detailed prescriptions, which included a whole set of regulations about possible grey areas (by considering, for instance, how a craftsman engaged in more significant trade might need to be treated), and was impossible to implement and control in a large city.[91]

But how effective were regulations in the select number of Germany cities in which they were more regularly issued? The following, final discussion focuses on two Lutheran cities in the south and north and then on Leipzig in the north-east of Germany.

The Case of Nuremberg

Lutheran Nuremberg might appear to be a case of continuous regulation and control, but the actual number of offenders was extremely low and privileges were lobbied for. Jutta Zander-Seidel has shown that the Reformation did not call for an intensification of sumptuary legislation. Nuremberg's leading reformer Andreas Osiander emphasised in 1525 that God had not laid down any laws about what should be worn – such outward laws were simply not essential to belief. Authorities were asked to regulate only extravagant excess. Nuremberg dress thus continued to

[87] Eisenbart, *Kleiderordnungen*, 26.
[88] STAH, 4/553–554, see Rublack, *Crimes of Women*, 39–40.
[89] Eisenbart, *Kleiderordnungen*, 43.
[90] Eisenbart, *Kleiderordnungen*, 48.
[91] Eisenbart, *Kleiderordnungen*, 64.

be varied and colourful.[92] The first proper sumptuary law dated from 1535 and – despite the IPO and with the exception of a few privileges for local patricians – distinguished solely between all urban men and women in distinction to the nobility and peasants. It was intact until 1560, when there was growing concern about how the sumptuousness of artisans' wives could be limited to a 'bourgeois mean' (*bürgerliches Maß*).

This led to an ordinance which distinguished between different status groups related to professions, which was updated in 1562, 1568, 1583, 1618 and 1657. These ordinances were read out in front of the town hall after Sunday services, and after 1583 ordinances were also printed. The 1583 ordinance was the first significant law. Patricians were at the top of the hierarchy, followed by merchants, common tradespeople and artisans and finally maidservants or house servants, without civic status. It did not consider the peasants in Nuremberg's extensive territory. The 1618 ordinance distinguished between merchants who were members of the great council; smaller tradespeople who were members of the great council and artisans who were members of the small council, followed by merchants; tradespeople and artisans who were not political representatives, as well as simple shopkeepers and artisans; and finally apprentices, journeymen and maidservants. Patricians in breach of these laws were to be heard directly by the council, whereas the rest of the population was heard by a lower 'council of five' and generally faced fines as punishment.

Lehner notes the surprising value of goods that even the lower classes were permitted during the seventeenth century, a time which has traditionally been seen as marking the city's decline. These allowances demonstrate considerable private wealth and a determination to mark distinction.[93] The town council meanwhile was under continuous pressure to respond with exceptional regulations to the status of individuals. A final ordinance was issued in 1693. By 1696, the patriciate received the formal right to decide about its membership. Lehner interprets this as the key reason why there was no need for further sumptuary laws to protect this elite.[94]

During the sixteenth century, by far the highest number of citizens were reprimanded in 1570, in response to the 1568 ordinance. That year twenty-nine citizens were targeted, especially women who wore overly expensive collars and velvet trims on their gowns. But in most

---

[92] Jutta Zander-Seidel, *Textiler Hausrat: Kleidung und Haustextilien in Nürnberg von 1500–1650* (Munich: Deutscher Kunstverlag, 1990), 297; see also Rublack, *Dressing Up*, chapters 4 and 5.

[93] Lehner, *Mode*, 172.

[94] Lehner, *Mode*, 6.

years there were fewer than five accusations that led to any punishment – and Nuremberg was one of Germany's largest cities, with a population of about 30,000 inhabitants.[95] Zander-Seidel's use of council minutes has moreover revealed the council's inconsistency in enacting laws, as when those charged with confiscating young women's pearl hair-bands above the considerable value of twenty florins in 1568 were told not to be 'overly strict', especially as the council recognised how difficult it was to be precise in evaluations. Magistrates moreover told officials that even journeymen were allowed to wear old velvet bonnets, whereas the sumptuary law prohibited anyone except patricians to wear velvet bonnets and berets. Officials were reprimanded not to punish anyone 'blindly' and not to be overly strict in relation to the velvet women used for trims.[96] Any suspect who belonged to the middling and lower classes was asked to appear before the council of five, who threatened with confiscation and a fine. Yet by 1587 there were complaints about the fact that badly paid officials were bribed by well-off citizens and that the laws mostly targeted the lower classes. Officials used a number of secret spies, whom the populace attacked as 'traitors'. In court, suspects produced elaborate arguments to justify their sartorial decisions and relied on a number of exemptions, for instance of gifts by higher-ranking people, or dress worn while high-ranking noblemen or dignitaries were visiting, as well as dress worn by foreign people or bought elsewhere. A key excuse for Nuremberg citizens of all classes was to argue that their dress items were old and that more precious fabrics therefore were lower in value, or that the fabrics were only imitations of silk. As a consequence, those reprimanded usually either did not have to pay a fine, or sometimes were allowed to keep wearing the item of dress.[97] They actively campaigned for their right to dress in ways which expressed their social aspirations.

Hanover

Hanover was a Lutheran North German city, whose population increased from 5,000 in 1500 to 9,000 by 1650.[98] From the fourteenth century, sumptuary laws attempted to differentiate urban citizens from noblemen and peasants. By the late fifteenth century this interest was replaced by the intention to differentiate further among urban citizens.

---

[95] Zander-Seidel, *Textiler Hausrat*, 296–297.
[96] Zander-Seidel, *Textiler Hausrat*, 292.
[97] Zander-Seidel, *Textiler Hausrat*, 295.
[98] Anne-Kathrin Reich, *Kleidung als Spiegelbild sozialer Differenzierung* (Hannover: Hahnsche Buchhandlung, 2005), 78.

As in Nuremberg, a key criterion in early modern Hanover turned out to be male political participation, which was rewarded with the privilege of greater sumptuousness. During the first half of the seventeenth century, higher taxation levels likewise guaranteed status privilege. Laws moreover served to discriminate against women considered less honourable, in terms either of their sexual licentiousness or of their occupation as maidservants. Reich rightly emphasises that this dual system enshrined gendered codes of honour, which identified male honour above all with political influence and wealth, and female honour with sexual restraint and belonging to a status-dominant, male-headed household. Men in official positions dressed not least to honour the city they belonged to.[99] This meant that allowances for furs were actually in breach of the IPO: from 1603 onwards they allowed the mayor, academics and the key urban diplomats any kind of fur.[100]

During the seventeenth century, emphasis on a man's academic rank further increased. From 1656 onwards, for instance, only those with a doctorate could use decorative ribbons on their gowns.[101] Most astonishingly, in 1688 the wives and daughters of university graduates were allowed to wear *white* mourning robes![102] This becomes comprehensible in relation to the fact that black had been increasingly linked to dress of the lower sorts, while women of the first estate, for instance, were allowed to wear white headdresses.

A further peculiarity of the Hanover legislation consists in the fact that it privileged the soldiers who guarded the city, who were allowed slashed clothing and during the seventeenth century were the only status group permitted to decorate their silken or woollen dress with gold or silver ribbons.[103]

The Hanover ordinances were not printed, but were meant to be posted next to the town-hall and read out annually, although it is difficult to imagine documents of several pages being read by individuals in public and memorised in detail, especially as their differentiation increased and they were issued during cold months, usually in February or early March.[104] It is now impossible to identify which institution exactly was entrusted to regulate the breach of these laws. But the regulations themselves specified precise fines that were meant to be paid, with the exception of the first ordinance in 1546, which mentioned maidservants and

---

[99] Reich, *Kleiderordnungen*, 178.
[100] Reich, *Kleiderordnungen*, 164, Tab. 13.
[101] Reich, *Kleiderordnungen*, 137, 153.
[102] Reich, *Kleiderordnungen*, 164.
[103] Reich, *Kleiderordnungen*, 166.
[104] Reich, *Kleiderordnungen*, 90–91.

threatened them, extraodinarily, with the loss of their life if they trimmed their dress with velvet in excess of a width of three fingers.[105]

The emphasis on fines in the regulation suggests that fiscal motives might have been relevant. Yet surviving registers of fines indicate an emphasis on regulating overly sumptuous behaviour at weddings and funerals; Reich mentions only four examples of fines in relation to normal sumptuary laws for the period 1628–1659.[106] Meanwhile new, small luxuries, such as handkerchiefs, offered further possibilities of distinction for all classes. Silk embroidery and gold lace were prohibited, but this still allowed for the use of silver metal thread and other precious decorations. Regulations for female jewellery became more restrictive during the seventeenth century, but also remained inconsistent. In 1623, for instance, the first estate was allowed six golden rings. This allowance was reduced to four in 1643 and then two in 1658. This extreme restriction, characteristically, must have caused intense lobbying, and was lifted in 1663. A new ordinance only prohibited the wearing of rings with precious stones worth more than twenty *Thaler* and thus allowed for as many rings as there were fingers.[107]

Between 1603 and 1651, moreover, there was a marked lack of precise regulation for the lower classes, as the ordinances were so intent on differentiating the upper middling and middling classes from top elites on the one hand and maidservants and journeymen on the other hand.[108] In 1603, the first estate was principally defined as consisting of the mayor, those with a doctoral degree, magistrates and patricians, the second estate as wealthy burghers; a third estate not very wealthy citizens; while in 1651 the first estate now also encompassed the Protestant clergy; the second estate comprised those paying annual taxes of 2,000 *Thaler* and those belonging to the merchants' chamber; the third estate those who paid 1,500 *Thaler* tax, or belonged to one of four main offices, or to one of a whole range of specified trades and highly reputable crafts, including goldsmiths, embroiderers of pearls and pharmacists. A fourth group distinguished them from those who served in less significant offices and trades, such as hatters and barbers, and paid 1,000 *Thaler* tax. A fifth estate comprised common citizens, journeymen and craftspeople such as carpenters and cooks. Servants, day-labourers and other common citizens made up a sixth estate, and maidservants were suddenly forbidden to wear any dress discarded by their mistresses.[109]

---

[105] Reich, *Kleiderordnungen*, 98, 170.
[106] Reich, *Kleiderordnungen*, 99.
[107] Reich, *Kleiderordnungen*, 157, Tab. 10.
[108] Reich, *Kleiderordnungen*, 116–117, Tab. 6.
[109] Reich, *Kleiderordnungen*, 171.

By 1663, however, this highly differentiated system had been simplified. There now existed four status groups: the fourth and fifth estates had merged into one group and servants were no longer mentioned, except that the ordinance now differentiated between maidservants from common families and those of middle- and upper-class origin, who might have needed to go into service because they were orphaned, for instance, and were allowed to wear clothes according to their higher status. Tax payments were no longer considered, which meant that social promotion was no longer connected to wealth through sumptuary privileges. This system was repeated by Hanover's final law in 1671.[110]

The Hanover laws thus are indicative of continuous efforts of negotiation, exemption and further differentiation, while the registers of fine suggest that they were not implemented. Social hierarchies were not frozen but kept on being re-negotiated through debates of these laws.

Leipzig: Regulations and Resistance

The case of Lutheran Leipzig, the centre of trade in the east of Germany, provides a final example which takes us from the fifteenth century through to the age of mercantilism. Leipzig had its important fair and distributed goods from the Atlantic trade on to Eastern Europe. In 1612, a first territorial ordinance resulted from years of discussion, and distinguished fourteen status groups. As in Hanover, it privileged academics with degrees – who would have been particularly present in this university town – and office-holders. When the ordinance was reinforced in 1628 it threatened extremely harsh punishments, directed especially against women and tailors. Alas, in 1640, the Leipzig council still bemoaned that there was almost 'not a month that went by without a new fashion'.[111] Civic sumptuary legislation started in the late fifteenth century to order the visualisation of rank. Six civic sumptuary ordinances had been issued up to 1625; a further eleven ordinances followed up to 1698. Delegated informers were responsible for naming offenders. But, as in Nuremberg, these collected very few fines, and those they did were almost exclusively from artisans' wives. Hence the actual surveillance measures linked to these exceptionally frequent ordinances proved extremely limited.[112]

---

[110] Reich, *Kleiderordnungen*, 117, Tab. 6.

[111] Thomas Weller, *Theatrum Praecedentiae: Zeremonieller Rang und gesellschaftliche Ordnung in der frühneuzeitlichen Stadt: Leipzig 1500–1800* (Darmstadt: Wissenschaftliche Buchgesellschaft, 2006), 109.

[112] Thus, in 1665/66 the council collected ten fines, in 1666/67 eleven, in 1667/68 only three and in 1674 only three as well. Weller, *Theatrum*, 361.

Civic legislation came to a halt by the end of the seventeenth century, while territorial sumptuary laws continued. At the same time, state officials systematically supported local luxury production.[113] By 1749, twenty-five Leipzig manufacturing firms produced silk and velvet, gold and silver decorations and brocade, and processed tobacco. In addition, English textiles as well as colonial goods traded by the Dutch and French became much more present at the Leipzig fair. In 1747, Saxon officials reported that common people preferred foreign silk.[114] Dresden, the seat of Saxony's territorial government, in turn had already begun to license a wider range of entrepreneurs in luxury wares. A Leipzig professor of philosophy helped local wholesale merchants to champion a politics of free trade.[115] Against this background, a new dress code was issued in 1750, to regulate who was allowed to wear what kinds of locally or foreign manufactured goods. Even day-labourers and farmers, for instance, were permitted to wear Saxon fabrics with some silk content.[116] Shop-keepers and craft masters were allowed hat buttons of pure gold, silk or silver.[117]

This code nonetheless alarmed numerous agents invested in the functioning of global markets. Wholesale merchants instantly argued that such restrictions would damage the fair and hence the well being of the whole city. Further appeals were received from local merchants in other Saxon cities and from several of the biggest German trading cities, such as Cologne and Hamburg. Even the British State Secretary wrote. They all claimed that the dress code would make the fair unattractive and cause far wider damage to others who had sold or bought fine fabrics in Leipzig.[118]

In response, the Dresden state officials decided to enforce the code only in 1752, by which time they reckoned that the domestic produc-tion of luxury would be sufficiently developed.[119] The dress code now served as a mercantilist measure. Yet the wholesale merchants' lobby argued that they relied on constant consumer demand for a wide selec-tion of fine wares to remain in business, because fashions changed quickly.[120]

---

[113] Robert Beachy, *The Soul of Commerce. Credit, Property, and Politics in Leipzig, 1750–1840* (Leiden: Brill, 2005), 26–27.
[114] Beachy, *Commerce*, 26.
[115] Beachy, *Commerce*, 27, Carl Günther Ludovici.
[116] Beachy, *Commerce*, 28, n.23.
[117] Beachy, *Commerce*, 28, n.23.
[118] Beachy, *Commerce*, 29.
[119] Beachy, *Commerce*, 29.
[120] Beachy, *Commerce*, 30–31.

Figure 1.6 Stall with gallant wares at the Württemberg 'Venetian Fair', Ludwigsburger Porzellan Manufaktur, c. 1765. Metropolitan Museum, New York.

Two state commissioners were duly sent to Leipzig to control sumptuary deviance. Over one hundred interrogations were conducted during the next six years.[121] Those interrogated showed no signs of guilt. They produced elaborate apologies to prove – in the usual manner – that they had had these items made before the new dress code, were unaware of a particular law, or that it did not apply to them. Many defended their view that their appearance manifested the rank they had achieved in society and hence due difference from social inferiors. By 1762, a governmental commission finally acknowledged that sumptuary competition was a 'social ill that is not to be directed through police-ordinances' (Figure 1.6).[122]

---

[121] Beachy counts 100 fines and 112 cases; see Beachy, *Commerce* 30 and n.29.
[122] Weller, *Theatrum*, 381.

Conclusion

In 1971 Mack Walker influentially distinguished 'two Germanys'. Hamburg, Leipzig, Frankfurt, Cologne, Dresden or Nuremberg made up the few dynamic 'mover-and-doer towns'. These contrasted well into the nineteenth century with an overwhelming majority of small 'hometowns' marked by their frozen social life and ideals.[123] In these German 'hometowns', Walker posited, even rules on what 'clothing who might wear did not actively assert rank and place so much as accept their existence and inhibit the race after status by the display of wealth'.[124]

As we have seen there is no evidence for this position, or the view that Germany's dynamic urban centres spurred on obsessive legislation. I have argued in addition that legislation needs to be understood in its materiality as text, as numbered or unnumbered, as hand-written or densely printed, as read out in public or left to be read by officials. There is no doubt that imperial legislation fossilised very quickly after 1548. It did not stand in the way of urban and territorial innovation in textile production and related trades such as ribbon- or hat-making. Leading towns and territories responded to the imperial legislation in very different ways, and some not at all, or not for many decades. Confessional belief did not impact on politics in any patterned ways. Modalities of control and punishment differed, too, and were subject to intense negotiation or sporadic attempts at enforcement by different interest groups in the population. It would be difficult to argue for any town or territory in Germany that it safely controlled sumptuary legislation and thus perceived it as a realistic tool to guarantee a good society. Many ordinances continued to focus on excessive expenses at festivities and sought to prevent private debt. They also served to enshrine the privileges of particular elites instead of closely controlling society at large. In Germany as elsewhere, legislation thus has to be read not just in terms of restrictions but also of the allowances that were often rather generously granted. Legislation could moreover provide a 'map of social assent' through the valorisation of particular fabrics and accessories as prestigious. Items of fashionable dress as well as brightly coloured clothes and accessories circulated far more widely

---

[123] Mack Walker, *German Home Towns: Community, State and General Estate, 1648–1871* (Ithaca: Cornell University Press, 1971).

[124] Walker, *Home Towns*, 135.

in sixteenth- and seventeenth-century Germany than historians have often led us to believe. Those who wore them and breached regulations could vocally defend their right to dress according to their perceived rank. Increasingly, however, innovative craftsmanship and fashionable consumption could be seen as essential for the well being of society.

2 Playing by the Rules? Dressing without Sumptuary Laws in the Low Countries from the Fourteenth to the Eighteenth Century*

Isis Sturtewagen and Bruno Blondé

Introduction

It is generally agreed that attempts to establish and restrain social transgressions in dress by means of legislative texts were largely absent in the late medieval Low Countries.[1] In 1932, A. de Ridder first collected a number of sixteenth- to eighteenth-century dress laws.[2] Paul De Win and Raymond van Uytven later added to this list a late fifteenth-century law issued by Philip the Fair,[3] while more recently Ronald van Belle was able to trace the first dress laws in this region back to the fourteenth century.[4] Not all of the dress laws brought together in these studies, however, were genuine sumptuary laws. In the late medieval and early modern Low

* The authors would like to thank Bert Watteeuw for his ideas and suggestions in the early stages of this paper, especially regarding moralistic literature and art, and Marieke de Winkel for her invaluable comments and contributions on the sumptuary legislation from the Dutch Republic.

[1] Among others: Frederik Buylaert, Wim De Clercq and Jan Dumolyn, 'Sumptuary legislation, material culture and the semiotics of "vivre noblement" in the county of Flanders (14th–16th centuries)', *Social History* 36/4 (2011): 401; Hester Dibbits, *Vertrouwd Bezit. Materiële cultuur in Doesburg en Maassluis 1650–1800* (Nijmegen: Boom uitgevers Amsterdam, 2001); Martha C. Howell, *Commerce before Capitalism in Europe, 1300–1600* (Cambridge: Cambridge University Press, 2010), 211–212.

[2] Alfred De Ridder, 'Contribution à l'histoire du costume et du luxe dans la Belgique d'autrefois', *Bulletin de la Société Royale d'Archéologie de Bruxelles* 5 (1932): 113–140.

[3] Paul De Win, 'De lagere adel in de Bourgondische Nederlanden', *Bijdragen tot de Geschiedenis* 68 (1985): 250; Raymond Van Uytven, 'Classes économiques, hiérarchies sociales et influence politique aux Pays-Bas du sud du XIVe au XVIIe siècle', in Annalisa Guarducci (ed.), *Gerarchie economiche e gerarchie sociali secoli XII-XVIII* (Florence: Le Monnier, 1990), 369–370; Raymond Van Uytven, *De Zinnelijke Middeleeuwen* (Leuven: Davidsfonds, 1998), 121–149; Raymond Van Uytven, 'Showing off One's Rank in the Middle Ages', in Wim Blockmans, and Antheun Janse (eds.), *Showing Status, Representation of Social Positions in the Late Middle Ages* (Turnhout: Brepols, 1999), 28–30.

[4] Ronald van Belle, *Vlakke grafmonumenten en memorietaferelen met persoonsafbeeldingen in West-Vlaanderen. Een inventaris, funeraire symboliek en overzicht van het kostuum* (Bruges: Uitgeverij Van De Wiele, 2006), 548.

Countries, dress laws were issued by a wide variety of political entities. Not only cities passed laws concerning the sartorial behaviour of their inhabitants, but also central authorities, including lords, counts, kings, emperors, stadtholders and regents, depending on the area and moment in time. Besides sumptuary concerns, dress laws targeted a variety of issues throughout the fourteenth to eighteenth centuries. In the late Middle Ages, many dress laws from the Low Countries aimed to regulate the use of uniform dress or livery.[5] The concern about livery was shared by civic and territorial governments alike. Princes, counts and dukes strove to maintain a monopoly through denying others – political factions, rival nobles and cities and their corporate organisations – the right to visually build power through clothes.[6] In the cities of the Low Countries, on the other hand, numerous laws were written in urban law books prohibiting citizens from wearing the livery of noblemen, thus limiting the display of noble power and influence within city walls and protecting the urban autonomy.[7] These regulations shared, nonetheless, one common purpose: rather than excesses of luxury, what was being restricted was the expression of political alliance and power. Before the sixteenth century, by far the majority of dress regulations from the Low Countries targeted precisely this (mis)appropriation of livery, rather than luxurious clothes and the ensuing transgressions of social rank.[8]

At the end of the sixteenth century, with the victory of Protestantism in the northern Netherlands, the wearing of Catholic religious habits became a topic of dress laws (for instance, a law passed in Amsterdam on the 21 November 1584).[9] Religious motives seem to have been strong in the Dutch Republic. Apart from prohibitions against Catholic habits, there were numerous dress laws issued by the Mennonites regarding

[5] The wearing of livery dress had been a prerogative of the nobility and their entourage, but during the fourteenth century uniform liveries with heraldic emblems and in specific colours became increasingly popular in urban contexts. Before this time cities had already appropriated the use of seals, coats of arms and banners from the world of chivalry: Wim Blockmans and Esther Donckers, 'Self-Representation of Court and City in Flanders and Brabant in the Fifteenth and Early Sixteenth Centuries' in *Showing Status, Representation of Social Positions in the Late Middle Ages*, 96–97; Louis Gilliodts-Van Severen, *Inventaire des Archives de la ville de Bruges* (Bruges: E. Gailliard, 1876), 14–16.

[6] Van Belle, *Vlakke grafmonumenten*, 548.

[7] An exception was usually made for wearing the livery of the rightful ruler of the area, and wearing livery was also allowed if one was indeed part of the household or retinue that the livery represented. Howell, *Commerce before Capitalism*, 211–212; Van Belle, *Vlakke grafmonumenten*, 547–549.

[8] It lies outside the scope of this article to discuss these regulations in detail here. The subject is touched upon briefly in Isis Sturtewagen, *All Together Respectably Dressed* (Unpublished PhD thesis, University of Antwerp, 2016).

[9] Hermanus van Noordkerk, *Handvesten ofte privilegiën, octroyen en willekeuren; mitsgaders costuimen ordonnantiën en handelingen der stad Amstelredam* (Amsterdam: Salomon en Petrus Schouten, 1748–78), i: 211.

the sober dress to be worn during worship.[10] In the 1630s the Jewish Mahamad (or congregation) issued stringent dress laws for all Jews in Amsterdam.[11] The motivations behind these two (self-inflicted) dress laws were quite contrary: the extreme sober lifestyle for the Mennonites would stand out and show other Protestants they were the better Christians, while for the Jews the motivation was not to stand out from the locals and to assimilate as much as possible.

The focus of this article, however, will be on sumptuary laws: laws that focused on excess of various kinds, including sartorial excess (both of fashionable forms and of luxurious and costly materials) as well as excessiveness in baptism celebrations, wedding parties, funerals and banquets. Perhaps due to their relative absence, the few known sumptuary laws have so far never been systematically scrutinised. Additionally, most of the current research has focused exclusively on the southern Netherlands.

This chapter aims to add to the map of Low Countries sumptuary legislation, and will try to contrast the retrieved sumptuary laws with the realities of dressing in the Low Countries of the Late Middle Ages and the early modern era.[12] What were the different judicial bodies that issued sumptuary laws, and how did the laws they passed differ from each other? What were the discourses used to justify sumptuary laws? What kinds of excesses, transgressions and social groups did they target? And, most importantly, how do these compare to everyday practices in late medieval and early modern cities such as Bruges and Antwerp? An assessment of a large body of sixteenth-century probate inventories and confiscations will allow us to examine whether the alleged lack of sumptuary legislation in the Low Countries was part and parcel of a market where empowered individuals enjoyed 'free choice', both economically and politically, to consume at liberty. Even in the absence of systematic sumptuary constraints, we will argue, social conventions were strong enough to shape the imperatives of conspicuous consumption, or at least to provoke a 'cultural discussion' on consumer behaviour. The relative

---

[10] See for instance Piet Visser, 'Een achttiende-eeuws afschrift van een verordening uit 1659 voor uiterlijk, kleding en huisinrichting bij de Groninger Oude Vlamingen', *Doopsgezinde bijdragen*, New series 27 (2001): 229–238 and Marcel Kremer, 'Teken aan de wand. Een onderzoek naar de naleving van Loppersummer voorschriften onder de Groninger Oude Vlamingen in de stad Groningen', *Doopsgezinde bijdragen*, New Series 27 (2001): 141–169.

[11] Wilhelmina Chr. Pieterse, 'De weelde bij de Portugese Joden te Amsterdam in het begin van de zeventiende eeuw', *De Opbouw* 17 (1963): 57.

[12] We have to admit that we will fail to offer a complete overview of sumptuary laws issued – especially of the laws issued by civic instances, because no sustained research has been conducted in municipal archives. The civic laws that will be discussed here will thus necessarily serve as an illustration and are not in any way intended as a complete overview.

absence of sumptuary legislation and opportunities for and limitations on consumption in an urban context will structure the following analysis of the social significance of dressing in the Low Countries.

Early Sumptuary Legislation in the Low Countries

During the fourteenth and fifteenth centuries, sumptuary legislation in the Low Countries was sparse and often very local. While a number of the late medieval sumptuary laws from this area were concerned with public display of wealth more generally, clothes themselves were not the most pressing matter. The town council of the Brabant city of Louvain, for instance, issued a sumptuary law in 1396, which was reissued in 1405. Rather than regulating dress it attempted to limit the amount of wine served at wedding parties, thereby restricting the number of guests and/or the duration of the festivities. In this piece of legislation the costliness of the bride's wedding dress was mentioned, yet it was predominantly used as a measure of social class and as a benchmark to determine the allowed amount of wine. In a similar vein, the town of Nijmegen limited the number of guests who were granted access to baptisms and weddings in the fifteenth century. In this case no reference to dress was made at all.[13]

However, a small number of urban sumptuary laws did discuss issues of dress more directly. Examples can be given for the mid-fourteenth-century northern Netherlandish Hanseatic towns of Zutphen (c. 1350) and Kampen (1366 and 1456). The Zutphen law targeted the length of sleeves and the width of fur trimmings on women's dress.[14] Kampen, moreover, limited the size of décolletage and the use of excessively fashionable veils for women.[15] The 1456 Kampen law prohibited women and girls from wearing mantles with overly long trains.[16] Rather than singling out particular social classes within the urban society, these civic dress laws of the northern Low Countries attempted to preserve general moral and decorous values and common sense in sartorial behaviour. The strategy used was the limiting of extravagance in the cut and shape of clothes. These early laws closely resemble many sumptuary laws from German towns during the fourteenth and fifteenth centuries.

---

[13] Paul Charles Guillaume Guyot, 'Een Oude Nijmeegse Weeldewet', in Isaac Anne Nijhoff (ed.), *Bijdragen voor Vaderlandsche Geschiedenis en Oudheidkunde* (Arnhem: Nijhoff, 1847), 276–283.

[14] Cornelis Pijnacker Hordijk, *Rechtsbronnen der stad Zutphen. Van het begin der 14de tot de tweede helft der 16de eeuw.* (Gravenhage: n.a., 1881), 11–12.

[15] W. E. J. Tjeenk Willink, *Boeck van Rechten der Stad Kampen, Dat Gulden Boeck* (Zwolle: n.a., 1875), 56.

[16] Willink, *Boeck van Rechten der Stad Kampen*, 19.

This is not surprising, however, as all of the Low Countries, except for the county of Flanders, were part of the Holy Roman Empire. In particular, the Hanseatic towns in the east of the present-day Netherlands were closely connected to, and shared cultural and political practices as well as economic interests with, the German Hanza cities. In the Low Countries, these moralistic dress regulations seem to have been, above all else, directed at women and female clothing styles.[17] Sumptuary legislation began to be occupied with limiting luxurious and costly clothes to fixed social groups only at the very end of the fifteenth century.

'*Vivre noblement*' in the Sixteenth Century

In 1497, Archduke Philip the Fair (1478–1506) commanded the drawing up of a sumptuary law – the first one of this kind to be issued by the central government in the Low Countries – that regulated the wearing of foreign textiles, including not just velvet and silk but also all woollen fabrics produced outside the realm.[18] Henceforth, the use of such exotic fabrics '*dont chacun veult user a sa voulente*' (that all want to use at their own will) was reserved to the high nobility and ducal officials; all others were forced to wear only clothes made from native cloth. It was forbidden to all '*de quelque estat ou condicion quilz soient*' (of whatever status or condition they are) except the knights of the Golden Fleece, barons and their wives to wear '*costes, robes, doublures ou bordures aucun velours, satin ou damaz de quelque coleur que ce soit*' (coats, robes, linings or guards in velvet, satin or damask of any colour). Men and women '*vivans noblement et destat*' (living nobly and of estate) were allowed to wear silks in doublets, berets and coats, on the condition that the coats did not use more than eight ells of such fabric. The wives and daughters of ducal officers, as well as their domestic servants, were granted the use of velvet, satin and damask in small items of dress such as *cottillettes* (partlets or collars).[19]

---

[17] See also Ulinka Rublack's Chapter 1 in this volume.
[18] Van Uytven, 'Showing off One's Rank', 29–30. Jean-Jacques Gailliard mentions an earlier sumptuary law in his posthumously published chronicle of the history of Bruges but does not provide a source reference. Allegedly, Philip the Good issued a law in August 1495 (he was 16 years old at the time) that prohibited people from dressing too luxuriously. The motivation for this law, according to Gailliard, was the fact that common people, thanks to the high wages and profit they made, could wear such costly clothes, challenged the wealthiest merchants and patricians to even greater splendour. Jean-Jacques Gailliard, *De Ambachten en Neringen van Brugge* (Bruges: Gailliard, 1849), 106.
[19] Gilliodts-van Severen, *Inventaire des Archives*, 481.

The 1497 sumptuary law limited the use not only of all costly foreign fabrics made of silk and precious metal, but also of cheap woollen fabrics which were imported from various European textile centres. Because the poor people of Flanders in particular depended on cheap imports for their clothes, an exception was made barely one month later: Irish mantles, kerseys and Scottish cloth were again permitted.[20]

Strikingly, in their translation of this sumptuary law, the authorities in Bruges assumed that citizens (*poorters*) living off their private means and even well-to-do artisans were allowed and able to permit themselves luxury clothing. In their regulation, dated 20 October 1497, the Bruges city council decreed that nobody, '*nichtemeer vrouwen dan mannen*', (women just as much as men) who did not 'live nobly', such as crafts-people and others, would be allowed to wear velvet, satin and damask in 'clothes, sleeves, mantles or any other things'.[21] The Bruges town council took advantage of the situation by stipulating that competing French woollen cloths were no longer allowed to be used for new clothes (existing garments were still allowed to be worn), and that the import of all woollen fabrics into the city would be strictly controlled.[22] The ordinance moreover explicitly adds that 'men zal de voorseide ons gheduchts heeren ordonnancien her executien legghen zonder dissimulacie' (we will execute our beforementioned formidable lord's ordinance without dis-simulation). Non-ennobled families of *poorters*, traders and successful entrepreneurial artisans strove to maintain a material culture that was also enjoyed by, or at least overlapped with, that of the nobility. That this lifestyle was socially accepted says much about the purchasing power and consumption attitudes of the wealthiest city dwellers. At the same time it implies that much more was needed than mere sartorial appearance and a *vivre noblement* (literally: living nobly) life-style for the recognition of noble standing.[23]

---

[20] Isidore L.A. Diegerick, *Inventaire analytique et chronologique des chartes et documents appartenans aux archives de la ville d'Ypres* (Bruges: Vandecasteele-Werbrouck, 1859), iv: 271.

[21] The document mentions *faelgen* instead of the more generic mantle. The *faelge* or *faille* was a female mantle typical for the Low Countries.

[22] Louis Gilliodts-Van Severen, *Cartulaire de l'Ancienne Estaple de Bruges* (Bruges: Impr. de L. de Plancke, 1904), 313.

[23] Buylaert et al., 'Sumptuary Legislation', 395–396, 401 discuss the issue of noble life-style or *vivre noblement* in the late medieval and early modern Low Countries in detail. They have shown that, in Flanders, costly forms of material production and con-sumption were not unilaterally charged with noble connotations, but were interpreted depending on the social context of their use. See also Wim De Clercq, Jan Dumolyn and Jelle Haemers, '"Vivre Noblement": Material Culture and Elite Identity in Late Medieval Flanders', *Journal of Interdisciplinary History* 38/1 (2007): 1–31.

The explicit aim of this law was to protect the local textile industry and prevent the outflow of bullion. However, Raymond van Uytven claimed that in practice it was as much the prince's intent to reaffirm the fine line dividing the clothing of the nobility and of wealthier citizens. Ronald van Belle, too, thought that 'sumptuary laws were no doubt the result of the rivalry between the nobility and the urban elites'.[24] Yet, as Buylaert et al. have already noted, this law had 'precious little interest in providing the noble order with exclusive sartorial privileges (...) its first preoccupation was with the social differentiation *within* the nobility'.[25] From the reaction of the Bruges town council, however, it becomes clear that, although economic protectionism was a real concern, there was also competition between the middling groups and the urban elites. The latter tried to appropriate noble styles of dressing while preventing the middling groups from doing the same. Clearly, the motives varied according to the different social bodies that produced dress regulations and that were influenced by their own political agendas. The fact that the law forbade the use not only of silk but also of all foreign fabrics, barely making an exception for those *de petit prys* (of little value), shows that the central government was concerned with more than merely visual displays of wealth.[26] As such, these sumptuary laws fit seamlessly into a wider context of late medieval craft guild strategies and protectionist laws against imported fabrics – particularly English and later French textiles, as well as fabrics from competing textile production centres within the Low Countries. A similar evolution took place at the end of the sixteenth century in England and in the early seventeenth century in France. Lawmakers were no longer primarily concerned with moral and social issues, but with the outflow of bullion: if a new fashion came into vogue, they preferred producing the necessary goods within the country – as opposed to importing new or cheaper products from abroad – to prohibiting their use altogether.[27] Already by the end of the fifteenth century, the Low Countries were developing local silk industries in Tournai and Bruges to replace foreign fabrics, and sumptuary laws then most likely functioned as a kind of 'infant industry protection'. While in Tournai the earliest evidence for the local production of silk fabrics dates to 1380, it took until the end of the fifteenth century for Bruges to open its own silk weaving

[24] Van Belle, '*Vlakke grafmonumenten*', 547.
[25] Buylaert et. al., 'Sumptuary legislation', 402.
[26] Gilliodts-van Severen, *Cartulaire*, 314.
[27] Herman Feudenberger, 'Fashion, Sumptuary Laws and Business', *Business History Review* 37/1–2 (1963): 43–44.

mills, and from 1496 onwards the Bruges satin weavers would become an independent guild.[28]

The cause of public welfare (*chose publique* = *res publica*) was referred to over and over again in sixteenth-century sumptuary laws. In October 1531 a substantive imperial law was issued at the court in Brussels, which was concerned not only with excesses in dress but also touched on various issues including heresy, bankruptcy, vagrancy, charity, marriages, baptism, public drunkenness, blasphemy and the import and export of horses. Everyone – princes, dukes, marquises and counts, however rich – was without exception prohibited from wearing textiles with gold and silver thread.[29] Gowns, mantles and coats of crimson velvet and satin, dyed with extremely expensive kermes, were not allowed to anyone situated below the station of knights and lower-ranking nobles.[30] All others could wear these only if they were able to buy and maintain two suitable cavalry horses that would be put at the disposal of the government in case of war. Velvet, satin and damask in all colours but crimson could be used on the condition that one managed a given number and quality of horses in accordance with the quality and expense of the fabrics and the garments made from them (and thus the yardage needed).[31] To avoid the detriment to public welfare, the law stated that 'those who have silk clothes should provide other apparel and that they who want to wear silk clothes should provide horses'. Perpetrators were to be punished with the confiscation of the garments and a fine equal to their monetary value. The church was called in for reporting transgressions. Half of the fine went to the parish church of the place of the crime, a quarter to the informant and another quarter to the court of justice that delivered the verdict. Every three months, a report on the inspections of those people who wore silk, supplied the central government with indispensable

---

[28] Alfons K. L. Thijs, *De zijdenijverheid te Antwerpen in de zeventiende eeuw* (Brussels: Pro Civitate, 1969), 62 and 79.

[29] Jules Lameere, *Recueil des Ordonnances des Pays-Bas, Deuxième Série, 1506–1700. Vol 3. 1529–1536* (Brussels: J. Goemaere, 1902), 265–273.

[30] In the same year a sumptuary law was issued by Charles V in Germany, but the two laws differed substantially. While they both tried most avidly to regulate the use of crimson or scarlet silks and textiles woven or decorated with metal thread, the German law went into much more detail for the lower social groups and for women. In the Low Countries the use of silk fabrics and especially velvet was less restricted than in Germany, where even the urban patriciate and noblemen were allowed to wear velvet only for trims. See Rublack's Chapter 1 in this volume.

[31] The ordinance differentiates between *robes* (gowns), *manteaulx* (mantles), and *sayes* (coats). The first two garments were much wider and usually also longer than the last one, and thus required much more fabric, resulting in a higher total material cost. Lameere, *Recueil des Ordonnances des Pays-Bas. Vol 3. 1529–1536*, 271–272.

information regarding the number of recoverable horses for military campaigns.[32]

That the ordinance of 1531 was, at most, moderately effective is shown by the many repetitions and specifications that followed on the orders of Mary of Hungary in 1542, 1545, 1546 and 1550.[33] Unsurprisingly then, in the sumptuary law of January 1545 there is a clear tone of frustration with the civil disobedience of sumptuary laws.[34]

In 1550 Emperor Charles opened yet another sumptuary law with the remark 'that the before-mentioned unruliness increases ever more on account of the diversity of clothes and the fashion of decorating them with gold and silver thread, fringe, embroidery, and various sorts of silk laces, stitching and other new inventions'.[35] This law barred not only cloth of gold and silver or metal thread passement-erie, but also all other imaginable decorations in which gold or silver was applied in any way. Just like the law of 1531, it meticulously spe-cified who could wear what, expanding the prohibition of silk clothes to livery as well as prohibiting the use of all kinds of silk in the dress of artisans, craftsmen and villagers. Instead of bargaining silk possession for horses, this time around there were only fines to be paid, of which one quarter went straight into the imperial treasury, at the expense of the church.[36]

These laws show that it was not only the import of exotic fabrics that worried the Spanish-Habsburg rulers in the Low Countries[37] – their need for money, brought on by an almost continuous state of war, inspired a form of sumptuary legislation that functioned as a conspicuous con-sumption tax (either in the form of war horses or simply as money) on the wearing of silk clothes, rather than forbidding it entirely. This motivation is given a clear voice by a sumptuary law on the wearing of silk clothes

[32] Ibid., 272.

[33] Jules Lameere, *Recueil des Ordonnances des Pays-Bas, Deuxième Série, 1506–1700. Vol 4. 1536–1543* (Brussels: J. Goemaere, 1907), 410–411; ibid., *Vol 4. 1536–1543* (Brussels: J. Goemaere, 1910), 213–14, 269; ibid., *Vol 6. 1549–1555* (Brussels: J. Goemaere, 1922), 81–82.

[34] Ibid., *Vol 4. 1536–1543*, 213.

[35] Ibid., *Vol 6. 1549–1555*, 81, original quote: 'dat de voorschreven ongheregheltheyt vermeerdert langhs zo meer: zoo overmids de diverscheyt van cleederen ende tfautsoen van dien met recamueren, gaut ende zelver draet, frenyen, borduerwerck ende meer andere soorten van zyde snoeren, sticsels ende andere nieuwe invention'.

[36] Ibid., *Vol 6. 1549–1555*, 80–83.

[37] In 1527 Margaretha of Austria complained in a letter to the town magistracy of Antwerp how the excessive consumption of silk contributed to a loss of about 300.000 ducats each year. Alfons K. L. Thijs, 'Les textiles au marché Anversois au XVIe siècle', in Erik Aerts and John M. Munro, (eds.), *Textiles of the Low Countries in European Economic History* (Leuven: Leuven University Press, 1990), 80.

issued by Willem of Orange in 1578.[38] It opens by noting that 'van noode is middelen te vinden om ghelt te hebben' (there is a need to find ways of obtaining money) and a few lines further down explains why: 'om te bewaren ende beschermen de voirseide landen tegens alle oppressien, ghewelt, forcen ende invasien' (to preserve and protect the aforesaid [Low] countries against all oppression, violence, force and invasions). Given the fact that 'de zotternije int volck te zeer verwortelt is' (the foolishness [of dress] is so deeply rooted in the people) there was no way to put into proper order the consumption of silk. Therefore the authorities decided 'datmen eenenyeghelijck taxeren soude na zyne qualiteyt ende graet ende dat zy voir eenen prijs voir een jaer' (that they would tax everyone, according to their quality and degree, a fixed price for the duration of one year). Within this one year for which the tax was paid, one was allowed to wear what one pleased.[39] What is different in this law from all the previous ones is that the tax was not levied according to the type and quantity of silk used, but rather according to the social status of the wearer, a clear sign of its predominantly fiscal preoccupation.

These princely luxury laws differ from other European sumptuary laws not only in their chronology – as in Germany (see Rublack's chapter in this volume) they appeared only at the very end of the Middle Ages – but also in the discourse used. Rather than targeting social emulation and the obscuring of social hierarchy, the laws were preoccupied instead with the implications of luxury consumption, more particularly of foreign textiles, on the domestic economy.

Playing by the Rules?

That the consumption of imported silk, which was at the heart of sixteenth-century luxury laws, was a widespread phenomenon in the Low Countries, regardless of sumptuary legislation, is clearly shown in the fact that these regulations alarmed both Italian and Antwerp silk merchants. This can be inferred from the private letters of Pieter van der Molen, the manager of the Antwerp Van der Molen merchant company. On 14 November 1540, Pieter wrote to Jeronimo Azeretto di Vivaldis, one of his Italian clients, that there were rumours that Emperor Charles V would publish a new law on velvet and silk cloth. Nothing happened,

---

[38] In its opening notes this placard refers to a regulation issued the previous year on the wearing of silk, which, however, as far as the authors are aware, has not been preserved.

[39] Christoffel Plantijn, *Listen vande generale middelen gheresolueert by zijn Alteze, mijn Heere den Prince van Orangnien, den Raedt van State, ende de generale Staten* (Antwerp: Christoffel Plantijn, 1578).

however, until February 1542, when Pieter wrote to Jeronimo again, this time to announce that 'the court has promulgated a new law: nobles or those who act like nobles who wear garments made of velvet, satin or damask, have to keep two horses of fifteen hands high to serve the court when necessary. So it will be too difficult for most to pay for silk garments and keeping two horses.' Pieter suggestively added to his last letter that probably this law would fade into obscurity as previous laws had done.[40]

Still, that silk merchants were quite nervous about sumptuary legislation confirms that the local demand of the urban upper and middling groups certainly had a notable effect on their volume of sales. That their customers, conversely, were not too troubled by sumptuary laws is clearly shown by the profusion of silk objects in probate inventories. On the basis of a sixteenth-century price list, Alfons Thijs voiced a rather pessimistic view of the potential of people of lower social groups to acquire even the cheapest silk textiles, despite the broad price range of silk and silk-blend textiles.[41] In his opinion urban middling groups would have had a more luxurious textile consumption pattern, which is confirmed by the probate inventory evidence we presently have at our disposal.[42] Indeed, in the middle of the sixteenth century, both silk and semi-silk (fabrics of mixed fibre content including silk) items were widespread among all social layers of the Antwerp society that is covered by our probate inventory evidence. Almost every household possessed at least one item in (semi-)silk.[43] As can be expected, people with lesser means were inclined to invest more eagerly in smaller items of silk, in cheaper silk products, as well as in locally produced semi-silks. Nonetheless, even clothing fabricated from the more luxurious velvet was not completely missing from the lower social categories of our probate inventory testators. In the 1560s almost 40 per cent of the more modest one-room dwellers in Antwerp owned velvet. In the middling layers of society this percentage varied between 33 and 70 per cent of all households (Figure 2.1).

---

[40] State Archives Antwerp, IB 2898, Copy-letterbook of Pieter Van der Molen 1538–1544, fol. 186r., fol. 225v. Translation taken from Jeroen Puttevils, 2015.

[41] Thijs, 'Les textiles au marché Anversois au XVIe siècle', 86.

[42] This data was drawn from a database constructed and described by Carolien De Staelen, *Spulletjes en hun betekenis in een commerciële metropool. Antwerpenaren en hun materiële cultuur in de zestiende eeuw* (Unpublished PhD thesis, University of Antwerp, 2007). The social stratification of the inventories in this database is founded on the number of rooms mentioned in the documents. Six social classes have been defined: class I with 1 room, II: 2–3 rooms, III: 4–7 rooms, IV: 8–11 rooms, V: 12–15 rooms and class VI with 16+ rooms.

[43] In probate inventories it is impossible to systematically distinguish between imported and locally produced silks.

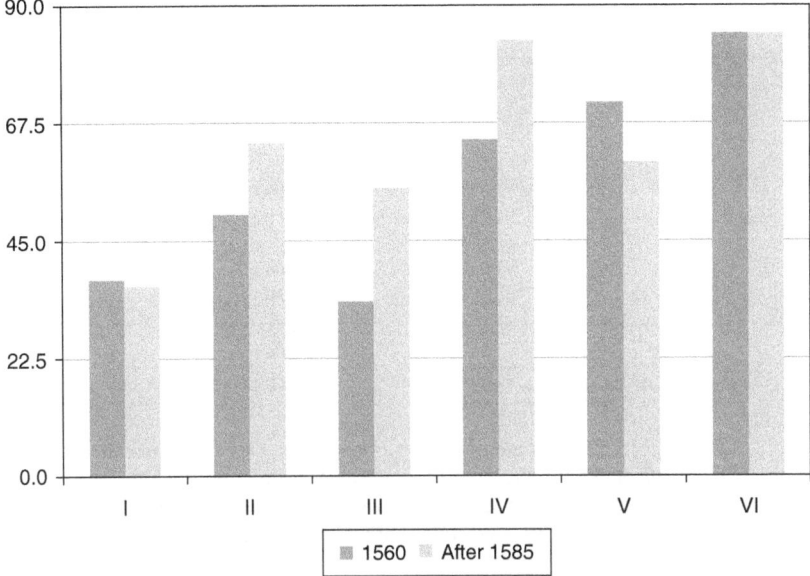

Figure 2.1 Percentage of Antwerp households with consumer items made from velvet, 1560 and 1585. Municipal Archives of Antwerp, Notariaat. Database Carolien De Staelen, University of Antwerp – Centre for Urban History.

In Bruges, which around this time was a city in decline, tormented by economic failure (thanks not least to Antwerp's competitive position) and religious conflict, the image of silk consumption seems much more modest.[44] Here, velvet appears only in the higher urban social levels, and in notable quantities only towards the end of the sixteenth century. However, cheaper varieties of silk, including satin (which was also locally produced from a combination of linen and silk), were recorded in inventories of the lower middling groups (Figures 2.2a and 2.2b). Even though the sumptuary laws generally speak of silk, the only types of silk ever specified in normative texts were the three most precious varieties: velvet, damask and satin. Cheaper silks such as ormesin and taffeta do not seem to have worried governments to such an extent as to deem

---

[44] This data was drawn from a database constructed by Inneke Baatsen, Julie De Groot and Isis Sturtewagen, containing post mortem and confiscation inventories from Bruges. The social stratification of the Bruges inventories was based on professional group (shopkeepers and artisans were defined as the core of the middling groups), house rent value and total number of objects per household.

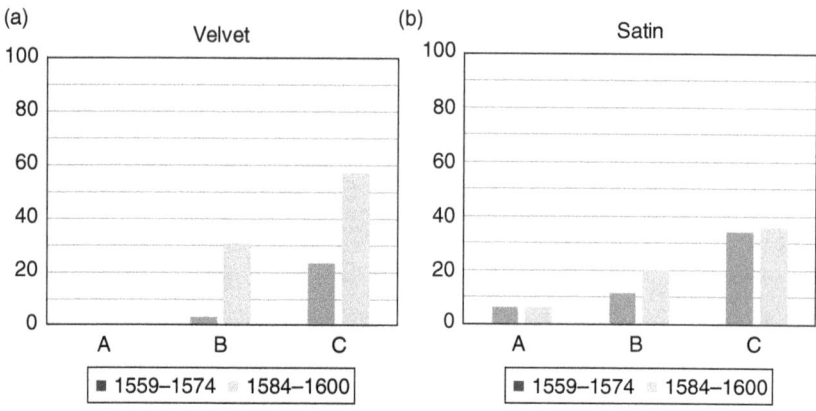

Figure 2.2a Percentage of Bruges households with consumer items made from velvet, 1559–1574, and 1584–1600. Municipal Archives of Bruges, Staten van Goed (1st and 2nd series) and Klerken van de Vierschaar. Database Inneke Baatsen, Julie De Groot and Isis Sturtewagen.

Figure 2.2b Percentage of Bruges households with consumer items made from satin, 1559–1574, and 1584–1600. Municipal Archives of Bruges, Staten van Goed (1st and 2nd series) and Klerken van de Vierschaar. Database Inneke Baatsen, Julie De Groot and Isis Sturtewagen.

them worth mentioning. Clearly, the low-end silks which were increasingly produced locally were tolerated, as was the use of more costly silks in smaller dress items – such as hats, partlets, belts and sleeves – or in the form of decorative trimmings and guards.[45] The sartorial order that the central government wanted to impose on its subjects was, if anything, old fashioned and almost counterfactual. It fell by the wayside in a society in which local silk production gradually developed from a substitute for imported silks into a successful industry, which by the sixteenth century catered for both local demand and foreign markets. While the Caroline

[45] Such decorative bands were not included in the above graphs, which only take into account the main materials that clothes and accessories were made of. In both Antwerp and Bruges this use of silk appears in lower middling group inventories in much higher numbers. In Bruges, for instance, 15 per cent of households in the lower middling groups (A) owned clothes with silk embellishments, almost 60 per cent of households in social group B and 82 per cent in group C in the period 1584–1600. In the earlier sample period the percentages were lower, but still included 8 per cent in group A; 22 per cent in group B; and 61 per cent in group C.

law of 1531 and later repetitions of it carefully guarded the status boundaries within the elites through the silk fabrics they were allowed to wear,
they hardly paid attention to the ascent of less expensive silk and semi-
silk fabrics, which by this time were fundamentally redefining the character of the concept of 'luxury' in the lower segments of the market.

Letters of clarification of sumptuary laws – such as the one concerning
the use of low quality woollens petitioned by the burghers of Bruges
mentioned above – show that both the nobility and urban citizens
constantly strived for a maximum exploitation of their rights. These
questions for clarification of certain details of the sumptuary laws came
from 'advocatz, procureurs, bourgois vivans de leurs rentes, marchans
en groz et leurs femmes' – precisely those segments of society that had
themselves increasingly portrayed in their best dress on panel or canvas.[46]
Clearly, these people were creative in finding ways to circumvent legislation. A way around the prohibition of metallic thread textiles was found
in the expanding industry for silk and metal thread passementerie.[47]
Both visual sources and probate inventories amply illustrate how such
ribbons and bands were used to decorate the edges of garments: hems
of skirts, necklines, wrists, along the buttoned opening of doublets, etc.
The edict of 1545 was a response to repeated questions about the decoration of collars and ruffs with gold and silver thread. The judgement
of Mary of Hungary was that since the Caroline law did not explicitly
forbid it, it was allowed. So too, she decided, was the use of gold and
silver buttons on clothing, which was another point that needed clarification. Similarly, doubt had arisen about the use of crimson velvet for small
dress items such as sleeves. The use of this expensive colour, which was
typically dyed in specialised northern Italian dyers' workshops at that
time, was not explicitly mentioned in the previous laws for sleeves, hence
was allowed for this specific purpose.[48]

On top of repeating the above points of discussion, a declaration
dated 3 December 1550 specified that this use of silk was also allowed
for artisans of the middling groups (les mechaniques), as was the use of
camlets and ostades. The wearing of crimson doublets for men and
kirtles for women, as well as silk linings, was permitted only to the
urban elites.[49] In sixteenth-century probate inventories from Bruges and
Antwerp, it is exactly these small items of dress, such as sleeves, partlets

---

[46] Lameere, *Recueil des Ordonnances des Pays-Bas, Vol 4. 1536–1543*, 128.

[47] Thijs, *De zijdenijverheid te Antwerpen*, 113–127.

[48] Lameere, *Recueil des Ordonnances des Pays-Bas, Deuxième Série, 1506–1700. Vol 5. 1543–1549*, 213–214.

[49] Lameere, *Recueil des Ordonnances des Pays-Bas. Vol 4. 1536–1543*, 128.

and hoods, or decorative bands on clothes, that most often were made from silk or half-silk fabrics.

It is clear that in this region there was no breeding ground for strict dress regulations restraining luxury consumption and luxurious displays. Sumptuary laws were negotiable to some extent, as is shown by the petitions for clarification addressed to the court. Town councils pressed the government explicitly to decriminalise certain practices at the fringes of legislation, such as the crimson sleeve.

A New 'Wave' of Legislation

It seems that no new sumptuary laws were issued from 1578 until well into the seventeenth century. The first new sumptuary law was instituted in 1632. On 26 January 1679, Carlos van Villa-Hermosa (the Spanish governor) renewed the more than century-old sumptuary law of 1550.[50]

In the seventeenth and eighteenth centuries, new legislative actions were issued, aimed at limiting display of wealth and at restricting specific types of dress or accessories for certain groups of people. These no longer showed concern with exotic fabrics and balances of trade. Dutch towns occasionally instituted sumptuary laws restricting the duration and size of banquets: three such laws were passed in Amsterdam in 1655 restricting marriage feasts, and in November 1672 aimed more generally at 'unnecessary and sumptuous banquets'.[51]

Throughout the seventeenth century, a number of edicts were issued in the Netherlands which regulated mourning, for instance in Amsterdam in 1637 and 1664[52] and in Flanders on 22 June 1696 (and later reissued in 1720). The latter stipulated that only the direct relatives of the deceased (ascendenten) were allowed to wear full mourning, consisting of a long black cloth mantle for men and dress for women, and a transparent crêpe veil; all others attending the funeral had to wear only a short mourning mantle. Moreover it was strictly forbidden to have domestic servants dress in mourning, or to wear mourning dress for a period longer than six months.[53] These laws seem to coincide with

---

[50] Veerle De Laet, *Brussel Binnenskamers. Kunst- en luxebezit in het spanningsveld tussen hof en stad, 1600–1735* (Amsterdam: Amsterdam University Press, 2011), 159.

[51] Willem Pieter Cornelis Knuttel, *Catalogus van de pamfletten-verzameling berustende in de Koninklijke Bibliotheek*, vol. II 1649–1667 (Den Haag: n.a., 1892), nr. 7687; Noordkerk, *Handvesten ofte privilegiën*, iii: 527.

[52] Noordkerk, *Handvesten ofte privilegiën*, 2: 2365.

[53] Georgius Fricx, *Vierde Placcaet-boec van Vlaenderen behelsende alle de placcaeten, ordonantiën, … geëmaneert voor de Provincie van Vlaenderen, sedert 't jaer 1684 tot ende met 1739* (Brussels: 1740), 1335, 1340.

spells of plague, which flared up numerous times, and might have been concerned with limiting the circulation of mourning dress, which was often bought second hand or rented, for fear of contamination. However, there was also clearly a concern with social display at funerals. Overly long garments were regulated not only in the context of mourning. An edict dated 1754 aimed to regulate, alongside mourning dress and multi-coloured livery for domestic servants, the use of long trains in clothing: 'Robben met slepende steirten en vermag niemant te draegen als de vrouwen van Hertogen, Princen ende Marcquisen, op Boete van ses hondert guldens' (Gowns with trailing tails are not allowed to be worn by anyone but the wives of dukes, princes, and marquises, on penalty of a fine of six hundred pounds).[54] Moreover, in the second half of the seventeenth century, several laws were issued that taxed and limited funeral and mourning expenses in various Flemish and Brabant towns, though mourning dress was not specifically targeted.[55] In 1664 the city of Antwerp introduced a tax on torches in funeral processions, and in 1685 the Council of Brabant decreed a new funeral ordinance which aimed to redress 'the excesses and abuses which occur daily during burials and funerals'. The new ordinance clearly articulated distinct 'funeral categories' and introduced a series of restrictions on showy items such as the ringing of bells, decoration of altars and the use of torches (the latter limited to 24 for a 'koorlijk', which was the highest funeral category). Financial restrictions also applied to the use of music. In this period similar funeral laws were issued for Mechelen (1692), Brussels (1692, 1699) and Ghent (1733).[56]

From the Northern Netherlands, particularly Amsterdam and Zeeland, there were a number of laws which tried to regulate the 'ongeregeltheden der dienstboden' (the unruliness of servants) in 1641, 1642 and 1679.[57] A specific issue with servant dress in Flanders was the appropriation of elements of military dress. In August 1765, a law prohibiting the recent fashion of using epaulettes in the livery uniforms of domestic servants was made public. These epaulettes were a distinctive mark of the army

---

[54] See the edict of 11 December 1754, *Vijfden Placcaet-boec van Vlaenderen geëmaneert van de Provincie van Vlaenderen*, Gendt (1763), 1034 – art. xxxii.

[55] Stefanie Beghein, *Kerkmuziek, consumptie en confessionalisering. Het muziekleven aan Antwerpse parochiekerken* (unpublished PhD thesis, University of Antwerp, 2014), 162–164.

[56] Stefanie Beghein, 'Music and funeral practices in Antwerp, c.1650–1750', in Stefanie Beghein, Bruno Blondé and Eugeen Schreurs (eds.), *Music and the City: Musical Cultures and Urban Societies in the Southern Netherlands and Beyond, c.1650–1800* (Leuven: Leuven University Press, 2013), 91–93.

[57] Noordkerk, *Handvesten ofte privilegiën*, ii: 2256; iii: 527; iv: 1080.

officers of the Crown, and everyone who did not belong to this rank was given one month to remove them from their clothes, or pay a fine of three hundred florins. Two months later, on 5 October, a supplementary law was issued regarding the decoration of swords in the military fashion, i.e. with gold tassels and black silk, which was now forbidden to anyone but the officers in the army, also punished by a fine of three hundred florins.[58]

Paradoxically, these examples of seventeenth- and eighteenth-century Netherlandish sumptuary laws were, much more explicitly than those in the sixteenth century, concerned primarily with the display of social status and rank. The development was quite unlike what happened in many other European countries. By this time sumptuary legislation in France and England was aimed primarily, or even solely, at preventing the outflow of bullion. The government of Louis XIV tried to support the French silk industry by limiting and banning the use of printed cottons, while England issued its so-called Calico Act in 1720.[59] Hence, even though the Low Countries adopted an economic approach to sumptuary legislation very early on,[60] it seems that in the late sixteenth and seventeenth centuries the legislators took on a more 'old-fashioned' conspicuous consumption discourse similar to the one that had been usual in the fourteenth-century Netherlands and until the sixteenth century in other European countries. No doubt this process was aided by the influence of the Reformation and Counter-Reformation, as well as by the introduction of new institutional trajectories of gaining noble status. Another important factor must have been the economic transformations that took place in the Low Countries during the seventeenth and eighteenth centuries.

Moralising Discourses

Buoyant luxury industries and a specific urban mentality geared towards serving the urban middle classes went hand in glove with poor sumptuary law restrictions and even poorer observance thereof: very little trace of

---

[58] De Ridder, 'Contribution à l'histoire du costume', 124. Algemeen Rijksarchief, Brussel, Conseil privé autrichien, carton n° 973.

[59] Feudenberger, 'Fashion, Sumptuary Laws and Business', 43.

[60] In most other European countries the change in sumptuary laws from dominantly moral and hierarchical to chiefly economic would take place about a century later. This has been discussed in detail for England by Margaret Rose Jaster, '"Clothing themselves in Acres": Apparel and Impoverishment in Medieval and Early Modern England', *Medieval Clothing and Textiles* 2 (2006): 93–95; and Susan Vincent, *Dressing the Elite: Clothes in Early Modern England* (Oxford: Berg, 2003), 117–143.

prosecution can be found in the Low Countries.[61] Moreover, the early sumptuary laws were heavily preoccupied with economic motives. Only in the second half of the seventeenth century does a more old-fashioned concern with refraining from overt 'conspicuous consumption' surface. Yet, the real significance of the few sumptuary laws that were issued in this period was that they were of only marginal importance. In fact, they touched upon limited manifestations of material culture. As a result, the Low Countries were an area where – implicitly or explicitly – 'freedom of consumption' was almost taken for granted.[62] Yet, as Patricia Allerston has already argued for sixteenth-century Venice, consumption, even in affluent urban societies and centres of luxury production, was seldom considered as culturally unproblematic.[63]

Indeed, sumptuary laws were but a small part of a larger regulatory environment in which unwritten rules and social pressure played an important part. In this light it is important to look beyond formal dress regulations and to consider the wider contemporary ideological discourses on clothes.[64] Moralising literature, paintings and caricature prints were common in the Low Countries, and in this contribution we cannot but superficially evoke some of their aspects by selectively and suggestively quoting from iconographic and literary sources. The writings of Bruges rhetorician Cornelis Everaert (c. 1480–1556), for instance, show that the negative effects of foreign textiles and other luxury goods on the domestic economy were also a concern outside court circles. Everaert, interestingly, shares a concern about foreign competition through imported fashion goods. This issue is the central problem in many of his plays written in the late 1520s and 1530s, for example the 'Spel van Ghemeene Neerrynghe' (Play of Common Trade), 'Esbatement van Arm in de Buerse' (Play of Poor in the Purse) and 'Spel van d'Onghelycke Munte' (Play of the Unequal Coin). All these plays centre on the socio-economic troubles in Bruges at that time, through personifications of the poor craftsmen, bourgeois consumers and the guilds. Everaert's plays attribute the poverty of the craftsmen and labourers to the exuberant lust

---

[61] With the exception of a fine of 20 s. 'zin cledre te draghene tieghen de kuere' (for wearing clothes against the law) mentioned in the Bruges city accounts of 1308, before the first known sumptuary law. Gilliodts-van Severen, *Inventaire des Archives*, 151.

[62] Jan de Vries, 'Luxury in the Dutch Golden Age in Theory and Practice', in Maxine Berg and Elizabeth Eger (eds.), *Luxury in the Eighteenth Century. Debates, Desires and Delectable Goods* (Basingstoke: Palgrave, 2003), 41–56.

[63] Patricia Allerston, 'Consuming Problems: Worldly Goods in Renaissance Venice', in ed. Michelle O'Malley and Evelyn Welch (eds.), *The Material Renaissance* (Manchester: Manchester University Press, 2007), 11–46.

[64] Jaster, 'Clothing themselves in Acres', 95.

of the urban consumer for foreign goods, which weakened and ultimately destroyed the guilds.[65]

Yet, from the fourteenth-century writings of Antwerp city clerk Jan van Boendale to later authors such as Desiderius Erasmus and the mystic poet Anna Bijns, the majority of moralist writings share one important characteristic: instead of focusing on class differentiation or trade balance, they concentrate on the cut and shape of garments, as well as their decoration. Jan van Boendale complained in his 'Bouc van der Wraken' (Book of Vengeance, c. 1346) that 'the women wear long clothes that gird them so tightly that the shape of their private parts becomes visible, by which they lead men into impurities'. Concerning men, Boendale remarked: 'The men wear clothing so short that it only just reaches their private parts'.[66]

Desiderius Erasmus advises the eleven-year-old Henry of Burgundy that 'having long trains is laughed at in women and despised in men'. Moreover, he warned that, although it was now accepted to wear loose clothes, it was seen as highly dishonourable if one's dress did not cover the private parts of one's body when kneeling or bending over.[67] Anna Bijns (1493–1575), although referring repeatedly to the increasingly sumptuously dressed commoners and peasants who now donned expensive silks, above all complained about the new shapes and styles of dress (*nieuwe sneden*) and the decoration of garments by slashing the fabric.[68] These moralist writings, very much like the dress laws from Kampen and Zutphen almost two centuries earlier, targeted purely decorative, and often impractical, elements in clothes. There is however a connotation of status present in such texts, in that these exaggerated forms seem to have been accepted for the nobility but considered foolish in urban contexts. Cornelia, the chairwoman of Erasmus's 'Women's Parliament', complains how women who married into knightly households immediately started wearing trains of fifteen ells long, and in this way not only

---

[65] Jacob Wijbrand Muller and Lodewijk Scharpé, *Spelen. Cornelis Everaert* (Leiden: E.J. Brill, 1920), 635–636.

[66] Original text: 'Vrouwen draghen cledre lanc, daer si in sijn ghepranct, datment daer dore merct ghereyt die vorme herre schamelheyt, daer si die manne mede leyden te gheloesder loesheyden' and 'Die manne draghen cledere mede cort tote hare scamelhede'. Ferdinand Augustijn Snellaert, *Nederlandsche gedichten uit de veertiende eeuw* (Brussels: M. Hayez, Drukker der Koninklijke Akademie, 1869), 372.

[67] Herman De la Fontaine Verwey, *Het boeckje van Erasmus aengaende de beleeftheidt der kinderlijcke zeden, Herdrukt naar de Latijns-Nederlandse uitgave van 1678* (Amsterdam: Universiteits-Bibliotheek, 1969), 23.

[68] Original quote: 'Sijde, laken, flueel en soude niet verslijten, Waert niet duerhouwen, duerhackelt, duersneden'. Willem Lodewijk Van Helten, *Refreinen van Anna Bijns, Naar de nalatenschap van A. Bogaers* (Rotterdam: n.a., 1875), 118 and 152.

pushed the boundaries of their own social class but also forced the wives of dukes and counts to wear even longer trains.[69]

Not only written accounts but also painting and print provided lively moralist commentary on fashion. The success of the starched ruff in the sixteenth century was a favourite topic of moralising images. The mid-sixteenth-century engravings designed by Pieter van der Borcht and Maerten de Vos depicted scenes of starchers' workshops operated by monkeys and demons, with the grim reaper waiting on the doorstep.[70] A polyptych from the same period, *De Levensfontein*, painted by Lucas II Horenbout for the Ghent beguinage church Onze-Lieve-Vrouw ter Hoyen, condemns a similar range of goods in a religious context and on a monumental scale.[71] In the central panel heretics and disbelievers have gathered around a worldly altar; the priestess who leads the mass is half woman, half monster, dressed in crimson with a wide ruff around her neck. The altar doubles as a market stall, and under the slogan 'Compt al by en coopt my' (Please come by, and buy me) offers the merry spender a wide array of fashionable goods including *portefraesen* (supports for starched collars and ruffs), masks, cutlery cases, silver and gold cups, jewellery and a pomander. Plays and paintings did not have the official character of legislative texts but, in reflecting on the daily practice of dressing, they did not constitute a law in writing as much as a law of the mind.

In a similar vein, the arrival of French fashion in the seventeenth century provoked serious concerns, both regarding the social and economic and the sexual and moral order of society – the latter closely connected to the seductive cut of the French fashion.[72] The Antwerp Jesuit Adriaen Poirters, for instance, complained about women wearing a little cross in between their partially uncovered breasts 'as Christ hanging between two murderers'.[73] Apart from sexually inspired frictions between the French culture and the Counter-Reformation, old-fashioned concerns about the social order of society loomed large as well. The humanist

---

[69] Jeanine De Landtsheer, *Erasmus: Vrouwengesprekken. Een keuze uit de Colloquia* (Amsterdam: Athenaeum-Polak & Van Gennep Salamander Classic, 2005), 143–153.

[70] Ger Luijten, 'Frills and Furbelows: Satires on Fashion and Pride around 1600', *Simiolus: Netherlands Quarterly for the History of Art* 24 (1996): 140–160.

[71] Anne De Breuck, *De Fonteyne des Levens van Lucas II Horenbault (ca. 1560-1626) in de klein begijnhofkerk O.-L.-Vrouw-ter-Hoye in Gent* (Leuven: 1988).

[72] Harald Deceulaer, *Pluriforme patronen en een verschillende snit. Sociaal-economische, institutionele en culturele transformaties in de kledingsector in Antwerpen, Brussel en Gent, 1585–1800* (Amsterdam: Stichting Beheer, 2001), 163–173; Ilja Van Damme, *Verleiden en verkopen: Antwerpse kleinhandelaars en hun klanten in tijden van crisis (ca. 1648-ca. 1748)* (Amsterdam: Aksant, 2007), 208–213; De Laet, *Brussel Binnenskamers*, 159–164.

[73] Deceulaer, *Pluriforme patronen*, 168.

Erycius Puteanus (1574–1646) satirically evoked maidservants that were inclined to dress as noblewomen, similar to the sumptuary laws on servant dress discussed above.[74] In the case of French fashion, finally, economic considerations still played a role as well.[75] Tellingly, the only sumptuary law from this period that has clear economic interests is a 1671 placard from Amsterdam prohibiting all 'Fransche manufacturen tot kleedinge' (French clothing items).[76]

This embarrassment did not prevent French fashion from becoming extremely influential around 1700. Strikingly, eccentric manifestations of the French courtly fashion, such as the periwig, were appropriated in bourgeois circles and adapted to a bourgeois lifestyle by moderating their shape and size.[77]

Yet, in the relative absence of harsh sumptuary constraints, moralistic literature, plays and satirical prints still played a role in demarcating and sustaining social boundaries. Satire does not have the ambition or the enforcing character of a sumptuary law, but, because it spread quickly in print, it was probably more effective in putting its message across to a larger group of people.[78] Although probate inventories and paintings indicate that people did not strictly comply with sumptuary legislation and certainly pushed the limits of what was socially accept-able, there was nevertheless a broad consensus and diverse discourse about what could be worn by whom. This consensus is visible in both the types of garments worn by people of different social standings and the materials used to make their clothes. Although silk appears in many lower-middling-group households, the quantities used were limited, and expensive varieties such as brocade and patterned velvets remained exclusive to the richest city-dwellers. A 'travel account' illustrates this point. In the French capital, Dutch elite travellers felt compelled to buy apparel that was appropriate for keeping up appearances in a Parisian context. However costly, at home these would be useless because, as Jan Teding van Berkhout recorded in the eighteenth century, the apparel bought was 'too beautiful to dare wear them in Holland'.[79] Clearly,

---

[74] De Laet, *Brussel binnenkamers*, 160.

[75] Ilja Van Damme, 'Middlemen and the Creation of a "Fashion Revolution": The Experience of Antwerp in the Late Seventeenth and Eighteenth Centuries', in Beverly Lemire (ed.), *The Force of Fashion in Politics and Society. Global Perspectives from Early Modern to Contemporary Times* (Aldershot: Ashgate, 2010), 21–39.

[76] Noordkerk, *Handvesten ofte privilegiën*, 3: 268.

[77] Michael Kwass, 'Big Hair: A Wig History of Consumption in Eighteenth-Century France', *American Historical Review* 111/3 (2006): 631–659; Deceulaer, *Pluriforme patronen*, 169.

[78] Aileen Ribeiro, *Dress and Morality*, 2nd ed. (Oxford and New York: Berg, 2003).

[79] Jan Teding van Berkhout (1713–1766) belonged to the bourgeoisie and was for some time the burgomaster of Delft and commander of the Dutch East India Company. In

bourgeois society imposed its own limits on consumption and material culture.

Conclusion

While a general tendency in European sumptuary legislation has been noted as becoming increasingly concerned with business and economic life during the seventeenth and eighteenth centuries, in the Low Countries this tendency did not develop along similar lines. Despite the still relatively limited number of sumptuary laws, the new probate inventory evidence discussed in this chapter clearly shows a contrary evolution. During the Late Middle Ages, a period when sumptuary legislation in France, Italy, Germany and England was targeting social and moral transgressions, the Netherlands hardly issued sumptuary laws. Conversely, from its first appearance at the very end of the fifteenth century princely sumptuary legislation was concerned with economic preoccupations, rather than occupied with demarcating social stratification. During the seventeenth century, however, legislators and moralists developed, on top of an economic argument, a more 'old-fashioned' and moralising take in their discourses, similar to the ones that had been usual during the fourteenth and fifteenth centuries in other European countries.

A comparison between sumptuary laws and other forms of written and visual sources shows that sumptuary regulation did not exist in a vacuum but rather interconnected with more generally held views and conventions on dressing. The case of the Low Countries suggests that changes in the rhetoric of sumptuary regulations are influenced strongly by the political, economic and religious context in which they are produced.

Sumptuary legislation, however important in some other regions, was a relatively insignificant building block of social conventions in the Low Countries. Yet, even in the relative absence of harsh sumptuary constraints, it is clear that social conventions shaped the imperatives of what historians of the seventeenth and eighteenth centuries have labelled as a 'bourgeois society'.

the original: 'qui sont trop beau pour oser les porter en Hollande'. Gerrit Verhoeven, *Anders reizen? Evoluties in vroegmoderne reiservaringen van Hollandse en Brabantse elites (1600–1750)* (Hilversum: Verloren, 2009), 271–272.

3   'Outlandish Superfluities': Luxury
     and Clothing in Scottish and English
     Sumptuary Law from the Fourteenth
     to the Seventeenth Century

Maria Hayward

In or around 1670, John Kennedy, 7th Earl of Cassillis (1653–1701),
lobbied the Scottish Committee of Trades to pass a new sumptuary law
'for the betterment of trade and the restraining of outlandish superfluities'.[1] In doing so he engaged in the ongoing debate about the threat
posed by imported luxury goods to Scottish domestic trade. While
Cassillis voiced his concerns in Edinburgh, his anxieties were shared by
many in London. However, although Scotland and England had been
joined by the Union of the Crowns with the accession of James VI to the
English throne in 1603, the two countries maintained separate sumptuary
laws.[2] Between 1337 and 1604 rich clothing was regulated in England
through a combination of acts of parliament and proclamations.[3] James
VI and I abolished English sumptuary legislation in 1604,[4] but he issued

---

[1] National Records of Scotland (henceforth NRS), GD25/8/601.
[2] He also acceded to the Irish throne. For this topic see: Mairead Dunlevy, *Dress in
Ireland* (Teaneck, NJ: Holmes and Meier Publishers, 1989), 46–59; and Susan Flavin,
Consumption and Culture in Sixteenth-Century Ireland: Saffron, Stockings and Silk
(Woodbridge: Boydell & Brewer, 2014), 118–130.
[3] For the key works on English sumptuary legislation see Frances E. Baldwin, *Sumptuary
Legislation and Personal Regulation in England* (Baltimore: Johns Hopkins University,
1926); Wilfred Hooper, 'The Tudor Sumptuary Law', *English Historical Review* 30/119
(1915): 433–449; and Negley B. Harte, 'State Control of Dress and Social Change in
Pre-industrial England', in D. C. Coleman and A. H. John (eds.), *Trade, Government and
Economy in Pre-Industrial England: Essays Presented to F. J. Fisher* (London: Weidenfeld and
Nicolson, 1976), 132–165. These all draw out the economic, social and moral implications
of the legislation. For a wider discussion of the economic significance of European sumptuary legislation see Martha C. Howell, *Commerce before Capitalism in Europe, 1300–1600*
(Cambridge: Cambridge University Press, 2010), 234–242. For an analysis of the role of
clothing prior to the acts of apparel, see Frederique Lachaud, 'Dress and Social Status in
England before the Sumptuary Laws', in Peter Coss and Maurice Keen (eds.) *Heraldry,
Pageantry and Social Display in Medieval England* (Woodbridge: Boydell Press, 2002),
105–123.
[4] Paul L. Hughes and James F. Larkin (eds.), *Stuart Royal Proclamations: Royal Proclamations
of King James I, 1603–1625* (Oxford: Clarendon Press, 1973), i: 253–257.

a series of proclamations on matters relating to luxurious clothing, and this continued under his son Charles I.[5] In contrast, James VI and I kept Scottish sumptuary law, which had begun in 1429/30, in place, and it continued until 1701.[6] As Marcia Pointon has demonstrated, the influence of sumptuary laws was felt well beyond 1700 with an Elizabethan statute being reprinted in a mid-eighteenth-century guide on the regulations to be observed when attending court.[7]

Both Scotland and England had sumptuary laws that applied to the whole nation rather than to specific cities, towns or burghs, although on occasion individual towns did produce their own regulations.[8] By seeking to regulate rich clothing, both countries acknowledged the sartorial value their citizens attached to being well dressed.[9] As a consequence, the high level of expenditure on clothing was considered detrimental to the wealth and well being of both nations. Rob Donn (1714–1778), writing in the mid-eighteenth century about the new clothes of the Scottish soldier and loyalist Hugh Mackay of Bighouse (d. 1770), summed the situation up when he observed that 'There is not a button nor a button-hole in it / That hasn't taken money off a poor man'.[10] While the form of these laws reveals points of similarity between the two countries, the structure and focus also uncover subtle differences. Most notable was their approach to the social hierarchy, with the English laws documenting the increasingly detailed gradations of rank from royal family to husbandman, while the Scots were divided into three estates in 1429/30 and just two in 1672.[11]

---

[5] This was not a new strategy – see Rudolph W. Heinze, 'The Pricing of Meat: A Study in the Use of Royal Proclamations in the Reign of Henry VIII', *Historical Journal* 12/4 (1969): 583.

[6] The historiography on Scottish sumptuary law is quite modest. Best known is F. J. Shaw, 'Sumptuary Legislation in Scotland', *The Juridical Review* 24 (1979): 81–115, which built on J. C., 'The Sumptuary Laws of Scotland', *Journal of Jurisprudence* 35 (1891): 290–297. Shaw suggests that Scottish sumptuary law may have begun earlier and that the legislation has been lost. Shaw, 'Sumptuary Legislation', 82.

[7] Marcia Pointon, 'Jewellery in Eighteenth-Century England', in Maxine Berg and Helen Clifford (eds.), *Consumers and Luxury: Consumer Culture in Europe 1650–1850*, (Manchester: Manchester University Press, 1999), 125.

[8] Alan Hunt, *Governance of the Consuming Passions: A History of Sumptuary Law* (New York: St Martin's Press, 1996), 211. He cites Coventry as an example of a town with its own clothing regulations.

[9] For Scottish dress in this period see R. M. D. Grange, *A Short History of Scottish Dress* (London: Burke's Peerage, 1966); and Rosalind K. Marshall, *Costume in Scottish Portraits, 1560–1830* (Edinburgh: Scottish National Portrait Gallery, 1986).

[10] Stana Nenadic, *Lairds and Luxury: The Highland Gentry in Eighteenth-Century Scotland* (Edinburgh: John Donald, 2007), 2.

[11] The broad three groups in 1429/30 were lords and knights with an income over two hundred merks, gentlemen and burgesses, and yeomen and commoners Thomas Thomson and Cosmo Innes, eds., *The Acts of Parliament of Scotland, 1124–1707*, 12 volumes (Edinburgh: HM General Register House, 1814–75) (hereforth *APS*), i: 18: 8–10; *Records of the Parliaments of Scotland to 1707* www.rps.ac.uk/trans/1430/12 (hereforth

In addition, while the English predominantly considered male clothing, the Scottish were more inclusive of women, with their laws often addressing men and women together. Finally, while both sets of legislation focused on the consumer, each country tried to tackle the other side of the problem in a different way. The Scots embraced suppliers in their sumptuary laws. In 1672 Scottish merchants were targeted for importing banned items, thereby recognising that merchants could drive the demand for luxuries just as much as the shopping population.[12] The English tried proclamations to regulate the tailoring trades. For instance in 1562 tailors and hosiers were limited to 1½ yards of cloth per pair of hose and were to be bound over by the sum of £40.[13] Not surprisingly some tailors and their customers were undeterred and on 24 January 1565 Richard Walweyn, a servant in London, was arrested for wearing 'a very monsterous and outraygous greate payre of hose'.[14]

For 247 years in England and for 271 in Scotland the parliaments at Westminster and Edinburgh sought to regulate 'monsterous and outraygous' clothing (Figure 3.1). Put another way, there was a period of approximately 150 years' overlap of sumptuary law in both countries, from 1450 to 1604, preceded by 93 years in England and followed by 97 in Scotland. As such, the focal period of the laws is in the long sixteenth century, couched in a broader period, which provides a view of changing ideas of and approaches to luxury in relation to clothing, fashion and textiles. This body of legislation is considered here in relation to three questions. First, what do the documents reveal about late medieval and early modern Scottish and English concepts of luxury?[15] Second, which goods were viewed as luxurious and what does this reveal about trade and taste in both countries? Third, what do the laws reveal about Scottish and English geographies of luxury? While both sets of sumptuary law

RPS) 1430/10–12 and the nobility and wealthy gentry as opposed to the rest of society in 1672, APS VIII, 71, c.21; RPS 1672/6/31.

[12] APS VIII, 71, c. 21; RPS 1672/6/31.
[13] Paul L. Hughes and James F. Larkin (eds.), *Tudor Royal Proclamations: vol 2, 1553–1587* (New Haven and London: Yale University Press, 1969), no. 493; Hunt, *Governance*, 120.
[14] Hooper, 'The Tudor Sumptuary Laws', 441; Amanda Bailey, *Flaunting: Style and the Subversive Male Body in Renaissance England* (Toronto: University of Toronto Press, 2007), 26.
[15] See Christopher J. Berry, *The Idea of Luxury: A Conceptual and Historical Investigation* (Cambridge: Cambridge University Press, 1994); and Woodruff D. Smith, *Consumption and the Making of Respectability, 1600–1800* (London: Routledge, 2002). For Scotland, see Nenadic, *Lairds and Luxury*. See also Clare Jackson, 'The Paradoxical Virtue of the Historical Romance: Sir George Mackenzie's Aretina and the Civil War', in *Celtic Dimensions of the British Civil Wars*, ed. John Young (Edinburgh: John Donald, 1997), 205–225.

Figure 3.1 Stylish cut and paning make this French doublet from the 1620s a prime example of the fashions legislators sought to control. Metropolitan Museum of Art, New York, 1989.196. The Costume Institute Fund, in memory of Polaire Weissman, 1989.

have been analysed separately in terms of trade, social hierarchy, gender relations or morality, this comparative focus on what they reveal about luxury and luxury goods provides a different approach.[16] It highlights some of the subtle, and not so subtle, differences between Scotland and England during this period. It suggests that while the union of the crowns might have brought the countries together under the rule of James VI

[16] See, for example, Lisa Jardine, '"Maketh thy doublet of changeable taffeta": Dress Codes, Sumptuary Law and Natural Orders', in Lisa Jardine (ed.), *Still Harping On: Women and Drama in the Age of Shakespeare* (Sussex: The Harvester Press, 1983), 141–168; John Scattergood, 'Fashion and Morality in the Late Middle Ages', in David Williams (ed.), *England in the Fifteenth Century: Proceedings of the 1986 Harlaxton Symposium* (Woodbridge: Boydell Press, 1987), 255–272. For discussions of morality see Cynthia B. Herrup, 'Law and Morality in Seventeenth-Century England', *Past & Present* 106 (1985): 102–123; and Aileen Ribeiro, *Dress and Morality* (London: B. T. Batsford, 1986).

and I and his Stuart successors, their relationships with luxury goods were not the same.

The Nature of Luxury in the Sumptuary Law

The concept of luxury, both as an idea and what that idea meant in relation to the range of desirable goods available to consumers, evolved from the mid-fourteenth century to the first few years of the eighteenth century. Magnificence, the acceptable face of medieval and early modern luxury for the social elite, was gradually replaced by the idea of beneficial luxury in the course of the long seventeenth century. According to writers such as Bernard Mandeville, a Dutch philosopher living in London in the 1680s, the demand for luxury goods – especially amongst the growing middling sort – would result in economic growth, especially when it promoted domestic industry over a reliance on foreign imports.[17] The court was often a catalyst for consumption but it was not without its critics. Sir George Mackenzie attacked the court as a source of luxury in his novel *Aretina* published in 1661. He believed that 'the mony which the poor country men buy with their sweat, must be sold for silk and spices'.[18] Attitudes towards luxury were also linked to, and tempered by, religious considerations. While both countries underwent the Reformation in the middle decades of the sixteenth century the results were very different, with Anglicanism and Puritanism in England and Presbyterianism and Episcopalianism in Scotland and small numbers of Catholics in both. Yet, as Rosalind Marshall has shown, Presbyterianism did not necessarily mean opposition to fine clothing. William Douglas, 3rd Duke of Hamilton (1634–1694), dressed in a magnificent style suited to his being the leading Scottish peer; he wore 'a new sute with gold buttons and brocade waistcoat' when he attended William III's birthday ball in 1689.[19] His wife Anne preferred dark, simpler clothes, but she made compromises with her dress choices when it was necessary to assert her place, and that of her husband, in public life.

The overt displays of luxurious extravagance demanded by public life were, according to Alan Hunt, at the heart of the thinking behind

---

[17] Nenadic, *Lairds and Luxury*, 12.

[18] Sir George Mackenzie, *Aretina, or The Serious Romance* (London: n.a. 1661), 224; cited in Jackson, 'The Paradoxical Virtue', 213.

[19] Rosalind K. Marshall, 'Conscience and Costume in Seventeenth-Century Scotland', *Costume* 6 (1972): 32–35; and in more detail in Rosalind K. Marshall, *The Days of Duchess Anne: Life in the Household of the Duchess of Hamilton, 1656–1716* (London: Harper Collins, 1973).

European sumptuary law in the late Middle Ages.[20] Yet the word 'luxury' was not used in the preambles to the Scottish and English acts and proclamations.[21] Instead, the Scots succinctly summed up the situation using the words 'sumptuous'[22] and 'costly'.[23] When more was required they settled for 'excess',[24] 'unnecessary sumptuousness',[25] and 'sumptuousness and prodigality'.[26] In 1581 they went further, noting that 'God has granted to this realm sufficient commodities for clothing of the inhabitants thereof within the self if the people were virtuously employed in working of the same at home'.[27] The English legislators opted for more variety and a slightly heightened level of disapproval, expressed in the terms 'outrageous and excessive',[28] 'inordinate',[29] and 'sumptuous and costly'.[30] They went further, inserting a moral dimension, asserting that luxurious clothing and accessories were selected by 'persons inclined to pride, mother of all vices'.[31] Stress was placed on:

the great, manifest and notorious detriment of the common weal, the subversion of good and politic order in knowledge and distinction of people according to their estates, pre-eminence, dignities and degrees, and to the utter impoverishment and undoing of many inexpert and light persons.[32]

The theme of pride was taken up by other commentators including the Puritan pamphleteer, Philip Stubbes, who denounced in 1585 the 'pride of apparel'.[33] And this pride in luxurious goods was more of a male failing than a female vice, as far as the English legislators were concerned, while the Scots were more even-handed in seeing men and women as equally culpable.

The desirability of novelty, both for consumers and producers, whether in the form of innovative goods or new styles of garments and accessories, was made evident in both sets of legislation. For instance, a Scottish

---

[20] Hunt, *Governance*, 34.
[21] For sumptuary law and luxury more broadly, see Catherine Kovesi Killerby, *Sumptuary Law in Italy, 1200–1500* (Oxford: Clarendon Press, 2002), 7. For a broader critique of luxury see Howell, *Commerce before Capitalism*, 214–227.
[22] In 1458 *APS* II, 49, c.13; *RPS* 1458/3/14.
[23] In 1581 *APS* III, 220, c.18; *RPS* 1581/10/37.
[24] In 1584 *APS* III, 354, c.15; *RPS* 1584/5/89.
[25] In 1621 *APS* IV, 625, c.25; *RPS* 1621/6/37.
[26] In 1672 *APS* VIII, 71, c.21; *RPS* 1672/6/31.
[27] *APS* III, 220, c.18; *RPS* 1581/10/37.
[28] In 1363 (37 Edw. III, cc. 8–14: Alexander Luders ed., *The Statutes of the Realm, 1101–1713*, 9 volumes, (London: Records Commission, 1810–1825) [*SR*] I, 380–381)
[29] In 1463 (3 Edw. IV, c.5; *SR* II, 399–402).
[30] In 1533 (24 Hen, VIII, c.13, *SR*, III, 430).
[31] In 1533 (24 Hen, VIII, c.13, *SR*, III, 430).
[32] 24 Hen, VIII, c.13, *SR*, III, 430.
[33] Philip Stubbes, *Anatomie of Abuses* (London; n.a., 1585), 70.

proclamation of 1686 banned 'the wearing of any new Invention'.[34] The significance of this was summed up in the early 1680s by the merchant Sir Josiah Childs when he observed that:

In all flowered Silks you change the fashion and flower every yeare, as much as you can – for English ladies, and they say the French, and other Europeans – will give twice as much for a new thing not seen in Europe before the worse, than they will give for a better Silke of the same fashion worne the former yeare.[35]

However, if royal legislation did not actually cite the concept of luxury and luxury goods, in 1592 the London authorities were more direct when they issued regulations to control 'the apparel of London apprentices' which they claimed were necessary because:

Luxury having greatly prevailed in this City amongst people of all degrees but in particular among Apprentices, in their apparel, etc, which then was justly apprehended might prove of dangerous consequence to their Masters.[36]

A male apprentice was not permitted to wear a hat in the city, fancy linens including ruffs, cuffs, or loose collars, coloured cloth or kersey in hose or stockings, no outer layer apart from a gown or cloak, a sword, dagger or other weapons or any rings or jewels. In addition, what the apprentice could wear was laid out in detail and it was practical and patriotic. He was permitted a woollen cap 'with no silk in or about the same', a ruff and collar made from no more than one and a half yards of fabric, a doublet (his upper body garment) made from canvas, fustian, sack-cloth, English leather or woollen cloth without any manner of gold or silver or silk, little breeches of the same stuff as the doublet which were not to be stitched, laced or bordered, shoes of English leather without being pinked, edged or stitched, and a knife.[37] This close scrutiny of adolescent male clothing reflected the part played by these young men, in an often volatile, adolescent street life.[38]

While this set of regulations emphasised what constituted luxury for apprentices, the royal wardrobes in Scotland and England acted as the benchmark for what was seen as ultimately luxurious or to use the

[34] NRS RH14/207.
[35] Quoted in Smith, *Consumption*, 52.
[36] John Nichols, *The Progresses and Public Processions of Queen Elizabeth* (London: Society of Antiquaries, 1823), 393. And compare with the growing discussion of luxury in contemporary literature; see Alison V. Scott, *Literature and the Idea of Luxury in Early Modern England* (Farnham: Ashgate, 2015).
[37] Nichols, *Progresses and Public Processions*, 393.
[38] A. L. Beier and Roger Finlay, 'Introduction: The significance of the metropolis', in A. L. Beier and Roger Finlay (eds.), *London 1500–1700: The Making of the Metropolis* (London: Longman, 1986), 21; Steven R. Smith, 'The London Apprentices as Seventeenth-Century Adolescents', *Past & Present* 61 (1973): 155–156.

preferred contemporary term, magnificent.[39] The English legislation increasingly defined the royal family in terms of exclusive access to certain items and these were specifically defined as purple silk, cloth of tissue and sable in 1533.[40] Analysis of Henry VIII's wardrobe accounts reveal purchases of all three items but in fairly modest amounts, indicating that these luxury goods were used carefully to create a specific effect on particular occasions when stressing royal authority really mattered.[41] In a similar vein, when the duke of Württemberg visited Elizabeth I's court in 1595 he recorded in his diary that 'At no other Court have I ever seen so much splendour and fine clothes'.[42]

In marked contrast, the Scottish legislation did not make purple or sable exclusive to the royal family. Indeed, there was no mention of purple at all. This did not mean that the Scottish monarchs did not wear purple, or sable. They did, as, for example, the accounts of James V (1512–42) reveal.[43] However, as the legislation of 1621 made clear, no constraints of any type, either positive or negative, were placed on 'the king's majesty, prince and their ordinary household servants', who were 'exempt from this act and all the clauses thereof'.[44] The king in question in 1621 was James VI and I, whose court was seen as opulent or luxurious according to the viewpoint of the observer.

Luxury Goods

While the word 'luxury' was not used in the sumptuary legislation, the documents recorded an ever-expanding list of 'luxury' goods. These were durable luxuries, as opposed to non-durable goods, such as food and wine, that could be appreciated when new, while retaining their value well as they aged. Consequently, they were often left as bequests and could be sold second-hand.[45] They could also be handed down, a factor noted in the Scottish legislation. For instance in 1621, in repetition of

---

[39] Maria A. Hayward, 'Luxury or Magnificence? Dress at the Court of Henry VIII', *Costume* 30 (1996): 37–46.

[40] 24 Hen, VIII, c.13, *SR*, III, 430.

[41] Maria A. Hayward, *Rich Apparel: Clothing and the Law in Henry VIII's England* (Aldershot: Farnham, 2009), 158–162.

[42] Victor von Klarwill, *Queen Elizabeth and some Foreigners* (London: Bodley Head, 1928), 376.

[43] Rosalind K. Marshall, 'To be the Kingis Grace ane Dowblett: The costume of James V, King of Scots', *Costume* 28 (1994): 14–21.

[44] *APS* IV, 625, c.25; *RPS* 1621/6/37, no. 5.

[45] Hunt, *Governance*, 33. For an example of how clothes could be pawned, see Reginald A. Foakes ed., *Henslowe's Diary* (Cambridge: Cambridge University Press [or. ed. 1961], 2002).

earlier legislation, 'It is always declared that it may be lawful for them [i.e. servants] to wear their master's or mistress's old clothes'.[46] Many of the items, such as cloth of gold tissue, were desirable because they were made from high value/precious materials, by craftsmen with high levels of skill who received high wages. There were three consequences of this. First, there was a split between luxury and semi-luxury goods, the latter being inexpensive or moderately inexpensive versions of elite luxuries for those with less disposable income (or, put another way, one man or woman's luxury was another's semi-luxury). Second, there were concerns about the quality of available items, and of their being genuine.[47] Third, novelty, innovation and limited availability also helped define what was seen as being luxurious. Most of the items that fell into these categories in this period in England and Scotland were imports.[48]

Not surprisingly, sumptuary laws concentrated on textiles and the broad context in both the Scottish and English legislation indicates that several clear distinctions with regards to luxury were being made.[49] Most important were the fabrics incorporating metal thread, which were usually but not exclusively silks, followed by the sub-divisions within the range of silks available, the wool–silk divide, the distinction between imported and domestically produced woollens and the range of imported linens, with the very fine, light-weight linens being the most highly prized (Figure 3.2).[50]

The chief difference between the Scots and the English was the level of detail recorded in relation to the range of silks being regulated. In 1581 'any cloth of gold or silver, velvet, satin, damask, [and] taffeta' was listed, while in 1621 the law was concerned with 'gold or silver cloth, or any gold or silver lace ... velvet, satin or other stuff of silk'.[51] In contrast, while the fifteenth- and early sixteenth-century English legislation referred to cloth of tissue, cloth of gold and silver, velvet, satin and damask, by the later sixteenth century, as the 1574 statute indicates, the

---

[46] *APS* IV, 625, c.25; *RPS* 1621/6/37, no. 6.
[47] On the changing value and visibility of moveable, consumable luxury goods, see Howell, *Commerce before Capitalism*, 14–15.
[48] John Styles, 'Product Innovation in Early Modern London', *Past & Present* 168 (2000): 124–169. And in 1579 in terms of 'the devising any new forms of apparel', Hughes and Larkin, *Tudor Royal Proclamations. Vol 2*, no. 624.
[49] Hunt, *Governance*, 70.
[50] For the range of Italian silks available see Lisa Monnas, *Merchants, Princes and Painters: Silk Fabrics in Italian and Northern Paintings 1300–1550* (New Haven and London: Yale University Press, 2008) and Lisa Monnas, *Renaissance Velvets* (London: V&A Publishing, 2012).
[51] *APS* III, 220, c.18; *RPS* 1581/10/37 and *APS* IV, 625, c.25; *RPS* 1621/6/37. For definitions of textile terms see Dorothy K. Burnham, *A Textile Terminology: Warp and Weft* (Sydney: Law Book Company of Australasia, 1982).

Figure 3.2 Fabrics with metal threads were popular for small accessories, which were not always covered by the legislation. Man's purse,
probably French, seventeenth century, silk satin, brocaded silk, metallic
thread, 11.43 × 7.62 × 6.35 cm. Los Angeles County Museum of Art
(LACMA), Costume Council Fund, M.83.108.4.

range of fabrics incorporating metal threads that no one under the rank
of countess could wear included:

Cloth of gold, cloth of silver, tinselled satin, satin branched with silver or gold,
satin striped with silver or gold, taffetas branched with silver or gold, taffetas
with gold or silver grounds, tinselled taffetas tufted or plain, tinselled cypresses,
Cypresses flourished with silver or gold, gold or silver camlets, networks wrought
with silver or gold and tabinets branched or wrought with silver or gold or any
other silk or cloth mixed or embroidered with pearl, gold or silver.[52]

The lack of detail in the Scottish accounts links more to their less closely
defined social hierarchy than to Scottish trade being more limited than
English trade. As Guicciardini noted the goods sent from Antwerp

---

[52] Hughes and Larkin, *Tudor Royal Proclamations. Vol 2*, no. 601.

to Scotland included 'silken cloths, all sorts of camlet, serge made in various ways, linen cloth and mercery'.[53] The volume of this trade was sufficient for the Scottish legislators to note in 1471 'the great expense and cost caused by the importing of silk into the realm' and it resulted in a long-term wish to produce silk in Scotland. The 1663 act 'In favour of silk weavers, printers etc' insisted that 'they shall take for apprentices as many of the natives of the kingdom as they can, and teach them faithfully their respective arts and trades'.[54]

By the end of the sixteenth century most notable was the range of very light-weight, translucent silks and linens used for veils and headwear that were available. Looking back to the list of fabrics forbidden to English countesses, 'tinselled cypresses, Cypresses flourished with silver or gold, networks wrought with silver or gold' were used primarily for veils, tires or attires for the head, and other female accessories. The function of these fabrics was to look good, a point the satirist, Stephen Gosson (1554–1624), stressed when he described the new fashion for gauze aprons:

> These aprons white of finest thread
> So choicely tied, so dearly bought,
> So finely fringed, so nicely spread,
> So quantlie cut, so richly wrought.[55]

This demand for fine linens encouraged shrewd Scottish producers to develop the scope of their domestic linen production and their success was indicated by the 1695 'Act anent the duty on Scots muslin'. This act indicated the range of fancy linen goods being produced when it stipulated that:

all muslin, plain or striped, or cambric and all sorts of linen under whatsoever name or designation, manufactured within the kingdom, shall at the exporting thereof pay custom only as Scots linen conforming to the book of rates.[56]

After sumptuous silks and fine linens, fur was a sought-after luxury. Even though fur was less fashionable in England by the sixteenth century than it had been a hundred and fifty years earlier, it was still a very important

---

[53] Richard H. Tawny and Eileen Power (eds.), *Tudor Economic Documents* (London: Longmans, Green and Co, 1924), iii: 168.

[54] *APS* VII, 466, c.25, *RPS* 1663/6/42. See Naomi Tarrant, '18th century English silks in Scotland', in Regula Schorta (ed.), *Seidengewebe des 18 Jahrhunderts: Die Industrien in England und in Nordeuropa /18th Century Silks: The Industries of England and Northern Europe*, Riggisberger Berichte 8 (Riggisberg: Abegg-Stiftung, 2000), 85.

[55] Quoted in Jane Ashelford, *Dress in the Age of Elizabeth* (London: Batsford, 1988), 36.

[56] *APS* IX, 417, c.30; *RPS* 1695/5/150.

mark of rank, and an expression of wealth, hence its use as a symbol of status on official robes.[57] Sable was identified in the legislation of 1337 as a highly desirable commodity and it retained this status well beyond the cut-off date for this chapter.[58] However, this was not the case with other furs, as demonstrated by the rise and fall in the interest in squirrel fur in the Middle Ages, or the rise in value of fox. Equally taste played its part. As Elspeth Veale has noted, women of the early Tudor elite preferred pale furs – miniver, ermine, lettice, lynx and the belly fur of the leopard – and this trend continued under Elizabeth I.[59] The Virgin Queen favoured white and by the end of her reign was ordering pure (miniver), white fox and swanskin.[60] In contrast, Scottish women had admired pale furs a century earlier, resulting in the 1458 law stating that 'no woman [should] wear … white weasel'.[61] The significance of fur in the fifteenth century was reflected by two other laws. The act of 1430 banned 'furs of pine-martens, beech-martens, purray nor great or richer furs' and in 1457 merchants were forbidden marten furs.[62] There were no further references to furs to line or trim clothes, but the quintessential male accessory, the beaver hat, did feature in 1621 when 'no beaver-fur hats [were to] be used or worn but by the privileged persons'.[63] Both countries sought to manage the appeal of expensive furs but struggled to stop the demand produced by changes in fashion.

After the materials, colour,[64] linked to the available dyes and the skill of the dyers, added extra value to fabrics and as a result the more expensive and rare dyes added an extra dimension of desirability and luxury. Several colours or colour/fabric combinations were stressed by the English – purple silk and blue velvet. Of these, purple was consistently

---

[57] For the significance of fur in the fourteenth century, see Stella M. Newton, *Fashion in the Age of the Black Prince: A Study of the Years 1340–1365* (Suffolk: Boydell Press, 1980).

[58] 11 Edw. III, c.2: *SR* 1, 280.

[59] Elspeth Veale, 'From Sable to Mink', in *The 1547 Inventory of King Henry VIII: Volume 2: Textiles and Dress*, ed Maria Hayward and Philip Ward (London: Harvey Miller for the Society of Antiquaries, 2012), 340–341.

[60] The National Archive, Kew (henceforth TNA) LC5/37, 150, 221, 256.

[61] *APS* II, 49, c.13; *RPS* 1458/3/14.

[62] *APS*, II, 18, 8–10; *RPS* 1430/12 and *APS*, II, 49: c.11, 13, *RPS* 1458/3/12, 1458/3/14.

[63] *APS* IV, 625, c.25; *RPS* 1621/6/37, no. 14. Beaver hats were also mentioned in 1672, see *APS* VIII 71, c.21; *RPS* 1672/6/31.

[64] Smith, 'Even colour, the most flimsy and superficial of all distinctions, becomes an object of his regard', cited in Maxine Berg and Helen Clifford, 'Introduction', in Maxine Berg and Helen Clifford (eds.), *Consumers and Luxury: Consumer Culture in Europe 1650–1850* (Manchester and New York: Manchester University Press, 1999), 8. For a broad overview see Susan Kay-Williams, *The Story of Colour in Textiles* (London: A & C Black Publishers Ltd, 2013). For colour in the Elizabethan context see, Jane Schneider, 'Peacocks and Penguins: The Political Economy of European Cloth and Colors', *American Ethnologist* 5 (1978): 413–438.

regarded as the colour that was representative of royal status,[65] while blue velvet was reserved for the Knights of the Garter. When purple silk was singled out in 1533, many individuals lower down the social order got round this prohibition by wearing violet – both silk and wool.[66] Scarlet was equally significant until the mid-sixteenth century when it lost ground to black, with a few exceptions such as scarlet mayoral robes.[67] Black could be found in clothing inventories of men and women across the social order because it conveyed a variety of ideas including elegance, respectability, professional integrity, piety and mourning.[68] After this, the evolving colour palate, in tandem with the increased accessibility of new red and black dyestuffs from the New World, including cochineal, brazilwood and logwood, making colour harder to control and define.[69]

Far more interesting is what the sumptuary law did not seek to control in relation to colour, and this was the rapidly increasing range of shades that were available from the mid-sixteenth century. Elizabeth I's wardrobe accounts and the gifts she received at the New Year indicate that, while black and white were important in her wardrobe, they were accompanied by a wide range of pastel, bright and muted shades.[70] While Raffield has noted that the Reformation ushered in a more muted palate for clothing 'based upon moderation [and] repression of excessive individualism', the queen did not share this view.[71] Neither did James VI and I, Charles I or Charles II.[72]

[65] The first reference to purple came in 1463 when 'no man under the estate of a lord [to] wear any manner of cloth or silk being of the colour of purple', 3 Edw. IV: c.5; *SR* 2, 399–402.

[66] Hayward, *Rich Apparel*, 344–345. This loophole, especially in relation to violet silks, was closed in the Elizabethan proclamations.

[67] John H. Munro, 'The Medieval Scarlet and the Economics of Sartorial Splendour', in Negley B. Harte and Kenneth G. Ponting (eds.), *Cloth and Clothing in Medieval Europe* (London: Heinemann, 1983), 13–71; and John H. Munro, 'The Anti-red Shift – to the Dark Side: Colour Changes in Flemish Luxury Woollens, 1300–1500', in R. Netherton and G. Owen-Crocker (eds.), *Medieval Clothing and Textiles* (Woodbridge: The Boydell Press, 2007), 55–96.

[68] Michel Pastoureau, *Black: The History of a Color* (Princeton: Princeton University Press, 2008). See also John Harvey, *Black: The Story of a Colour* (London: Reaktion, 2013) and his earlier work John Harvey, *Men in Black* (London: Reaktion, 1997).

[69] For studies on the significance of red, see Amy B. Greenfield, *A Perfect Red: Empire, Espionage and the Quest for the Colour of Desire* (London: Black Swan, 2011).

[70] For a different view of dyeing in Elizabethan London see Jane Schneider, 'Fantastical Colours in Foggy London: The New Fashion Potential of the Late Sixteenth Century', in Lena Cowen Orlin (ed.), *Material London, ca. 1600* (Philadelphia: University of Pennsylvania Press, 2000), 109–127. For the importance of black and white see Grant McCracken, 'Dress Colour at the Court of Elizabeth I: An Essay in Historical Anthropology', *Canadian Review of Sociology and Anthropology* 22 (1985): 515–533.

[71] Paul Raffield, 'Reformation, Regulation and Image: Sumptuary Legislation and the Subject of Law', *Law and Critique* 13/2 (2002): 127–150.

[72] See, for example, Roy Strong, 'Charles I's Clothes for the Years 1633 to 1635', *Costume* 14 (1980): 73–89.

There was remarkably little mention of colour in the Scottish legislation. It mostly focused on the colour of professional and parliament
robes and was used to regulate the lower ranks in relation to work and
holiday wear. The statute of 1457 stated that labourers, husbandmen and
their wives had to wear grey or white on work days, reserving light blue,
green and red for holidays.[73] By 1621 the rules were more restrictive,
stating that 'the husbandmen and labourers of the ground [could] wear
no clothing but grey, white, blue and self black cloth made in Scotland'.[74]
This makes an interesting point of contrast with the legislation passed by
Charles V in 1530 which made no attempt to regulate the colours worn
by the day-labourers and peasants in the German lands.[75] The length
of time covered by the Scottish legislation also serves to demonstrate
that by the end of the seventeenth century fashionable developments
in clothing and textiles were more concerned with pattern than colour,
as reflected by the 1681 law which sought to regulate 'all flowered,
striped, figured, chequered, painted or printed silk stuff or ribbons (in
no way comprehending changing coloured or watered stuff or ribbons)'
(Figure 3.3).[76]

Decoration and embellishment on outer garments came under
increased scrutiny because a modest wool gown or pair of hose could
be converted into something much more flamboyant, and expensive,
with the liberal application of lace, embroidery, slashing and pinking.[77]
A Scottish law of 1430 forbad use of 'embroidery nor pearl nor bullion'
while a proclamation of 1686 banned 'all Embroideries of Hair, Threed,
Buggle, except what is embroidered within this Kingdom'.[78] During the
course of the seventeenth century ribbon emerged as an essential means
of enhancing clothing and the Scottish legislation charted this in detail.
In 1672 the legislators focused on 'any gold or silver laces of whatsoever kind, buttons, ribbons, tracings, fringes or looping made of gold or
silver', with further references to 'plain taffeta ribbons' and 'plain satin
ribbons'.[79] In 1698: 'any clothes stuffs, ribbons, fringes, tracing, loops,
agréments, buttons or anything pertaining to apparel, made of silver or

---

[73] *APS* II, 49, c.13; *RPS* 1458/3/14.
[74] *APS* IV, 625, c.25; *RPS* 1621/6/37, no. 16. For life at the lower end of society see Stana
Nenadic, 'Necessities: Food and Clothing in the Long Eighteenth Century', in Elizabeth
Foyster and Christopher A. Whatley (eds.), *A History of Everyday Life in Scotland, 1600–
1800* (Edinburgh: Edinburgh University Press, 2010), 137–163.
[75] See Ulinka Rublack's Chapter 1 in this volume.
[76] *APS* VIII, 348, c.78; *RPS* 1681/7/36.
[77] See for example, Janet Arnold, 'Decorative Features: Pinking, Snipping and Slashing',
Costume 9 (1975), 22–26.
[78] *APS*, II, 18, 8–10; *RPS* 1430/12.and NRS RH14/207.
[79] *APS* VIII, 71, c.21; *RPS* 1672/6/31.

Figure 3.3 This love of pattern can be seen on this pair of embroidered shoes, French, 1690–1700. Metropolitan Museum of Art, New York, 06.1344a, b, Rogers Fund, 1906.

gold thread, wire or filigree, or wherein there is any silver or gold thread, wire or filigree, or the counterfeits thereof'.[80]

Fine linen shirts and smocks, decorated at the neck with ruffs or falling bands and at the wrists with ruffles or cuffs, also received increased levels of attention, demonstrating that luxury could be linked to the time taken, and skill required, to prepare and maintain clothes, as well as to the garments themselves.[81] The 1562 proclamation denounced 'the outrageous double ruffs which now of late are crept in' and were popular with men and women alike.[82] It had little effect, and the potential for ruffs with matching wrist ruffles to make a luxurious display is evident from

[80] *APS* X, 150, c.7; *RPS* 1698/7/114.
[81] See Janet Arnold, Jenny Tiramani and Santina Levey, *Patterns of Fashion 4: The Cut and Construction of Linen Shirts, Smocks, Neckwear, Headwear and Accessories for Men and Women, c. 1540–1660* (Basingstoke: Macmillan, 2008).
[82] Hughes and Larkin, *Tudor Royal Proclamations. Vol 2*, no. 493.

twelve sets ordered in 1617–1618 for James VI and I which required 'xxvij elnes of very fine cambricke, ccclxix yards lace, xj and a half elnes holland stocke'.[83] This evidence of royal opulence was compounded by this being just one of several orders placed annually. Four years after James VI and I's progress to Scotland in 1617 a law was passed seeking to restrict 'pearling or ribboning upon their ruffs, sarks [shirts], napkins and socks except the persons before privileged'.[84] It also demonstrated the range of linens available in Scotland, which included 'lawn or cambric... tiffanies, cobwebs, lawns or slyres', and was as good as in England.[85]

Geographies of Luxury

Turning now to the geography of luxury as revealed by these acts and proclamations, it is possible to consider it in three ways: firstly, the specific domestic geography covered by the legislation. For example, the English act of 1337 stipulated that 'no man nor woman, great or small … of what estate or condition he be, the King, Queen and their children only except, shall wear no cloth … other than is made in England, Ireland, Wales or Scotland'.[86] By 1510 Scottish goods were excluded so that 'none under the degree of gentleman to use or wear any furs from outside England, Ireland or Wales'.[87] The acts and proclamations stressed the worth of goods produced on English soil, and in the wider context of the British Isles, especially woollen cloth and furs. In contrast, the Scottish legislation generally focused on promoting Scottish goods, such as the 1621 act which required 'the pearling and ribboning' on shirts and other body linens to be 'of those made within the kingdom of Scotland'.[88] On occasion bans were placed on 'the importation of English cloth and other English wares', as in 1597, when the poor quality of the goods was given as justification.[89] Even when considering national concerns, Scotland was placed in a wider European context as in 1458, when there were attempts to regulate women's short caps with little hoods hanging down at the back 'such as are used in Flanders, England and other countries'.[90]

---

[83] TNA AO3/3248/45.
[84] *APS* IV, 625, c.25; *RPS* 1621/6/37, no. 2.
[85] *APS* IV, 625, c.25; *RPS* 1621/6/37, no. 4.
[86] 11 Edw. III, c.2; *SR* I, 280.
[87] 1 H8, c.14; *SR* III, 8–9.
[88] *APS* IV, 625, c.25; *RPS* 1621/6/37, no. 2.
[89] *APS* IV, 135, c.21; *RPS* 1597/11/28. Although a wish to retain bullion in Scotland was just as important a consideration; see Jenny Wormald, *Court, Kirk and Community: Scotland, 1470–1625* (London: Hodder Arnold, 1981), 41–45.
[90] *APS* II, 49, c.13; *RPS* 1458/3/14.

However, most luxury goods were imported, with the different groups of luxury products being brought from a variety of locations. This wider geography was summed up in the 1581 Scottish act as 'foreign countries'.[91] More precisely, imported furs came from the Baltic States, France, Italy, Russia, Scandinavia and Spain.[92] Most high-quality silks came from Italy – especially Florence, Lucca and Venice,[93] along with some from France and Spain – with fine linens coming from the Low Countries. While these luxury goods indicate the influence of Europe, a study of Elizabeth I's gift rolls or the accounts of James VI's Treasurer of the Chamber reveal payments for ivory fans and ostrich feathers.[94] Such items indicate that not all of the luxury goods available in Scotland and England were included in the legislation and that there was a much wider trade network in luxury goods than encompassed in the early laws. Equally, in 1681 the new Scottish law focused on the European rivals to Scottish linen production and the cotton goods shipped from the Indies: 'any foreign Holland-linen, cambric, lawn, dornick, damask, tyking, bousten or damety, tufted or striped Holland, calico, Selesia or East India linen, and all other foreign cloths and stuff made of linen or cotton, wool or lint'.[95] The Scottish legislation also incorporated foreign clothing or clothing made abroad, thereby acknowledging the scope of Scottish trade and links with Europe as a result of education and travel. In 1681 the act banned 'all wearing clothes made abroad, for men, women or children (excepting wearing clothes and linen brought home by persons for their own use who have been abroad and used by them, and made of such cloths, stuffs and furniture as are by this act allowed to be worn within this kingdom)'.[96]

Next was the potential divide between urban and rural spaces which again highlights points of similarity and difference between Scotland and England. Urban streets were important as places where an individual could show off their fine clothing, and they were the setting for the rapidly growing urban population with its access to wealth and new ideas. English towns, such as Bristol, Norwich and York, and Scottish burghs

---

[91] *APS* III, 220, c.18; *RPS* 1581/10/37.
[92] Hayward, *Rich Apparel*, 102.
[93] See Henry S. Cobb (ed.), *Petty Customs Account 1480–81* (London: London Record Society 27, 1990), 95. Ludovico Bonvisi, merchant of Lucca, imported one piece of velvet containing 9 yards, eleven pieces of satin containing 174 yards, six pieces of damask containing 87 yards, five pieces of sarsenet containing 79 yards and twelve pieces of baudekyn costing £83.
[94] For Elizabeth I's gifts, see Jane Lawson (ed.), *The Elizabethan New Year's Gift Exchanges, 1559–1603* (Oxford: Oxford University Press for the British Academy, 2013).
[95] *APS* viii 348, c.78; *RPS* 1681/7/36.
[96] *APS* viii 348, c.78; *RPS* 1681/7/36.

including Aberdeen, Glasgow and Perth were home to the increasingly wealthy, numerous and influential urban groups – merchants, and the medical and legal professions – who came now under close scrutiny in relation to their appearance.[97] In 1455 'all men of law who are forespeakers, for the cost, have habits of green in the fashion of a tunic, and the sleeves be open like a tabart'.[98]

Not all of the attention was negative, as indicated by the increased emphasis being placed on the livery of civic officials including mayors, sheriffs and aldermen.[99] This acted as a display of the 'cultural capital' of those English towns that were large and influential enough to be permitted a mayor.[100] The style of the long, English scarlet, fur-trimmed, sleeved mayoral gowns can be seen in Lucas de Heere's watercolour; their social significance is reflected by their depiction with a Knight of the Garter and a yeoman of the Guard, two other groups identified in the legislation and who helped assert royal magnificence.[101] In 1621 the 'provosts, bailies, dean of guild and treasurer within the burgh of Edinburgh' were permitted 'apparel of velvet, satin or other stuff of silk'.[102] As Philip Stubbes noted, using expensive materials to assert the authority of civic government was for the good of society: 'The majestrats also, & Officers in the weale publique, by what title soever they be called (according to their abilities) may were (if the Prince, or Super-intendent do Godly command) costlie ornaments and riche attire, to dignifie their callings, and to demonstrate and shewe forth, the excelency, and worthines of their offices, and functions'.[103] This was true whether it was in Scotland or England.

London, both a capital and a court city, was at the heart of the English luxury trade. As John Stow observed London was a 'citty filled more aboundantly with all sorts of silkes, fine linnen, oyles, wines & spices, perfection of arts, and all costly ornaments and curious workmanship,

[97] Sylvia Thrupp, *The Merchant Class of Medieval London* (Chicago: Chicago University Press, 1948); and Heather Swanson, *Medieval Artisans: An Urban Class in Late Medieval England* (Oxford: Wiley Blackwell, 1989). Also see John H. Baker, 'A History of Judges Robes', *Costume* 12 (1978): 27–39.

[98] *APS* II, 43, c.12; *RPS* 1455/8/13. Also see Gordon Donaldson, 'The Legal Profession in Scottish Society in the Sixteenth and Seventeenth Centuries', *Judicial Review* 21 (1976): 1–19.

[99] 24 Hen, VIII, c.13, *SR*, III, for example, citizens and burgesses could wear 'suche hoodes of Clothe and of suche colours as they have heretofore used to weare except that it is not lawful for them to wear velvet, damask or satin of crimson, violet, purple or blue'.

[100] For cultural capital, an idea put forward by Pierre Bourdieu and Jean-Claude Passeron, see Hunt, *Governance*, 71.

[101] Lucas de Heere, *Beschrijving der Britische Eilanden*, c. 1570, British Museum.

[102] *APS* IV, 625, c.25; *RPS* 1621/6/37, no. 1.

[103] Stubbes, *Anatomie of Abuses*, sig. C2r.

then any other province, so as London well deserves to beare the name of the choicest storehouse in the world'.[104] In 1613 the Merchant Taylors guild made clear the distinction between clothes worn in London and elsewhere when they stipulated that no member should 'use or weare any costly array, Garments or apparell within this City, otherwise than shall be decent, meete and fit for his degree and calling as a Citizen and Merchant man ought to have and under such manner and forme as it shall be adjudged and deemed by the Maister, Wardens and other Assistant of the said fraternity'.[105]

In addition, the city of London and Westminster became increasingly important as the places where luxury goods were most readily available, with ever-increasing shopping opportunities on offer.[106] The appeal of shopping at the Royal Exchange for small luxuries was evident from the inventory of Thomas Deane's shop.[107] The area in and around St Paul's was equally important, as indicated in Thomas Middleton's *The Black Book* of 1604, in which Lucifer went to London's cathedral 'to see [the] fashions'.[108]

If Lucifer had gone to St Giles's cathedral in Edinburgh he would have encountered the fashionable there too. As the capital, seat of government and home to the royal officials, Edinburgh was very significant. However, in terms of size Edinburgh was not as dominant as London was by the 1690s. Having approximately 4.7 per cent of the Scottish population, in comparison with London which had about 10 per cent of the English people, Edinburgh did not dominate over Scotland's regional towns, so giving them more independence and resulting in a sense of

---

[104] John Stow, *Abridgement of the Chronicles of England* (London, 1611), dedication. For London see Frederick J. Fisher, 'The Development of London as a Centre of Conspicuous Consumption in the Sixteenth and Seventeenth Centuries', *Transactions of the Royal Historical Society*, 4th series, 30 (1948): 37–50; Caroline Barron, *London in the Later Middle Ages: Government and People 1200–1500* (Oxford: Oxford University Press, 2005); and Ian W. Archer, 'Material Londoners?', in Orlin (ed.), *Material London*, 174–192.

[105] Quoted in Diana de Marly, *Working Dress: A History of Occupational Clothing* (London: Batsford, 1986), 12.

[106] See Derek Keene, 'Sites of Desire: Shops, Selds and Wardrobes in London and other English Cities, 1100–1550', in Bruno Blondé, Peter Stabel, Jon Stobart and Ilya van Damme (eds.), *Buyers and Sellers: Retail Circuits and Practices in Medieval and Early Modern Europe* (Turnhout: Brepols, 2006), 125–153; and Nancy Cox, 'Beggary of the Nation: Moral, Economic and Political Attitudes to the Retail Sector in the Early Modern Period', in John Benson and Laura Ugolini (eds.), *A Nation of Shopkeepers, Five Centuries of British Retailing* (London: I. B. Tauris, 2003), 26–51.

[107] Kay Staniland, 'Thomas Deane's Shop in the Royal Exchange', in Ann L. Saunders (ed.), *The Royal Exchange* (London: London Topographical Society, 1997), 59–67.

[108] Bailey, *Flaunting*, 106–107, 111. Arthur H. Bullen (ed.), *The Works of Thomas Middleton* (London: John C. Nimmo, 1886), viii: 32. Other examples of male 'flaunting' at St Paul's are given in Ashelford, *Dress in the Age of Elizabeth*, 44.

localism.[109] That said, the importance of all the burghs as a means of disseminating the sumptuary law was evident from the proclamation dated 24 April 1684, which required that it was read out at 'the Mercat Cross of Edinburgh, and remanent Mercat Crosses of the head Burghs of the Shires of the Kingdom, and other places needful'.[110] In turn the people looked to Edinburgh for news about new legislation, including the sumptuary laws. On 13 August 1698 David Crawford wrote from Edinburgh to James Hamilton, Earl of Arran (1658–1718), telling him that parliament had been debating the sumptuary law.[111] They needed to keep abreast of changes in order to ensure that their clothes were appropriate. In 1601 the Edinburgh tailor Patrick Nimmo made a set of clothes for the laird of Stanehouse, which he described in his account book as being made from 'Scots claith' costing £48 11s 7d.[112] These appear to have conformed with the sumptuary regulations of the time. However, in 1673, Alexander Heriot paid 'for a horse to myself to go to Edinburgh to get some new furnishing' for the clothes of his employer, Alexander Gilmour of Craigmillar, which had to be changed in order to comply with the new sumptuary law.[113]

The Scottish legislation sometimes distinguished between the burghs and elsewhere, as in 1458 when it noted activity 'especially within burghs'.[114] However, it more usually did not differentiate, as in 1430 when the law sought to ban activity 'in burghs nor in the land', or in 1458 ('especially within burghs and the commoners to landward'), or in 1681 ('either in burgh or landward and outwith burghs').[115] In contrast the English legislators singled out the countryside for regulation. The sumptuary legislation reflected the fifteenth-century change in terminology

[109] Ian D. Whyte, *Scotland's Society and Economy in Transition, c.1500–c.1760* (London: Palgrave, 1997), 117. For the significance of Edinburgh, see Michael Lynch, 'Crown, Capital and Metropolis. Edinburgh and Canongate: The Rise of a Capital and an Urban Court', *Journal of Urban History* 32/1 (2005): 22–43. John J. Brown, 'Merchant Princes and Mercantile Investment in Early Seventeenth-Century Scotland', in Michael Lynch (ed.), *The Early Modern Town in Scotland* (London: Croom Helm, 1987), 125–146; Helen Dingwall, *Late Seventeenth Century Edinburgh: A Demographic Study* (Aldershot: Scolar Press, 1994).

[110] NRS RH14/135; John H. Burton (ed.), *Register of the Privy Council of Scotland* (Edinburgh: HM General Register House, 1877), 7: 496–497.

[111] NRS GD406/1/4259. Also see NRS GD406/1/4337. He became the 4th duke of Hamilton in 1698.

[112] NRS RH9/1/7; Margaret H. B. Sanderson, *Mary Stewart's People: Life in Mary Stewart's Scotland* (Edinburgh: James Thin, The Mercat Press, 1987), 75–90.

[113] NRS GD122/3/2, no. 56.

[114] *APS* II, 49, c.13; *RPS* 1458/3/14.

[115] *APS*, II, 18, c. 10; *RPS* 1430/14; *APS*, II, 49, c.13; *RPS* 1458/3/14 and *APS* VIII, 348, c.78; *RPS* 1681/7/36.

to describe the lower, and aspirational, groups in society, shifting from free and un-free to yeomen, husbandmen and labourers.[116] The yeoman could hold up to, and above, 80 acres and as such could, and did, aspire to a variety of luxury goods.[117] Further changes took place to patterns of landholding in the sixteenth century and the ways in which land could be exploited financially.[118] As a result local markets and travelling chapmen facilitated access by the gentry, as well as the yeomen and husbandmen, to new luxury goods.[119] As Joan Thirsk has noted the growing availability of buttons, pins, stockings and trimmings, especially home-produced items, was linked to ways of tapping labour resources.[120] It was also the site of the country homes of the elite, which were centres of conspicuous consumption and the display of rich clothing. When James VI and I visited Audley End in Essex he felt that it 'was too much for a King, though it might do very well for a Lord Treasurer'.[121]

Finally, the specific site of luxury was the human body. Scottish and English legislators targeted the male body across the social spectrum, and that of his male servants, and his horse, as well as its harness and saddle. While women came and went from the English legislation, they were under more consistent scrutiny in Scotland. Even so, it was luxurious clothing displayed on the adult and adolescent male body that threatened the well being of the state and the individual. Concern over the latter was evident in a proclamation of 1574 which referred to 'the wasting and undoing of a great number of young gentlemen'.[122] Young men of this type rarely lived or travelled alone, and their male servants and retainers, especially those visible outside the household, were often provided with rich livery.[123] Attempts to control expenditure on livery were not restricted to England and Scotland, as is clear from the Milanese ban on embroidered silk liveries in November 1565.[124] Horse ownership

---

[116] William G. Hoskins, *The Making of the English Landscape* (Harmondsworth: Penguin Books, [1970] 1985), 155.

[117] Ibid., 154–163.

[118] Deborah Youngs, 'Estate Management, Investment and the Gentleman Landlord in Later Medieval England', *Historical Research* 73/1 (2000): 124–141.

[119] Margaret Spufford, *The Great Reclothing of Rural England: Petty Chapmen and their Wares in the Seventeenth Century* (London: The Hambledon Press, 1984).

[120] Joan Thirsk, *Economic Policy and Projects: The Development of a Consumer Society in Early Modern England* (Oxford: Clarendon Press, 1978), 6.

[121] Quoted in Hoskins, *Making*, 167.

[122] Hughes and Larkin, *Tudor Royal Proclamations. Vol 2*, no. 646.

[123] As Hunt noted, livery was first addressed under Richard II and there were over twenty proclamations and statutes over the next 120 years, ending in 1514. Hunt, *Governance*, 86.

[124] For this legislation and the protests against it, see Chapter 7 by Catherine Kovesi in this volume.

was a sign of wealth and the ownership of a horse from Italy or Spain could be seen as the ultimate luxury. Henry VIII was keen to improve the size, strength and appearance of native horses and passed legislation 'concernyng the breeds of Horses' in 1535, 1540 and 1541–1542.[125] A similar wish for the Scots to have access to good horses was echoed in legislation of 1424 when all Scottish men with an income of £20 or more were expected to have a suitable horse 'as a gentleman ought to'.[126] In both countries, a fine horse was not a luxury but a patriotic duty.

Swords and daggers were discussed in growing detail in the sixteenth-century English legislation. This was partly in relation to the range of expensive decorative techniques, including gilding, silvering and damascening, but the right to carry a sword was also linked to growing problems with violence and duelling amongst young men.[127] A precursor to this came in 1420 when silvering (silver plating) was restricted to a knight's spurs and 'all the apparel that pertaineth to a baron and above that estate'.[128] In contrast, the 1429 act in Scotland was concerned with the yeomen 'with £20 in goods' being well armed so that they could undertake their national duty and fend off unwelcome aggressors, including the English. They were to have a bow, arrows, sword, buckler and knife, and any yeoman that 'is no archer, and cannot draw a bow' was to have 'a sword and buckler, and a good axe, or else a pointed staff'.[129] However, by 1672 the emphasis had changed and a Scottish man's weapons provided an opportunity for luxurious display, reflected by the 'buttons, buckles and hilts of swords of goldsmith work, which the privileged persons after-expressed are allowed to wear'.[130]

However, other bodies were considered under the legislation, including the royal body and the female body.[131] Royal bodies could legitimately be clothed in luxury goods and they were distinguished from the rest of the society by exclusive access to certain items. The impact of there being a woman on the English throne for the second half of the sixteenth century

---

[125] 27 Hen. VIII, c.6; *SR* III, 535–536; 32 Hen. VIII, c.13; *SR* III, 758–760; 33 Hen. VIII, c. 5; *SR* III, 830–832. Hunt suggests that by the 1580s legislation encouraging horse ownership had a military angle reflecting anxieties about fears of invasion; Hunt, *Governance*, 317.

[126] *APS*, II, 18, 8–10; *RPS* 1430/12–14.

[127] For example, Hughes and Larkin, *Tudor Royal Proclamations. Vol 2*, nos. 542, 611.

[128] 8 Hen. V, c.3; *SR* II, 203.

[129] *APS* II, 18: 11–12; *RPS* 1430/16.

[130] *APS* VIII, 71, c.21; *RPS* 1672/6/31.

[131] Prior to Elizabeth I's reign, references to women were limited. For example, in 1363 wives were not to wear clothing exceeding the value of their husband's clothes and their veils could not cost more than 12d each, 37 Edw. III: cc. 8–14: *SR* I, 380–381; Newton, *Fashion*, 132.

may help explain the inclusion of women in the legislation from 1574. Hunt sees this as a consequence of increased tension between old and new money but it can also be linked to Elizabeth I wishing to control female rivals who challenged her place as the best-dressed woman in England.[132] Her feelings on the matter were evident when she reprimanded Lady Mary Howard, one of her ladies in waiting, for wearing a 'rich border powdered with gold and pearl, and a velvet suit belonging thereto' that the queen felt was too good for her, noting that 'if it become me not as being too short, I am minded it shall never become thee as being too fine'. It was the luxurious nature of the border that displeased the queen, 'who thought it exceeded her own'.[133]

During her brief period of rule, Mary Queen of Scots was exempt from the legislation; like Elizabeth she carefully managed her appearance.[134] However, much more interesting is the developing role of Scottish women in this period in business and as consumers of luxury goods.[135] Scottish female consumers come under official scrutiny for a range of infringements. First among these was the use of luxury fabrics in excessive quantities, so in 1430 'commoners' wives nor their servants' were not permitted 'either long tail, nor side necked hoods, nor pouches on their sleeves, nor costly caps such as lawn or rens'.[136] While in 1471 'men's wives worth less than £100 [should] wear no silk as a lining, except on the collar and sleeves alone under the same pain'.[137] A second infringement involved going out in disguise. The 1429 statute forbade women to go to church or market with their faces covered 'that sho may nocht be kende'.[138] A third concerned wilfully flouting the law, as indicated by the proclamation dated 24 April 1684: 'yet several Women, even in Our Capital City of Edinburgh, and elsewhere throughout this Our Kingdom, have presumed to go abroad with Cloathes made of the said prohibited Stuffs, upon Pretext that they are only Night-Gowns, Undress or Mantois'.[139] The idea that women took a natural interest in clothing

---

[132] Hunt, *Governance*, 236; Simon Adams, 'Eliza Enthroned? The Court and its Politics', in Christopher Haigh (ed.), *The Reign of Elizabeth I* (Basingstoke: Palgrave, 1984), 72–74; Susan Vincent, *Dressing the Elite: Clothes in Early Modern England* (Oxford: Berg Publishers, 2003), 137–138.

[133] Henry Harrington (ed.,) *Nugae Antiquae, Being a Miscellaneous Collection of Original Papers by Sir John Harrington* (London: Edward Jeffery, 1797), 2: 139–140.

[134] For example, NRS E23/3, no. 24.

[135] Helen Dingwall, 'The Power behind the Merchant? Women and the Economy in Late Seventeenth-Century Edinburgh', in Elizabeth L. Ewan and Maureen M. Meikle (eds.), *Women in Scotland c.1100–c.1750s* (East Linton: Tuckwell Press, 1999), 152–162.

[136] *APS*, II, 18, 8–10; *RPS* 1430/14.

[137] *APS* II, 100, c.7; *RPS* 1471/5/7.

[138] *APS* II, 49: 13; *RPS* 1458/3/14.

[139] NRS RH14/135.

lies behind an undated printed poem from the late seventeenth century called 'The Ladies Petition to the Parliament against the passing of the Sumptuary Act'.[140] Whether it was truly presented by women is not as important as the message of the petition, which was that outmoded sumptuary laws seriously interfered with a woman's right to fashionable, and ideally luxurious, French clothing.

Conclusion

The appeal of luxury goods was summed up by Wulfstan, bishop of Worcester (d. 1095). When his friends tried to reassure him that modestly priced cat or rabbit fur was more suitable for a man of God than expensive lambskin, he replied 'Believe me, men sing oftener of the Lamb of God than of the cat of God'.[141] As the period of approximately 350 years covered by the Scottish and English sumptuary laws indicates, the people of both countries followed in Wulfstan's footsteps in their appreciation of luxury goods. While the legislators did not use the word luxury, they had a clear idea of what it was (a problem), what goods embodied it, where they came from and where they were to be encountered. There were some differences, including that the Scots considered men and women equally susceptible while the English predominantly focused on men's luxurious tendencies. The Scots were also less concerned about the finer points of the social hierarchy, a hierarchy that the English invested a lot of time and money in defining in terms of clothing and appearance. Yet, silk, in the form of textiles, accessories, trimmings and thread, was the primary and enduring luxury for both countries. The continuation of the Scottish legislation during the seventeenth century revealed the growing importance of fashionable change in driving ideas of what was luxurious and linking it to ever more closely defined details of colour, weave, pattern and decoration. It also hinted at a potential rival to silk in the form of cotton. The generation and management of the sumptuary laws were linked to the royal courts, the social elites and court cities of London and Edinburgh, which all served to drive an interest in luxury. This was an interest that spread throughout all levels of society, except the very poor, and into rural and urban areas alike. While both countries shared a predominantly Eurocentric view of luxury, the Scottish documents hint at the wider world of luxury goods that was opening up during the course of the seventeenth century. However, while these were

---

[140] NRS GD150/3377 and printed in full in Shaw, 'Sumptuary Legislation', 113–115.
[141] Cited in Elspeth Veale, *The English Fur Trade in the Later Middle Ages*, London Record Society (Oxford: Oxford University Press, 1966), 4.

the goods that John Kennedy, 7th Earl of Cassillis, saw as 'outlandish superfluities', the 'Ladies Petition' saw them as a woman's right:

> Let poor born maids have privilege to wear
> Their pleasure, let the silks be ne're so dear.
> This is the summ of what we now can say,
> Grant it, and your petitions shall pray.[142]

---

[142] NRS GD25/8/60 and Shaw, 'Sumptuary Legislation', 115.

4 Regulating Sumptuousness: Changing Configurations of Morals, Politics and Economics in Swiss Cities in the Seventeenth and Eighteenth Centuries

André Holenstein

Introduction

In 1773, the canon and Catholic Enlightenment philosopher Franz Philipp Gugger (1723–1790), from Solothurn in northwestern Switzerland, spoke to the Helvetic Society (*Helvetische Gesellschaft*) about the connections between the history and the political economy of republics. He argued that republics had emerged in places where nature was harsh, driving people to work hard and effectively, but never in places where nature was fertile and made possible a life of abundance. Gugger based his theory on historical evidence: 1,300 years ago, on seventy-two boggy islands,

Providence had, through a marvel of human industriousness, taken up residence in order to wield a free sceptre over the Adriatic Sea ... Opposite, in a region where Europe's famous rivers flow into the North Sea through marshy soils from which no grain will grow, Liberty sought and found its prosperity through a product of industriousness ... And in the same way, Liberty has risen amidst sky-high cliffs ..., in our fatherland [i.e. in the Swiss Confederation]. In a word, riches, splendour and abundance are not the sources from which republics have sprung: Contrariwise, they were the reason for their decline, and a deadly poison to them. A truth which sad observation ... places plainly and clearly before all republicans! Thus we must hear how Greece ... with the Persian riches, and Rome after its conquests, through the introduction of sumptuousness, won the sources of their own downfall ... Seeing that republics have their origin in moderation, in a nature entirely separate of any sumptuousness; in a word, in virtue: it follows that republicans in particular must honour virtue as their most important maxim of state'.[1]

---

[1] Franz Philipp Gugger, 'Das Wesen des Republikaners', in *Verhandlungen der Helvetischen Gesellschaft in Schinznach im Jahr 1773* (Basel), 41–106, here 86–89.

It was not by pure chance – so went Gugger's argument – that Venice, the Netherlands and the Swiss Confederation – the three most prominent republics in old Europe – had emerged in places where people had had to work hard and fight the forces of nature to gain freedom and prosperity. But republics were doomed to fall once wealth and abundance gained the upper hand. Ancient Greece and Rome provided sufficient evidence of this.

In the Christian tradition, excessive and ostentatious consumption of material goods was criticised as sinful wastage up until the eighteenth century. But 'luxury' was also considered reprehensible in economic and political respects.[2] In the eighteenth century, however, the globalisation of commodity flows, the spread of colonial produce and increasing prosperity awakened the desire among large parts of the population to refine their standard of living. 'Luxury' became the keyword in an intellectual controversy that redefined the relations between morals, politics and consumption. This controversy was carried on with particular intensity in small commercial republics such as the Protestant cities of the Swiss Confederation, because trade dynamics and growing prosperity in them collided head-on with the classical image of a republic as a community of virtuous citizens, and especially with the traditional mythical self-stereotype of the Swiss as frugal, pious peasants.

This contribution examines the changing configurations of morals, politics and economics in the seventeenth and eighteenth centuries. The aim is to show how the luxury debate in Switzerland's city republics fits into the older tradition of religious and moral criticism of consumption. This critical attitude towards consumption manifests itself in the cities' sumptuary laws – as considered in the second part of this chapter – and in the establishment of special courts of justice tasked with supervising them (so-called reformation chambers) in the seventeenth century. Finally, it will be shown how, in the controversy over luxury debated by Swiss authors, the classical republican concept of virtue clashed with a novel appreciation of luxury as a motor of economic development and an asset in dealing with social issues and poverty.

[2] Christopher J. Berry, *The Idea of Luxury: A Conceptual and Historical Investigation* (Cambridge: Cambridge University Press, 1994); Sandro Guzzi-Heeb, 'Luxus', in *Historisches Lexikon der Schweiz. Vol 8. Locarnini-Muoth* (Basel: Schwabe, 2009), 132–134; Renata Ago, 'Luxus', in *Enzyklopädie der Neuzeit* (Stuttgart and Weimar: Metzler, 2008), vii: 1046–1052.

Sumptuary Laws in the Swiss Confederation

From the late Middle Ages onwards, Swiss cities, like many other governments, issued laws to limit the consumption expenditure of their citizens and subjects. In particular, these sumptuary laws defined the types of dress people were allowed to wear in line with the estate they belonged to and their gender.[3] Beginning in the sixteenth century, regulations were increasingly refined to reflect social differences. In Geneva, for example, permissible expenditure was graded according to whether the persons in question were 'people of quality' (*gens de qualité*), 'lesser or mediocre people' (*gens moindres ou médiocres*), or 'mechanical craftspeople and other people of a low condition' (*artisans mécaniques et autres gens de basse condition*).[4]

Dress regulations were originally framed by religious considerations. The Reformation further reinforced this motivation. The sumptuary laws of Geneva characterised the place as a 'city of God' (*cité de Dieu*), whose inhabitants were expected to orient their way of life according to the requirements of Christian morals. Sumptuary laws remained primarily founded on religious principles until the middle of the seventeenth century in Geneva, and even longer in Bern. A theology of retribution was particularly important: people needed to be prevented from arousing the wrath of God with their sinful behaviour.[5] In addition, by disallowing wasteful living, the councils intended to prevent the impoverishment of households and limit the growth of poor relief expenditure. In the seventeenth century, sumptuary laws were also influenced by mercantilist concerns; the authorities proscribed the wearing of fine fabrics on the grounds that the import of foreign goods had a negative effect on the trade balance.

---

[3] Diethelm Klippel, 'Aufwandsgesetze', in *Enzyklopädie der Neuzeit. Vol 1. Aa-Basel* (Basel: Schwabe, 2002), 840–844; Gabriele Mentges, 'Kleiderordnung', in *Enzyklopädie der Neuzeit. Vol. 6. Haab-Juon* (Stuttgart and Weimar: J.B.Metzler, 2009), 746–749; Katharina Simon-Muscheid, 'Kleidung', in *Historisches Lexikon der Schweiz. Vol. 7. Jura-Lobsigen* (Basel: Schwabe, 2008), 258–260; Peter Ziegler, 'Sittenmandate', in *Historisches Lexikon der Schweiz. Vol. 11. Schaichet-StGB* (Basel: Schwabe, 2012), 549–551.

[4] Corinne Walker, 'Les lois somptuaires ou le rêve d'un ordre social. Evolution et enjeux de la politique somptuaire à Genève (XVIe-XVIIIe siècles)', *Equinoxe* 11 (1994): 111–129, here 121. In the seventeenth century, Bern's sumptuary laws distinguished three groups: noble and patrician citizens; craftspeople, grocers and officials; and servants. *Sammlung Schweizerischer Rechtsquellen, Kanton Bern*, ed. H. Rennefahrt (Aarau: Sauerländer, 1961), vi, part 2: 946–951 (4 July 1664).

[5] Walker, 'Les lois somptuaires', 115; Philipp Gut, 'Eine Religion der ständischen Ordnung: Kleidermandate', in André Holenstein et al. (eds.), *Berns mächtige Zeit* (Bern: Stämpfli Verlag, 2006), 216–218.

The Reformation Chambers (*Reformationskammer;*
chambre de la Réforme)

The gradual decrease in the importance of religious motives in Protestant authorities' sumptuary laws is also reflected in the establishment of so-called reformation chambers in Zurich in 1627, in Geneva in 1646 and in Bern in 1676.[6] Unlike the moral courts which had been created immediately after the Reformation in the 1520s and 1530s, and whose tasks also included the enforcement of sumptuary laws, these new special courts were comprised exclusively of secular councillors and did not include members of the clergy.[7] The reformation chambers were conceived as expert committees and special courts for regulating public consumption behaviour, and as such, they were tasked with advancing the population's *reformatio morum*. In Bern, the chamber was not only responsible for overseeing the sumptuary laws but also monitored adherence to regulations concerning taverns and inns (excessive alcohol consumption, gambling, dancing) and acted as an arbitrator and court in employment-related conflicts between masters and their servants.[8] Specifically tasked city officials were to report transgressors of the relevant laws to the chamber. In 1676, the Bernese reformation chamber obliged the city's fire wardens, clerks and messengers to do this job, their strong public presence making them, it was thought, well suited to undertake such work. The court promised them one-third of the fine as a reward for their diligence. But they proved negligent in the fulfilment of their task, and after only one year, they were replaced with secret inspectors.[9] By protecting the anonymity of its informants, the chamber sought to ensure that transgressions were reported even though the city of Bern, with a population of around 14,000, was a fairly small community in which social relations were largely transparent. Nonetheless, the chamber's work remained dependent upon the diligence and the credibility of its

---

[6] John Martin Vincent, *Costume and Conduct in the Laws of Basel, Bern, and Zurich, 1370–1800* (Baltimore: Johns Hopkins Press, 1935). For Zurich, see Christoph Wehrli, *Die Reformationskammer. Das Zürcher Sittengericht des 17. und 18. Jahrhunderts* (Zurich: Winterthur: 1963). For Geneva, see Corinne Walker, 'Images du luxe à Genève. Douze années de répression par la Chambre de la Réformation (1646–1658)', *Revue du Vieux Genève* 17 (1987): 21–26; Id., 'Les lois somptuaires'. For Bern, see F. Studer, 'Aus den Verhandlungen der Reformationskammer von 1676–1696', *Berner Taschenbuch auf das Jahr 1879* (Bern: B. F. Haller, 1878), 207–241; Regula Wyss, 'Zu hohe Kappen, zu lange Perücken: die Justizpraxis der Berner Reformationskammer 1694–96', in André Holenstein et al. (eds.), *Berns mächtige Zeit* (Bern: Schulverlag blmv/Stämpfli, 2006), 215.
[7] Walker, 'Les lois somptuaires', 120 f.; Wyss, *Reformationskammer*, 215.
[8] Studer, *Verhandlungen*, 227f., 229–231.
[9] Studer, *Verhandlungen*, 235–239; Wehrli, *Reformationskammer*, 92–99, 121–123.

informants, who were required to repeat their charge on oath in court if the alleged transgressor denied the offence. By imposing the oath on the informant the chamber wanted to exclude any suspicions of false charges that might be based on personal motives. For historians, however, the strict secrecy in the Reformation chamber's records regarding the identity of informants has the disadvantage of making it impossible to trace the social relationships between informants and transgressors, or possible motives for the charge.

The records, which survived only for certain periods,[10] show that the Reformation chambers in Zurich, Geneva, Basel and Bern convened often, though at highly irregular intervals. In some years they met nearly every week, in other years less than once a month. The Genevan reformation chamber dealt with 863 cases between 1646 and 1658. In this period, nearly a thousand individuals – almost ten per cent of Geneva's population – were requested to appear before the chamber.[11] The Reformation chamber in Basel held 41 sittings in 1727, during which it convicted as many as 219 individuals of violating dress regulations, whereas in 1745, in the same number of sittings, it sentenced no more than 39 individuals.[12]

The transgression of sumptuary laws was clearly a female offence. Even in Bern, where men were summoned to appear before the chamber more frequently than in the other cities, 77 per cent of the cases handled in the periods from 1676 to 1682 and from 1692 to 1696 for which the records have survived concerned women.[13] During the first half of the eighteenth century, the chambers of Basel and Zurich summoned almost exclusively women.[14] Likewise, the 863 cases handled by the Genevan reformation chamber between 1646 and 1658 were very unevenly distributed among women (598 cases) and men (216 cases); in addition, the chamber summoned 49 children whose hair had been too sumptuously dressed.[15]

Contrary to a widely held view in the literature, it was not mainly commoners' wives and maids who were summoned to answer charges of violating sumptuary laws. On the contrary, disproportionately many members of the upper ranks were accused of such offences – people whose financial standing, estate and need for distinction enabled or

---

[10] Vincent, *Costume*, 158; Wehrli, *Reformationskammer*; Walker, 'Images du luxe à Genève'; Id., 'Les lois somptuaires'; Wyss, *Reformationskammer*, 215.
[11] Walker, 'Images du luxe à Genève', 23–24.
[12] Vincent, *Costume*, 154–153.
[13] Philipp Gut, 'Das Bemühen um 'gute Ordnung' in Kleiderangelegenheiten. Kleiderordnungen und die Reformationskammer im 17./18. Jahrhundert in Bern' (Unpublished, Lizentiatsarbeit Historisches Institut der Universität Bern, 2004), 37.
[14] Vincent, *Costume*, 155, 157.
[15] Walker, 'Images du luxe à Genève', 23.

even required excessive expenditure. The Bernese chamber regularly summoned council members and bailiffs (*Landvögte*), or rather their female family members, and curates, and did not shy from questioning the daughter of the governing mayor (*Schultheiss*). The daughters of Bern's political elite frequently came into conflict with the law because they wore overly high fur caps, pinned up their hair or wore dresses made of fine fabrics and decorated with precious ornaments.[16] In Geneva, likewise, members of the political and social elite appeared in court more frequently than any other group in the middle of the seventeenth century. Taken together, the *citoyens* and the *bourgeois* – the two legally privileged groups in Geneva's society – accounted for 87 per cent (63 and 24 per cent, respectively) of individuals summoned, while the *natifs* and the *habitants*, who had fewer rights, were clearly under-represented, at four and nine per cent of the cases, respectively.[17]

The Reformation chambers served as an instrument of self-disciplining for the cities' governing elites. To limit and restrain the distinctive consumer behaviour of people of rank was part of the ruling technique of the patriciates, who, in the course of the seventeenth century, succeeded in asserting their exclusive claim to positions in government and in the bailiwicks (*Vogteien*), thereby excluding large groups of citizens from sharing in power and acquiring lucrative positions in the republic.[18] Inwardly, with a view to strengthening social cohesion within the citizenry, the Reformation chambers sought to uphold the idea of equality within a community of citizens that was increasingly differentiated socially and politically.[19] The chambers wanted to convey an image of a solicitous authority and underline its role as a model, particularly towards their rural subjects, by prosecuting excessive expenditure among members of the governing elite. This aim is confirmed in the restrictions which the Bernese city council imposed on the ceremonial installation of newly elected bailiffs in the sixteenth and seventeenth centuries. They were no longer permitted to hold lavish banquets in their bailiwick with numerous guests from among their relatives and their guild; instead, they

[16] Wyss, *Reformationskammer*, 215; Gut, *Kleiderordnungen*, 38. From 1694 to 1696 the Bernese reformation chamber summoned 342 individuals, of which 193 (56%) belonged to the upper class, 49 (14%) were servants, 45 (13%) were craftspeople and 11 (3%) were scholars; 44 of the accused (13%) belonged to other groups. Ibid.

[17] Walker, 'Images du luxe à Genève', 24. In the decade from 1650 to 1659, the *citoyens* and *bourgeois* accounted for 51 per cent, the *natifs* for 17.7 per cent, and the *habitants* for 31.3 per cent of the Genevan population. Alfred Perrenoud, *La population de Genève du seizième au début du dix-neuvième siècle* (Geneva: A. Jullien, 1979), 193.

[18] Daniel Schläppi, 'Patriziat', in *Historisches Lexikon der Schweiz* (Basel, 2010), ix: 570–573.

[19] David Wyss, *Politisches Handbuch für die erwachsene Jugend der Stadt und Landschaft Zürich* (Zürich: Bey Orell, Gessner und Compag.,1796), 414.

were required to strive for the utmost modesty and respectability at this public event.[20]

The punishments meted out by the Reformation chambers likewise confirm the hypothesis that these courts mainly focused on the consumer behaviour of members of the upper ranks. Between 1694 and 1696, the Bernese reformation chamber handled a total of 342 charges and passed judgement in 261 cases. In 97 cases the defendants were acquitted; in 142 cases they were sentenced to a fine; and in the remaining cases they were sentenced to a short term of imprisonment, to corporal punishment or to expulsion from the city. Neither the acquittals nor the fines indicate any privileged treatment of members of the upper ranks. On the contrary, craftspeople and servants were acquitted more often and fined more rarely than members of the upper ranks. In addition, high fines were rarely if ever imposed on craftspeople and servants.[21]

The sumptuary laws and the Reformation chambers' judicial practice were aimed at regulating people's consumption habits in the public sphere. This was known to those men and women who, after having been reported to the Bernese reformation chamber, justified their incriminated behaviour by stating that they had merely worn the piece of clothing in question in front of their own house, or that someone had only seen their prohibited headdress because they had looked out of the window of their own house. Junker Abraham Tscharner appeared before the chamber on 13 February 1679 because his daughter had worn an excessively long, silken Casaque (long-armed blouse). He argued that she had only worn it standing outside their home, but had to pay a 2 pound fine (equivalent to two-and-a-half days' wages for a horseman) as she had in fact been seen walking on the street by the informant. One week later, Rudolf von Graffenried had to pay the same fine because his daughter had likewise been spotted with an excessively long 'Gassaggen [Casaque] and hanging braids [Haarzopf] on the street'. He added that she had 'reformed' her headdress in the meantime, so as to conform to the regulations.[22]

The boundary between the domestic private sphere and the legally controlled public sphere was negotiated between the judges and the defendant in each specific case. The idea of the coexistence of two fundamentally different spheres also influenced the considerations of the

---

[20] André Holenstein, *Die Huldigung der Untertanen* (Stuttgart/New York: Gustav Fischer, 1991), 458–460.

[21] Regula Wyss, 'Von zu hohen Kappen und zu dicken Perücken. Eine quantitative Untersuchung über die Justizpraxis der bernischen Reformationskammer' (Unpublished, Seminararbeit Historisches Institut der Universität Bern, 2003), 20–22.

[22] Burgerbibliothek Bern, Mss. Hist. Helv. III.261, fol. 52 (*Proceedings of the Bernese Reformation Chamber*, 13–20 February 1679).

Bernese city council committee during the revision of the sumptuary law in 1727, when they proposed that members of the Reformation chamber, who were invited to a social gathering in their role as private individuals, should report the wearing of proscribed dress only when it concerned other guests, and not when it concerned the host, as the host, unlike his guests, had not left the private sphere and his proscribed apparel had not become visible to the public.[23]

Such considerations reveal how socially sensitive the principle of reporting others was. The possibility of reporting someone to a court based on a breach of regulations opened up the opportunity for individuals to use criminal justice for their own personal interest, for example to take revenge. In the revised sumptuary law of 1728, Bern's city councils defined more precisely the situations and social relationships that exempted them and other city officials from reporting a breach of the law. The list exempted individuals from the duty to report an offence if their relation with the offender was so close that it obliged them to abstain from voting in relevant council elections, or if they lived in the same house. Remarkably, servants and maids were expressly forbidden to report their male and female masters or their children.[24]

Several observations indicate that the Bernese reformation chamber increasingly came under pressure to justify its existence. Although the councils continued to issue detailed laws about permissible pieces of clothing and their adornment with precious stones, gold and silver thread, lace or fur,[25] nearly no breaches of the dress rules were reported during the last period for which the reformation chamber's records have survived, from 1781 to 1797. The chamber had markedly shifted the focus of its activities in the course of the eighteenth century. At the end of the *Ancien Régime*, it was mainly concerned with labour contract disputes between masters and their servants, as well as with the authorisation of dances and the prosecution of violations of bans on dancing.[26] The city's small council and the chamber were forced to admit that prosecution by means of secret and official inspectors failed to have the desired effect, and that the authority's regulatory efforts were to no avail because the development of fashion was always a step ahead.[27]

---

[23] Gut, *Kleiderordnungen*, 76–77.
[24] *Sammlung Schweizerischer Rechtsquellen, Kanton Bern*, ed. H. Rennefahrt (Aarau, 1961), vi, part 2: 979 (6 September 1747).
[25] Ibid., 991–999 (29 January 1766).
[26] Tina Adam, 'Arbeitskonflikte in Berner Haushalten. Die Justizpraxis der Reformationskammer 1781–1787', *Berner Zeitschrift für Geschichte* 79 (2017): 3–37.
[27] Gut, *Kleiderordnungen*, 79–83.

Controversies over Fashion and Luxury in Republics

The sumptuary laws and the records of the Reformation chambers of Swiss cities give an impression of the new kind of material culture that was gaining ground among the city elites. In the seventeenth and eighteenth centuries the consumer behaviour of the members of the upper ranks reflected their desire for cultural distinction as well as their taste, which they had refined on the model of the French court.[28] The records of Bern's reformation chamber document the emergence of gender-specific fashions and consumption patterns in the last quarter of the seventeenth century. Women were mainly reported for wearing overly high or expensive caps, overly valuable fur trimmings, an overly low-cut décolleté or overly short sleeves, whereas men tended to be reported for the shape and size of their wigs and for gold ornaments. Proscribed coiffures and clothing made of overly lavish fabrics and laces were reported equally often with respect to both sexes.

Among the cases for which the court records indicate the place or event at which the informant had noticed the breach of a dress rule, many mention the church. This was the city's central public site where the community regularly came together. The weekly Sunday services were important social events for the city's inhabitants. Although the sumptuary laws allowed people to dress more expensively on Sundays than on working days, they nonetheless stipulated strict dress rules for churchgoers of both sexes. Women were required to wear a veil (*tüchli*) without lace that covered the neck, hair and ears; men were required to wear a coat and collar.[29] In December 1678 the Bern chamber noted that women mostly wore caps in church rather than tüchli, and therefore instructed those in charge of fire safety to visit every house and ensure that mothers and daughters who were to go to church on Sundays or Christmas and take communion should not wear caps but the traditional (*alt gewoohnte*) 'veil', and otherwise would be accused.[30]

---

[28] Walker, 'Lois somptuaires', 123. John Brewer and Roy Porter (eds.), *Consumption and the World of Goods* (London and New York: Routledge, 1993); Maxine Berg and Helen Clifford (eds.), *Consumers and Luxury. Consumer Culture in Europe 1650–1850* (Manchester: Manchester University Press, 1999); Michael Prinz (ed.), *Der lange Weg in den Überfluss. Anfänge und Entwicklung der Konsumgesellschaft seit der Vormoderne* (Paderborn: Schöningh, 2003); Reinhold Reith and Torsten Meyer (eds.), *Luxus und Konsum. Eine historische Annäherung* (Münster, 2003); Maxine Berg et al. (eds.), *Luxury in the Eighteenth Century* (Basingstoke: Palgrave, 2007); Ruedi Brassel-Moser, Konsumverhalten *Historisches Lexikon der Schweiz* (Basel: Schwabe, 2008), vii: 393–396.

[29] Gut, *Kleiderordnungen*, 39–42, 49–52.

[30] Burgerbibliothek Bern, Mss. Hist. Helv. III.261, fol. 42f. (Proceedings of the Bernese Reformation Chamber, 19 December 1678).

A table of around 1782 to 1783 detailing annual imports and the value of imported goods documents how strongly the consumption needs of Bern's inhabitants already depended on the city's participation in global trade:[31] It includes cotton from India and the Orient worth more than 1 million livres, silk and velvet from France, Italy, Holland and Eastern Switzerland worth 330,000 livres, fashion goods for men and women from Paris, London, Lyon, Geneva and Neuchâtel worth 100,000 livres, hair powder and perfumes from France worth 20,000 livres, jewellery from England, France, Holland and the Piedmont worth 50,000 livres, hardware (*quincaillerie*) and haberdasheries from England, France and Holland worth 0.5 million pounds, sugar from the seaports of Holland and France worth 300,000 pounds, coffee from the Levant, Martinique, France, Holland, England and Italy worth 200,000 pounds, tea from Holland, England and France worth 80,000 pounds, chocolate from Milan, Turin and Venice worth 20,000 pounds and tobacco and snuff from Holland, Spain and France worth 300,000 pounds.[32]

How did these products get to the inhabitants of Bern? The Bernese *Ancien Régime* saw a growth in the number of markets and marketplaces, particularly in the countryside.[33] Around 1790, 87 towns and villages in the republic of Bern had an annual fair, and 48 had a weekly market. Many of these markets had been authorised by the Bernese council's commerce-chamber upon request by the relevant communities.[34] Moreover, peddlers played an important role in supplying rural households with special and novel goods.[35]

The increasing differentiation and refinement of consumption was by no means limited to wealthy circles. It is true that wealthy people were the first to buy products of the emerging luxury industry: they practised the new lifestyle of 'douceur de vivre' by lavishly decorating their living quarters with tapestries, dressing tables, chairs, crystal glasses and porcelain objects, or by purchasing coaches.[36] But the emerging material

---

[31] Erika Flückiger, Anne Radeff, 'Globale Ökonomie im alten Staat Bern am Ende des Ancien Régime', *Berner Zeitschrift für Geschichte und Heimatkunde* 62 (2000): 5–40.

[32] Ibid., 28–30.

[33] Anne Radeff, *Du café dans le chaudron. Economie globale d'Ancien Régime* (Lausanne: Société d'Histoire de la Suisse Romande, 1996), 399, 406–407.

[34] Anne Radeff and Beat Kümin, 'Markt-Wirtschaft. Handelsinfrastruktur und Gastgewerbe im alten Bern', *Schweizerische Zeitschrift für Geschichte* 50 (2000): 1–19, here 8, 12–14.

[35] Radeff, *Du café*, 204–206, 305–307.

[36] Michael Stürmer, 'Luxusgüter in der Knappheitsgesellschaft. Handwerkskultur und höfisches Leben im 18. Jahrhundert', *Francia* 6 (1978): 319–365; Ulrich-Christian Pallach, *Materielle Kultur und Mentalitäten im 18. Jahrhundert* (München: R. Oldenbourg, 1987).

culture was no less tempting for ordinary people and was acquired by large parts of the population, within the limits of their respective financial capabilities: 'It is not only wealthy people or even … workers … who engage in consumption, but also the large mass of farmers … These numerous consumers not only purchase objects comparable to those of their ancestors (sheets from wool or hemp, farming tools, pans); when they can, they also choose new products (cotton fabric, coffee, window panes, etc.)'.[37]

The fact that many new products came from the colonies gave them a high symbolic value, and their consumption by ordinary people elicited particularly critical comments from among the political and cultural elite. For example, Rudolf Holzer (1760–1781), a student of theology in Bern, observed in 1779 in a critical description of the Bernese administrative district of Laupen that here there was 'hardly a farmer's wife [left] whose kitchen is not adorned with tea and coffee pots, pewter plates, and the like; the surest signs that the cities' lavish splendour, luxury, and weaknesses have found their way to the countryside'.[38]

The changing consumption patterns of large parts of the population in the eighteenth century were the subject of controversial discussions within the debate about the harmfulness or usefulness of luxury. In Switzerland, this debate was conducted mainly by members of the cultural and political elites, many of whom were members of one or several of the many learned societies founded in the eighteenth century. In terms of a rough typology, we can distinguish two opposing views on the effects of luxury on the political economy of the Swiss republics. The advocates of the traditional view were categorically opposed to luxury, justifying this position with classical republican arguments from the ancient world and civic humanist arguments from the Italian Renaissance. Their view centred on the key concept of virtue. The newer view was based on economic and social arguments. Its proponents put fundamental criticism of luxury into perspective by regarding the material expenditure of the upper classes as a prerequisite not only for the Swiss commercial republics' economic prosperity, but also for the continued employment of the lower classes and for effective alleviation of poverty.[39]

---

[37] Radeff, *Du café*, 136–135.
[38] Quoted after Georg C. L. Schmidt, *Der Schweizer Bauer im Zeitalter des Frühkapitalismus* (Bern: Paul Haupt, 1932), ii: 159*, fn. 293. Regarding the genre of topographic descriptions, see Gerrendina Gerber-Visser, *Die Ressourcen des Landes. Der ökonomisch-patriotische Blick in den Topographischen Beschreibungen der Oekonomischen Gesellschaft Bern (1759–1855)* (Baden: Hier und Jetzt, 2012).
[39] Simone Zurbuchen, 'Patriotismus und Nation: Der schweizerische Republikanismus des 18. Jahrhunderts', in M. Böhler et al. (eds.), *Republikanische Tugend. Ausbildung eines Schweizer Nationalbewusstseins und Erziehung eines neuen Bürgers* (Geneva, Slatkine,

'A Deadly Poison': Luxury in the Classical Republican Discourse on Virtue

Swiss proponents of the Enlightenment criticised excessiveness in material regards based on a classical concept of the republic in which theory of government and morality were inseparably linked.[40] Their criticism manifested itself in many ways, including in numerous speeches by chairmen of the Helvetic Society in the last third of the eighteenth century, whose patriotic republicanism was modelled on ancient Sparta, the ancient Roman republic and above all the heroic founding fathers of the Swiss Confederation.[41] In the middle of the eighteenth century, this school of thought had received new impetus from Jean-Jacques Rousseau's theories of government and critique of civilisation, which were enthusiastically greeted by young members of the Swiss intellectual and political elite.[42]

The rationale was that a republic was necessarily based on a certain degree of equality among its citizens. Too much material inequality and consumption of luxury goods among the wealthy classes would arouse envy and jealousy among the citizens, fragmenting the community and thereby putting at risk the republic's internal stability.[43] Unlike large monarchies, republics – which, in pre-revolutionary theories of government, were always conceived of as small communal states – built on their citizens' willingness to sacrifice their personal interests for the common weal. The citizens of a republic were expected to voluntarily subject

2000), 151–181, here 156; Béla Kapossy, 'Introduction. From Republicanism to Welfare Liberalism', *Schweizerische Zeitschrift für Geschichte* 50 (2000): 275–303; Daniel Tröhler, 'Kommerz und Patriotismus. Pestalozzis Weg vom politischen zum christlichen Republikanismus (1764–1780)', *Schweizerische Zeitschrift für Geschichte* 50 (2000): 325–352.

[40] Eight presidential speeches discussed the issue of luxury in front of the Helvetic Society. Ulrich Im Hof, *Die Entstehung einer politischen Öffentlichkeit in der Schweiz. Struktur und Tätigkeit der Helvetischen Gesellschaft* (Frauenfeld: Huber, 1983), 158–162. André Holenstein, 'Frugalität und Virilität. Zur Mythisierung kriegerischer Gewalt im republikanischen Diskurs in der Schweiz des 18. Jahrhunderts', in C. Ulbrich et al. (eds.), *Gewalt in der Frühen Neuzeit* (Berlin: Duncker and Humblot, 2005), 117–130.

[41] François de Capitani, 'Die Antike im schweizerischen Staatsdenken des 18. Jahrhunderts', in E. Giddey (ed.), *Vorromantik in der Schweiz?* (Fribourg: Editions Universitaires Fribourg Suisse, 1982), 217–236; Im Hof, *Helvetische Gesellschaft*, 180–181; Guy P. Marchal, 'Die "Alten Eidgenossen" im Wandel der Zeiten. Das Bild der frühen Eidgenossen im Traditionsbewusstsein und in den Identitätsvorstellungen der Schweizer vom 15. bis ins 20. Jahrhundert', in *Innerschweiz und frühe Eidgenossenschaft* (Olten: Historical Association of the Five Cantons, 1991), ii: 338–352.

[42] Daniel Tröhler, 'Der Zürcher Rousseau-Kult der 1760er Jahre', in J. Reiling et al. (eds.), *Zwischen Vielfalt und Imagination. Praktiken der Jean-Jacques Rousseau-Rezeption* (Geneva: Slatkine, 2013), 83–101.

[43] Walker, 'Lois somptuaires', 124.

themselves to their community's laws and, if necessary, to risk their lives as soldiers in defence of the republic.[44] Citizen virtue was the moral and political fundamental category of classical republican patriotism.[45]

From an economic point of view, virtue necessarily had to be coupled with a frugal material culture. Self-sufficient agriculture was the type of political economy congenial to a republic. A republic's economy was 'oikonomic' in the sense of the ancient economic theory; that is, its paramount aim was to secure the household's subsistence rather than to make a profit on the market and in trade.[46]

From the standpoint of this interpretation of political economy, luxury was a deadly poison for any republic. It corrupted citizens' virtue and would inevitably lead to the republic's downfall.[47] Excessive consumption spoiled the citizens, aroused new desires in them, and made them susceptible to corruption.[48] In addition, the desire to satisfy refined, sensuous pleasures made citizens soft and weak, causing them to fail as soldiers and rendering the republic easy prey for aggressive neighbours in the event of a war.[49] Glutz von Blotzheim of Solothurn reminded his audience at the Helvetic Society of the ancient Romans:

> Poverty, or rather, owning no more than what is necessary, was a virtue which adorned Rome's greatest heroes – Cincinnatus, Fabricius, Regulus. They went from triumph to the plough and from there back to the head of the army if their fatherland called them. They feared idleness far more than their enemies. Accustomed to work from an early age, they were unable to think of sensual pleasure, which might have emasculated their courage and weakened their body: instead, they hardened the latter against the toils of the Solothurn war, just as they steeled their courage against war's perils.[50]

But the old Confederates were even better suited than the ancient Romans to be cited as heroic paragons of republican virtuousness by the

---

[44] Gugger, *Wesen*, 48–49.

[45] Herfried Münkler, 'Die Idee der Tugend. Ein politischer Leitbegriff im vorrevolutionären Europa', *Archiv für Kulturgeschichte* 73 (1991): 379–403.

[46] Kapossy, *Introduction*, 287; William James Booth, *Households. On the Moral Architecture of the Economy* (Ithaca: Cornell University Press, 1993).

[47] Johann Heinrich Schinz, 'Wiederbelebung der alteidgenössischen Tugenden', in *Verhandlungen der Helvetischen Gesellschaft in Schinznach im Jahr 1768* (Basel), 11–49, here 32–33; Gugger, *Wesen*, 85; Urs Joseph Niklaus Alois Glutz von Blotzheim, 'Die antike Republik als Vorbild für die Schweiz', in *Verhandlungen der Helvetischen Gesellschaft 1787* (Basel), 11–43, here 14–16; Jacob Sarasin, 'Vom Glück des Schweizertums', in *Verhandlungen der Helvetischen Gesellschaft 1794* (Basel), 9–84, here 46–47.

[48] This applied, for example, to the doctor, politician and enlightenment thinker Laurenz Zellweger of Appenzell. See Paulfritz Kellenberger, *Laurenz Zellweger von Trogen 1692–1764* (Zürich: Universität Zürich, 1951), 102–103.

[49] Schinz, *Tugenden*, 42.

[50] Glutz, *Republik*, 26.

Swiss patriots of the eighteenth century. The founding myth portrayed
the Confederates' freedom as a result of the successful struggle of 'pious,
noble peasants' from the three founding cantons against the tyranny
of the foreign Habsburg nobility.[51] A view which was symptomatic of
this national ideology in the Helvetian discourse on luxury was that the
evil of luxury was, at bottom, alien to the Swiss national character and
invaded the country from abroad. Particular blame for the imitation of
harmful consumption habits and their introduction to Switzerland was
placed on young people's journeys abroad.[52] The increasing integration
of Swiss trading cities into the global economy led Schinz of Zurich
to refer to peace and trade as silken ropes that fettered the Swiss and
constrained their republican freedom.[53] Jakob Sarasin (1742–1802) of
Basel – a successful merchant – said in 1794 that even the mountains
had not protected the Swiss against the 'toxic fumes' of luxury, 'since
frequent emigrations, foreign military service, and the spread of trade
chained us to foreign countries to a greater degree than what would have
been conducive to the simplicity of our habits'.[54]

Sarasin's verdict reveals the ideological nature of the eighteenth-
century classical republican discourse on virtue. Sarasin was not the only
member of the Helvetic Society who had gained his wealth from trade in
luxury goods but nonetheless praised the old Confederates' frugal culture, criticised civilisation and lamented the decadence of his time to
his like-minded patriotic audience of fellow society members. Johannes
Zellweger (1730–1802) of Trogen (Appenzell) is another example:[55] in
his role as president of the Helvetic Society he gave a fiery speech against
luxury, yet he was the owner of a successful trading company, belonged
to the richest group in his country and demonstrated his wealth, among
other things, by building the palace-like houses that line the central
square in Trogen to this day.[56]

The imploring pathos of the republican discourse on virtue was
not least due to the fact that the patriots saw the spread of wealth and
luxury as a sure sign of the Confederation's impending fall. This diag-
nosis, rooted in a critique of civilisation, inevitably led to the question of

[51] Salomon von Orelli von Baldingen, 'Sozial- und Kulturgeschichte der Schweiz', in
Verhandlungen der Helvetischen Gesellschaft 1790 (Basel), 7–95, here 13–14. In general,
see Marchal, *Die 'Alten Eidgenossen'*, 338–352.
[52] André Holenstein, *Mitten in Europa. Verflechtung und Abgrenzung in der Schweizer
Geschichte* (Baden: Hier und Jetzt, 2014), 178–193.
[53] Schinz, *Tugenden*, 43.
[54] Sarasin, *Glück*, 38.
[55] Im Hof, *Helvetische Gesellschaft*, 161.
[56] Johannes Zellweger, 'Das Problem des Luxus', in *Verhandlungen der Helvetischen
Gesellschaft in Schinznach im Jahr 1776* (Basel), 41–106.

what could be done to combat luxury. Opinions regarding appropriate treatments diverged widely. While some still relied on the deterrent effect of sumptuary laws,[57] others had lost faith in the power of such laws to regulate people's behaviour. Much in line with enlightened thinking, they turned to pedagogy and emphasised the importance of 'the most highly regarded and richest families' as role models, the 'careful education of young people' and 'public appreciation of honest industriousness'.[58] Fiscal measures were considered as well: Isaak Iselin from Basel proposed high duties on luxury imports.[59] Others wanted to forbid young people from travelling abroad, especially to Europe's major capital cities, because they returned from there with a pernicious taste for luxury.[60] And yet others believed in the effectiveness of appeals to highly esteemed and wealthy citizens to voluntarily limit their own consumption.[61]

Those republican patriots who chose not to ignore the population's growing wealth, and who accepted luxury as a matter of fact, searched for ways of reconciling material wealth with virtue as a guiding norm. They argued that the wealthy should invest their capital in charitable projects instead of private consumption, for example in 'institutions for the education of young people, for the encouragement of diligence, and for honouring meritorious achievements', or in the erection of monuments and in funding prizes for useful inventions.[62] The legitimate need for diversion and amusement could be satisfied with 'simple, public celebrations which entailed lower costs and less luxury, and which corrupted the mores less than anything that is concealed and nonetheless happens in private homes'.[63]

Prosperity, Marketing and Social Policies in the Swiss Commercial Republics: Luxury in Late-Enlightenment Philanthropic Discourse

While the classical republican patriots, with their discourse on virtue, aimed to slow the growing economic dynamics and prevent the republic's

---

[57] Niklaus Emanuel Tscharner, *Ueber die Nothwendigkeit der Prachtgeseze in einem Freystaate* (Zürich: Bey Orell, Gessner und Compag., 1769).

[58] Wyss, *Politisches Handbuch*, 413–414.

[59] Isaak Iselin, *Palämon oder von der Ueppigkeit* (Zürich: Bey Orell, Gessner und Compag., 1769), 73.

[60] Holenstein, *Mitten in Europa*, 186–189.

[61] So e.g. Laurenz Zellweger (Kellenberger, *Zellweger*, 103); Schinz, *Tugenden*, 36–39; Sarasin, *Glück*, 63–64.

[62] Iselin, *Palämon*, 78–79; Tscharner, *Prachtgeseze*, 40–41.

[63] Johann Heinrich Heidegger, *Über den zürcherischen Luxus*, ed. L. Weisz (Zürich: Orell Füssli, 1933), 112–113.

political economy from being integrated into the increasingly globalised international economy, other authors from among the intellectual elite took a more sober stance on luxury. They saw it not only as an inevitable social and economic fact, but also as a sign of general progress. In their view, the production and consumption of luxury goods opened up prospects for overcoming pressing social and economic problems of their time.

This position becomes apparent, for example, in the treatises which were awarded a prize in a 1779 competition organised by the Basel Encouragement Society (*Basler Aufmunterungsgesellschaft*) and were printed in 1781. The Society had presented the learned public with the following question: 'To what degree is it appropriate to limit the expenditure of the citizens of a small republic whose prosperity is based on trade?'[64] The award winners included the popular philosopher Leonhard Meister (1741–1811) and Johann Heinrich Pestalozzi (1746–1827), later a famed pedagogue, both from the economically thriving commercial republic of Zurich.

Leonhard Meister considered trade, commerce and industry to be the 'cornerstones of the newer republics':

In every state, as in every household, life itself must first be ensured before we ensure its comfort. If the population is larger than what the land can support, arts and trade must replace the land. A smaller population means smaller military power and lower public and customs revenues; less food will lead to a smaller population; and food will be less if arts and trade are less widespread. These are to a great extent the cornerstones of the newer republics; the Genevans' republic largely rests on the tips of the clock's hands; Venice on playing cards; the Netherlands on spices and tea leaves; several Swiss cantons on bolts of silk and cotton. Commerce and factories expand the country's natural borders; they enable us to harvest fields that we have not ploughed, and fruit that we have not planted.[65]

He did admit that 'The fewer people's needs, the smaller are their troubles and worries; the less inequality there is, and the more freedom'. But this was counterposed with the following advantages:

---

[64] *Ueber die Aufwandgesetze. Sammlung einiger Schriften, welche bey der Aufmunterungs-Gesellschaft in Basel eingeflossen sind, über die Frage: In wie fern ist es schicklich dem Aufwande der Bürger in einem kleinen Freystaate, dessen Wohlfahrt auf die Handelschaft gegründet ist, Schranken zu setzen?* (Basel: Johann Jacob Flick, 1781); Rudolf Braun, *Industrialisierung und Volksleben* (Winterthur: Keller, 1960), 109–17.

[65] Leonhard Meister, 'Abhandlung über die Frage: In wie fern ist es schicklich dem Aufwande der Bürger, in einem kleinen Freystaate, dessen Wohlfahrt auf die Handelschaft gegründet ist, Schranken zu setzen?', in *Ueber die Aufwandgesetze* (Basel: Johann Jacob Flick, 1781), 15–16.

(...) the greater the refinement and the multiplication of needs, the more skills and strengths develop. If we look at a rich man's table laid with porcelain and silver, and we smell the sweet fragrance of foreign nectar or aromatic herbs, we not only seem to hear the worker moaning in his workshop and the Negro in his plantation; in our mind's eye we picture the geometer calculating the length of the sea; without mechanics there can be no shipping; no trade can develop without natural history and financial science; and without all that, there can be no sumptuous table!

Growing material needs, industrious trade and research mutually stimulated each other and advanced humankind.[66]

Pestalozzi added that the cultivation of refined tastes was necessary to enable the domestic industry to produce competitive goods that were in line with current fashion trends and met consumers' needs:

A nation which has to make a living from industry must have plentiful experience regarding the peculiarities of taste and the situation, knowledge, and follies of purchasers – skills needed to adapt the outfit of one and the same thing in multiple ways (...). And in this way expenditure also facilitates the sales of goods processed by industry – for the more refinement, elaboration, industriousness and flexibility the nation's spirit will contain – the more perfect and attractive its processed goods will be, and that in turn will provide the basis for guaranteed sales.[67]

Meister and Pestalozzi viewed luxury as beneficial to population growth and social cohesion in the republic, because the luxury industry integrated the growing lower classes into the working process and helped to solve increasingly pressing social issues. 'And the same way in which expenditure appropriately educates the national spirit to meet the needs of domestic industry, it also secures and multiplies the number of hands needed as tools to work this industry – by naturally increasing the state's population to the same extent as it throws revenues among the people.'[68] With regard to people's employment and the rapidly growing non-farming population, Pestalozzi wrote

that once the wealthier inhabitants' measure of expenditure, which has been established as long as anyone can remember, becomes interwoven with the sources of income and professions of the common inhabitants – one cannot, without committing an act of injustice against the common man, noticeably limit this established measure of expenditure; at that time every careful common

---

[66] Meister, *Abhandlung*, 17.
[67] Johann Heinrich Pestalozzi, 'Abhandlung über die Frage: In wie fern ist es schicklich dem Aufwande der Bürger, in einem kleinen Freystaate, dessen Wohlfahrt auf die Handelschaft gegründet ist, Schranken zu setzen?', in *Ueber die Aufwandgesetze* (1781), 10–11, 14.
[68] Pestalozzi, *Abhandlung*, 13–14.

father of a family, in choosing his children's profession, will look towards those branches of industry which, according to the current tone of our mores, will be most likely to earn them a living.[69]

Pestalozzi opposed the restriction of wealthy families' '*aisance*' (affluence) by means of sumptuary laws. Instead he thought that by relinquishing such laws, the authorities should aim to tie wealthy households to the fatherland. He observed that:

A small trading town inevitably needs its wealthy families to stay. It is these families and their funds that provide a living for the inhabitants, so it must necessarily be a main concern of such small trading towns' policies that these families should love their fatherland, and want to remain its citizens; and if a government should arbitrarily and narrowly limit such families' expenditure, it would be certain to act contrary to the town's essential real needs, to the benefit which the fatherland receives from industry and from these families' expenditure.[70]

Pestalozzi believed that the government of a small commercial republic should orient its economic policies toward the interests of its wealthiest citizens, given that patriotism no longer sufficed to tie them to their fatherland:

If such families regard a country as the place in which their property shall be put to work, the openness of this place towards industry is necessarily a concern of their own economy. The general prosperity of the place – its affluence, its population and the prosperity of the middle and low ranks – ensures them the use of their funds before their very eyes. It gives them the opportunity to securely put their money to use among their fellow citizens; the wealth and the credit of their fellow citizens thus becomes a matter that concerns their own funds. (…) Thus is the importance, in the current situation, of the great and wealthy families' attachment to the fatherland. And since in our century one may not count on the pure motives of patriotism and the gratitude to which all rich Swiss families owe the magnificence of our secure and free constitution – as many such families, owning great riches, look down with pride and contempt on the constitutions under which their ancestors, as common inhabitants, laid the foundations of their excellent fortune – and because a rich man generally only attaches himself to low creatures' weal as long as it is his own interest, it is very important that the governments of small commercial states fully recognise the influence which wealthy citizens' free expenditure can have on tying them in the best and most secure way to the interests of the fatherland.

If one acknowledged, however, 'that the palaces, gardens, and estates of the wealthy can secure the prosperity of a small commercial town in a very comforting way, one will, from this perspective, also have to tolerate

---

[69] Ibid., 15.
[70] Ibid., 16–17.

these people's horses and hairdressers; for they will hardly build palaces in a place where one would think to restrict their stables and divest them of the tassels and fringes on their harnesses'.[71]

Pestalozzi summarised the favourable consequences of the unlimited luxury consumption of wealthy citizens for the republic as follows:

I see bread and joy – and a rich blessing flow down on the tables and into the cottages of low citizens from wealthy people's expenditure. Overall, I see sums of money of such greatness fall down into the common ranks as a result of this expenditure, that their lack, given the people's current needs, would lead to misery, destitution, emigration, and the stoppage of industry. (...) I see, in the closer linkage of the interest of rich commercial houses with the interest of the fatherland, the source and security of national prosperity and the development of most people's industriousness; and so it appears to me that wealthy families' expenditure is indispensable to the fatherland, and a true beneficence for their fellow citizens.[72]

Meister and Pestalozzi, as well as Isaak Iselin, the author of the prize question announced in 1779 in Basel, saw the economic and social potential of luxury and commerce as a welcome excuse for adapting the ideal of virtue to the needs of their time: 'Moderate Swiss Christians were keen to rescue luxury from such moral criticism and redescribed it as compatible with virtue provided economic rationality was preserved'.[73] In the views of these authors, patriots of the classical republican tradition were backward; their outdated, isolationist concept of society offered no prospects for economic and social policies that were capable of both securing the country's economic competitiveness and guaranteeing social justice.[74] Iselin, instead of viewing economic prosperity as a threat to virtue, regarded it as a prerequisite for a virtuous society. His anti-Rousseauist concept of virtue included the cultivation of manners and the appreciation of the sciences and arts, which he viewed as necessary preconditions for sustainable economic prosperity.[75] If noble and wealthy citizens refined their wealth through science and scholarship, wealth and affluence would no longer be expressed in the barbaric passions of coarse souls or in boisterous luxury, but in the 'more noble and appealing comforts of social exchange and domestic life'.[76]

---

[71] Ibid., 19–22.
[72] Ibid., 22–23.
[73] Kapossy, *Introduction*, 296.
[74] Ibid., 297–298.
[75] Béla Kapossy, *Iselin contra Rousseau. Sociable Patriotism and the History of Mankind* (Basel: Schwabe, 2006).
[76] Zurbuchen, *Patriotismus und Nation*, 176–177.

Only under the beneficial influences of economic prosperity does the human soul rise to grand and charitable efforts and to the higher truths through which it comes to know its dignity and its destiny. As wealth spreads out, the necessity and the value of order become more critical; and it becomes easier to spread enlightenment and charitable attitudes. Even the evils which grow from soil fattened under the influence of riches alongside the latter's better fruit, and often threaten to suffocate them; even these evils become a means to develop, practise, and test the citizen's virtue.[77]

How do the two positions fit into the European debate about luxury, wealth and consumption in the eighteenth century?

First, the eighteenth-century Swiss patriots' discourse on virtue is a variant of classical republicanism. The historical influence of the republican ideal of virtue in Europe stretches from Italian civic humanism to Montesquieu and Rousseau, who both had a strong influence on republican thinking among the Swiss patriots of the eighteenth century. However, we can also trace a genuinely Swiss variant of the republican ideal of virtue. In the fifteenth century, when the Confederation was confronted with Habsburg Austria's criticism that it had ousted the rightful rulers and taken their place, the old Confederates' virtue became the centrepiece of a Swiss legitimisation strategy. Since then, the Swiss have justified their freedom and the expulsion of the aristocracy by pointing out that the aristocrats had ceased to be 'noble' and had become corrupted, while virtue had passed to the 'pious, noble peasants' of the Confederation.[78] The battle victories in the late Middle Ages were interpreted as divine judgements in favour of the Confederates; they testified to the fact that God had placed this chosen people under His special protection. Both lines of argument – the stylisation of their own virtue into the keystone of their political legitimacy, as well as the idea of being chosen by God – were incompatible with a corrupt way of life. Unsurprisingly, therefore, from the late fifteenth century onwards, upholding a frugal material culture and abhorring luxury were core elements of Swiss self-justification.

Second, Leonhard Meister's and Johann Heinrich Pestalozzi's discriminate views on luxury have several European precursors, including the writings of people like Bernard Mandeville, Jean-François Melon and Voltaire, who had already arrived at a more favourable assessment of luxury and the enjoyment of material pleasures in the first half of the eighteenth century. In the writings of these authors, the condemnation

---

[77] Isaak Iselin, *Versuch über die gesellige Ordnung* (Basel: J. Schweighauser, 1772), 92–93.
[78] Marchal, *Die 'Alten Eidgenossen'*, 316.

of luxury gave way to its consideration as a product of human nature and psychology, and its appreciation as a positive factor in economic and social development.[79]

Mediation between 'wealth and virtue' was also a matter of particular concern to the Scottish moral philosophers. Adam Ferguson rejected the connection between luxury and the corruption of virtue which was axiomatic in classical republican thinking. In his view, in a society based on trade and commerce, people's virtue was no more in danger of corruption than in any other society. Even in a 'commercial society', people were in a position to prove their virtuousness.[80]

The idea that people were naturally less inclined to concern themselves with the public weal than to pursue their personal interests and improve their particular situation was an important starting point for such reasoning. 'The desire of bettering our condition [is] a desire … which comes with us from the womb and never leaves us till we go into the grave.'[81] Unlike the classical discourse on virtue, which conceived of a political community's cohesion as based on citizens' efforts to promote the common weal, the concept of interests granted individuals the right to protect their particular concerns.[82] According to David Hume's or Adam Smith's philosophy of history, in the eighteenth century humankind had, in the most advanced parts of the world, reached the stage of a 'commercial society'. In this stage of human history, people owed their relative wealth to trade and commerce, and to the advanced division of labour. The militarily frugal Sparta was no longer an appropriate model for such a society – especially when one considered the fact that the exercise of political rights in the Spartan polis was restricted to the propertied, free patresfamilias, while the constitution was based on a slave economy, in violation of the principle of natural freedom. In this new understanding, 'wealth and virtue' were by no means mutually exclusive; trade and luxury actually came to be seen as preconditions for a state's growth and success and for a happy and virtuous society.[83]

---

[79] Berry, *Luxury*, 126–176; Winfried Schulze, *Vom Gemeinnutz zum Eigennutz. Über den Normenwandel in der ständischen Gesellschaft der Frühen Neuzeit* (Munich: Historisches Kolleg, 1987).

[80] Marco Geuna, 'Richesse, commerce et corruption dans la pensée d'Adam Ferguson', in Jacques Berchtold and Michel Porret (eds.), *Être riche au siècle de Voltaire* (Geneva: Droz, 1996), 81–95, here 89.

[81] Adam Smith, *Wealth of Nations*, quoted after Berry, *Luxury*, 153.

[82] Münkler, *Tugend*, 379.

[83] Berry, *Luxury*, 142–158.

Conclusion

Sumptuary laws mirrored the changing configurations of morality, politics and economy in communal-republican discourse. Over time, political and economic arguments were uncoupled from religious-moral perspectives which sought to regulate behaviour, yet even the idea that God might punish superfluous consumption remained present in legal ordinances well into the eighteenth century. The restriction of luxury was increasingly legitimated with reference to social and economic arguments, especially in relation to the fight against poverty and concerns about a trade deficit. Criticism of luxury had been in any case a fundamental part of the construction of Swiss identity since the fifteenth century. A critique of the nobility went hand in hand with the idea that the Swiss were pious, noble peasants who lived frugally and bought only necessities. This notion of political and economic virtue founded on communal-republican liberty and at times included an ethnicised rejection of foreign cultures represented in dress or food. The literary-cultural movement of eighteenth century Helvetism supported proto-nationalist ideas which became the intellectual basis of the Swiss political nation between the ephemeral Helvetic Republic (1798–1803) and the foundation of the modern Swiss Confederation in 1848. Yet during the eighteenth century ideas of republican virtue were increasingly challenged by developments in trade.

Zürich, Basel, Geneva, St. Gallen and Schaffhausen were flourishing republics of trade and part of a globalising economy with a particular focus on textile- and watch-production. Those who were wealthy began to stress the convenience and refinement which luxury consumption facilitated and began to justify the physical and sensuous needs of consumers by arguing that the lower classes found employment through producing luxury and were taught to appreciate industry and work as bourgeois values.

5   Dangerous Fashions in Swedish Sumptuary Law

Eva I. Andersson

Introduction

Swedish sumptuary legislation has a long history. While not starting particularly early – the first example is from the fourteenth century – sumptuary laws continued to be issued until the nineteenth century. The Swedish sumptuary laws included rules on food, funerals, carriages, foreign language teachers, horse trappings, coffee, and, of course, clothing. Clothing was one of the most important ways in which medieval and early modern people claimed and displayed their position in society. Through fine materials and the latest designs, wealth and status could be made visible to all. Clothing was therefore a way to make society legible by differentiating between genders and classes.

Scholars turn to sumptuary laws for many reasons. For some, they provide a way to study the development of economic thought or trade policies. For others, the objects in them hold the most interest. What did they mean? How were they used to send messages? Why were they forbidden, or allowed? This article discusses the role of dress regulations in controlling and creating order in society by upholding distinction between the sexes, between the estates, between moral and immoral women, and between Swedes and foreigners. It is, however, not just a study of the ideas behind the sumptuary laws, but also of the material reality of the forbidden items of clothing, and of those wearing them. Thus, both the disorderly subjects of the Swedish king and the disorderly *objects* will be addressed. Whose consumption of clothing caused disorder, and which were the garments that had the power to threaten the order in society?

Sweden in the Middle Ages and Early Modern Period

While the kingdom of Sweden existed already in the early Middle Ages, its borders were not the same as today. The largest difference between medieval and modern Sweden is that the provinces of Scania, Blekinge and

Halland in the south and southwest belonged to Denmark, while Bohuslän in the southwest, north of Gothenburg, and Jämtland and Härjedalen in the northwest, were part of the kingdom of Norway. In the thirteenth century, Finland was incorporated into the Swedish realm, though the Swedish presence in Finland was mostly confined to the western and southern areas.

The fourteenth and fifteenth centuries were a period of political upheaval and change in the Nordic countries. Sweden joined Denmark and Norway in the so-called Kalmar Union in 1397. The period from the 1430s onwards was characterised by social unrest and civil strife, as Sweden eventually left the Kalmar Union and became an independent state again. The sixteenth century saw the creation of the early modern Swedish state: a hereditary kingdom with a growing administration, the birth of parliament and the conversion to Lutheranism.

For most of the period discussed in this chapter, the Swedish population was small and the level of urbanisation low. The capital, Stockholm, was founded in the thirteenth century, but remained small. At the beginning of the sixteenth century it had only around 7,000 inhabitants. Other towns were even smaller: in the Middle Ages most Swedish towns had not more than a thousand inhabitants. In the seventeenth century, however, Stockholm increased in size and became an important European city. In 1621 the Swedish state also finally succeeded in founding a permanent settlement on the west coast: Gothenburg, which became the country's port to the west and home to the Swedish East India company, which was founded in 1731.[1] Stockholm's rapid growth is connected to what was attributed as 'Sweden's era of greatness'. During this period, war led Sweden to incorporate parts of Denmark-Norway, northern Germany and the Baltic states into its realm, making Sweden a multilingual realm.

Unlike their European counterparts, the Swedish parliament and society were divided into four estates: the nobility, the clergy, the burghers and the farmers. This reflects the strong political influence gained by the Swedish farmers during the political strife and civil wars of the late Middle Ages, when Sweden left the Kalmar Union and emerged as a national state. The Swedish Four-Estate Parliament endured until 1865, but the division of society according to medieval estates became increasingly difficult to uphold in the early modern period, as is visible in the sumptuary legislation and the debates on luxury and consumption in the seventeenth and eighteenth centuries.[2]

---

[1] Christian Koninckx, *The First and Second Charters of the Swedish East India Company (1731–1766): A Contribution to the Maritime, Economic and Social history of North-western Europe in its Relationships with the Far East* (Kortrijk: Van Ghemmert, 1980).

[2] Leif Runefelt, *Att hasta mot undergången: anspråk, flyktighet, föreställning i debatten om konsumtion i Sverige 1730–1830* (Lund: Nordic Academic Press, 2015); Maria Cavallin

Medieval and Early Modern Sumptuary Legislation in Sweden

Internationally, sumptuary laws have been the object of study for a very long time. Early studies often took a critical tone. Written by proponents of free trade and modern capitalism, these works describe sumptuary laws as 'medieval', 'backwards' and 'anti-democratic'. These early studies, however, failed to understand the role that sumptuary laws played in the economic, political and moral discourses of the period.[3] More recent scholarship, such as the works of Alan Hunt, Maria Hayward, Susan Vincent, Evelyn Welch and Catherine Kovesi Killerby, shows a much more nuanced view of the laws, placing them within the contemporary debate on luxury and consumption, as well as studying spoken and unspoken ideas of class, gender and race.[4]

Swedish research on sumptuary laws is no different from that of other European countries. The laws have been studied by ethnologists primarily as sources about the dress of the people, and by historians asking questions about consumption, trade policies, their effect on the economy, or about economic and moral thought. In 1959, the ethnologist Bo Ek identified four main motivations in Swedish sumptuary laws, motivations that changed over time. According to his model, sixteenth-century sumptuary laws were mainly concerned with upholding the differences between the estates, the main motives of the seventeenth-century laws were religious or fiscal, and the eighteenth-century laws were above all intended to improve the national economy and balance of trade. Historian Christer Ahlberger uses a similar model in his study of the consumer revolution in Sweden, in which he examines the period from the 1750s to the early twentieth century.[5] Ahlberger's study is not primarily about sumptuary law, but about changing practices and conceptions of consumption. It focuses on the consumption of selected

Aijmer, *I kungens och folkets tjänst: synen på den svenske ämbetsmannen 1750–1780* (Göteborg: Göteborgs Universitet, PhD thesis, 2003).

[3] Susan Vincent, *Dressing the Elite: Clothes in Early Modern England* (Oxford: Berg, 2003), 117–118; Alan Hunt, *Governance of the Consuming Passions: History of Sumptuary Law* (Basingstoke: Macmillan, 1996).

[4] Hunt, *Governance*; Maria Hayward, *Rich Apparel: Clothing and the Law in Henry VIII's England* (Farnham: Ashgate, 2009); Catherine Kovesi Killerby, *Sumptuary law in Italy, 1200–1500* (Oxford: Oxford University Press, 2002); Vincent, *Dressing the Elite*; Evelyn S. Welch: *Shopping in the Renaissance: Consumer Cultures in Italy, 1400–1600* (New Haven: Yale University Press, 2005).

[5] Sven B. Ek, 'Dräktförordningarnas samhälleliga bakgrund', in *RIG*, häfte 4 (1959), 104–105; Christer Ahlberger, *Konsumtionsrevolutionen 1. Om det moderna konsumtionssamhällets framväxt 1750-1900* (Göteborg: Humanistiska Fakulteten, Göteborgs Universitet, 1996), 58–63.

'modern' goods, both among the middling and lower classes in Sweden's western trade port Gothenburg, and also among the rural population in the surrounding region. Ahlberger questions previously accepted conceptions about both the attitude to modernity and the agency of the peasantry in the late-eighteenth and early-nineteenth century, arguing that the positive attitude among the peasantry towards sumptuary laws in the late-eighteenth century should not be seen as a sign of political weakness in relation to the three higher estates but rather, in the context of struggles about consumption and status within the rural community, between the landed and the landless.[6]

The concept of luxury and the luxury debates in Sweden have been studied by many historians. Recently, Håkan Möller and Leif Runefelt have published on discourses of luxury in the seventeenth and eighteenth century, respectively. Neither of them is concerned with sumptuary law in particular, though they include them as a part of the bigger picture.[7] Even if there is not a large number of studies that focus on Swedish sumptuary law, it is still somewhat surprising that a gender perspective has rarely been applied in those that do exist.[8] This is something that will be addressed in this article. In attempting to remedy the absence of a gender perspective in previous analysis of Swedish sumptuary laws by discussing underlying ideas of gender in the dress regulations, I would like to stress that this is not a study of the history of ideas, such as Möller's or Runefelt's works on the discourses of luxury, economy and of consumption in early modern Sweden.[9] Instead, my aim is to stay close both to the objects (the clothes themselves), and to the subjects (the people who wore them). Rather than the debate on luxury and its connection to the sumptuary laws, it is the practice of dress regulation which is drawn into focus.

The first Swedish example of sumptuary legislation is the so-called 'Statute of Tälje' (*Tälje stadga*) from 1345. This is roughly half a century

[6] Ahlberger, *Konsumtionsrevolutionen 1*.

[7] Håkan Möller, *Lyx och mode i stormaktstidens Sverige: Jesper Swedberg och kampen mot perukerna* (Stockholm: Atlantis, 2014); Runefelt, *Att hasta mot undergången: anspråk*.

[8] My own article on medieval Scandinavian dress regulations is one of the exceptions. Eva I. Andersson, 'Inget scharlakan för dåliga fruntimmer: dräktregleringar och sexuella normbrytare i medeltidens Skandinavien', in *Det våras för medeltiden: vänbok till Thomas Lindkvist* (Göteborg: Institutionen för historiska studier, Göteborgs Universitet, 2014), 57–70.

[9] Möller, *Lyx och mode i stormaktstidens Sverige*; Leif Runefelt, *Hushållningens dygder: affektlära, hushållningslära och ekonomiskt tänkande under svensk stormaktstid* (Stockholm: Almqvist & Wiksell International, PhD thesis, Stockholm University, 2001); Leif Runefelt, *Dygden som välståndets grund: dygd, nytta och egennytta i frihetstidens ekonomiska tänkande* (Stockholm: Stockholms Universitet, 2005); Runefelt, *Att hasta mot undergången: anspråk*.

later than in Denmark and Norway (at this time separate kingdoms), where sumptuary laws were issued in 1283 and 1306, respectively.[10] The Statute of Tälje was enacted by King Magnus Eriksson and was concerned with the requirements and privileges of the nobility. A list of requirements that each noble estate had to fulfil/obey makes up most of the statute. But there were also regulations dictating the nobility's consumption on festive occasions, especially weddings, of which dress is an important subtopic. First, the statute placed a limit on the cost of the garments worn both by the bride and groom and by the guests. Second, an attempt was made to limit the value of clothing given to the entertainers at the wedding.[11] It was the custom for the bride to give away her wedding clothes to the entertainers. As we all are aware, clothing was very costly and these garments could be re-sold for cash, or worn by the entertainers themselves. Since clothing at the time was fairly unisex in cut, the fact that the entertainers were men would not have hindered them from using the bride's clothes, either as they were, or made over.[12]

The first regulation of dress which indicated a distinction between social groups is found in a 1436 document directed to the burghers of Stockholm.[13] This statute was followed by another six dress regulations in the sixteenth century. Most of these are not what we generally think of as sumptuary laws – specific laws issued to curb consumption – but are part of protocols or regulations covering a variety of topics concerning the governance of the city of Stockholm.[14] As I will discuss later, until the end of the century the distinction between groups in these statutes was based not on estate, but instead on moral conduct. More general admonitions that commoners should not ape the dress of their betters are of course also to be found in the sixteenth century, such as the Statute of Uppsala (*Uppsalastadgan*) of 1546.[15] I have, however, excluded these from the discussion, since they do not specifically list what was forbidden

---

[10] Herluf Nielsen, 'Luksusforordning', in John Granlund (ed.), *Kulturhistoriskt lexikon för nordisk medeltid från vikingatid till reformationstid*, 11 (Malmö: Allhem, 1966). Bror Emil Hildebrand (ed.), *Svenskt iplomatarium. Bd 5, Åren 1341–1347, D. 1*, Utg. (Stockholm, 1858), nr 3972.

[11] Ibid.

[12] Eva I. Andersson, *Kläderna och människan i medeltidens Sverige och Norge* (Göteborg: Göteborgs Universitet, PhD thesis, 2006), 260–305 (in Swedish), 336–341 (in English).

[13] *Privilegier, resolutioner och förordningar för Sveriges städer. Första delen* (Stockholm: P.A. Norstedt & söner, 1927), hereafter *Privilegier 1927*, 82.

[14] *Privilegier 1927*, 82; *Privilegier, resolutioner och förordningar för Sveriges städer. Andra delen* (Stockholm, P.A. Norstedt & Söner, 1932), hereafter *Privilegier 1932*, 88; *Privilegier, resolutioner och förordningar för Sveriges städer. Tredje delen* (Stockholm: P.A. Norstedt & söner, 1939), hereafter *Privilegier 1939*, 56, 146, 289, 446, 533–534 and 661–665.

[15] Ek 1959; Ahlberger, *Konsumtionsrevolutionen 1*, 58–59.

or allowed. By the very end of the century we also find dress regulations directed at the nobility, such as Johan III's 1590s statute for the nobility. Like his statute for the burghers of Stockholm from 1589, this document made distinctions between estates in regards to which materials were allowed.[16] That most dress regulations directed at the people from this time only concern Stockholm is not a coincidence; with the small population in Sweden and low urbanisation, Stockholm was probably the only city where the problem of distinguishing between people and classes through dress could arise.

In the seventeenth century proper sumptuary laws were issued, addressing the whole of Sweden, though not always all parts of society. For example, the 1664 sumptuary laws came in three different versions, one for each of the three higher estates in Sweden: the nobility, the clergy and the burghers (Figure 5.1).[17] Including these different versions, ten sumptuary laws regulating dress were issued in the seventeenth century. A strong element of seventeenth-century dress regulation is a deep concern about the fact that fashions were changing, that one could not just once and for all decide how people should dress, and that people did not stick to a fixed form of dress. This is not unique to Sweden; attempts were made in other European countries to stop the vagaries of fashion. This probably reflects a real increase in the pace at which fashions changed.[18] The desire to maintain status quo in dress is, of course, much older than the seventeenth century. For example, Saint Bridget of Sweden claimed that people abandoning the kind of dress she herself wore in her youth lay behind the arrival of the Black Death in Sweden.[19] The last three sumptuary laws of the seventeenth century – issued in 1688, 1693 and

---

[16] Uppsala University Library, Nordiska samlingen, N238:2 13-37, *Konung Johans stadga för adlen d. 2 Maÿ 1590*, § 13; *Privilegier*, 1939, 661–665.

[17] *Kongl. May.tz Stadga och Påbudh, Öfwer åthskillige Oordningars affskaffande, vthi Klädedrächter, så hoos Adel, som andre Ståndz-Personer här i Rijket. Datum Stockholm den 30. Augusti, Åhr 1664* ([s.n.]: [s.l.], 1664). Hereafter *Kongl. May.tz* 1664:1; *Kongl. may. tz Stadga och Påbudh, Öfwer åthskillige Excesser och Oordningars affskaffande widh Adelige Troloffningar, Gästebudh, Barndoop och Begraffningar., Tryckt i Stockholm, af Ignatio Meurer, kongl. booktr. Åhr 1664.* Hereafter *Kongl. May.tz* 1664:2, *Kongl. Majts stadga och påbud över åtskillige excesser och oordningars avskaffande vid rikets prästerskaps trolovningar, bröllop, barndop och begravningar samt klädedräkter. Tryckt i Stockholm av Ignatio Meurer, kunglig boktryckare år 1664* (Stockholm 1664). Hereafter *Kongl. May.tz* 1664:3; *Kongl. May.tz Stadga och Påbudh, Öfwer åthskillige Excesser och Oordningars affskaffande widh Rijkszens Borgerskaps Trolofningar, Gästebudh, Barndoop och Begrafningar, sampt Klädedrächter., Tryckt i Stockholm, af Ignatio Meurer, kongl. booktr. åhr 1664.* (Stockholm, 1664) Hereafter *Kongl. May.tz* 1664:4.

[18] Jennifer M. Jones, *Sexing La* mode*: Gender, Fashion and Commercial Culture in Old Regime France* (Oxford: Berg, 2004), 37–38.

[19] *Sancta Birgitta Revelaciones. Skrifter utgivna av Svenska fornskriftssällskapet. Serie 2, Band VII:8* (Stockholm: Svenska fornskriftssällskapet, 2002), ch. 57.

Figure 5.1 The 1664 sumptuary law directed at the nobility, forbidding 'diverse excesses and disorders at Noble betrothals, feasts, baptisms and funerals'. From *Kongl. may.tz Stadga och Påbudh, Öfwer åthskillige Excessers och Oordningars affskaffande widh Adelige Troloffningar, Gästebudh, Barndoop och Begraffningar*. Tryckt i Stockholm, af Ignatio Meurer, kongl. booktr. Åhr 1664.

1699, respectively – presented an innovation: they explicitly forbade specific materials such as patterned silks, though provided little detail on dress itself.[20]

---

[20] *Kongl. May:tz Förbud, Angående Införslen af Façonnerade Gull- Silfer och Silkes Tyg och Band, sampt gemene Hattar, med allehanda slagz Knappar, Snören, Frantzar, Galoner, Spetzar och Knyttning, aff Gull, Silfwer, Silke, Trå, Redgarn, Vll och Håår giorde; Daterat Stockholm den 3 aprilis, åhr 1688.*, tryckt hoos Niclas Wankijf, kongl. booktryckiare (Stockholm, 1688). Hereafter *Kongl. May:tz 1688*; *Kongl. May:tz Förnyade Placat Och Stadga, Angående Förbudne Sijden-Tyg och andre slijke Wahrur. Daterat Stockholm den 4 Februarii Åhr 1693* (Stockholm: Kongl. Booktryckerijet, hoos Sal. Wankifz Änkia., 1693). Hereafter *Kongl. May:tz 1693*; *Kongl. May:tz Placat Och Förbud, Angående Åthskillige slags Sijdentygs och Brocaders bärande och brukande til Kläde-Drächter, wid alfwarsamt Straff tilgiörandes,*

The debate about luxury was lively in the eighteenth century, and so was the issuing of sumptuary laws.[21] Including the various amendments and 'explanations', more sumptuary laws were issued in the eighteenth century than in the previous three centuries combined: fifty-eight in all, though not all of them were concerned with dress.[22] The most numerous of these were amendments to previously issued laws, as what was allowed and what was forbidden changed quite often. One reason explaining the frequent changes was that the state wished to encourage domestic production and, when fabrics or other fashionable trimmings could be produced in Sweden, the laws had to be changed to make them legal. A good example is the amendment of 28 September 1736, which declared that since the Swedish manufactures had improved so much it was now allowed for everyone to wear half-silks made with wool, linen, camel hair or cotton, as long as it was domestically produced.[23] Other laws and proclamations such as the acts of 1722, 1731, 1732 and 1746 included detailed descriptions of allowed and forbidden garments and styles, down to the placement of buttons and the number of folds allowed at the sides of men's coats.[24] Models of approved garments were also

---

Gifwit Stockholm den 20 Martii, Anno 1699 (Stockholm: K. B. hos Sal. Wankifs Enkia., 1699). Hereafter *Kongl. May:tz* 1699.

[21] Bo Peterson, 'Yppighets nytta och Torftighets fägnad' Pamflettdebatten om 1766 års överflödsförordning', *Historisk Tidskrift* 1 (1984): 3–43; Leif Runefelt, *Att hasta mot undergången.*

[22] Ahlberger, *Konsumtionsrevolutionen 1*, 62.

[23] 'Den. 28. Sept. Angående inrikes tillwärkade siden-warors friare bruk, än de förre förordningar mot yppighet innehålla'. in Modée, Reinhold Gustaf, Lindhielm, Hedvig Eleonora & Fougt, Elsa (red.), *Utdrag utur alle ifrån den 7. decemb. 1718./1791 utkomne publique handlingar. Stockholm. 1–15. 1742–1829=. [Del 2], Utdrag utur alle ifrån 1729. års slut utkomne publique handlingar, placater, förordningar, resolutioner och publicationer, som riksens styrsel samt inwärtes hushållning ock författningar i gemen, jämwäl och Stockholms stad i synnerhet, angå; med nödige citationer af alle paralel-ställen, som utwisa, hwad ändringar tid efter annan i ett eller annat mål kunnat wara giorde. Hwarförutan de uti desze handlingar åberopade äldre acters innehåll kortelingen anföres, så ofta nödigt warit. Följandes efterst wid hwar del ett fullkomligit orda-register öfwer des innehåll. Andra delen til år 1740. Med hans kongl. maj:ts allernådigste privilegio* (Stockholm: tryckt hos Lorentz Ludwig Grefing, 1746).

[24] *Publication Angående Förordningens Wärckställande, Om Yppighets och Öfwerflödighets afskaffande, dat. den 3 Junii 1720. sampt om Mode på Kläder. Gifwen Stockholm i Råd-Cammaren den 3. Aprilis Åhr 1722* (Stockholm: Kongl. Tryckeriet uplagd, hos Johan Henrich Werner, 1722). Hereafter *Publication 1720; Kongl. Maj:ts Resolution Och Förklaring, Uppå Justitiæ Cancellerens, wälborne Baron Gabriel Stierncronas, underdånige förfrågan, i anledning af Cämners-Rätternes ingifne Memorial, uti några stycken, angående den, til en och annan Yppighetz och Öfwerflödighetz afskaffande giorde Förordning af den 3 Junii 1720. så ock den beträffande wärckställigheten däraf utgångne Publication af den 3. sidstl. April, samt om Mode på Kläder. Gifwen Stockholm i Råd-Cammaren den 22 Junii 1722* (Stockholm: Kongl. Tryckeriet, 1722). Hereafter *Kongl. Maj:ts Resolution Och Förklaring 1722; Kongl. maj:ts Ytterligare nådige Förordning Til hwarjehanda Yppig- och Öfwerflödighets afskaffande. Gifwen Stockholm i Råd-cammaren den 22. septembr. 1731* (Stockholm: Kongl.

made, and prints showing the designs sent out to the town magistrates and province governors.[25] The attempts to halt the change of fashion thus continued into the eighteenth century. Distinction in dress between social groups also remained an issue for the law-makers in the eighteenth century, as can be seen by the many attempts to regulate the dress of lower class women, to which we will now turn.

Throughout the history of Swedish sumptuary law, fines and the confiscation of illegal goods were normal penalties for breaking the law, but women were sometimes also subjected to punishments intended to shame. For most of the period discussed in this article the state apparatus was not large enough to ensure that the citizens actually followed the regulations. Informants reporting their fellow countrymen and women to the authorities were instead the main way for transgressions to be punished. Informing was economically advantageous for the informer, since they received a percentage of the fine.

In the eighteenth century, the ways to control dress became more formalised. As mentioned above, models and pattern drawings were distributed to local authorities in towns and counties responsible for the compliance of citizens within their jurisdiction. The frequent issuing of amendments and clarifications, which explicitly referred to questions regarding the interpretations of the law submitted by officials, show that magistrates and other officials were actively concerned with the enforcement of sumptuary laws. It also demonstrates that concerns expressed by officials and other influential citizens could influence the King and parliament in these matters. One example of this is the explanation given by the King in March 1732 concerning the 1731 law, which stated that while the usage of panniers (hoop skirts) was allowed for ladies of the upper classes, wearers should be registered at the annual census and would be liable to pay an extra tax.[26] This example shows a new way of looking at luxury consumption: as a source of revenue rather than something that should be forbidden for the good of the people.

His Majesty's merciful warning against luxury and sumptuousness of 1792 [*Kongl. Maj:ts Nådiga Warning Emot Yppighet och Öfwerflöd. Gifwen*

Boktryckeriet, 1731). Hereafter *Kongl. Maj:ts* 1731; *Kongl. Maj:ts Nådige Resolution Och Förklaring Öfwer Justitiæ Cantzlerens Wälborne Baron Johan Cederbielckes Giorde underdånige Påminnelser och Förfrågningar Wid Kongl. Maj:ts Förordning Af den 8 Novemb. 1731. Til hwarjehanda Yppig- och Öfwerflödighets affskaffande. Gifwen Stockholm i Råd-Cammaren den 15. Martii 1732* (Stockholm: Kongl. Boktryckeriet, 1732). Hereafter *Kongl. Maj:ts* 1732:1; *Kongl. maj:ts Förnyade Förordning Emot En och annan Yppighet. Gifwen Stockholm i Råd-Cammaren then 20 januarii 1746* (Stockholm: Kongl. Tryckeriet, 1746). Hereafter *Kongl. Maj:ts* 1746.

25 *Kongl. Maj:ts* 1731
26 *Kongl. Maj:ts* 1732.

152   Eva I. Andersson

Drottningholms Slott den 11 augusti 1792] shows a further change in Swedish sumptuary regulation. In it, the King no longer threatened his subjects with fines or the seizure of the offending goods, but instead expressed his hope that the good character of the Swedes would prevent them from excessive consumption of foreign goods and vanity in dress.[27] However, fines did not disappear immediately; in the 1794 sumptuary law, fines remained.[28] Similarities with the patriotic pleas of 1792 are found also in later statutes on the subject of dress. The law of 1817 stated that the King would prefer not to legislate on the dress of individuals, appealing instead to the patriotism of the Swedish citizens and in particular to the good example provided by the higher classes.[29]

As such changes demonstrate, the argument presented by Ek, and developed by Ahlberger, is overly linear. Female sexuality and honour were foregrounded in concepts of class distinction which were an important component in late sixteenth century dress regulations. In the eighteenth century there was still an urge to regulate women's dress according to estate, even if Ek and Ahlberger argue that sumptuary laws by this time were guided primarily by economic motives, and were less concerned with difference between the estates. Morals and religion – where luxury was thought to lead to other vices, weaken moral fibre and anger the Christian god – appear to have been motives mainly found in the seventeenth century, as Ek and Ahlberger rightly noted. However, women's honour remained an issue in dress regulations from the Middle Ages to the eighteenth century. Even after sexual purity disappeared from legal texts, public shaming remained as a punishment for women who broke sumptuary laws. Throughout centuries of Swedish sumptuary laws, women's right to dress was thus always in some way connected to honour and to shame.

Sumptuary Laws, Dress and Shame

In the medieval and early modern period, women's access to consumption was generally dictated by their fathers' and husbands' professions or birth. The regulation of dress in relation to sexual morality was, however,

[27] *Kongl. Maj:ts Nådiga Warning Emot Yppighet och Öfwerflöd. Gifwen Drottningholms Slott den 11 augusti 1792* (Stockholm: Kongl. Tryckeriet, 1792). Hereafter *Kongl. Maj:ts* 1792.
[28] *Kongl. Maj:ts Nådiga Förordning, Til hämmande af Yppighet och Öfwerflöd. Gifwen Stockholms Slott den 1 Januarii 1794* (Stockholm: Tryckt i Kongl. Tryckeriet, 1794). Hereafter *Kongl. Maj:ts* 1794.
[29] *Kongl. maj:ts nådiga Kungörelse, Angående Nödwändigheten af inskränkning uti införsel och förbrukning af Utländske Yppighets-Waror; Gifwen Stockholms Slott den 30 april 1817* (Stockholm: Kongl. Tryckeriet, 1817). Hereafter *Kongl. Maj:ts* 1817.

an important exception. For most of the time that Sweden had laws regulating dress, a woman's sexual morals were a deciding factor in her 'right to dress'. This is especially true for dress regulations in the fifteenth and sixteenth centuries. The 1436, 1529, 1563, 1570 and 1575 laws only concerned women who were defined as 'loose', 'whores' and as 'living an evil life'. Exactly what was meant by these terms is problematic, and it is anachronistic and misleading to use them as synonyms for the modern term prostitute. The regulations were directed at a wider group of women, not all of whom were engaged in prostitution. In her studies of prostitution in medieval and early modern England, Ruth Mazo Karras prefers the expression 'common women' or 'whores', since these appellations had broader contemporary meaning that included a variety of forms of sexual and social transgression.[30] These are also appropriate points of reference for Scandinavia. Here, like in England, women described as 'loose' could have been performing sexual acts for payment, but they could also have been women who had pursued sexual relationships with the wrong men, such as married men or (before the Reformation) priests. Women who disrupted the social order in other ways, such as by being scolds or gossiping, were also deemed 'loose'. In magistrate's records in late medieval Stockholm, such women were denied 'honourable dress' and luxurious materials and ornaments as a punishment for lying and malicious gossip.[31] Crimes of 'unruliness' were seen as a consequence of natural female weakness. According to contemporary ideas, failure to control this feminine unruliness could damage society as a whole.[32]

From a European perspective, Alan Hunt has claimed that it was not until the early modern period that dress regulations become primarily directed at women.[33] The increased propensity to regulate women's dress could be seen as the first sign of the gradual 'feminisation' of fashion.[34] This development in the regulation of dress has been associated with a decline in the status of women after the Reformation that included a more serious view of, and harsher punishment for, sexual offences. This is generally seen as a widespread European development which included the Nordic countries. Norwegian historian Anne Irene Riisøy, however, found that in Norway there was a strong continuity in how sexual

[30] Ruth Mazo Karras, *Common Women: Prostitution and Sexuality in Medieval England* (Oxford: Oxford University Press, 1996), 131; Ruth Mazo Karras, 'The Regulation of Brothels in Later Medieval England', *Signs* 14/2 (1989): 399–433.
[31] Andersson, 'Inget scharlakan för dåliga fruntimmer'.
[32] Carol Lansing, 'Gender and Civic Authority: Sexual Control in a Medieval Italian Town', *Journal of Social History* 31/1 (1997): 33–59.
[33] Hunt, *Governance*, 27.
[34] Jones, *Sexing* La mode.

'offences' were viewed from the thirteenth to the seventeenth century. For example, dress regulations remained the primary way of controlling 'whores' and other female sexual transgressors throughout the period.[35] Looking at dress regulations, Sweden shows a similar continuity between the Middle Ages and the early modern period as that observed by Riisøy for Norway. It is also notable that while specific statutes regulating the clothing of 'common women' disappeared by the end of the sixteenth century, the sexual behaviour and morals of women continued to be a component in Swedish sumptuary law in the seventeenth century.

In the seventeenth century, it was the dress of the bride which was regulated according to her sexual purity. The birth of a child conceived out of wedlock (even if born after marriage) would incur a fine if the woman had donned the dress of honourable women at her wedding.[36] While in theory the crime was equal for men and women, there were no such regulations of the groom's dress. Women's sexual status had to be *visible*, not only to make sure that no mistakes could be made when assessing a woman's worth, but also as a punishment, publicly exposing her shame. While the identification of dishonourable women was the most common function of the medieval and early modern dress regulations directed at women who transgressed sexual norms, public shaming through dress was also an important factor.[37]

The regulation of women's dress according to sexual honour – or lack thereof – ostensibly ended in the seventeenth century, but public shaming was still a factor in attempts to control women's consumption of fashionable clothing in the eighteenth century. A statute dated 26 June 1766 decreed that 'loose womenfolk' and female servants under the age of forty who were not in service and 'sat by themselves' were forbidden to wear silk caps.[38] The term 'loose' in this case did not refer to sexual immorality, but to vagrancy. However, it is significant that it was only women whose right to fashionable clothing was curtailed by a lack of a steady employment or fixed abode. Men in the same position were not

---

[35] Anne Irene Riisøy, *Sexuality, Law and Legal Practice and the Reformation in Norway* (Leiden: Brill, 2009).

[36] *Kongl. May.tz Stadga och Påbudh, Öfwer Åthskillige Miszbruckz och Oordningars affskaffande widh the Trolofningar, Brölop och Barndoop, och Begraffningar, sampt Klädedreckter, hwilka häreffter aff Clericiet eller Prästeståndet föröfwas böre. Gifwen i Stockholm den 1. Martij Åhr 1669* (Stockholm, 1669). Hereafter *Kongl. May.tz*. 1669; *Kongl. May.tz* 1664:4; *Kongl. May:tz* 1699.

[37] Mazo Karras, *Common Women*, 37; Nickie Roberts, *Whores in History: Prostitution in Western Society* (London: HarperCollins, 1992), 79.

[38] *Kongl. Maj:ts Nådige Förordning, Emot Yppighet och Öfwerflöd. Gifwen Stockholm i Råd-Cammaren then 26. Junii 1766* (Stockholm: Kongl. Tryckeriet, 1766). Hereafter *Kongl. Maj:ts* 1766:1.

Figure 5.2 Silk cap from the 1760s, worn by a peasant woman in Dalecarlia. Currently in the collections of the Nordic museum, Stockholm. NM.0012059A-B. Photograph: Elisabeth Eriksson.

targeted at all. Shame also remained an integral part of the punishment, since the breach of the law meant not just a fine of 20 *daler silvermynt*, which was a considerable sum at the time – a male farm hand had to work four weeks to achieve it – but also a stint in the pillory. Men who broke the sumptuary laws in the eighteenth century were sentenced to fines, and the forbidden clothes were usually impounded, but there was no additional punishment intended to shame them.

It is also significant that silk caps were targeted in particular. These caps were the only garments made from silk or half-silk that were allowed for plebeian women, and were also an important part of rural and popular fashion at the time (Figure 5.2). As headwear, they carried more connotations than fashionability. Since medieval times, the covered head was the sign of the honourable wife, and while silk caps were worn by both married and unmarried women in the eighteenth century, there was still a perceived connection between a covered head and chastity and honour. In early modern England forcibly removing a woman's headwear cast doubt upon her virtue.[39]

---

[39] Tim Reinke-Williams, 'Women's Clothes and Female Honour in Early Modern London', *Continuity and Change* 26/1 (2011): 69–88.

Dress Regulations and an Ordered Society

The perceived connection between sexual and other misdemeanours committed by women does not mean that regulation of sexuality was the main objective of dress regulations. The regulations must instead be seen primarily as a way for the authorities to secure societal order. The threats to the common order posed by 'loose' women were wide-ranging, such as honourable matrons and maidens being mistaken for common women, or that areas in which prostitution took place were also associated with other disturbances such as drinking or fighting. More fundamentally, social order was threatened by the fact that prostitutes in luxurious clothing suspended the connection between status and material appearance, a connection that was taken for granted in the Middle Ages and the early modern period. In a society where the nobility was assumed to both have and deserve better and more expensive clothing than a burgher, and a burgher to have and deserve better clothing than a farmer, a low-status woman in luxurious clothing upset the ideas of the natural order in society. It also challenged the norm that sin should be punished, not rewarded.

The concern with order was not only valid for the regulations specifically aimed at 'loose' women, but was a factor in all dress laws from this period. A recent study of the medieval Swedish legal system emphasises that the laws and the legal system served above all to preserve order in society. The driving force behind the law was not to punish wrongdoers, but to limit and control private violence and provide alternative solutions to conflicts. Laws were also seen as a contract between the King and his subjects, most notably the peasantry.[40] From the mid-sixteenth century onwards the Swedish state increased and institutionalised its power and by the seventeenth century the state's monopoly of violence was consolidated, though the need to curb private violence remained. Laws regulating consumption can be seen as one way to prevent conflict, since conspicuous consumption – or consumption that broke the norms set for one's estate – could cause envy and tension in society. Such tension could, in turn, lead to violence.

Historians have argued that across Europe societal order was achieved through legal acts regulating women's dress, the frequency of which increased in times of social disorder. One example is Carol Lansing's study of the regulation of dress in the Italian city of Orvieto in the Middle Ages. Lansing argues that in times of crisis, regulation of women's

---

[40] Christine Ekholst, *A Punishment for Each Criminal: Gender and Crime in Swedish Medieval Law* (Leiden: Brill, 2014), 12–17 and 76–78.

dress was motivated not so much by practical considerations but by a perceived female 'irrationality'. By regulating the behaviour of women, rational order could be restored.[41] It is hard to observe this rationale in Swedish dress regulations. Many of the seventeenth-century sumptuary laws were issued in periods when Sweden was at war, but such acts were directed at both women and men. The civil unrest of the late fifteenth and early sixteenth century only produced two local statutes, and while both were about the dress of 'dishonourable' women, they are not sufficient to corroborate this theory. It is undeniable, however, that women's consumption and dress were perceived as potentially more disruptive than men's. In late medieval and early modern dress regulations, men are mentioned only as the legal custodians of women and as sellers of the forbidden goods, demonstrating that even when sexual morals were not at the core of regulations, it was the dress of women and not that of their male counterparts that threatened established social order.

At the beginning of the seventeenth century, however, the dress of both sexes was addressed and regulated. The estate of the wearer now became the most important concern, though other categories such as geographic origin also shaped Swedish dress regulations. The statutes of 1583, 1589, 1664 and 1669 exempted foreign citizens resident in Sweden, mostly of German or Dutch origin, from the law, presuming that they followed the sumptuary laws of their home countries. These foreigners were not necessarily short-term visitors to Sweden, but could be permanent residents of the realm. It was therefore possible that of two merchants or artisans living next to each other, or engaged in the same trade, one might be allowed fabrics and garments forbidden to the other, due to their geographical origin. Naturally it was nearly impossible for the Swedish authorities to control foreign citizens who broke the sumptuary laws of their home countries, especially since these differed from town to town as in the case of the German Empire.[42] The texts of the sumptuary laws acknowledge this problem, stating that this exemption was frequently abused both by foreign citizens who dressed above their station, and by Swedish women who claimed to be of foreign origin.[43]

---

[41] Lansing, 'Gender and Civic Authority'.

[42] Constanze Eisenbart, *Kleiderordnungen der Dutschen Städte zwischen 1350 und 1700: ein Beitrag zur Kulturgeschichte des Deutschen Bürgertums* (Göttingen: Musterschmidt, 1962).

[43] 'Kungl. Majts stadga och påbud över åtskillige excessers och oordningars avskaffande vid rikets prästerskaps trolovningar, bröllop, barndop och begravningar samt klädedräkter. Tryckt i Stockholm av Ignatio Meurer, kunglig boktryckare år 1664' and 'Kungl. Majts stadga och påbud över åtskillige excessers och oordningars avskaffande vid rikets borgerskaps trolovningar, bröllop, barndop och begravningar samt klädedräkter.

In the eighteenth century sumptuary laws changed in format and motives. The declared objective of the laws became primarily to secure the economic welfare of the realm. However, class and gender remained important criteria in the sumptuary legislation of the eighteenth century. There are more than ten laws targeting lower class women, whose consumption of foreign goods, given the size of that consumption hardly was a threat to the national economy. These regulations forbade their use of jackets made from materials other than domestic worsted or wool, clothes from silks and half-silks, and the use of calicoes or other cotton textiles.[44] This is interesting since, as Runefelt notes, while women's vanity, capriciousness and pursuit of fashion were standard tropes in a general discourse on luxury and consumption in the second half of the eighteenth century, in Sweden women's dress was more often an afterthought in the proposals and discussions leading to regulation. In the Swedish debate, men's dress was seen as more important than women's in upholding the difference between the estates. It was also claimed that attempts at controlling women's fashions were ineffective, since women were inventive by nature, and would soon find new types of luxury. Even if the role of women was seen in negative terms, their actions were not considered serious enough to deserve the full attention of the law, even in

Tryckt i Stockholm av Ignatio Meurer, kunglig boktryckare år 1664' in Anders Anton von Stiernman, *Samling utaf kongl. bref, stadgar och förordningar &c. angående Sweriges rikes commerce, politie och oeconomie uti gemen, ifrån åhr 1523. in til närwarande tid. Uppå hans kongl. maj:ts nådigesta befallning giord af And. Anton von Stiernman Tredje del* (Stockholm: Kungl. Tryckeriet, 1753), 258–287.

[44] *Kongl. maj:tz nådige Påbud, Att Ryttare- Dragoune- Soldate- och Båtzmäns-Hustrur samt Tienstepigor, ey måge hafwa frihet att bära andra Tröjor, än dem som här i Riket af Regarn och Ull tillwärckas. Gifwit Stockholm i Råd-cammaren den 17. octob. 1727* (Stockholm: Kongl. Tryckeriet, 1727); *Kongl. Maj:ts nådige Förklaring Öfwer Påbudet af den 17. Octobr. 1727. att Ryttare- Dragoune- Soldate- och Båtsmäns Hustrur samt Tienste-Pigor ej måge hafwa Frihet att bära andra Tröjor än dem, som här i Riket af Regarn och Ull tilwärkas. Gifwen Stockholm i Råd-cammaren den 15. maji 1732* (Stockholm: Kongl. Boktryckeriet, 1732). Hereafter *Kongl. Maj:ts 1732:2. Sammandrag Utaf Kongl. Maj:ts tid efter annan utgångne Nådige Förordningar Och Förklaringar, Angående Wisze Tyger och Klädebonader, som de Gemena och Tienstefolket i anledning der af, antingen är tillåtit eller förbudit at bära.* (Stockholm: Kongl. Boktryckeriet, 1733). Hereafter *Kongl. Maj:ts 1733*; *Kongl: maj:tz nådige Förordning, Angående Inrikes tilwerckade Sidenwarors friare bruk och nyttiande, än the för thetta om Yppig- och Öfwerflödighets afskaffande, utfärdade Förordningar innehålla. Gifwen Stockholm i Råd-Cammaren then 28. sept. 1736* (Stockholm: Kongl. Tryckeriet, 1736). Hereafter *Kongl. Maj:ts 1736*; Rutger Fuchs (ed.), *Publication, angående the Cattuners och Bomulls-lärfters bruk- och bärande, som hwita införskrifwas, och här innom Riket tryckas. Gifwne Stockholm then 13. novembris år 1741* (Stockholm: Kongl. tryckeriet, 1741); *Kongl. Maj:ts 1766:1*; *Kongl. Maj:ts Nådige Förklaring, Öfwer Wisze delar af then Yppighets och Öfwerflöds hämmande then 26 Junii sistl. utfärdade Förordningen. Gifwen Stockholm i Råd-Cammaren then 11. Decemb. 1766* (Tryckt uti Kongl. Tryckeriet, 1766). Hereafter *Kongl. Maj:ts 1766:2.*

the realm of fashion.[45] However, one group of female consumers of fashionable clothing was considered problematic enough to warrant repeated legislation. At the bottom of the hierarchies of both estate and gender, the capriciousness and inventiveness of lower-class women was apparently a threat to the social order.

Dangerous Foreign Objects

This chapter suggests that some objects could be perceived as more dangerous and more disorderly than others. A survey of forbidden dress materials and ornament in Swedish dress regulations shows a continuity in consumption habits of what was considered desirable between the later Middle Ages and the sixteenth century. Silks, scarlet cloth, fine woollen cloth (*kläde*), vair (squirrel fur), other valuable fur and ornaments of gold or gilded silver were sought after and prohibited.[46] A comparison between dress regulations and the garments listed in wills and magistrate's records from medieval Sweden shows that the same materials and garments in legislation were the most prized items of dress. The fifteenth-century magistrates' records of the town of Arboga report, for example, a valuable man's gown made from blue woollen cloth and lined with the backs of squirrels. This would have belonged to a burgher, and since he was not a 'loose woman', the only group targeted in Swedish sumptuary laws from this century, he had the full right to wear this costly garment.[47] In addition to luxurious materials, the veils and wimples of respectable women were forbidden to those perceived as 'dishonourable'.

Different tastes emerged from the end of the sixteenth century, in particular in the town of Stockholm. While silks, scarlet cloth, woollens and gold cloth were still found, the lists of forbidden (and allowed) items show the emergence of a class of burghers asserting their status and even, at times, competing with the nobility and courtiers.[48] In late sixteenth-century regulations the category of 'silk' is broken down into atlas (a satin weave), damasks and velvets, with a distinction made between garments worn 'over or under the belt', that is to say between whole gowns or skirts, which (obviously) included parts worn under the belt, and doublets or the small shoulder capes called *kragha*. Many more wool

---

[45] Leif Runefelt, *Att hasta mot undergången: anspråk*, 99–109.

[46] *Privilegier* 1927, 82; *Privilegier* 1932, 88; *Privilegier* 1939, 146, 289–290.

[47] Andersson, *Kläderna och människan i medeltidens Sverige och Norge*; Eva Andersson, 'Clothing and Textile Materials in Medieval Sweden and Norway', *Medieval Clothing and Textiles* 9 (2013): 97–120.

[48] *Privilegier* 1927, 82; *Privilegier* 1932, 88; *Privilegier* 1939, 56–57, 146, 289, 446, 533–534 and 661–665.

fabrics were mentioned than ever before. Scarlet and woollen cloth were still present, but says, wool grosgrain, wool, camlet, *macheyer* (originally a Low German word meaning a coarse wool fabric) and Turkish *macheyer* (which, presumably, differed from ordinary macheyer in some way that was perceived as 'Turkish') were also listed. These wool fabrics were all allowed for burgesses, though scarlet cloth was not to be used for whole gowns, and a distinction was made between the 'best' and the 'lesser' of the burghers when it came to which silk fabrics were allowed.[49]

This increasing refinement of the categories of forbidden fabrics and garments continued into the seventeenth century, when silks were classified into no less than fifteen types, including half-silks. More detail is also found regarding other objects for adornment, such as ribbons, lace, feathers, jewellery and other accessories. Woollen cloth disappeared from the lists of forbidden fabrics in the seventeenth century. This probably reflects the lessened status of wool fabrics and, along with the increase in the types of silk fabrics, a change in fashions. The same change can also be observed in seventeenth-century probate inventories in Stockholm, where the variety of materials and the range of terms used to describe garments became much greater towards the end of the century. Hans Peter Rulandt, a wealthy merchant who died in 1677, had doublets, cassocks and coats made from woollen cloth, serge, barchent, a fabric with linen warp and cotton weft, camlet *Hollande*, polymite, a multi-coloured, often striped fabric of camel hair mixed with wool, or wool mixed with linen, grosgrain, plush, and plain and patterned atlas, as well as breeches made of woollen cloth, plush, and chamois leather, and underwear made of parkum, a linen or cotton twill, and Holland and Swedish linen.[50]

Since clothing is fundamentally symbolic, it is no surprise that the use of foreign cloth or the donning of foreign garments was seen as potentially dangerous. Foreign clothes and fashions could not only destroy the finances of both the nation and individuals, but also corrupt the morals and character of citizens, both individually and as a community. While sumptuary laws generally did not grade the danger of the forbidden items, some appear to have been of more concern than others. In the sixteenth century, velvet caps decorated with pearls, beads and metal ornaments were perceived as a dangerous usurpation of the rights of the nobility when worn by non-noble women.[51] The consumption

[49] Eva I. Andersson, 'Women's Dress in Sixteenth-Century Sweden', *Costume* 45 (2011): 24–38.
[50] Justitiekollegium 1637–1856, Förmyndarkammaren 1667–1924, Rådhusrättens 1:a avdelning 1850–1924, SE/SSA/0145A/F 1/F 1 A/5.
[51] *Privilegier* 1939, 446.

of fashionable clothing by the burgesses of Stockholm also had other adverse effects on the order of society: according to a statute from 1589 by King Johan III (ruled 1568–1592), it led to an increase in the price of silks, making it impossible for the nobility to clothe their wives and daughters according to their rank.[52] Another example of the perceived dangers of fine dress worn by the wrong people can be found in the 1496 regulation of prostitutes in the town of Malmö, then in Denmark, where their unlawful displays of fine dress were thought to encourage young women to became prostitutes.[53]

A special kind of disorder was created by those objects that pretended to be something they were not. Jewellery made of glass was forbidden; sumptuary laws observed that since the law restricted the use of precious stones, gold and silver, some women had taken to wearing imitation jewellery. This was considered a breach of the law, according to the principle that a person's status should be easily identifiable. The general dislike of that which purported to be something that it was not extended from fake jewellery, to make-up and, in some sense, to clothing itself.[54] According to the Swedish legislators, Swedes were especially susceptible to being fooled by imitations and fakes due to their simplicity. Examples of this gullibility were given in the laws and included cases of consumers who bought 'Bohemian diamonds', rock crystal or glass, believing them to be real 'Oriental' diamonds.[55]

Most of the dangerous objects were foreign in origin. In the age of mercantilism in the late seventeenth and eighteenth centuries, any import was viewed with suspicion, but imports of fashionable fabrics and items were especially dubious since they were connected not only to luxury and the foreign, but also to *change*. Seventeenth-century Swedish sumptuary law showed a deep concern over the fact that fashions were changing; that one could not just once and for all decide how people should dress. The Swedish authorities tried in vain to stop changes in fashion by describing which garments were allowed and how they should look, and by forbidding both new and foreign inventions in regard to dress.

While the influences may have been foreign, Swedes themselves also contributed to changing fashions. This was caused either by wanting to dress above their estate or, in the case of the nobility, because they were curious and thus continuously changed their manner of dress. According

[52] Andersson, 'Women's Dress in Sixteenth-Century Sweden', *Privilegier* 1939: 446, 533–534, 661–665.
[53] Andersson, 'Inget scharlakan för dåliga fruntimmer' Aage Andersen (ed.), *Den danske rigslovgivning 1397–1513* (Köbenhavn: Reitzel, 1989), 168–169.
[54] Jones, *Sexing* La mode, 16.
[55] *Privilegier* 1939, 661–665.

to the legislators, this created a spiral of ever-changing fashions, as the burghers tried to outdo the nobility, and they in turn tried to defend the exclusive rights to conspicuous clothing whilst also competing for status within their own estate. Remarkably, this did not affect the view, often repeated in various forms, that the Swedes were characterised by a 'traditional honourable simplicity', as one law of 1794 put it.[56] Changing fashions and luxury consumption were instead seen as disturbances caused by specific external circumstances. If these could be made to disappear, the Swedes' true nature would reawaken, and they would return to their old, simple, honourable way of dressing. Foreign fashions and foreign objects were believed by legislators to be powerful and dangerous enough to suppress the true nature of a whole people.

Conclusion

In regards to sumptuary law, Sweden is both typical and atypical. The arguments and motivations behind Swedish sumptuary laws conform to what we find in most European countries in the early modern period. However, the practice of regulating consumption through sumptuary laws continued longer than in other European countries. A further difference is that dress regulations that were intended to enforce distinctions in dress according to rank were not introduced until the late sixteenth century in Stockholm. The most plausible explanation for this late date is the low rate of urbanisation in Sweden. Stockholm was by far the largest town in a country with a small, mostly rural population. In a small community one does need to rely on clothes, or other external signs, to recognise the people one meets. It was not until the late sixteenth century that an economically strong burgher class could – or at least was perceived to be able to – challenge the sartorial exclusivity of the nobility. Even then, this phenomenon was probably restricted to urban Stockholm, as indicated by the fact that most of the fifteenth- and sixteenth-century dress regulations were directed at the burghers of Stockholm. The first sumptuary law covering the whole of Sweden that tried to enforce distinctions in dress according to estate was enacted only in 1664. By that time, Sweden was a great military and political power, and Stockholm a large city even by European standards.

---

[56] *Utdrag utur alla ifrån och med år 1791 utkomne publique handlingar, placater, förordningar, resolutioner, och publicationer, som riksens styrsel samt inwärtes hushållning och författningar i gemen, jemwäl ock Stockholms stad i synnerhet angå: med ett fullkomligt orda-register öfwer desz innehåll; jemte förtekning, efter åratalen, på alla de publique handlingar och acter, som denna femtonde delen innehåller. Femtonde delen till 1794 års slut. Med hans kongl. maj:ts allernådigste privilegio* (Stockholm: Kongl. Tryckeriet, 1829), 550–560.

Distinction according to estate was not the only motivation behind the Swedish sumptuary laws. In the fifteenth and sixteenth centuries, a series of statutes concerned with distinguishing women based on their perceived respectability emerged. Women's morality was a constant theme in dress regulations up to the end of the seventeenth century, and even beyond that date, shaming remained a punishment for women breaking sumptuary laws. Not only was women's dress often regulated according to (perceived) sexual purity, but transgressions of gendered norms, sexual and otherwise, could also be punished by a loss of the right to wear garments that were fashionable or signified respectability. In contrast, men's sexuality was never a criterion for dress regulations, their rights to dress depended on estate, not perceived morality. This concern with women's sexuality and its expressions in sumptuary laws has remained largely unnoticed, due to the lack of a gender perspective in previous scholarship.

However, while women are more commonly described as irresponsible and unruly in the laws, it is obvious that men's consumption could also be problematic. Leaving aside those regulations connected to perceptions of sexual honour and morality, we find that from the time when national sumptuary laws began to be issued, men's consumption was as much the focus as women's. Sumptuary laws were not only about consumption, imports and economy; like other laws of the period, they were also conceived in order to preserve order in society. The state tried to decrease tensions and avoid conflicts caused, or exacerbated, by envy and status by enforcing distinctions in dress according to estate, or by limiting the spending within an estate. Since men were more prone to violence than women, there was every reason to control their consumption too.

Nationality was another category which affected one's right to types of dress in early modern Sweden. Sumptuary laws made exceptions for foreigners living in Sweden, exceptions which opened up loopholes in the laws and led to the problem of people (particularly women) pretending to be of foreign origin solely for the purpose of wearing forbidden fashions.[57] Interestingly, despite this and other descriptions of Swedes obviously trying to circumvent the laws, the legislators still claimed that luxury in itself was something foreign to the Swedes. Luxury objects were perceived to be introduced by foreigners either because of their own wish to dress luxuriously, or to trick the Swedes to exchange the riches of their homeland for foreign fashions and trinkets.[58]

---

[57] *Kongl. May.tz* 1664:1; *Kongl. May.tz* 1664:2; *Kongl. May.tz* 1664:3; *Kongl. May.tz* 1664:4.
[58] *Kongl. May.tz* 1664:1.

When studying Swedish sumptuary legislation, it becomes clear that the simple scheme of changing motivations proposed by most earlier research is exactly that: too simple. A wider, cultural history perspective which includes not only gender and class but also the materiality of the regulated objects reveals a more complex picture, and the intersecting hierarchies of early modern Sweden.

Part II

Enacting Sumptuary Laws in Italy

6   Sumptuary Laws in Italy: Financial Resource and Instrument of Rule

Maria Giuseppina Muzzarelli

'Laudable Expedients'

The earliest sumptuary laws in Italy date back to the second half of the thirteenth century, and they continued to be issued until the late eighteenth century.[1] Their declared purpose was the curtailing of luxuries and, in particular, of imports in order to protect local economies. Another, and far from secondary purpose concerned the preservation of social hierarchies and the assurance of good governance and social harmony.[2] The laws established the dress of each social category and they were to be strictly applied. A third, undeclared but important, purpose was to fill the public coffers through the fines imposed on offenders. Whatever the lawmakers' original or prevailing purpose might have been, sumptuary laws were useful instruments of rule.

The sumptuary laws issued by specific cities, areas or even entire countries are a rich repository of sources that provide important insights on economic and social circumstances, city and state projects, and the inner functioning of a society. This chapter considers sumptuary laws as instruments of rule and focuses in particular on the systems adopted in several Italian cities to enforce the laws, or at least benefit from their non-compliance. Lawmakers frequently referred to their disillusionment in being able to use sumptuary laws as an instrument to discipline the consumption of luxuries. Yet, despite the admission that the lawmakers' attempts to curtail expense, and the illicit appropriation of elements of dress that were supposed to belong exclusively to specific social strata,

[1] Diane Owen Hughes, 'Sumptuary Law and Social Relations in Renaissance Italy' in John Bossy (ed.), *Disputes and Settlements. Law and Human Relations in the West* (Cambridge: Cambridge University Press, 1983), 69–99; Catherine Kovesi Killerby, *Sumptuary Legislation in Italy, 1200–1500* (Oxford: The Clarendon Press, 2001); Maria Giuseppina Muzzarelli, 'Le leggi suntuarie', in Carlo Marco Belfanti and Fabio Giusberti (eds.), *Storia d'Italia. Annali 19: La moda* (Turin: Einaudi, 2003), 185–220.

[2] Alan Hunt, *Governance of the Consuming Passion. A History of Sumptuary Law* (Basingstoke: Palgrave Macmillan, 1996).

was bound to fail, sumptuary laws were repeatedly enacted for more than five centuries. This fact testifies to the evident usefulness of these measures, partly represented by the revenue secured by the fines imposed for each infringement of the regulations. In the Middle Ages, and in the following centuries, there was a clear understanding that both men and women would never relinquish luxury and vanity which they loved to exhibit with pleasure, if provided with the means to do so.

In 1427, while expounding on the sin of 'novelty' involved in vanities, Bernardino da Siena (1380–1444) remarked that 'con fatiga' (with great difficulty) city governments tried to 'ponare rimedio e ordinare' (find solution and order) by deliberating that 'no silver over a given amount should be worn, nor wool cloth more than established; and that the sleeves should never be so wide and large to make one fly, straight to Hell'.[3] In essence, the Friar Minor noted that '… this law will not impose any regulation, as each of you will want to do what the other does. So I say to you, as I would not be able to do otherwise: act as you see it fit, on your own'.[4] A century and a half later Michel de Montaigne (1533–1592) reached the same conclusion when in 1580 he published the first two books of his *Essays*.[5] For both Bernardino da Siena and Montaigne sumptuary laws were useful in theory but essentially useless in practice.

Almost everyone agreed with them. As one of the late nineteenth-century commentators observed, sumptuary laws had little or no value: 'from a legal and moral viewpoint, these laws seem to point only to a painful and fruitless work'.[6] However sumptuary laws continued to be enacted and to include a wide range of measures aimed at punishing the infringement of regulations. The payment of sometimes conspicuous fines, increases in the taxation rates applied to offenders and the seizure of forbidden items provided revenues which justified the repeated iteration of bans limiting expenditure on clothing, weddings, funerals and banquets. However, it remains difficult to assess how much revenue was actually collected via these means. Testimonies are scarce and lacking in detail, as are the relevant documentation on tax proceeds.

---

[3] Che non si possi portare se non tanto ariento adosso; e che non si possa mettare se non tanto panno per vestire; e che non si facci tanto le maniche grandi, e ale, che ti faranno anco volare a lo 'inferno'. Bernardino da Siena, *Prediche volgari sul Campo di Siena. 1427*, ed. Carlo Delcorno, 2 vols. (Milan: Rusconi, 1989), i, 'predica XXXVII', 1068–1098, esp. 1087–1088.

[4] Ibid., 1087–1088: 'questa legge non vi farà regolare, che così vorrà fare uno come un altro. Unde io vi dico, ch'io non vi saprei già dar modo: datevelo voi, fate da voi'.

[5] Michel de Montaigne, *Saggi*, ed. Fausta Garavini (Milan: Adelphi, 1966), 349.

[6] Agostino Zanelli, 'Di alcune leggi suntuarie pistoiesi dal XIV al XVI secolo', *Archivio Storico Italiano*, series 5, 16 (1895): 206–224, at 206: 'sotto l'aspetto giuridico e morale queste leggi non ci additano altro che un penoso ed infecondo lavoro'.

Later interpretations of sumptuary laws continued to emphasise their fiscal value. In a late nineteenth-century essay dedicated to the sumptuary laws of the city of Pisa, the philosopher Giovanni Gentile (1875–1944) considered them as inescapably doomed to failure.[7] However, he made an argument for their relevance, as he thought that they were 'considered as an additional revenue, almost a tax, a purview ... a source of city contribution', which shows indirectly that their application had an important fiscal effect.[8] According to this interpretation, Gentile separated their general and summative effectiveness (or lack thereof) from their particular application that brought about economic benefits for the state.

Creative Taxation

The assumption is that the Italian cities repeatedly issued and re-issued sumptuary laws as one means to cope with a growing need for money. The contribution generated by the fines and other fiscal impositions related to sumptuary matters could be of substantial importance to the smooth running of public affairs. It was believed that whether or not the laws curbed despicable habits, at least by exercising some creative taxation additional funds could end up in the public coffers.[9] To ascertain whether the fines were collected can be quite hard to establish. However, the systematic indication of fines and the variety of measures conceived to ensure that the laws were enforced and complied with (and the consequent penalties incurred by offenders) are all useful elements in our analysis. It may be presumed that revenues were expected and were thought of as an important asset at a political level. After all, consensus could be won and maintained by means of the tax lever, thus enabling the redistribution of wealth and the public use of at least a portion of privately-owned assets.

If the intent of 'filling the coffers' is more than plausible, the difficulty of showing that the expected outcome was truly met is a real problem, due to the scarcity of documentary evidence for the collected fines.

---

[7] Giovanni Gentile, 'Le leggi suntuarie nel Comune di Pisa', contribution to the seminar of Amedeo Crivellucci, 3 April 1894 unpublished at the time and later printed in Carlo Bonomo, *La prima formazione del pensiero di Giovanni Gentile* (Florence: Sansoni, 1972), 187–211.

[8] Ibid., 205–206: 'considerate come un'entrata straordinaria, quasi una tassa, una prestanza ... una fonte di contribuzione comunale'.

[9] Mario Ascheri, 'Tra vanità e potere: donne, lusso e miti (di ieri e di oggi)', in Maria Assunta Ceppari Ridolfi and Patrizia Turrini (eds.), *Il mulino delle vanità. Lusso e cerimonie nella Siena medievale* (Siena: Il leccio, 1996), ix-xx, esp. xi.

The systematic collection of evidence pertaining to Emilia-Romagna and Umbria enables us to partly reconstruct the dialogue taking place between lawmakers and the people who were the targets of the legislation.[10] This allows us to see what might have happened – and in some instances did certainly happen – to those acting '*contra formam ... statutis*' (against the writ of the law). Even the resistance against the regulations and their constant re-issuing provide us with indications of the dialectic nature of sumptuary laws which, in many instances, demanded a softening of the norms to make them more acceptable. In 1376, for example, the city of Perugia in central Italy granted permission for its inhabitants to wear accessories forbidden by the law, for a limited amount of time. This rare measure recognised that, as such accessories were already owned, additional expenditure required for buying new ones could be avoided, and be in line with the law.[11] Sumptuary systems were designed to make regulations acceptable, whether by discounting fines or by granting permission to wear garments owned before the issue of a new law. They testify to the will of the lawmakers to design a supple, acceptable instrument, suited to extant circumstances, which had to be administered with care and discretion. However, the reconstruction of this dialogue between lawmakers and citizens remains impersonal, and cannot help in describing precise situations or specific forbidden items. Only by bringing together different sources that include the laws, but also fines and cases brought against the wearers of forbidden items, can one come closer to both the people and the objects integral to sumptuary processes.

The 1335 statutes of the city of Bologna, under 'De pena portancium ornamenta', mandated fines between 10 and 25 *lire* for different kinds of infringements pertaining to sumptuary laws.[12]

Tailors who dared to produce garments made from forbidden cuts were fined 10 *lire*. The same fine was applied to the wearers of garments made from a forbidden fabric. The husbands or fathers of women who flaunted more gold or silver than allowed, or women over 40 walking outdoors without covering their heads, had to pay 25 *lire*, equal to a

---

[10] Maria Giuseppina Muzzarelli (ed.), *La legislazione suntuaria. Secoli XIII-XVI. Emilia-Romagna* (Rome: Ministero per i beni e le attività culturali. Direzione generale degli archivi, 2002); Maria Grazia Nico Ottaviani (ed.), *La legislazione suntuaria. Secoli XIII-XVI. Umbria* (Rome: Ministero per i beni e le attività culturali. Direzione generale degli archivi, 2005).

[11] 'Perugia, 5 September 1376, Riformanze', in Nico Ottaviani, *La legislazione suntuaria. Secoli XIII-XVI. Umbria*, 88.

[12] 'Bologna, 1335, Statuti', in Muzzarelli (ed.), *La legislazione suntuaria. Secoli XIII-XVI. Emilia-Romagna*, 78–80.

125-day wages of a labourer.[13] Only the wives of knights and physicians, who certainly were a minority, were exempted.

Such regulations were re-issued with little or no variation in the following years and led to the collection of fines that were recorded in a specific ledger for the period between July 1365 and June 1366 which has survived to this day.[14] The ledger records the name of the person found wearing a forbidden dress and the amount of the fine. The amounts are always under 5 *lire*, a lower and different figure than the one dictated in the Statutes. The discrepancy was probably the result of a discount granted to those willing to pay the fine up front. This can be reasonably inferred from the fact that in 1355 the city of Florence mandated that whoever paid within 10 days from the reported charge could benefit from a 50 per cent discount on the penalty.[15]

Sources for Bologna record that on Sunday 13 July 1365 five people were fined, all were men whose wives had been found wearing prohibited items. They were reported by the notary Luchino da Cremona, who was in charge of recording the fines in the ledger, by the appointed official for the enforcement of sumptuary laws, and a *nuncio* (clerk). In all the five instances, the items concerned were silver-gilded 'afublaturis', namely the fastenings of dresses composed of small silver-gilded buckles or buttons, most likely in these cases exceeding their allowed weight of 3 ounces. The law prohibited 'maspillos de auro vel de argento … ad collum et ad manichas pro afublatura' (gilded and silver ornaments … on the collar and sleeves [used] as fastenings) exceeding 3 ounces in weight and established a penalty of 25 *lire* for those infringing the rule. The husbands of the five guilty women lived in different areas of town, and the occupation of one of them was given as a haberdasher. They were summoned and given three days to appear in front of the tribunal to present their case, but if they failed to do so, they were to be fined 5 *lire*. We know, for instance, that on the 3 August 1365 an apothecary and another

---

[13] At that time, the cost of making a doublet amounted to 1 lira (20 soldi), a sum corresponding to two days' wages for a master craftsman. A full skirt and cloth garment of medium quality was worth about 22 lire, while a silk belt with golden silver thread was worth a little more than 3 lire. Maria Giuseppina Muzzarelli, 'Consumi e livelli di vita: gruppi socio-professionali a confronto', in Franco Franceschi (ed.), *Storia del lavoro in Italia, Il Medioevo. Dalla dipendenza personale al lavoro contrattato* (Rome: Castelvecchi 2017), 457–459 and 462–464; Elisa Tosi Brandi, *L'arte del sarto nel Medioevo. Quando la moda diventa un mestiere* (Bologna: il Mulino, 2017), 124.

[14] 'Bologna, July 1365 – June 1366, Multe', in Muzzarelli (ed.), *La legislazione suntuaria. Secoli XIII-XVI. Emilia-Romagna*, 84–101.

[15] Pietro Fanfani (ed.), *Legge suntuaria fatta dal Comune di Firenze l'anno 1355 e volgarizzata nel 1356 da ser Andrea Lancia* (Florence: Società tipografica sulle Logge del Grano, 1851), 30.

man of unknown occupation were fined 5 *lire* for 'frexios deauratos contra formam statutorum comunis Bononie' (gilded ornaments in contravention of Bologna sumptuary laws) and for 'cuculgis de ariento deaurato ad manicas' (silver-gilded ornaments for sleeves) (Figure 6.1).[16] On 5 August of the same year, five people were also fined 5 *lire* each: a butcher, a ragman, a notary and two other men whose occupation was not given. The ledger includes more than 90 cases accruing around 450 *lire* worth of fines. In this case at least, we can be sure of the fact that these bans were enforced and benefitted the town's coffers.

The *Provisio super ornatu mulierum* issued in January 1401 is a further way to investigate the relationship between the law and its actual application.[17] The *Provisio* banned a series of garments and ornaments, ranging from gold and silver belts and fur borders to rings and velvet dresses, by imposing fines from 5 to 10 *lire*, and in many cases also prescribing the seizure of the forbidden items. This was therefore a strict legislation mandating the recording, in a specific ledger, of the dresses found to be 'in contravention of the allowed shapes' (contra formam predictam), in other words prohibited by the 1401 legislation, but already manufactured and owned at the time the sumptuary law came into force. Certainly these precious and probably much loved garments would not have been relinquished by their owners without a fight. Therefore the lawmakers, facing failure if the law was to be enforced, found a sensible solution: the forbidden garments could still be worn if they were reported to the authorities and made recognisable by a specific seal. This was not a new measure: in Bologna tagging seals had been also imposed by the 1389 regulations, and in Florence a few decades earlier, there had been experiments with this practice.[18] In the city of Pistoia as well, more than fifty years earlier, a similar strategy had been imposed in the attempt to strike a balance between public utility and private interest. Pistoia's 1332 sumptuary provisions allowed the display

---

[16] 'Bologna, July 1365 – June 1366, Multe', in Muzzarelli (ed.), *La legislazione suntuaria. Secoli XIII-XVI. Emilia-Romagna*, 85–86.

[17] 'Bologna, January 1401, Statuto Suntuario', in Muzzarelli (ed.), *La legislazione suntuaria. Secoli XIII-XVI. Emilia-Romagna*, 127–136. See: Maria Giuseppina Muzzarelli, '"Contra formam statutorum": regole, controlli e provvedimenti sanzionatori in materia suntuaria. Il caso di Bologna', in Didier Lett (ed.), *Statuts, écritures et pratiques sociales dans les sociétés de la Méditerranée occidentale à la fin du Moyen Âge (XIIe-XVe siècle). Les statuts vus de l'extérieur: les références à la norme dans les sources de la pratique* (Rome: École Française de Rome, 2019).

[18] For Bologna see: 'Bologna, January 1401, Statuto Suntuario', in Muzzarelli (ed.), *La legislazione suntuaria. Secoli XIII-XVI. Emilia-Romagna*, 120. For Florence, see: Catherine Guimbard, 'Appunti sulla legislazione suntuaria a Firenze dal 1281 al 1384', *Archivio storico italiano* 150/551 (1992), disp. 1, 57–81 and 64.

Figure 6.1 Portrait of a woman, possibly Ginevra d'Antonio Lupari Gozzadini, attributed to Maestro delle Storie del Pane, c. 1494. 50.2 x 37.1 cm. Robert Lehman Collection, 1975. Metropolitan Museum of Art, 1975.1.96.

of forbidden ornaments if branded within a period of two months with a seal placed on a robe near the side opening, and on a cloak and skirt, where the lady best wished. The name of the woman and her husband had to be recorded in a special ledger together with the chapel of residence and details of the dress.[19]

---

[19] 'Con marcho di piombo, nel quale da un lato sia li scacchi e dal autro lo nicchio'. Paolo Peri, 'Le leggi suntuarie pistoiesi del XIV e XV secolo e le testimonianze figurative', in Laura Dal Prà and Paolo Peri (eds.), *Dalla testa ai piedi. Costume e moda in età gotica* (Trento: Provincia Autonoma di Trento, 2006), 368–433, see 379.

The 1401 Sumptuary Statute for the city of Bologna detailed what had to be recorded, but did not clearly state whether fees had to be paid or not, and if so, how much was charged for each recording and related tagging. We do not even know what the seal on the garments looked like. The ledger includes 211 reported charges which, similarly to the fines of 1365–1366, testify to the fact that words were put into action.[20] These records provide a window into women's lives through their dresses, as in the majority of cases it was the woman owning the forbidden garment that reported it. Only in rare instances did men perform this task. Therefore we come to know the identity of these women, at times we even learn about their husbands' professions and, most importantly, we can almost picture the tagging thanks to detailed description. The garments reported on 25 January 1401, for instance, were all 'sacchi' (sacks), namely lined and richly trimmed surcoats for winter wear which, as stated in the recurrent formula, were tagged with the prescribed seal. These were garments in wool cloth, velvet or silk in different colours, and partially or completely lined in fur (squirrel, ermine), with fringes around the collar. Often these garments were made of patches and stripes in several contrasting colours with richly embroidered or winged sleeves. Many women reported only one dress, but some reported two, three and in one case even five. The latter is donna Giovanna, wife of Giovanni Boccadiferro. One of her five surcoats was made of crimson high-pile wool velvet with figures. Her second garment was in gilded wool cloth in grain-colour satin (*zetanino*) with woven gold figures and trees; the third was made of white crimson cloth (*cremisino*) also with figured and compass patterns; and a fourth was in green velvet with vair-lined sleeves. The last surcoat was made of a running wave pattern with striped red wool cloth and silver stars.[21]

One woman reported a surcoat in dark green wool cloth with gold embroideries depicting birds, deer and trees, while another reported an extraordinary grain-coloured velvet dress with gilded and scarlet leaves combined with velvet in running waves.[22] The ladies who wore these garments brought them to be recorded, but it was their husbands who

---

[20] 'Bologna, January 1401, January, Registro della bollatura delle vesti', in Muzzarelli (ed.), *La legislazione suntuaria. Secoli XIII-XVI. Emilia-Romagna*, 137–147. For the Italian version of the 1401 law and the list of the reported dresses with an introduction, see: Maria Giuseppina Muzzarelli (ed.), *Belle vesti, dure leggi: 'In hoc libro continentur et descripte sunt omnes et singules vestes'* (Bologna: Costa editore, 2003).

[21] Muzzarelli (ed.), *Belle vesti, dure leggi*, 48.

[22] Ibid., 46 and 57.

paid, possibly by drawing the needed amount from their wives' dowries.[23] In order to continue wearing these expensive garments the applicants would certainly have had to pay a sort of tax of which however we do not have any evidence. We know instead that the Bologna Statute of 1401 imposed fines of 5 to 10 *lire* to the wearers of garments 'against the law' ('contra formam legis') and that this fine was in addition to the more onerous, and therefore much feared, seizure of the forbidden asset – hence the rush by many women to report their garments that otherwise could be confiscated. Just to give an idea of the size of the possible revenue from the tagging of seals, one has to consider a minimum of 5 *lire* (the minimum amount of the fine imposed in 1401) for each of the 211 garments recorded. The resulting amount of 1,055 *lire* was surely not negligible – even if it was 'una tantum' (one-off) – if we think that a simple clerk earned 60 *lire* a year.

The 1401 law waged war against novelties and in particular 'new garments and new shapes'.[24] The term 'new' is repeated twice, but the records of the already-owned dresses recorded show that these were relatively new fashions: many of the garments brought in for tagging are in fact described as being made 'with scales and waves' ('a scaglie e a onde'). The same hostile reaction towards new fashions is shown in the regulation issued in Venice in 1506: tailors producing new designs were required to pay fines of 25 ducats in addition to six months in jail and three years banishment; if a tailor was reported by his assistant, the latter was entitled to 25 ducats from the offender's property besides securing the title of master of the shop.[25] Lawmakers thought tailors were responsible for new and extravagant shapes and designs, and were therefore perceived as the promoters of fashion. In his *Nuova Cronica* Giovanni Villani, though never mentioning tailors, remarked that the 1330 Florentine sumptuary laws were 'of great detriment to silk-men and goldsmiths who found new and different ornaments every day to make a profit'.[26]

---

[23] Catherine Kovesi Killerby, 'Practical Problems in the Enforcement of Italian Sumptuary Law, 1200–1500', in Trevor Dean and Kate J.P. Lowe, eds., *Crime, Society and the Law in Renaissance Italy* (New York: Cambridge University Press, 1994), 103.

[24] 'vestes novas factas ad turlos, scaglias, undas vel ad intaglios vel ad aliam formam seu figuram novam'. 'Bologna, January 1401, Statuto Suntuario', in Muzzarelli (ed.), *La legislazione suntuaria. Secoli XIII-XVI. Emilia-Romagna*, 129. See also Maria Giuseppina Muzzarelli, '"Vesti bollate": The Italian Fashion Gazette of the Fourteenth and Fifteenth Centuries (Shapes, Colours, Decorations)', in Catherine Kovesi (ed.), *Luxury and the Ethics of Greed in Early Modern Italy* (Turnhout: Brepols, 2018).

[25] Archivio di Stato di Venezia (Henceforth ASV), Sen.Terra, R.15, cc.86v-87r.

[26] 'Grande danno de'setaiuoli e orafi, che per loro profitto ogni dì trovavano ornamenti nuovi e diversi'. This quote from Villani's *Nuova Cronica* is to be found in 'Appendix I' of *Draghi rossi e querce azzurre. Elenchi descrittivi di abiti di lusso (Firenze, 1343–1345)*,

The 1504 Venetian laws allowed the wearing of garments and ornaments worth a maximum of 25 gold ducats (the parameter of reference was in this case value and not quantity) and established that the same amount, 25 ducats, was to be paid as a fine by infringers who had also to relinquish the item. The artisan who had made the forbidden item had to pay the same fine as the customer, though in addition he had also to serve time in prison. If a dress was made using more than 3 *braccia* of fabric, the tailor had to pay a fine of 10 ducats and the owner of the garment would see it seized.[27] In the case of a garment with a forbidden train ('cauda') the tailor was given a fine of 25 ducats and 2 months in prison, while the owner had to pay 25 ducats and had the garment confiscated.[28] In 1535 it was decreed that for destitute tailors the fine would be replaced with flogging, jail and banishment.[29] In Venice the law established that fines should be allocated to the town's coffers, although in the case of forbidden sleeves, the owners were deprived of the sleeves and had pay a fine of 25 ducats to the benefit of the city's convents.[30] The authorities in Venice appear to have been quite strict in imposing heavy fines of 25 ducats, equivalent to eight times the monthly fee paid to the notary charged with the handling of procedures pertaining to sumptuary law enforcement. It may therefore be inferred that substantial income was derived from such fines as well as from seizures. Attempting to picture how these seized properties were dealt with is not easy: perhaps they were stored all piled up in some public warehouses, and later auctioned off, or taken apart. In 1559 the city of Parma ordered that 'robbe proibite' (forbidden garments) which had been confiscated were to be allocated to the Ospedale della Misericordia, while the city of Reggio Emilia in 1550 by a decree 'established that forbidden items were to be taken apart publicly in the square and then have them donated to the said hospital [Ospedale dei Bastardi]'.[31]

Cui Prodest – Whom Does It Profit?

The hypothesis explored in this article is that sumptuary laws had limited effect, and therefore were constantly reiterated. Yet they also had

---

trans. and ed. Laurence Gérard-Marchant (Florence: SISMEL-Edizioni del Galluzzo, 2013), xxxv.

[27] A *braccio* is equivalent to 55–60 centimetres.

[28] ASV, Sen. Terra, R.14, cc. 196v–197r and R.15, cc. 37r–38r.

[29] ASV, Sen. Terra, R.28, cc.160r–163r.

[30] ASV, Sen. Terra, R.15, cc.190r–190v.

[31] 'Con declaratione che le cose prohibite publicamente in piazza s'habbiano a discusire in pezzi e poi donarle al predetto hospitale'. 'Parma, 1559, Prammatica', in Muzzarelli (ed.), *La legislazione suntuaria. Secoli XIII-XVI. Emilia-Romagna*, 462; and 'Reggio Emilia, 7 March 1550, Provvigioni', 631.

a revenue-raising function, though it is difficult to ascertain the exact amounts that were collected. But who was in charge of collecting such fines? In the city of Genoa the Gabella (tax collection) derived from sumptuary measures was contracted out. Between 1408 and 1445 the income generated from the farming of this revenue was 500 *lire* per year on average.[32] This was a substantial amount of money if we consider that the making of a gown cost 1–2 *lire*, depending on the fabric, and that a simple wool garment was worth about 5 *lire*.[33]

In Bologna the 1288 laws tell us that the Podestà could count on 'secretos denuntiatores pro qualibet capella' (secret informers).[34] Several inquisitions for this city survive for the period between 1 May and 2 October 1300.[35] In a single day, 5 May 1300, five people were summoned and questioned; another four were called the following Sunday, and then another five the following Sunday, and so on. Witnesses were identified and summoned, however nobody had anything to declare: all defendants stated 'that they knew nothing' ('se inde nichil scire'). It reveals a great resistance to collaborating with the authorities, something that could probably be overcome only by keeping the charges secret, or by promising parts of the fine to the informer. Therefore, the 1376 Bologna regulations established that anyone could report transgressors to the Podestà or the People's Captain, either anonymously or in person. The town authorities were bound, if so required, to keep secret the names of informers; informers were entitled to half of the fine paid by offenders.[36]

Whistle-blowing played a central role in a town's judicial system.[37] A successful prosecution – and sumptuary laws were no exception – entailed not only monitoring and punishing, but also pursuing and rewarding collaboration. As for Bologna, the 1327 sumptuary regulations for the city of Modena also established that half of the fine was to be given to the informer.[38] In 1445, the city of Perugia decreed that half of

---

[32] Luigi Tommaso Belgrano, *Della vita privata dei Genovesi* (Rome: Multigrafica editrice, [Genoa, 1875] 1970), 253–254.

[33] Jane Bridgeman, '"Pagare le Pompe": Why Quattrocento Sumptuary Laws did not Work', in Letizia Panizza (ed.), *Women in Italian Renaissance Culture and Society* (Oxford: European Humanities Research Centre, 2000), 209–226, 216–217.

[34] 'Bologna, 1288, Statuti', in Muzzarelli (ed.), *La legislazione suntuaria. Secoli XIII-XVI. Emilia-Romagna*, 55.

[35] 'Bologna, 1 May – 2 October 1300, Inquisizioni', in Ibid., 60–69.

[36] 'Bologna, 1376, Statuti', in Ibid., 110.

[37] Andrea Zorzi, 'The Judicial System in Florence in the Fourteenth and Fifteenth Centuries', in Dean and Lowe (eds.), *Crime, Society and Law*, 40–58, at 42.

[38] 'Modena, 1327, Statuti', in Muzzarelli (ed.), *La legislazione suntuaria. Secoli XIII-XVI. Emilia-Romagna*, 392.

the value of forbidden dresses made of gold or silver cloth, gold or silver brocade, velvet or silk was to be split equally between the bailiff and the informant.[39]

A decree issued in Perugia in 1460 established that a memorial stone 'bearing the charges against infringers' should be placed in the Church of San Lorenzo.[40] The same measure also indicated that fines, or the proceeds from the seized goods, were to be split in four equal parts: one quarter was allocated to the Apostolic Chamber, one quarter to the bailiff, one quarter to the informant, and the last quarter was used for repairs or improvements to public buildings and the city chapels. If there were no informants, the quarter that was their due was allocated to maintenance projects.[41] These kinds of fiscal allocations benefitted the entire community. In Assisi in 1468 the fine was assigned to the Camera del Comune which allocated a portion to the repairs of the church of S. Maria degli Angeli, while in 1450 in Foligno a woman found wearing a dress with 'a train longer than four fingers' had to pay 25 *lire* every time she infringed the law. Half of the fine went to the repairs of the Podestà's palace.[42] Such allocations, all described in detail, suggest that the fines were collected. In Orvieto in 1576 the quarter of the fine assigned to Magnifica Comunità was allocated 'to the works of the illustrious Magistrate's palace' ('fabrica del palazzo dell'illustre signor magistrato') while the other three quarters went to the Apostolic Chamber, the bailiff and the informer, respectively.[43]

The recourse to informants was a practice regularly included in the measures and certainly taken advantage of, although the extent of its application cannot be fully ascertained. What is definite is that it was never questioned whether the informer should be compensated. The only exception is the regulation issued in 1430 by Amadeus VIII of Savoy.[44] In this regulation the lawmakers set precise regulations, not just for women but also for their husbands, brothers and fathers. The

---

[39] 'Perugia, 18 March 1445, Costituzioni', in Nico Ottaviani (ed.), *La legislazione suntuaria. Secoli XIII-XVI. Umbria*, 125.

[40] 'Perugia, 29 April 1460, Decreto', in Ibid., 131: 'in quo ponantur denuntie in scriptis in contrafacientes'.

[41] Ibid., 132.

[42] Respectively in 'Assisi, 25 May 1468, Riformanze', in Nico Ottaviani, *La legislazione suntuaria. Secoli XIII-XVI. Umbria*, 266; and 'Foligno, 29 March 1450, Riformanze', in Ibid., 410.

[43] 'Orvieto, 20 September 1576, Statuti', in Nico Ottaviani, *La legislazione suntuaria. Secoli XIII-XVI. Umbria*, 1099.

[44] *Gli Statuti di Amedeo VIII di Savoia del 31 luglio 1430* (Turin: E. Accademia delle Scienze, 1940). A new edition entitled *La Loi du Prince*, ed. Franco Morenzoni with Mathieu Caesar, is in press. See II: *Compendium Statutorum Generalis Reformacionis Sabaudie* (Turin: Édition critique par Chantal Ammann-Doubliez, and Deputazione Subalpina di Storia Patria, in press).

law also refers to the relationship between the value of a forbidden item and the fine to be paid, which was fixed at one quarter of the value of the former. Finally, once a quarter had been set aside for the cost of administration, the money raised from fines was given to 'charitable uses' ('in pios usus').[45] This allocation was applied to all fines, and not solely to those pertaining to infringements of sumptuary regulations, and 'as the money collected from fines is generated by an offense against God, this money must be used to produce works of piety in honour of God and not become part of our treasury'.[46] In essence, the ducal administration claimed not to want to benefit from the infringement of the law, giving away to charities three-quarters of the money raised. In reality, the state administration benefitted indirectly because such charities provided aid to the poor, the ill and other needy people, and therefore spared the public coffers substantial sums and helped the keeping of the public peace.

The Savoyard Statutes are unique. Sumptuary laws coeval with Amadeus VIII's measures aimed in most cases at drawing a direct benefit from the infringement of the law by exchanging so-to-speak disloyalty with expediency. This was so much so that fines ended up by being perceived as a sort of useful tax on luxury used to meet all kinds of public financial needs. The 'Statuta Sabaudiae', where virtue seems to prevail over expediency, established instead that fines were to be recorded in a special ledger for alms (compulsory for all penalties concerned with the infringement of sumptuary laws). Unfortunately this ledger has not survived. This was not a new idea. In France, as early as the second half of the thirteenth century, the proceeds of the fines had already been decreed to be allocated in favour of the community, including to 'pious causes'. In Montpellier anyone infringing the 1255 matrimonial and clothing laws had to contribute 1,000 bricks for the repairs of the city walls.[47] In Montauban, for infringements concerning dress regulations,

---

[45] *Compendium Statutorum*, 197. See also Maria Giuseppina Muzzarelli, 'Regole per tutti. Confronti nel campo della legislazione suntuaria a partire dalla normativa sabauda', in Morenzoni with Mathieu Caesar, eds, *La Loi du Prince. Vol. I. Les Statuts de Savoie d'Amédée VIII de 1430. Une œuvre législative majeure*, in press.

[46] 'Quia ex offensa dei procedunt et per consequens ad ejus honorem et opera pietatis sunt convertende, per erarium nostrum non exigantur'. Ibid., 5. See: Neithard Bulst, 'La législation somptuaire d'Amédée VIII', in Bernard Andenmatten and Agostino Paravicini Bagliani (eds.), *Amédée VIII – Félix V: premier duc de Savoie et pape (1383–1451)* (Colloque International Ripaille-Lausanne, 23–26 October 1990. Bibliothèque historique vaudoise, 103) (Lausanne: Fondation Humbert II et Marie José de Savoie, 1992), 191–200.

[47] N. Bulst, 'La legislazione suntuaria in Francia (secoli XIII-XVIII)', in Maria Giuseppina Muzzarelli and Antonella Campanini, eds, *Disciplinare il lusso. La legislazione suntuaria in Italia e in Europa* (Rome: Carocci, 2003), 121–136, at p. 131.

1,000 bricks had to be provided for the building of the church of St.-Jacme or the city bridge, while in Amiens in 1583 the poor were allocated one-third of the fines for violations of the sumptuary laws.[48] In Italy, however, allocations of this kind started to appear, with rare exceptions, in the sixteenth century and young orphan girls, the 'shameful poor', hospitals and Monti Pii (pawnbrokers managed by the Church) are listed among the recipients.

Quantum – How Much?

A major problem in addressing the issue of sumptuary fines is that we do not know how many people were fined, how much they paid, or even if they paid at all. We also do not know how much the seized items were sold for, and how much the 'administrative machine' in charge of monitoring compliance with the law and of the collection of fines cost. At the most what we can do is to compare the fines applied in different cities and the procedures to find and punish offenders by considering the period spanning from the fourteenth to the late fifteenth century.

In Bologna in 1335 the official fine amounted to 10 *lire*, but the fine actually paid in 1365–1366 amounted to half that sum.[49] Under the 1376 law fines ranged from 20 to 40 sous, and the informants were allocated half the fine. According to the same law, the Podestà and Captain were bound to carry out the necessary investigation and were entitled to 2 sous out of every lira of fine.[50] The investigations had to be carried out with great care, without arresting women for whatever reason. The authorities were cautious in their investigations, perhaps due to the high social standing of many of these ladies 'sovravestite' (excessively dressed). Potential informants were even more careful, to the point that although lured by the money of the fine, they probably did not collaborate with the authorities frequently. A *bando* (public notice) issued in Bologna in 1570 stated that the authorities 'proceed without any exception against those who do not obey' the law,[51] but a *Riformanza* issued in Foligno in 1589 reports that 'there is no man brave enough to speak out'.[52]

---

[48] Ibid.
[49] 'Bologna, 1335, Statuti', in Muzzarelli (ed.), *La legislazione suntuaria. Secoli XIII-XVI. Emilia-Romagna*, 80; and 'Bologna, July 1365 – June 1366', Multe', in Ibid., 84–101.
[50] 'Bologna, 1376, Statuti', in Ibid., 110.
[51] 'Bologna, 3–5 July 1570 Bandi', in Ibid., 223: 'a contra gli inobedienti si procederà senza rispetto di persona alcun'.
[52] 'Foligno, 12 May 1589, Riformanze', in Nico Ottaviani (ed.), *La legislazione suntuaria. Secoli XIII-XVI. Umbria*, 540: 'non ci è huomo ch'abbia ardire di parlare'.

The 1453 law promoted by Cardinal Bessarione in Bologna appears to move away from its predecessors, and is based on the hierarchical structure of society in which each social rank was identified by appropriate dress and accessories for women. The husbands or fathers of offenders were fined 10 *lire*, while tailors had to pay 5 *lire*.[53] Some twenty years later, in 1474, the new law set the same fines but also introduced the excommunication of anyone who did not comply with the imposed restrictions.[54] The excommunicated were not allowed to go to church and, if attempting to do so, would be driven out.

In Pistoia in 1332, as in many other cities, fines were set at a flat rate of 25 *lire*. This applied not only to the wearers of pearls, enamels and precious stones, but also to those displaying dresses with fretwork (interlaced decorative designs) and embroidered with letters or patterns.[55] In Siena in 1274 fines amounted to 100 *lire*, increasing in 1330 to 200 *lire*, in addition to the confiscation of the forbidden item; tailors as well had to pay hefty fines. In order to mitigate the severity of the norm, in Siena the use of the already-owned dresses was allowed for two years after the passing of the law but only if they were reported to the official in charge.[56] The measures were often modified and even reprieved – for example during a visit by important personalities or for lordly weddings – but were renewed at times when non-compliance was seen to have increased. The law was also invoked when a city's finances were in trouble due to war or famine, another example of the usefulness of these laws for the smooth running of public affairs.[57]

In Florence the husbands of women wearing forbidden dresses had to pay a fine of 50 *lire* corresponding to around one-quarter of the cost of the dress, though the proportion was often much lower. One may ask whether a fine of this kind truly represented a deterrent or was simply a way to compensate for not having complied with a regulation which – instead of being enforced – was circumvented to the benefit of the city coffers.[58] In Milan in 1396 the wearers of dresses embroidered with pearls were fined 100 *lire*, an amount probably equal to a quarter of the value of the pearls themselves. The wives of knights and physicians were exempted from the restrictions, though men wearing pearl ornaments

---

[53] 'Bologna, 23 March 1453, Provvisioni', in Muzzarelli (ed.), *La legislazione suntuaria. Secoli XIII-XVI. Emilia-Romagna*, 148–152, esp. 151.

[54] 'Bologna, 11 May 1474, 3 July 1474 and 14 Nov. 1474, Provvisioni', in Ibid., 154–161. See also: Kovesi Killerby, *Sumptuary Law in Italy*, 138.

[55] Peri, 'Le leggi suntuarie pistoiesi', 379.

[56] Ceppari, Ridolfi and Turrini, *Il mulino delle vanità*, 79–86.

[57] Ibid., 89.

[58] Bridgeman, 'Pagare le pompe', 219–220.

were not and could also be fined 100 *lire*. The same fine was set for garments excessively long or trimmed with fur, while for embroideries the fine was 25 *lire* and 10 *lire* for tailors cutting and sewing dresses 'in contravention of the content and purpose of this law' ('contra formam et intentionem presentium capitulorum').[59] The Podestà who did not perform all acts necessary for the prosecution of the perpetrator was to be fined 50 *lire*, and double this amount was imposed on the prostitutes caught wearing the 'coazzone', a very popular hairstyle with a braid interspersed with ribbons and other decorations that only women of repute were allowed to wear. In Milan the law envisaged also a 100-*lire* increase for the husband's tax evaluation when his wife was found wearing a forbidden item. The tax increase was a penalty established elsewhere as well, for instance in Bologna in 1398.[60]

In Florence in 1355 the fines ranged from 25 to 200 *lire*. Whoever wore forbidden dresses in samite, hoods with gold or silver or precious coronets exceeding 10 gold florins in value, had to pay fines as high as 200 *lire*.[61] The fine imposed on the wearer of a fur-lined cape was 100 *lire* while the fine was 25 *lire* for people wearing more than two rings. For parti-coloured and chequered dresses one had to pay a fine of 100 *lire* besides the loss of the garment, which was requisitioned by the city of Florence. Whoever refused to pay lost their right of access to the city's public buildings: a form of additional 'civic' penalty.[62] The city official in charge of enforcing the regulations was bound to perform this task through inspections of the city's main spaces, such as churches, during holidays, to spot possible infringers. He was entitled to 2 sous for every lira paid in fine. The allocation of a portion of the fine to the official in charge was the norm, as it allowed the law-enforcing magistrature to cover its costs. The case of Florence is worthy of analysis because of its distinctive features. The first consists in its pragmatic policy, adopted since 1299, at the time of the first sumptuary measures in Florence, envisaging – in exchange for an annual tax – the permission to wear supposedly forbidden dresses and precious ornamentations.[63] Florence's approach

---

[59] E. Verga, 'Le leggi suntuarie milanesi', *Archivio Storico Lombardo*, 9, Year 25 (1898), 5–79, 9–10 concerning the 1396 fines against those who wore embroidered garments and pearls and at p. 25 concerning fines against tailors.

[60] 'Bologna, 18 July 1398, Provvisioni', in Muzzarelli (ed.), *La legislazione suntuaria. Secoli XIII-XVI. Emilia-Romagna*, 124.

[61] On dresses in Florence, see Carole C. Frick, *Dressing Renaissance Florence: Families, Fortunes, and Fine Clothing* (Baltimore: Johns Hopkins University Press, 2002).

[62] Fanfani (ed.), *Legge suntuaria fatta dal Comune di Firenze*, 23. See also Kovesi Killerby, 'Practical Problems', 103.

[63] Laurence Gérard-Marchant, 'Aspetti della moda femminile a Firenze nella "Prammatica" del 1343', in *Draghi rossi e querce azzurre*, ix-xvi, at p. x.

has been seen by historians as blending prevention and compromise.[64] Florence was the first city to consider taxation as a possible measure.[65] Levies were established on three types of female ornamentations: by paying 50 *lire* a year one was entitled to wear what would, without the payment, have caused a fine of 100 *lire*. In order to wear in public what she wished, a woman had to declare the possession of forbidden dresses and ornaments, and the tax had to be paid, followed by tagging with a seal. The Statutes of the early fourteenth century replaced earlier collaboration, as represented by the 1299 taxes, with repression; but in 1330 the old policy of tagging of forbidden clothes was resumed. It was after the expulsion of the Duke of Brienne, when a regime open to 'new men' was established in Florence in September 1343, that the sumptuary restrictions were revamped. A period of unprecedented democratisation was then initiated, which aimed at limiting the use of precious fabrics and refined styles in dresses. A norm aimed at targeting the wealthy, fell like an axe on the makers of those products, namely the 'new men' who often belonged to the social groups of manufacturers of dresses and accessories. An extraordinary source provides information on this phase of the Florentine laws: the 1343 Prammatica recording the large-scale tagging of forbidden dresses. The measure that established the recording of these luxury dresses has not survived and therefore there is no certainty about the criteria of reporting and the possible, almost certain, payment of a tax that permitted the continued wearing of these clothes. However, five different lists of 'marked' dresses survive, which are just a small part of a certainly much larger series of forbidden garments which were owned and reported. These documents detail almost 7,000 dresses and 2,400 different women reporting them. This is an exceptional repository of knowledge drawn from a likewise extraordinary fiscal source. If just 25 *lire* for each 'tagged' dress was paid (the same amount of the fine established by the 1355 measures for some sumptuary restrictions in Florence) the impressive figure of 175,000 *lire* could be collected.

Conclusion

Sumptuary laws were a useful political instrument, and were used to keep in check an opposing party by depriving them of demonstrating the marks of their power and privilege. These regulations were also

---

[64] Christiane Klapisch-Zuber, 'I freni al lusso nella Firenze del Trecento', in *Draghi rossi e querce azzurre*, xvii-xxxviii, at p. xviii.
[65] Bridgeman, 'Pagare le pompe', 220–221.

useful to government, as they highlighted status and power. Power could be preserved by building and strengthening a specific hierarchy, with different standings determined by birth or social function. Undoubtedly dress and ornamentation facilitated the work of differentiation and recognition. Sumptuary regulations reveal how rulers adopted this semiology to compensate, distinguish, separate and keep in check individuals and groups, and therefore govern. Through the skilful control of appearances, limiting what could be worn by even the wealthiest, these laws contributed to the government of society. The measures issued not only referred to precious items but also scrutinised and prohibited what exceeded the boundaries of the dress and ornamentation granted to each level of society.

Rulers attempted to maintain their control by preventing changes that might set their parties at a disadvantage, limiting infighting and protecting local economies while also drawing an economic benefit from infringement of the law. The goals of deterring dissipation and fostering solidarity in favour of the needy pertained more to preachers than lawmakers. Yet civic legislators and rulers found common ground with religious preachers on matters of sumptuary measures. By opposing dissipation moral and economic motivations converged. This explains why the money raised from the fines inflicted on offenders were allocated to the benefit of religious institutions or Monti di Pietà.

Sumptuary laws tell us a great deal about a society and the idea that such a society had of itself. They reveal the importance assigned to aesthetics, to marks of recognition provided by dress and ornamentation and to the passion for abundance.[66] These laws speak also about a system set up to strengthen city governments through taxation.[67] It was a matter of playing on consumption by at times favouring local production and curtailing exports, and at other times steering people away from consumption and towards the acquisition of more durable assets which preserved capital.

This essay has shown that sumptuary laws were not just aimed at stopping consumption or reducing expenditure. Perhaps acknowledging the impossibility of achieving such aims, they often included provisions for the collection of taxes that helped fill a city's coffers, and fostered wealth redistribution. Fines and the confiscation and recording of

---

[66] Gerhard Jaritz, 'Social Grouping and the Languages of Dress in the Late Middle Ages', *Medieval History Journal* 3/2 (2000): 235–259.

[67] See Giuliano Pinto, *Città e spazi economici* (Bologna: Clueb, 1996), P. Mainoni, 'Finanza pubblica e fiscalità nell'Italia centro-settentrionale fra XIII e XV secolo', *Studi Storici* 40 (1999): 449–470; Patrizia Mainoni, *Politiche finanziarie e fiscali nell'Italia settentrionale (secoli XIII-XV)* (Milan: Unicopli, 2001).

forbidden dresses were all instruments used to shift economic resources from the private to the public sphere. In many instances, though not always, acceptance of paying a fine meant that infringers could wear what they wanted. Therefore fines and seal tagging became a sort of tax collection through which at least a portion of the wealth of the proud, vain and well-to-do could reach the needy or be used to pursue the public good. Money from these fines could be put to good use in paving the roads or helping hospitals, underlining a course of action that brought together private ambitions and public virtues. One might therefore argue that fiscal motivations were one of the most powerful drivers of the policies adopted to regulate luxuries and appearances.

7   Defending the Right to Dress: Two Sumptuary Law Protests in Sixteenth-Century Milan

Catherine Kovesi

In the early modern period, the numerous city states of the Italian peninsula were seemingly more disquieted than any other part of the world by new expenditure on clothing among an increasingly wide section of their social classes. The evidence for such an assertion is a large corpus of legislation, passed by more than thirty city governments of all political persuasions, in a rather crude attempt to constrain and control such expenditure – the so-called sumptuary laws. More than three hundred Italian sumptuary laws are extant for the period 1200 to 1500, a greater number than in all other areas of Europe combined.[1] This great number is partly explained by the numerous self-governing entities in the Italian peninsula, each with its own law code, but is also symptomatic of Italy's central role in a new commercial world of trade and consumption, which meant the peninsula was at the forefront of the economic, social and political effects of new wealth. Although Italian sumptuary laws were directed against all manner of expenditure, the overwhelming number of laws focused on clothing – its cost as well as its style, its wearers as well as its producers.[2] The legislative record left behind is an immensely rich but largely static one, and it is often hard to get a sense of how sumptuary laws were received by their targets.

The history of this legislation in Italy is punctuated, however, by intermittent appeals against individual laws, and these provide fragmentary glimpses as to their reception. For the most part, these protests were generated by, or written on behalf of, elite women, outraged at restrictions on their personal right to dress as they pleased. However, in the mid-sixteenth century, two anonymous protests appeared in Milan, unique in

---

[1] For a general survey of the Italian sumptuary legislation see Catherine Kovesi Killerby, *Sumptuary Law in Italy, 1200–1500* (Oxford: Clarendon Press, 2002); also Maria Giuseppina Muzzarelli and Antonella Campanini (eds.), *Disciplinare il lusso: la legislazione suntuaria in Italia e in Europa tra Medioevo ed età moderna* (Rome: Carocci, 2003).

[2] For a comparison of the various concerns of Italian sumptuary laws see the graph in Kovesi Killerby, *Sumptuary Law*, 38, Figure 2.1.

the history of such protests for their probable origin in the world of the artisanal producer. This chapter seeks to place these Milanese protests within the longer trajectory of arguments about, and attitudes toward, appropriate consumption in the period. It argues that these petitions mark a singular theoretical departure in the nascent debate on luxury in the Italian, and possibly European, context.[3] For the first time an argument is made that the purchase and wearing of sumptuous clothing – so often demonised, debated, ridiculed and parodied – is instead a moral, material and financial good for all stakeholders in Milanese society; for the first time an argument is made on behalf of merchants, artisanal producers (including nuns), unemployed youth and the poor of a city; for the first time an argument is made for the continued freedom of the economy in Milan (whether real or imagined), as expressed through the right of freedom of dress for all (again, whether real or imagined).

Milan is unusual amongst Italian cities in this period in that it passed very few sumptuary laws, and the ones it passed were initially quite half-hearted and lacked the useful minutiae that sumptuary laws from other cities provide in such depth and detail. The earliest Milanese sumptuary statute appeared only in 1396 under Giangaleazzo Visconti, and no further law was passed for a full century until 1498, under the redaction of Ludovico Sforza.[4] Over the succeeding two centuries Milan passed only a further six laws, a total of eight laws in three centuries.[5] By contrast, the Florentines passed 61 laws and the Venetians 42 laws in a similar time period.[6]

---

[3] For the history of the use of the term 'luxury' in Italy see Catherine Kovesi, 'Luxury in the Renaissance: A Contribution to the Etymology of a Concept', in Machtelt Israëls et al. (eds.), *Renaissance Studies in Honor of Joseph Connors* (Florence: Leo S. Olschki, 2013), 228–234; and Catherine Kovesi, 'What is Luxury? The Rebirth of a Concept in the Early Modern World', *Luxury: History, Culture, Consumption* 2/1 (2015): 25–40.

[4] See Ettore Verga, 'Le leggi suntuarie milanesi: gli statuti del 1396 e del 1498', *Archivio Storico Lombardo* 25 (1898): 5–79.

[5] Ettore Verga, 'Le leggi suntuarie e la decadenza dell'industria in Milano 1565–1750', *Archivio Storico Lombardo* 27 (1900): 49–116.

[6] For the best summary of the Florentine legislation see Ronald Rainey, 'Sumptuary Legislation in Renaissance Florence' (Unpublished PhD thesis, Columbia University, 1985), and his 'Dressing Down the Dressed Up: Reproving Feminine Attire in Renaissance Florence', in John Monfasani and Ronald G. Musto (eds.), *Renaissance Society and Culture: Essays in Honor of Eugene F. Rice, Jr.* (New York: Italica Press, 1991), 217–237. For Venice see Giulio Bistort, *Il magistrato alle pompe nella Repubblica di Venezia* (Miscellanea di Storia Veneta edita per cura della R. Deputazione Veneta di Storia Patria, series 3, vol. 5, Venice, 1912), also M. M. Newett, 'The Sumptuary Laws of Venice in the Fourteenth and Fifteenth Centuries', in T. F. Tout and James Tait (eds.), *Historical Essays by Members of the Owens College, Manchester* (London: Longmans Green, 1902), 245–277. For a comparison of laws passed by cities throughout the Italian peninsula see the table in Kovesi Killerby, *Sumptuary Law*, 28–29.

The protests that are the subject of this chapter appeared in response to the new Milanese sumptuary law of 21 November 1565. To call it 'Milanese' needs some qualification, as it was the first sumptuary law to be passed during the period of the Spanish domination of Milan. Although this law was formulated by the Tribunale di Provvisione at the instigation of the Senate, this was only done after an order by the Spanish Governor of the Duchy, Gabriel de la Cueva y Girón, 5th Duke of Alburquerque, on behalf of Philip II of Spain. Such laws seem to have been part of a wider strategy on the part of Philip II, eventually reaching to all parts of his extensive realm. By 1575, for example, sumptuary laws were being imposed on colonial Inca subjects in the Viceroyalty of Peru by Viceroy Francisco de Toledo.[7] This new wave of sumptuary laws was also symptomatic of the flood of goods arriving in Spain from the Americas which thrust Spain prematurely into 'the luxury debates' that were to become a feature of other European countries, especially England and France, in the eighteenth century.[8]

The Tribunale delle Provvisione gave the task to the Consiglio Generale, which, in turn, appointed a special Giunta to formulate a Provision.[9] The law that this Giunta produced was quite unlike the previous two laws passed in Milan. This new law was quite severe, full of detail, and is really the first Milanese law that bears comparison with what had been and was still being passed elsewhere in the peninsula. This law was strictly hierarchical and gender specific. There were clauses for noblemen, for noblewomen, for *borghesi*, for courtesans, for peasants and foreigners. It covered what could be consumed at feasts, what ritual to follow at baptisms and at funerals, as well as providing detailed provisions concerning clothing – in other words all the usual suspects of sumptuary

---

[7] See Elena Phipps, 'Garments and Identity in the Colonial Andes', in Elena Phipps et al. (eds.),*The Colonial Andes: Tapestries and Silverwork, 1530–1830* (New York: The Metropolitan Museum of Art; New Haven and London: Yale University Press, 2004), 27.

[8] For a discussion of these arguments, especially the monetarist theories of the theologians Martín de Azpilcueta and Tomás de Mercado at the University of Salamanca, see James Casey, *Early Modern Spain: A Social History* (London and New York: Routledge, 1999), 68 ff. The first major contribution to the luxury debates in Spain was that of Juan Sempere y Guarinos, *Historia del luxo y de las leyes suntuarias de España*, 2 vols. (Madrid: Emprenta Real, 1788). For the eighteenth-century luxury debates see Maxine Berg and Elizabeth Eger (eds.), *Luxury in the Eighteenth Century: Debates, Desires and Delectable Goods* (Basingstoke: Palgrave, 2002), and especially the overview provided in Maxine Berg, *Luxury and Pleasure in Eighteenth-Century Britain* (Oxford: Oxford University Press, 2005).

[9] See Verga, 'Le leggi suntuarie e la decadenza dell'industria', 54, citing Archivio Storico Civico di Milano, *Dicastri, Cameretta*, 31 May 1564, c. 109.

laws.[10] Significantly for the protesters, this law also had strict prohibitions for clothing which included any gold or silver cloth, or ornaments of the same, and in particular gold, crystal, silver, pearl, bejewelled or embroidered buttons; all products for which Milan was famous.

Whilst the majority of Italian sumptuary laws concentrated on prohibitions for clothing worn by women, this Milanese provision had lengthy restrictions also for men. Men were forbidden any item of clothing (robes, tunics, capes, doublets, stockings, berets and hats) incorporating any fabric of gold or silver thread. They were forbidden any extravagant ornaments, especially buttons of gold, of crystal with gold or silver, pearls or jewels, embroidery or trimmings or fringes of gold, silver or silk. In decorating their robes, men were not to use more than a quarter of the fabric used in the robe itself. Also prohibited was clothing with slashings,[11] not just for everyday use, but also at masked balls. Liveries of silk with embroidery or with more than one border of decoration were also forbidden, as were retinues of more than six servants, household staff members or pages. Saddlecloths of velvet or silk were also prohibited, as was the use of any accoutrement for horses or mules that used embroidery, or metal worked with gems. Such ornamented metalwork was also prohibited for swords, daggers and whips. Servants were also not to be dressed in the livery of either the groom or bride's household on the occasion of weddings.

Noblewomen were similarly forbidden the use of cloth of gold, ornamentations of embroidery or trimmings, buttons and rosettes or other precious items. Long trains were forbidden, as were linings of sable, ermine or lynx. Berets and hats were also prohibited except in cases of rain or sickness, and no cloth or silk was to be used that incorporated work in gold or silver thread. Lacework was also restricted for shirts.[12] Only three rings were to be worn, and no precious ornament was to be worn on the head or on sleeves, nor was sable to be worn on the head, on collars or within wide fan-shaped sleeves. No belts, crowns or bracelets made of paste of amber and no musk or other perfumes were permitted, nor necklaces of gold above the value of 100 *scudi*,[13] and enamel was

---

[10] The provisions of the law are summarised by Verga, 'Le leggi suntuarie e la decadenza dell'industria', 54–57.

[11] 'Frappati o frastagliati' are the words used, which could also indicate jagged and pointed cuts to clothing.

[12] The word used is 'retegini', which Verga assumes is 'reticella/reticello', a kind of needlepoint lace.

[13] The *scudo* was a silver coin used in the Duchy of Milan until 1796. It was first minted in 1551 under Charles V. It was further subdivided into 6 *lire* (each of 20 *soldi*), or 240 *denarii*.

excluded above all.[14] Noblewomen were not to be accompanied by more than two ladies-in-waiting (in addition to a chaperone),[15] and these ladies were not to wear silk. Little carriages, chariots and litters were not to be ornamented with gold and silver, nor to be carved or bevelled in any manner except for the knobs and the family coat of arms. The coverings of these modes of transport were to be decorated only with plain silk, with no use of gold or silver.

For artisans, shopkeepers and workers in general, silk and any ornament of gold was forbidden, except for a necklace worth no more than 25 *scudi*. Men in these classes were allowed only a doublet of silk, and woollen stockings lined with sendal (a light silk cloth). Courtesans were instructed to dress with the most rigorous simplicity, identifying themselves with a white mantle over their heads, and a red belt. They were not permitted carriages, nor pageboys. Foreigners, however, were exempt from the provisions of the law for the first six months of their residency in the city.

There were also provisions for banquets (a banquet being defined as any meal at which more than eight people were present). At such banquets, no one was to consume peacocks, pheasants, guinea fowl nor young poultry in wintertime, nor wild boar, capriole or antelope. They could, however, freely consume salami of veal, aspic, blancmange ('biancomangiare')[16] and pasta dishes. No more than two courses of meat and of pies ('torte') were to be served. If you served meat then you were not to serve fish at the same time, and vice versa. All sweet confections were prohibited, as were elaborate statues and decorations carved from sugar.

No refreshments were to be provided at baptisms, no gifts were to be given to the godparents and visits to the newborn were restricted. At funerals, only the mother, father, sons, wife and brothers and sisters of the deceased were permitted to wear mourning clothes. Servants were forbidden from wearing mourning clothes, the cathedral bell was not to be rung and the house was not to be draped in black cloth (other than at the door, as a sign that someone within had died).

---

[14] One of the most authoritative discussions of the details of costume in Milan in this period is that of Rosita Levi-Pisetzky, *Storia del costume in Italia. Vol. 3. Il Cinquecento. Il Seicento* (Milan: Istituto Editoriale Italiano and Fondazione Giovanni Treccani degli Alfieri per la Storia di Milano, 1964–1969).

[15] 'Donna di governo'.

[16] For a discussion of 'biancomangiare' and 'gelatina', or aspic, see Allen J. Grieco, 'From the Cookbook to the Table: A Florentine Table and Italian Recipes of the Fourteenth and Fifteenth Centuries', in Carole Lambert (ed.), *Du manuscrit à la table: Essais sur la cuisine au Moyen Âge et répertoire des manuscrits médiévaux contenant des recettes culinaires (Études Médiévales.)* (Montréal: Presses de l'Université de Montréal, 1992), 29–38.

The penalties for infraction of any part of this law, other than loss of the offending item/s, was a monetary fine, varying from 25 to 50 *scudi*. For recidivists, this penalty was doubled, and a flogging was added. Any tailors who contravened were also subject to penalties, and were to be imprisoned.[17]

The law was quite moralistic in tone, based upon two fundamental concepts: that extravagant consumption caused the ruin of families as it fostered jealousy and rancour; and that such consumption also led to a decline in population as no one could afford the expenses associated with marriages.[18]

It was in the following year, 1566, that the two anonymous petitions against this law appeared. As noted earlier, this in itself is not new. Almost from their inception, we have indications in chronicles that sumptuary laws were protested against by their targets, and therefore by women in particular.[19] From the early fifteenth century these protests gained momentum with petitions from women, or from men on behalf of women, in particular against sumptuary laws that included excommunication as a penalty for their infraction. In 1437, for instance, the Venetian Cristina Corner wrote to the pope, asking that she be allowed exemption from a recent sumptuary law because of her noble blood, for the honour of her parents and because of her great beauty.[20] A group petition by five other Venetian noblewomen was presented to the pope in the same year, and in 1470 the Venetian noble Andrea Gritti wrote on behalf of twelve female relatives.[21] In 1452,

[17] Imprisonment was a very rare penalty for infraction of a sumptuary provision. Significantly it was a punishment meted out only to producers who had no social clout, such as tailors, as here, and also shoemakers. See the instance in Venice, in a law of March 1430, in which shoemakers who made shoes, or *pianelle*, with a platform higher than half of a *quarta* (about three-and-a-half inches), were to be imprisoned: Archivio di Stato, Venice, Maggior Consiglio, Reg. Ursa, XXIX, 2 March 1430, and also ASV, Complizationi leggi, Busta 305, Filza T, 2 March 1430, with discussions in Kovesi Killerby, *Sumptuary Law*, 51–52, and Newett, 'The Sumptuary Laws of Venice', 274, amongst several others citing this law.

[18] The link between consumption, marriages and declining population is one of the most recurrent motifs in sumptuary law preambles throughout Italy. See Kovesi Killerby, *Sumptuary Law*, 41–60. See also the discussion in Julius Kirshner, 'Li emergenti bisogni matrimoniali in Renaissance Florence', in William J. Connell (ed.), *Society and Individual in Renaissance Florence* (Berkeley, Los Angeles, London: University of California Press, 2002), 79–109, esp. 82 ff. Verga argues that after 1623, Milanese sumptuary laws become more strictly focused on economic regeneration. See Verga, 'Le leggi suntuarie e la decadenza dell'industria', 51.

[19] See Catherine Kovesi Killerby, '"Heralds of a Well-Instructed Mind": Nicolosa Sanuti's Defence of Women and Their Clothes', *Renaissance Studies* 13/3 (1999): 256, n. 4 for references to earlier protests against sumptuary laws.

[20] Ibid., 257.

[21] Ibid.

the learned Sienese woman, Battista Petrucci, delivered an oration in the presence of Emperor Frederick III's fiancée, Eleanora of Portugal. When the Emperor offered her a reward for her eloquence, Petrucci chose the right to wear her clothes and jewels, notwithstanding the city's sumptuary law, and the city's councillors reluctantly granted the request.[22] In 1453, a lengthy protest against a sumptuary law was made by the Bolognese noblewoman and one-time lover of Sante Bentivoglio, Nicolosa Sanuti.[23] She protested against the sumptuary law of Cardinal Bessarione, papal legate to Bologna. Amongst other arguments she asserted that clothing was a mark of honour, and that those who passed the law placed love of money before love of the honour of the city, and therefore were guilty of avarice. 'I also am moved not a little', she said, 'when I behold the insatiable appetites of certain men who, not considering women's condition and circumstances, wish that to be forbidden by law which their own avarice was preventing'.[24] Most of all, she was incensed that a noblewoman, who had no other recourse than her garments to display her status and honour, was now to be deprived of her clothing. As Sanuti expressed it: 'who would be so torpid or idle, what woman so unlearned, what female so pusillanimous, that she would decline to speak in favour of the restoration, defence and preservation of her ornaments?'[25]

The two Milanese protests, however, mark a singular departure in this tradition of sumptuary law protest. For the first time it is the merchants, gold workers, silk workers and embroiderers of the city who are championed, and the arguments made in their defence are broader, on behalf of the health of the economy of the city as a whole, and not simply motivated by personal outrage at individual deprivation of clothing.

These two appeals have not been published before, and remain in manuscript in the Archivio di Stato in Milan in a fondo with an assortment of later documents relating to issues of luxury in the city.[26] These protests are alluded to briefly in the work of Ettore Verga and

---

[22] See Orlando Malavolti, *Historia del Sig. Orlando Malavolti de' fatti e guerie de' Sanesi, cosi esterne come Civili* ... (Venice: Per Salvestro Marchetti in Siena all'insegna della lupa, 1599), parte 3, libro secondo, 38v. For the context see Kovesi Killerby, 'Heralds of a Well Instructed Mind', 258.

[23] For a discussion of this protest and a translation of the treatise see Kovesi Killerby, 'Heralds of a Well Instructed Mind', 255–282. See also the excellent discussion in Jane Bridgeman, 'Pagare le pompe: Why Quattrocento Sumptuary Law Did Not Work', in Letizia Panizza (ed.), *Women in Italian Renaissance Culture and Society* (Oxford: European Humanities Research Centre, Oxford University, 2000), 209–221.

[24] Kovesi Killerby, 'Heralds of a Well Instructed Mind', 273.

[25] Ibid.

[26] Archivio di Stato di Milano, *Fondo araldica, p.a.*, no. 139 [1566].

of Claudio Donati,[27] but otherwise have not, to my knowledge, been discussed in any detail elsewhere. They are both anonymous, written in the same hand, and have similar content, but their argumentative style is quite distinct. The first petition is relatively short (twelve pages), and is quite impassioned in tone. The second is longer (sixty-six pages), more measured, and adds more flesh to the arguments of the first.

There are various possibilities of authorship raised by the two documents. Verga simply assumes that they were written by manufacturers of the forbidden items and, from their content, this certainly seems to be the case. It could be that they were penned by two different authors but written out by the same copyist (and hence the reason for the same hand). It could also be that the authors knew each other, and discussed the issues at hand together, and hence the similarity in arguments. What seems more probable, however, is that they are two versions of an argument produced by the same author; the shorter, more impassioned piece functioning as a kind of draft for the second, more measured one. Indeed both documents contain the same recurrent phrases, and the second makes internal references to passages present in the first. Perhaps the author felt that the shorter draft was not articulated well enough and was too emotionally charged to convince the authorities to revoke the law.[28] Whilst both protests are discussed in what follows, due to its more substantive content and clearer articulation of the issues, a translation of the lengthier of the two protests has been appended here below.

The first petition begins, in the customary manner, with an appeal to the otherwise just good sense of its target. It praises the ruling governor and his prudent care for the good of the state, not just for the public but also the private good: 'The actions of Your Excellency in this state are well known in the world', it begins, for being not only 'very just but also most prudent', and these actions proceed 'not only most judiciously but also circumspectly always having regard to the public and private benefit'. But unlike other such petitions, this writer emphasises the governor's care 'most particularly' for the good 'of the merchants of this city and the infinite poor people dependent upon them', emphasising that 'they are all faithful servants of His Catholic Majesty and of His Excellency' the governor.[29]

---

[27] Verga, 'Le leggi suntuarie e la decadenza dell'industria', 61–63; and Claudio Donati, *L'idea di nobiltà in Italia. Secoli XIV – XVIII* (Rome and Bari: Editori Laterza, 1988), 134–135.

[28] I am grateful to Gianluca Caputo for suggesting this possibility to me.

[29] 'Anchor che l'ationi di vostra eccellenza così in questo stato come altrove siano state tale che habbino fatto conoscere al mondo che ella non solo è giustissima ma anco prudentissima et che sole procedere non solo giudiciosamente ma anco circonspettamente havendo sempre riguardo et al publico et al privato comodo e incomodo e intindendo il

From its opening paragraph therefore this petition sets itself apart from all those that have gone before it. This is not a noble pleading for the maintenance of long-held privileges for him or herself, but an individual writing on behalf of the merchants of the city, and on behalf of the poor of the city whose well being depends on their industry. Indeed despite later references in the petition to more nuanced hierarchies in the city, for the first two pages, the writer divides the city quite simply into nobles, merchants and the poor.

The second unusual aspect of this petition is its emphasis on an historical absence of distinction in clothing in Milan according to station and rank. The writer argues instead for the historic freedom of dress in the city. Although, as we have seen, Milan had passed only two prior sumptuary laws, the writer of this petition seems blithely unaware even of these, and emphasises instead that the historical experience of the Milanese has been one of complete freedom in dress. Moreover the writer indicates that not even natural hierarchies of clothing operated in the city. As the writer states, 'not just from memory of present times, but also from the memory of the most ancient writers of this city ... it has always been the case that there has been freedom of dress for everyone without distinction'.[30] In the absence of a larger corpus of Milanese sumptuary law it is hard to verify this assertion, but equally, on the same basis, it is possibly true and might indicate that the two previous sumptuary laws had remained dead letters.

This freedom of dress for all is then linked by the author to Milan's stability and social cohesion. Whereas other Italian cities sought to use differentiation in dress to maintain class distinctions as a stabilising force, the writer of this petition argues that such distinction in dress achieves the very opposite. To institute this law, the writer argues, would be most damaging for the populace of Milan because now, for the first time, you would have divisions between people, as their items of clothing would be regulated according to station. Now, the writer argues, you would pit nobles against knights, knights against merchants, merchants against plebeians and you would cause 'without doubt the greatest contestations, discords, controversies, and seditions in this most tranquil and most

mal potria occorer' nondimeno trattandosi di cosa è stato importante non solo al servitio di S[ua] M[aestà] Catt[olica]: del che vostra eccellenza hanno creduto li sup[lican]ti del che vostra eccellenza ne fien cura molto particularmente et diligentemente, ma anco al servitio del publico di questa citta et stato ma molto più particularmente delli mercanti di questa citta et infiniti poveri dependenti da loro ...'.

[30] 'Vostra Eccellenza ha da saper che non solo a memoria de passati tempi ma ne anco a memoria de antichissimi scrittori non si è mai trovato che in questa fosse constituita pragmatica ma sempre si è lassata questa libertà del vestir ad ognuno indifferentemente ...'.

quiet of cities which would of course be the most displeasing occurrence for any virtuous and most gracious Prince'.[31]

What is fascinating here is that every other Italian city made the opposite argument in its sumptuary laws, in other words that vestimentary codes are essential for order and stability and certainty of station in the city. Yet, whether true or not, here the writer clearly indicates that this had never been needed in Milan.

The bulk of the petition is then devoted to issues of trade and wealth. First, the writer argues, this law would stop, or at least greatly diminish, mercantile traffic in Milan. From this it follows that the tariffs from trade which are the nerve of the city's patrimony,[32] and all the other tariffs relating to personal clothing would diminish even more greatly because ceasing the commerce of the city would mean ceasing the commerce of foreigners who, in the greatest numbers, bring so much trade to Milan.

From this follows the next reason: 'nothing is dearer to a prince than to have his citizens rich and the city opulent'.[33] Such wealth had been essential in particular in times of war, so that the heavy imposts of warfare could be met with ease by its wealthy citizens. And, the argument continues, there is no better means to maintain the opulence of the city than to maintain the crafts and industries of the city, the products of which are bought not only by those within the city but by traders from far away. In particular cloth of silk and gold is singled out: 'The ingenuity of the Milanese in conceiving of, and creating, the most beautiful work not just suitable for ordinary persons, but also for Princes, Kings, and Emperors, means that His Majesty should glory in having in His states such industrious subjects'.[34]

---

[31] 'Non restarò anco di dirli che havendo questa legge a portar divisioni et distintioni da persona a persona da nobili et cavalieri principali da nobili a mercanti da mercanti a plebei et ignobili senza dub(b)io causereb(b)e grandissime contentioni discordie lutti dispareri et seditioni in questa tranquillissima et quietissima città il che quanto fosse dannoso e spiacevole ad ogni virtuoso e Leg[iadrissi]^mo principe Vostra Eccellenza che è nata principe e destinata a governi de nobilissimi stati lo può giudicare'.

[32] ' ... li datii di mercantia di questa città che sono il nervo del patrimonio region di questo stato patiriano ...'.

[33] 'Si aggiunge che niuna cosa deve essere più cara al principe che haver li suoi sudditi ric[c]hi et le città sug[g]ette opulente et dannarose ...'. Here 'dannarose' is understood as 'danarose', that is, moneyed.

[34] ' ... li ingegni de milanesi molto accomodati et industriosi in concertar bellissimi lavori foggie et altri concerti non solo accomodati a persone mediocre[i] ma anco a principi regi et imperatori la qual causa altra l'utilità dovervi esser in molta consideration presso ognuno et si doveria Sua Maestà gloriar di haver nelli stati suoi sog[g]etti industriosi et armati di mirabile ingegno ...'.

Here the writer inserts a little history lesson for the Governor. It is for this reason, the petition continues:

that in the city of Milan illustrious princes in the past, and Senates of old, considering how important and how useful it was for the city of Milan to have these crafts, prohibited through public laws and statutes, under the most severe penalties, any artisan, especially those tirelessly working in creating cloth of silk and gold, from going outside the city of Milan to teach their craft, knowing that if these crafts had been taught outside this city, its industry and greatness would have been much diminished.[35]

If this current law is carried out, however, then what are these workers to do except leave the city and teach others their skills? This would then have the highly undesirable result that nearby cities would become industrious mercantile centres and therefore wealthy, whilst Milan would become 'poor, negligent and lazy' ('povero, negligente et ocioso').

This is the first time, as far as I know, that an argument has been made in the Italian context against a sumptuary law on the basis of encouraging the industry of a city. Previously it is sumptuary law provisions themselves that have maintained that passage of the law would be to the benefit of the commerce of the city. In Venice, for instance, a sumptuary law of 1360 declared: 'our state has become less strong because money that should navigate and multiply ... lies dead, converted into vanities'.[36] Whereas Nicolosa Sanuti argued that the ornaments of a city and the display of its wealth are a source of honour, here, the writer continues, it is the industry of Milan itself that is honourable. Every station of person in the city – men and women, the most lowly to the highest, young as well as old, laymen as well as religious – by means of

honest crafts in gold as much as in silk works in honest labours for the desire of earning a living, ... but removing freedom of dress in the city will mean the loss of any occasion to work and to exercise these crafts and these people will be forced to abandon this country as they will have no other mode of life ... With freedom of dress, however, her mercantile industries prosper, the city flourishes and becomes fat [grassa] and opulent.[37]

---

[35] ' ... et per questa causa illustrissimi principi passati et li senati antichi considerando di quanta importanza di quanto utile fosse nella città de molto haver le arti per pudice leggi et statuti prohibirno [sic] sotto gravissime pene che niuni artifice et particularmente quelli che si affaticheno a fabricar drappi di setta et oro non dovessero andar fuori del molto ad insegnar tal arti non insegnassero se non a milanesi vedendosi che se a li arti fossero imparate fuori di questa città che saria scemata della industria et grandezza de molto ...'.

[36] Cited by Bistort, *Il magistrate alle Pompe*, 66, n. 2.

[37] ' ... viveno con il mezzo d' honeste arti così d'oro quanto seta et travagliandosi in honesti exercitij per desiderio di guadagno se astengano dalle male operationi le quali lasciandosi

The writer also believes that the industry of Milan has two other highly practical benefits for the city. The first is that it keeps youth off the streets and engaged in honest activity, and this, of course, brings honour to the city, and stops these youths from thinking of, or doing, bad things. The second benefit is one that seems obvious, but is a new argument as far as sumptuary law protest is concerned; the industry of Milan, it is argued, is not only of the greatest public and private benefit and a cause of growth for the city, but, it gives a living to the 'infinite poor people' ('infiniti poverelli') who would otherwise be forced to disperse elsewhere.

The second petition, translated here below, is similar in many respects, but, in addition to the practical arguments about the perceived damage to the industry of Milan that this law brings in its wake, it elaborates an ethic of consumption whereby consumption in and of itself becomes a moral good. It begins by invoking God in a way that is novel in arguments that have been gaining pace in the previous two centuries in Italy about greed and acquisition. Firstly, the writer argues, God gave man the gift of ingenuity and industry, and you can therefore get a glimpse of the divine in the rich clothing made here on earth, and even perhaps in those who wear such clothing judiciously. God, in other words, leaves his trace in the work of the artisan. Such an argument is in stark contrast to that advanced by Tertullian, and often invoked by legislators, who had argued many centuries earlier that if God had meant men and women to wear coloured clothing, He would have created blue sheep.[38]

More pertinently, the writer continues, you cannot pass a law that is only of benefit to a few, namely the nobles ('gentilhuomini'), who are by this law given the greatest freedom in clothing. Echoing the other petition, this writer states that it is a well-known fact that there has always been liberty of dress for all in Milan and that this has led to the city becoming wealthier than any other city in Italy. The real cause of problems in the city arises not from giving people freedom of dress, but from the vice of ambition. And, given that ambition is an act of the will, against which no law can do anything, you cannot argue that this same ambition would disappear just because you now had laws restricting clothing.

---

la libertà del vestire perderiano le occasioni del lavorar del travagliar si nel suo exercitio et sarebbeno sforzati ov[v]ero abandonar questi paesi ov[v]ero non havendo né modo de viver né patrimonio impiegar la vita sua per male operationi et far tutti li mali che poria secco, l'otio allo incontro stando la libertà del vestire come prima la quiete vive et si conserva la città resta florida industriosa mercantile grassa e oppulenta ...'.

[38] Tertullian, *On the Apparel of Women*, trans. S. Thelwall in Alexander Roberts and James Donaldson (eds.), *Ante-Nicene Fathers: Translations of the Writings of the Fathers Down to A.D. 325* (Buffalo: The Christian Literature Publishing Co., 1885), vol. 4. This proscription is in ch. 8.

Moreover, if you restrict the possibilities for people to buy clothing with their wealth, then you run the risk that they may use their money instead for other more sinful purposes.

It is God-given, man-made skill that is emphasised as the foundation of Milanese greatness. Because of the diligence of the Milanese workers, even the countryside has undergone 'a marvellous metamorphosis' from the sterile place that nature made, into a fertile man-made place, which has not just doubled but tripled the value of the lands to the great benefit of the nobles, of the merchants, of the workers and the whole city. And for this reason the city's forefathers had given to the craftsmen of the city not just freedom, but also privileges to encourage them to stay in the city and not share their secrets. From all of these great trades in the city the workers earn not only their own maintenance but also that of those dependent upon them: fathers, mothers, wives and spouses of their children, and also the infinite number of nuns who in their convents practice these crafts. Indeed, this writer goes so far to assert, a third of the mouths of the city are maintained due to the arts of gold and silk and other crafts.

As in the first petition, this writer also directly addresses the issue of vestimentary codes, and places it once again within a moral framework:

If one should say that it suits the city's decorum to be able to discern at first sight the non-nobles from the nobles, and the lesser nobles from the greater, we would reply that this means nothing. Even if we could eliminate ambition, we would not be able to find anybody actually willing to adopt that sort of decorum ... Moreover, if we did not already have freedom of dress, it would be wise to introduce it, if only in order to stimulate men to show openly their status, displaying their superior qualities not in the way they dress, but rather through their virtuous deeds.[39]

Liberty of dress is good, it is argued, because it animates in the souls of men a desire to strive toward industry, which is 'the foundation and soul of this city' ('il fundamento et l'anima di questa città'). The self-evident benefits to social order are stressed further because, through such attention to dress, young people, occupying themselves in thoughts of how to dress, have less time to think about adultery, or homicides, betrayals or other excesses.

This writer concludes with an impassioned plea: to disrupt the industry of the city in this unprecedented way would cause its downfall, especially 'when people are faithful and loving, as the inhabitants of Milan are, and where the Prince knows how to maintain the love of His subjects'. That love is fragile, however:

---

[39] Donati, *L'idea di nobiltà*, 135, argues that this sumptuary law was thereby in the interests also of impoverished nobles as it removed the visible competition fostered by the wealth of those lower down the social scale.

In order to preserve that love, He needs to avoid ruining matters that would thereby disrupt the peace of His citizens, particularly the freedom and extent of trade. If the law were to be adopted in this city, its overall wealth would be greatly diminished, since without the trade of the crafts of gold and silk, all other related activities would be terminated, or nearly so, as we have demonstrated. The great and honourable way with which to multiply the money of this city would be over. In addition, all those people who would suffer much as a result would try to take out of the city the greatest amount of money.

These two petitions express a whole new paradigm regarding consumption and its expression through clothing in Italy that had clearly been gaining momentum over the previous century. Here consumption of expensive textiles and all of the accoutrements of clothing is not merely a practice that should be reserved for elites, but a widespread universal practice with implications for everyone from the poorest in the city up to the highest levels. This consumption, and all those involved in its production, in and of itself, was argued to be an honourable thing.

Appendix: Text of Milanese petition against sumptuary laws[40]

In the name of God

We declare in the name of all those who might be affected by this matter, that the imposition of the law[41] concerning the dress of people in this city would be beneficial to no one, or only to the smallest minority, and would harm countless people, not just in particulars but also more generally, as well as harming the city and His Majesty himself, and should therefore not be allowed in any manner. To which matter we adduce the following reasons and considerations:

The first is that, pursuant to God,[42] although the matter pertains to theologians, speaking openly and submitting oneself to each and every better opinion, one could nevertheless say that, just as those who, through investigating the almost infinite works of [2] nature, come to

---

[40] Archivio di Stato di Milano, *Fondo araldica p.a.*, no. 139 [1566]. I am indebted to Gianluca Caputo for his careful work in transcribing the original text, and in assisting with its translation. The translation has attempted to preserve, as far as possible, the style and idiom of the Italian original, whilst rendering it into contemporary English. The original is almost entirely without punctuation, with long sentences consisting of a series of connected clauses. Punctuation and paragraphs have therefore been inserted to aid in clarity, and the frequent repetition of 'and' and 'but' has in many cases been removed. There are no folio numbers in the original, but numbers in square brackets inserted here indicate the folio breaks in the original.

[41] 'Pragmatica'. This refers to the pragmatica of 1565. This has been rendered simply as 'law' throughout the text.

[42] Lit. 'secondo dio' (lower case 'd' in the original).

some comprehension of the excellence of the great God, Creator and Protector of that same nature, so those who are more ignorant, contemplating the marvels of art, raise themselves in some way to a consideration of God's great wisdom, who infuses such knowledge into men, thereby comprehending in some way the great bounty of the self same God who, through His benignity, bestows ingenuity and industry on them; so they also glimpse the boundless and unintelligible Majesty of the self same God in Heaven upon seeing the majesty that rich garments and accessories[43] confer [3] upon earth, and perhaps they then favour anyone who uses them judiciously.

The second is that, pursuant to worldly matters, one first has to make three premises: The first is that not all laws befit all places, no matter how good they are. The second is that, whereas an ordinance cannot be beneficial to all those whom it affects, one should at least ensure that it will favour the majority and the most important people. The third is that, whenever an ordinance may generate good and evil, evil and good need to be counterbalanced diligently, and one has always to deliberate the ordinance in order to achieve the greater good, whilst avoiding the greater evil.

Now, moving on to the matter regarding the law. [4] If one were to infer that freedom of dress should cause universal detriment to the city, we would reply that this might be true for those cities where the purchasing of clothes involves sending money to other regions, because it weakens and impoverishes cities in many respects. But this is not true in our city, in which all those products relating to clothing are made here with the greatest abundance, such that not only does money stay in the city but also we make even more money by trading with foreigners, so that the law, which would be much more beneficial to those other cities, would be exceedingly harmful in ours. And this is so because where the conditions differ [5] so greatly, the laws should likewise differ.

But we entrust this truth to experience. Freedom of dress has been in place for such a long time [in Milan] that, if it were to harm the city, it would by now have been completely ruined. Whereas, on the contrary, we see in reality that year by year it has become ever greater, more popular, and more famous, and it is renowned in many places. It is surrounded by sturdy ramparts, and embellished inside and out with new and rich buildings. All this has occurred at the very peak of the greatest expenditure on clothing in general; an unmistakable sign that freedom of dress

[43] 'Apparati'.

not only does not harm the city, but, on the contrary, is distinctly beneficial to it, [6] as we will say in due course.

If one should assert that some cities have laws concerning clothing,
and yet textiles are still being manufactured in spite of them, we would
reply that it just so happens that there is not a city in the world that
produces such a great quantity of cloth of gold and of silk, and in so
many designs, and of such gold and silver, and that weaves so many
embroidered fabrics, and that makes numerous other sorts of products
with gold and silk, as are made in this one. And that, furthermore, the
cities that have such laws suffer greatly because of them, although not as
much as Milan would suffer due to the numerous types of work related
to the clothing industry that are made in this city (as we have said), and
also due to the fact it has been [7] well versed in this process since its
inception. Milan would suffer from limitations to freedom of dress more
than those cities that were founded, as it were, with such laws on their
heads, since their inhabitants have been used to them since birth, and,
adapting to them, have learned how to lead their lives accordingly. Truth
be told, if one thinks carefully about it, amongst others [...][44] although
those blessed cities, whomever they are, still produce cloth, whether of
silk or of gold, if one attentively and fully considers the matter, they
are not to be compared to this one neither in terms of greatness, nor in
industry, nor in the number of workers, nor [8] in the number of their
inhabitants, nor in wealth. Therefore, it would not be appropriate for
this city, which in freedom of dress stands above others, to be rendered
inferior to these others as a result of adopting this law, as this city where,
as we have said, men are accustomed differently, with such a sudden and
great change, would not be able to adapt.

If one should say that the aforementioned freedom in dress harms
many particular individuals, especially noblemen, we would reply that,
if it is true that it is a form of freedom, it is not therefore any form of
obligation[45] and cannot thereby harm anybody. If then one would rebut
that, although that freedom is not compelling in itself, it nonetheless [9]
has led to the creation of a compelling and harmful custom, we would
reply to this that it is not true that this custom was the consequence of
the abovementioned freedom. On the contrary, it sprang from ambition,
since it originates from the use of free will, which cannot be forced by any
law, nor by any lack of legislation. That this is the truth may be clearly
appreciated by the fact that this custom is not so stable as not to be subject to great change, as it was recently reformed and moderated in time

---

[44] This small section of the text is illegible.
[45] The expression in the original is: 'non obligation obligando'.

and place, both for men and women, since it is imprudent to follow it in many regards.

In addition, this is either a good, or a bad custom. If it is good, we should not try to change it or talk about it any further. If it is bad, it does not follow [10] as a consequence that freedom of dress is likewise bad, since we have shown above that the custom is not the consequence of this same freedom, but rather of ambitious will; therefore, it will become known as bad and shunned without taking the abovementioned freedom of dress away. Even if it will not be considered bad and shunned by everybody, it will at least be shunned by wise and prudent noblemen, who represent the majority of those who know well how to provide for and organise their matters without being harmed by the aforementioned freedom, which is good, or by that custom no matter how bad it is.

If one should say that we need also to look after those noblemen who, although they are very prudent, as a result of this custom nevertheless see fit to condescend in various and good respects [11] to expenditures which could be avoided with the adoption of this law (adding that it is also appropriate to look after those, assuming there are any, who spend inconsiderately and without measure on clothing, perhaps more than their wealth would allow, thus ruining their households in this and other respects), we would reply it would be great to remedy everything but, since this is impossible, we should remedy the most pressing matters, as we made clear in the first three assumptions.

Even if we grant for the sake of argument that the law might be beneficial to some noblemen, their number, meaning the number of those who could benefit from it, is so small, and therefore correspondingly small the good that might arise from it, [12] that their number is not to be compared with the number of those who would be harmed by it, following the damage to which the law could lead. In addition, those who might decide to spend recklessly if unable to spend on clothing as a result of the law, would without doubt spend their money on a thousand other, possibly less appropriate, things, and in a thousand other more harmful ways. But what matters the most is the particular harm that would be inflicted upon a nobleman by the universal harm the law would cause to all these cities.

It follows that one can with proven reasons and sensible conjectures foresee that he [i.e. the nobleman] would spend less by far without the law, [13] since everybody knows that the artisanal trades[46] render every city better and greater in some way when they are practised within it.

---

[46] 'Arti'. This can mean 'guilds', but in this context it is used for the various artisanal crafts and trades associated with the gold, cloth of gold and silk industries.

Hence, we see everywhere that artisanal creators[47] are sought after and held dear by Princes, and their merchandise and crafts much appreciated. Artisanal crafts do not just make our city of Milan great and powerful. In fact, all its greatness rests on the industry of its inhabitants. Since we do not have here wools, silks, cottons nor any sort of metal from our own mines and as primary materials, we would not have any products were it not for our industry, which by lively force[48] brings here all the afore-mentioned things in such quantities that could not be found in the territories where [14] they are normally produced. The things brought here in their primary and raw form are then, through our industry, turned into numerous and ingenious creations adapted for living comfortably and honestly.

Not only master craftsmen and managers[49] support themselves by virtue of the aforementioned industry, and their infinite workers, but this industry also fattens the marrow of the city, increases the number of inhabitants, and, in a manner of speaking, forces foreigners to bring their money here into our own pockets. This generates an increase in the consumption of grains and other provisions produced in our state, and so their price stays stable. And from this good another one springs; seeing that their assets are extremely profitable and do not lose value, the noblemen [of this city] [15] take pride and go to great lengths to find ways diligently to improve their agricultural lands, as one can appreciate in seeing the marvellous metamorphosis undergone by our country which, sterile by nature, has become very fertile, thus increasing the value of the land threefold.[50] All of this does not solely benefit the nobleman, or the merchant, or the worker, but all of them together, as well as all the city, since money, as we have said, does not leave the city but, in an endless cycle of change, the merchant gives it to the worker, the nobleman to the merchant, and the merchant and the worker to the nobleman. Actually, one could say that it is the nobleman [16] who benefits the most from it, since the much-increased value of his land is a stable element,[51] whereas the merchandise, meaning the merchant's money, is unstable.[52] The goods that the nobleman has to sell are goods of necessity, and as a consequence their sale is guaranteed, whereas the goods of the merchant

---

[47] 'Arteficii'.
[48] 'A viva forza'.
[49] 'Capi'.
[50] 'Triduplicato'. The meaning of this is not clear; it could mean either 'triplicato' (three-fold), or 'tri-duplicato' (increased sixfold). Classical Latin dictionaries register the past participle 'triplicato', (triplicāre).
[51] 'Immobile'.
[52] 'Mobile'.

are optional,[53] and as a consequence their sale is uncertain. Therefore, clearly and tangibly, one can see that the true essence and proper soul of this city is the industry of its inhabitants.

Being fully cognisant of this fact, our ancestors not only always ensured our artisanal trades were practised freely, but that they were granted privileges. In addition, they always strived to attract foreigners bringing new ideas with generous offers. And the production of gold and silver threads, which originates in this city, although it was attempted and started [17] in many other places, in none other does it flourish and is it considered on an equal level as it is by those here who have always favoured it, and cared for it as the principle [industry] and of the greatest profit and reputation to both the private and the public sector. And they have been exceedingly jealous of this production, granting generous privileges to the creators of this industry, and, what is more, with the most severe punishment forbidding anybody from taking their craft somewhere else, especially those that were of the greatest importance, honour and benefit, such as are those who, were the law to be imposed, would collapse to the ground, that is those of the gold and silk crafts, which feed almost one-third of the mouths in this city.

Nor should this come as any surprise to those willing to consider the high number of gold merchants, [18] embroiderers, shopkeepers, veil makers[54] and other gold and silk workers such as the silver and goldbeaters, and the gold and silver wire pullers[55] and chain makers,[56] the female master silk pullers, the spinners, weavers, the male and female warp threaders,[57] weavers who shape and work the gold threads, young people and shop boys, and finally all of those who, through their professional activities, sustain not only themselves, but also their fathers, mothers, wives, husbands, offspring and their families. Added to this is the infinite number of nuns, the offspring of Milanese noblemen, who in their convents attend to the aforementioned activities. So we realise that is was not an overstatement to have said [19] that one-third of the mouths of this city feed themselves thanks to the artisanal crafts of gold and silk, as well as the other things that are made with gold and silk, which are the precise activities that would be damaged by the law.

From all that we have demonstrated thus far, one should draw a firm conclusion: the harm of many is not to be compared with the benefit of

[53] 'Voluntarie'.
[54] 'Artefici di velami'.
[55] 'Tiratori'.
[56] 'Le filere'.
[57] 'Orditori' and 'ordinarie'.

a few noblemen. On the contrary, one can clearly see that the law would be more disadvantageous than advantageous even to those noblemen, since, if the law were to be instituted, we know with absolute certainty that they too would begin to doubt its efficacy, seeing that imposing on the many would result in the elimination of all, or nearly all, of the abovementioned crafts.

One should firmly believe that all other regions, [20] having seen the adoption of this law by us, where in many other cities with much honour, utility, greatness and reputation the inhabitants make their own textiles, and do all the other abovementioned activities related to clothing without paying excise duties nor transport costs, would decide immediately to make an example of our law, or dress according to its precepts, without adopting it.

It goes without saying that, if the production of gold thread and cloth of gold should decline, the production of silk cloth would increase. Since the Milanese gold thread and cloth of gold are the most excellent and wonderful that can be found, in general terms, it follows that a great number of foreigners come here regularly, many of whom come in order to buy such gold thread and cloth of gold who, for convenience sake, since they are already here, also buy silk cloth [21] according to their needs. If the law were to be adopted in this city (thus putting an end to the production of gold thread and cloth of gold), these foreigners would also no longer come here to buy silk cloth. On the contrary, they would elect some other city, and there are many, where the silk cloth is equal to ours or even slightly superior, due to either a better availability of raw materials, or to a secret skill and grace in that place. Therefore, there would be no spaces for silk production left here, nor the usual workplaces of those crafts, so that they would be completely, or nearly, extinguished.

Furthermore, being unable to sustain themselves in any other way, workers, artisans, and merchants would be forced to leave the city and go to practice their professions somewhere else. Nor would there be a shortage of places they could go to, [22] since there is no prince in any nearby city who would not willingly accept them and who, at the first available opportunity, would not go ably and astutely to attract them with notable gifts and privileges, inviting those merchants and craftsmen of ours who in his opinion, with some honourable gift and useful negotiation, could bring benefit and honour to some of his cities and territories.

There is one fine example of this, possibly more than one, and even if a few merchants and artisans decided to remain here, they would lose their usual profit, and we would surely see bankruptcies following from it. These bankruptcies would cause immense damage to countless interested parties, to both noblemen and others likewise. Such that the provisions of noblemen, due to the decline in the city's inhabitants, [23] due to the loss of earnings and of trade, and due to the bankruptcies, would also be among those who, through force of circumstance, would be unable to sustain themselves. Amongst others would also be those who grow mulberry leaves,[58] from whom this law would also take away their livelihood. In other words, removing the expense of three things would result in removing the income of four others. In addition, almost all merchants manage the capital of some noble friend; if they were unable to carry out their usual trades as a result of the law, they would also be unable to help that same nobleman in keeping and managing his capital, and giving him the agreed profit.

Those reasons would still be valid even if one were to object that dressing grandly[59] [24] causes dowries to increase uncontrollably. Even if we assume that it is true that this blessed notion of dressing grandly makes dowries escalate, it also increases the profit and earnings even of workers in the field; such that if the dowry used to be 50 *scudi*,[60] and now it is 100, so one who needed to sell 50 moggia[61] of grain to make 50 *scudi*, now needs to sell 100, thus giving to his son-in-law fifteen or twenty *pertiche*[62] of land, on the top of the aforementioned 50 *scudi*, as he has now to give him an additional 100 *scudi*. As it is, if the person who receives the dowry wishes to adopt this custom, he has to spend twice as much as he used to in clothes, therefore the dowry he receives is twice as much [25] as it used to be, and all that money will stay in the city, as we have repeatedly said.

Moreover, if the law were to be adopted, the nobleman and any other person would promptly start feeling its harmful effects, since he would have to dress not only himself anew, but his wife, and his family in line with the law, whilst rendering useless[63] the garments of cloth of gold in his house, or disposing of them with an ensuing great loss. Therefore, as we said at the beginning, the law would benefit no one, and it would damage countless others, as we have shown above.

If one should say that, nonetheless, justice and virtue demand the governors of cities to legislate such that each individual should comply with

---

[58] 'Foglie de moroni'. These are mulberry leaves from the *Morus alba*, or white mulberry, essential to the silk industry as they are the food of silk worms.
[59] 'Largamente'.
[60] See n. 13 above.
[61] The 'moggio' (plural 'moggia') is a measurement of grain. It was equal to 24 staia (one staio = 24.7 litres).
[62] The 'pertica' (plural 'pertiche'), or 'perch', can be a measurement of length, area, or volume. Here, as, a measurement of land, it is approximately 25.29 square metres.
[63] 'Morti', literally 'dead'.

the standards of their status,[64] we would reply that, even if we stretch it to the point of saying that this is part of justice, it would still be a very weak part, since it essentially does not concern [26] anyone's loss, and it would not be appropriate to have it as any special consideration, since adopting it would cause all the many evils[65] we have shown above.

If one should say that it suits the city's decorum to be able to discern at first sight the non-nobles from the nobles, and the lesser nobles from the greater, we would reply that this means nothing. Even if we could eliminate ambition, we would not be able to find anybody actually willing to adopt that sort of decorum. In any case, it would also be extremely surprising that, under such untenable pretension, one would be keen on trying such a pernicious thing, since this city has never seen such a disorderly way of dressing as not to be able to recognise, in same way, a distinction in people's quality. Moreover, if we did not already have freedom of dress, it would be [27] wise to introduce it, if only in order to stimulate men to show openly their status displaying their superior qualities not in the way they dress, but rather through their virtuous deeds. On the contrary, it seems that it should weaken the reputation of a city if the only way to recognise nobles would be through their clothing, as if nobility depended only on clothing and they were unable to make themselves known through other means.

After having replied to the reasons that could support the adoption of the law, and having demonstrated in various ways that freedom of dress is good, and the law is bad, for the sake of argument we will make below some relevant considerations, speaking finally about the harm his Majesty would suffer from it.

Freedom of dress is good because it sparks in the souls of men a [28] certain virtuous desire to make an impression, which stimulates and persuades each one, in line with his status, to industriousness which is, as we said, the foundation and soul of this city.

It is good because sensible young people, directing their thoughts as to how to dress, have less time to think about adulteries, men,[66] betrayals and other excesses.

It is good because from the freedom and diversity of dress of each person, we can easily come to distinguish men of arms and intellect from those who are not, which is a valuable asset for princes.

The law is bad because, since it would destroy the trades, as we have said, it would leave many young people of our city, who virtuously

---

[64] 'Grado'.
[65] 'Mali'.
[66] This is most likely a reference to sodomy.

commit to those trades, idle and wandering about, and nothing could be worse than that. [29]

It is bad because, no matter how much diligence is put into drafting it, it will never be so justly measured as not to give rise, due to differences in clothing, to confusion, contentions, animosity, and hatred between one level of society and another, and perhaps even among those within the same status, hence we would incur the risk of provoking those parts [of the population] that have already been provoked in this city, which would lead to innumerable deaths and the ruin of the citizens.

It is bad because it is incompatible with the strictest ordinances that the merchants, craftsmen and workers of the abovementioned gold and silk guilds have imposed on themselves to practise. If the law were imposed, the prince would either have to grant them permission to continue practising their professions, thus going against the law and the public good, or forcefully keep them here without granting them that permission, which would be unjust. [30]

Moving on to the harm His Majesty would suffer from it, it will be easy to demonstrate that He will suffer greatly in all the three benefits that this city, along with any other, can confer on its prince.

The first benefit consists in the number of inhabitants, since with them the city is preserved for the prince and defended from enemies in any pitched battles or sieges. With the adoption of the law, the number of inhabitants will diminish greatly, as we have shown above, since countless workers, craftsmen and merchants, who would no longer be able to sustain themselves and their families, would then be forced to leave their homes and would resettle somewhere else. [31]

The second consists in the income and revenues of the prince's financial Chamber,[67] because with these he sustains himself, accumulates wealth, and remunerates others. With the adoption of the law, the income and revenues of this Chamber would vanish, since lacking trade and the crafts, as we have shown above, excise duties would not be paid anymore, neither on raw materials brought here, nor on the innumerable products that are made with them. Since the majority of those products are sold in other states, this implies the payment of two excise duties, sometimes even three, because it just so happens that many goods are shipped through other territories, in addition to this state in which the duty is paid. [32]

Nor would His income and revenues suffer solely from the decrease in merchandise, but also as a consequence of the ensuing decrease in the number of inhabitants, because every person consumes salt, wine, bread,

---

[67] 'Camera'. In Milan top administrative matters were entrusted to a *consilium secretum*, or Privy Council. A special section of this Council, the Camera, dealt with the administration of finance under the Masters of the Entries ('Maestri delle entrate straordinarie').

meat and other foods on which taxes are paid, either wholesale, or retail, or both wholesale and retail, and this brings to His Chamber a considerable profit. It follows that if the number of the inhabitants of this city decreases notably, so do the revenues on levies, and the resultant profit.

This harm will be acknowledged as even greater when one considers that countless foreigners will cease to come, foreigners who come according to their needs[68] to buy and trade in the goods of the aforementioned guilds. They stay here days and weeks, eating [33] and drinking, consuming goods subject to our levies and taxes.

The third benefit for the prince consists in the overall wealth of the inhabitants, of which He makes use as the need arises. He can rely on this, especially when people are faithful and loving, as the inhabitants of Milan are, and where the prince knows how to maintain the love of His subjects. In order to preserve that love, He needs to avoid ruining matters that would disrupt the peace of His citizens, particularly the freedom and extent of trade. If the law were to be adopted in this city, its overall wealth would be greatly diminished, since without the trade of the crafts of gold and silk, all other [34] related activities would be terminated, or nearly so, as we have demonstrated. The great and honourable way with which to multiply money in this city would be over. In addition, all those people who would suffer much as a result would try to take out of the city the greatest amount of money.

It follows that, not just all three great harms taken together, but each one individually, should suffice for a rejection of the imposition of the law in this city. Everybody benefits from being wealthier, and the law would cause other major damages, both particular and universal, and many inconveniences, and dangers, as we have shown above. [35]

As seal and conclusion of this reflection, we wish to say two more things:

The first is that, since we appreciate that industry is the soul of this city, any damage or burden imposed on it, as well as any obstacle placed against the free trade of those goods it produces, will evidently lead to the ruin of this city.

The other is that many of our lords and princes, in fact almost all of them, previously persuaded by some particular person to disturb the marvelous industry of Milanese tradesmen [36] through taxation of merchandise, either through the adoption of a law, or something else, in the end became aware and touched upon the truth of all the aforementioned arguments we have wisely discussed, and decided to leave the esteemed Milanese industry in hereditary possession of its innate freedom.

---

[68] 'Alla giornata', that is, 'whenever they need to'.

8   Against the Law: Sumptuary Prosecutions in Sixteenth- and Seventeenth-Century Padova

Luca Molà and Giorgio Riello

For the *Censori* sopra le Pompe, the magistrates in charge of upholding the sumptuary laws of the City of Padova in the Republic of Venice, 16 April 1564 was a busy day. Two of the Censori stood at San Lorenzo Bridge, just behind the University and not far from the Palazzo della Ragione, the main civic building in Padova, while a third magistrate escorted the *Podestà*, the city's chief of justice (Figure 8.1a). They were accompanied by a notary and an assistant (*precone*). The surviving documentation states that their aim was 'to see and enquire anyone passing through wearing any sort of items against the sumptuary legislation'.[1] They did not have to wait long. They stopped passers-by who they believed were in breach of the city's sumptuary rules. They caught Giustina, wife of Doctor Antonio Musiano, 'who was wearing a gold chain attached to her fan', as a certain Giovanni de Cornalibus confirmed.[2] Elena, wife of Bortolomeo Enselmo, was also apprehended for wearing 'earrings with pearls' (Figure 8.1b).[3] Two men, Dotto di Dotti and Marco da Corno, were also stopped because they were donning velvet trimmed cloaks with embroideries.[4]

By now the news that the Censori were patrolling the entrance to the city centre must have spread across Padova, explaining their transfer to another prominent location in the city. They moved to the Church of Santa Chiara, where they stopped several more people. Among them was Alessandro Soncino, who was wearing 'a gold band around his cap and a pair of hose of light blue satin all striped with white ribbons'.[5]

---

[1] Archivio di Stato di Padova, Giudici del Maleficio (hereafter ASPGM), b. 30/2, reg. 3, fol. 3r: 'causa et occasione videndi et inquirendi an aliquis transiret, qui contrafaceret in aliquo partibus captis contra immoderatos ornatus'.

[2] ASPGM, b. 30/2, reg. 3, fol. 3v: 'qual haveva una cadena d'oro attacada al ventagio'.

[3] ASPGM, b. 30/2, reg. 3, fol. 4r: 'rechini di perle alle orechie'.

[4] ASPGM, b. 30/2, reg. 3, fols. 5r–6v: Dotto di Dotti 'haveva una capa con veludo a torno et rechami sopra il veludo a torno a torno' and Marco da Corno 'haveva una capa listada a torno a torno di veludo et sopra ditto veludo recamo de cordelline o altro'.

[5] ASPGM, b. 30/2, reg. 3, fol. 10r: 'qual hava un cordon d'oro a torno la beretta et un paro de calzoni de raso azuro tutti designadi de cordoni over altro bianchi'.

(a)   (b)

Figure 8.1 'Podestà di Padova' (a) and 'Gentildonna padovana' (b), from the *Album Amicorum* of a German soldier, Italy, 1595. Gouache on paper, 15.56 x 11.43 cm. Los Angeles County Museum of Art, Gift of the 1991 Collectors Committee (M.91.71.1-.101).

Another man, Enselmo de Enselmis, was wearing 'a cloak with ornament or ormesin strings, or of another type with decorations all around the garment'.[6] Dozens more men and women were stopped by the Censori that year and hundreds more faced prosecution for disrespecting Padova's sumptuary laws, as recorded in a series of trials in the city's archives. Our brief excursus on a day in the life of a city and its sumptuary concerns provides an entry point on how sumptuary laws came to shape people's sartorial choices. The cases of Marco da Corno, Giustina and Elena raise a series of questions about how sumptuary laws were not just enacted but also upheld.

The study of sumptuary regulation has relied on extensive published and unpublished sources. The body of legislation governing early modern expenditure on dress, banquets and ceremonies has been key to the understanding of what we might call 'the sumptuary phenomenon'.

---

[6] ASPGM, b. 30/2, reg. 3, fol. 11r: 'qual havea una capa con dopioni over cordoni de ormesino, o de altra sorte con gasi a desegno a torno a torno essa capa'.

Dozens – sometimes hundreds – of detailed laws have allowed historians to interrogate the nature of sumptuary regulation, its functions and aims, and its material and conceptual remits. Yet, a focus on legislative documentation has equally proven to be a limitation as it can only capture the prescriptive nature of the law, rather than how sumptuary laws were experienced and negotiated on an everyday basis.

This chapter focuses on the city of Padova in northern Italy, for which a substantial number of prosecution cases have survived. Padova was an important economic, cultural and political centre in the Veneto region in the northeast of Italy, well known for its university (founded in 1222) and as a prosperous Commune and later Signoria before becoming part of the mainland (*terraferma*) possessions of the Venetian Republic in 1405. Like many other Italian cities, Padova enacted several sumptuary laws, especially in the fifteenth and sixteenth centuries, with major acts issued in 1536, 1555, 1561 and 1569. Sumptuary enactments continued over the seventeenth and the first half of eighteenth centuries, though less frequently and comprehensively. Unlike other cities, however, Padova's legislators seem to have been rather more zealous in implementing sumptuary regulations, at least if we consider the high number of prosecutions deposited in the Paduan archives.

Prosecutions exist for other Italian cities but they very often consist of only short reports stating the names of the accused and the garments that were disputed by the authorities. This is the case for Florence considered by Giulia Calvi, where between 1638 and 1640 more than 160 women and 40 men were prosecuted for infringing the sumptuary regulations of the city. Among them were rich and poor people alike (notaries and craft masters, but also simple peddlers, hatters, shoemakers and even peasants) found in breach of the law. Men were wearing collars with white trimmings (very fashionable in the first half of the seventeenth century) longer than the measure allowed by law. Women were guilty of wearing dresses embellished with trimmings or were at times wearing jewellery with pearls and diamonds.[7] These Florentine prosecutions tell us about the crime committed but provide only limited insights into how people were apprehended, their reasons for wearing forbidden garments and accessories and the actual prosecution. By contrast, the sumptuary prosecutions for the city of Padova provide a fuller picture as they include extensive summaries of each recorded prosecution, sometimes extending over several pages. They state not just the accusation

---

[7] Giulia Calvi, 'Leggi suntuarie e la storia sociale', in Maria Giuseppina Muzzarelli and Antonella Campanini (eds.), *Disciplinare il lusso: la legislazione suntuaria in Italia e in Europa tra Medioevo ed età moderna* (Rome: Carocci, 2003), 213–230.

but also the testimonies of third parties and the defence by the accused. Although they only rarely include explanations as to whether the accused was found guilty and asked to pay a fine, these documents reveal a complex world of practices, attitudes to the law and the ultimate experience of the sumptuary regime.

This contribution thus aims to consider the ways in which sumptuary laws were experienced on an everyday basis. Rather than relying on an extensive body of sumptuary regulation, our chapter shows how prosecutions can be used to understand sumptuary practices. Our argument is that at least in the case of Padova – though such an argument could be extended to other Italian cities for which prosecutions are currently being studied – sumptuary laws were occasionally upheld through the action of specific magistracies.[8] Prosecution cases show however the difficulty of bringing offenders to justice and the resistance of both magistrates and common citizens in acknowledging the law. We start with a short overview of the sumptuary laws and their enforcement in the Veneto, followed by an analysis of the Paduan sumptuary legislation. The main part of this chapter will be dedicated to prosecutions, especially in the period between 1560 and 1620, when Padova's wealth and prosperity was at its highest and sumptuary enactments proliferated. We consider in particular the main actors of sumptuary prosecutions (magistrates, accused parties and witnesses), the situations from which prosecutions arose and the garments and accessories disputed.

Sumptuary Laws in the Veneto

An interest in sumptuary legislation in the medieval and early modern Veneto emerged during the final decades of the nineteenth century and – in line with a trend shared by other Italian regions – continued until the 1920s. In that period scholars and local antiquarians expanded their interests beyond traditional political and military history to include various aspects of urban society, everyday life and costume, topics frequently subsumed under the broad heading of 'private life'.[9] This first wave of research saw the publication of a large part of the sumptuary

---

[8] Documents attesting prosecutions for breach of sumptuary laws, at different points in time, have remained for Florence, Perugia, Siena, Venice, Ferrara, Bologna, Lucca and Viterbo. Catherine Kovesi Killerby, *Sumptuary Law in Italy, 1200–1500* (Oxford: Clarendon, 2002), 152–160.

[9] See, for instance: Luigi Tommaso Belgrano, *Della vita privata dei Genovesi* (Genoa: R. Istituto Sordo-Muti, 1875); Pompeo Molmenti, *La storia di Venezia nella vita privata dalle origini alla caduta della Repubblica*, 3 vols. (Trieste: Edizioni Lint, 1880); Luigi Frati, *La vita privata di Bologna dal secolo XIII al XVII con appendice di documenti inediti* (Bologna: Nicola Zanichelli, 1900).

legislation issued in the main cities of the Veneto: those of Venice, Padova, Vicenza and, to a lesser extent, Treviso. These texts were accompanied by ample commentaries on the nature, structure and functions of sumptuary laws in these cities.[10] From the 1920s onwards, however, interest in the history of luxury consumption declined both for the Veneto and for Italy more widely. With the exception of two essays dedicated to the city of Verona's sumptuary laws,[11] it was only at the end of the 1980s that interest in this field resurfaced, inspired by the growth of research in early modern consumption especially among Anglo-American scholars.[12]

This analysis of the sumptuary laws of the Veneto alerts us that Padova was an important but not unique city in the territories of the Republic of Venice. Between 1299 and 1600 Venetian councils produced well over a hundred decrees, some of them rather long and detailed. From the fifteenth century onwards, Padova's sumptuary laws were informed by the legislation issued in Venice. This is not surprising, considering that

---

[10] On Venice, see: Cesare Foucard, *Lo statuto inedito delle nozze veneziane, emanato nel 1299* (Venice: Nozze Marcello-Zon, 1853); Emilio Motta, 'Leggi suntuarie del 1476', *Archivio Veneto* n.s., 36 (1888): 244–246; M. Margaret Newett, 'The sumptuary laws of Venice in the fourteenth and fifteenth century', in T. F. Tout and J. Tait (eds.), *Historical Essays First Published in 1902 in Commemoration of the Jubilee of the Owens College Manchester* (Manchester: Longmans, Green and Co., 1907), 245–277; Giuseppe Giomo, 'Il lusso: leggi moderatrici – pietre e perle false', *Nuovo Archivio Veneto*, n.s. 16 (1908): 103–114; Giulio Bistort, *Il Magistrato alle Pompe nella Repubblica di Venezia. Studio storico* (Venice: R. Deputazione Veneta di Storia Patria, 1912; reprinted in Bologna: Forni Editore, 1969). On Vicenza, see: *Legge suntuaria vicentina tratta dal libro Provisioni esistente nell'archivio di Torre* (Vicenza: Tipografia Paroni, 1882); Domenico Bortolan, *Il lusso e le leggi suntuarie a Vicenza nel secolo XVI* (Vicenza: Tipografia Paroni, 1891). On Padova, see: Antonio Bonardi, *Il lusso d'altri tempi in Padova. Studio storico con documenti inediti* (Padova: R. Deputazione Veneta di Storia Patria, 1910). On Treviso, see: Federico Stefani, *Legge suntuaria circa il vestire degli uomini e delle donne ordinata intorno all'anno 1432 dalla città di Treviso* (Venezia: Nozze Galvagna, 1880); and Leone G. Pelissier, 'Notes et documents d'histoire d'Italie. Loi sumptuaire de Trévise en 1507', *Nuovo Archivio Veneto* 14 (1897): 52–57.

[11] Luigi Simeoni, 'Statuto suntuario a Verona nel XIV secolo', *Studi Storici Veronesi* 2 (1949–50): 235; Angelo Magnano, 'Documenti per una storia delle leggi suntuarie veronesi', *Atti e Memorie dell'Accademia di Agricoltura, Scienze e Lettere di Verona*, 6th series 22 (1970–71): 247–401.

[12] Stella Mary Newton, *The Dress of the Venetians 1495–1525* (Aldershot: Scolar Press, 1988); Piergiovanni Mometto, '"Vizi privati, pubbliche virtù". Aspetti e problemi della questione del lusso nella Repubblica di Venezia (secolo XVI)', in Luigi Berlinguer and Floriana Colao (eds.), *Crimine, giustizia e società veneta in età moderna* (Milan: Giuffré, 1989), 237–271; Federica Ambrosini, 'Cerimonie, feste, lusso', in Alberto Tenenti and Ugo Tucci (eds.), *Storia di Venezia dalle origini alla caduta della Serenissima, V. Il Rinascimento: società ed economia* (Rome: Fondazione Treccani, 1996), 441–520; Patricia Fortini Brown, 'Behind the Walls: The Material Culture of Venetian Elites', in John Martin and Dennis Romano (eds.), *Venice Reconsidered. The History and Civilization of an Italian City-State, 1297–1797* (Baltimore and London: Johns Hopkins University Press, 2000), 295–338; Luca Molà, 'Leggi suntuarie in Veneto', in Muzzarelli and Campanini (eds.), *Disciplinare il lusso*, 47–57.

Venice was one of the largest cities (with a population ranging between 100,000 to 170,000 in the period under consideration) and probably one of the most important markets for luxury goods and conspicuous consumption in Europe. Other cities of the Veneto, such as Verona (c. 50,000 inhabitants in the sixteenth century), Padova (40,000), Vicenza (30,000) and Treviso (20,000), all had autonomous but fragmentary sumptuary legislation before the end of the fourteenth century. In Padova a first law on weddings issued in 1277 was followed by a second one on funerals – decreed by its lord Francesco Novello da Carrara – as late as 1398.[13] The number of laws, however, grew everywhere in the region after the early fifteenth century, as a response to the increase of luxury consumption.

The early fifteenth century coincided also with the expansion of Venice on the mainland. Sumptuary laws were thus restructured and re-issued by the various cities of the Veneto and eventually updated on a regular basis every twenty-five to thirty years. A look at the statutes shows that between the mid-fifteenth century and the end of the sixteenth century, sumptuary laws were reissued on at least five occasions – in 1456–1460, 1502–1507, 1533–1536, 1559–1562 and 1590–1595 – suggesting that each generation was keen to update sumptuary legislation to keep it in line with the times. This chronology explains why the laws of the different cities of the Veneto informed each other and in turn were informed by the Venetian legislation. For instance the sumptuary laws of 1488 and 1504 for Padova refer explicitly to laws recently enacted in Venice, as do other decrees issued afterward.[14] This is not surprising, as any sumptuary decision by the civic councils of the cities of the Terraferma had to be taken in the presence of the representative of Venice and had to be later ratified by the Republic's Senate. This was no rubber stamping exercise: in 1459 a new law was proposed in Padova by the *Deputati ad utilia*

---

[13] Bonardi, *Il lusso di altri tempi*, 9–11.

[14] Bonardi, *Il lusso d'altri tempi*, 161–162, decree of 16 June 1504: 'La natura et condition del sexo femineo, pien de vanità per l'ocio, cason de molti mali, et la poca prudentia de chi mal misura i fati soi e le dannose spese in nove foze et superflui ornati, conduse questa povera città de Padoa a gran miseria [...] E questo intervien che niun vuol apparer inferiore del compagno; e molti sono astreti a far più de quelo porta le sue condictioni; e a tal partito la città se impie de povertà. E le cosse vano de mal in pezo: et questo tollerato inconveniente cesseria chi metesse qualche regola, la qual non se partendo dal honesto havesse a refrenar li immoderati et dannosi apetiti, come novamente ha fato la Illustrissima Signoria nostra, la qual ha troncato queste dannose superfluità, stranie foze et excessive spese cun insoliti portamenti d'habiti [...] Onde imitando lo sapientissimo esempio de coloro soto al cui governo et protectione se vive, che da ferma speranza de esser exaudite le preghiere et sancte provision fatte per ben de questa soa fidelissima cità, la qual gie diè esser cara'. The reference here is to the sumptuary law issued by the Venetian Senate on 3 January 1504; Archivio di Stato di Venezia, Senato, Terra, reg. 14, fols. 196v–197r.

(the Podestà's advisors) and approved by the city Council. However, the Senate in Venice refused to ratify the law. The bone of contention was the fact that the new Padova law allowed two silk garments to the wives, daughters and daughters-in-law of noblemen, knights, doctors and merchants, but only one silk garment to women belonging to artisans' families. Eventually a new version was approved by the Senate in Venice in 1460 but only after 'all women [in Padova] whether married or not and of whatever status and condition' were allowed two silk garments each.[15]

The period between 1530 and 1570 is particularly rich in sumptuary enactments and prosecutions. The revived economic position of the city led many to question the new riches of its inhabitants. This explains why in 1536 the City Council passed a sumptuary law specifically targeting the dress and luxury of men, in contrast to previous laws that had legislated only on the dress of women. This law applied to every man and forbade any garment with zibeline linings, or with slashes, strings, embroideries, gold or silver fringes. Silk could be used on sleeves and to cover buttons, but not more than four *braccia* could be used. Men could not wear hose of gold or silver cloth, velvet, satin or damasks (including their linings). Gold and silver ornaments were generally not allowed with the exception of rings. Silk shirts or shirts with gold and silver threads were also forbidden. Simple berets of velvets were allowed for men. The 1561 law equally forbade men of whatever station all ornaments in gold, silver, pearls, jewellery and enamels to be worn, not just on their person but also as paraments for their horses and mules (in this case with the exception of cavaliers according to their grade). No slashing, embroidery, pleating or embossing in gold and silver were allowed. A maximum length of silk cloth was established for coats, doublets and capes as well as for hose (which could only have simple taffeta and ormesin linings). The law also established that tailors, designers and embroiderers had to pay a high fine if found guilty of supplying forbidden items.[16]

Similar regulations are to be found in the sumptuary laws issued in the same year, 1561 in Bologna and in Venice in 1562, which were addressed to both men and women. The main concern of the legislators, as in Padova, was that all apparel and accessories (including bonnets, hats, coifs, gloves, belts, etc.) should be plain (*schietti*), without embroidery,

---

[15] 'Mulier sive nupta sive non, cuiscumque status et conditionis existat'. Bonardi, *Il lusso d'altri tempi*, 23–31, here p. 23. See also Archivio di Stato di Venezia, Senato, Terra, reg. 4, fols. 143v–144v, 20 May 1460.

[16] See Bonardi, *Il lusso d'altri tempi*, 51–52, 170–180 (1538 law) and 195–203 (1561 law).

enamel, gold and silver thread or perfumed with musk and amber. Venetians declared that fabrics employed in dressing should be woven in a single colour, and prohibited the use of patterned cloth (*a opere*) or with a new design (*invenzione*). Taffeta, ormesin and satin were generally allowed, while even items of simple velvet clothing were limited in number. All these laws expressed a particular concern for very expensive velvet with piles of different heights (*velluto altobasso*), and in Padova the 1561 decree specified punctiliously the many forbidden variations of velvet cloth, showing incidentally the incessant evolution of this type of highly fashionable fabric during the sixteenth century and the difficulties in controlling new fashions.[17]

Whilst the Venetian sumptuary legislation in the 1560s and 1570s gave one year of immunity to all foreigners who established themselves in the city, those of Bologna and Padova exempted from the restrictions all foreign students attending their famous universities as they were of major importance for the local economy.[18] Their attire would have contrasted starkly with that of the young members of the Paduan nobility, had the latter strictly followed the dictates of the law. This, however, was unlikely to have happened considering the political and social evolution of Padova in the sixteenth century, where a restricted number of patrician families acquired growing power until they were finally able to monopolise civic offices by the early seventeenth century. The Paduan nobility detached itself from trade and productive activities and aimed at living as *rentiers* out of their estates in the countryside. A new mentality saw all mechanical work as degrading, and families went to great lengths to demonstrate their ancient noble lineage. The concepts of civility and honour became prevalent among this group, as did the necessity of dressing in a

---

[17] Such velvets included 'veluti figurati, stampati, alti bassi, veluti rizzi, pelosi, franzati, stochati, disfilati, faldati o puntizati, paerte tessuti et parte non, parte di veluto parte di raso, et ogni altra foza nova'. Bonardi, *Il lusso d'altri tempi*, 197; Bistort, *Il Magistrato alle Pompe*, 373–414; Maria Giuseppina Muzzarelli (ed.), *La legislazione suntuaria, secoli XIII-XVI. Emilia-Romagna* (Rome: Ministero per i Beni e le Attività Culturali, Direzione Generale per gli Archivi, 2002), 203–209.

[18] In Bologna the law of 1561 stated that: 'Non intendando compresi nella presente provisione li scolari forestieri, né gli altri forestieri che al presente sono o verranno in questa città, quali si tolleranno et tolleraranno in quelli habiti che a loro piacerà' ['The present law does not include foreign students, or other foreigners that at present or in the future will come to this city, whom are and will be allowed the clothes that they best please']. In Muzzarelli (ed.), *La legislazione suntuaria*, 207. In Padova a sumptuary law of 1575 specified: 'Che li forestieri che staranno in questa città per tre anni con la sua famegia siano sottoposti a questa parte, eccettuando li scolari forestieri et li dottori leggenti forestieri' ['That foreigners who have lived with their families in this city for three years be subjected to the sumptuary law, except foreign students and foreign professors']. Bonardi, *Il lusso d'altri tempi*, 92, and 219.

manner that could demonstrate their superior status, causing continuous tensions with a body of sumptuary laws aimed at limiting conspicuous consumption for all social groups.[19]

Enforcing the Law

Historians have long argued that sumptuary laws remained a 'dead letter' and were not often enforced. This assessment seems to be confirmed by the frequent reiteration of laws. Interpretations as to why enforcement was unsuccessful differ between those historians who consider it an impossible task, due to the complexity of controlling people's consumer choices, and those who point instead to a distinctive lack of intention on the part of legislators for enforcing laws that were obviously unpopular both among the elite and the lower ranks of society.

Catherine Kovesi observes that archival sources might suggest that enforcement was far from uncommon though it might not have been systematic. First, the laws themselves included references on their implementation that appeared early in Italy compared to other European cities and nations (Figure 8.2). Far from being ineffective or simply moralising legal acts, Kovesi argues that sumptuary laws were applied and had a real impact on people's lives.[20] Their importance can be seen in the fact that they were often published (as in the case of Padova) and read publicly as new sumptuary laws were enacted.

Second, the laws relied on specific bodies enforcing the rules that they contained. This was often done through existing magistracies and notaries. In thirteenth- and early fourteenth-century Bologna and Siena, for instance, it was the Podestà of the Comune who was entrusted with supervising compliance with sumptuary regulations.[21] Later on the officials in charge of the actual application of the law were especially appointed, as in the case of the *ufficiali dell donne* (officials on women), an office established in Florence in 1333.[22] Separate magistracies were established in other cities such as the short-lived official position of the *donnaio* in Siena in the 1320s. The 'professionalisation' of sumptuary enforcement was however a rather late and

---

[19] The social and political evolution of Padova in the early modern period has been surprisingly little researched. The best overview for the growing divide among social groups remains Angelo Ventura, *Nobilità e popolo nella società veneta del Quattrocento e Cinquecento* (Milan: Unicopli, 1993), 189–251.

[20] Kovesi Killerby, *Sumptuary Law in Italy*, ch. 7.

[21] Muzzarelli (ed.), *La legislazione suntuaria*, 5, 50–73; Maria Assunta Ceppari Ridolfi, 'Un caso toscano: Siena', in Muzzarelli and Campanini (eds.), *Disciplinare il lusso*, 60–61.

[22] Carole Collier Frick, *Dressing Renaissance Florence: Families, Fortunes and Fine Clothing* (Baltimore: Johns Hopkins University Press, 2004), 183.

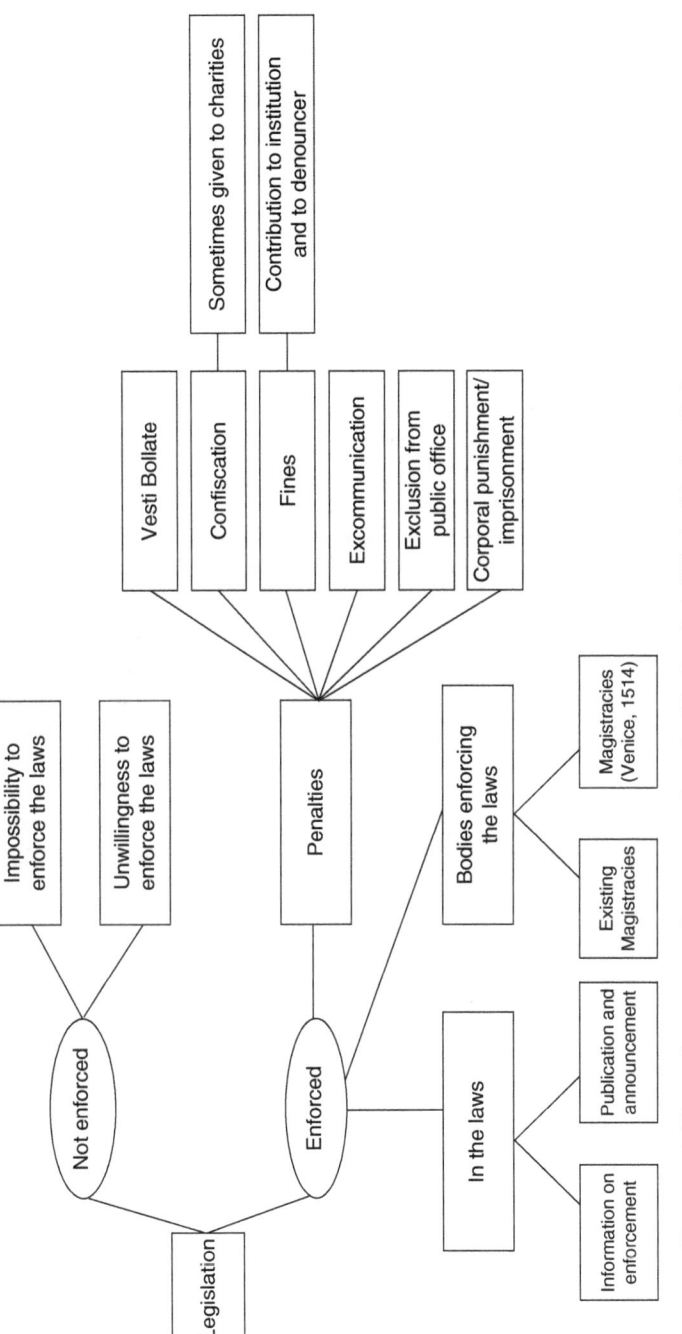

Figure 8.2 The enforcement of sumptuary laws in Medieval and Early Modern Italy.

partial phenomenon. In the case of Venice, for instance, the separate institution of the Magistrato alle Pompe (Sumptuary Magistrate) was established only in 1514 whereas in Vicenza the office of the Censori was first created in 1536.[23]

Finally, sumptuary laws established a series of precise penalties, the most common of which were fines, the confiscation of the forbidden goods and the taxation of exempted items. The latter – often referred to as 'vesti bollate' (sealed garment) – granted exemptions to existing garments from a new law by paying a certain amount of money and registering the specific items.[24] This has been seen as a quasi-tax.[25] Confiscation was also not uncommon, as the item was used as proof in an eventual prosecution and could be used for charitable ends. Fines were the most common measure in enforcing sumptuary laws.[26] These were paid both by consumers/wearers and producers. Rare forms of prosecution included the excommunication of those proved guilty and, in the case of men, their exclusion from public office for specific periods.[27] Corporal punishment and imprisonment were seldom used, though – as the case of Venice shows – they could be inflicted in special circumstances.[28]

The enforcement of sumptuary laws in Padova was established in the very text of the laws through the indication of specific penalties and by minutely regulating the remit of action of the sumptuary magistracy (Magistrato alle Pompe). Padova is an important case not just because of the unique survival of prosecution cases, but also because the city followed the pattern of sumptuary enactment of other Italian cities. As we have already seen, the first regulation forbidding large wedding banquets was enacted as early as 1277. A century later, in

---

[23] Bistort, *Il Magistrato alle Pompe*; Mometto, 'Vizi privati', 260–261.

[24] A list of all garments allowed as 'vesti bollate' for the city of Bologna was compiled in 1401 and has been edited by Maria Giuseppina Muzzarelli (ed.), *Belle vesti, dure leggi: 'In hoc libro continentur et descripte sunt omnes et singules vestes'* (Bologna: Costa editore, 2003).

[25] This was the case of the 1415 Florentine statutes that established that on payment of 50 florins to the city's exchequer, a lady could wear any prohibited attire, embroidery or jewellery for a year. Jane Bridgeman, ' "*Pagare le pompe*": Why Quattrocento Sumptuary Laws did not Work', in Letizia Panizza (ed.), *Women in Italian Renaissance Culture and Society* (Oxford: European Humanities Research Center, 2000), 219–220.

[26] On fines and denunciations see: Maria Giuseppina Muzzarelli, 'Il corpo spogliato. Multe, scomuniche e strategemmi per il rispetto delle leggi suntuarie', *Micrologus* 15 (2007): 399–423.

[27] Maria Giuseppina Muzzarelli, 'Reconciling the Privilege of a Few with the Common Good: Sumptuary Laws in Medieval and Early Modern Europe', *Journal of Medieval and Early Modern Studies* 39/3 (2009): 609–610.

[28] Kovesi Killerby, *Sumptuary Law in Italy*, ch. 7.

1398, further laws were enacted to regulate expenditure on baptisms and funerals.[29] Padova therefore was not an early implementer of sumptuary laws but followed the examples of larger and more politically influential cities such as Florence and Bologna. It was only in the second half of the fifteenth century, after being conquered by the Venetian Republic, that Padova started enacting comprehensive sumptuary laws. Two major laws were produced in 1440 and 1460. Between 1440 and 1684 around twenty laws were enacted altogether. Following the political and economic crisis of the first two decades of the sixteenth century, from the 1530s to the end of the sixteenth century the city was particularly active in enacting detailed laws in 1536, 1555, 1561 and 1569. Such laws, often thirty to forty pages long, were comprehensive in their coverage as we have seen for the case of the 1536 and 1561 laws. These were also the periods in which the bulk of prosecution took place.

If from a chronological point of view the Paduan sumptuary laws are unremarkable, the same cannot be said about their structure. Throughout the period considered they were 'generic' rather than 'selective' laws. This means that unlike sumptuary laws in France and in several other Italian cities such as Perugia and Bologna, the Paduan sumptuary laws did not distinguish between people of different social and economic standing but forbade or allowed garments, foods and accessories for the entire population without social distinction.[30] Like the Venetian laws by which they were inspired, the sumptuary laws of Padova were not conceived as a way to distinguish the rising bourgeoisie from the nobility – both groups were equally prosecuted.[31] This did not mean that sumptuary laws in Padova ignored social hierarchy or sartorial competition. Bonardi, writing in the early twentieth century, observed that especially in the sixteenth century the Paduan bourgeoisie was getting richer while the nobility was declining. He therefore

---

[29] Antonio Bonardi, *Il lusso di altri tempi in Padova: studio storico e documenti inediti* (Venice: Tipografia Libreria Emiliana, 1909), 9 and 11.

[30] Bonardi, *Il lusso di altri tempi*, 17.

[31] This principle had already been applied to Venice in the so-called 'prima serrata' of the Maggior Consiglio in the late thirteenth century that divided Venetian society into three groups: nobles, citizens and populace. Eventually this hierarchy was extended to other cities of the Veneto. By the 1460s the sumptuary laws of Venice and the other cities of the Veneto did not distinguish between social or professional groups applying the laws to all inhabitants. See Frederic C. Lane, 'The Enlargement of the Great Council of Venice', in J. G. Rowe and W. H. Stockdale (eds.), *Florilegium Historiale: Essays Presented to Wallace K. Ferguson* (Toronto: University of Toronto Press, 1971), 237–274; Stanley Chojnacki, 'Social Identity in Renaissance Venice: The Second Serrata', *Renaissance Studies* 8/4 (1994): 341–358.

proposed the argument that sumptuary laws were a tool on the part of the nobility to impose 'equality' with other rich citizens. If the nobility could not outdo the rising bourgeoisie, sumptuary laws prevented the bourgeoisie from outdoing the nobility.[32]

Bonardi might have had a point if we consider another peculiarity of the sumptuary laws of Padova: they were less concerned with quantities (number of dresses for instance) and paid instead more attention to the quality of the textiles used, the types of garments and the value of jewellery worn. The use of silk, trimmings, necklaces, and other accessories and jewellery was at the core of both sumptuary regulations and prosecutions. A further specificity of the sumptuary laws of Padova is that over time they moved from the regulation of dress and accessories to paying increasing attention to the use of carriages, to banquets and food, the dress of prostitutes and also nuns, the dress of servants and their public visibility and the regulation of seamstresses and tailors.

Over time, the laws also came to articulate the legal processes that supported them. Fines were established for those who did not respect the laws, which increased in cost over the course of the fifteenth and sixteenth centuries. In 1488, for instance, anyone found in breach of sumptuary regulation was fined 200 *lire* and had the items confiscated. Half a century later, in 1536, fines were raised to the substantial sum of 50 ducats.[33] At the heart of any prosecution was the Magistrato alle Pompe, a body formed of five Censori who were selected from the notables of Padova. These were salaried positions and their holders were given in addition between a quarter and a third of the value of fines. They were at times helped by the Capitani and soldiers, who were not paid for their services, though their expenses were reimbursed.

As we have seen, it was not uncommon for the Censori to initiate a legal case simply by stopping suspects during one of their occasional patrols in the streets of Padova. If instead a denunciation was sent to the magistrates, the Censori had the right to summon the person accused. Denunciations could be made in person or in writing to the office of the Censore. In both cases, the identity of the denouncer was kept secret in all following legal proceedings. An example is found in an anonymous denunciation of 1623 (Figure 8.3): 'Signora Girolima Conte: coloured sleeves, long pearl necklace; Countess Emilia S. Bonifazia: coloured sleeves with flowers, gold and pearls and a long necklace' that the denouncer saw in the house of the Cavalier Capo di Vaca in San Stefano,

[32] Bonardi, *Il lusso di altri tempi*, 19.
[33] Bonardi, *Il lusso di altri tempi*, 37 and 52.

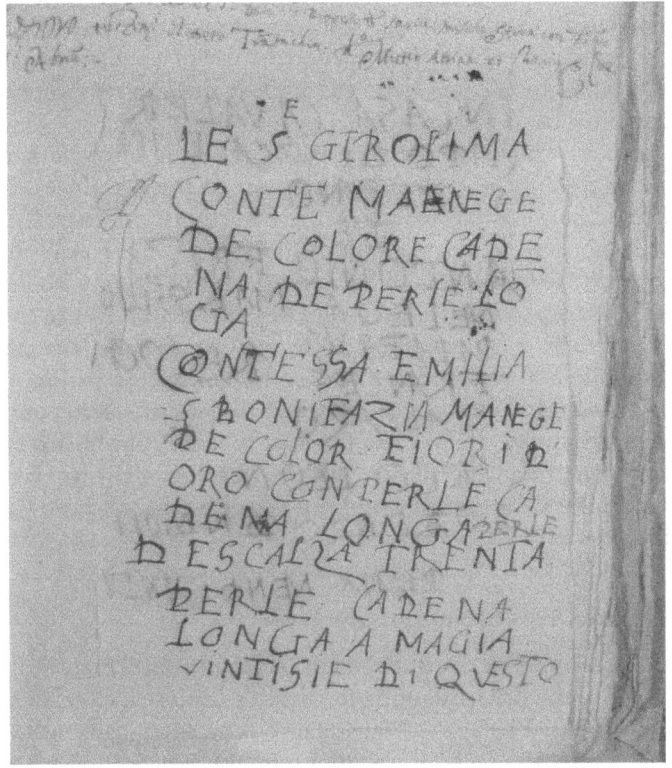

Figure 8.3 Anonymous denunciation, ASPGM, 30/5, 7 January 1623.

citing also a list of testimonies and asking the prosecutor to devolve the
fine to beggars.[34]

It was not uncommon for denouncers to place messages like this in a
small box (*cassetta*) in front of the Palazzo del Capitanio, the office of the
authority of the Republic of Venice. When an accusation was received, the
Censori had no more than two weeks to summon the party and initiate
the prosecution (otherwise the Censori themselves were liable to be fined
25 *lire*). The trial itself was at the heart of the prosecution procedure.

---

[34] ASPGM, 30/5, 7 January 1623, loose sheet inserted in the register: 'Le S.e Girolima
Conte manege de colore cadena de perle loga; contessa Emilia S. Bonifazia manege de
color fiori e oro con perle cadena longa; zerie descalza trenta perle cadena longa a magia;
vinstisie di questo in case Cavalier Capo di Vaca e in S. Stefano. te(stimoni) Antonio
Frizimelega, Marssilio Papafava, Frances(co) Relogi Galeazo Checo Leoni, Lorenzo
Bingioli. Pena mendicanti'.

The accused or one of his/her representatives could call for witnesses to testify on their behalf, while the Censori called in witnesses for the prosecution. A verdict was reached through the use of a ballot box. The entire procedure had to last less than a month. If the Censori were too slow, they could be fined 100 *lire*.

In cases in which the accused was found guilty, he/she had to pay the fine to the ufficio of the Censore (part of the tax office). This sum was divided between the accuser, the Censore and charities. If the guilty party did not pay, it was the task of the Censori once again to inform the Capitano within a month to avoid a fine of 25 *lire*. The laws also established a process of appeal chaired by the Rettori of the city who, if in disagreement, could ask the help of the Camerlengo (the city's fiscal authority). The appeal process had to be completed in less than two months. Meanwhile, the guilty party had to deposit a sum equivalent to the fine with the Monte di Pietà (civic or religious pawnbrokers). It was also established that the Rettori did not have the right to overturn the decision of the Censori but could send the case back to the Censori to be reconsidered.[35]

The Lives of Sumptuary Laws

This complex system of enforcement was more than mere words, as in the course of the sixteenth and seventeenth centuries it led to hundreds of prosecutions. The rest of this chapter considers sumptuary laws in practice by focusing on prosecutions in the period 1560–1620. Our concern is not to prove the effectiveness of the law.[36] It is evident that, as in the case of Florence and other cities for which we have evidence, prosecutions cluster in the years following the enactment of new laws or the reiteration of existing ones, with long periods in which there were no prosecutions at all. The law is here interpreted instead as a socio-cultural phenomenon in which the motivation of both legislators and citizens and the avoidance strategies and resistance of the latter are seen as part of the everyday practices surrounding conspicuous consumption, the challenging of established social hierarchies and the administration of the law. We concentrate here on sartorial consumption and focus in particular on three main issues. First we wish to consider the spatial nature of enforcement in a city like Padova that was large but was not a metropolis of the

---

[35] Bonardi, *Il lusso di altri tempi*, 82–83.

[36] This has been a common approach to sumptuary prosecutions, though Hunt admits that 'The relationship between effectiveness and enforcement is complex'. Hunt, *Governance of the Consuming Passions*, 328.

size of Rome, Paris or London. Second, we analyse the ways in which sumptuary laws were negotiated and even opposed in their implementation and highlight the role played by witnesses. And finally we conclude by considering which consumer goods were targeted by the laws and discuss in detail an intriguing case of a new type of consumer product.

The Space of Sumptuary Laws

We have already encountered the Censori surveilling the streets of Padova. The magistrati alle pompe's authority was manifested – and one might say was visually and physically confirmed – in the space of early modern streets and city squares. Yet this does not mean that the process of what we might call 'sumptuary application' was at all straightforward. The Censori faced several problems, among which was whether their authority would be challenged.

The Censori were not necessarily able to stop everyone passing in the streets of Padova. Several accusations against people on board coaches and carriages that could not be stopped are recorded. On the 16 April 1564, Donna Daula, wife of Count Borse San Bonifacio, for instance, was seen wearing 'a string of pearls round her neck and another long string of pearls' while travelling in a carriage.[37] Paola Borromea, wife of Francesco Borromeo, was also seen passing though in a carriage decorated in gold (against the laws), wearing forbidden earrings.[38] In these, and other, cases in which the offenders were actually apprehended, the forbidden items had to be deposited within days to avoid large fines. Visits to private residences by the magistrates could follow, as in the case of Elena, wife of Bortolomeo Enselmo, whom we have already encountered, who was seen wearing pearl earrings. Three weeks after the episode, the magistracy's clerk went to see Elena at her home and a written document was later submitted by one of the lady's representatives to the magistracy. Similarly, anonymous denunciation was followed by visits to private homes by the magistrates.

These cases alert us to the fact that the implementation of sumptuary laws happened in communities where people knew each other personally. An anonymous denunciation might not remain such for long, thus raising questions about who might be one's enemy or friend. To walk around town wearing items forbidden by the law was a risk, as neighbours, friends and other fellow citizens might think it worth reporting to the

---

[37] ASPGM, b. 30/2, reg. 3, fol. 8v: 'qual havea un fillo de perle strette al collo, et una filza de perle longhe'.

[38] ASPGM, b. 30/2, reg. 3, fol. 8r: 'et era sopra un cochio dorado torno a torno'.

authorities. This was the case for Cassandra, wife of Alessandro da Lion, accused of wearing forbidden bracelets while walking with her servants near her home. On the 27 May 1562 a certain Giulio Vigonza testified:

one day last week – I cannot remember if it was Thursday or Friday – I was in the company of monsignor Francho, messer Beneto de Dotori, messer Riccardo Trevisan and messer Raffaele Novellino and we were doing some exercise walking along the [city] walls between S. Benedetto and S. Lunardo. And so we reached a lady [walking] with two servants, and I asked who she was as I did not know her, and I was told [by the companions] that she is the wife of messer Alexandro Leono, sister of messer Jacopo Brunello. And so passing through, one of our group – I cannot remember whom – said: "it is not right, she is in breach of the law", or something similar. And so I turned and looked at the lady, and I thought that she was hiding her hands so that they could not be seen. And she swiftly entered a door through the back of the walls. And our group thought that she had bracelets or chain bracelets, but I did not see them. I cannot remember who said so: "do not hide them", or similar words, but it was one of our group.[39]

Other members of Vigonza's party testified that Cassandra 'was in breach of the sumptuary laws as she was wearing bracelets'. We have here a small vignette of the dangers of sumptuary infractions, in this case brought against a woman walking in a relatively safe place far away from the city's main squares. Cassandra must have panicked on being challenged by these four men and their servants. One of these servants testified that 'I saw that she took off something from her arms, and put these things in her pocket. But what these were I cannot say, as I was behind my master, and I could not see [...] I heard the gentlemen saying [...] that she had bracelets on her hands'.[40] There is clearly a gendered dimension

---

[39] ASPGM, b. 30/2, reg. 2, fol. 105v, 27 May 1562: 'Io non scio questo altro se non che ritrovandami un giorno de la setimana passada, et non vi saperei dir certo se fosse la zobia o venere, in compagnia del reverendo monsignor Francho, excellente messer Beneto de Dotori, l'excellente messer Ricardo Trivisan, messer Raphaelo Novellino, et caminavamo in atto de exercitio drieto alle mure che vano dal ponte de S. Benedetto a quelle de S. Lunardo. Et così fra via agiongemo una gentildonna con due massare, la quale non cognoscendo io, dimandai chi era, et mi fu ditto questa è la mogliere de messer Alexandro Leono sorella de messer Jacopo Brunello. Et così passando noi inanci uno de la compagnia, qual non saperia ben dir chi fosse, disse: non le valle, io ho ben veduto quello che passa la parte; over simile parole. E alhora mi voltai e vidi questa gentildonna, che a mio guidicio paria che ne ascondesse le mani, a fine che non li fosseno vedute. Et entrò subito in una porta che è lì drieto a queste mure. E mi parse intender nella compagnia che ella havesse li manilli over maglie, ma io però non li vidi ... Io non saperia ben dir chi fosse quello dicesse: non li valle a scondere, o simil parole, ma fu uno de la compagnia'.

[40] ASPGM, b. 30/2, reg. 2, fol. 106r, 27 May 1562: 'Ser Leandro q. Dominici de villa Bogioni, servitor ex.s doctor dominus Iulii de Vigoncea [...] respondit: Io andando dredo al mio parron, se ben mi ricordo zobia passada verso sera, drieto le mure vechie del ponte de S.Benetto, agiongessimo una gentildona [...] io non conosco la gentildona, et visi solum che essa si tolse via non so che cosa dai brazi, et se messe presto in la

to this story as one reads the increasingly embellished deposition by the six men. While some of them had hardly seen her, others had greeted her. Raffaello Novellino, a member of the group, claimed to have heard one of his companions saying '"Madam, you are infringing the sumptuary law, as you wear bracelets on your hands" [...] though I did not look at her hands but I looked at her face, and I heard one of the group saying "do not hide the bracelets"'.[41]

The case of Cassandra points to the murkiness of the spatial remit within the law. It is well known that sumptuary officers had no access to churches as they were considered to be outside the jurisdiction of temporal law.[42] More difficult to evaluate is whether sumptuary laws could be enforced solely in public spaces, or even how a public space was defined. The Censori, for instance, could enter private residences and check that sumptuary laws concerning banquets were upheld.[43] On the 5 June 1561, Giulia, wife of Roberto de Conti, was seen on her sister-in-law Alessandra Pigia's balcony, and in Alessandra's house during a party. Giulia was accused of wearing a white dress with gold trimmings and some gold and pearls, all of which were prohibited. It is not known how the accusation reached the magistracy, but the Censori sent an officer to seize the said dress.[44] Giulia did not oppose the seizing, though a week later, on 14 June, her husband appeared in front of the magistrates claiming to be acting on behalf of his wife. He argued that the prosecution was unfair: the items were clearly forbidden by the law, but Giulia had not worn them in public and claimed that 'in one's own house it must be licit to wear whatever one wants'. Rebuked for the fact that Giulia was not in her own house, he argued that she was in the house of her father-in-law that could be reached from Giulia's house through

---

gagioffa. Ma che de cosa fosse io non scio, perchè io era dredo a mio parron, et non possè così vedere [...] Io sentii a rasonare a essi gentilhomeni [...] che ditta gentildonna havea li manilli alle mani'.

[41] ASPGM, b. 30/2, reg. 2, fol. 106v, 30 May 1562: '"Madona, voi passati la parte, che haveti manilli alle mani" [...] Io non li hebi fantasia alle mani, ma la guardai in el viso; e sentire a dir similmente da uno de la compagnia: "Non vale a sconder li manilli", o simili parole'.

[42] Collier Frick, *Dressing Renaissance Florence*, 183.

[43] The documentation for Padova reports several such cases. For other cities see Maria Giuseppina Muzzarelli, '"Ponere una certa regola et modestia": il canone del consentito e del proibito nei banchetti cittadini fra Medioevo et Età moderna', in *'Per una severa maestra': dono a Daniela Romagnoli* (Fidenza: Unisa, 2014), 124.

[44] ASPGM, b. 30/2, reg. 2, fol. 66r, June 1561: 'Imperò hano deliberato essi Magnifici Signori [Censori] che sia processo contra di essa donna Iulia et inquirido, aciò ritrovata colpevole sia punita iuxta la forma de le parte, aciò la pena sua sia exempio ad altri. Et mandorno a Bortholamio di Zanin comandador che andar debia alla casa de ditta d. Iulia a dimandar la prefatta ruba biancha qual havea indosso nelli lochi sopradetti'.

a connecting door and not the public street. Yet, the meaning of public was not necessarily about public spaces. The Censori objected to the fact that Giulia was seen wearing the forbidden items at a party (*fieret tripudium publicum*) that was not necessarily private but attended by a variety of people. The response was that this was not a public festivity but a 'private gathering with six of seven married ladies who went to the house of d. Paolo [Giulia's father-in-law] so as to see the procession of Corpus Christi'.[45]

The spatial remit of the law was challenged in other ways. Only rarely were the laws upheld outside the city perimeter. Yet exceptions were made, especially if they related to Paduan citizens. This is the case for four noble ladies who on 10 September 1589 were seen wearing dresses trimmed in gold and silver as well as gold necklaces, jewellery and other forbidden items at the Zocco Fair in a small village ten miles from Padova.[46] Some of the accused claimed that, although citizens, they were coming from 'abroad' (another city), where they had been unknowingly wearing forbidden items. In the 1560s a tailor called Francesco defended himself saying that 'the legal action against me, poor Francesco the tailor, has been caused by hate ... Your excellencies surely know that messer Francisco Buzacharini came to see me to have a suit made similar to that that I made for messer Zorzi Contarini. I told him that I did not want to make it as he would have breached the sumptuary laws. And he told me that I could produce it for him as he did not want to wear it in his territory [Padova] but in Rome where he had to go and that he would not wear it in Padova as it would have been against the law'.[47] A similar excuse was made by Marco da Corno, whom we encountered wearing a velvet cloak decorated with trimmings, who was told that he had to deposit the item at the Sumptuary Office within three days or face a fine of 25 *lire*. His excuse was that 'This clothing is the same as that I wore before I returned to Padova. And I was not aware of any laws. And if

---

[45] ASPGM, b. 30/2, reg. 2, fol. 66v, 14 June 1561: 'In domibus propriis quibus debet esse licitum portare quicquid volunt'; 'Hac non esse verum, cum tripudium esset satis privatum, cum sex aut septem matronis tantum, quae eo die accesserunt ad domum ipsius d. Pauli pro videnda processione Corporis d. nostri Yehsus Christi huius civitatis'.

[46] Bonardi, *Il lusso di altri tempi*, 104.

[47] ASPGM, b. 30/4, reg. 2, without date and folio numbers, around 1563: 'la querella instituita [...] contra di me povero Francesco sartore è stata ingiustamente instituita et per solo odio et non altramente. Le magnificentie vostre sapiano che già mesi sei vene a trovarmi messer Francesco Buzacharino, qual mi pregò volesse farli uno habito della sorte che haveva fato al magnifico messer Zorzi Contarini. Io li resposi che non lo voleva far perché saria stato condenato. Lui mi dise che lo dovesse far sopra de lui perché non lo voleva portar in questa città né suo territorio, ma lo voleva portar a Roma ove haveva d'andar, e che in Padova non l'haria portato perché saria stato condenato'.

I had known of the sumptuary laws, I would have not worn it, but I am happy to oblige as a good son of this city'.[48] As in the case of Venice, admonitions must have been more common than prosecutions.[49]

Witnesses and Disputations

When on 16 April 1562 the Censori of Padova stopped a certain Alessandro Soncino in front of the church of Santa Chiara, they claimed that he was wearing 'a gold band around his cap and striped hose with bands which were not white'.[50] This was confirmed by a witness, though a second one, Lionello di Marco Crivellari, said that 'I have seen and I still see, the said Alessandro, wears hose all trimmed in white, though I cannot say what they are made of as I cannot see closer, and he wears around his cap a gold band'.[51] Clearly the testimony was recorded on the spot, though Crivellari raised doubts in the attempt to extricate himself from such an embarrassing situation. Passers-by were asked to act as witnesses to corroborate the Censori's accusations but they showed little willingness to testify against their neighbours and other citizens. This was the case of a certain Bernardino de Zuffis who on 26 April 1565 was asked by the Censori to act as a witness. In the words of De Zuffis: 'on Tuesday night, I was near the church of S. Agata. Piero da Lion et Annibal Buzacharin [the Censori] asked me to look at the ladies who accompanied the Rettoresse inside the church, [to ascertain] if they were wearing things forbidden by the sumptuary laws. I said that my eyesight is not good, though I saw the esteemed Chiara Zacha, spouse of messer Bortholo Zacho, who was wearing a belt with gold buttons', though he could not say if she was wearing coral.[52]

---

48 ASPGM, b. 30/2, reg. 3, fol. 6v, 16 April 1562: 'Questi habiti sono quelli medemi quali haveva avanti venisse a ripatriar a Padoa. Et non sapea de parte alcuna. Et quando io havesse saputo della parte delle pompe, io non l'haveria portato, ma de contro io son contento ad obedir come figliolo di questa città'.

49 For Venice, see Hunt, *Governance of the Consuming Passions*, 350.

50 ASPGM, b. 30/2, reg. 3, fol. 10r, 16 April 1562: 'qual havea un cordon d'oro a torno la beretta et un paro de calzoni de raso tutti designadi de cordoni over altro bianchi'.

51 ASPGM, b. 30/2, reg. 3, fol. 10r: 'Io ho visto et vedo tuttavia, mostrando ditto d. Alessandro, qual ha un paro de calzoni lavoradi tutti de biancho, ma però non vi saperia dir di che fosseno se non li andasse apresso, et quello che ha atorno alla beretta è un cordon d'oro'.

52 ASPGM, b. 30/2, reg. 3, fol. 16v, 26–27 April 1565: 'Marti di sera, ritrovandomi in la giesia de S. Agatha apresso li mag.ci messer Pieo da Lion et Annibal Buzacharin doctori [the Provveditori], fui advertido da essi che dovesse guardar quelle gentildonne che acompagnano le Cl.me Rettoresse lì in la giesia, se havevano cosa a torno che fosse prohibito per le parte de le pompe. Alli quali io dissi che io non havea tropo bona vista, pur vidi alla mag.ca madonna Chiara Zacha, consorte del ma.co messer Bortholo Zacho, la qual havea una cerna de botoni d'oro'.

Witnesses were key to any prosecution, though their reluctance to come forward or support the magistracy's accusations is evident in a context of close social relations in which people knew each other personally. This is compounded by the fact that most accused belonged to the city's social elite and were therefore well-known citizens, sometimes with important public offices. Notwithstanding occasional public patrols, even the Censori might not have been keen on the task for which they were appointed. A certain Antonio dall'Aquila said that during the Fair of St Anthony (early June) in 1565 he was walking in the company of Giulio di Pegna around 10 o'clock. In front of them were Cavalier Giacomo Zabarella and the Provveditore Piero da Lion 'and walking through the fair the said Cavalier [Zabarella] said to the said Piero Lion "You Sumptuary Officers see only small and trivial things, and do not want to see the important ones". And he [Lion] excused himself and said that it was not his task to seek people out, but that his office and job was to pursue people who had been sued. The Cavalier replied that this was an excuse and that his Excellency [Lion] saw many at the Fair who did not follow the law, and that it was his duty to discharge his office, and many other words. And I believe that they were having a laugh, as they often do together'.[53]

It appears that the Censori did not always apply the letter of the law but preferred to act only in response to an accusation. Indeed, they might themselves have been victims of anonymous accusations, as can be observed in one received in 1562 that denounced before the sumptuary officers the wife of one of their own membership: 'Signora Isabella, spouse of the Magnificent Matio Buzacarini, himself a Sumptuary officer – giving very bad example to all other women in this city – has made such an affront as to wear all sorts of dress and ornament against the sumptuary laws that were recently re-enacted'. The accuser explained that on 17 March Signora Isabella was seen 'while waiting in her coach in St. Stephen's Square with the Honourable Capitanio … wearing gold bracelets or ornaments around her arms that are prohibited by your Law. Moreover, this year she wore zibeline cuffs and gold necklaces and fastenings and clothing with parts that are embroidered and decorated'

---

[53] ASPGM, b. 30/2, reg. 3, fol. 35r–v, 11 July 1565: 'Et andando per la Fiera il ditto magnifico Cavalier disse verso ditto d. Piero Lion: Voi Signori sopra le Pompe vedeti se non bagatelle et minucie, et non volete veder le cose importante. Et lui excusandosi diceva non esser suo officio de andar vedendo, ma che era suo officio et carigo di espedir questi quali fossero quereladi, replicando il Cavalier che era una scusa, et V.Ecc. ha visto molti in Fiera che passeno le parti, et havete rispetto a far l'officio vostro, et molte altre parole. Et credo che burlasseno insieme come spesse volte soleno far'.

Figure 8.4 'Carrozza padovana' (Carriage in Padova), from the *Album Amicorum* of a German soldier, Italy, 1595. Gouache on paper, 15.56 x 11.43 cm. Los Angeles County Museum of Art, Gift of the 1991 Collectors' Committee (M.91.71.1-.101).

(Figure 8.4).[54] There was clearly a sense of unease on the part of the Censori and Provveditori in targeting acquaintances, friends and even members of their own families, which might draw scrutiny on their own behaviour.

Sumptuary laws could also be challenged and at times even made a mockery of. On 23 March 1587, for instance, an anonymous denunciation was found in the sumptuary box saying that Francesco, son of Zuan Piero Paganello 'wears against the law "a jacket of silver cloth"'.[55]

---

[54] ASPGM, b. 30/4, May 1562 (n.d.): 'Denuncio io a voi magnifici signori sopra le pompe qualmente la signora Isabella consorte del magnifico messer Matio Buzacharini, ancora lui signore supra dicte pompe, dando malissimo exempio a tute le altre done di questa città, ha hauto ardire di portare diverse sorte de habiti et di adornamenti contra le legi et parte vostre nuovamente prese et confirmate [...] et questo in diversi tempi e lochi, ma ultimamente ali 17 mazo 1562, il dì delle pentecoste, in chochio sul sagrà de San Stefano quando se aspettava il Cl.mo Capitanio haveva la sodeta signora Isabella magie d'oro over come volgiamo dir manili attorno li brazi, adornamento prohibito dalla vostra parte. Oltra del tuto questo anno ha portato il zebellino ancora dinsvoltato nelle mani et cadene d'oro sì al colo come cinte et liste de intalgio over recamo alle veste et altro'.
[55] ASPGM, reg. 30/3, reg. 4, fols. 73r, 23 March 1587: 'Denuntia inventa in cassella [...] "Messer Francesco fiolo de messer Zuan Piero Paganello: Denontia ha hauto ardimento

Several witnesses were called all of whom confirmed that Francesco had indeed the previous day been wearing this jacket inside the Palazzo del Capitanio. He had been warned by dottor Barbo 'that said jacket was against the sumptuary laws, and that he would be punished. But he [Francesco] responded that he thanks God he had enough to pay the fine'. He was heard to laugh at the accusation and to say that 'he had ways to wear the jacket, and also the means to pay for it more than other people'.[56]

The Material Culture of Sumptuary Laws

In reading the sumptuary prosecutions against the inhabitants of Padova, one is struck by the recurrent appearance of specific garments and accessories. Venetian legislators – like their counterparts in other parts of Europe – established the number of silk garments a lady could own. Yet, one can observe a progressive 'inflation' as the number of dresses allowed increased over time. In 1460, for instance, Paduan ladies could only legitimately own two silk garments. Yet in 1535 Venetian ladies could own six such garments, the ladies of Verona five in 1548, and the ladies of Treviso in 1559 four silk garments – and in 1602 they were allowed ten. They could also own two garments of each fabric including velvet, satin, damask, tabi and ormesin.[57]

Legislators were all too aware of the vagaries of fashion and new laws often updated the old to include the latest products and fashions. This is particularly evident in the case of accessories and decorative items. In the 1530s sumptuary laws, new *stratagli*, fringes and trimmings were detailed, whilst in the 1590s they concentrated on new strings, ribbons and other silk accessories. Sumptuary laws are the mirror of a changing consumer culture. It is not by chance that in 1593 a new guild of trimming-makers (*passamaneri*) was established in Venice. By the first decade of the seventeenth century the production of trimmings in Padova used 26,000

---

contra la forma delle pompe de questa magnifica città, portar un giupone di tella d'argento"'.

[56] ASPGM, reg. 30/3, reg. 4, fol. 74r, 23 March 1587: 'il signor dottor Barbo gli disse che esso zipon era contra le parte delle pompe, et chel seria condenato. Qual respose che haveva per gratia di Dio de pagar essa condanason, et [...] disse che haveva il modo di portar tal zipon, et ancho di pagar più de qualche d'uno d'altro'.

[57] Si veda la conferma veneziana delle delibere prese nei Consigli di Padova, Verona e Treviso in: Archivio di Stato di Venezia, *Senato, Terra*, reg. 4, fols. 143v–144v, 20 May 1460; *ivi*, reg. 28, fol. 176r, 29 July 1535; *ivi*, reg. 36, fols. 98v–105r, 6 April 1549; *ivi*, reg. 42, fols. 145r–149r, 16 March 1560; *ivi*, reg. 72, fols. 213r–217v, 20 December 1602.

pounds of silk per year, and as much as 70,000 were used in Verona, where more than 1,400 looms were employed in this expanding sector.[58]

The portrait of an anonymous lady by the Paduan artist Chiara Varotari provides an important record of what sumptuary laws were fighting against (Figure 8.5). It is a rare example of the work of a female artist, and pays perhaps a greater attention to the subject's clothing and jewellery than is found in the work of her male counterparts. The lady was clearly a member of one of the most prestigious noble families in the Republic of Venice and is adorned in a variety of items that were forbidden by the Paduan sumptuary laws. This portrait was painted at a time when the fortunes of Padova – and the entire Italian peninsula – were once again under strain.

A sumptuary law enacted by the Consiglio of the city in May 1619 claimed that conspicuous expenditure on women's dress was leading 'to the total misery and annihilation of the most important families of this poor city'.[59] It imposed greater restrictions on women's dress than any previous laws:

First. To be prohibited to all women outside their home and around the city to dress in any other colour than black, except for wives in the first year of their marriage.

2°. That any person whatever is prohibited to wear gold or silver cloth, either woven, inserted over embroideries or drawn with gold, [and is prohibited to wear] silk and any other type of cloth that has gold on any part of the person.

3°. That no one is allowed to wear more than one string around one's neck or a gold chain, but ... not [both] ... at the same time. They are allowed gold buttons up to a maximum number of 40, a gold belt that should not hang, bracelets and jewels real or fake with the exception of earrings, that can have some pearls, and rings that can have jewels.[60]

---

[58] See Luca Molà, *The Silk Industry of Renaissance Venice* (Baltimore and London: Johns Hopkins University Press, 2000), 306–307; Id., 'Le donne nell'industria serica veneziana del Rinascimento', in Luca Molà, Reinholld C. Mueller and Claudio Zanier (eds.), *La seta in Italia dal Medioevo al Seicento. Dal baco al drappo* (Venice: Marsilio, 2000), 423–459.

[59] 'sarà la total desolazione et esterminio della maggior parte delle famiglie di questa povera città'. In *consilio mag. cae civitatis Paduae de anno domini 1619 indictione secunda die martis XI maii*. Cit. in Bonardi, *Il lusso d'altri tempi*, 235.

[60] 'Primo. Sia prohibito a tutte le donne il vestir di altro colore fuori di casa per la città, che di negro, eccettuate le spose per il primo anno.2°. Che ad ogni sorte di persone sia che esser si voglia sia prohibito li drappi d'oro e di argento sia tessuto, o postovi sopra li rechami e dissegnati d'oro, di seta et di qualunque altra sorte et sopra ogni altra cosa con oro sia che parte si voglia della persona.3°. Che non possino portar più di un fillo di perle strette al collo overo una cadena d'oro, purchè non portino la cadena et le perle nell'istesso tempo. Li sii anco permesso una bottonadura d'oro al numero di 40, una centa d'oro che non penda, li manili et orechini, ma il tutto senza sogie buone et false eccettuato alli orecchini, che possino haverli qualche perla et nelli annelli le sue zoglie'. In Bonardi, *Il lusso d'altri tempi*, 235–236.

Figure 8.5 *Portrait of a Lady*, by Chiara Varotari, c. 1630 (1584–1663), oil on canvas. Musei Civici agli Eremitani, Padova. Cameraphoto/Scala, Florence – Photo Scala, Florence, courtesy of the Ministero dei Beni e delle Attività Culturali e del Turismo.

The laws continued by stating that women were not allowed to wear fur, or have pinked or slashed clothes. They were also not allowed to have more than one servant with them or travel in coaches with gold decorations or with silk or velvet upholstery.

By contrast we see here the lady wearing not one but two strings of large pearls, and another necklace made of three strings of smaller pearls (Figure 8.5). She is also wearing a gold chain around her neck and waist. Clearly in defiance of sumptuary laws, she is dressed not in black, but in an expensive silk dress with a gold and silver background and decorations, as well as several gold buttons. She also wears an elaborate headdress (repeatedly forbidden by the Paduan laws if worth more than 5 ducats), an extravagant collar and embroidered cuffs. Perhaps the only items that are not directly against the sumptuary laws are her rings (possibly with jewels) and her bracelets (*manilli*), forbidden in previous laws but allowed by the 1619 sumptuary laws.

Visual evidence allows us to question the effectiveness of the law but also provides material expression as to what was perceived as desirable attire for a lady of the elite. Over the centuries the Censori paid a great deal of attention to gold jewellery, as a final case shows us. On the 7 May 1619, exactly a year after the new sumptuary laws were enacted, messer Alvise Gagliardi, husband of Lucietta, appeared in front of the Censori of Padova saying that 'he intends to prove that the necklace that his wife wore the last day of Easter in the house of Antonio Frizimelega was a necklace of glass made yellow with saffron'.[61] He objected to the accusation that his wife wore an expensive and forbidden gold necklace. In the same deposition, he also denied other accusations, and in particular that his wife's gloves were forbidden by the sumptuary regulations, that she had gold hairpins, and that the necklace that she wore on the day of Santa Croce (3 May) in the church of S. Agostino was made of gold with zephyrs.

Messer Alvise was defending his wife's honour in a sumptuary proceeding in which she played only a minor part, as at no point did she appear in front of the magistrates. Alvise's wife was not even stopped in the street by the Censori but was the victim – so her husband argued – of false accusations. This legal proceeding was initiated by an anonymous message: 'on Tuesday 5 April 1620, the sumptuary

---

[61] ASPGM, b. 30/5, trial n. 10, folios not numbered, 7 May 1620: 'Dice et esser la verità provar intende che la cadena che haveva la signora sua consorte al colo l'ultima festa di Pasqua in casa del molto Ill.mo signor Antonio Frizimelega era cadena di vero fatta zalla con il zafrano', adding that 'et è quella apunto che sarà mostrata alli testimonii, et che hora si presenta' (and it is this that is shown to the witnesses, as here presented).

box (*cassetta delle pompe*) at the Palazzo [del Capitanio] was opened and a denunciation was found inside: 'the wife of Alvise Gagliardo, who lives near the Embankment, has taken the liberty of wearing a gold or gold-plated necklace ... and also a gold [unreadable] with pearls on her neck, and embroidered pinked gloves with gold bands and gold pendants and hair-pins made of gold or silver that is gold-plated'.[62]

The denouncer did not explain where and when Alvise's wife had made show of such forbidden items. The Censori however had to take action, as it appeared that Lucietta's necklace had not passed unnoticed. Several witnesses were called in to testify whether Lucietta had indeed worn a forbidden piece of jewellery. Antonio Marzelani, a citizen of Padua living in the contrada of Savonarola, said that on the third Sunday before Easter he was on his way to the church of Sant'Agostino to visit his friend Fra Desiderio when he passed in front of the house of messer Frizimelega 'and I saw a coach with two ladies who were descending and entering the house and, believing that there was a party, I followed the ladies and went upstairs to the house in the main reception room'. He remained there until the ladies left. The last of them was Lucietta, wife of Alvise Gagliardo, 'and while she descended the staircase, I noticed her hairstyle and I saw very well the hairpins made of white silver and none of them were made of gold'. He was presented with the necklace and he confirmed that it was the necklace worn by Alvise's wife: 'and I recognised it very well as I had seen before one of these yellow chains of fake gold', adding that 'I said to Alvise with surprise that such a thing [the necklace] is of fake gold and he replied to me "I have another one that is even better" and I asked him to show it to me and he immediately went upstairs to fetch it and he showed it to me and I realised that it was made of glass painted with saffron and that it looked remarkable'.[63]

---

[62] ASPGM, b. 30/5, trial n. 10, folios not numbered, 5 April 1620: 'A dì marti 5 aprile 1620. Fu alla presenza delli Signori Sopracensore et Censore per me nodaro apperta la cassella delle Pompe in Palazzo nella qual fu trovata l'infrascripta denuncia: 1620. Si da in notta comme la moglie del signor Alvise Gagliardo, sta su l'Arzere, si ha fatto lecito di portar contra la parte una cadena di oro overo di mesturra sopra indorata, et ancho un [unreadable] d'oro con le perle all collo, et guanti con ricamo fereti alle stringe [...] d'oro straforati con cordelle con oro, et agi da testa de oro overo di arzento sopra dorati'.

[63] ASPGM, b. 30/5, trial n. 10, folios not numbered, 7 May 1620: 'Ser Antonio Marzelani qd Paulo, habita in Padoa in contrà della Savonarolla [...] Sopra il quarto risponde: "con occasione che andavo la 3a festa di Pasqua a S. Agustino a visitare il reverendo padre fra Desiderio mio amico dell'ordine suddetto di S. Agustino. Nell'andare passai davanti la casa dell'illustre signor Frizimelega, et vi vidi una coppia di carozze con due gentildone che smontavano et entravano in casa de esso signor Antonio, et io credendo che si facesse festa mi aviai dietro esse gentildone et andai di sopra in casa nella salla di esso signor Antonio, nella qual vi era due gentildone, et steti ivi fino che si partirono, et partendosi le lasciai andare avanti, et ne restò una in ultima che era la moglie del signor Alvise Gagiardo nominata Lucietta, alla qual mi aviai dietro giù per la scala, et mentre si veniva

Ser Zuane Galvan, son of Sebastian, another citizen of Padua, also confirmed that the necklace was the one that Alvise's wife was wearing on the last Sunday before Easter when she was at the Frizimelega house and that it was made of glass and saffron, and that he himself had commissioned it in Venice. He also confirmed that the gloves shown were those worn by signora Lucietta and that the hairpins were not made of gold.[64] Another witness, Ottonello Descalzo, said that '… I have very good knowledge [of such necklaces] as I had seen it before as they were brought [to Padua] from Venice by Dr Galvan of Venice whom I work with'.[65] Alvise Bagnago was also at the Frizimelega house and recounted that he had discussed with Ottonello Descalzo 'the topic of sumptuary regulations … and I said that the necklace and pearls were against the regulations but I said it laughing and Ottonello too started to laugh as it was clear that it was made of glass'.[66] Several other witnesses were called in and reported that the gloves were 'ordinary', that the hairpins were of silver and not gold, and that Lucietta did not have embroideries of any kind. Ser Carlo Antonio Forteza testified that the glass necklace

giù di essa scala andavo considerando quel conciero di testa et diversità delle cordelle che haveva, et li vidi li agi d'arzento bianchi benissimo, né ve ne haveva nissuno d'oro. Sopra il quinto risponde: "la cadena mostratami è quella a punto che haveva la moglie del suddetto signor Alvise in S. Agustino il giorno della Crose la matina, et la conobbi benissimo perchè altre volte, con occasione che ero sopra la porta del signor Alvise, che passò per la contrà una gentildona che haveva una di queste cadene de sida zalla finte d'oro, et io verso esso signor Alvise gli disse: 'Guardate – maravigliandomi – come quella cosa è ben finta de oro'. Lui me rispose: 'Ne ho una che è più bella et fa più mostra di quella', et io lo pregai che me la mostrasse et di subito andò di sopra et la portò giù a mostrarmela, et mi accorsi che era di vetro inzafranata et faceva bella vista, et è aponto quella che la moglie di esso signor Alvise porta ordinariamente"'.

[64] ASPGM, b. 30/5, trial n. 10, folios not numbered: 'La cadena che mi havete mostrato … è di vero fatta zalla con il zaffrano, et io per apunto l'ho fatta fare questa Quadragesima passata in Venecia'; 'essendo dall signor Antonio Frizimelega la 3a festa di Pasqua il doppo disinare, capitai in sala di essa casa dove erano molte gentildone in piedi, dove osservai particularmente la signora Lucieta Gagiarda per veder se la cadena sopranominata faceva bella vista, et vidi che se l'accomodava ne l man, nelle quali haveva a ponto li guanti che mi havete mostrato'; 'et per curiosità osservando se questa parte delle pompe si osservava, attendendo li concieri di testa de varie gentildone, et in particulare osservai questo de questa signora Gagiarda, la qual vidi che haveva in testa varie cordelle pontade con agi d'arzento, et osservando se alcuna di quelle cordelle havesse oro vidi che non ne havevano, et non haveva agi d'oro'.
[65] ASPGM, b. 30/5, trial n. 10, folios not numbered: '… et di quella ne ho bonissima praticha perché l'havevo veduta altre volte con occasione che essendo venuto il signor Dottor Galvan da Venecia, con il quale pratico ordinariamente'.
[66] ASPGM, b. 30/5, trial n. 10, folios not numbered: '… et cominciassimo a discorer de dette cose, tra le quali fu della materia de queste parte delle Pompe, et io con l'occasione che la signora Gaiarda all'hora passò con la carozza partendosi dalla casa delli signori Frizimelega, dissi che quella signora passava la parte perchè haveva colana e perle, et lo dissi ridendo, et perchè il signor Ottonello si misse a rider anche esso, et darmi la burla sopra la colana perchè era di vetro'.

presented by the provveditori was that worn by Lucietta and this and others were brought to Padua from Venice by his brother-in-law Galvan.

Several elements in this sumptuary proceeding are helpful to us, including the fact that the trial against Lucietta did not reach its natural conclusion and she was informally acquitted. We are told that on 9 May 1620 the Censori decided to vote on the case with the usual procedure ('those who think she is innocent, put the ball in the green container, those who think her guilty in the red'), but they never recorded the result, nor the final verdict, leaving the rest of the page blank.[67] It was probably decided that Lucietta was not breaching any sumptuary laws but simply wearing a fashionable item made of glass coloured in yellow that looked like gold. This was not one of the luxuries that sumptuary laws attempted to prohibit but what today we might call a 'populuxe', a cheaper copy that, although it confounded people, did not fall within the sumptuary remit. Clearly Messer Alvise had mobilised trustworthy witnesses for the defence. Their role was very important in any sumptuary prosecution and was often the reason why it was difficult to convict any of the accused.

Conclusion

This chapter attempts to contextualise a large and hitherto unexplored source detailing the sumptuary prosecution cases of the city of Padova in the sixteenth and early seventeenth centuries. This chapter provided an overview of the ways in which sumptuary laws were applied in order to understand the sumptuary application not from a prescriptive perspective, but from the point of view of those involved in prosecutions, such as the accused, the accuser and witnesses. We have also discussed the conceptual, practical and spatial remit of sumptuary laws and the many strategies adopted by all parties involved to cope with laws that were clearly perceived as intrusive and divisive. Prosecutions are rare in Italian and European archives. In most cases they simply list the names of the people prosecuted and the garments involved. Padova stands out as a special case: the richness of the materials allow us to understand how sumptuary laws and their enactment shaped public life in the late sixteenth and seventeenth centuries. These materials also show that

---

[67] ASPGM, b. 30/5, trial n. 10, folios not numbered, 9 May 1620: 'L'andarà parte che la magnifica signora Lucietta Gagiarda sia condenata giusta la legge; a chi piace che sia condenata metti le balle nel bussollo verde, a chi non piace nel rosso. La qual parte balotada furon trovade: nel verde per la parte balle [blank], nel rosso contra la parte balle [blank]. Et cusì fu [blank]'.

sumptuary laws were unsystematically applied and that in most cases they did not lead to any conviction. Yet, to simply dismiss the laws as ineffective would be incorrect. Clearly a sumptuary regime existed and was put in practice at regular intervals. It might have not achieved its aim but it was among the many tools used by legislations in the everyday administration of an early modern city.

Part III

The European Maritime Powers and
Their Empires

9 Spanish Fashion and Sumptuary Legislation from the Thirteenth to the Eighteenth Century*

Amanda Wunder

Sumptuary laws regulated the production, sale and public use of luxury goods in the Spanish kingdoms for more than 500 years. Between the mid-thirteenth and early eighteenth centuries, the Crown and Cortes (parliament) promulgated sumptuary laws 'to restrain overindulgences in food and excesses in clothing, furnishings, fashions, and other branches of luxury', as the Enlightenment historian Juan Sempere y Guariños explained. He defined luxury as 'the use of things that are not necessary for subsistence, because of vanity or voluptuousness'.[1] Sumptuary laws governed different kinds of consumption and display – including feasts, funerals and weddings, servants and coaches[2] – but were concerned most of all with the luxurious fabrics and trims that were used for personal dress and adornment in public. The laws also forbade fashions that were not necessarily luxurious but were deemed otherwise scandalous and threatening to public order. Spanish sumptuary laws worked in conjunction with clothing laws to distinguish royals from commoners, soldiers from civilians, Christians from Jews and Muslims, and married women from prostitutes.[3] The Spanish government issued paternalistic sumptuary

---

* I am grateful to James Amelang, Abigail Balbale, María Barrigón, Cristian Berco, José U. Bernardos Sanz, María Judith Feliciano, Richard Kagan, and Tara Zanardi for sharing their insights and bibliography on a wide range of subjects for this chapter. This research was made possible by digitized versions of archival and rare printed materials on two websites maintained by the Spanish Ministry of Education, Culture and Sport: Legislación Histórica de España (LHE), http://www.mcu.es/archivos/lhe/; and the Portal de Archivos Españoles (PARES), http://pares.mcu.es/.

[1] Juan Sempere y Guariños, *Historia del lujo y de las leyes suntuarias de España*, ed. Juan Rico Giménez (València: Institució Alfons el Magnànim, 2000), 71: 'para contener los excesos en la comida y las demasías en los trajes, muebles, modas y demás ramos de lujo'; 75: 'el uso de las cosas no necesarias para la subsistencia, por vanidad o voluptuosidad'.

[2] On the regulation of coaches, see Alejandro López Álvarez, 'Coches, carrozas y sillas de mano en la monarquía de los Austrias entre 1600 y 1700: Evolución de la legislación', *Hispania: Revista Española de Historia* 66, no. 224 (2006): 883–908.

[3] As explained in the Introduction to this book by Ulinka Rublack and Giorgio Riello, clothing laws required people to wear certain garments, whereas sumptuary laws forbade them.

laws to stop individuals from spending more than they could afford and protectionist laws banning luxury imports to bolster the national economy.

Like neighbouring France, Spain had a long, unbroken record of centralised state-issued sumptuary legislation, yet the history of Spanish sumptuary laws (which has been written almost exclusively in Spanish) has for the most part been excluded from scholarship beyond the Pyrenees.[4] The first and only comprehensive history of Spanish sumptuary legislation remains Sempere y Guariños' *History of Luxury and of Sumptuary Laws in Spain* (*Historia del lujo y de las leyes suntuarias de España*), which was first published in 1788. Sempere y Guariños published previously unpublished laws in two volumes chronicling the rise and fall of sumptuary legislation from the mid-thirteenth century to his own times. By recounting the history of Spanish sumptuary laws over the centuries, Sempere y Guariños built a case against sumptuary legislation as detrimental to Spain's economic development. Subsequent Spanish scholarship has focused on the social and political roles that sumptuary laws played at particular historical moments.[5] The present volume offers an opportunity to revisit the history of sumptuary legislation in Spain as it developed over half a millennium and to integrate that story into a truly global history.[6]

This chapter outlines a new cultural history of sumptuary legislation in Spain from the mid-thirteenth to the eighteenth centuries. When they are re-read in the twenty-first century, the primary sources that Sempere y Guariños first brought to light in the late eighteenth century offer fresh

---

[4] Alan Hunt, *Governance of the Consuming Passions: A History of Sumptuary Law* (New York: St. Martin's Press, 1996), 36.

[5] On the history of Spanish sumptuary laws in the Middle Ages, see: José Damián González Arce, *Apariencia y poder: La legislación suntuaria castellana en los siglos XIII–XV* (Jaén: Universidad de Jaén, 1998). On the era of the Catholic Monarchs, see: Carmen Bernis, *Trajes y modas en la España de los Reyes Católicos*, 2 vols. (Madrid: Instituto Diego Velázquez del Consejo Superior de Investigaciones Científicas, 1978–1979). On the Habsburg era (sixteenth and seventeenth centuries), see: Carmen Bernis, *Indumentaria española en tiempos de Carlos V* (Madrid: Instituto Diego Velázquez del Consejo Superior de Investigaciones Científicas, 1962); Antonio Álvarez-Ossorio Alvariño, 'Rango y apariencia: El decoro y la quiebra de la distinción en Castilla (siglos XVI–XVIII), *Revista de Historia Moderna: Anales de la Universidad de Alicante* 17 (1998–99), 263–278; Saúl Martínez Bermejo, 'Beyond Luxury: Sumptuary Legislation in 17th-Century Castile', in Günther Lottes, Eero Medijainen, and Jón Vidar Sigurdsson (eds.), *Making, Using and Resisting the Law in European History* (Pisa: Plus – Pisa University Press, 2008), 93–108; and Ruth de la Puerta, 'Sumptuary Legislation and Restrictions on Luxury in Dress', in José Luis Colomer and Amalia Descalzo (eds.), *Spanish Fashion at the Courts of Early Modern Europe*, 2 vols. (Madrid: Centro de Estudios Europa Hispánica, 2014), i: 209–231. On the eighteenth century, see Álvaro Molina and Jesusa Vega, *Vestir la identidad, construir la apariencia: La cuestión del traje en la España del siglo XVIII* (Madrid: Ayuntamiento de Madrid, Área de Gobierno de las Artes, 2004).

[6] Chapter 10 on Portugal by Francisco Bethencourt and Chapter 12 on Spanish America by Rebecca Earle offer especially relevant comparisons to the Spanish case presented in this chapter.

insights into the ways in which Spanish sumptuary laws evolved to confront shifting concerns about class, religion, gender and national identity over the centuries. The question of whether and when those laws were actually enforced is a thorny issue. Isolated individual cases are cited in the pages that follow, but there is not yet enough information to draw general conclusions. The focus here is primarily on Castile, the kingdom in central Spain that rose to become the governing centre of the Spanish Empire, and on laws that regulated textiles, fashions and personal adornments. The history of Spanish sumptuary legislation follows the same patterns that have been observed in other European cultures and nations, but the laws operated within a set of historical circumstances that were uniquely Spanish.[7] What constituted luxury – the kinds of objects that were subjected to sumptuary laws and the meanings ascribed to them – was shaped by Spain's singular history, beginning in the militaristic multi-confessional era of the late Middle Ages.

Sumptuary Laws and Social Order in Reconquest Spain

The history of Spanish sumptuary legislation begins in the mid-thirteenth century, when the Christian and Islamic kingdoms of the Iberian peninsula were still engaged in the protracted military struggle (711–1492) that the victorious Christian side would later designate the Reconquest (*Reconquista*). By the end of this period, the small and disparate Christian kingdoms of the north had expanded and consolidated into the modern Spanish nation. Late-medieval Spain and Portugal were distinguished from the rest of Europe by their coexisting populations of Christians, Muslims and Jews.[8] Almost eight centuries of contact and exchange with the Islamic world had a profound impact on luxury production and consumption in Spain, where Castilian-speaking Christians used the Arabic-derived words *alhaja* and *axuar* (*ajuar*) to describe the luxuries that they used to adorn their persons, homes and churches (both terms were translated as 'all manner of houshoulde stuffe' in a 1599 Spanish–English dictionary; *axuar* could also signify a woman's dowry).[9] Islamic luxury goods – most of all the fine silks woven in

---

[7] See the pattern of sumptuary legislation across Europe (excluding Spain) described in Martha Howell, *Commerce before Capitalism, 1300–1600* (New York: Cambridge University Press, 2010), 208–260.

[8] On the historiographical debate over coexistence in medieval Spain, see Maya Soifer, 'Beyond Convivencia: Critical Reflections on the Historiography of Interfaith Relations in Christian Spain', *Journal of Medieval Iberian Studies* 1, no. 1 (2009): 19–35.

[9] Sebastián de Covarrubias Orozco, *Tesoro de la lengua castellana o española* (Madrid: Luis Sánchez, 1611), ed. Felipe C. R. Maldonado, rev. by Manuel Camarero (Madrid: Editorial Castalia, 1995), 36 and 62. John Minsheu, *A Dictionarie in Spanish and English, First Published into the English Tongue by Ric. Perciuale Gent. Now Enlarged and*

Andalusia – were coveted by their Christian and Jewish neighbours.[10] In the twelfth-century epic *Poem of the Cid*, for example, the hero Rodrigo Díaz de Vivar promises to return from a military expedition with a 'fine red fur-lined Moorish tunic' for a Jewish money-lender.[11] Luxury textiles travelled fluidly across confessional lines in medieval Spain, where rich silks inscribed with Arabic script in praise of Allah were used to bury Christian royalty and celebrate Christian saints. An exceptionally sumptuous example is the Almohad silk that was used to make vestments for the feast day of San Valerius at the cathedral of Roda de Isábena in Aragón (Figure 9.1).[12] Silk fabrics enriched with precious metals did not only signify wealth and status: they also functioned as external signs of virtue and honour in medieval society.[13] Beginning in the 1250s, the Castilian Crown began to deploy sumptuary legislation controlling the use of silk and other luxuries as part of a concerted effort to consolidate royal power, reward the military class and distinguish among the peoples of the three religions.

Amplified with Many Thousand Words ... (London: Edmund Bollifant, 1599; www.ems .kcl.ac.uk/content/proj/anglo/dict/pro-anglo-dict-main.html), 18 and 39. On the importance of *alhajas* in seventeenth-century religious consumption, see Amanda Wunder, *Baroque Seville: Sacred Art in a Century of Crisis* (University Park: The Pennsylvania State University Press, 2017), 15.

[10] For a survey of Islamic textiles made in Spain (940–1492), see Louise W. Mackie, *Symbols of Power: Luxury Textiles from Islamic Lands, 7th-21st Century* (Cleveland: Cleveland Museum of Art, 2015), 167–209.

[11] *The Poem of the Cid*, trans. Rita Hamilton and Janet Perry (London: Penguin Books, 1975; reissue 1984), 31.

[12] On Christian uses of Islamic textiles, see María Judith Feliciano, 'Muslim Shrouds for Christian Kings? A Reassessment of Andalusi Textiles in Thirteenth-Century Castilian Life and Ritual', in Cynthia Robinson and Leyla Rouhi (eds.), *Under the Influence: Questioning the Comparative in Medieval Castile* (Leiden and Boston: Brill, 2005), 101–131. On the San Valerius textiles, see: Maryam Ekhtiar et al. (eds.), *Masterpieces from the Department of Islamic Art in The Metropolitan Museum of Art* (New York: The Metropolitan Museum of Art, 2011), 78–80. The Museo de Ricas Telas Medievales de las Huelgas has an extraordinary collection of royal Castilian burial garments made from Andalusi textiles: *Vestiduras Ricas: El Monasterio de las Huelgas y su época, 1170–1340* (Madrid: Patrimonio Nacional, 2005). Silks and other luxury domestic objects with origins in the Islamic world remained hallmarks of wealth and taste among Andalusian elites after the conquest of Granada in 1492; see: José Luis Gasch-Tomás, 'Asian Silk, Porcelain and Material Culture in the Definition of Mexican and Andalusian Elites, c. 1565–1630', in Bethany Aram and Bartolomé Yun-Casalilla (eds.), *Global Goods and the Spanish Empire, 1492–1824: Circulation, Resistance and Diversity* (London: Palgrave MacMillan, 2014), 153–173, here at pp. 161–162.

[13] On the association between luxury fabrics and virtue in medieval clerical vestments, see: Maureen C. Miller, *Clothing the Clergy: Virtue and Power in Medieval Europe, c. 800–1200* (Ithaca, NY: Cornell University Press, 2014).

Figure 9.1 Textile fragment from the dalmatic of San Valerius inscribed in Arabic: 'Good luck and glory and exaltedness and magnificence'. Green, blue, red and white silk brocaded with gold-wrapped threads. Made in Spain, thirteenth century. Metropolitan Museum of Art, New York City. Fletcher Fund, 1946. Inv. no. 46.156.10.

Luxury, Virtue and Valour

In 1258, early in the reign of King Alfonso X of Castile and León (r. 1252–1284), the Cortes of Valladolid issued what has been called 'the first effective sumptuary legislation in Spanish history'.[14] The laws differentiated among members of the king's household by limiting the materials that men of different ranks and occupations were allowed to wear and the number of garments they could own; they also forbade anyone at court from spending more on food or clothing than the king and queen, and restricted the consumption of silks, furs, silver and gold to the magnates (Spain's highest-ranking nobility).[15] King Alfonso's famous seven-part law code, the *Siete Partidas* (1250s–1260s), explains the theory behind the law: kings were obligated by the virtue of their office to wear 'garments of silk, adorned with gold and jewels' and 'crowns of gold, richly decorated with magnificent jewels', and to ride horses with bridles and saddles 'ornamented with gold, silver and precious stones',

---

[14] 'A Thirteenth-Century Castilian Sumptuary Law', *Business History Review* 37, no. 1–2 (1963): 98–100, quote on p. 99. On the sumptuary laws issued by Alfonso X's predecessors in the first half of the thirteenth century, see: Sempere y Guariños, *Historia del lujo*, 134–143.

[15] The nobility was divided into two categories: the *ricos hombres* (magnates) who attended the king's court, and the *caballeros* (knights) who were the vassals of the magnates. Joseph F. O'Callaghan, *A History of Medieval Spain* (Ithaca, NY: Cornell University Press, 1975), 287.

in order to distinguish themselves from their subjects and to 'indicate the splendor of Our Lord God, whose position they occupy on earth'.[16] Thirteenth-century manuscript illuminations invariably depict Alfonso X wearing a gold crown and dressed in sumptuous silk fabrics, sometimes adorned with patterns that can be matched to actual garments excavated from royal tombs.[17]

Colour was a form of luxury that was strictly regulated according to the wearer's status and occupation. Only the king could wear a cloak made from a fine red wool called 'escarlata'.[18] Scribes, crossbowmen, falconers and other men in the king's household were forbidden from wearing scarlet hose, while clergy could wear only dark-coloured hose of blackish or brownish hues. A squire was forbidden from wearing cloth dyed any colour at all.[19] Knights, on the other hand, were expected to wear brightly coloured clothes of red, yellow, green or purple, 'in order that their dress might be elegant, and that they might be cheerful and their hearts be emboldened, so as to render them more valiant', as stated in the *Siete Partidas*.[20] A knight's colourful clothing communicated the privileged status of military men in 'a society organized for war', as medieval Castile has been called.[21]

In the fourteenth century, sumptuary laws incentivised men to join the cavalry by granting their wives special privileges to consume luxury goods.[22] The Seville city ordinances of 1348, for example,

---

[16] Alfonso X, *Las Siete Partidas*, trans. Samuel Parsons Scott and ed. Robert I. Burns, 5 vols. (Philadelphia: University of Pennsylvania Press, 2001), ii: 288.

[17] Gonzalo Menéndez Pidal, *La España del siglo XIII leída en imágenes* (Madrid: Real Academia de la Historia, 1986), 37–42.

[18] Alfonso X, 'Ordenamiento de las Córtes celebradas en Valladolid en la era MCCXCVI (año 1258)', article 14, in *Cortes de los antiguos reinos de León y de Castilla, publicadas por la Real Academia de la Historia*, 5 vols. (Madrid: Rivadeneyra, 1861–1903), i: 54–63, here at p. 57. On the thirteenth-century fabric known as 'escarlata', see: Rosa María Dávila Corona, Montserrat Durán Pujol, and Máximo García Fernández, *Diccionario histórico de telas y tejidos: Castellano-catalán* (Salamanca: Junta de Castilla y León, Consejería de Cultura y Turismo, 2004), 78–79. On the historical significance of red as a power colour, see: Amy Butler Greenfield, *A Perfect Red: Empire, Espionage, and the Quest for the Color of Desire* (New York: Harper Perennial, 2005); and Carmella Padilla and Barbara Anderson (eds.), *A Red Like No Other: How Cochineal Colored the World: An Epic Story of Art, Culture, Science and Trade* (New York: Skira/Rizzoli, 2015).

[19] Alfonso X, 'Ordenamiento de las Córtes celebradas en Valladolid ... (año 1258)', articles 4, 5 and 22, pp. 55 and 59.

[20] Alfonso X, *Las Siete Partidas*, 2: 427. On the chivalrous ideals of the *Siete Partidas*, see: González Arce, *Apariencia y poder*, 142–153.

[21] Derek W. Lomax, *The Reconquest of Spain* (New York: Longman, 1978), 177.

[22] Earlier laws, such as one issued by King Alfonso VIII (r. 1158–1214) in 1212, temporarily restricted spending on luxury dress and adornments to stimulate spending on arms; see: Sempere y Guariños, *Historia del lujo*, 134–135. On the dress privileges of knights,

forbade the wife of 'any resident of Seville who does not maintain a horse' from wearing sendal (which is a fine silk fabric).[23] A similar law issued in the kingdom of Valencia ten years later restricted the wearing of silk and cloth of gold, embroidery with pearls and precious stones, and fur linings to those men who kept arms and horses, and to those men's wives.[24] As these sumptuary laws indicate, a woman's right to dress was determined by her husband's status.[25] As external signs of virtue, luxuries could be worn only by virtuous women and thus were forbidden to prostitutes.

Clothing laws further distinguished between virtuous and dishonest women. Priests' mistresses, for example, were required by law to wear an identifying marker – a russet-coloured linen cloth three-fingers wide – over their headdresses.[26] All across Europe, women's clothing and adornments performed an important social function by displaying the wealth and honour of their families and communities.[27] But the social benefits of publicly exhibiting an opulently dressed woman conflicted with the imperative to protect her virtue and reputation (and that of her entire family) by keeping her out of public view. The competing pressures for women to be exposed or enclosed remained problematic in Spain through the early modern period.

see: María Martínez, 'Indumentaria y sociedad medievales (ss. XII-XV)', *En la España Medieval* 26 (2003): 35–59, especially pp. 40–41 and 54. See Chapter 10 by Francisco Bethencourt on special privileges granted to knights in Portugal.

[23] Alfonso XI, 'Ordenamiento de peticiones de las Córtes celebradas en Alcalá de Henares en la era MCCCLXXXVI (año 1348)', article 119, in *Cortes de los antiguos reinos de León y de Castilla* 1: 593–626, here at p. 624: 'qualquier vezino de Seuilla que non mantouiere cauallo'.

[24] Juan Vicente García Marsilla, 'Ordenando el lujo: Ideología y normativa suntuaria en las ciudades valencianas (siglos XIV y XV)', in Sophie Brouquet and Juan V. García Marsilla (eds.), *Mercados del lujo, mercados del arte: El gusto de las élites mediterráneas en los siglos XIV y XV* (València: Universitat de València, 2015), 561–591, here at p. 568.

[25] On the history of women and sumptuary legislation, see: Diane Owen Hughes, 'Regulating Women's Fashion', in Christiane Klapisch-Zuber (ed.), *Silences of the Middle Ages*, vol. 2 of Georges Duby and Michelle Perrot (eds.), *A History of Women in the West* (Cambridge, MA: Harvard University Press, 1992), 136–158.

[26] Peter I, 'Cuaderno primero otorgado á peticion de los procuradores de las ciudades y villas del Reino en las Córtes celebradas en Valladolid en la era MCCCLXXXXIX (año 1351)', article 24, in *Cortes de los antiguos reinos de León y de Castilla*, ii: 1–74, here at pp. 14–15; John I, 'Cuaderno otorgado á peticion de los procuradores del Reino en las Córtes en Soria de la era MCCCCXVIII (año 1380)', article 9, in Ibid., 301–310, here at p. 304. On sumptuary laws governing prostitutes, and on prostitutes' relations with the clergy, see: Marie A. Kelleher, *Measure of Woman: Law and Female Identity in the Crown of Aragon* (Philadelphia: University of Pennsylvania Press, 2010), 105–106.

[27] See Chapter 1 by Ulinka Rublack on the public role of women's attire in Germany.

Dress and Religious Difference

Sumptuary and clothing laws identified members of religious minorities and marked their status as second-class citizens in the Christian and Islamic kingdoms of medieval Spain. Islamic laws required Christians and Jews to wear identifying belts around their tunics and prohibited them from wearing Islamic headdresses. Across Christian Europe, a plethora of clothing laws were issued after the Fourth Lateran Council (1215) that required Jews and Muslims in Christian territories to wear distinctive clothing so that Christians would not accidentally engage in sexual relations with non-Christians. In Spain, Alfonso X ordered 'that all Jews male and female living in our dominions shall bear some distinguishing mark upon their heads so that people may plainly recognize a Jew, or a Jewess', since, it was claimed, 'many crimes and outrageous things occur between Christians and Jews because they live together in cities, and dress alike'.[28] The specifics of what that mark looked like varied by time and place; in 1405, for example, the Cortes of Valladolid required Jewish men and women to wear a russet-coloured badge on their right sleeve.[29] Muslims living in villages populated with Christians had been required to wear 'long beards as their law mandates' in 1258 by the Cortes of Valladolid, which also forbade Muslims or Jews from wearing white fur, colourful fabrics or fine silks, unless they had special permission from the king.[30] Almost a hundred years later, at the Cortes of Valladolid in 1351, King Peter I of Castile (r. 1350–1369) complained that those laws were not being observed or enforced, which was an offence to God and caused great harm to the land: 'There are many Jews and Moors at my court and in my kingdoms who call themselves by Christian names and dress in striped and parti-coloured cloth and with adornments, in a guise that makes them unrecognizable'. The Cortes thus decreed that Jewish or Muslim males aged thirteen and older who were caught using Christian names or wearing gold or silver would be flogged for a first offence. A second offence would result in the death penalty.[31]

---

[28] Alfonso X, *Las Siete Partidas*, 5: 1437.

[29] Henry III, 'Ordenamiento sobre judios y usuras, otorgados en las Córtes de Valladolid del año de 1405', article 9, in *Cortes de los antiguos reinos de León y de Castilla*, 2: 544–554, here at pp. 552–553.

[30] Alfonso X, 'Ordenamiento de las Córtes celebradas en Valladolid ... (año 1258)', articles 26–27, p. 59: 'baruas luengas como manda su ley'.

[31] Peter I, 'Cuaderno ... Córtes celebradas en Valladolid ... (año 1351)', article 32, in *Cortes de los antiguos reinos de León y de Castilla*, 2: 1–74, here at p. 19: 'muchos judios e moros andan en la mi corte e en los mis rregnos que se llaman nonbres de christianos, e visten panos de viado e a meytad e con adobos, en guisa que sse non pueden conosçer ...'.

Trying to soothe relations with the Christian majority, Jewish leaders issued sumptuary laws for their own community that limited the luxurious clothes and jewels that Jewish women could wear.[32] *Conversos* – Jewish converts to Christianity – occupied a precarious position in Spanish society that worsened after 1478 when the Spanish Inquisition was founded by the so-called Catholic Monarchs, Isabella I of Castile (r. 1474–1504) and Ferdinand II of Aragón (r. 1479–1516). The stated objective of the Inquisition was to root out 'Judaizers' – insincere converts to Christianity who, it was feared, would infect good Christians with their heresies. Individuals found guilty by the Inquisition had to wear a *sanbenito* (also spelled *sambenito*), a tunic made from coarse cloth, during their sentencing, which might require them to wear the humiliating garment in public for a specified number of years.[33] When the French-born sculptor Esteban Jamete was convicted of heresy in 1558, he was sentenced to wear a yellow *sanbenito* for three years; one year into his sentence, Jamete's father-in-law denounced him to the Inquisition for complaining about the *sanbenito* and going out without it.[34] It was widely believed in Spain that heterodox religious beliefs were passed by blood from generation to generation.[35] The Inquisition publicly marked and perpetually punished contaminated families by forbidding the children and grandchildren of convicted heretics from wearing luxury fabrics and adornments. Catalina Hernández, whose grandfather had been convicted of heresy, found herself called before the Inquisition of Toledo when she was caught wearing a velvet skirt in 1573.[36] The pervasive belief in the power of blood continued to shape clothing and sumptuary laws in Spain even after the conquest of Granada and expulsion of the Jews (1492) and the forced conversion

---

[32] On sumptuary laws issued within the Jewish community in 1432, see: Moisés Orfali, 'Del lujo y de las leyes suntuarias: Ordenanzas sobre la vestimenta femenina en su contexto social y halájico', in Yolanda Moreno Koch (ed.), *La mujer judía* (Córdoba: Ediciones El Almendro, 2007), 161–179, here at pp. 162 and 171–172.

[33] On the *sanbenito*, see Henry Charles Lea, *A History of the Inquisition of Spain*, 4 vols. (New York: The MacMillan Company, 1906–1907; repr. 1922), iii: 162–172.

[34] Richard L. Kagan and Abigail Dyer, *Inquisitorial Inquiries: Brief Lives of Secret Jews and Other Heretics*, 2nd ed. (Baltimore: Johns Hopkins University Press, 2011), 60–62.

[35] On the theory of blood purity (*limpieza de sangre*), see James S. Amelang, *Parallel Histories: Muslims and Jews in Inquisitorial Spain* (Baton Rouge: Louisiana State University Press, 2013), 98–109.

[36] 'Proceso de fe de Catalina Hernández' (1573), Archivo Histórico Nacional (AHN), Inquisición 119, Exp. 34 (PARES). This section of the archive contains other cases of individuals caught wearing luxuries forbidden to the descendants of heretics.

of Spanish Muslims (1502) brought an end to the era of religious coexistence.

Luxury and Novelty in Imperial Spain

The number of sumptuary laws rose significantly during the sixteenth century in Spain, as in most of Europe.[37] This spike in sumptuary legislation is associated with the growth of global commerce, the increasing availability of a greater diversity of goods to a broader consumer base, and the accelerating pace of change in the world of fashion.[38] Spain was at the centre of those changes after Christopher Columbus's first trans-Atlantic voyage in 1492. Even before Columbus set sail, the production and consumption of luxury goods had begun to change in Spain in the late fifteenth century when Italian-style velvets, satins and damasks woven with large pomegranate-like patterns and enriched with silver and gold thread began to supplant traditional Andalusi silks as favoured markers of distinction.[39] In the sixteenth century, vast quantities of long-coveted luxuries and exotic new goods travelled from the Americas to Spain's port at Seville: precious metals and gemstones, pearls and furs, and expensive dyestuffs like indigo and logwood (used to produce a rich jet black). Luxury goods became more accessible than ever and could be found in the homes of urban artisans and beyond the cities in rural areas by the 1530s.[40] In 1538, the local government of Valverde (Segovia) forbade women from wearing silver jewellery worth more than twenty-two reales, apparently in response to the arrival of such luxuries in that rural community.[41] Isabella and Ferdinand, followed by their daughter Joanna (r. 1504–1555) and their grandson Charles V (r. 1516–1556), attempted to contain the dissemination of luxury goods through sumptuary laws, but the rapid pace of change left the laws always chasing two steps behind the fashions.

---

[37] According to Alan Hunt's tabulations, the number of sumptuary laws rose from the fifteenth to the sixteenth centuries in Venice (a 155 per cent increase), France (217 per cent), Germany (233 per cent), England (500 per cent) and Spain (800 per cent), but not in Florence or other Italian cities. Hunt, *Governance of the Consuming Passions*, 29, Table 2.1.

[38] Howell, *Commerce before Capitalism*, 208 and 232.

[39] *L'Art dels Velluters. Sedería de los siglos XV-XVI*, exhibition catalogue (València: Generalitat Valenciana, 2011), 94.

[40] On the consumption of luxuries by the artisan class in Seville, see: Blanca Morell Peguero, *Mercaderes y artesanos en la Sevilla del descubrimiento* (Seville: Diputación Provincial de Sevilla, 1986).

[41] *Ordenanzas de la Cuadrilla de Valverde, comunidad y tierra de Segovia, sobre la plata y paños de las bodas y otras cosas* (Madrid: Rivadeneyra, 1894), 18.

Sumptuous Silks and Social Disorder

The focus on social hierarchy and religious difference in late medieval sumptuary laws shifted to moral and economic concerns in post-Columbian Spain. Expensive fabrics were a gateway to sin, according to Queen Isabella's personal confessor, Fray Hernando de Talavera, who wrote a treatise denouncing excesses in clothing and shoes. Talavera claimed that the fineness and softness of sumptuous fabrics led people to 'the sin of luxury and of excessive pleasure'. The desire for fine fabrics engendered pride and vainglory, and encouraged consumers to reach above their social rank: 'Now there is hardly even a poor farmer or craftsman who does not dress in fine wool and even silk', Talavera complained.[42]

The first sumptuary law of Isabella and Ferdinand's reign was a 1494 ban on brocades (rich fabrics woven with patterns in silver or gold threads). In a striking break with medieval precedent, the new law applied equally to all social classes (except for the Church, as discussed below). 'You know well and it is evident to all', the law begins, 'how much in recent times our subjects and people of all estates and occupations go about excessive and disproportionate in their garments and apparel and trimmings and trappings without adjusting their expenses each according to their estate or with their way of living'.[43] The law was supposed to stop Spaniards from squandering their estates on sinful luxuries, especially on foreign goods. A two-year ban was imposed on imported brocades, cloth of gold and embroidery with silver or gold thread, and Spanish artisans were forbidden from making new clothes or horse trappings with those fabrics, or from gilding or silvering secular objects.[44] Isabella and

---

[42] Written in 1477, Talavera's treatise was first published in 1496. Hernando de Talavera, 'De vestir y calzar: Tractado provechoso que demuestra cómo en el vestir é calzar comúnmente se cometen muchos pecados y aun también en el comer y en el beber', in *Escritores místicos españoles*, vol. 16.1 of *Nueva Biblioteca de Autores Españoles* (Madrid: Bailly Bailliére, 1911), 57–78, here at p. 66: 'pecado de mollicie y de sobrado deleite'; 'ya no hay pobre labrador ni oficial por maravilla que no viste fino paño y aun seda'.

[43] Isabella I and Ferdinand II, 'Que por dos años ningu[n]o pueda traer ni meter de fuera del reyno brocado en pieça ni en ropas', in *Libro de las bulas y pragmáticas de los Reyes Católicos*, 2 vols. (Alcalá de Henares: Lâçalao Polono, 1503; facs. ed., Madrid: Instituto de España, 1973), ii: ff. 272r–273v, here at ff. 272r–272v: 'Bie[n] sabedes y a todos es notorio quanto de pocos tiempos a esta parte todos estados y profisiones de personas nuestros subditos y naturales se ban desmedido y desordenado en sus ropas y trajes y guarniciones y jaezes no midiendo sus gastos cada vno con su estado / ni co[n] su manera de biuir'.

[44] See the discussion of horse trappings as a site of luxury in Chapter 3 by Maria Hayward.

Ferdinand ordered that the law be pronounced at 'the customary plazas and markets' in all of their jurisdictions so it would 'come to the attention of everyone and no one is able to claim ignorance'.[45] The 1494 law was reissued by the Catholic Monarchs with more severe punishments in 1495 and 1496, by Queen Joanna in 1515, and again by Emperor Charles V in 1534.[46]

After the ban on brocades, the widespread wearing of silks continued to cause 'great disorder' in Spain, according to a 1499 law promulgated to control the problem. Hearkening back to earlier sumptuary laws that discriminated by class and occupation, this one rewarded military men and their families with the privilege of wearing silk. In a break with tradition, however, colour was no longer controlled. Men who kept horses, and their sons up to age fourteen, were permitted to wear doublets and hoods made from silk of any colour, which could be adorned with one silk strip no more than four fingers wide. The wives and unmarried daughters of men who 'continually maintain horses' were allowed to wear a silk bodice and a skirt or dress that could be adorned with a limited amount of decorative trim. Since the Muslim population of Granada was not permitted to own horses, a special provision of the law allowed them to wear silks, according to custom.[47]

When Muslims in the Kingdom of Castile were forced to convert to Christianity in 1502, the Crown reneged on the surrender treaty that had promised the Muslims of Granada that they would retain their traditional rights and customs – including the right to dress. A series of new sumptuary and clothing laws was issued in the sixteenth century to govern the appearances of the Moriscos, as converted Muslims and their descendants were called.[48] It seems that Morisco men were for the most part assimilated to wearing local Old Christian styles of dress, but some women continued to wear the traditional *almalafa*, a white garment

---

[45] Isabella I and Ferdinand II, 'Que por dos años …', f. 273v: 'las plaças y mercados acostu[m]brados'; 'venir a noticia de todos y persona alguna dello no pueda pretender ygnorancia'.

[46] Sempere y Guariños, *Historia del lujo*, 228, 234, 237.

[47] Isabella I and Ferdinand II, 'Que p[er]sonas puede[n] traer seda, y de que manera la pueden traer', in *Libro de las bulas y pragmáticas de los Reyes Católicos*, 2: ff. 265r–266v, here at f. 265r: 'gran desorden'; f. 265v: 'continnamente mantuuieren cauallos'. Fashions worn during the reign of Isabella and Ferdinand are described and illustrated in: Bernis, *Trajes y modas en la España de los Reyes Católicos*; and Ruth Matilda Anderson, *Hispanic Costume, 1480–1530* (New York: Hispanic Society of America, 1979).

[48] On the intersection of sumptuary legislation and clothing laws governing Moriscos in the sixteenth century, see: Javier Irigoyen-García, *'Moors Dresses as Moors': Clothing, Social Distinction, and Ethnicity in Early Modern Iberia* (Toronto: University of Toronto Press, 2017).

Figure 9.2 Moriscas (left) and Old Christian women (right) in Granada. Detail from the view of Granada in Georg Braun and Frans Hogenberg, *Beschreibung vnd Contrafactur der vornembster Stät der Welt*, vol. 3 of *Civitates orbis terrarum* (Cologne, 1582), fol. 5v. Alfredo Dagli Orti / Art Resource, NY.

that they used to veil their faces.[49] In 1526, Charles V issued a decree on Granada that forbade Moriscas from using *almalafas* to cover their faces and ordered them to give up the garments or at least to break with tradition by dyeing them a colour.[50] Old Christian women were also forbidden from covering their faces with the dark mantles and hats that they wore. Both styles of head-covering – the Morisca *almalafa* and the Old Christian mantle and hat – can be seen in the view of Granada that was published in Cologne in 1582 as part of Georg Braun's cities-of-the-world series (Figure 9.2). Moriscos were able to evade the laws banning traditional dress by paying a tax until 1567, when Philip II

---

[49] On the *almalafa*, see: Olivia Remie Constable, *To Live Like a Moor: Christian Perceptions of Muslim Identity in Medieval and Early Modern Spain*, ed. Robin Vose (Philadelphia: University of Pennsylvania Press, 2018), 47–55.

[50] Charles V, 'Cédula sobre lo que debía de hacerse en el reino de Granada en virtud de las visitaciones hechas y de lo acordado en la Congregación celebrada en la Capilla Real (7 diciembre 1526)', doc. 31 in Antonio Gallego y Burín and Alfonso Gámir Sandoval, *Los moriscos del Reino de Granada según el Sínodo de Gaudix de 1554* (Granada: Universidad de Granada, 1968), 198–205, here at pp. 202–203.

(r. 1556–1598) reissued the laws along with a new provision explicitly forbidding Moriscos from wearing silk. As Javier Irigoyen-García has argued, the ban on silk effectively treated all Moriscos like convicted heretics and made them second-class citizens of the Spanish Crown, regardless of the status they held within their own community.[51] The enforcement of punitive clothing laws has long been considered a contributing factor in the Moriscos' armed uprising of 1568, which resulted in their dispersal and ultimate expulsion from Spain.

The Catholic Church was exempt from all the sumptuary laws issued by the Spanish Crown.[52] Unaffected by restrictions on precious metals, ecclesiastical vestments for the celebration of the mass and processions like Corpus Christi became more lavish than ever. Liturgical silverwork and vestments richly embroidered in silver and gold reached their artistic apogees in the sixteenth century at the royal monastery of the Escorial and in cathedral cities like Salamanca and Burgos.[53] The Church was responsible for policing its own consumption of luxury and the dress of its clerics. In the wake of the Council of Trent (1545–1563), bishoprics across Spain published detailed dress codes ordering the clergy to wear plain black garments without any decorative trims or jewellery when they were not performing official functions.[54] Bishops were also responsible for making sure that the clothes and accessories used to dress sacred images, including life-size wooden processional sculptures, conformed to the Council of Trent's order to avoid adorning images 'with a seductive charm'.[55] Religious leaders and moralists were especially vexed by the popular practice of dressing sculptures of the Virgin in contemporary secular fashions, which were changing ever more rapidly in the second half of the sixteenth century.[56]

---

[51] Irigoyen-García, *'Moors Dressed as Moors'*, 112.

[52] The Catholic Monarchs did take steps to control clerical dress in other ways. The Spanish Pope Alexander VI granted them authority to punish clerics who failed to wear clerical dress and the tonsure. Ángel Fernández Collado, *Historia de la iglesia en España: Edad moderna* (Toledo: Instituto Teológico San Ildefonso, 2007), 44–45.

[53] Marta M. Laguardia Álvarez, 'Liturgical Embroidery and the Embroiderers of Salamanca in the Sixteenth Century', *Datatèxtil* 7 (2002): 28–43; Aurelio A. Barrón García, 'Renaissance Embroidery in Burgos', *Datatèxtil* 30 (2014): 2–22; María Barrigón Montañés, 'Hilos de oro tendidos, cortaduras y matiz: Joyas del obrador de bordados de El Escorial', *Reales Sitios* 198 (2013): 40–69.

[54] See, for example, the regulations on clerical dress issued by Archbishop Juan Bautista Acevedo of Valladolid, *Constitvciones Synodales: Fechas y promulgadas en la primera Synodo q[ue] se celebró en la Ciudad y Obispado de Valladolid ...* (Valladolid: Juan de Bustillo, 1607), ff. 81r–82r.

[55] *The Canons and Decrees of the Council of Trent*, trans. H. J. Schroeder (Rochford, IL: Tan Books and Publishers, 1978), 216.

[56] Susan Verdi Webster, *Art and Ritual in Golden-Age Spain: Sevillian Confraternities and the Processional Sculpture of Holy Week* (Princeton: Princeton University Press, 1998), 119–124.

Figure 9.3 Man's cloak made in Spain from Italian red silk cut velvet, lined with linen, decorated with a border of yellow satin appliqué outlined with silk cords, and edged with silk fringe, c. 1580–1590. Victoria & Albert Museum, London. Inv. no. 832–1904.

'Friends of Novelties': Artisans and Fashion Innovations

Luxury begat novelty in sixteenth-century Spanish fashion.[57] New styles of garments with stiff geometric shapes and wide hems were made to show off rich fabrics with large patterns and yards of silk ribbons, fringe and other luxury trims – as seen on a late-sixteenth century red velvet man's cloak in the collection of the Victoria & Albert Museum (Figure 9.3).[58] Military-style slashings, which

---

[57] On fashion innovations in early modern Europe, see Evelyn Welch (ed.), *Fashioning the Early Modern: Dress, Textiles, and Innovation in Europe, 1500–1800* (Oxford: Oxford University Press, 2017).

[58] The techniques used to make a rich embroidered silk Spanish cloak are reconstructed by Claire Thornton in Melanie Braun et al., *17th-Century Men's Dress Patterns, 1600–1630*

revealed sumptuous silk linings beneath rich outer layers of fabric, were adapted to civilian use for men's and women's clothing. As Spain reached the height of its imperial powers, the rich and rigid Spanish style of dress was disseminated around the globe and could be seen at the European courts of London, Milan, Brussels, Stockholm, Prague and beyond.[59] Spanish sumptuary legislation became more specific and complicated during the reign of Charles V as lawmakers tried to outwit the artisans who were inventing new trends, but their efforts inadvertently accelerated the pace of change by stimulating new fashion innovations in response to the legislation.

On 29 December 1551, a new law was published to defend previous pragmatics and eliminate the latest 'inventions of tailors and artisans, and other friends of novelties'.[60] Novelty (*novedad*) was considered to be inherently threatening, defined in the first Castilian dictionary (1611) as 'a new and unaccustomed thing' that 'tends to be dangerous because it brings change to the old custom'.[61] The six densely printed pages of the 1551 law detailed the amounts and kinds of trimmings that were permitted on particular garments and accessories for men and women. No one of any class or station was allowed to wear garments made from brocade, embroidered or otherwise embellished with silver or gold thread, silk cording, braid, ruffles or fringes. Men's and women's garments could be adorned with a silk band measuring no more than one-eighth of a *vara* wide (10.5 cm or 4.125 inches) or up to three narrow strips of silk at the hem, which had to be attached with plain backstitches (decorative stitching was forbidden). Hats could not be adorned with decorations made from real or fake silver or gold. Owners of banned goods could continue to use them for up to eight months if they first registered them with local officials. A person caught violating the new law would lose the offending skirt, cloak, doublet, breeches or hat, and be charged a fine equal to its value. A similar penalty would be issued to an artisan who was caught making an offending garment for the first time, but repeat

---

(London: Thames & Hudson/V&A, 2016), 134–141. More surviving garments and accessories from the period appear in *La moda española en el Siglo de Oro*, exhibition catalogue (Toledo: Fundación Cultura Deporte Castilla-La Mancha, 2015).

[59] See the essays in Colomer and Descalzo (eds.), *Spanish Fashion at the Courts of Early Modern Europe*.

[60] Charles V, *Las prematicas y ordenanzas que sus Magestades ordenaron sobre los trajes, Brocados, Oros y Sedas en el año de mil y quinientos y cincuenta y vno* (n.p.: Juan de Brocar, [1551]), Biblioteca Nacional de España (BNE) R/14370/9, ff. 70r–72v, here at f. 70v (LHE): 'inuenciones de sastres y officiales: y otras gentes amigos de nouedades'.

[61] 'Novedad' in Covarrubias Orozco, *Tesoro de la lengua castellana*, 780: 'Cosa nueva y no acostumbrada. Suele ser peligrosa por traer consigo mudanza de uso antiguo'.

offenders were threatened with much harsher punishments: lashings and a two-year exile for a second offence, and six years rowing on the king's galleys for a third.[62]

In response to the 1551 law banning silk passementerie, artisans invented new wool trimmings to take their place.[63] Charles V denounced 'the malice of the artisans' who were defrauding the law and issued another law in October of 1552 that applied the same limitations and restrictions as on silk to the new wool trimmings.[64] The 1551 and 1552 laws depicted tailors as adversaries of public order and charged them with enforcing sumptuary laws that ran counter to their economic interests. The laws also strictly limited the artisans' own consumption of luxury goods: tailors, shoemakers, tanners, weavers and their fellow craftsmen were not allowed to wear any silk except for their hats and other head-coverings, and their wives were limited to using silk for a bodice and one silk strip decorating a wool mantle.[65] Early modern Spanish writers complained that the wives of artisans were going out so finely dressed that they had become indistinguishable from the wives of noblemen.[66] A Polish visitor to Seville in 1595 was astonished to see the wife of a tailor going to church dressed in pearls worthy of royalty.[67] The laws of 1551–1552 highlight the unique relationship that artisans had with sumptuary legislation, which effectively punished them twice as makers of luxuries and novelties who were also their consumers.

Dress Reform and Decline in Late Sixteenth- and Seventeenth-Century Spain

In the second half of the sixteenth century, King Philip II set an example of sartorial restraint for his subjects and came to be known for dressing

---

[62] Charles V, *Las prematicas y ordenanzas* [1551], ff. 70v–72r.

[63] Sempere y Guariños, *Historia del lujo*, 238.

[64] Charles V, *Las prematicas y ordena[n]ças que sus Magestades ordenaro[n] sobre los trajes, Brocados, Oros y sedas en el año de mil y quinie[n]tos y cincuenta y vno: con la declaracion deste año de mil quinie[n]tos y cincuenta y dos; Juntamente con la vltima declaracion para que no se hagan guarniciones ni cortaduras de paño, con otras cosas tocantes alos dichos trajes* (n.p., [1552]), BNE, R/14090(17), ff. 225v–226v, here at f. 225v (LHE): 'la malicia delos officiales'.

[65] Charles V, *Las prematicas y ordenanzas* [1551], f. 71v.

[66] Antonio Álvarez-Ossorio Alvariño, 'Leyes suntuaries y circulación de élites: El consumo suntuario frente a la sociedad estamental (siglos XVI-XVII)', in *Actas del I Congreso de Jóvenes Geógrafos e Historiadores* (Seville: Escuela Libre de Historiadores, 1995), 267–273, here at pp. 268–269.

[67] Marzenna Adamczyk, 'Diario de una peregrinación por España, 1595', *Hispania* 45, no. 160 (1985): 387–429, here at p. 427.

exclusively in black after the death of his third wife in 1568.[68] Modest
black clothing became the ultimate status symbol in Philip II's Spain,
but luxury continued to thrive in sumptuous details like the gold buttons
and expensive lace ruffs that can be seen on members of the De la Llana
family in their 1586 illuminated letter of nobility (Figure 9.4). Luxurious
dress came under fire during the period of national soul-searching that
followed the defeat of the supposedly invincible Spanish Armada by
Elizabeth I's England in 1588.[69] In the wake of the disaster, the critic
Martín González de Cellorigo called for the restoration of an ancient
Roman law that had restricted women's display of wealth during the
Second Punic War. According to González de Cellorigo, Spanish women
were spending so much on luxuries that men could not afford to marry
them – and the population was declining as a result. He also claimed that
Spanish men had become lazy and unproductive thanks to easy New
World money.[70] New gender-specific sumptuary laws were designed to
bring men and women back in line with ideals of masculinity and femininity from a romanticised past when men had distinguished themselves
as warriors and women had honoured their families by staying out of
public view.[71] Whereas previous generations of sumptuary legislation had
restricted luxury fabrics and trims in general, laws issued between the
1590s and 1630s tried to control specific kinds of garments and the ways
that men and women wore their clothes and styled their hair. The success
or failure of those laws was largely determined by the degree to which the
Habsburg kings and queens followed their own rules.

Legislating Masculinity and Femininity

'Some men appear through their finery to be sorry to have been born
male', Francisco de Quevedo wrote in the early 1600s. 'The end result is

[68] William N. Ambler, 'The Portrait Workshop at the Court of Philip III of Spain' (Unpublished PhD thesis, Institute of Fine Arts, New York University, 2014), 102; José Luis Colomer, 'Black and the Royal Image', in Colomer and Descalzo (eds.), *Spanish Fashion at the Courts of Early Modern Europe* 1: 77–112, here at pp. 86–91.
[69] On the phenomenon of criticism (*arbitrismo*) that followed the Armada's defeat in Spain, see: J. H. Elliott, 'Self-Perception and Decline in Early Seventeenth-Century Spain', *Past & Present* 74 (1977): 41–61.
[70] See the translated selection from Martín González de Cellorigo's *Memorial de la política necesaria y útil restauración a la república de España* ... (1600) in Jon Cowans (ed.), *Early Modern Spain: A Documentary History* (Philadelphia: University of Pennsylvania Press, 2003), 133–140.
[71] On gender ideals for men and women, respectively, see: Elizabeth Lehfeldt, 'Ideal Men: Masculinity and Decline in Seventeenth-Century Spain', *Renaissance Quarterly* 61, no. 2 (2008): 463–494; and Mariló Vigil, *La vida de las mujeres en los siglos XVI y XVII* (Madrid: Siglo XXI de España, 1986).

Figure 9.4 Fashionable black garments worn with white ruffs during the reign of Philip II. *Letter Patent of Nobility of Francisco de la Llana, Resident of Antequera* (Granada, 1586). Hispanic Society of America, New York City.

that their gender is uncertain ... which has been the grounds for the promulgation of new laws', the famous satirist explained.[72] Laws governing Spanish men's appearances in the late sixteenth and early seventeenth centuries targeted trends that were considered to be effeminate. Nothing symbolised the purported decline of Spanish manhood more than a man

---

[72] Francisco de Quevedo, *España defendida y los tiempos de ahora* (1609), translated in: François Soyer, *Ambiguous Gender in Early Modern Spain and Portugal: Inquisitors, Doctors and the Transgression of Gender Norms* (Leiden and Boston: Brill, 2012), 19.

wearing a large decorated ruff. Men's ruffs, which had grown larger and more ostentatious over the years, inspired numerous laws between the 1580s and the 1620s. In 1586, the Cortes of Madrid passed a law declaring that 'no man, of any estate, condition, quality, or age' was allowed to wear a collar or cuffs decorated with ornamental openwork, gold or silver wire, or stiffened with starch.[73] In 1594, Philip II ordered the men in his kingdoms to comply with the Cortes's restrictions on ruffs, to which he added a ban on any colour except for white and a precise restriction on their width to one-twelfth of a *vara* (that is, 7 cm or 2.75 inches).[74] Like Charles V's 1551–1552 laws on trimmings, Philip II's laws on ruffs included detailed descriptions of forbidden decorations. Directed exclusively at men, the ruff laws introduced a new emphasis on gender that would become a key feature of Spanish sumptuary legislation in the decades that followed.

The laws on ruffs were strictly enforced in the 1590s, when men like Alonso García – a muleteer from Villena – were jailed for exceeding the size limits or violating the rules for decorations.[75] A reprieve came with the accession of Philip III (r. 1598–1621), who issued a sumptuary law in 1600 that took the unusual step of loosening previous restrictions by increasing the legal width of men's ruffs to one-eighth of a *vara*.[76] The court of Philip III came to be known for its sartorial decadence even as Spain's fortunes and international standing plummeted.[77] When Philip IV (r. 1621–1665) came to the throne, dress reform was a top priority. Under the guidance of the Count of Olivares, the new king issued a set of twenty-three reforms (*Capítulos de Reformación*, 1623), twelve of which dealt with consumption and the physical appearances of his subjects. The most radical change was an order for men of all classes to replace their ruffs with a plain and flat white collar (*valona*).[78] Shortly after the

[73] Cortes de Madrid (1586–1588), ch. 52, in *Actas de las Cortes de Castilla*, vol. 9 of 61 (Madrid: Hijos de J. A. García, 1885), 445–448; quote on p. 447: 'ningun hombre, de qualquier estado, condicion, calidad y edad que sea …'.

[74] Philip II, *Prematica en que se manda guarder lo proueido por vn capitulo de las Cortes, del año de ochenta y seis: En que se prohibio que los hombres no puedan traer en los cuellos, ni en puños, guarnicion alguna, ni almidon, ni gomas, ni filetes: Sino sola la lechuguilla de olanda, ò lienço, con vna, ò dos vaynillas, y se declara q[ue] sean de vn dozauo de vara de medir, y q[ue] las vaynillas y filetes no sean de color sino blancas: Y se acrecientan las penas contra los que excedieren* (Madrid: Pedro Madrigal, 1594), BNE R/5251(3) (int. 3c).

[75] 'Ejecutoria del pleito litigado por el fiscal del rey y Antonio Martín, alguacil de Salamanca, con Alonso García, arriero, vecino de Villena (Valencia) y preso en la cárcel pública de Salamanca, por haber incumplido las leyes y pragmáticas al vestir un cuello más grande de lo estipulado', Archivo de la Real Chancillería de Valladolid (ARCHV), Registro de Ejecutorias, Caja 1806, 15 (PARES).

[76] Philip III, *Prematica en que se prohiben colgaduras y adereços de casas de brocados, y telas de oro y plata y bordado, y hechura de joyas de oro y pieças de plata, y se da la forma en ella contenida, y se permite traer cuellos de ochaua con almidon* (Madrid: Pedro Madrigal, 1600), BNE R/23919 (int. 3b), f. 39r.

[77] On the fashions of Philip III's era, see: Carmen Bernis, *El traje y los tipos sociales en El Quijote* (Madrid: El Viso, 2001).

[78] Philip IV, *Capitvlos de reformacion, qve sv Magestad se sirve de mandar guardar por esta ley, para el gouierno del Reyno* (Madrid: Tomas Iunti, 1623), 14–15.

Figure 9.5 Men wearing the *golilla* and *valona* imposed by Philip IV.
*Letter Patent of Nobility of Don Francisco and Don Fernando Ramírez de
la Trapera of the City of Úbeda* (Granada, 1633). Hispanic Society of
America, New York City.

law was passed, a stiff neckband (*golilla*) was invented to support the
collar and raise it higher on the neck. Women were still permitted to wear
ruffled collars and cuffs, albeit with limited decorations. A 1633 portrait
of the Ramírez de la Trapera family, from the southern town of Úbeda,
reflects the new dress policy: the men wear a *valona* over a *golilla*, while
the women continue to wear large decorated ruffs (Figure 9.5).[79] Philip

---

[79] See the classic essay by Ruth Matilda Anderson, *The Golilla: A Spanish Collar of the 17th
Century* (New York: Hispanic Society of America, 1969); and the theme revisited in
Amanda Wunder, 'Innovation and Tradition at the Court of Philip IV of Spain (1621–
1665): The Invention of the Golilla and the Guardainfante', in Welch (ed.), *Fashioning
the Early Modern*, 111–133.

IV's ban on ruffs stands out among sumptuary laws for its immediate and long-term effectiveness, which can be attributed to the fact that the king himself adopted the new collar that he was requiring his subjects to wear.[80] The stiff, starched white collar atop a *golilla* became a defining feature of seventeenth-century Spanish menswear and remained an official garment for government employees well into the eighteenth century.

In the spring of 1639, Philip IV issued a trio of gendered sumptuary laws.[81] One forbade men from wearing long hair and quiffs (*guedejas y copetes*), which were blamed for causing scandal in the Spanish kingdoms.[82] No man wearing his hair in such an effeminate fashion would be permitted in the presence of the king, it was declared. The other two laws applied to women, who were forbidden from covering their faces with their mantles or wearing the wide-hipped farthingale (*guardainfante*) and low-cut bodice (*escotado*) that had become fashionable in the 1630s.[83] Critics claimed that women were subverting the authority of their fathers and husbands by appearing in public anonymously beneath their mantles and hiding illicit pregnancies under their voluminous skirts.[84] Requiring many yards of costly fabrics starched

---

[80] Martínez Bermejo, 'Beyond Luxury'; and Javier Portús Pérez, 'Control e imagen real en la corte de Felipe IV (1621–1626)', *Studia Aurea* 9 (2015): 245–264, here at pp. 249–250.

[81] On the controversies of this era, see: Rafael González Cañal, 'El lujo y la ociosidad durante la privanza de Olivares: Bartolomé Jiménez Patón y la polémica sobre el guardainfante y las guedejas', *Criticón* 53 (1991): 71–96.

[82] Philip IV, *Pregon en qve sv Magestad manda, qve por qvanto el abvso de las gvedejas y copetes con que andan algunos hombres, y los rizos con que componen el cabello ha llegado à hazer escandalo en estos Reynos, ningun hombre pueda traer guedejas ni copete* (Madrid: Francisco Martínez, 1639), Harvard Law School Library (HLSL). On the definition of 'guedejas', see: Carmen Bernis, 'La moda en los retratos de Velázquez', in Javier Portús (ed.), *El retrato en el Museo del Prado* (Madrid: Anaya, 1994), 271–301, here at pp. 278–279.

[83] Philip IV, *Prematica en qve sv Magestad manda, que ninguna muger ande tapada, sino descubierta el rostro, demanera que pueda ser vista, y conocida, so las penas en ella contenidas, y de las demas que tratan de lo susodicho* (Madrid: Pedro Tazo, 1639), HLSL; Philip IV, *Pregon en qve sv Magestad manda, que ninguna muger de qualquier estado y calidad que sea pueda traer, ni traiga guardainfante, ò otro instrumēto, ò trage semejante, excepto las mugeres que con licencia de las justicias publicamente son malas de sus personas* (Madrid: Francisco Martínez, 1639), HLSL. The anti-*tapada* law of 1639 repeated a law that had been issued by the Cortes in 1586 and published as a royal decree by Philip II in 1590; see *Actas de las Cortes de Castilla* 9: 440–442.

[84] Laura R. Bass and Amanda Wunder, 'The Veiled Ladies of the Early Modern Spanish World: Seduction and Scandal in Seville, Madrid, and Lima', *Hispanic Review* 77/1 (2009): 97–144; Amanda Wunder, 'Women's Fashions and Politics in Seventeenth-Century Spain: The Rise and Fall of the *Guardainfante*', *Renaissance Quarterly* 68/1 (2015): 133–186.

at great expense to cover it, the *guardainfante* was criticised for being 'costly and superfluous' – the very definition of luxury.[85] The 1639 law was designed to shame women out of wearing wide-hipped farthingales and low-cut bodices by permitting only prostitutes to wear them in public, but Philip IV's own wives and daughters wore the exaggeratedly feminine style, which only grew in popularity – and in size – over the following decades. The *guardainfante* reached enormous proportions by the 1660s (Figure 9.6) before falling out of fashion towards the end of the seventeenth century, no thanks to sumptuary legislation. The cleavage-baring bodices that had been banned in 1639 remained so commonplace at the century's end that one cleric facetiously claimed that a foreigner visiting Spain who had heard that only prostitutes were permitted to wear low-cut bodices would have to ask, 'in this land are all women prostitutes?'[86] Churchmen and lawmakers seeking to control women's appearances frequently resorted to the threat that any woman seen in public ran the risk of being mistaken for a prostitute – who was, by definition, a 'public woman' (*muger pública*). But how women dressed behind closed doors was beyond the scope of sumptuary laws. This was tacitly admitted by a 1600 law, which forbade prostitutes from wearing silk dresses, gold, pearls and jewels in public but did not restrict the luxuries that a 'public woman' enjoyed in the privacy of her own home.[87]

Spanish Fashion and Economic Protectionism

The new fashions that emerged during Philip IV's reign – exemplified by the *golilla* for men and the *guardainfante* for women – became a national costume that distinguished Spanish dress from the French trends that prevailed in the rest of Europe. At the same time, Spanish sumptuary laws began to focus more than ever on the protection of national economic interests. In 1657, Philip IV passed a law prohibiting his subjects of all ranks from wearing any clothes or textiles manufactured in the enemy nations of France, England or Portugal (which had separated from

---

[85] Alonso Carranza, *Rogacion en detestacion de los grandes abusos en los traxes y adornos nueuamente introducidos en España* (Madrid: María de Quiñones, 1636), ff. 3r–5v, 'costoso y superfluo'.

[86] Antonio de Ezcaray, *Vozes del dolor, nacidas de la mvltitvd de pecados, que se cometen por los trages profanos, afeytes, escotados, y culpables ornatos* ... (Seville: Tomás López de Haro, 1691), 262: '*En esta tierra todas son mugeres publicas?*'.

[87] Philip III, *Prematica y nveva orden de los vestidos y trages, assi de hombres como de mugeres* (Madrid: Pedro Madrigal, 1600), BNE R/23919 (int. 3a), f. 31r.

Figure 9.6 An exceptionally large *guardainfante*. Juan Carreño de Miranda, *Portrait of Doña Inés de Zúñiga, Countess of Monterrey*, c. 1660–1670. Museo Lázaro Galdiano, Madrid. Inv. no. 1518.

Spain in 1640). The law permitted merchants who already had the forbidden goods in stock to dispose of their inventory by shipping it to the Indies. Tailors who made clothing from illegal imports were threatened with fines, public shaming and exile.[88] Yet contraband goods – especially luxury textiles from France – continued to make their way to the court, where they were a sign of class distinction for those who could afford to purchase them.[89] Around the time of Philip IV's death in 1665, Spanish men began to adopt the frock coat and cravat that were popularised by King Louis XIV.[90] Philip IV's successor, Charles II (r. 1665–1700), reissued the law of 1657 multiple times and added requirements for legally imported fabrics to meet the same standards of quality that were imposed on textiles produced domestically.[91] This kind of protectionist legislation, inspired by mercantilist economic theory, continued to thrive up to the late eighteenth century, even as laws restricting luxury per se were coming to an end.

Dressing Spanish in Bourbon Spain

The death of Charles II in 1700 brought an end to the Habsburg dynasty in Spain and ushered in a new era after the contested accession of the first French Bourbon king of Spain, Philip V (r. 1700–1746), was settled by the Peace of Utrecht in 1713. The Spanish court definitively shifted to French fashions, but Philip V maintained continuity with his Habsburg predecessors by repeating old sumptuary legislation. In 1723, he reissued a 1691 law banning brocades and other fabrics or decorations made with silver or gold and forbidding the importation of laces and silks from enemy nations. Men and women were permitted to wear velvet,

---

[88] Philip IV, *Prematica qve sv Magestad manda pvblicar sobre conservacion del contrauando, reuocacion de las permissiones, prohibicion del vso de las mercaderias, y frutos de los Reynos de Francia, Inglaterra, Portugal, y reformacion de trajes, y vestidos, y otras cosas* (Madrid: Pablo de Val, 1657), BNE R/23879(9), 5–6 and 9–10.

[89] Manuel Herrero Sánchez, 'La política de embargos y el contrabando de productos de lujo en Madrid (1635–1673). Sociedad cortesana y dependencia de los mercados internacionales', *Hispania* 59, no. 201 (1999): 171–191.

[90] Amalia Descalzo Lorenzo, 'Vestirse a la moda en la España moderna', *Vínculos de Historia* 6 (2017): 105–134, here at p. 122. On the relationship between Spanish and French dress in the second half of the seventeenth century, see: Arianna Giorgi, *España viste a la francesa: La historia de un traje de moda de la segunda mitad del siglo XVII* (Murcia: Universidad de Murcia/Editum, 2016).

[91] Charles II, *Pragmatica qve sv Magestad manda pvblicar sobre la reformación en el Escesso de Traxes, Lacayos, y coches, y prohibicion del consumo de las mercaderias de Francia, y sus Dominios, y otras cosas* (Madrid: Julian de Paredes, 1674), BNE R/23879(18); Sempere y Guariños, *Historia del lujo*, 314–316.

damask, taffeta, and other silks of any colour as long as they were made in Spain or in friendly nations. As set forth in previous legislation, artisans including tailors were only allowed to wear silk on their sleeves, hose and hat linings. To the pre-existing laws Philip V added a new one requiring officers of the court in Madrid and throughout the realm to dress exclusively in black.[92] Three years earlier, the king had ordered all magistrates to wear the *golilla*.[93] Thus it was that Spain's first Bourbon monarch turned the unofficial uniform of Spanish noblemen in the Habsburg era into a legally-mandated costume for civil servants.[94]

Philip V's 1723 law was the last general sumptuary law governing luxury consumption in Spain, but the Crown continued to issue new clothing laws and protectionist legislation regulating consumption by its subjects and their appearances throughout the eighteenth century.[95] Following the economic model established by Jean-Baptiste Colbert in Louis XIV's France, Philip V and his successors banned foreign imports and established royal manufactories for silk, fine woollens, tapestries, porcelain, mirrors and glass, and other luxury goods.[96] Spanish silk production – which had declined precipitously in the seventeenth century – was revived under Bourbon rule. In 1726, Philip V declared that Spanish looms were producing enough high-quality fabric to dress the entire nation, and thus ordered all his subjects without exception to dress exclusively in silks and woollens made in Spain.[97] New protectionist legislation responded to the increasing globalisation of commerce in the eighteenth century. Philip V banned silks and other textiles imported from China or elsewhere in Asia in 1718.[98] When Indian muslin became a popular material for making women's head-coverings, Charles III

---

[92] Philip V, *Pragmatica sancion, que su Magestad manda observer, sobre Trages, y otras cosas* (Madrid: Juan Sanz, 1723), BNE R/23879(39), ff. 1r–5v.

[93] Archivo de la Corona de Aragón, Real Audiencia, registro 7 (22 June 1720), f. 47r (LHE).

[94] Anderson, *The Golilla*, 16–17.

[95] Alan Hunt argues that sumptuary legislation did not die out in the eighteenth century, but rather underwent 'a process of transfiguration' with laws banning 'moralized objects' replaced by 'protectionist economic regulation'. Hunt, *Governance of the Consuming Passions*, 361.

[96] On the revival of industry under Bourbon rule, see Richard Herr, *The Eighteenth-Century Revolution in Spain* (Princeton: Princeton University Press, 1958), 123–147.

[97] Philip V, [Untitled; first words of text: 'Don Phelipe, por la gracia de Dios, Rey de Castilla ... teniendo presente lo que se han adelantado las fabricas de sedas . . .'.] (Madrid: Imprenta de la Calle de la Paz, 1726), AHN, Consejos, Lib. 1477, núm. 16, f. 34 (LHE).

[98] Philip V, [Untitled; first words of text: 'Manda sv Magestad, qve por qanto se ha reconocido que de poco tiempo à esta parte se han introducido, è introducen en estos Reynos las ropas, sedas, y texidos de la China . . .'.] (Madrid: n.p., 1718), AHN, Consejos, Lib. 1476, no. 10, f. 33 (LHE).

(r. 1759–1788) issued a royal order stating that 'absolutely no mantles or mantillas may be worn in my kingdom other than those made only of silk or wool, which is what was and has been for many years now the costume typical of the Nation'.[99]

What constituted typical Spanish costume was a charged political question in the eighteenth century.[100] This was a fertile period for the invention of dress traditions that gave rise to the phenomenon of *majismo* – an untranslatable term referring to urban elites who dressed up in outfits that were supposedly inspired by traditional lower-class costumes.[101] Two women dressed as *majas* wear the lace mantillas that became synonymous with Spanish femininity in a painting attributed to Francisco de Goya (Figure 9.7).[102] The two men behind them wear long cloaks and broad-brimmed hats (*chambergos*), which they use to cover their faces. Like the covered women (*tapadas*) of the Habsburg era, covered men – called *embozados* – were blamed for causing 'many scandals and excesses' at the Bourbon court.[103] For fifty years, starting in 1716, the government passed ineffective legislation prohibiting men at court from hiding their faces with hats or other covers.[104] An effort to enforce the laws against *embozados* in 1766 was so unpopular that a riot broke out in Madrid and forced the king to flee the capital. In 1784, yet another royal order was issued to stop men from 'the abuse of disguising themselves by day and night', this time using a coarse brown cloak decorated with colourful embroidery. The law tried to discourage 'persons of distinction' from

---

[99] Charles III, *Pragmatica sancion de su Magestad, por la que se sirve mandar, que no se use absolutemente en el Reyno de otros Mantos ni Mantillas, que los de solo Seda, o Lana, con lo demas que contiene* (Madrid: Antonio Sanz, 1770), Google Books, 3: 'no puedan usarse absolutamente en mi Reyno otros Mantos ni Mantillas, que los de solo Seda ó Lana, que es el que era y ha sido de muchos años á esta parte el trage proprio de la Nacion'.

[100] On the 'clothing question' in eighteenth-century Spain, see: Molina and Vega, *Vestir la identidad, construir la apariencia*.

[101] See the definition of 'majismo' in Tara Zanardi, *Framing Majismo: Art and Royal Identity in Eighteenth-Century Spain* (University Park: Pennsylvania State University Press, 2016), 4.

[102] On the mantilla and Spanish identity, see Tara Zanardi, 'Crafting Spanish Female Identity: Silk Lace Mantillas at the Crossroads of Tradition and Fashion', *Material Culture Review* 77/78 (2013): 139–157.

[103] Philip V, *Vando del Rey N. Señor (que Dios guarde) en que prohibe Gorros calados, y todo genero de Embozo, que oculte el rostro* (Madrid: Juan Sanz, 1723), in Vicente Salva, *Colección General de Cortes, Leyes y Cédulas Reales: Reinado de Felipe V desde 1701 hasta 1735*, vol. 31, Real Academia de la Historia, ff. 181r–v, here at f. 181r (LHE): 'muchos escandalos, y excessos'.

[104] Philip V's law against *embozados*, first issued on 9 July 1716, was repeated in 1723 and again in 1745. *Tomo tercero de autos acordados* (Madrid: Juan Antonio Pimentel, 1745; repr., *Nueva recopilación*, Valladolid: Lex Nova, 1982), v: 341.

Figure 9.7 *Majas* and *embozados*. Attributed to Francisco de Goya y Lucientes, *Majas on a Balcony*, c. 1800–1810. Metropolitan Museum of Art, New York City. H. O. Havemeyer Collection, Bequest of Mrs. H. O. Havemeyer, 1929. Inv. no. 29.100.10.

wearing the garish garment by warning that they would be confused with the gypsies, smugglers, bullfighters and butchers who were traditionally associated with it.[105] The fashions that became popular in the eighteenth

---

[105] Charles III, Royal Order of 5 May 1784 quoted in *Novísima recopilación de las Leyes de España: dividida en XII libros* ... 6 vols. in 4 (Madrid: [n.p.], 1805–1807), 3: 193, n7: 'el

century may have been new, but the Bourbon government responded in a familiar way: by legislating against them.

As the era of European sumptuary legislation came to an end, critics declared that laws against luxury had done more harm than good.[106] 'Sumptuary Laws have been partially to blame for the ruin of our most valuable industries', wrote Pedro Rodríguez de Campomanes, an economist who served the government of Charles III. 'It would be a grave political error to fall back into such a trap, and it is not expected now in this enlightened century.'[107] In his *History of Luxury and of Sumptuary Laws in Spain*, Juan de Sempere y Guariños denounced laws like Isabella and Ferdinand's ban on brocades, which he claimed had reduced the artisan class 'to idleness and indigence'. Spain would have been better off, he said, if the Catholic Monarchs had taken advantage of the silver and gold coming from the Indies and encouraged the domestic production of brocades instead of banning the luxury fabrics altogether. His stance against sumptuary laws did not mean that Sempere y Guariños advocated the consumption of luxury, which he called 'an abhorrent vice' that causes 'moral and civic damages' to society. He supported legislation outlawing styles that were 'obscene and provocative' (like low-cut bodices), restricted the movement of the body (like ruffs and large farthingales), or hid the face (like *tapadas* and *embozados*).[108] Sumptuary legislation was incompatible with Enlightenment, according to Sempere y Guariños and his contemporaries, but the imperative to regulate dress and consumption remained steadfast even in the century of lights.

Conclusion

As this overview of five hundred years of sumptuary legislation in Spain reveals, laws governing consumption were a flexible tool. The laws, which originated in the thirteenth century as a means of distinguishing social and religious hierarchies, evolved in response to changing social

---

abuso de disfrazarse de dia y noche'; 'personas de distincion'. Cited in José Cepeda Adán, 'Tipos populares en el Madrid de Carlos III', in *Coloquio internacional Carlos III y su siglo: Actas*, 2 vols. (Madrid: Universidad Complutense, Departamento de Historia Moderna, 1990), 2: 481–503, here at p. 495.

[106] Hunt, *Governance of the Consuming Passions*, 359.

[107] Pedro Rodríguez de Campomanes, *Discurso sobre la educacion popular de los artesanos, y su fomento* (1775), quoted in Sempere y Guariños, *Historia del lujo*, 378: 'las Leyes Suntuarias han sido causa parcial de destruirse nuestras manufacturas mas preciosas. Seria grande error político incidir de nuevo en semejante escollo: y no es ya de esperar en las luces de este siglo'.

[108] Sempere y Guariños, *Historia del lujo*, 227, 'a la ociosidad y a la indigencia'; 75: 'un vicio detestable', 'los daños morales y civiles'; 373: 'indecentes, y provocativas'.

and political concerns over the centuries. With the completion of the Reconquest and the rise of Spain as an imperial power, sumptuary laws were applied generally without making class distinctions and their purview was expanded to include all kinds of novelties as well as pure luxuries. As Spain's fortunes faded, from the 1580s through the seventeenth century, the Crown and Cortes tried to turn things around by reforming Spanish society through gender-specific laws legislating men's and women's appearances. Some things changed while others remained much the same. The protectionist policies put in place by Isabella and Ferdinand in the 1490s, when they issued the first ban on imported brocades, continued throughout the eighteenth century, well after the last ban on luxury consumption was issued in 1723.

This chapter has outlined a cultural history of Spanish sumptuary legislation based on the laws themselves – which inevitably privilege the perspective of the lawmakers. Many questions remain to be answered about the impact that these laws had on the governed – on the makers, sellers and consumers of luxury goods – and the role that sumptuary legislation played in Spanish society. To what extent were the laws actually enforced? Who was prosecuted for violating the laws, and what were their punishments? How did sumptuary laws affect local artisans and industries? Conventional wisdom claims that sumptuary laws were reissued repeatedly because they were so ineffective, but new archival research could challenge this assumption. The ongoing digitisation of Spanish archives now makes it possible to locate cases of individuals who were prosecuted for violating sumptuary laws across the kingdom. These were men and women like Diego de Valladolid, a merchant accused of selling an illegal brocade in 1496; Luisa of Madrigal, who had a skirt confiscated in 1516 by local authorities who claimed that its silk trim was too wide; and master tailor Francisco Portillo, who allegedly made garments violating restrictions on ornament in 1675.[109] These are just a few of the individuals whose lives and livelihoods were affected by sumptuary laws in early modern Spain, and whose stories remain to be told.

---

[109] 'Ejecutoria de sentencia a favor de Diego de Valladolid, mercader, vecino de la villa de éste nombre, absolviéndole de la pena en que había incurrido por haber vendido brocado pelo morado al Conde de Melgar para cubrir la tumba de la condesa' (16 April 1496), Archivo General de Simancas, RGS, LEG, 149604, 15 (PARES); 'Pleito de Luisa de Madrigal, de Madrigal: Sobre Luisa de Madrigal contra la justicia de dicho lugar, por haberle quitado una raya que tenía unas tiras de seda más anchas de lo que la pragmática recomendaba' (1516/17), ARCHV, Pleitos Civiles, Escribano Fernando Alonso (F), Caja 541, 6 (PARES); 'Causa contra Francisco Portillo, maestro sastre, por haberle hallado haciendo vestidos en contraversión de la Pragmática sobre ornamentos en el vestido' (1675), ARCHV, Causas Secretas, Caja 4, 21 (PARES).

10 Sumptuary Laws in Portugal and its Empire from the Fourteenth to the Eighteenth Century

Francisco Bethencourt

Medieval and early modern sumptuary laws have so far been primarily discussed as mechanisms to ensure social distinction: they contributed to defining and perpetuating hierarchies.[1] Lower and middling social groups were prohibited from emulating the appearance of higher-status groups and female clothing was regulated.[2] Economic aims, particularly a reduction in the high level of imported goods, have also been considered among the explanations for the extensive legislation on luxury.[3] Finally, state-building has been identified as motivating such legislation, which increased in Europe and other parts of the world from the Middle Ages to the end of the Ancien Régime. The regulation of clothing increased the presence, and the impact, of the state in everyday life; disciplinary power went along with assertion of rank.[4] However, the question remains to what extent these laws were implemented, since their frequent publication suggests inefficiency in enforcing them, even if recent studies have revised or at least nuanced this view.[5]

Although these generalising arguments are useful to consider in the majority of cases, they fail to account for the wide range of sumptuary

---

[1] Maria Hayward, *Rich Apparel: Clothing and Laws in Henry VIII's England* (Farnham: Ashgate, 2009).

[2] Catherine Kovesi Killerby, *Sumptuary Laws in Italy, 1200–1500* (Oxford: Clarendon Press, 2002); Maria Giuseppina Muzzarelli (ed.), *Disciplinare il lusso: la legislazione suntuaria in Italia e in Europa tra medioevo ed età moderna* (Rome: Carocci, 2003).

[3] Negley B. Harte (ed.), *The New Draperies in the Low Countries and England, 1300–1800* (Oxford: Oxford University Press, 1997).

[4] Alan Hunt, *Governance of the Consuming Passions: A History of Sumptuary Laws* (Basingstoke: Macmillan, 1996).

[5] The uselessness of sumptuary laws was lamented by early modern jurists. In the eighteenth century, this became the main argument against legislation that, it was claimed, would leave the state in disrepute: see Juan Sempere y Guarinos, *Historia del luxo y de las leyes suntuarias de España* (Madrid: Imprenta Real, 1788), who presented this legislation as an historical curiosity. More recently, work in the archives has revealed periods of implementation of sumptuary laws: see Hilary Doda, '"Saide Monstruous Hose": Compliance, Transgression and English Sumptuary Law to 1553', *Textile History* 45/2 (2014): 171–191.

laws – running into hundreds – published in many parts of the world, which addressed many different situations and were driven by a variety of purposes. In medieval Aragon, for instance, representatives of the three orders in assembly, particularly the third order, targeted royal expenses and asked the king to reduce them.[6] It is only surprising that the same argument was not made elsewhere, since conspicuous consumption linked to royal weddings was one of the main causes of financial depletion. The point remains that different social agents could be interested in regulating sumptuousness.

This leads to a theoretical issue that must be addressed from the very beginning: I do not agree with the notion of separation between state and society that many interpretations assume.[7] The state is embedded in society, and results from an extraordinarily complex mix of interactions and interdependencies, although the development of royal bureaucracy led to the assertion of an interest group. We shall see that many sumptuary laws were suggested by local and regional authorities, representatives of the third estate in parliament, or even by members of the upper social strata seeking to avoid internal competition and financial stress.

This makes the case of Portugal and its extensive empire particularly significant, because of the plurality and hierarchy of competing centres of power linking together different territories at varied real-time distance.[8] It provides material for a reflection on European developments confronted with specific colonial conditions. This means that the following questions need to be addressed: what were the main political, social, economic and financial purposes of sumptuary laws? How did they relate to other policies of the Crown? Did they respond to specific conjunctures? How did their content evolve in time and space in relation to the different parts of the Portuguese empire?

My argument is that sumptuary laws reflected the financial and military needs of the Crown, but also expressed the political, social and economic dynamics of the Portuguese and colonial societies. My research suggests that sumptuary laws were related to economic and financial policies from the very beginning, although this dependence became

---

[6] See José Damian Gonzalez Arce, *Aparencia y poder. La legislación suntuária castellana en los siglos XII-XV* (Jaén: Universidad de Jaén, 1998). The reform of the expenses of the royal house was called into question in 1238 under the king of Aragon and Catalonia, Jaume I.

[7] A critique of the separation between state and society was persistently formulated by Norbert Elias, particularly in *What is Sociology?*, trans. Stephen Mennell and Grace Morrissey (London: Hutchinson, 1978) and *The Society of Individuals*, trans. Edmund Jephcott (Oxford: Blackwell, 1991).

[8] Francisco Bethencourt, 'Political Configurations and Local Powers', in Francisco Bethencourt and Diogo Ramada Curto (eds.), *The Portuguese Oceanic Expansion, 1400–1800* (Cambridge: Cambridge University Press, 2007), 197–254.

much more acute in the seventeenth century, due to the long war of independence against Castile. They were also shaped by traditional Jewish and Christian discussions of luxury, and by notions of austerity inherited from classical antiquity, so well voiced by Fénelon at the end of the seventeenth century. Fénelon considered that luxury corrupts customs, and criticised the idea that luxury nourishes the poor, since they are more useful working the land, while the rich would be weakened by voluptuous refinements.[9] The new evaluation of luxury articulated in the eighteenth century by philosophers and economists from Bernard Mandeville to Adam Smith provoked a disruption in this traditional reasoning;[10] it took time to be absorbed, but we will see its impact on the debate around the last important Portuguese sumptuary law from 1749. We have significant documents showing not only successful resistance to this law, but also derision among the ruling elite over later attempts to reinstate this kind of legislation.

I will limit my chapter to legislation regarding excessive expenditure or conspicuous consumption. Rules governing the dress and religious symbols to be worn by Jews and Muslims lasted until 1497, when those subject to such rules were either forced to convert or expelled from Portugal, but are outside the scope of sumptuary legislation. Nor will I deal with the penitential dress imposed by the Inquisition on condemned heretics. I will analyse the series of sumptuary laws passed in Portugal in chronological order, since there has been no overall study of these, and available articles focus on specific laws, leaving enormous gaps.[11] More work remains to be done on implementation of sumptuary laws, as well as on the parallels between this legislation and other ways of regulating behaviour, which were also extensively embodied in legislation, socially segmented and adapted through time.[12]

---

[9] Fénelon, *Les aventures de Télémaque* [1699], ed. Jacques Le Brun (Paris: Gallimard, 1995), esp. 368–369.

[10] Bernard Mandeville, *The Fable of the Bees: or Private Vices, Publick Benefits* [1714–1729], ed. F. B. Kaye, 2 vols. (Oxford: Clarendon Press, 1924) was the first to articulate a systematic and bold amoral vision of the economic benefits of luxury; see Maxine Berg, *Luxury and Pleasure in Eighteenth Century England* (Oxford: Oxford University Press, 2005). Adam Smith, *An Inquiry into the Nature and Causes of the Wealth of Nations* [1776], ed. R. H. Campbell and A. S. Skinner, text editor W. B. Todd, 2 vols. (Oxford: Oxford University Press, 1976) integrates this reasoning.

[11] I thank Diogo Ramada Curto, José Pedro Paiva and Lurdes Rosa for bibliographical information. It is surprising that the excellent *História da Vida Privada em Portugal*, ed. José Mattoso (Lisbon: Círculo de Leitores, 2011), vols. i and ii on medieval and early modern periods, addressed neither clothing nor sumptuary laws.

[12] See for example Luís Filipe Lindley Cintra, *Sobre "formas de tratamento" em língua portuguesa. Ensaios* (Lisbon: Livros Horizonte, 1972).

Medieval Legislation

The first significant sumptuary law was published in 1340 by King Alphonse IV, under pressure from the Portuguese *cortes* (a parliament formed of representatives from the three orders) gathered in Santarém. It was written alongside laws concerning gambling, usury, the payment of debts, the desertion of lords by their servants and abusive behaviour by privileged people. The main purpose of this *cortes* was to lend money to the king for a major expedition against the Muslims, in alliance with the Castilians, and this was to lead to the decisive battle of Salado. The export of gold coins was also forbidden at this point, indicating that resources of money and manpower were at stake. Among the twenty-seven articles of the law, six imposed restrictions on luxury food, twenty on dress and one on the number of animals kept for transport.[13]

The law was explicitly justified in relation to the excessive expense that weakened the vassals of the king. The number and quality of clothes and ornaments permitted were proportionally related to the social hierarchy of *ricos homens* (upper noblemen), knights, squires, citizens – meaning the bourgeois of the cities, classified by the level of their income, which could be higher than that of the aristocratic categories – servants and labourers, alongside women and children of each rank. A final addition concerned the quality and quantity of dress items prostitutes were allowed. Social hierarchy was certainly asserted, but noble ranking was confronted with the financial capacity of social groups outside the nobility, since one of the main features of the Portuguese (and Iberian) aristocracy was precisely its loose definition in terms of lifestyle and its fantasised genealogies.[14] This vision of social hierarchy is also interesting from the point of view of the history of social perceptions, because the notion of the three orders was absent: clergymen were excluded as they had their own code of appearance; the nobility was segmented by status, and non-noble occupations were ranked; while women and children were placed according to the husband's and father's position, which showed the subordination of both female and minors.

The king reserved for his own and his family's use fabrics with gold thread and the best quality cloth from Flanders. For different social

---

[13] A. H. de Oliveira Marques, 'A pragmática de 1340', *Revista da Faculdade de Letras de Lisboa* XXII, 2nd series, 2 (1956): 130–154 (original text of the law published 145–154).

[14] José Mattoso, *A nobreza medieval portuguesa: a família e o poder* (Lisbon: Estampa, 1981); see for the early modern period Mafalda Soares da Cunha and Nuno G. Monteiro, 'Aristocracia, poder e família em Portugal, séculos XV-XVIII', in Mafalda Soares da Cunha and Juan Hernández Franco (eds.), *Sociedade, família e poder na Península Ibérica: elementos para uma história comparativa* (Lisbon: Colibri, 2010), 47–75.

categories, the items permitted were categorised by a decrease in the number of fabrics and the amounts to be used, as well as by the expenditure estimated to be involved. There were restrictions on the amounts of silk and the numbers of ornaments made of gold, silver, enamel or pearls that could be used, not only for dresses, belts and shoes, but also for saddles, bridles and spurs. Boots, particular types of hose, and small capes were limited to men who owned horses. The number of servants and horses accompanying prelates and *ricos homens* in their travels to meet the king was also limited, to avoid aggravating the people forced to lodge them.

Instead of a top-down royal prescription of allowed or prohibited items, we find an intervention by the three orders to control expenses that could lead to increased private debt and bankruptcy. This intervention to regulate behaviour and appearance can be seen as helping to shape state-building, but not in the usual top-down, centralising manner conceived of by most historians. It expressed the elites' vision of the social order as a political community supporting and supported by the king. The most interesting aspect is that the numbers of attendants for notable men were limited because these would put a burden on local populations. We can see the interest that the third estate had in restricting the exaction of support by landlords and notables. It was also interested in limiting the expenditure of citizens, servants and labourers, to avoid spiralling ostentatious consumption.

Competition among the upper echelons of noblemen probably played a role in this law too: we know that many of them could hardly keep up their standard of living, and would have benefitted from royal intervention to limit their spending on clothing and the provision of food.[15] The king was obviously interested in controlling private expense, since he needed, at that period, the support of *ricos homens* in recruiting local troops. The bankruptcy of landlords would lead to failure to provide military support, and social disorder in their domains would follow any increase in fiscal demands. This law represented an effort to reinforce social hierarchy, but it also responded to various requirements to guarantee social order, especially the nobility's performance of established duties and service to the king.

The new dynamics of fashion in the fourteenth century Europe certainly influenced this law.[16] It is not accidental that 74 per cent of the

---

[15] Mattoso, *A nobreza medieval portuguesa;* José Mattoso, *Identificação de um país: ensaio sobre as origens de Portugal*, 2 vols., 3rd ed. (Lisbon: Estampa, 1988).

[16] A. H. de Oliveira Marques, chapter on 'Dress', in *Daily Life in Portugal in the Late Middle Ages*, trans. S. S. Wyatt with drawings by Victor André (Madison: The University of Wisconsin Press, 1971), 39–96; Id., *Portugal na crise dos séculos XIV e XV*

articles promulgated concerned clothing and appearance. The three estates responded to changes to the basic items of clothing, which had been relatively stable up to the thirteenth century in Europe. There were new items in the form of caps, hoods, cloaks, coats, overcoats, robes, jackets, skirts, bodices, shirts and hose, each with different lengths and fabrics, including silk, all mentioned by the law, as well as ornaments of gold and silver thread, or pearls. The work of tailors had also become more complex and costly, due to the use of imported fabrics and new cuts in clothes, which could be lined with different materials and decorated with embroidery, lacework or other rich fabrics, among which brocade is specifically mentioned. Dressing had become much more expensive than eating, which was why it was particularly targeted by the law.

The Black Death and the political instability of the last decades of the fourteenth century – the war with Castile, which invaded Portugal; the revolution of 1383–1385, which brought a dynastic change; and Portuguese military incursions into Castile to support the House of Lancaster's claims to the throne – did not stimulate any new laws on luxury. During the fifteenth century, one of the most stable periods of Portuguese history, in which economic development stimulated the beginning of oceanic expansion, there is no sign of new sumptuary laws either, which is more surprising.[17] The new wealth acquired, at least by the urban elite and nobility involved in overseas expansion, does not seem to have triggered further sumptuary laws. However, the compilation of laws ordered by King D. Duarte (r. 1433–1438) integrated the text of the pragmatic sanction of 1340.[18]

The Impact of Overseas Expansion

The next series of sumptuary laws were published during the long period of overseas expansion, which saw an extraordinary increase in commodities traded into Europe, but also the first signs of economic crisis, particularly in 1545–1452 and 1570–1580.[19] Duarte Nunes do Lião's

(Lisbon: Presença, 1987), 466–469. For an analysis of queens' dowries, collections, and art and architecture patronage see: Ana Maria Rodrigues, 'The Treasures and Foundations of Isabel, Elisenda and Leonor. The Art Patronage of Four Iberian Queens in the Fourteenth Century', in *Reassessing the Role of Women as 'Makers' of Medieval Art and Arquitectura*, ed. Therese Martin (Leiden: Brill, 2012), 903–936.

[17] Vitorino Magalhães Godinho, *A expansão quatrocentista portuguesa*, revised ed. (Lisbon: Dom Quixote, 2007).

[18] Martim de Albuquerque and Eduardo Borges Nunes (eds.), *Ordenações Del-Rei D. Duarte* (Lisbon: Fundação Calouste Gulbenkian, 1988), 448–459.

[19] See Vitorino Magalhães Godinho, 'A "revolução dos preços" e as flutuações económicas no século XVI', in *Ensaios*, II (Lisbon: Sá da Costa, 1968), 155–174; Jorge Pedreira, 'Costs and Financial Trends in the Portuguese Empire, 1415–1820', in Bethencourt and

compilation of *Leis Extravagantes*, printed in 1569, included sumptuary laws published in 1535, 1537, 1538, 1560, 1565, 1566 and 1567.[20] These laws open Part Four of Lião's compilation, followed by rulings on arms regulation, robbery, forbidden types of gambling, crimes committed by slaves (significantly including Muslims and Jews), smuggling of livestock to Castile, the illegal export of gold and silver, trade and prices for meat and bread, interest on money, forbidden negotiations with the Pope contrary to the jurisdiction of the king, foreigners, beggars, vagrants and paupers, hunting and fishing, responsibility for the royal treasure, penalties for different types of sexual relations, adulterers and prostitutes, the detention of people and responsibility for those detained, banishment, and special areas in which criminals might be kept.[21] It seems at first sight a haphazard compilation, but economic and financial issues clearly dominate; conspicuous consumption was regulated along with gambling, contraband trading and marginal behaviour.

The law published by King John III in 1535 focused on fabrics and ornaments related to dress, but also covered the decoration of houses and churches, flags and emblems, arms and apparel for horses. A general prohibition of the use of the most valued items of gold, silver, enamel and silk at the beginning was followed by exemptions, a common legal practice of the ancien régime. The law showed the enormous complexity in Renaissance tailoring techniques, particularly backstitch, and the use of ornaments such as fringing, ribbons, piping and tassels. What is notable is the explosion not only of veils, but also of hats, caps and head-dresses, whose silk lining was regulated. References to shoes, slippers, purses, bags and perfumed gloves reveal an increased variety in the accessories available. The attention given to the lining of many items is perhaps the most striking development, particularly in relation to sleeves.

Knights and other upper-class owners of horses remained the key social category to enjoy access to the most valued items of apparel and ornaments for arms and horses. *Fidalgos* (noblemen) of the royal house also enjoyed this distinction, as well as the queen's ladies. Women in

---

Ramada Curto (eds.), *Portuguese Oceanic Expansion* 49–87; Isabel dos Guimarães Sá, 'The Uses of Luxury: Some Examples from the Portuguese Courts from 1480 to 1580', *Análise Social* 46/192 (2009): 589–604.

[20] Duarte Nunes do Lião, *Leis extravagantes* (Lisbon: António Gonçalves, 1569), facsimile edition with an introduction by Mário Júlio de Almeida Costa (Lisbon: Fundação Calouste Gulbenkian, 1987). There were laws from the reigns of John II and Manuel I not included in this compilation, but the available references are summarised below; see footnote 32. This is a compilation of laws not included in the famous compilation commissioned by King Manuel and published in 1510–1514. Duarte Nunes do Lião was an important jurist and chronicler.

[21] Lião, *Leis extravagantes*, fl. 111r–178v.

general were allowed to wear all kinds of veils and head-dresses made out of silk, but this material was excluded from dresses. Penalties for breaking the law were quite harsh, including heavy fines from ten to fifty cruzados and two years of exile to Africa.[22] In those years the vast population of workers and artisans earned less than 20 cruzados (roughly equivalent to ducats) a year; in 1583 the inquisitors earned 300 cruzados a year and the top judges of the royal court, *Desembargo do Paço*, 750 cruzados.[23] The leniency towards women is striking as they were less penalised for wearing silk than in other parts of Europe, probably due to a relatively better position concerning inheritance and management of property, both at aristocratic and popular levels, reinforced by extraordinary male emigration.[24]

This law was updated and adapted in 1537–1539, first allowing foreigners to wear silk for six months after their arrival, then reducing the length of dresses, and finally regulating the clothing of students at the University of Coimbra.[25] Students were forbidden to wear striped and pleated fabrics; and they were only allowed to wear round caps and open or closed coats, never capes with hoods, probably to avoid confusion with some members of the clergy, including professors. The law prohibited slashed or pinked hose, as well as coloured ornaments or even white shirts or handkerchiefs. The use of a mule or horse was limited to students with an income (or family allowance) of more than two hundred cruzados. They were allowed to have one servant, two if they owned a mule, three if they owned a horse. They were forbidden to receive guests, except a father or brother, or to play games.

In 1560, Queen Catarina, regent of the kingdom, reduced the restrictions on clothing imposed on ladies in waiting at the court, and the wives of *fidalgos*, judges, knights of the royal house and distinguished owners of horses.[26] Catarina was interested in luxury and her decision was among the few laws specifically directed at noblewomen. However, wives of artisans were explicitly excluded. These allowances are in line

---

[22] Lião, *Leis extravagantes*, fl. 111r–113v.

[23] Francisco Bethencourt, *The Inquisition. A Global History, 1478–1834* (Cambridge: Cambridge University Press, 2009), 104.

[24] Darlene Abreu Ferreira, 'A Status of Her Own: Women and Family Identities in Seventeenth Century Aveiro, Portugal', *Journal of Family Studies* 34/1 (2009): 3–24; Id., *Women, Crime and Forgiveness in early modern Portugal* (Farnham: Ashgate, 2015); Margarida Durães, 'Providing Well-being to women through Inheritance and Succession: Portugal in the 18th and 19th Centuries', in Margarida Durães et al. (eds.), *The Transmission of Well-Being: Gendered Strategies and Inheritance Systems in Europe (17th–20th Centuries)* (New York: Peter Lang, 2009), 201–228.

[25] Lião, *Leis extravagantes*, fl. 115r–v and 165v–166r.

[26] Lião, *Leis extravagantes*, fl. 113v–115r.

with mid-fifteenth-century claims, voiced by Nicolosa Sanuti among others, that noblewomen should be allowed to wear elaborate dress, since, through this means, they would enhance and project the civic dignity of their cities or royal courts.[27] This law highlights the fact that women were not especially targeted by Portuguese legislation on luxury: the ladies of the court and noblewomen received the same exceptions as their husbands and, as in this case, they could be particularly favoured. The extraordinary role of Queen Catarina in organising Habsburg royal collections with exotica brought to Europe by Portuguese merchants has to be underlined.[28]

In 1565–1566 new developments in hose were addressed: 'imperial' hose and hose with rigid structures (*calças de rocas*) to hold ribbons, made out of silk or other fabric, were forbidden, but *fidalgos* and knights were permitted hose of silk and other fabrics with slashes, as long as they did not have rigid structures, cotton lining, stripes, ribbons, fringes or other ornaments.[29] We have to note that the hose was identified separately as *calças*, *calções* and *ceroulas*, which denotes an early diversification. In the same years, the number of attendants for people of 'quality' was limited to two standing pages, two riding men and one slave with a jacket and a small rough cape. Special capes with hoods were reserved for high judges of the royal court. The law insisted on the precise length of different pieces of clothing. At the same time, the prohibition of silk was reinforced, as well as that of leather in specific items, particularly in blankets for horses and mules. Men were prohibited to wear gloves and other items of perfumed leather – all perfume was forbidden. Amber and musk were explicitly mentioned, which reveals increased sophistication. This is perhaps the first time in the Portuguese case that sumptuary laws were used to define masculinity, then a matter of discussion due

---

[27] For the case of Nicolosa Sanuti from Bologna, see Catherine Kovesi Killerby, '"Heralds of a Well-instructed Mind": Nicolosa Sanuti's Defence of Women and Their Clothes', *Renaissance Studies* 13/3 (1999): 255–282.

[28] See Anne-Marie Jordan, 'The Development of Catherine of Austria's Collection in the Queen's Household: its Character and Cost' (Unpublished PhD thesis, Brown University, 1994); Id., 'Portuguese Royal Collections after 1521: The Choice between Flanders and Italy', in K. J. Lowe (ed.), *Cultural Links between Portugal and Italy in the Renaissance* (Oxford: Oxford University Press, 2000), 265–293. For a larger approach see Nuno Vassalo e Silva and Helmut Trnek (eds.), *Exotica. Os descobrimentos portugueses e as câmaras de maravilhas do Renascimento* (Lisbon: Museu Calouste Gulbenkian, 2001) and the articles by Rui Manuel Loureiro, Bruno Werz, Hugo Miguel Crespo, Annemarie Jordan Gschwend and Kate Lowe, in Annemarie Jordan Gschwend and K. J. P. Lowe (eds.), *The Global City on the Streets of Renaissance Lisbon* (London: Paul Holberton, 2015).

[29] Lião, *Leis extravagantes*, fl. 115r–v.

to the crisis of the Portuguese Empire in India and the idea that luxury corrupted the Portuguese.[30]

The detailed regulation of dress for the mourning of close relatives (parents, siblings, children and in-laws) is to be noted. It permitted cloaks with hoods, open capes reaching to the mid-leg, and coats reaching to the knees, but forbade large sleeves – a prohibition repeated in other laws. Mourning apparel on mules and horses was excluded. Mourning was limited to six months.[31] Royal funerary practices were highly ritualised and filled with symbolic meaning, but this intervention in private funerary practices is an interesting phenomenon that had its roots in Roman sumptuary laws. There is an indication that King Manuel I issued a pragmatic sanction against excessive expenditure on mourning and funerals on 27 June 1504.[32] This reveals wide changes in the sixteenth century, driven by conspicuous consumption and competition for distinctive investment in funerary rituals, including the mourning of deceased relatives. The extension of sumptuary laws to mourning rituals means that a section of the nobility found itself unable to cope with increased competition in this domain. It is in this light, in a century of inflation, that we need to interpret an increased control of clothing and regulation of accessories, including the number of servants and the use of mules and horses, then so important for transport.

The reign of Sebastian (1557–1578) ended with an excruciating defeat at the battle of Ksar el-Kbir, in Morocco, in which the king lost his life and thousands of noblemen died or were captured. Impoverishment of the aristocracy and the bourgeoisie due to their lost investment in war was aggravated by the enormous ransoms demanded by the victors.[33] Two years later the union of crowns between Portugal and Spain imposed by Philip II was welcomed by most Portuguese noblemen and merchants, and the re-establishment of an independent Portugal occurred only in 1640.[34] The financial recovery of these social groups is well expressed

---

[30] Lião, *Leis extravagantes*, fl. 116v. Among a growing bibliography on this subject, see Kim M. Philips, 'Masculinities and the Medieval English Sumptuary Laws', *Gender and History* 19/1 (2007): 22–42.

[31] Lião, *Leis extravagantes*, fl. 116r–117v.

[32] Luís Fernando de Carvalho Dias, *Luxo e pragmáticas no pensamento económico do século XVI* (Coimbra: Coimbra Editora, 1958), 73. This is mentioned by a judge asked to give his opinion on a new sumptuary law in 1749; he summarises the whole series of Portuguese sumptuary laws, some of them not included in available compilations of legislation.

[33] Maria Augusta Lima Cruz, *D. Sebastião* (Lisbon: Círculo de Leitores, 2006); Amélia Polónia, *D. Henrique* (Lisbon: Círculo de Leitores, 2005).

[34] Vitorino Magalhães Godinho, '1580 e 1640: da União Dinástica à Restauração', in *Ensaios e Estudos. Uma maneira de pensar*, 2nd ed. (Lisbon: Sá da Costa, 2009), i: 421–468; Fernando Bouza, *D. Filipe I* (Lisbon: Círculo de Leitores, 2006).

by the new sumptuary law published in 1609, in which excessive private expenditure on clothing was clearly indicated as a justification for royal action against it in the preamble.[35]

The set of prohibited items followed those of previous laws, but imports from India were specifically included, which meant that the economic benefits of the colonies were not taken on board in this law, or considered exclusively as items for re-export to Europe. Exceptions within the hierarchy again focused on knights, *fidalgos* registered in the king's books and judges of the royal court. This law seems to confirm the widespread use of silk, not only in caps, cloaks, capes and jackets, but also in hose and the linings of various items. Women's dresses, veils and headdresses were also regulated in regard to the use of silk, gold and silver. In general, the law was more permissive than previous ones, allowing the limited use of silk in the lining of hats and of ornament on various pieces of clothing, particularly accessories such as buttons. There was more regulation of lace and embroidery, which increased their presence as distinct fashion items in the late sixteenth and early seventeenth centuries.

The novelty of this law lies in its reference to urban transport in litters and chairs, which was reserved for licenced enfeebled noblemen. Age had been mentioned in previous laws, to exclude young noblemen from the privileges of their parents; but now the use of covered chairs was reserved for authorised noblemen over the age of sixty. The wives of *fidalgos* and judges were authorised to use covered chairs as a means of transport in the city, and the use of silk in the curtains and seats of these was allowed, while other women could use open chairs. The change in urban modes of transportation is thus dramatically highlighted; we can also recognise the impact of overseas practices, mainly those imported from Asia.

The same sumptuary law of 1609 addressed the interior decoration of houses for the first time; it prohibited the use of silk from curtains, bedcovers, bed pavilions and tablecloths. No gold or silver was allowed to gild leather wallpaper. Previous regulations governing mourning were restated, as well as special arrangements for foreigners and the number of servants that noblemen could have attending them. Soldiers were specifically excluded from the regulations. As in previous laws, penalties addressed not only consumers, but also tailors and jewellers.[36] The extension of sumptuary laws to the decoration of

[35] José Justino de Andrade e Silva (ed.), *Colecção chronologica da legislação portugueza, 1603–1612* (Lisbon: Imprensa de J. J. A. Silva, 1854), 275–276.

[36] Andrade e Silva (ed.), *Colecção chronologica da legislação portugueza, 1603–1612*, 275–281.

houses reveals a new trend in consumption thirty years after the disaster of 1578, which had now apparently been absorbed. But there is another policy that also needs to be highlighted: the apparent increased status of soldiers.[37]

In response to the 1609 law, the city of Porto, an important port in northern Portugal, recorded declarations of forbidden clothing.[38] According to this law, and following previous practice, people who had forbidden items were permitted to wear them for a certain period of time (or until they were worn out) if they registered them. The register, apparently the only one to have survived, proves that the law was implemented in some places, and provides an exceptionally good insight into specific types of consumption. The items registered show, among other things, the contrast between coloured clothing for travelling and black clothing for urban wear, but the most interesting items concern the profusion of oriental textiles, mainly Indian bedspreads and Chinese mantillas, but also jackets and other pieces of dress, both for men and women, made of Indian textiles, particularly silk with silver embroidery, or printed cotton, like chintz and calico.[39] The increased import of textiles from India had clearly had an impact on standards of consumption.[40]

There is little evidence that sumptuary laws were published in the colonies, or even of efforts to extend overseas metropolitan pragmatics. The main reasons for this relative silence must be related to sheer geographical distance, dependence on mixed-race local elites, competing local ethnic

---

[37] The impact of the *regimento de ordenanças* published in 1570, which created regular militias and military training all over the kingdom, still needs to be assessed. António Camões Gouveia and Nuno Monteiro highlighted the importance of this law in the long run in 'A milícia', in António Manuel Hespanha (ed.), *História de Portugal*, vol. IV. *O Antigo Regime, 1620–1807* (Lisbon: Círculo de Leitores, 1993), 197–203, while the real implementation of this structure was questioned by António Manuel Hespanha, 'A administração militar', in António Manuel Hespanha (ed.), *Nova História Militar de Portugal* (Lisbon: Círculo de Leitores, 2004), ii: 169–176.

[38] See the excellent study of this register by Hugo Miguel Crespo, 'Trajar as aparências, vestir para ser: o testemunho da pragmatica de 1609', in Gonçalo Vasconcelos e Sousa (ed.), *O luxo na região do Porto no tempo de Filipe II de Portugal (1610)* (Porto: Universidade Católica Editora, 2012), 93–148.

[39] Crespo, 'Trajar as aparências, vestir para ser: o testemunho da pragmatica de 1609', esp. 124–127 and 131–135.

[40] There is not much on dress in the early modern period and the impact of the empire. See the superficial and problematic surveys by Fernando Oliveira, *O vestuário português ao tempo da expansão, séculos XV e XVI* (Lisbon: Ministério da Educação, 1993); Maria João Lourenço Pereira, 'Vestuário', in João José Alves Dias (ed.), *Portugal do Renascimento à crise dinástica* (Lisbon: Presença, 1998), 627–633. I highlight here the study on Indian bedspreads exported to the Portuguese market by Barbara Karl, *Embroidered Histories. Indian Textiles for the Portuguese Market during the Sixteenth and Seventeenth Centuries* (Vienna: Böhlau Verlag, 2016).

groups and blurred hierarchies due to forced conversion and complex social mobility. However, we can chart a certain level of local discussion on excessive spending on clothing, transportation and servants, all of which were considered to drain resources. Transport by litter, which was typical of China and India, became a target for the viceroys of the Estado da Índia from the late sixteenth century. They apparently lamented the undistinguished social use, the expense on fine materials, decoration and service, the blurred frontiers between native and Christian habits. Vice-regal legislation limited the use of litters (*andores* and *palanquins*) in 1591, 1603 and 1636.[41] This set of legislation seems to have been legitimised by the king himself: there is a reference to a royal decree prohibiting the use of litters in the Estado da Índia in 1615.[42] But royal intervention in overseas conspicuous consumption is ambiguous, to say the least. The use of silk was forbidden in India in 1623 by the viceroy, but the king intervened the following year to revoke this sumptuary law, which most probably meant that he had received petitions against the disruption of Indian silk production and consumption, although we cannot discard the possibility that he simply did not want the viceroy to usurp his jurisdiction.[43] Even less information concerning sumptuary laws in Brazil is available for this period, but the limited reach of colonial society in coastal enclaves can explain the silence.

Legislation on luxury in Portugal did not develop further until the restoration of independence in 1640. In this final period under the shared rule of the Spanish kings sumptuary laws were apparently not considered an important tool for governance. Probably the Habsburgs were conscious of the fact that they were seen as a foreign power and decided to avoid unnecessary social unrest through intervention in people's appearance. They had their hands full with the management of fiscal impositions and military recruitment in what was a general period of crisis for the Spanish empire in Europe, plagued by the emergence of riots in the 1630s that contributed to the restoration of Portuguese independence in 1640.[44]

---

[41] Nandini Chaturvedula, 'In the Precipice of Ruin: Consumption, Sumptuary Laws, and Decadence in Early Modern Portuguese India', *Journal of World History* 26/2 (2015): 355–384, esp. 375.

[42] João Pedro Ribeiro, *Indice chronologico remissivo da legislação portugueza posterior a publicação do codigo filippino com hum apendice* (Lisbon: Academia Real das Sciencias, 1820), vi: 164.

[43] Andrade e Silva (ed.), *Coleccão chronologica da legislação portugueza, 1620–1627*, 112. Also mentioned in Ribeiro, *Indice chronologico remissivo da legislação portugueza*, vi: 171.

[44] António de Oliveira, *Poder e oposição política em Portugal no período Filipino, 1580–1640* (Lisbon: Difel, 1991).

The Impact of War

In 1643, a new sumptuary law was published, in which the need to curb excessive spending was explicitly related to the war to defend the restored independence of the kingdom against Castile. The prohibition on using gold, silver or silk on clothing and accessories was extended to the whole population, including servants, and came to include horse accoutrements. This law was the shortest and simplest of all: the major novelty was that the law did not indicate any exemptions relating to social rank, specially privileged groups or gender.[45] The effort needed for the war did not allow exceptions: a return to normality came only after the peace treaty with Spain, celebrated on 13 February 1668, in which the independence of the kingdom was implicitly recognised.

The regency and reign of D. Pedro II (1667–1706) is the richest in sumptuary laws and reveals new developments in consumption unleashed by the peace with Spain. In 1668, immediately after the peace treaty with Spain, the regent, D. Pedro, summoned the cortes and was urged by the three orders to publish a new sumptuary law that extended previous regulations to cover the length of ribbons, and included new ornaments with slashes, stripes and lacework. The *vestia*, a kind of waistcoat, was prohibited, but the dictionary of Moraes Silva published in 1789 still had an entry for the noun, which means that the garment had a long life.[46]

Walking sticks now made their appearance in sumptuary laws, and were reserved for the use of officers of the militia, while sleeves of leather or fur covering the hands were reserved for women. This is one of several significant cases in which sumptuary laws were used to define masculinity and femininity. Exceptions for particular social groups were not introduced in the 1668 law, although the titled nobility and counsellors could be attended by more than four pages besides their coach driver. The regulation for attendants allowed four in the case of royal feasts, and twelve in the case of people involved in bull fighting, although ornaments of gold, silver or silk were forbidden.

The law also regulated litters and coaches, whose use was reserved for the titled nobility, counsellors of state, large landowners, military governors of towns, judges and *fidalgos* whose names appeared in the royal registers, and their wives.[47] Litters had already been included in

---

[45] Andrade e Silva (ed.), *Colecção chronologica da legislação portugueza, 1640–1647*, 215–216.

[46] Antonio de Moraes Silva, *Diccionario da lingua portugueza* (Lisbon: Officina de Simão Thaddeo Ferreira, 1789), ii: 522.

[47] Andrade e Silva (ed.), *Colecção chronologica da legislação portugueza, 1657–1674*, 147–149. The prohibition of mules for personal transport, except for clergymen, was published in

the sumptuary law of 1609, but coaches made their first appearance here. This obviously represents a development in both urban and rural means of transportation that had a clear impact on consumption. The social environment is also to be noted, since titled nobility are expressly mentioned, alongside counsellors of state, military governors, judges, registered *fidalgos* and their wives. The law reveals the reorganisation of the nobility that took place during the War of Restoration and beyond, due to the defection to Spain of some titled noblemen, followed by the expropriation and distribution of their lands and the issuing of new titles by the king.[48] The definition of nobility was also a matter for consideration at this time, as recognised *fidalgos* were recorded in the royal registers. Royal counsellors and judges had been exempted from sumptuary laws since the sixteenth century, but the status of military governors was raised during the War of Restoration (1640–1668).

D. Pedro II's second major law in this field, published in 1677, is one of the most comprehensive enacted. Excessive expenditure on clothing was addressed alongside the decoration of houses, the keeping of coaches, the employment of servants (and their number), vanity in funerals, and mourning dress. The impoverishment of the nobility and the ruin of their heirs were the main justifications for the law, which lamented damage to existing customs, and urged the common good of the country and its preservation. The traditional prohibition of gold, silver and silk was retained, although for the first time there was an openness to mercantilist policies: the use of imported fabrics, laces, belts, straps and hats was forbidden, but specific lacework was allowed when produced within the kingdom, while silk and ornaments of gold and silver produced in the *Estado da Índia* were also allowed. The introduction of mercantilist policies in this law is in line with other European countries at the time; and it also coincided with new policies for stimulating manufacturing from the 1670s to the early 1700s.[49]

Specific dress codes for clergymen, judges and students were reinstated in this law of 1677. Fabrics for funerals were regulated even more strictly than before. The use of silk in vehicles for urban transport, particularly coaches and litters, was also regulated, as well as the number of mules or

---

1669, in order to promote horse breeding, claimed to be in decline after the peace with Spain: see p. 175. This law would later be invoked as part of the set of sumptuary laws.

[48] On the reorganisation of the aristocracy, see Leonor Freire Costa and Mafalda Soares da Cunha, *D. João IV* (Lisbon: Círculo de Leitores, 2006) and Angela Barreto Xavier and Pedro Cardim, *D. Afonso VI* (Lisbon: Círculo de Leitores, 2006).

[49] See Leonor Freire Costa, Pedro Lains and Susana Münch Miranda, *An Economic History of Portugal, 1143–2010* (Cambridge: Cambridge University Press, 2016), esp. 109–163.

horses used (a maximum four, with special exceptions) and the number of attendants (two to four, when a couple travelled together).

Finally, the prohibition of gambling and penalties for houses in which it took place were included in this law. The regulations made the royal porter responsible for supervising the clothing of people attending audiences in the palace, but all legal officials were required to enforce the implementation of this law.[50] This is one of the major sumptuary laws enacted in Portugal, published nine years after peace with Spain was re-established. Its main new feature was the acknowledgement of mercantilist policies: this was the point at which there was a shift from a wartime economy to a peacetime economy, implying the encouragement of investment in manufacturing. Other laws that were generally promulgated or compiled together with sumptuary laws were integrated in this law, mainly those dealing with gambling, which confirms the importance and significance of the legislative environment.

The sumptuary laws of 1686, 1688, 1690 and 1698 generally confirmed the law of 1677; they were also guided by mercantilist policies, since the protection of national industries was explicitly indicated as one of the main concerns, as well as the protection of products from the colonies. Foreign hats made from beaver and other furs were explicitly prohibited. The prohibition of mules as a mean of personal transport was subject to exceptions for judges and physicians. The law of 1698 is perhaps the strictest of all, since it imposed common patterns for clothing, with prints included in the law to prevent a growing diversity of forms. The shape of pockets (a new issue) and sleeves was dealt with, as well as slashes and pinking, alongside materials allowed for buttons and buttonholes.[51]

It is not by chance that the extraordinarily detailed regulations for the production of fabrics in Portugal were published in the middle of this run of laws, in 1690.[52] However, there was some backtracking, since the prohibitions on importing hats, textiles, porcelain and glass were made less stringent in 1692, with the argument that national production did not yet respond to demand, and this was inconvenient for the Portuguese customers, while tax revenues had declined.[53] This is an important issue, since Portuguese mercantilist policies had to take account of traditional sources of income for the royal finances, particularly the revenues raised by customs houses and taxation on imported goods. The restriction of

[50] Andrade e Silva (ed.), *Colecção chronologica da legislação portugueza,1675–1680*, 25–27.
[51] Andrade e Silva (ed.), *Colecção chronologica da legislação portugueza, 1685–1700*, 64–65; 165; 419–421.
[52] Andrade e Silva (ed.), *Colecção chronologica da legislação portugueza, 1685–1700*, 213–233.
[53] Andrade e Silva (ed.), *Colecção chronologica da legislação portugueza, 1685–1700*, 271.

imports, or heavy taxation on them, risked causing a sharp decline in the royal income. However, the treaty with England signed in 1703, known as the Methuen Treaty, changed the conditions for mercantilist policies, since it allowed the import of English textiles without taxation against low taxation for Portuguese wines.[54]

It is in this transitional period, in the late seventeenth and early eighteenth centuries, that we find some references to sumptuary laws concerning the colonial world. In 1696 King Pedro II wrote two letters, in response to a request from the governor of Brazil, in which he forbade slave women from wearing silk and embroidery, as well as rings of gold or silver. In 1702, the Bishop of Rio de Janeiro asked the king to rule against the circulation of black and mulatto women in the city at night, and also to forbid these women to use luxury items of dress they received from their masters. The king agreed in 1703, but the following year there was still a consultation with the Overseas Council on the matter, which raises the issue of the decision being implemented. In 1709, a petition from the municipality of Salvador, in Bahia, complained about the excess use of luxury items of dress among blacks and mulattos, forcing the king to extend the rule already applied to Rio to the whole of Brazil.[55] We have no information about the degree to which this law was actually implemented, but it is obvious that gender and racial mobility were at stake.

In the Estado da Índia, Francisco de Távora (1681–1686) appears to have been the most active viceroy concerning publication of sumptuary laws; he reflected the new set of legislation produced in Portugal in those years, but also arrived in Goa with precise instructions from King Pedro II to tackle excessive expense among the population. In 1682 the viceroy banned the *vigílias*, a lavish ritual of birth celebration that blurred Christian and Hindu practices.[56] In 1683, the prohibition of litters was renewed with the explicit purpose of stimulating the Portuguese practice of horse-riding and the development of cavalry, useful in time of war. However, there were exceptions for the infirm or disabled, old vassals, noble women, judges of the *Relação*, ministers of the treasury, military officials and ecclesiastics.[57] The redirection of this policy from economic austerity and social hierarchy to racial and religious distinction occurred

---

[54] José Luís Cardoso *et alii*, *O tratado de Methuen, 1703: guerra, diplomacia, política e economia* (Lisbon: Livros Horizonte, 2003).

[55] See Silvia Hunold Lara, 'Sedas, panos e balangandãs: o traje de senhoras e escravas nas cidades do Rio de Janeiro e Salvador (século XVIII)', in Maria Beatriz Nizza da Silva (ed.), *Brazil: colonização e escravidão* (Rio de Janeiro: Nova Fronteira, 2000), 177–191.

[56] Chaturvedula, 'In the Precipice of Ruin', 380.

[57] Chaturvedula, 'In the Precipice of Ruin', 377–378.

in 1714, when King João V prohibited the Hindus to use litters (*andores*). In 1715 the bishop of Cochin prohibited Christians boys from carrying Hindus in portable litters under threat of excommunication; the decision was supported by the king at first but reversed in 1731 upon advice of the viceroy João de Saldanha da Gama.[58] Under the enormous political and military threat posed by the Marathas, it did not seem advisable to deepen internal divisions in the Estado da Índia. To complete the picture, it is interesting to note that a proposal of a general sumptuary law by the viceroy Vasco Fernandes César de Meneses in 1715, due to pervasive conspicuous consumption, was discussed by the Overseas Council, but King João V did not support it.[59] In general, it does not seem that dress was consistently regulated by sumptuary laws in the Estado da Índia.

The End of Sumptuary Laws

This busy period for the publication of successive sumptuary laws was disrupted in 1703, when the Treaty of Methuen imposed the import of English textiles to Portugal free of tax. Portuguese law acknowledged this crucial change, revoking the pragmatic sanction of 1677 insofar as it concerned the import and use of English textiles.[60] This did not prevent the creation of new sumptuary laws in the following years, but these were limited in scope. The law of 1702, published before the Treaty of Methuen, reinforced the prosecution of infringements, while a law of 1708, at the beginning of the reign of John V, introduced new exceptions.[61]

The final sumptuary laws were enacted at the end of the long reign of John V (1689–1750, reigned 1707–1750). In 1742, a law that applied to the kingdom of Angola prohibited the use of velvet, ornamented silk and gold, except for captains and higher-ranking military officers.[62] There is no evidence to confirm the implementation of this law. In this case, what is interesting to note is the importance of high-ranking military officers in Angola, whose status in a colony run by a very limited number of Portuguese people who were basically occupied in the slave trade was seen as in danger of being eroded by the widespread use of velvet, ornamented silk and gold in clothing. The absence of an economy based

---

[58] Chaturvedula, 'In the Precipice of Ruin', 379–380.
[59] Chaturvedula, 'In the Precipice of Ruin', 355–359.
[60] João Pedro Ribeiro, *Indice chronologico remissivo da legislação portugueza* (Lisbon: Academia Real das Sciencias, 1805), i: 283.
[61] Ribeiro, *Indice chronologico remissivo da legislação portugueza*, i: 280, 288, 289; and José Roberto Coelho e Sousa, *Systema, ou colecção dos Regimentos Reais* (Lisbon: Francisco Borges de Sousa, 1783), v: 397–398.
[62] Ribeiro, *Indice chronologico remissivo da legislação portugueza*, i: 333.

on plantations in Angola at this time limited the diversity of the social elite, which did not include owners of significant properties and sugar mills as in Brazil.[63]

The most elaborate text of the series of Portuguese sumptuary laws was published in 1749.[64] Significantly, it was the last one to be enacted. It was preceded by a consultation with members of the royal court. Three judges' opinions have come down to us. The first, by José Vaz de Carvalho, repeated the traditional Christian refusal of luxury as unproductive and promoting moral corruption. This judge praised agriculture and animal breeding as emanations of natural law and necessary for the sustenance of society. Curiously, he did not express concern about the protection of national production and colonial trade, which at that time supported the Portuguese imperial state – not only the gold from Brazil, then at its peak, but also spices arriving from India, Brazil and West Africa, textiles from India, and porcelain from China, not to mention the major dividends from the slave trade.[65] The judge advocated not only the renewal of previous sumptuary laws, but also excluding free mulattos and black people from wearing expensive clothing, a policy that had not been regularly implemented before. Finally, judge Vaz de Carvalho reverted to the old policies implemented from the fourteenth to the sixteenth century – called *sesmarias*, the royal right to distribute unexploited land – concerning the useful ownership of land by vassals, which condemned the abandonment of property and favoured its redistribution into productive hands. This means that Vaz de Carvalho's reasoning was not entirely conservative; he challenged the logic of seigneurial privilege over land when there was a failure to mobilise investment, work and production. He also condemned excessive taxation by landlords, which overburdened peasants, and favoured partition of communal land.[66]

The other two judges whose opinions have come down to us had, in one case, a contrasting (and exceptionally up-to-date) perspective on

[63] See Adriano Parreira, *Economia e sociedade em Angola na época da Rainha Jinga, século XVII* (Lisbon: Estampa, 1989); and José Carlos Venâncio, *A economia de Luanda e hinterland no século XVIII* (Lisbon: Estampa, 1996).

[64] Still useful is the extensive study by Luís Fernando de Carvalho Dias, *Luxo e pragmáticas no pensamento económico do século XVI* (Coimbra: Coimbra Editora, 1958), even if the history of economic thought has changed significantly since that time. The author studied and published the main consultations and the law that we analyse here. The law is transcribed at pp. 97–109.

[65] Freire Costa et al., *An Economic History of Portugal, 1143–2010*, 164–227; Leonor Freire Costa, Maria Manuela Rocha and Rita Martins de Sousa, *O ouro do Brasil* (Lisbon: Esfera dos Livros, 2013).

[66] Dias, *Luxo e pragmáticas no pensamento económico do século XVI*, 39–48 (I have drawn here on the published consultations). The only references to national industry concerned uniforms for domestic servants and timber for coaches and furniture.

economic policies, while the other developed an even more traditional reasoning than his first colleague. Let us start with the latter judge. Nicolau Francisco da Silva placed the moderation of luxury at the centre of his reasoning, to avoid the impoverishment of vassals and the ruin of the kingdom, while explicitly defending the protection of social hierarchies, in which he privileged his own noblesse de robe. From his point of view, the wide use of expensive clothing by different social groups blurred hierarchies that he considered crucial for a properly ordered society. He was the only legal adviser who clearly expressed the idea that a new sumptuary law should be used to reinforce social hierarchy and regulate appearance according to social rank. He departed from a moral vision of luxury as corruption, which was alien to his thought.[67]

The third judge was Manuel de Almeida Carvalho and an exception here. He must have read or discussed the most recent developments in political economy in other European countries, since he was the only adviser to praise conspicuous consumption as economically productive, as it expanded the workforce and increased social well-being. He placed industry at the same level as agriculture, contrary to the developments that would be promoted by the physiocrats in the third quarter of the eighteenth century and beyond. He also took on board the commercial interests of the empire, highlighting the need for mercantilist policies, which meant increased taxation for imported commodities not originating in the colonies and lowered taxation for exported or re-exported commodities. He discussed the idea of private property as part of the *ius gentium* that preceded the institution of monarchy, in which the sovereign had the right to repossess and redistribute land not in use. He thus agreed with his colleague José Vaz de Carvalho in a critique of seigneurial rights, here made much more explicit. Almeida Carvalho also highlighted the uselessness of sumptuary laws, since they had scarcely been implemented in the past; he argued that more attempts at creating new sumptuary laws would erode the reputation of law and royal power. It would be futile to oppose the increase of luxury, which benefitted the inventor, the artist and the manufacturer.[68]

---

[67] Dias, *Luxo e pragmáticas no pensamento económico do século XVI*, 54–88. Nicolau Xavier da Silva presents an elaborate but biased analysis of this series of Portuguese sumptuary laws. Some of these I was unable to find in the main collections of legislation, particularly concerning the reigns of John II and Manuel I.

[68] Dias, *Luxo e pragmáticas no pensamento económico do século XVI*, 49–53. The opinion of Diogo Marchã Temudo – another judge of the *Desembargo do Paço*, the highest appeal royal court in Portugal – expressed in 1698, half a century before this consultation, confirms the long-term critique of seigneurial rights, including the entailing of property to the Church and the proposal to privatise communal land. This opinion was also published in Dias, *Luxo e pragmáticas no pensamento económico do século XVI*, 113–121.

The king, who by now was at the end of his long reign, decided to follow the conservative advice of José Vaz de Carvalho. The resulting sumptuary law of 1749 is very interesting, because it is the longest of all Portuguese series, and reveals the significant developments in fashion that had taken place over the previous generation. It gathers together all the major prohibitions (and some exceptions) already present in other laws. However, this strict limitation of consumption by law, which prescribed social and racial exclusions – black and mulatto people could not wear expensive clothing in any of the colonies – then proved to be unacceptable from an economic and a social point of view.

The law raised enormous protest immediately after its publication, which led to its partial revocation. The main group involved in this powerful protest was the merchants, who formed the *Mesa do Bem Comum do Comércio* (literally Table of Trade Common Good). They pointed out the significant damage to colonial trade, to customs revenues, to national manufacturing and to the employment of young women. They claimed that reciprocal trade between Portugal and other countries would be damaged and in turn this would contribute to the decline of exports and re-exports. Moreover, the merchants stressed the economic and political consequences of the law in Brazil, where Portuguese interests depended on blacks and mulattos, the vast majority of the population in that colony. The exclusion of these crucial segments of the population from consumption of a significant number of items of clothing would not only damage trade but also undermine these groups' attitudes and the political support they offered. The merchants also indicated that the law would downgrade the status of mulattos, who had made the republic respectable as valuable vassals, and who had been dispensed by the king from enquiries into the purity of their blood when it came to joining military orders. They also contested the prohibiting of those who were not noblemen or their servants from using swords, stating that merchants needed to defend themselves while travelling.[69]

This is an extraordinary document, the only existing one, to my knowledge, with a clear anti-racist stance – obviously for economic and commercial reasons that suited the merchants – written by white men in that period of time in Portugal. The document also shows a sharp economic and social vision capable of taking an overall view of different parts of the Portuguese empire and pointing out the damaging consequences of the implementation of this law. The employment of women, surprisingly, is favoured, which reveals a precocious sensitivity to social issues that

[69] Dias, *Luxo e pragmáticas no pensamento económico do século XVI*, 89–94.

was otherwise insufficiently integrated into contemporary economic and political thought.[70]

This law was immediately repealed by laws enacted in 1749 and 1751 that dealt with the articles criticised by the merchants – but this swift change of mind probably meant that the political legitimacy that would have enabled the implementation of all the other aspects of it was lacking.[71] To put it plainly, this last sumptuary law, extremely ambitious in scope, ended up being partly withdrawn, and thus compromised any further attempts to publish similar laws. Instead of counteracting the increased trend towards wider consumption of luxury goods, which blurred the frontiers of distinction in appearance, the failure of the sumptuary law of 1749 announced the end of a long sequence of legislation on consumption. A late complaint, in 1780, from the members of the Senate of Goa, who only then had access to the law thirty-one years after its publication, was immediately accepted by an embarrassed Overseas Council.[72] This episode shows the traps inherent in communications between Lisbon and the capital of the Estado da Índia, the latter having probably been excluded from information about a law that several members of the royal councils had immediately felt to be problematic.

Enlightenment Derision

The correspondence on sumptuary laws between D. Miguel da Anunciação, Bishop of Coimbra and Paulo de Carvalho Mendonça, produced in 1762, is an interesting issue that has not generally been included in studies of the controversies that surrounded the bishop during his lifetime. D. Miguel da Anunciação was born in 1703, became a clergyman, and was elevated to the bishopric of Coimbra in 1741, continuing in this role until his death in 1779. He was involved in the polemic of the late 1740s concerning 'sigilism' – that is, the accusation that many confessors were betraying the secrets of the confession to obtain denunciations of the sinners' accomplices, thus interfering with the competences and jurisdiction of the Inquisition.[73] Twenty years

---

[70] See José Luís Cardoso, *O pensamento económico em Portugal nos finais do século XVIII, 1780–1808* (Lisbon: Estampa, 1989); Id., *História do pensamento económico português* (Lisbon: Horizonte, 2001).

[71] The laws of 1749 and 1751 repealing the previous law were also dealt with in Dias, *Luxo e pragmáticas no pensamento económico do século XVI*, 110–111.

[72] See Silvia Hunold Lara, 'Customs and Costumes: Carlos Julião and the Image of Black Slaves in Late Eighteenth-Century Brazil', *Slavery and Abolition* 23/2 (2002): 125–146, esp. 132 and 145.

[73] António Pereira da Silva, *A questão do sigilismo em Portugal no século XVIII: história, religião e política nos reinados de D. João V e D. José* (Braga: s.n., 1964), António Pereira

later, in November 1768, the same prelate decided to publish a pastoral condemning books he considered heretical. In that same year, seven months earlier, the king had created the *Real Mesa Censória* for the censorship of books, involving laymen, theologians and commissioners of the Inquisition. The bishop was thus considered a rebel under the new jurisdictionalist stance adopted by the Marquis of Pombal, the main secretary of state of Portugal in 1750–1777, to assert the State against the Church. He was arrested in his palace and brought to Lisbon, where he was condemned to a long prison sentence, from which he was released by King Joseph only in 1777.[74]

Paulo de Carvalho Mendonça (1702–1770) was a brother of the Marquis of Pombal, and was involved in Pombal's policies to control the Church and keep the royal family on their side. He accumulated important secular positions, such as those of President of the Senate of Lisbon, and supervisor of the house and property of the Portuguese Queen, Mariana Victoria de Borbon y Farnesio, who was the daughter of the Spanish King Philip V. As a clergyman, he also obtained important ecclesiastical positions, such as Grão-Prior of the Colegiada de Guimarães, canon of the cathedral of Lisbon and member of the General Council of the Inquisition.

D. Miguel da Anunciação must have addressed Paulo de Carvalho Mendonça due to the latter's informal position as a mediator between his brother, the Marquis of Pombal, and the Church in Portugal. The bishop of Coimbra had sent letters to check the possible receptiveness of Paulo Mendonça to new sumptuary laws, which in his view were necessary to reduce the excess of luxury that was demoralising the country. He also suggested the suppression of opera, then arousing great enthusiasm. Their contrasting attitudes to consumption are visible in this correspondence, although we have only the final response from Paulo Mendonça. He pointed out to his correspondent that operas were performed without the participation of women, in contrast to what happened in Rome under the auspices of the Pope. Concerning the reform of luxury, Mendonça cited the military campaign, in Pará, Brazil, of his brother, the governor Francisco Xavier de Mendonça Furtado, who had sent troops 600 miles into the interior, among naked natives, where they experienced the same troubled feelings as those that might be stimulated by court ladies wearing ornaments. Mocking the bishop, he concluded that 'it is not the

---

da Silva, 'Sigilismo', in *Dicionário de História Religiosa de Portugal*, ed. Carlos Moreira de Azevedo, vol. P-Z (Lisbon: Círculo de Leitores, 2001), 233–236.

[74] Manuel Augusto Rodrigues, 'Pombal e D. Miguel da Anunciação, bispo de Coimbra', *Revista de História das Ideias* 4/1 (1982): 207–298.

ornament that moves the spirit, but the difference of sex'.[75] This correspondence allows us to understand better the politics of the government
of Pombal, its departure from previous systems of values, and the resistance of conservative members of civil and ecclesiastical society.

Conclusion

Sumptuary laws in Portugal were inspired by legislation on luxury
produced in other European countries. The financial concerns of the
Crown regarding the impoverishment or bankruptcy of vassals due to
conspicuous consumption were designed to guarantee military service
and prevent excessive rents demanded of peasants. These concerns
were seen as equally important by the cortes or parliament, where the
representatives of the third estate pushed for limitations on the expenses
of royal officers and noblemen, including on the number of servants
and horses or mules used, in order to control the burden of lodging
these people. Restrictions imposed by the king on luxury consumption
targeted both citizens and peasants, and sought to avoid the blurring of
social frontiers as regarding appearance; but they also included different
strata of the nobility. It is probable that the regulation of luxury, including
clothing, interior decoration, means of transport, mourning and vanity in
funerals, had been pushed by noblemen incapable of sustaining competition under conditions of inflation or the long-term stagnation of rural
rents. Privileged exceptions favoured both a stable hierarchy and financial capacity.

The vision of social hierarchies expressed by theses laws did not
match the perception of the three orders. In many cases, they were
driven by occupations in which the noblesse de robe, particularly royal
judges, played a significant role. Women were not especially targeted in
the Portuguese case; they had an equivalent status to their husbands
or fathers, but in some cases, particularly that of the ladies in waiting,
women benefitted from special privileges. Certain laws contributed to
defining masculinity and femininity through the regulation of clothing.
Overseas expansion resulted in an extraordinary increase in the import
of fabrics and clothing from India and China, transforming habits of
consumption and styles of dress. The register recording the implementation of the 1609 law in Porto shows the variety of items available and the
extensive use of foreign garments in a significant town.

---

[75] Dias, *Luxo e pragmáticas no pensamento económico do século XVI*, letter reproduced in
123–125, quote p. 125.

The colonial world was not particularly targeted by this series of sumptuary laws. Although colonial authorities, namely governors, bishops and even (but rarely) municipal councils, convinced the king to promulgate laws against luxury among black and mulatto people, mainly in the late seventeenth and early eighteenth centuries, the royal councils generally resisted publishing special sumptuary laws for, or extending existing ones to, the colonies. The cases identified were not very significant, and the only clear case of the application of a law to the entire colonial world, in 1749, was one that excluded black people and mulattos from wearing expensive clothing. This was immediately revoked under pressure from the merchants in Lisbon and, presumably, from targeted groups in the colonial world.

Central authorities felt that ethnic competition in the matter of appearance could not be contained by law, while there was a sharp consciousness that the survival of the empire rested on the promotion of mixed-race elites. Dress was commonly recycled in the colonies, while the domestic slaves of prominent households were paraded as expensive accessories wearing lustrous garments and jewels. The depictions of colonial human types and processions of confraternities of black people by Carlos Julião or Jean-Baptiste Debret show diversity and richness of appearance as an expression of the multiple identities and layers of fashion that slaves and freed people proudly carried with them.[76] In the nineteenth and twentieth centuries, colonial legislation abandoned restrictions on the wearing of expensive clothing by blacks and mulattos to concentrate on naked bodies and native appearance, as in the law concerning the Estado da Índia published on 26 October 1878.[77]

The right to dress as they pleased, claimed by men and women from the upper, middle and even the lower strata of the population, can thus be observed through these repeated pieces of legislation. Social competition was usually at stake; but there were important periods, particularly that of the war of independence against Castile in 1640–1668, when restrictions on luxury were imposed in general terms, without allowing exceptions or privileges even for titled noblemen or royal judges. It is

---

[76] See the profuse illustrations of daily life and the variety of human types in Brazil by Jean Baptiste Debret, *Voyage pittoresque et historique au Brésil* 3 vols. (Paris: Firmin Didot, 1834–1839); on Carlos Julião see Manuela Tenreiro, 'Military Encounters in the Eighteenth Century: Carlos Julião and Racial Representations in the Portuguese Empire', *Portuguese Studies* 23/1 (2007): 7–35.

[77] João José da Silva, *Repertório alphabetico e chronologico ou indice remissivo da legislação ultramarina desde a época das descobertas até 1882* (Macau: Seminário de S. José, 1886). This law replicates late eighteenth-century legislation in Brazil: see the chapter on 'Trajo' in Maria Beatriz Nizza da Silva, *Vida privada e quotidiano no Brasil na época de D. Maria I e D. João VI*, 2nd ed. (Lisbon: Estampa, 2004).

true that, since their beginning, sumptuary laws had been entangled with economic and financial policies; but the change from a wartime economy to a peacetime one triggered new economic concerns, this time based on a mercantilist stance that lasted until the Treaty of Methuen signed with England in 1703. The promotion of national industry in periods of commercial crisis, starting with the period of 1670–1690, played a major role in the new political atmosphere of the eighteenth century.

The last significant Portuguese sumptuary law, issued in 1749 and immediately withdrawn, symbolised the end of this series of legislation, already under attack as useless and contrary to the well-being of the population. Praise of luxury as an economic benefit replicated Mandeville's vision of private vices as public benefits, and reversed the traditional vision of luxury as moral corruption and idleness. The letter of Paulo de Mendonça Carvalho, written on 4 December 1762 to the bishop of Coimbra, D. Miguel da Anunciação, openly derided the pretence that luxury could be legislated against. By that time, sumptuary laws were already a thing of the past.

11 'Splendour and Magnificence': Diplomacy and Sumptuary Codes in Early Modern Batavia

Adam Clulow

In 1632, a new Governor-General arrived in Batavia to a lavish welcome. The appointee, Hendrik Brouwer, had been tasked with taking charge of the Dutch East India Company's (*Vereenigde Oost-Indische Compagnie* or VOC) sprawling operations across Asia. As he disembarked, cannon fire boomed out from the vessels assembled in the harbour. While the shots were still reverberating across the water, they were answered by Batavia Castle, the looming fortification that dominated the port city.[1] Approaching the castle, Brouwer moved through the long lines of soldiers assembled to welcome the new arrival. Waiting for him was his honour guard, a contingent of halberdiers gorgeously attired in red and yellow, the bright colours of their sumptuous clothes contrasting with the threadbare outfits of the regular garrison soldiers. Once he reached the castle, Brouwer formally assumed the office before a large crowd of townspeople, soldiers and other residents of the port, all of whom swore to serve the new Governor-General faithfully.

Such ceremonies with their echoes of royal coronations were not an accident, the product of a personal whim or a love of the trappings of the office. Rather, they functioned to boost the status of the Governors-General, transforming these officials into kinglike figures capable of engaging in diplomacy with diverse polities scattered through the region. The VOC's 1602 charter had granted it the right to 'enter into agreements and contracts with princes and potentates' across the region.[2] Yet, even if such privileges had been awarded in Europe, they did not translate automatically to Asia, where the first Governors-General – as the senior officials in a company of merchants – had struggled to assert themselves

---

[1] H.T. Colenbrander (ed.), *Dagh-register gehouden int Casteel Batavia vant passerende daer ter plaetse als over geheel Nederlandts-India. Vol. 2: 1631–4* (The Hague: Martinus Nijhoff, 1898), 96. Hereafter *Batavia Dagregisters*.

[2] J.A. van der Chijs, *Geschiedenis der stichting van de Vereenigde O.I. Compagnie* (Leiden: P. Engels, 1857), 130.

in a diplomatic world dominated by emperors, kings and sultans. To overcome these barriers, the Company relied on the systematic deployment of what is broadly labelled in VOC sources as 'pracht en praal', usually translated as 'pomp and circumstance' or 'splendour and display'.[3] Enveloping the Governor-General within royal ceremonies remade him from just another merchant, as these officials were contemptuously dismissed by one local ruler, into quasi-kings, who could engage effectively with polities across the region.[4]

But even as Brouwer was welcomed to Batavia with appropriate ceremony, he carried with him a charge from his superiors in Europe, the *Heren XVII* or Gentlemen 17 (hereafter referred to as the *Heeren* 17), to cut back on the kingly props that were such an indispensable component of the Governor-General's self-presentation. One target of their wrath was the sumptuously dressed halberdiers, the ever-present companions of the Governors-General in Batavia. The *Heeren* 17's instructions would be repeated again and again over the coming decades: reduce extravagance and, they believed, unnecessary expenditure on personal display, on 'pracht en praal' and the ostentatious performance of status. As such the instructions to Brouwer anticipate a string of sumptuary laws that were promulgated in Batavia in 1647, 1680, 1704, 1719, 1729 and 1733, before culminating in a sprawling code consisting of 124 articles issued by Governor-General Jacob Mossel on 30 December 1754. Although these included a focus on dress, initially only ornaments such as jewellery and gold buttons but later clothes themselves, they were arguably more concerned with accessories such as parasols and carriages, which were the subject of repeated injunctions.

Such laws were not unique to Batavia. As this volume demonstrates, sumptuary codes were common in both Europe and Asia, where they were issued with striking regularity.[5] But if such codes were widely promulgated, it is also the case that the versions issued in Batavia had certain features drawn from the colonial city's peculiar position in Asia that set them apart. Batavia was a hybrid political space characterised by contradictions. It was a sovereign enclave carved out by a commercial organisation, the VOC, in Asia. It was a European metropolis dominated by imposing Dutch architecture that might have been transplanted from

---

[3] J.A. van der Chijs, *Nederlandsch-Indisch Plakaatboek* (Batavia: Landsdrukkerij, 1885–1900), ii: 111. The last translation comes from Robert Ross, *Clothing. A Global History: Or, The Imperialists' New Clothes* (Cambridge: Polity, 2008), 41. For the purposes of this chapter, I have translated 'pracht' as splendour and 'praal' as magnificence.

[4] *Batavia Dagregisters, Vol. 1: 1624–29*, 80.

[5] Surprisingly such orders were not promulgated in the United Provinces.

the streets of Amsterdam but one whose prosperity depended on a large Chinese population.[6] And, most relevant for this chapter, it was home to a Governor-General who seemed to many observers to wield the power of a king, but who was also subordinate to the *Heeren* 17, a distant body that met three times a year thousands of miles away in Europe. The ongoing contest between autonomy and control generated a perennial tension between a Governor-General, who complained that only officials on the ground were capable of understanding and reacting to conditions in Asia, and the *Heeren* 17, who attempted to rein in what they saw as the excesses of their subordinates. This tension was central to how Batavia functioned; it is also key to understanding the nature of the sumptuary codes promulgated there.

The Batavian sumptuary laws have been the subject of a number of ground-breaking studies by Jean Gelman Taylor, Robert Ross, Marsely Kehoe and others.[7] These scholars have analysed a string of orders issued in Batavia, clearly showing how the Company sought to regulate and restrict display in its Asian headquarters and, by extension, its other colonies. The starting point for this chapter is with a different and more basic question: although these sumptuary codes were promulgated in Batavia, who exactly was driving them? Answering this requires us to look beyond a familiar set of sources. For decades now, scholars have relied on Van der Chijs's monumental compilation, *Nederlandsch-Indisch Plakaatboek*, which collects the thousands of laws and edicts (including a string of sumptuary codes) issued in Batavia in seventeen massive volumes.[8] While indispensable, Van der Chijs's remarkable work is also limited, often providing, for example, summaries punctuated by quotations rather than

---

[6] Leonard Blussé, 'Batavia, 1619–1740: The Rise and Fall of a Chinese Colonial Town', *Journal of Southeast Asian Studies* 12/1 (1981): 159–178.

[7] Jean Gelman Taylor, *The Social World of Batavia: Europeans and Eurasians in Colonial Indonesia*. 2nd edn. (Madison: University of Wisconsin Press, 2009); Robert Ross, 'Sumptuary Laws in Europe, the Netherlands and the Dutch colonies', in Nigel Worden (ed.), *Contingent Lives: Social Identity and Material Culture in the VOC World* (Cape Town: Rondebosch, 2007), 382–390; Marsely L. Kehoe, 'Dutch Batavia: Exposing the Hierarchy of the Dutch Colonial City', *Journal of Historians of Netherlandish Art* 7/1 (2015). doi: 10.5092/jhna.2015.7.1.3 Available at https://jhna.org/articles/dutch-batavia-exposing-hierarchy-dutch-colonial-city/. There has also been important work on the ramifications of these laws for the Cape. See: J. J. F. Joubert, '*Die Kaapkolonie onder Ryk tulbagh, 1751–1771*' (Unpublished MA thesis, Stellenbosch University, 1942). Stan Du Plessis, '"Pearls worth Rds4000 or less": Reinterpreting Eighteenth-Century Sumptuary Laws at the Cape', *ERSA Working Paper* 336 (2013). Available at https://econrsa.org/system/files/publications/working_papers/working_paper_336_0.pdf; Liza-Mari Coetzee, '*Clothing, Gender and Social Identity at the Cape of Good Hope, 1652–1795*' (Unpublished MA thesis, University of Johannesburg, 2014).

[8] J. A. van der Chijs, *Nederlandsch-Indisch Plakaatboek*, 17 vols. (Batavia: Landsdrukkerij, 1885–1900).

the full text of these codes. More importantly for the purposes of this chapter, however, looking only at the *Plakaatboek* ignores the hundreds of letters dispatched by the *Heeren* 17 to their chief subordinates in Asia, as well as the resolutions taken in Batavia Castle in which commands from Europe were discussed and acted upon.[9] Examining these sources reveals the central role played by the *Heeren* 17 in propelling the sumptuary codes that were issued in Batavia's name.[10]

This chapter uses such sources to make three arguments. First, the push towards sumptuary codes pre-dated the 1647 law that is conventionally taken as the first iteration of these laws. In fact, the *Heeren* 17, outraged at the extravagant display they believed was commonplace in their Asian colonies and factories, had been prodding the Governor-General to take action for decades before the first code was issued. Second, the *Heeren* 17 remained the driving force behind the Batavian sumptuary codes throughout the seventeenth century. Faced with an insistent drumbeat from their superiors in Europe, successive Governors-General either did nothing, stalled or acquiesced depending on the degree of pressure, while seeking to carve out or defend their own privileges of rank. In this way, the sumptuary codes became a contested site, marked by low-level but persistent clashes between the *Heeren* 17 and their representatives in Asia. And third, this underlying dynamic started to shift only in the eighteenth century when successive Governors-General began, in response to their own, more localised concerns, to take a more active role in drafting and promulgation. Mossel's sprawling 1754 code represented the culmination of this process. It was both a reaction to pressure from the *Heeren* 17 but also, and arguably more importantly, an attempt by a reforming Governor-General to use such codes to re-establish domestic

---

[9] Net-generale resoluties en -incidenteel- net-secrete resoluties, 1613–1810, Arsip Nasional Republik Indonesia, Archief van de gouverneur-generaal en raden van Indië (Hoge Regering) van de Verenigde Oostindische Compagnie en taakopvolgers, 1612–1811, inv.nr 853 1182. These resolutions can now be accessed via the pioneering *Sejarah Nusantara* online platform developed by the National Archives of the Republik of Indonesia and the Corts Foundation (https://sejarah-nusantara.anri.go.id). Kopieboek van uitgaande missiven, instructies en andere papieren van de Heren XVII en de kamer Amsterdam aan de kantoren in Indië 1614–1795, Nationaal Archief, De archieven van de Verenigde Oostindische Compagnie, 1602–1795, inv.nr 312–344.

[10] I am by no means the first to suggest that the impetus for these laws came from the *Heeren* 17. Ross writes that the Governor-General was 'Encouraged and to some extent required by the Heren XVII' when it came to sumptuary laws. Ross, 'Sumptuary Laws', 386. Kehoe explains that such regulations were 'in many cases in response to complaints from the Heeren XVII (advisory board, headquartered in the Republic) of the Dutch East India Company', Kehoe, 'Dutch Batavia', 24. The goal of this chapter is to explore the nature of the dynamic between the Governor-General and the *Heeren* 17 and how it influenced the Batavian sumptuary codes.

hierarchies in VOC operations in Asia which had been loosened by the opening up of intra-Asian trade. This combination of external pressure and internal factors helps explain the 1754 law's monumental scope and scale.

Dual Centres of Authority

As it grew and expanded, the VOC developed two connected centres of authority, one in Europe and a second in Asia. In the first years after the Company's formation in 1602, the *Heeren* 17, a body based in the United Provinces, constituted the organisation's primary command structure.[11] Consisting of 17 directors (*Bewindhebbers*) drawn from the six chambers that made up the VOC, they met for extended periods (typically more than a week) three times a year at rotating locations in the United Provinces.[12] The fleets that departed for Asia were placed under the control of an admiral who was commissioned to lead his ships to the region and once there to take command of the Company's operations across the region. As the VOC expanded and more and more ships arrived in Asia, it became clear that such arrangements were not sustainable and in 1609 the *Heeren* 17 elected to overhaul this system. Their solution was to create a separate office, the Governor-Generalship (*Gouveneur-Generaal*), that was to be based permanently in Asia and to take control of operations there. The decision pushed the VOC onto a different path from its English rival, which continued to rely on a model organised around individual fleets, and brought it more in line with the Portuguese system with its central authority in Goa.[13] To fill the new office, the *Heeren* 17 selected Pieter Both, an experienced merchant who was instructed to assume control over VOC activities in Asia.[14]

In addition to creating a centralised office, the directors recognised that they needed to establish a permanent headquarters in Asia from

---

[11] After an initial trial phase, the Company settled into an organisational model with 60 *bewindhebbers* or directors. The six chambers that made up the VOC each dispatched representatives for the meetings of the *Heeren* 17. The Amsterdam chamber sent eight Directors, the Zeeland chamber sent four, and the four smaller chambers sent one each, with the seventeenth post rotating. Femme Gaastra, *The Dutch East India Company: Expansion and Decline* (Zutpen: Walburg Pers, 2003), 21.

[12] Femme Gaastra, 'The Organization of The VOC', in G. L Balk et al. (eds.), *Indonesia. The archives of the Dutch East India Company (VOC) and the local institutions in Batavia (Jakarta)*, (Leiden and Boston: Brill, 2007), 19.

[13] Gaastra, *The Dutch East India Company*, 39–40.

[14] Pieter van Dam, *Beschrijvinge van de Oostindishe Compagnie*, ed. F.W. Stapel. (Rijksgeschiedkundige Publicatiën, The Hague, 1927–1954), i: 517–531.

which the Company's affairs could be directed. Their choice eventually settled on Jayakarta, a port city located near Banten that was under the control of a minor prince. In 1610, an agreement was reached that allowed the Company to set up operations there, but relations quickly deteriorated and within a decade there was open war. By the time the dust had settled, the prince had been deposed and his dominion claimed as VOC territory. The establishment of Batavia, as the settlement was later named, permanently altered the trajectory of the Company's development by creating a sovereign space in which it could operate unhampered by external authority.[15] It had the added consequence of creating a rival centre of power within the organisation itself. From the beginning, the slow pace of communication between Europe and Asia gave officials in Batavia considerable freedom to operate independently. On the ground, successive Governors-General protested that they were the only ones who could understand conditions in Asia and act effectively.[16] Antonio van Diemen, who held the office from 1636 to 1645, laid out a more general position, writing that 'We have said and we confirm with this that we *must be trusted with the matters of the Indies*, and therefore cannot wait for orders if we are to do the Company's service'.[17]

Across the two centuries that the VOC operated, the *Heeren* 17 and successive Governors-General clashed repeatedly over a set of connected issues. From their vantage point in Europe, it seemed to the Directors as if Batavia barrelled too readily into conflict with other Asian powers or European rivals without considering either the expenses involved in protracted war or the political consequences.[18] In addition, the *Heeren* 17 fretted continually about private trading, which was rife throughout VOC areas of operation, about corruption and the related problems of conspicuous consumption and lavish display in Asia. It was these last concerns that provided the backdrop to the initial push for a sumptuary code.

---

[15] May 30, the anniversary of 'the conquest of the kingdom of Jakatra', became an annual celebration for VOC officials in Asia. For one such celebration, see *Batavia Dagregisters, Vol. 1: 1625–1629*, 257.

[16] H.T. Colenbrander and W. Ph. Coolhaas (eds.), *Jan Pietersz. Coen: Bescheiden Omtrent Zijn Bedrijf in Indië*, 9 vols. (The Hague: Martinus Nijhoff, 1919–1954) i: 439. This letter was written just before the conquest of Jayakarta.

[17] J. K. J. de Jonge (ed.), *De opkomst van het Nederlandsch gezag in Oost-Indië: verzameling van onuitgegeven stukken uit het oud-koloniaal archief* ('s-Gravenhage: Nijhoff, 1862–1909), 5: 248–249. Emphasis in original.

[18] In particular, the *Heeren* 17 complained that Batavia was too focused on its prestige and hence too ready to use violence to assert its role in the region. Colenbrander and Coolhaas (eds.), *Jan Pietersz. Coen*, iv: 539.

Regulation and Order

Studies of Batavian sumptuary codes generally commence with an ordinance directed at 'pracht en praal' dated 9 March 1647.[19] In fact, the *Heeren* 17 had been urging successive Governors-General to pass such laws for decades, dating to before the conquest of Jayakarta and the establishment of Batavia. In 1617, thirty years before the first actual ordinance was issued, the *Heeren* 17 took aim at the 'extraordinary splendour' of their servants in Asia.[20] To suppress this extravagant display, the Governor-General was instructed to enact 'sumptuary statutes, ordinances and instructions'. It was a remarkable demand for an organisation that was less than two decades old and which still lacked a permanent headquarters in Asia or a secure foothold in local trading networks, and yet the *Heeren* 17 were convinced that action must be taken immediately to curtail the excesses they saw in Asia.

When no such laws were forthcoming, the *Heeren* 17 returned to the same concern in a letter dated 23 November 1631. They started, in what would become a standard refrain, by explaining that they had heard from 'various people [of] the splendour among everyone there, namely in India'.[21] It was common for returnees from Asia to comment on the lavish nature of Batavian life and its extravagant rituals. One such account, which can be taken as broadly typical, described the 'rich and excessive lives of the Hollanders in the Indies', which both fascinated and appalled visitors.[22] Faced with such reports, the *Heeren* 17 explained that these excesses were 'a plague (*pest*) in Batavia and over the whole of the Indies'.[23] This time they were not satisfied with simply urging the Governor-General to take some sort of action. Instead, they targeted the 'wearing of jewels, diamonds, gold chains, gold or silver trimmings' on clothes and, in another version of the same instructions, gold buttons, all of which were to be prohibited on penalty of forfeiture and fines.[24] Such

---

[19] Van der Chijs, *Nederlandsch-Indisch Plakaatboek*, ii: 111.

[20] Pieter Mijer (ed.), *Verzameling van instructiën, ordonnanciën en reglementen voor de regering van Nederlandsch Indië, vastgesteld in de jaren 1609, 1617, 1632, 1650, 1807, 1815, 1818, 1827, 1830 en 1836, met de ontwerpen der Staats-Commissie van 1803 en historische aanteekeningen* (Batavia: Ter Lands-Drukkerij, 1848), 31.

[21] Letter from the *Heeren* 17 to the Governor-General and Council, 23 November 1631, VOC 315, unfoliated. The key paragraph of the 1631 letter is also reproduced in the Batavia resolutions from 1680. 5 July 1680, ID-JaAN, Hoge Regering inv. nr 892.

[22] *Beschryving van Batavia, met des zelfs kasteel en publyke gebouwen* (Amsterdam: Dirk Swart, 1741), 26.

[23] Letter from the *Heeren* 17 to the Governor-General and Council, 23 November 1631, VOC 315, unfoliated.

[24] Ibid. The reference to buttons comes from a quote from the original 1631 letter, reproduced in a 1676 missive. De Jonge (ed.), *De opkomst van het Nederlandsch gezag in Oost-Indië*, vi: 165.

penalties were to apply not only to VOC employees but also to the 'free people of Batavia', a group usually referred to as the free burghers (*vrij-burger*). Originally consisting of former VOC servants who had received permission to settle in the Company's colonies in Asia, the free burghers were both dependant on the organisation and frustratingly beyond its constraints.[25]

In their letters, the *Heeren* 17 targeted extravagant displays in ornaments and dress worn by VOC employees and free burghers. That such fashions were common among those who could afford them is confirmed by contemporary depictions and accounts of Batavia. A well-known painting from the period, 'Pieter Cnoll and His Family', produced by J. J. Coeman in 1665 and now hanging in the Rijksmuseum, shows Cnoll, a VOC *opperkoopman* or upper merchant with his half-Japanese wife, his daughters and their servants (Figure 11.1).[26]

A confident figure, Cnoll is depicted in black, wearing gleaming gold buttons and a beautiful embroidered gold sash, while his wife, Cornelia, is adorned with gleaming pearls and jewels – all objects prohibited in one way or another by the *Heeren* 17's commands. Cnoll worked for the VOC but contemporary descriptions of the free burghers invariably highlighted their lavish lifestyles. One author explained that burgher wives and daughters looked more like princesses than the members of trading families.[27] Another observer noted that a guard had to be placed on the church in Batavia, which was famous as a site of ostentatious display, as an especially bold group of thieves had attempted to rob the churchgoers of the 'gold, pearls and precious stones' they wore in abundance.[28]

While their 1631 letter had urged Batavia to reduce 'splendour', the *Heeren* 17 were presented with a more concrete opportunity to take action when they drew up instructions for Hendrik Brouwer, who had been dispatched to replace Jacques Specx as Governor-General. Brouwer was issued with comprehensive instructions consisting of 96 articles touching on all aspects of VOC operations in Asia.[29] Article 7 of these instructions

---

[25] The first mention of this community dates back to 1616, when Governor-General Jan Pietersz. Coen explained that he had approved the discharge of Company employees to live and work in VOC settlements. Taylor, *The Social World of Batavia*, 9. Although he permitted this, Coen complained frequently that the free burghers were totally 'unsuitable for the planting of colonies'. Colenbrander and Coolhaas (eds.), *Jan Pietersz. Coen*, i: 644.

[26] For a superb discussion of this and other paintings from this period, see Jean Gelman Taylor, 'Meditations on a Portrait from Seventeenth-Century Batavia', *Journal of Southeast Asian Studies* 37/1 (2006): 23–41.

[27] *Beschryving van Batavia*, 36.

[28] Frederik Bolling, 'Friderici Bollingii Oost-Indisch reisboek', trans. J. Visscher. *Bijdragen tot de Taal-, Land- en Volkenkunde van Nederlandsch Indië* 68 (1913), 333.

[29] Mijer, *Verzameling van instructiën, ordonnanciën en reglementen*, 49–70.

Figure 11.1 *Pieter Cnoll, Cornelia van Nijenrode and their Daughters,* by Jacob Coeman, 1665. Rijksmuseum, SK-A-4062, Amsterdam.

noted that 'excesses' had increased exponentially in places like Batavia and that great 'pracht' had affected the 'high and low servants of the Company in the Indies'.[30] Reminded of the 1617 regulation, which had called for clear laws to halt such practices, Brouwer was urged to pass his own sumptuary ordinances.

Alongside this repetition of their previous instructions, the *Heeren* 17 had a specific target in mind where such reforms could productively start. This was the contingent of halberdiers that formed the honour guard for every Governor-General in Batavia and which was costing, the *Heeren* 17 complained, more than 5,000 guilders a year. It was not simply a question of wages; rather they were outraged by the halberdiers' ostentatious livery, which required a bloated budget simply to maintain. The only way to resolve this problem was by cutting the number of halberdiers and Brouwer was instructed to take such actions immediately.[31] It was a demand that struck at the heart of the Governor-General's kingly

---

[30] Ibid., 51.
[31] Mijer, *Verzameling van instructiën, ordonnanciën en reglementen,* 56; Van der Chijs, *Nederlandsch-Indisch Plakaatboek,* i: 271. The *Heeren* 17 took aim at a group consisting of six halberdiers, four guards and an unspecified number of youths.

presentation. The halberdiers were not conventional soldiers recruited to fight in one of the Company's perennial conflicts. Instead they functioned as vital props for the office.

The King of Jaccatra

When it was created in 1602, the VOC was authorised to engage in diplomacy, to dispatch its own embassies and to negotiate directly with local potentates. From the beginning, however, the Company struggled to find a stable position within Asian diplomatic orders. As the employees of a company of merchants led by a merchant, VOC agents found it difficult to explain who exactly they represented, why they should be taken seriously and what exactly they wanted. To make things more difficult, the Company could not simply look towards Europe to borrow legitimacy from institutions there. The Dutch Republic was a political newcomer governed by an unruly parliament and itself occupying an uncertain position on the European diplomatic landscape. It lacked a monarch, a readily translatable figure capable of being inserted into negotiations with Asian rulers. Because of this, the Company's ambassadors were compelled to rely on improvisation and invention.

Although they came from a republic, the first VOC envoys and ambassadors to arrive in Asia claimed to represent the 'king of Holland', a fictive monarch designed to serve as a royal figurehead. The first VOC officials to make contact with Japan, for example, were clear that they represented 'our King (*onsen Coninck*) and Princely Excellence, Duke Maurijtius of Nassau'.[32] The king in question was in fact Prince Maurits, the *Stadhouder* of a number of Dutch provinces and the highest-ranking aristocrat in the United Provinces. Although a powerful actor in Dutch politics, Maurits operated in the shadow of republican institutions and his position in no way approximated that of a monarch. For VOC agents, however, invoking the 'king of Holland' provided a kind of royal disguise that could be draped over the Company's activities, thereby obscuring the unfamiliar nature of the organisation, while also facilitating diplomatic interactions by boosting the status of Dutch envoys and providing them with a familiar framework for exchange.

As the Company entrenched its position in Asia, however, its diplomatic strategy began to shift away from Europe and the *Stadhouder* to a new focus on Batavia and the Governor-General. This was in part a pragmatic response to the rapid expansion of the organisation's activities and

---

[32] F.C. Weider, *De Reis van Mahu en De Cordes door de Straat van Magalhães naar Zuid-America en Japan, 1598–1600* (The Hague: M. Nijhoff, 1923), iii: 81–84.

reach. By the 1620s, the Company was engaged in ongoing negotiations with a range of emperors, kings, sultans and other rulers across Asia. The sheer volume of diplomatic traffic meant that it could no longer afford to wait for letters from the *Stadhouder*, which could take years to obtain. At the same time, some within the Company began to suspect that a reliance on a figure in Europe for endorsement undermined the Governor-General's own position. As it expanded within Asia, the organisation was increasingly obsessed with its own reputation, viewing it as a vital instrument needed to lure allies closer to Batavia while keeping rivals in check.[33] A strong Governor-General able to command respect from the 'feigned friends and declared enemies' that surrounded Batavia was, it was believed, crucial to the organisation's survival, and persistent references to a more senior figure in Europe could only undermine this status.[34] Addressing this point directly, one official commented that his superiors should no longer procure letters from the *Stadhouder* as 'the respect for the Governor-General is markedly lessened (to the Company's disadvantage)'.[35]

The problem was, however, that early Governors-General were not especially impressive figures. While the Princes of Orange were not kings, they looked every bit the part, requiring only a minor blurring around the edges to present them as monarchs. Portraits of Prince Maurits, which were presented to rulers in Asia, depicted a magnificent figure whose prestige had been buttressed by a string of impressive military victories. One surviving portrait shows the *Stadhouder* attired in gleaming gold armour presented to him by the States-General after his triumph at Nieuwpoort.[36] With the insignia of the Order of the Garter that he received from the English crown around his neck, he stands in an imperious pose, one hand resting on his sword, while the other holds a staff of office. In contrast, the first Governors-General were far more modest figures all too easily dismissed by local rulers. One summed up a more general attitude when he proclaimed that sending an embassy to meet with the Governor-General 'would be in conflict with his honour. If prince Mauritius [Maurits] was here, he would send [an envoy] to

---

[33] Niels Steensgaard, 'The Dutch East India Company as an Institutional Innovation', in Maurice Aymard (ed.), *Dutch Capitalism and World Capitalism* (Cambridge: Cambridge University Press, 1982), 255.

[34] Leonard Blussé, 'Amongst Feigned Friends and Declared Enemies', in Sølvi Sogner (ed.), *Making Sense of Global History: The Nineteenth International Congress of the Historical Sciences Oslo 2000 Commemorative Volume* (Oslo: Universitetsforlaget. 2001), 154.

[35] *Batavia Dagregisters, Vol. 5: 1641–42*, 75.

[36] See for example the portrait of Maurits, Prince of Orange, c. 1613–1615, by Michiel Jansz. Van Mierevelt, Rijksmuseum, Amsterdam, SK-A-255-00.

him as to a brother, but he would not stoop to [send an embassy] to the General, who was just the overseer of merchants'.[37] To counter this, the Company engaged in a deliberate process to transform the Governor-General from a merchant among merchants into, as these officials later became known, 'the Raya de Jaccatra of the Hollanders, that is the king of Jaccatra'.[38]

The primary mechanism for doing this was by surrounding the Governor-General with the accoutrements of kingship. Johan Nieuhoff, who accompanied a Dutch embassy to China, wrote admiringly that the Governor-General 'lives in no less Pomp and State than the Princes of *Europe*'.[39] Francois Valentijn, the long-time chronicler of the Dutch East Indies, explained that the Governor-General 'displays absolutely the splendour and state of a distinguished sovereign. Not only does he reside in an impressive palace, but his entire state, train and government is kingly'.[40] The most astute observers noted just how important this monarchical presentation was to the VOC's strategy in Asia. Jean-Baptiste Tavernier, the famous French traveller, who visited Batavia around the middle of the seventeenth century, commented that the 'Company to maintain their Authority and Commerce in the *Indies*, believe it to be to their advantage, that the General ... should keep up the Port of a Prince'.[41]

But what exactly was the 'Port of a Prince'? Given their position as the representatives of a trading organisation, the Governors-General could not wear a crown or drape themselves in regal robes. Instead portraits of early incumbents show them looking far closer to prosperous merchants than kinglike figures (Figure 11.2).[42] Because of this, it was the honour guard that surrounded the Governor-General at all times that provided the props of kingship or what one observer called the visible 'marks of

[37] *Batavia Dagregisters, Vol. 2: 1625–29*, 80.
[38] Friderici Bollingii, 'Friderici Bollingii Oost-Indisch reisboek', trans. J. Visscher, *Bijdragen tot de Taal-, Land- en Volkenkunde van Nederlandsch Indië* 68 (1913): 331.
[39] Johannes Nieuhof, *An Embassy from the East India Company of the United Provinces to the Grand Tartar Cham Emperor of China deliver'd by their excellencies, Peter de Goyer and Jacob de Keyzer, at his imperial city of Peking* (London, 1673), 27. Emphasis in the original.
[40] Francois Valentijn, *François Valentijn's oud en nieuw Oost-Indien* ('s Gravenhage: H.C. Susan, 1856–1858), iii: 548.
[41] John Baptista Tavernier, *A collection of Several Relations & Treatises Singular and Curious of John Baptista Tavernier* (London:printed by A. Godbid and J. Playford for Moses Pitt, 1680), 65.
[42] For an analysis of the portraits of these officials, see David van Duuren, 'Governors-General and Civilians: Portrait Art in the Dutch East Indies from the Seventeenth to the Nineteenth Century', in Marie-Odette Scalliet et al. (eds.), *Pictures From the Tropics. Paintings by Western Artists during the Dutch Colonial Period in Indonesia* (Wijk en Aalburg: Pictures Publishers, 2000).

JAQUES SPECKS.
GOUV ᴿ:GENERᴸ. VAN INDIA.

Figure 11.2 *Portrait of Jacques Specx, Governor-General of the Dutch East Indies*, by anonymous artist (copy after), 1750–1800. SK-A-3760, Rijksmuseum, Amsterdam.

Grandeur'.[43] And arguably the most important component of these was the halberdiers, who functioned as proxy symbols, royal emblems that surrounded an unroyal figure.[44]

Visitors to Batavia invariably commented on the gorgeously attired halberdiers that formed the most conspicuous part of the Governor-General's entourage (Figure 11.3). Tavernier explained that an honour guard of twelve halberdiers accompanied these officials whenever they travelled outside the castle. Like so many others, Tavernier fixated on their 'sumptuous' attire, explaining that 'His Halberdiers wear their yellow Satten Doublets, Scarlet Breeches lac'd with Silver Lace, and their Silk Stockins'.[45] Such descriptions were common. Frederik Bolling, a Danish soldier who entered VOC service and visited Batavia in the 1670s, explained that the halberdiers wore red scarlet with silver braiding.[46] Christoph Frick (sometimes Fryke), a German who served as a VOC surgeon, wrote that the guard consisted of 'twelve Halbardiers, drest much after the manner of our Yeoman of the Guard but in Red and Yellow'.[47] The contrast with the other soldiers employed by the VOC was arresting. Whereas the 'General's Guards' were gifted with gorgeous attire that might rival the honour guard of any European king, the soldiers that were dispatched to man the Company's scattered forts and outposts wore little more than rags. It 'is a great pity', Tavernier wrote, 'to see how poorly they [VOC garrison soldiers] are attir'd, and how meanly fed'.[48]

The most detailed account was provided by François Valentijn, who described the richly dressed soldiers that accompanied the Governor-General whenever he left the castle:

He has a guard of 12 halberdiers, who are the most handsome and sharpest young men among the soldiers. They wear a yellow damask jerkin with silver buttons that is always kept half open. Underneath they wear very wide scarlet trousers with a bunch of long, silk ribbons on both sides and 3 trimmings of 2.5

[43] Guy Tachard, *A Relation of the Voyage to Siam* (London, 1688), 117.
[44] While their numbers fluctuated, most accounts suggest there were around twelve halberdiers. While this may not seem like an especially large number, particularly in comparison to the massive entourages that sometimes accompanied Asian monarchs, it should be viewed in the context of Batavia's relatively small European population, which numbered just a few thousand. It was also the case that the halberdiers were just the most prominent part of a much larger military establishment that was regularly paraded through Batavia. For details of Batavia's population, see Susan Abeyasekere, *Jakarta: a history* (Singapore and New York: Oxford University Press, 1987), 19
[45] Tavernier, *A Collection of Several Relations*, 65.
[46] Bolling, 'Friderici Bollingii Oost-Indisch reisboek', 331.
[47] *A Relation of Two Several Voyages Made into the East-Indies by Christopher Fryke and Christopher Schewitzer* (London, 1700), 34. Frick was less impressed by the Governor-General's retinue than some other observers.
[48] Tavernier, *A collection of several relations*, 65.

Figure 11.3 *The Great Hall of the Central Government in Castle Batavia*, by Johann Wolfgang Heydt, 1738–c. 1800. Rijksmuseum, RP-P-1961-473, Amsterdam.

fingers wide. They also have a belt of grey leather and a sword with a silver hilt, hook and buckle on their side and wear scarfs of muslin. They have (when they go out) a handsome hat on their heads, wear pearl coloured or other silk stockings and new, neat shoes. I saw [people] among them wearing golden buttons on their waist-coats, large golden buckles in the shoes and garters with diamond buckles.[49]

As is clear from such descriptions, the halberdiers' ceremonial function far outweighed any military role. Such troops were not designed to fight, rather they surrounded the Governor-General as concrete reminders of his regal status.

In addition to accompanying the Governor-General, the halberdiers played a prominent role in the reception of ambassadors. When foreign

[49] Valentijn, *François Valentijn's oud en nieuw Oost-Indien*, iii: 548.

envoys arrived in Batavia, it was one of the halberdiers who accompanied them, in 'the same carriage, in the countenance of the ambassador'.[50] When they reached the castle, envoys handed over letters from their sovereign to another of these soldiers, who placed it on a silver or gold platter covered in satin and held under a yellow 'parasol of state'.[51] In this way, they became conduits for royal letters that were passed from ambassadors, themselves royal proxies, to the Governor-General, who asserted his status as a commensurate figure.

If the halberdiers with their ostentatious livery formed a key part of the Governor-General's self-presentation, they also presented an obvious target for the *Heeren* 17, who consistently believed that too much money was being wasted on extravagant display. Compelled by his instructions, Brouwer took swift action, writing back soon after arriving that he had cut the number of halberdiers in half with the result that the 'splendour of Batavia [was] greatly reduced'.[52] It seemed like a victory for the *Heeren* 17 and their attempts to reduce unnecessary expenditures, but the halberdiers were too central to the office's public display to remain depleted for long. By 1636, Brouwer was out and their number swiftly inflated again, creeping back up to the original total and then steadily increasing as successive Governor-Generals moved to expand their retinue by creating new roles that mirrored the personnel of a royal court.

The result was that these soldiers with their sumptuous attire remained a constant source of friction between the Governors-General and their superiors in Europe. In 1661, exactly three decades after the initial instructions to Brouwer, Joan Maetsuycker, who had assumed the office in 1653, decided to take action. Responding, we presume, to ongoing criticism from Europe, he moved to cut back on expenses.[53] By this year, the Governor-General's court had swelled still further to fifteen individuals: a chamberlain (*hofmeester*), stablemaster (*stalmeester*), groom (*stalknecht*), coachman (*cochier*), six halberdiers, two bodyguards, a trumpeter, a cook and a tailor. All fifteen wore the same sumptuous red and yellow livery as the halberdiers, requiring a lavish cost to outfit and maintain. Determined to offer some show of economy without undercutting the foundations of the kingly image, Maetsuycker suggested to his superiors that five of the fifteen – the chamberlain, stable master, groom, cook and tailor – should no longer be provided with livery, thereby

[50] *Batavia Dagregisters, Vol 23: 1675*, 60.
[51] Ibid., *Vol 27: 1679*, 621.
[52] De Jonge, *De opkomst van het Nederlandsch gezag*, v: 197–198.
[53] Van der Chijs, *Nederlandsch-Indisch Plakaatboek*, ii: 343

reducing the budget required for upkeep. It was a saving measure certainly but it did nothing to cut the retinue's overall numbers and it still meant that the remaining ten would all receive payments to cover their plush uniforms.

Not surprisingly, such a minor economy measure does not seem to have impressed the *Heeren* 17. Undeterred, one of Maetsuycker's successors, Johannes Camphuys, decided it was better, in the absence of a firm command from his superiors, simply to take action on his own initiative. In 1690, the government in Batavia resolved that even though they had received no final guidance from the *Heeren* 17 they would reduce the number of 'liveried servants' to twelve.[54] Concealed in what was supposedly an economising measure was another increase: from the 10 liveried servants proposed in 1662 to 12, including a new position, the 'first halberdier', who was given the rank of cornet, along with six halberdiers, two bodyguards, a coachman, a trumpeter and steward, all of whom would be provided with funds to purchase their own livery. The result was to entrench the halberdiers' ceremonial role in Batavia and to ensure they would remain an indispensable part of the Governor-General's retinue and self-presentation. More importantly, the intermittent skirmish over the honour guard reveals a basic dynamic that runs through the sumptuary codes issued in the seventeenth century: even as they were compelled to respond to pressure from the *Heeren* 17, the Governors-General worked to draw clear lines around their ceremonial privileges.

Orders from Europe

It took thirty years of sporadic pressure from Europe to produce the first sumptuary law in Batavia. Signed by Governor-General Cornelis van der Lijn, the 1647 order began by referencing the *Heeren* 17, who had heard disturbing reports from 'overcomende personen' – that is, individuals recently arrived from Asia – concerning the lavish habits of the Batavian elites.[55] Such news, alongside their own investigations, had convinced the *Heeren* 17 of the 'costliness of the clothing and the splendour' both of VOC servants and of the free burghers.[56] Although he had been instructed to issue strict ordinances regulating consumption and display, Van Der Lijn opted instead for a general warning about costly clothing and gold and silver ornaments. This was coupled with a caution that if

[54] Van der Chijs, *Nederlandsch-Indisch Plakaatboek*, iii: 258.
[55] 9 March 1647, ID-JaAN, Hoge Regering inv. nr 863.
[56] Ibid.

such warnings were not followed, VOC authorities would be forced to respond with a 'precise order and regulation of state'.[57]

In the 1647 order, Van der Lijn took aim as well at another much-noted feature of Batavian life, parasols or *kieppesollen*. Adopted initially from Javanese aristocrats, these had spread widely through Batavia, where a range of residents employed a slave to hold a parasol above their heads 'without regard for quality or condition'.[58] Often beautifully decorated, parasols crowded public spaces in Batavia, congesting thoroughfares and impeding free movement.[59] In his order, Van der Lijn explained that such objects were deployed for magnificent display rather than to meet a real need for shelter. Crucially, however, the *kieppesollen* were not to be banned entirely. Instead the Governor-General had determined that only his own office and the remaining members of the Council of the Indies were allowed to have a parasol carried by a slave. Anyone else found with such a covering would face confiscation of the offending item and a substantial fine.

Although it was not included in the final edict, the council in Batavia also debated the issue of carriages, another perennial point of contention between officials in Asia and the *Heeren* 17. The council had received instructions from their superiors to cut back on what was perceived as the frivolous use of carriages by, among others, the wives of the Governor-General and the Council of the Indies.[60] While the council acquiesced to the order, its members did push back, explaining that such carriages were used to give 'lustre to the state of Honourable Company before the Indian nations'. It was a reminder that many of the privileges that the *Heeren* 17 considered wasteful expenses were viewed in Batavia as central to doing business in Asia. It is telling, therefore, that even as Van der Lijn took aim at conspicuous display, he was careful to carve out exemptions for himself and the members of the Council of the Indies.

The next Governor-General to issue sumptuary orders was Rijklof van Goens in 1680. As before, his action was preceded by a steady stream of letters from the *Heeren* 17. In a letter dated 16 October 1676, its members wrote to Batavia urging action to be taken against

---

[57] 9 March 1647, ID-JaAN, Hoge Regering inv. nr 863

[58] Van der Chijs, *Nederlandsch-Indisch Plakaatboek*, ii: 111. They were known in Java as *payongs* or *songsongs*. Kees Zandvliet (ed.), *The Dutch Encounter with Asia, 1600–1950* (Zwolle: Waanders, 2002), 313. For a fascinating discussion of parasols as 'malleable exotic icons', see Benjamin Schmidt, 'Collecting Global Icons: The Case of the Exotic Parasol', in Daniela Bleichmar and Peter C. Mancall (eds.), *Collecting Across Cultures: Material Exchanges in the Early Modern Atlantic World* (Philadelphia: University of Pennsylvania Press, 2011), 31–57; 292–296.

[59] *Beschryving van Batavia*, 37.

[60] 9 March 1647, ID-JaAN, Hoge Regering inv. nr 863.

'splendour and magnificence'.[61] In particular, they demanded immediate restrictions on carriages, both open and hooded, which should be limited to the Governor-General and the Council, and clothing and ornamentation, including, in a repeat of the 1631 injunction, the 'wearing of pearls, diamonds and other costly stones' as well as gold or silver lace and buttons. Just five days later, on 21 October, the *Heeren* 17 wrote again to the Governor-General. They were prepared to allow the members of the Council of the Indies to have their own carriages but were adamant that the 'costs and burdens' of these conveyances would not be covered by the Company.[62] Instead, only the Governor-General would be permitted to maintain a carriage at VOC expense.

It was an issue that continued to preoccupy the *Heeren* 17 in their regular meetings. In November 1678, they wrote again, laying down a line that should not be crossed: 'We have forbidden', they explained, 'the keeping of carriages or covered carriages in our said letter of 21 October 1676 and the attached regulation, outside of the ones that are specially permitted. We do not find any reason to make any kind of dispensation. On the contrary, we still think this should be precisely executed and followed.'[63] It was, it seems, a reprimand of Batavia's persistent attempts to carve out special exemptions for its administrative elite and a clear indication that the *Heeren* 17 would not tolerate any bending of the rules when it came to carriages.

In July 1680, Van Goens finally moved to put these instructions into action.[64] In a striking example of how much authorities in Batavia simply parroted directives from Europe, Van Goen's order consisted overwhelmingly of lengthy quoted extracts of letters and rules from the *Heeren* 17 from 1631, 1676 and 1680. But, as was typical, the Governor-General also inserted key exemptions for high-ranking members of the Batavian government. Whereas the *Heeren* 17 had been insisting for decades that no-one should be permitted lavish clothing or jewellery, the 1680 order stipulated that this prohibition did not apply to the wives, children and widows of the Governor-General and of the members of the Council of the Indies.[65] By the close of the seventeenth century, then, the template was well established: the *Heeren* 17 issued letters instructing their subordinates to take action, while the Governors-General, when they

---

[61] De Jonge, *De opkomst van het Nederlandsch gezag*, vi: 165–166.
[62] Letter from the *Heeren* 17 to the Governor-General and Council, 21 October 1676, VOC 320.
[63] Ibid., 1 November 1678, VOC 320.
[64] Van der Chijs, *Nederlandsch-Indisch Plakaatboek*, iii: 47.
[65] 5 July 1680, ID-JaAN, Hoge Regering inv. nr 892; Van der Chijs, *Nederlandsch-Indisch Plakaatboek*, iii: 4.

decided to yield, dutifully repeated their superiors' rhetoric even as they fended off any incursions on their own privileges. In the early eighteenth century, however, there was a discernible shift as, for the first time, the Governors-General began to take a more direct role in authoring sumptuary orders.

The Eighteenth-Century Shift

In 1704, a new Governor-General, Joan van Hoorn, issued another sumptuary law – but this time the impetus seems to have come from Batavia. Unlike the orders that had preceded it, the 1704 regulation started by referencing not the *Heeren* 17 in Europe but the Council of the Indies in Batavia. It explained that the Council was unhappy about the number of carriages kept by VOC servants and free burghers as well as the 'inappropriate racing and tearing along (*rennen en rossen*) of the carriages through the city, especially at night'. Because of this, they had decided to take action to prevent the abuse of such carriages. The chosen mechanism was a system of fines that would serve as well to enlarge the 'funds of the Heemraden [District Council] of Batavia and its hinterlands, to compensate the daily costs of building and repairing bridges, general roads etc.'.[66] While it took aim at a familiar object, the use and misuse of carriages, the 1704 order was not directed in the first place at the reduction of conspicuous consumption. Rather, it was intended, as Van Hoorn makes clear, to maintain order by stopping the racing of carriages through the city while, as an added benefit, raising funds for the District Council through a system of fines and imposts. In this way, it diverges from the *Heeren* 17's standard concerns by placing an emphasis on order rather than extravagance. The decree went on to establish a hierarchy of fines that had to be paid depending on the size of the carriage and the number of horses that were pulling it.

By attaching a series of fines, Batavia Castle hoped to place strict limits on the use of carriages. It did not prove successful, however, and by 1719 a new Governor-General, Hendrik Zwaardecroon, moved to update the order. The new regulation began by acknowledging that the earlier iteration had failed. Rather than serving its intended function, Van Hoorn's order had succeeded only in laying a platform for further crowding. Unperturbed by the Company's injunctions, the residents of Batavia had simply paid the necessary duties and continued their old habits 'as if the payment of the said impositions gave them the right for misuse,

[66] Van der Chijs, *Nederlandsch-Indisch Plakaatboek*, iii: 536–538.

luxury and insolence'.[67] This had a direct impact on the Council of the Indies, who found their ability to move around the city's 'bridges, gates and narrow passages' restricted by the press of competing carriages.[68] The crowding of vehicles also had adverse implications for the safety of Batavia as it prevented the garrison's soldiers from easily entering and exiting the castle, which they were sworn to defend in the event of an attack.

The 1704 and 1719 orders were the first sumptuary orders tied more closely to the Governor-General than the *Heeren* 17. Although focused on a familiar target, they were concerned primarily with reducing congestion in Batavia's narrow roads and bridges instead of cutting back on 'pracht en praal'. As such, they stand apart from the earlier orders. This began to change in 1729 when a new Governor-General, Diederik Durven, moved to issue a far more expansive order that specifically targeted the question of display.[69] Durven's order began with a standard target, lamenting that 'the amount of carriages has increased so much that the entire colony is filled and stuffed with them'.[70] While this was a familiar complaint, the order went further by specifically targeting the question of display. The lavish decoration of carriages with gold, silver or gilt made it impossible to distinguish different social levels and to mark off the VOC elite.[71] To deal with this problem, Durven ordered that all gold and silver should be stripped from the offending carriages within two months from the publication of the edict.[72] He took aim as well at the widespread use of parasols, which were now to be subjected to further restrictions. While European women were permitted such items, their use by Chinese officials, including the Trustees for the Deceased Estates, was strictly forbidden.[73] The 1729 order went further than past edicts; it was also more widely distributed, with Durven ordering that it be translated into Portuguese, Malayan, Javanese and Chinese 'so no one can pretend to be ignorant'.[74]

Twenty-five years after Durven's intervention, a new Governor-General, Jacob Mossel, issued the most ambitious of the Batavian

---

[67] Ibid., iv: 136.
[68] Ibid.
[69] Van der Chijs, *Nederlandsch-Indisch Plakaatboek*, iv: 239–244.
[70] Ibid., 239.
[71] Ibid., 239–240.
[72] Ibid., 243.
[73] The Board of Trustees for Chinese Deceased Estates, also known as the Deceased Estates Chamber, was established by the High Government of the VOC in 1640 to fight fraud in the inheritance of the estates of Chinese and non-Christians. It was composed of two Dutchmen and two Chinese officials.
[74] Ibid., 244.

sumptuary codes, the 'Measures for Curbing Splendour and Magnificence'.[75] While it targeted the usual list of suspects, Mossel's code marked a sea-change in Batavia's use of sumptuary codes. It was far longer, far more detailed and far more insistent than anything that had come before. Accounting for its sprawling scope and scale requires a broader consideration of what was happening in Batavia around the midpoint of the eighteenth century and the circumstances that drove Mossel to depart from the more limited models preferred by his predecessors.[76]

Measures for Curbing Splendour and Magnificence

By the time he penned the sumptuary code that would become permanently bound up with his name, Mossel had entered the fourth year of an extended term as Governor-General that would last from 1750 until his death in office in 1761. Praised by modern historians as a reforming and effective Governor-General, Mossel was famous for the deluge of laws, codes and other edicts that poured forth from Batavia Castle during his tenure.[77] A measure of this can be found in volume 6 of Van der Chijs's *Plakaatboek*, which covers just the first phase of Mossel's term in office, from 1750 to 1754, but includes over eight hundred printed pages of regulations touching on every aspect of life in Batavia and the Company's other colonies and factories.[78]

One reason why Mossel was so prolific was because he assumed the office of Governor-General during a period of rapid change. His predecessor, Gustaaf Willem, baron Van Imhoff, who had served as Governor-General from 1743 to 1750, had lifted restrictions on private trade, loosening the Company's monopoly and opening up the intra-Asian market. These reforms allowed VOC servants and subjects to participate legally in trading networks that had previously been off limits. As Chris Nierstrasz explains in his important study of this previously neglected period, the VOC under Van Imhoff believed it could make up for income lost via the surrender of its monopoly through new tolls and by gaining a clearer sense – and hence, hold over – private fortunes previously

---

[75] I have not discussed another law dated 28 January 1733 that primarily addressed parasols. Van der Chijs, *Nederlandsch-Indisch Plakaatboek*, iv: 333–336.

[76] For an excellent discussion of Mossel's edict, see Ross, 'Sumptuary Laws in Europe, the Netherlands and the Dutch colonies'.

[77] For one of these more positive assessments, see W. Ph. Coolhaas, 'Zijn de Gouverneurs-Generaal van Imhoff en Mossel juist beoordeeld?', in *Bijdragen tot de Taal-Land-en Volkenkunde* 114 (1958): 29–54.

[78] Van der Chijs, *Nederlandsch-Indisch Plakaatboek*, vol. 6.

accumulated in the shadows.[79] To support this shift in policy, Van Imhoff established new institutions such as the Bank van Lening, which was chartered in 1745 to lend to private merchants.[80] While Mossel continued some of Van Imhoff's innovations, he also pulled back, implementing new restrictions on private trade and cutting back on concessions and privileges granted by his predecessor.[81] The 'Measures for Curbing Splendour and Magnificence' issued in December 1754 form one part of this wider process.

Consisting of 124 articles divided into twelve sections, the new code regulated every aspect of carriages, dress and display down to the most minute detail.[82] The first section, fully 29 articles in total, provided detailed rules for carriages and the horses that pulled them. It reserved a 'glass carriage' (*glaze koets*) for the Governor-General as well as the right to use six horses and European horsemen.[83] Section two, comprised of a pair of articles, regulated parasols and wax umbrellas, which were forbidden to anyone below the rank of *onderkoopman* (under-merchant) although 'European women, with no distinction' were permitted to make use of them.[84] Section three took aim at men's clothing in nine highly detailed articles, stipulating that only the High Government that controlled Batavia were permitted to wear clothes with gold or silver embroidery or braid, while only VOC officials holding the rank of upper-merchant or higher were permitted to have 'solid golden buttons'.[85] The fourth section, eight articles in total, turned its attention to women's clothing and the wearing of jewels. Only the wives and widows of the Governor-General, Director-General and the members of the Council and the president of the Council of Justice were permitted to carry gold or silver betel boxes decorated with precious stones or to wear double pearl necklaces. Any infringement of this would earn a swift fine of 500 rijksdaalders.[86] Article 45 declared that 'Velvet clothing, decorated or embroidered with gold or silver, will not be allowed to be worn by any of the women, except the wives, widows and children of the high government and the president of the council'.[87] The fifth section, just three

---

[79] Chris Nierstrasz, *In the Shadow of the Company: The Dutch East India Company and its Servants in the Period of its Decline (1740–1796)* (Leiden: Brill, 2012), 82.

[80] Ibid., 81.

[81] Ibid., 85.

[82] Van der Chijs, *Nederlandsch-Indisch Plakaatboek*, vi: 773–795. As Taylor has noted this law focused especially on dress and included dozens of precise edicts regulating clothing for men and women. Taylor, *The Social World of Batavia*, 67.

[83] Van der Chijs, *Nederlandsch-Indisch Plakaatboek*, vi: 775.

[84] Ibid., 784.

[85] Ibid., 785.

[86] Ibid., 786.

[87] Ibid., 786.

articles, focused on slaves, both their number and dress. It stipulated that only the 'wives and widows of the high Indies government as well as those of the president of the Council of justice, will be allowed to take three maids with them' and specified what sort of clothes and necklaces they could wear, including a prohibition on pearls and diamonds.[88] The sixth section continued the focus on slaves, specifying the kind of livery that slaves could wear. Only the highest officials were allowed to dress their horsemen and other servants in rich clothes embroidered with lace. The seventh and eighth sections, eight articles in total, addressed weddings, restricting, for example, the use of decorative arches set up before individual houses to the most senior officials. The ninth, tenth and eleventh sections focused on a diverse set of topics including meals, baptism and funerals, while the final section pushed beyond Batavia by providing detailed regulations for other settlements where the VOC operated. In Bengal, for example, only the Director was permitted to have an open carriage or a 'coach with glass' made in the European style.[89]

The sheer level of detail down to the tiniest of points makes for numbing reading. It also raises an obvious question. What accounts for such a detailed code promulgated with such lavish attention to the minutiae of clothing and attire? The answer is provided by the law's lengthy preamble, which clearly lays out its rationale. This was, first of all, a response to instructions from Europe. The Mossel edict started by explaining that the *Heeren* 17 had expressed 'their displeasure in an explicit manner in their letter of 8 October 1753'.[90] It went on to cite letters and instructions stretching all the way back to 1631, when the *Heeren* 17 had first called the display of extravagant wealth a 'plague' on their possession in Asia. In recent years, such excesses had been further exacerbated, reaching a 'pinnacle' (*toppunt*) that compelled action.

While important, there was nothing new here and it does not explain why Mossel diverged from the far more limited codes preferred by his predecessors. Instead, the 1754 sumptuary code functioned at the same time as a tool for what Mossel believed was a necessary process of social re-engineering. Van Imhoff's opening up of private trade had pushed the Company into uncharted waters, opening up new opportunities that were quickly seized by the Batavian elite to both accumulate and display wealth. By 1753, a year before Mossel's code was issued, the VOC, as Nierstrasz explains, 'felt in a position to draw more trade in

---

[88] Ibid., 787.
[89] The Plakaatboek does not include the articles directed at VOC operations outside of Batavia. These can be found in *Nederlandsche Jaarboeken* 9/2 (1755), 969–979.
[90] Van der Chijs, *Nederlandsch-Indisch Plakaatboek*, vi: 773.

under monopoly again'.[91] This did not mean the complete abolition of Van Imhoff's reforms, but rather the restriction of a previously expansive remit for free trade. In tandem with this, Mossel moved aggressively to re-establish hierarchies by ensuring that the capacity to display wealth became tied once again to office in the VOC.

All of this was laid out in the preamble to the 1754 code. Order in the Company's sprawling empire depended, it explained, on 'distinction, according to position and subordination'.[92] When this most basic of 'pillars' began to shake and collapse, the 'good of the Company' was endangered. Van Imhoff's sweeping reforms had meant that low-ranking VOC servants and the free burghers sought always to 'match the status in outward appearance of the first ministers of the Dutch company'. It was a familiar complaint but one that recent reforms had significantly magnified. High-ranking VOC officials, who lacked the means to compete, were forced to confront the extravagant display of wealth from their social inferiors, bringing about rampant 'decline and disrespect'. If such individuals were allowed to match or exceed their superiors, then proper order would collapse, imperilling the colonial establishment. The way to fix this was through regulation that mapped privilege precisely onto rank within the VOC. As Nierstrasz explains, the 'VOC introduced measures to impose the hierarchy as stringently as possible by linking remuneration unequivocally to position and by regulating the social status a particular position entailed in fairly explicit terms'.[93] Viewed in this context, Mossel's 1754 law was designed to repair the frayed lines of Batavian society and re-establish hierarchy after a period of rapid change. Because of this, the 1754 code was more concerned with reserving certain rights of display than it was with simply banning 'pracht en praal'. In its copious detail and attention to the smallest of points, the order sought to regulate every aspect of dress, performance and transportation in a way that would serve to reinforce the position of senior VOC officials.

Conclusion

Mossel's regulation is by far the best known of the sumptuary laws promulgated in Batavia, but viewed in the long trajectory of these orders it was not typical. Rather earlier iterations of the sumptuary laws were the

---

[91] Nierstrasz, *In the Shadow of the Company*, 212.

[92] Van der Chijs, *Nederlandsch-Indisch Plakaatboek*, vi: 773–774.

[93] Nierstrasz, *In the Shadow of the Company*, 139. Nierstrasz explains further that the 'principal objective of Mossel's policy was to ensure that its employees palpably felt that they were dependent on the VOC if they were to make their fortunes'.

product primarily of pressure from the *Heeren* 17, who sought to curb the excesses they saw in Batavia. In contrast, VOC officials, particularly the early Governors-General who struggled to establish a place in diplomatic circuits, were far more aware of the importance of ceremony and display. One remarked that 'in these countries (where I never been before) I had to look through different eyes and speak a different tongue. Everybody I encountered told me how important the display of worldly splendor was for the interest of the Company'.[94] For much of the seventeenth century, it seemed as if the *Heeren* 17 and the Governors-General were in fact speaking different languages, one emphasising the importance of display to boost the VOC's stature, the other the need to save money by curtailing 'pracht en praal'. It was only in the eighteenth century that the Governors-General began to assume a more active role by using sumptuary codes as a tool to impose order. This reached a climax in Mossel's vast 1754 code, which attempted to force Batavian society back into strict hierarchical lines. Tracking Batavia's long history of sumptuary codes requires us therefore to consider the range of different forces and pressures that drove them forward. There was nothing monolithic about these orders. Rather their content and priorities shifted as Batavia and the concerns of successive Governors-General changed.

---

[94] Quoted in Rene Barendse, *The Arabian Seas, 1640–1700* (Leiden: CNWS, 1998), 403.

12 Race, Clothing and Identity: Sumptuary Laws in Colonial Spanish America

Rebecca Earle

The Scandalous Excesses

On holidays and other festive occasions, Andean peoples in the Spanish Viceroyalty of Peru liked to dress up. According to sixteenth-century documents, wealthy Amerindians in Lima, Quito and other colonial cities enjoyed wearing a combination of European and Andean garments, sometimes made of silk and other expensive, imported fabrics. Their sartorial exuberance annoyed local Spaniards, who issued repeated orders prohibiting Amerindians from wearing a range of garments containing silk, velvet, Holland cloth, lace and other embellishments. The indigenous elite did not accept these prohibitions without protest. In 1593, members of the Amerindian community in Quito wrote to Emperor Philip II to complain that 'as conquered people it sometimes happens that officials and other people undress them and take their clothing, saying that they can wear only cotton, which causes them much trouble and vexation'.[1] The monarch agreed that Amerindians should be allowed to wear what they pleased, as long as it did not violate existing legislation regulating excessive dress. He therefore instructed colonial administrators to prevent these seizures and ensure that 'the Indians are not vexed'.

---

[1] Fernando Montesinos, *Anales del Perú*, c. 1652, ed. Víctor Maurtua, 2 vols. (Madrid, 1906), ii: 16, 95–96; and R.C. a la Audiencia de Quito remitiendole lo que piden los indios de aquella provincia, de que no se les impida el traer vestidos como los españoles, 22 November 1593, *Colección de documentos para la historia de la formación social de Hispanoamérica, 1493–1810*, ed. Richard Konetzke, 3 vols. (Madrid: Consejo Superior de Investigaciones Científicas, 1962), ii pt. 1: 11 (quote). See also Juan Sempere y Guarinos, *Historia del luxo, y de las leyes suntuarias de España*, 2 vols. (Madrid, 1788), ii: 42. Indigenous participation in Andean festivals is discussed in Carolyn Dean, *Inka Bodies and the Body of Christ: Corpus Christi in Colonial Cuzco, Peru* (Durham: Duke University Press, 1999); David Cahill, 'The Inca and Inca Symbolism in Popular Festive Culture: The Religious Processions of Seventeenth-Century Cuzco', in *Hapsburg Peru: Images, Imagination and Memory*, eds. Peter Bradley and David Cahill (Liverpool: University of Liverpool Press, 2000): 87–144; and Karine Perissat, 'Los Incas representados (Lima–siglo XVIII): ¿Supervivencia o renacimiento?', *Revista de Indias* 60/220 (2000): 623–649.

A few decades later, in 1628, Philip II's grandson Philip IV ordered that 'no Indian may wear clothing made of [imported] fabric, own a sword, dagger, lance, harquebus or gun, nor ride on horseback with saddle and reins, on pain of the loss of the garment, weapon, saddle, reins and horse'.[2] This ordinance, which applied specifically to two provinces in southern Mexico, was one of a number of regulations aimed at restricting the adoption of certain Spanish practices by Amerindians. A century later, officials in Peru expressed dismay at the ineffectiveness of legislation aimed at 'moderating the scandalous excesses in the clothing worn by blacks, mulattoes, Indians and mestizos of both sexes', which they believed caused 'frequent robberies committed to maintain such costly garb'.[3] Similar rulings, which sought, in sometimes contradictory fashion, to regulate the clothing worn by 'blacks, mulattoes, Indians and mestizos' in Spain's New World colonies, were issued repeatedly from the sixteenth century until the end of colonial rule in the early nineteenth century.

Legislation aimed at controlling sartorial display was a common feature of the medieval and early modern world, as the contributions to this volume demonstrate. So too was hand-wringing about the social disorder provoked by excessive or overly luxurious costume, whether worn by elites or subalterns. Less familiar perhaps is the explicit association between clothing and race that lies at the heart of the examples cited above. This chapter explores the close connections between sumptuary laws and embodied identity in colonial Spanish America. What a person wore materially shaped their status as a Spaniard, Amerindian or any of the other 'castes' or 'conditions' into which colonial society was divided. Since colonial governance was predicated on these divisions, the history of sumptuary laws in Spanish America is inevitably entangled with colonial regulation of caste or race. The chapter first reviews current understandings of Spanish American racial or caste categories, which demonstrate the dynamic relationship between clothing and caste. It concludes by situating the persistent efforts to regulate dress within the broader ambitions of Spanish imperial governance, which were both wide-reaching and fundamentally contradictory.

Scholarship on sumptuary legislation in Europe has long noted the efforts made by officials to regulate the dress of different social classes and genders. Beyond the distinctive badges imposed on Jews in medieval

---

[2] Ordenanzas para el bueno gobierno de los indios en las Provincias de Soconusco y Verapaz, 29 September 1628, *Colección de documentos*, ed. Konetzke, ii pt. 1: 321.

[3] R.C. aprobando un bando del Virrey del Perú para moderar el exceso en los trajes que vestían los negros, mulatos, indios y mestizos, 7 September 1725, *Colección de documentos*, ed. Konetzke, iii pt. 1: 187.

England, the use of dress to demarcate ethnic divisions has received less attention. A growing body of research on early modern Europe and the Islamic world however demonstrates the persistent efforts by Jewish, Muslim and Christian legislators alike to prescribe the sorts of garments permitted to members of different religious groups.[4]

This work greatly extends our knowledge of the use of clothing to police the frontiers between purity and pollution, and between different religions. Medieval and early modern theologians and legal experts from all three religious traditions devoted serious attention to whether outsiders should be obliged to wear distinctive clothing, or prohibited from adopting the region's usual dress. They pondered the moral and corporeal consequences of wearing clothing associated with other faiths. Concerns over impurity for instance prompted jurists from several Islamic legal schools to ban the wearing of undergarments previously owned by Jews or Christians. Jewish laws dating back to Leviticus, in turn, had long condemned fabrics containing both wool and linen, or other mixed fibres, as defilements. Christian, Jewish and Islamic scholars also explored the circumstances under which it was permissible to deviate from such stipulations. The close connections between clothing and embodied religious identity were matters of particular concern. In medieval and early modern Europe and the Islamic world wearing the wrong clothing thus constituted not simply a violation of legal norms. It might also alter the wearer's body, rendering it impure. In sum, research into the early modern regulation of clothing in the Old World has begun

---

[4] Cecil Roth, 'Sumptuary Laws of the Community of Carpentras', *Jewish Quarterly Review* 18/4 (1928): 357–383; John Edwards, ed. and trans., *The Jews in Western Europe, 1400–1600* (Manchester: Manchester University Press, 1994), 88–92; José Damián González Arce, *Apariencia y poder. La legislación suntuaria castellana en los siglos XIII y XV* (Jaén: Universidad de Jaén, 1998), 170–177; Yedida Kalfon Stillman, *Arab Dress. A Short History from the Dawn of Islam to Modern Times*, ed. Norman Stillman (Leiden: Brill, 2000), 23–25, 39–40, 83–84, 101–119; Magda Teter, *Jews and Heretics in Catholic Poland: A Beleaguered Church in the Post-Reformation Era*, (Cambridge: Cambridge University Press, 2006), 71–79; Maria Filomena Lopes de Barros, *Tempos e espaços de mouros. A minoria muçulmana no reino português (séculos XII a XV)* (Braga: Fundação Calouste Gulbenkian, 2007), 182–198; Milka Levy-Rubin, *Non-Muslims in the Early Islamic Empire: From Surrender to Coexistence* (Cambridge: Cambridge University Press, 2011); Anver Emon, *Religious Pluralism and Islamic Law: Dhimmis and Others in the Empire of Law* (Oxford: Oxford University Press, 2012), 131–136; and John Tolan, 'The First Imposition of a Badge on European Jews: The English Royal Mandate of 1218', in Douglas Pratt et al. (eds.), *The Character of Christian-Muslim Encounter* Leiden: Brill, 2015), 145–166; as well as the unpublished conference papers delivered at the Université de Nantes, 5–6 June 2014 by Camilla Adang ('Legal Texts on Wearing Clothing Belonging to, Manufactured, or Sold by non-Muslims'); and Nadezda Koryakina ('Les vêtements de chrétiens portés par des juifs pour se protéger'); for details see the website of the RELMIN project ['Le Status Légal des Minorités Religieuses dans l'Espace Euro-Méditerranéen (V-XV siècle)']: www.cn-telma.fr/relmin/index/.

to explore how and why dress was able to modify the corporeal condition of the person it swathed.

In colonial Latin America, in contrast, scholars have long recognised clothing's ability to alter embodied identity. As the anthropologist Joanne Rappaport put it, in the colonial Indies 'clothing had a "transnaturing power" that did not just reflect identity, but helped constitute it'.[5] The following section explores this transnaturing power, which helps explain why sumptuary legislation from the early modern Hispanic world was so often concerned with issues of race, as the opening vignettes intimate.

Performing Race in Colonial Spanish America

Scholarship on the meaning and origins of race as a cultural category is vast. Nonetheless, it is possible to identify a sea change in how scholars approach the concept. For decades the scholarly consensus was that medieval and early modern ideas about difference were fundamentally distinct from later ideas about race. Early modern distinctions between, say, Christians and Muslims were not considered examples of racial thinking, but rather reflections of cultural prejudices. Because an individual could in theory adopt a different faith, hostility towards those of different religions was said to reflect a more flexible, 'cultural' model of differentiation not based on permanent, embodied attributes. Only systems of difference based on supposedly inflexible, physical characteristics were to be considered 'racial'. As the historian Kathleen Wilson explained, race in this sense was understood to concern 'fixed, inherent difference, articulated through and signified primarily by physical appearance and the "science of surfaces"'.[6] Race, in this perspective, was a creation of the late eighteenth century that reached its zenith in the long nineteenth century, and its nadir in Auschwitz.

A more recent body of research has questioned this firm distinction between 'cultural' and 'racial' models of difference. A rich and varied scholarship now suggests either that early modern 'cultural' distinctions were not as flexible as they might appear – that the ability of individuals to move from one category to another was far more limited than had been recognised – or that the very distinction between cultural/religious

---

[5] Joanne Rappaport, *The Disappearing Mestizo. Configuring Difference in the Colonial New Kingdom of Granada* (Durham: Duke University Press, 2014), 52–55 (quote p. 52).

[6] George Fredrickson, *Racism: A Short History* (Princeton: Princeton University Press, 2002), 5–13; Kathleen Wilson, *The Island Race: Englishness, Empire and Gender in the Eighteenth Century* (London: Routledge, 2003), 11–15 (quote p. 15); and Benjamin Isaac, *The Invention of Racism in Classical Antiquity* (Princeton: Princeton University Press, 2004), 1–51.

and 'physical' explanations for difference is unhelpful. After all, as the anthropologist Peter Wade has observed, the widespread belief that culture is itself innate and inherited undermines any division between systems of difference based on culture and those based on the physical body.[7] From the perspective of such research, medieval sumptuary legislation limiting the right of non-Muslims to wear garments previously owned by Muslims, or requiring Jews to wear distinctive clothing, qualifies as racial. Yet other scholars parse the vocabulary employed to discuss different sorts of divisions between different populations, and prefer to use terms such as 'caste' to refer to earlier models, thus preserving 'race' to refer only to the post-Enlightenment manifestations of human categorisation.[8]

Scholarship on the Hispanic world has played an important role in these debates in part because of the evident centrality of 'caste' or 'race' to the structuring of these early modern societies.[9] Colonial Spanish America was organised along explicitly ethnic lines; innumerable laws regulated whether Spaniards could reside in indigenous villages, whether Amerindians were subject to the Inquisition, whether mulattos could attend university, and many other matters of greater or lesser moment. Generally speaking, Peninsular Spaniards – those born in Europe – were

---

[7] Peter Wade, 'Afterword: Race and Nation in Latin America: An Anthropological View', in Nancy Appelbaum et al. (eds.), *Race and Nation in Modern Latin America* (Chapel Hill: University of North Carolina Press, 2003), 263–282.

[8] See for instance *Journal of Medieval and Early Modern Studies* 31/1 (2001): special issue on 'Race and Ethnicity in the Middle Ages'; Mary Floyd-Wilson, *English Ethnicity and Race in Early Modern Drama* (Cambridge: Cambridge University Press, 2003); Isaac, *The Invention of Racism in Classical Antiquity*; Margaret Greer, Walter Mignolo and Maureen Quilligan (eds.), *Rereading the Black Legend: The Discourses of Religious and Racial Difference in the Renaissances Empires* (Chicago: University of Chicago Press, 2007); and Miriam Eliav-Feldon, Benjamin Isaac, and Joseph Ziegler (eds.), *The Origins of Racism in the West* (Cambridge: Cambridge University Press, 2009).

[9] James Sweet, 'The Iberian Roots of American Racist Thought', *William and Mary Quarterly* 54/1 (1997): 143–166; Jorge Cañizares Esguerra, 'New Worlds, New Stars: Patriotic Astrology and the Invention of Indian and Creole Bodies in Colonial Spanish America, 1600–1650', *American Historical Review* 104/1 (1999): 33–68; Jorge Cañizares Esguerra, *Nature, Empire, and Nation: Explorations of the History of Science in the Iberian World* (Stanford: Stanford University Press, 2006); María Elena Martínez, *Genealogical Fictions: Limpieza de Sangre, Religion, and Gender in Colonial Mexico* (Stanford: Stanford University Press, 2008); Jorge Cañizares Esguerra, 'Demons, Stars and the Imagination: the Early Modern Body in the Tropics', in Eliav-Feldon et al. (eds.), *The Origins of Racism in the West*, 313–325; Ruth Hill, 'Entering and Exiting Blackness: A Color Controversy in Eighteenth-Century Spain', *Journal of Spanish Cultural Studies* 10/1 (2009): 43–58; Max S. Hering Torres, María Elena Martínez and David Nirenberg (eds.), *Race and Blood in the Iberian World* (Vienna: LIT Verlag, 2012); Rebecca Earle, *The Body of the Conquistador: Food, Race and the Colonial Experience in Spanish America, 1492–1700* (Cambridge: Cambridge University Press, 2012); and Kimberly Anne Coles, Ralph Bauer, Zita Nunes and Carla L. Peterson (eds.), *The Cultural Politics of Blood, 1500–1900* (London: Palgrave Macmillan, 2015).

accorded most privileges, while those with any degree of African ancestry were subject to the most constraints. Caste categories were thus deeply imbricated in the structures of colonial power. For this reason the Spanish administration expended considerable effort in recording the caste of individual members of the colonial population.[10] Therefore, in theory, it should be possible to determine someone's caste status simply by locating any document in which they were mentioned.

In reality, the situation was not so straightforward. These bureaucratic records were neither harmonious nor internally consistent. Different officials at times classified the same population in different ways.[11] Moreover, records are replete with examples of what the historian Robert McCaa called 'racial drift'. One study from late eighteenth-century Chile found that over a twelve year period nearly half the male heads of household in Valparaiso were ascribed different caste statuses in different official documents.[12] Sometimes changes were noted explicitly, as when individuals claimed that their birth had mistakenly been recorded in the wrong register, but sometimes people silently moved (or were moved) from one classification to another. The historian Ann Twinam for instance describes a family which in a mere five years arranged to have baptismal records altered such that the hitherto plebeian mother retrospectively acquired an honourific title, the father was reclassified from mulatto to Spaniard, and three of their four children also appeared as Spaniards, despite the fact that both parents had earlier been classified

---

[10] The state began recording peoples' ethnic status haphazardly from the earliest days of the conquest, and systematically from the mid-sixteenth century, after the Council of Trent made it obligatory to maintain records of baptisms, marriages and similar life events. Parish records were often organised by caste, so that separate books of baptisms, marriages and deaths were commonly used for Spaniards, Indians and the 'castes' – an umbrella term that referred to people of mixed ethnicity. Tribute rolls ostensibly listed all indigenous men, who were required to pay the special head tax – the 'Indian tribute' – levied on them, and colonial officials periodically carried out population censuses, which likewise classified people as Spaniards, enslaved or a variety of other categories. In addition, judicial records usually stated an individual's 'caste', 'condition' or 'quality'.

[11] See for example Robert Jackson, *Race, and Status: Indians in Colonial Spanish America* (Albuquerque: University of New Mexico Press, 1999), 106–109.

[12] Robert McCaa, Stuart Schwartz and Arturo Grubessich, 'Race and Class in Colonial Latin America: A Critique', *Comparative Studies in Society and History* 21/3 (1979): 422. See also Patricia Seed, 'Social Dimensions of Race: Mexico City, 1753', *Hispanic American Historical Review* 62/4 (1982): 592–600; Robert McCaa, 'Calidad, Clase, and Marriage in Colonial Mexico: The Case of Parral, 1788–90', *Hispanic American Historical Review* 64/3 (1984): 479–480, 497–499; Martin Minchom, *The People of Quito: 1690–1810: Change and Unrest in the Underclass* (Boulder: Westview Press, 1994), 174; and Karen Graubart, 'The Creolization of the New World: Local Forms of Identification in Urban Colonial Peru, 1560–1640', *Hispanic American Historical Review* 89/3 (2009): 476.

as mixed race.[13] Scholars continue to debate the degree of agency that individuals exercised in these transformations, but it is evident that as an individual made their way through life it was possible for their caste status to change.

This was particularly the case for women. For example, although marriage records often omitted the bride's caste altogether, the historian Elizabeth Anne Kuznesof has observed that,

when the ethnicity of the bride was recorded it was not uncommon for [it] to differ from that of her birth record. In other words, the ethnicity of the bride was often excluded from the marriage record, and when it was included, the priest often recorded her as being of the same ethnic background as the groom.[14]

This practice of adjusting the bride's status to match her husband's makes it difficult to interpret the racial endogamy that, according to such records, characterises marriage in the Indies. More profoundly, it indicates the flexibility of caste categories.

Caste categories, in other words, were inherently relational, reflecting the hierarchies and relationships that shaped the colonial world, as the anthropologist Laura Lewis has demonstrated. They were thus simultaneously statements about ancestry and about reputation.[15] In legal disputes witnesses might be asked whether the defendant was 'held and reputed' to be white, not whether they *were* white. In reply witnesses might affirm that they considered an individual to be Spanish because they had 'heard it said' that they were. Equally, witnesses might insist that an individual was agreed to belong to a caste category that appeared to contradict their reputed ancestry.[16] Caste identity was therefore the result of a complex, intersectional interplay between ancestry, appearance, reputation,

[13] Ann Twinam, *Purchasing Whiteness: Pardos, Mulattos, and the Quest for Social Mobility in the Spanish Indies* (Stanford: Stanford University Press, 2015), 140–141. Or see Magali Carrera, *Imagining Identity in New Spain: Race, Lineage, and the Colonial Body in Portraiture and Casta Paintings* (Austin: University of Texas Press, 2003), 1–21.

[14] Seed, 'Social Dimensions of Race: Mexico City', 592–600; Elizabeth Anne Kuznesof, 'Ethnic and Gender Influences on "Spanish" Creole Society in Colonial Spanish America', *Colonial Latin American Review* 4/1 (1995): 163 (quote); Laura Lewis, *Hall of Mirrors: Power, Witchcraft, and Caste in Colonial Mexico* (Durham: Duke University Press, 2003), 33, 76; and David Wheat, '*Nharas* and *Morenas Horras*: A Luso-African Model for the Social History of the Spanish Caribbean, c. 1570–1640', *Journal of Early Modern History* 14/1–2 (2010): 147–148.

[15] Lewis, *Hall of Mirrors*; Rappaport, *The Disappearing Mestizo*; and Rebecca Earle, 'The Pleasures of Taxonomy: Casta Painting, Classification, and Colonialism', *William and Mary Quarterly* 73/3 (2016): 427–466.

[16] See for instance Verónica Undurraga Schüler, 'Españoles oscuros y mulatos blancos: Identidades múltiples y disfraces del color en el ocaso de la colonia chilena. 1778–1820', in Rafael Gaune and Martín Lara (eds.), *Historias de racismo y discriminación en Chile* (Santiago: Editorial Uqbar, 2010), 356, 359; and Twinam, *Purchasing Whiteness*, 62.

lifestyle and social standing, none of which had much meaning when taken in isolation.

Caste might best be viewed as a reflection of overall habitus. The importance of clothing in creating this flexible yet embodied identity can be seen clearly in a court case from 1759 New Granada. When asked to describe a certain Clara Reina, one witness responded that 'from her appearance she didn't seem to him to be a mulatta and because she wore a certain type of skirt and a little shawl he didn't think she was white but rather a mestiza'.[17] Likewise, simply wearing certain characteristic garments such as the indigenous *huipil* or smock shown in Figure 12.1 might be sufficient to establish an individual as Amerindian. These garments determined how the wearer was perceived, and therefore who they were.[18]

Because of clothing's importance in creating caste, early modern Spanish Americans were very attuned to nuances of dress. 'Even Indians, black people and lowly persons wear silks and striped clothing', noted the Augustinian friar Antonio de la Calancha in his seventeenth-century description of Lima. He added that prohibitions had little effect; as a result artisans were constantly endeavouring to pass themselves off as noble by dressing in velvets and fashionable black capes.[19] 'The lowest class of Spaniards are very ambitious of distinguishing themselves from [mestizos], either by the colour or fashion of the clothes', observed the eighteenth-century Spanish travellers Jorge Juan and Antonio de Ulloa.[20] The colonial archive is full of complaints about individuals who changed their clothing or living habits, and thereby 'became' a different race. As one priest lamented in late seventeenth-century Mexico City, when an Amerindian put on a cloak, shoes and stockings, and grew his hair, he quickly became a mestizo, 'and in a few days a Spaniard, free of tribute'.[21]

---

[17] Jaime Jaramillo Uribe, *Ensayos sobre historia social colombiana* (Bogotá: Universidad Nacional de Colombia, 1969), 195, 211 (quote).

[18] Rappaport, *The Disappearing Mestizo*, 52–55. For illuminating discussion of the relationship between clothing, perceived appearance, and identity see also Valentin Groebner, *Who Are You? Identification, Deception, and Surveillance in Early Modern Europe* (New York: Zone Books, 2007); and Nancy E. van Deusen, 'Seeing *Indios* in Sixteenth-Century Castile', *William and Mary Quarterly* 69/2 (2012): 205–234.

[19] Antonio de la Calancha, *Corónica moralizada del orden de San Agustín en el Perú* (Barcelona, 1638), 67.

[20] Jorge Juan and Antonio de Ulloa, *A Voyage to South America*, trans. John Adams (1806; repr. New York: Knopf, 1964), 137 (quote); and Rebecca Earle, "Two Pairs of Pink Satin Shoes!!": Clothing, Race and Identity in the Americas, 17th-19th Centuries', *History Workshop Journal* 52 (2001): 175–195.

[21] José de la Barrera, Santa María de la Redonda 1 July 1692, 'Sobre los inconvenientes de vivir los indios en el centro de la ciudad', *Boletín del Archivo General de la Nación* 9/1 (1938): 20.

Figure 12.1 *De Español, y Yndia, sale Mestizo* [*From a Spanish Man and an Indian Woman, Comes a Mestizo*], early eighteenth century, by anonymous artist. Brooklyn Museum, bequest of Samuel E. Haslett and Charles A. Schieren, gift of Alfred T. White and Otto H. Kahn through the Committee for the Diffusion of French Art, by exchange, 2011.86.1.

This 'casta painting' depicts a family scene; the painted caption tells us that the Spanish man and indigenous woman are the parents of the little mestizo boy. The woman is dressed in an elaborate *huipil*, or smock. In such paintings *huipiles* are worn solely by Amerindian women; it is the *huipil*, as much as the caption or the women's appearance, that determines their identity as indigenous.[22]

Sumptuary Laws and Conquered Peoples

Clothing's powerful ability to transform an individual's caste explains why sumptuary laws in Spanish America so often sought to regulate the dress of different castes. To be sure, this legislation also addressed other

---

[22] As the anthropologist Joanne Rappaport commented with regard to indigenous dress in colonial New Granada (present-day Colombia), 'the very fact of wearing native clothing made these women into Indians': Rappaport, *The Disappearing Mestizo*, 53.

social divisions. As in Europe, in the Americas sumptuary laws frequently stressed the importance of preserving social distinctions. Legislation aimed at the 'common people who without having sufficient wealth wish to dress like the wealthy' was issued regularly until the end of the eighteenth century.[23] Regulations also stipulated what accoutrements different categories of official could display at religious services and other public functions, so as to ensure the visibility of hierarchical differences in rank. Individual officials who deviated from the required dress code faced a stiff reprimand, perhaps from the monarch himself. Clothing was moreover included in the laws governing commerce and travel to the Indies. The importation of clothing from China was repeatedly prohibited on the grounds that the trade encouraged smuggling, and the number of garments individual travellers and sailors were permitted to take in their luggage was limited, again to discourage the evasion of customs duties. The first Spanish American sumptuary law (or at least the first I have located), issued in 1509, banned 'all persons of whatever position, status, or condition' from sporting a wide range of fabrics and decorations in the name of preventing wasteful expense.[24] In this regard colonial regulations reflected the well-established themes of European sumptuary legislation.

At the same time, this corpus of legislation also aimed specifically at preventing unsanctioned caste reclassification via dress. Such caste-inflected legislation persisted throughout the colonial era precisely because the cultural and legal structures that viewed caste as an embodied condition themselves persisted. Restrictions on the garments and accoutrements permitted to specific castes were issued from the 1550s, when free and enslaved people of colour were banned by local ordinances in Lima from wearing silk, jewels and other adornments. Very similar legislation deploring the 'scandalous excesses' of the city's mestizos and other castes was issued nearly two centuries later.[25] Dozens

[23] The quotation is from a 1648 appeal by the Audiencia of Chile: Cecelia Salinas, *Las chilenas de la colonia: virtud sumisa, amor rebelde* (Santiago: LOM Ediciones, 1994), 114. Or see the legislation from 29 December 1679, 9 October 1684, 26 November 1691 and 10 February 1716 in *Colección de Documentos*, ed. Konetzke, ii pt. 2: 693–694; iii pt. 1: 124–134.

[24] On the dress of officials see for instance *Colección de Documentos*, ed. Konetzke, ii pt. 2: 625–626 (for a reprimand), iii: 1, 235, iii: 2, 573; and Alejandro Cañeque, *The King's Living Image: The Culture and Politics of Viceregal Power in Colonial Mexico* (New York: Routledge, 2004). The *Recopilación de leyes de los reynos de las Indias* (Madrid, 1791), vol. 1 reproduces many of the regulations governing the importation of 'ropa de China' and the like. The 1509 pragmatic is reproduced in *Colección de Documentos*, ed. Konetzke, i: 23–25.

[25] R.C. aprobando un bando del Virrey del Perú para moderar el exceso en los trajes que vestían los negros, mulatos, indios y mestizos, 7 September 1725, *Colección de documentos*, ed. Konetzke, iii pt. 1: 187; Tamara Walker, *Exquisite Slaves: Race, Clothing and Status*

of laws banning Amerindians, mulattos, mestizos and other non-whites from carrying swords or similar weapons were issued repeatedly from the 1530s to the end of the seventeenth century.[26] Legislation specifically regulating the dress of non-Spanish women was also common. Black and mulatto women in seventeenth-century Mexico were for instance prohibited to wear 'any gold, silver, or pearl jewellery, nor any Castilian garments, nor silk shawls, nor gold or silver passamanterie'. These regulations were reiterated in subsequent centuries; similar legislation was also issued for Peru.[27] Although such laws sometimes exempted the indigenous nobility from conforming to these restrictions, native elites in any event regularly petitioned for permission to wear Spanish clothes, carry swords and engage in other displays of respectability.[28]

The eighteenth-century painting shown in Figure 12.2 depicts the modest dress such rulings directed Afro-Mexicans to adopt. The woman, likely enslaved, wears a simple laced bodice and locally-produced shawl that contrasts with the imported fabric of the elegant banyan worn by the Spanish man. The eighteenth-century Spanish slave code for Santo Domingo similarly prohibited both the enslaved and free people of colour from wearing 'pearls, emeralds, and other precious stones', and, equally significantly, banned them from wearing the Spanish mantilla in place of the African head-cloth.[29]

in *Colonial Lima* (Cambridge: Cambridge University Press, 2017); and Chapter 9 by Amanda Wunder in this volume.

[26] Josephe and Francisco Mugaburu, *Chronicle of Colonial Lima. The Diary of Josephe and Francisco Mugaburu, 1640–1697*, trans. Robert Miller (Norman: University of Oklahoma Press, 1975), 32, 59, 82–83, 124, 217; Juan Francisco de Montemayor de Cuenca, *Recopilación sumaria de algunos mandamientos y ordenanzas del gobierno de esta Nueva España* (Mexico City, 1787), 74; and *Colección de Documentos*, ed. Konetzke, i: 167–168, 292–293, 420, 479, 580; ii pt. 1: 183–184, 317, 321; ii pt. 2: 417, 427–428, 514–515.

[27] Mugaburu and Mugaburu, *Chronicle of Colonial Lima*, 32, 59, 82–83, 124, 217; R.C. aprobando un bando del Virrey del Peru, *Colección de Documentos*, ed. Konetzke, iii pt. 1: 187; Ordenanza y Auto, 14 April 1612, Juan Francisco de Montemayor de Cuenca, *Recopilación sumaria de algunos mandamientos y ordenanzas del gobierno de esta Nueva España* (Mexico City, 1787), 74 (quote); R.C. al presidente de la Audiencia de Guadalajara sobre que observe las ordenes y leyes que prohiben traer armas los indios, mestizos, negros y mulatos, Madrid, 30 December 1692; and Pragmática contra el abuso de trajes y otros gastos superfluos, Madrid, 10 February 1716; *Colección de Documentos*, ed. Konetzke, iii pt. 1: 27, 124–134, respectively. Walker, *Exquisite Slaves*, provides a clear analysis of the Peruvian legislation.

[28] See for instance *Colección de Documentos*, ed. Konetzke, i: 580; ii pt. 2: 757; and Yanna Yannakakis, *The Art of Being In-between: Native Intermediaries, Indian Identity, and Local Rule in Colonial Oaxaca* (Durham: Duke University Press, 2008), 36.

[29] Extracto del Código Negro Carolino, Santo Domingo, 14 March 1785, *Colección de Documentos*, ed. Konetzke, iii pt. 2: 562. See also Médéric-Louis-Élie Moreau de Saint-Méry, *Description topographique, physique, civile, politique et historique de la partie française de l'isle Saint-Domingue* (1797; repr. Paris: Société de l'Histoire des Colonies Françaises, 1958), 93.

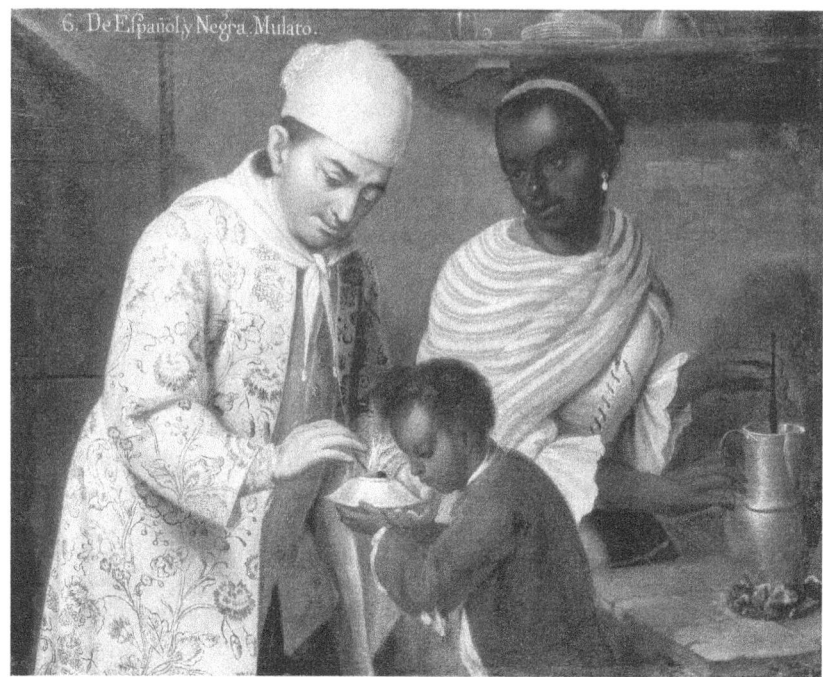

Figure 12.2 *De Español y Negra, Mulato* [*From a Spanish Man and a Black Woman, Mulato*], attributed to José de Alcíbar, c. 1760–1770. Denver Art Museum.

The mother and son in this painting adopt reassuringly deferential poses in the presence of the Spanish man, who the caption tells us is the boy's father. The mother's modest garments conform to the regulations governing the dress of black and mixed-race women, although her pearl earrings violate a 1612 Mexican ordinance that 'no black woman … may wear any jewellry of gold, silver [or] pearls'.[30]

Some of these laws explicitly reflected the reality that marriage materially altered a woman's caste. For instance, in sixteenth-century Mexico, black women were barred from wearing gold, pearls, silk or other luxurious goods, unless they were married to a Spaniard – precisely the circumstances that were likely to result in a readjustment of their 'quality' to better match that of their husband, as noted earlier. They were similarly prohibited from wearing indigenous garb unless married to an Amerindian. Most Amerindian women were at the same time banned

---

[30] Montemayor de Cuenca, *Recopilación sumaria*, 73–74.

from adopting Spanish dress. 'Castas', or mixed-race women, were not to dress as Amerindians unless married to indigenous men. This mattered to the colonial state because once dressed in indigenous garb, these women would more easily become indigenous themselves, and that would entitle them to certain legal protections. The correct classification of such 'mestizas dressed as Indians' flummoxed colonial courts.[31]

Other legislation conversely spelled out that racially-inflected sartorial restrictions applied even to women married to Spaniards, in vain attempts to halt the transformative potential of such marriages.[32] These regulations were accompanied by multiple ordinances stipulating who was permitted to wear garments made of silk, prohibiting inadequate or indecent dress, and regulating the spread of particular fashions such as the identity-concealing (and figure-hugging) clothing of 'tapadas', or veiled women. The latter was described as particularly worrisome because it permitted women to display their feminine curves while hiding their caste from admirers. Indecent garments of this sort were blamed for a range of disorders, including the devastating earthquake-tsunami that flattened Lima in the mid-eighteenth century.[33]

Sumptuary legislation, in short, was premised on the interconnections between caste, morality, gender and status. Writers, priests and officials in both Spain and the Indies worried throughout the early modern era that, left unregulated, fashion would 'induce moral laxity and social disorder', as Marta Vicente has noted. Low-cut bodices, snug veils, and tempting fabrics assailed the virtue of women and the resolve of men. Vicente recounts the plight of a young servant in Barcelona who exchanged sexual favours for a length of calico, and the anxiety of Mexican viceroys that

---

[31] Berta Ares Queija, 'Mestizos en hábito de indios: ¿estrategias transgresoras o identidades difusas?', in Rui Manuel Loureiro and Serge Gruzinski (eds.), *Passar as fronteiras. Il coloquio internacional sobre mediadores culturais, séculos XV a XVIII* (Lagos: Centro de Estudios Gil Eanes, 1999), 133–146; and Rappaport, *The Disappearing Mestizo*, 52–55.

[32] Walker, *Exquisite Slaves* discusses both such laws and their persistent failure to modify behaviour.

[33] Consulta del Consejo de las Indias sobre una representación del ... Fr. Mariano de Junqueras Madrid, 25 August 1789, *Colección de Documentos*, ed. Konetzke, iii pt. 2: 660–666; Gonzalo Aguirre Beltrán, 'The Integration of the Negro into the National Society of Mexico', in Magnus Mörner (ed.), *Race and Class in Latin America* (New York: Columbia University Press, 1970), 24; Douglas Cope, *The Limits of Racial Domination: Plebeian Society in Colonial Mexico City, 1660–1720* (Madison: University of Wisconsin Press, 1994), 16; Pilar Gonzalbo Aizpuru, 'De la penuria y el lujo en la Nueva España, siglos XVI-XVIII', *Revista de Indias* 65/206 (1996): 49–75; Julia Tuñón Pablos, *Women in Mexico. A Past Unveiled*, trans. Alan Hynds (Austin: University of Texas Press, 1999), 26–28; Charles Walker, *Shaky Colonialism: The 1746 Earthquake-Tsunami in Lima, Peru, and its Long Aftermath* (Durham: Duke University Press, 2008); and Laura Bass and Amanda Wunder, 'The Veiled Ladies of the Early Modern Spanish World: Seduction and Scandal in Seville, Madrid, and Lima', *Hispanic Review* 77/1 (2009): 97–144.

the colony's ladies would succumb to similar temptations. To be sure, some philosophers (and merchants) embraced new ideas suggesting that private vices might support public benefits, but colonial hierarchies were premised on the assumption that honour, reputation and caste were, if not interchangeable, at least closely correlated. The transformative potential of a change of costume obscured the divisions between elites and plebeians, Spaniards and mulattas, the virtuous and the debased.[34]

Sumptuary legislation at times reflected the demographic contours of the local population in according particular attention to those groups whose sartorial fluidity was seen as most destabilising. Legislators in Lima for instance devoted particular care to regulating the dress of enslaved men and women, as Tamara Walker has shown. In the case of this vice-regal capital, the delight colonial officials took in bedecking enslaved entourages in luxurious outfits inspired repeated prohibitions and also guaranteed their failure. The importance of fine clothing to the enslaved themselves prompted further legislative backlashes from Lima's colonial administration.[35] Local context certainly shaped the specific contours of sumptuary legislation in the colonial Indies. At the same time, persistent recourse to sumptuary laws across Spanish America, over the three centuries of colonial rule, by both local and imperial officials, reminds us of the need to look beyond purely contingent or local factors when making sense of this body of legislation. Having issued its first colonial sumptuary law in the early sixteenth century, the Spanish state promulgated dozens of orders, pragmatics, cédulas and other ordinances aimed at channelling and controlling New World sartorial practices until the very end of the colonial era.[36] These laws reflect broader features of the colonial experience in their sustained efforts to manage and regulate the social and ethnic hierarchies that underpinned Spanish control.

---

[34] Marta Vicente, *Clothing the Spanish Empire: Families and the Calico Trade in the Early Modern Atlantic World* (Basingstoke: Palgrave Macmillan, 2006), 68–83 (quote 69); and, on Spanish luxury debates, also see Sempere y Guarinos, *Historia del luxo*; Juan Rico, 'Criptoburguesía y cambio económico en la Ilustración española', *Cuadernos Hispanoamericanos* 408 (1984): 25–56; and Manuel Pérez-García, '*Vicarious Consumers': Trans-national Meetings between the West and East in the Mediterranean World (1730–1808)* (New York: Routledge, 2016). On honour and caste see Asunción Lavrin (ed.), *Sexuality and Marriage in Colonial Latin America* (Lincoln: University of Nebraska Press, 1989); Ramón Gutiérrez, *When Jesus Came, the Corn Mothers Went Away. Marriage, Sexuality and Power in New Mexico, 1500–1846* (Stanford: Stanford University Press, 1991); and Lyman Johnson and Sonya Lipsett-Rivera (eds.), *The Faces of Honor: Sex, Shame and Violence in Colonial Latin America* (Albuquerque: University of New Mexico Press, 1998).

[35] Walker, *Exquisite Slaves*.

[36] In 1805 the Consejo de Indias for instance ruled on the quantity of gold embroidery that officials in Mexico City might use to adorn their uniforms: *Colección de documentos*, ed. Konetzke, iii pt. 2: 810–813.

The formal stipulations of colonial legislation resonated with the deeply held convictions of many colonists. Recall the attempts by settlers in sixteenth-century Quito to impose an informal dress code on Amerindians with which this chapter opened. The 'officials and other people' who objected to the festive dress worn by local indigenous elites insisted that 'as conquered people' they should wear only cotton, and certainly never European garments.[37] Moralising critics such as the Andean writer Felipe de Guaman Poma de Ayala concurred that the adoption of European dress caused unwelcome changes in indigenous mores. Guaman Poma, a Quechua-speaking writer from central Peru, was descended from local indigenous nobility, and witnessed first-hand the transformations wrought on indigenous culture by colonial settlement. In the early seventeenth century he composed a lengthy manuscript chronicle documenting human history from its earliest days to his own lifetime. He illustrated his text with hundreds of drawings, including Figure 12.3 of 'creolised Indians', who, he complained, spent too much time frolicking, to the cost of their souls (Figure 12.3). Throughout his chronicle Guaman Poma was critical of indigenous people, and particularly women, who embraced Spanish culture with too much enthusiasm. The heedless couple shown here sport hybrid costumes that combine Spanish breeches, shoes and hats with Andean tunics and jewellry. The woman's sleeves, for instance, are wholly European, while her cloak is fastened with an indigenous *tupu*, or shawl pin. Her tunic is likewise adorned with the checkerboard *tocapu* design typical of elite Incaic garments. From Guaman Poma's perspective the European elements of her costume signal her dissolute lifestyle. From the perspective of colonial settlers they would perhaps demonstrate her greater degree of civility, or alternatively might have constituted an irritating provocation of the sort that prompted settlers in late sixteenth-century Quito to confiscate the European garments worn by indigenous elites.[38] As Guaman Poma's caption to his drawing insisted, these people 'spend their time singing and amusing themselves, rather than serving God'. Guaman Poma was a sharp critic of Spanish colonialism, yet he agreed with Spanish settlers that it was pernicious for Amerindians to embrace European customs and wear European clothing.

Belief that it was pernicious for 'conquered people' to adopt European dress was expressed repeatedly during the colonial era. Commentators suspected that such behaviour provoked 'social disruption and the disintigration of colonial hierarchies', as the historian

---

[37] R.C. a la Audiencia de Quito, *Colección de documentos*, ed. Konetzke, ii pt. 1: 11.
[38] Ibid.

Figure 12.3 Felipe de Guaman Poma de Ayala, *Nueva corónica y buen gobierno* (1615–1616), Drawing 321: 'Creolized Indians spend their time singing and amusing themselves, rather than serving God'. Det Kongelige Bibliotek, Copenhagen.

In the early seventeenth century Guaman Poma composed a monumental illustrated chronicle focused on his native Peru, which included an extensive critique of the dissolute lifestyle of the 'creolised Indians' depicted here, who adopted Spanish cultural practices. His drawing of their reprehensible behaviour illustrates exactly the sort of hybrid dress snatched from indigenous people in Quito: 'shirts, cloaks, *anacos* [an indigenous tunic], and silken garments'.

Nicole von Germeten has observed.[39] Colonists for instance concurred that a major riot in 1692 Mexico City could be blamed in part on the lax attitude of officials who permitted Amerindians to wear Spanish capes and other European accoutrements. Dressed in such splendid garments the wearers were bold and rebellious, in the view of priests and officials.[40] Acculturated Amerindians, particularly those living in cities, were invariably depraved and troublesome, insisted a Guatemalan priest writing over a hundred years later. For this reason he thought it was a mistake to encourage them to adopt European dress.[41] Uncontrolled blurring of sartorial lines was persistently associated with all manner of social disorder. Sumptuary laws thus reflected a deep current of hostility to the embrace of the dominant European culture by subalterns.

At the same time, these efforts to police the sartorial frontiers between Amerindians and colonists flew in the face of a fundamental aim of Spanish imperial policy: the conversion of the indigenous population into a reasonable facsimile of the Spanish population. Innumerable laws and exhortations required officials and priests to do all in their power to make indigenous people more like Spaniards. In the words of one sixteenth-century official, settlers should do everything possible to ensure that Amerindians adopted 'our customs in eating, drinking, dressing, cleanliness and personal conduct ... and finally our language'.[42] Similar efforts were underway in Spain itself, where following the fifteenth-century Reconquista of the Islamic states in southern Spain, and the sixteenth-century defeat of remaining pockets of resistance, the Catholic monarchy endeavoured to force Muslim converts to embrace not only Christianity but also Spanish surnames, table manners and dress. The policies advocated for both regions reflected a shared conviction that being Christian required far more than a change

---

[39] Nicole von Germeten, *Violent Delights, Violent Ends: Sex, Race, and Honor in Colonial Cartagena de Indias* (Albuquerque: University of New Mexico Press, 2013), 149–150.

[40] Fray Bernabe Nuñez de Paez, Informe, Doctrina de San Pablo, 4 July 1692, Archivo General de la Nación, Mexico City, Historia, vol. 413, fols. 10, 11, 13; Cope, *The Limits of Racial Domination*, 125–160; Lewis, *Hall of Mirrors*, 27; and Cañeque, *The King's Living Image*, 227. Thanks to Frank Eissa Barroso for the material from the Archivo General de la Nación.

[41] Antonio Larrazabal, *Apuntamientos sobre la agricultura y comercio del Reyno de Guatemala* (Nueva Guatemala, 1811), 42–43.

[42] Carta de Tomás López a los reyes de Bohemia, Guatemala, 9 June 1550, Archivo General de Indias, Seville, Audiencia de Guatemala, legajo 9A, N. 68, R.17, fols. 5, 9 (quote); and Carta de Tomás López Medel, 25 March 1551, Archivo General de Indias, Seville, Audiencia de Guatemala, legajo 9A, R. 18, N. 77, fol. 10. The transformative effects ascribed to European clothing, and the broader dream of Hispanising the indigenous population, are discussed in Earle, *The Body of the Conquistador*.

of faith. It also demanded the adoption of Christian culture more generally.[43]

As with communities of Muslim converts in Spain, many writers recommended that Amerindians should be required to wear Spanish clothing. The Spanish jurist Juan de Matienzo explained in a sixteenth-century legal treatise how this would bring multiple benefits:

Wearing Spanish clothing not only is not bad, but indeed is good for many reasons. Firstly, because [Amerindians] will thereby grow to love us and our clothes; secondly because they will thereby begin to be more like men ...; thirdly, being dressed as Spaniards they will be ashamed to sit together in the plaza to eat and drink and get drunk and fourthly, because the more they spend, the more silver they will extract from the earth, and that much more Spanish merchandise will be sold, which will all be to the benefit of the treasury.[44]

Wearing European dress would thus help Amerindians become civilised, or, as Matienzo put it, 'more like men'. It would also facilitate colonial rule, by building bonds of affection between colonisers and colonised. Colonial jurists persisted for the remainder of the colonial era in recommending that Indians should be encouraged to adopt Spanish habits 'in dressing, and in clothing and other laudable customs'.[45] As colonial rule was drawing to its close learned societies in the New World continued to offer prizes for essays demonstrating the benefits of Amerindians dressing in Spanish garb.[46] Such Indians, proclaimed numerous voices, were more intelligent, more civilised and more Catholic than those left to their own sartorial devices.

Colonisers in short vacillated over whether their aim was to transform indigenous society, and indigenous people, into more European societies, and peoples, or whether good governance lay precisely in preventing this from occurring. The inconsistencies between the various royal orders cited at the chapter's start illustrate this vacillation. In 1593 the Spanish crown determined that Amerindians in Quito were permitted to wear the

---

[43] José María Martín Ruíz, 'Política y moral en el siglo de oro: el memorial del Morisco Francisco Nuñez Muley', *Baetica. Estudios de Arte, Geografía e Historia* 17 (1995): 391–402; Mary Elizabeth Perry, *The Handless Maiden: Moriscos and the Politics of Religion in Early Modern Spain* (Princeton: Princeton University Press, 2005); and Chapter 9 in this volume by Amanda Wunder.

[44] Juan de Matienzo, *Gobierno del Perú*, ed. Guillermo Lohmann Villena (1567; repr. Paris and Lima: Institut Français d'Études Andines, 1967), 69–70.

[45] Juan de Solórzano Pereira, *Política indiana*, 2 vols. (1647; repr. Madrid, 1736), i: 30, 196–197 (quote); Bernardo Ward, *Proyecto económico, en que se proponen varias providencias, dirigidas á promover los intereses de España* (Madrid, 1787), 266; and Vicente, *Clothing the Spanish Empire*, 78–83.

[46] *Junta pública de la Real Sociedad Económica de Amantes de la Patria de Guatemala celebrada en 12 de Diciembre de 1796* (Nueva Guatemala, 1796), 19–20.

same garments as Europeans, and were subject to the same sumptuary legislation. Less than four decades later indigenous residents of southern Mexico were subject to a sweeping range of restrictions that greatly impeded their ability to dress as Europeans. This reflects not legislative carelessness or the targeting of specific communities, but rather the fundamental uncertainties at the heart of early modern colonialism.

To be sure, colonial sumptuary laws reflected diverse and changing concerns. In some regions missionaries struggled to outlaw what they regarded as nudity by stipulating what clothing should be worn during religious services.[47] Other writers, like the jurist Juan de Matienzo, hoped that obliging Amerindians to wear European clothing would benefit Spanish commerce and industry. At times, such as after the anti-colonial Tupac Amaru Rebellion, which convulsed the Andes in the late eighteenth century, certain indigenous garments were viewed as subversive, and were accordingly prohibited on political rather than economic or moral grounds.[48] The nature of the Spanish state, and its overall approach to the regulation of economic and social practices, dress included, as well as the relative availability of different commodities, also experienced significant change from the sixteenth to eighteenth centuries, as other contributions to this volume demonstrate. The forces shaping New World sumptuary legislation, in short, varied over the three centuries of colonial rule. Nonetheless uncertainty over whether colonial rule required firm divisions between colonisers and colonised, or instead ever closer integration, characterised Spanish policy throughout the early modern era. Sumptuary legislation formed part of a larger body of persistently contradictory colonial regulation because this contradiction lay at the core of early modern colonialism.

The art historian Carolyn Dean has labelled this the coloniser's quandary: 'the paradoxical need to enculturate the colonized and encourage mimesis while, at the same time, upholding and maintaining the difference that legitimizes colonization'.[49] Scholars such as Homi Bhabha have likewise reminded us of the discomfort caused to colonisers by too close an imitation of their ways by wily colonised people, and of the persistent efforts by colonial legislators to prohibit, contain and neutralise

---

[47] Víctor Manuel Patiño, *Historia de la cultura material en la América Equinoccial*, vol. 4: *Vestidos, adornos y vida social* (Bogotá: Instituto Caro y Cuervo, 1990).

[48] Charles Walker, *Smoldering Ashes: Cuzco and the Creation of Republican Peru, 1780–1840* (Durham and London: Duke University Press, 1999), 53–54.

[49] Dean, *Inka Bodies and the Body of Christ*, 47 (quote); Carolyn Dean and Dana Leibsohn, 'Hybridity and its Discontents: Considering Visual Culture in Colonial Spanish America', *Colonial Latin American Review* 12/1 (2003): 5–35; and Earle, *The Body of the Conquistador*.

the destabilising effects of colonial mimicry. As Bhabha writes, 'it is as if the very emergence of the "colonial" is dependent for its representation upon some strategic limitation or prohibition *within* the authoritative discourse itself'.[50] The contradictory nature of colonial recommendations regarding indigenous dress reflects well the persistent underlying tensions inherent in Europe's colonising endeavours, both in the Americas and in Europe itself.

Conclusions: Reprehensible Imitation and Unauthorised Transformations

Racially-inflected sumptuary legislation was enacted, or at least advocated, in many of Europe's New World colonies. Settlers in eighteenth-century Brazil repeatedly asked the Portuguese crown to legislate against the perceived excesses of the clothing worn by non-whites, and the metropolis obliged – although, as Francisco Bethencourt shows in Chapter 10 of this volume, this legislation did not go uncontested. In the French colony of Saint Domingue sumptuary legislation specifically banned free people of colour from the 'reprehensible imitation' of the clothing, jewellery and hairstyles worn by whites. Free people of colour were instead required to dress in accordance with 'the simplicity of their condition'.[51] Comparable legislation affecting enslaved people was issued in South Carolina and the Dutch Antilles.[52]

The widespread recourse to such legislation suggests a broader recognition of clothing's transformative potential, and in particular its ability to transport the wearer across the frontiers of caste. Clothing, as

[50] Homi Bhabha, 'Of Mimicry and Man: The Ambivalence of Colonial Discourse', *October* 28 (1984): 127 (quote); Homi Bhabha, 'Signs Taken for Wonders: Questions of Ambivalence and Authority under a Tree outside Delhi, May 1817', *Critical Inquiry* 12/1 (1985): 144–165; and Robert Young, *Colonial Desire: Hybridity in Theory, Culture and Race* (London: Routledge, 1995).

[51] Silvia Hunold Lara, 'The Signs of Color: Women's Dress and Racial Relations in Salvador and Rio de Janeiro, ca. 1750–1815', *Colonial Latin American Review* 6/2 (1997): 205–224; Réglament provisoire des Administrateurs, concernant le Luxe des Gens de couleur, 9 February 1779, in Médéric-Louis-Élie Moreau de Saint-Méry, *Loix et Constitutions des Colonies Françoises de l'Amérique sous le vent*, 6 vols. (Paris, 1784–90), v: 855–856; and Chapters 10 by Francisco Bethencourt and 13 by Robert DuPlessis in this volume. See also Nandini Chaturvedula, 'On the Precipice of Ruin: Consumption, Sumptuary Laws, and Decadence in Early Modern Portuguese India', *Journal of World History* 26/2 (2015): 355–384.

[52] William Wiecek, 'The Statutory Law of Slavery and Race in the Thirteen Mainland Colonies of British America', *William and Mary Quarterly* 34/2 (1977): 268; Neville Hall, *Slave Society in the Danish West Indies: St. Thomas, St. John and St. Croix*, ed. B.W. Higman (Baltimore: Johns Hopkins University Press, 1992), 116, 148–149; and Chapter 13 by DuPlessis in this volume.

scholars of early modern Europe increasingly recognise, did not simply reflect identity but actively helped produce it.[53] Does this in turn reflect a shared understanding of the nature of caste, or race, in early modern Europe and the Atlantic world? The growing scholarship on the importance of clothing in marking out the boundaries between Jews, Christians and Muslims suggests precisely this. It was important, perhaps, to prevent bodies from wearing the wrong sorts of clothing not simply because this might mislead others, or provoke disorder, or encourage wasteful spending or incite immorality. Perhaps unauthorised sartorial crossings, in Europe as in Mexico, also activated clothing's 'transnaturing power' through its ability to change the bodies of the wearers.

This, in turn, suggests the inadequacy, or insufficiency, of distinctions between embodied conditions, on the one hand, and cultural practice on the other, between inside and outside, between bodies and clothes, when considering early modern ideas about corporeal difference, or what we might call race. Perhaps rather than disputing whether early modern models of physical difference are best labelled as racial, or by some other term, we should instead focus on the features that characterised these mutable bodies and their fluid relationships to their cultural environment. Sumptuary legislation, viewed from this perspective, helps reveal how, for many hundreds of years, the body and its garments merged smoothly into one, to the enduring consternation of legislators' and officials, who sought, Canute-like, to control the disruptive potential of a change of clothes.

---

[53] See for instance Claire Sponsler, *Drama and Resistance. Bodies, Goods, and Theatricality in Late Medieval England* (Minneapolis: University of Minnesota Press, 1997); Martha Howell, *Commerce Before Capitalism in Europe, 1300–1600* (Cambridge: Cambridge University Press, 2010), esp. 243–245; and Ulinka Rublack, *Dressing Up: Cultural Identity in Renaissance Europe* (Oxford: Oxford University Press, 2010).

13 Sartorial Sorting in the Colonial Caribbean and North America

*Robert S. DuPlessis**

Sumptuary legislation is most frequently envisaged as state-sponsored restriction on expense and ostentation in dress as materialised in rich fabrics, costly ornamentation and exaggerated styles. Statutes of this type existed in seventeenth- and eighteenth-century British, French and Dutch North American and West Indian colonies, but they were few in number. Yet 'rules of conduct or procedure established by custom, agreement or authority' aimed at 'regulating or limiting personal behavior', notably sartorial expression—to quote more expansive definitions of 'law' and 'sumptuary'—were ubiquitous in those settlements.[1] Promulgated by religious and secular institutions, entailing unwritten and written ordinances, and as likely to involve provision as consumption of attire, collectively they addressed many groups within the varied colonial populations, and some engaged nearby indigenous societies.

In the colonies, as in the European metropoles, sumptuary measures presumed that perceptible sartorial distinctions expressed and helped constitute a social order. But whereas European laws mainly focused on gender, class, wealth and profession as the salient criteria of difference, New World enactments more often fixated on legal status and race. Metropolitan regulations challenged what authorities perceived as immoderate and immoral demand on the part of at least formally free people. The same concerns animated some North American and Caribbean regulations. But other laws applied to the substantial and increasing numbers of the populace in permanent and temporary bondage, individuals who only exceptionally pursued sartorial excess (or allegedly did so). Legally and economically hobbled against exercising choice about what they wore, such men and women were most likely to experience sumptuary intervention in the form of mandates about supply. For most slaves and indentured servants, for most of the time, the right to dress meant a claim to some modicum of clothing the satisfaction

* Thanks to Chris Densmore, Curator of the Friends Historical Library, Swarthmore College, for help in locating illustrations of Quaker dress.
[1] *The American Heritage College Dictionary*, 3rd ed. (Boston: Houghton Mifflin, 1993), ss.vv.

of which was granted not to them but to those who possessed them. So often, however, was that claim fulfilled inadequately or not at all that laws were deemed necessary not to restrict slave and servant dress, but simply to ensure they received even rudimentary attire.

'Excesse in Apparrell': Legislating Acceptable Dress

In continental North America, the sole instances of European-style sumptuary laws appeared early – only a few years, in fact, after the foundation of the Massachusetts Bay (est. 1630) and Connecticut (est. 1636) colonies. Like metropolitan acts, the ordinances issued by these colonies' assemblies (known as 'General Courts') were justified by a combination of moral, religious and financial reasons; concentrated on pricey and showy adornments and accessories; and, in their final and most complete iterations, were particularly concerned to maintain a proper correspondence between social standing and sartorial performance.

Decrying 'greate, ... & unnecessary expences', 'the nourishing of pride & exhausting of mens estates', and 'evill example to others', initial Massachusetts Bay 'Orders' of 1634, 1636 and 1639 attributed these scourges both to unspecified 'newe & immodest fashions' and to 'the ordineary [frequent] weareing' of a list of items including gold, silver, silk and bone 'laces, girdles, hatbands &c'; wide and slashed sleeves and breeches; cutwork, other needlework and embroidered caps, sashes and 'rayles' (scarves or shawls); ruffs; beaver hats; even long hair. Established markers of class, wealth, pomp and (often) royalism in England, in Puritan New England these styles and accoutrements were summarily dismissed as 'superfluities tending to little use or benefit', condemned as 'uncomely, or preijdiciall to the common good', and banned. No particular group of offending consumers was identified: indeed, the 1639 law put on notice 'all ... of what quality or estate soever they may bee'. But the orders did bar everyone (while singling out tailors) from making garments with sleeves short enough to bare the arm or (though only if for women) more than half an ell wide. They also forbade adding lace or points to any attire – unless (a faint echo of European sumptuary laws that sought to protect or promote local economic interests, as noted in the introduction to this volume) the item was to be taken out of Massachusetts Bay. The civil authorities did not appoint special sumptuary officials, instead summoning clergy and congregants to enforce their decrees in order to repress 'disorders in apparrell' and 'attaine a generall reformation'.[2]

---

[2] Nathaniel B. Shurtleff (ed.), *Records of the Governor and Company of the Massachusetts Bay in New England*, 5 vols. in 6 (Boston: W. White, 1853–1854), i: 126, 163, 274–275. All quotations here and subsequently are *sic*.

Vain hopes, it seems, since when nearby Connecticut – a direct offshoot of Massachusetts Bay – enacted an attempt at a sumptuary ordinance in 1641, the text conceded that a previous (lost) edict 'conserneing the restraint of excesse in apparrell' had been flouted, and (perhaps tacitly acknowledging the failure of ecclesiastical discipline) vested enforcement of the new directive solely with town constables.[3] Whether reflecting a similar despair at controlling, much less remaking, sartorial habits or (what seems less likely in light of 1639 laments about 'excessive wearing' of unacceptable apparel) a conviction that it had successfully done so, in November 1644, without warning or explanation, the General Court of Massachusetts Bay repealed 'all former orders made about apparrell and lace'.[4] Whatever its cause, the hands-off mood proved evanescent. In 1651, the colony returned to the sumptuary lists with its most comprehensive law; moreover, following Connecticut's lead – its brief 1641 order had warned residents that their dress must not 'exceede their condition and ranks' – Massachusetts Bay now focused on attire's social signification.

To be sure, neither colony wholly abandoned religious/moral justifications for combatting what magistrates deemed extravagant dress. Even in the later seventeenth century, each defined itself as professing the Gospel in a 'wilderness condition', wherein showy attire dishonoured God while corrupting settlers.[5] Yet it can hardly be coincidental that in the 1650s to 1670s, a period of often painful economic adjustment, confusing social change and political tensions, both Massachusetts Bay and Connecticut decreed sumptuary laws that condemned 'excesse in apparriell' for disrupting hierarchies of wealth, status and authority and endorsed 'sober and moderate' dress.[6] The enactments did not broaden the definition of censured sartorial behaviour beyond showy accessories

---

[3] J. Hammond Trumball and Charles J. Hoadly (eds.), *The Public Records of the Colony of Connecticut*, 15 vols. (Hartford: Brown & Parsons et al., 1850–1890), i: 64.

[4] Shurtleff (ed.), *Records of the Governor and Company of the Massachusetts Bay*, ii: 84.

[5] Ibid., iv, pt. 2: 41 (1662): Trumball and Hoadly (eds.), *The Public Records of the Colony of Connecticut*, ii: 283 (1676).

[6] Except as noted, all quotations from Shurtleff (ed.), *Records of the Governor and Company of the Massachusetts Bay*, iii: 243–244 (1651), 261 (1652 insertion of an omitted phrase), repeated in iv, pt. 2: 61–62; Trumball and Hoadly (eds.), *The Public Records of the Colony of Connecticut*, ii: 283 (1676), which copied much of the language and all of the tone and focus of the 1651 and 1662 Massachusetts Bay ordinances; OED, s.v. For contemporary conditions, see Jackson Turner Main, *Society and Economy in Colonial Connecticut* (Princeton: Princeton University Press, 1985); and Marsha L. Hamilton, *Social and Economic Networks in Early Massachusetts. Atlantic Connections* (University Park, PA: Penn State University Press, 2009).

and adornments, nor denounce additional items save 'great bootes'. But magistrates now avowed, at length and repeatedly, their 'utter detestation and dislike' when persons 'of meane condition' had the impudence to 'take upon them the garbe of gentlemen'. It was 'intollerable', Massachusetts Bay officials intoned, that such individuals should dare to bedeck themselves in items 'allowable to persons of greater estates, or more liberall education'. It was a punishable offence, their Connecticut counterparts added, for individuals to 'make or ware or buy any apparell exceding the quality and condition of their persons and estates or that is apparently beyond the necessary end of apparell for covering or comelyness [propriety or decency]'. According to the anxious authorities, clothing's function of embodying and sustaining the correct social structure was being eroded.

In order to prevent such blatant disregard of rank-appropriate sartorial performance – in order to ensure that colonists would dress so as not to 'exceed their ranckes and abillitie in the costlynes or fashion of theire apparrill in any respect' – donning items repeated from the 1630s lists was forbidden to anyone with an estate valued at less than £150 (Connecticut) or £200 (Massachusetts Bay).[7] The strictures did, however, exempt public officials and their immediate families, military officers and soldiers in active service, those privileged by 'education & implojyments … above the ordjinary degree', and individuals 'whose estates have bineene considerable, though now decayed'. Clergy were not, however, mentioned as deserving to be maintained within the sartorial elite. Interestingly, gender continued to play a minor role in the sumptuary imaginary of authorities in these colonies – both 'men and weomen' were arraigned and the dress of both was to be regulated – while class, or at least wealth and socio-cultural capital, became of primary importance.

In 1675, Massachusetts Bay leaders noted ruefully the 'neglect of due execution' of their 'wholesome lawes … for restreyning excesse in apparrell', not to mention the popularity of 'vajne, new, strainge fashions' ('naked breasts and armes' and 'superstitious ribbons both on hajre & apparrell').[8] But as they and their Connecticut colleagues well knew, resistance to sumptuary edicts had existed for as long as they had been promulgated, no matter whether the authorities appealed to religious dictates, to financial prudence, or to a hypothesised social

---

[7] A 1662 Massachusetts 'adition' extended the constraints to children and servants and to tailors who fashioned their apparel. Shurtleff (ed.), *Records of the Governor and Company of the Massachusetts Bay*, iv pt. 2: 41–44.

[8] Ibid., v: 59–60.

order. Perhaps in response, but seeking to realise at least a monetary benefit from their ordinances, both colonies introduced a graduated schedule of fines that had the potential, at least, to turn the colonial sumptuary laws into a luxury tax system that would provide revenue, on the model of some European states (as discussed in Maria Muzzarelli's Chapter 6 and Matthew Romaniello's Chapter 9 in this volume). But even that project seems to have been half-hearted: in Massachusetts Bay county courts were allowed to impose fines 'at their discretion'.[9]

The General Courts cast their regulations as means of stemming the advance of fashion as a criterion governing dress behaviour throughout their colonies. Yet their specific ordinances actually accepted a modicum of sartorial novelty, if grudgingly, tacitly and only for a select few, while seeking to prevent its adoption by groups whose fashionable dressing would confound what officials took to be a desirable socio-sartorial order. By identifying attire that defined social difference, and trying to restrict its consumption, the Courts created a right to dress freely for a sartorially privileged elite and a right of permissible dress defined by limits and exclusions for the majority. From all evidence, however, these distinctions mattered little in practice; 'poore & rich' adopted 'strainge fashions', and officials' 'excesse' became the norm. It is not surprising, therefore, that no other North American mainland colony of Britain, France or the Netherlands ventured such laws against free settlers, and indeed only one passed a general sumptuary measure directed at any group of settlers whatsoever. That exception was a 1735 South Carolina law.[10] Like the earlier New England statutes, it was animated by concerns about men and women who 'wear clothes much above the[ir] condition'. But that condition was slavery, and those who dressed 'above' it were accused not of pride or immorality but of using 'sinister and evil methods' to obtain their improper garb. Whereas the Massachusetts and Connecticut measures emerged from within the free-settler communities at which their rules were directed, moreover, the South Carolina sumptuary regulation was one element of an increasingly comprehensive body of slave law in a colony where the number of men and women in bondage

---

[9] Ibid., v: 60.
[10] 'An Act for the better ordering and governing Negroes and other slaves', 29 March 1735, in David James McCord (ed.), *The Statutes at Large of South Carolina*, 8 vols. (Columbia: A. S. Johnston, 1840), vii: 396, Art. XXXVI. The act was renewed in 1740 in the wake of the fearsome Stono Rebellion, and again in 1783 after the disruptive revolutionary years; see 'An Act for the better Ordering and Governing Negroes and other Slaves in this Province', 10 May 1740, [Art.] XL, in John Faucheraud Grimké, *The Public Laws of the State of South-Carolina* (Philadelphia: W. Aitken & Son, 1790), 173–174. The 1783 renewal is in Ibid., 175.

had risen dramatically as rice and indigo cultivation expanded.[11] In addition, that single article commanded much broader restrictions than all the New England acts combined, as it forbade every slave 'to have or wear any sort of apparel whatsoever' made up from fabrics 'finer, other, or of greater value than' any of ten enumerated varieties of cheap linens, woollens and cottons.

Significantly, the South Carolina measure did not outlaw all costly or modish attire or ornaments from slave bodies. On the contrary, its strictures specifically exempted 'livery-men and boys' – that is, slaves whose costumes publicly displayed their owners' wealth and station.[12] For the great majority of the enslaved, however, the law decreed that their clothing was to be made only of inexpensive, generally unfashionable textiles, no matter whether supplied by masters or by the slaves' own labour.[13] Adding injury to insult, the act 'authorised, empowered and required' any free person to confiscate any and all offending attire from the enslaved 'for their own use, benefit and behoof', irrespective of 'any law, usage or custom to the contrary'. The rubric did not seek to establish distinctive slave dress, and apart from Negro cloth, inventories show none of the fabrics was racially coded or worn only by slaves.[14] But while revealing that whites considered cloth a transparent marker of status, the law clearly intended to brand slaves as worthy only of the most basic garb unless serving as components of their masters' public self-presentation.

The remaining colonial sumptuary laws redolent of metropolitan precedents were promulgated in the Caribbean as plantation agriculture and labour developed rapidly during the economic boom after the Seven Years' War.[15] The initial ones targeted specific aspects of the

[11] See Peter Coclanis, *The Shadow of a Dream. Economic Life and Death in the South Carolina Low Country 1670–1920* (New York: Oxford University Press, 1989); Peter Wood, *Black Majority. Negroes in Colonial South Carolina from 1670 through the Stono Rebellion* (New York: Knopf, 1974); Jack P. Greene, Rosemary Brana-Shute and Randy J. Sparks (eds.), *Money, Trade, and Power. The Evolution of Colonial South Carolina's Plantation Society* (Columbia: University of South Carolina Press, 2001).

[12] On slave livery, see also Linda Baumgarten, *What Clothes Reveal: The Language of Clothing in Colonial and Federal America* (New Haven: Yale University Press, 2002), 128–132, and figs. 37, 182–186.

[13] On slave modes of earning money for clothing, and the apparel they purchased, see Robert S. DuPlessis, *The Material Atlantic. Clothing, Commerce, and Colonization in the Atlantic World, 1650–1800* (Cambridge: Cambridge University Press, 2016), 75–77, 135–137, 151–159. South Carolina's permitted fabrics were Negro cloth (also known as plains or kendal cottons), duffel, coarse kersey and Scots plaid woollens; oznabrig (ozenbrig), blue, check and coarse garlix linens; calico and checked cottons (the latter actually a linen-cotton blend). To guarantee that slaves would only wear cheap cloth, check, plaid, garlix and calico could cost no more than 10 shillings a yard.

[14] See ibid., 137–140.

[15] Trevor Burnard and John Garrigus, *The Plantation Machine. Atlantic Capitalism in French Saint-Domingue and British Jamaica* (Philadelphia: University of Pennsylvania Press,

dress of enslaved men and women in Dutch Surinam, beginning with a 1760 prohibition on slaves wearing hats in public; in 1769, shoes and stockings lengthened the list of forbidden garb. Eight years later most gold finery and jewellery were also banned, though gold earrings and small gold clasps on necklaces and bracelets were expressly permitted.[16] Elements of ever more comprehensive acts policing the enslaved, these proscriptions aimed at making clear and formalising the demarcation of slaves from the colony's growing population of free people of colour by putting a statutory imprimatur on widely acknowledged, if erratically implemented, status-based sartorial distinctions.[17]

More ambitious in scope and racial rather than status-based in inspiration and orientation were French Caribbean sumptuary laws regarding *gens de couleur*, politically and socially liminal but economically and militarily significant individuals of mixed ancestry as well as formerly enslaved men and women who had earned or been granted freedom.[18] Not isolated enactments, the statutes formed part of a larger campaign to signal, stigmatise, separate and subordinate the largest, wealthiest and most rapidly expanding group of free people of colour in the New World colonies according to racialised notions of public behaviour and sartorial presentation that whites considered appropriate.[19] The offensive restricted carrying of weapons, forbade use of 'white' surnames, blocked access to professions and complicated inheritance, among many other vexations. It gathered force from the 1760s with the arrival of a wave of new settlers and officials from Europe influenced by the teachings of

---

2016); Trevor Burnard, *Planters, Merchants, and Slaves. Plantation Societies in British America, 1650–1820* (Chicago: University of Chicago Press, 2015).

[16] Jacob Adriaan Schiltkamp and Jacobus Thomas de Smidt (eds.), *West Indisch Plakaatboek: Plakaten, Ordonnantiën en Andere Wetten, Uitgevaardigd in Suriname, 1667–1816*, 2 vols. (Amsterdam: S. Emmering, 1973), i: 690 (no. 574); ii: 820 (no. 701); ii: 927 (no. 778).

[17] That particulars of dress were used to differentiate the two groups is indicated by a 1799 Surinam decree (reissued 1804) that forbade all slaves (save those under government orders) and free people of colour ('unless they wear shoes and stockings') to appear in public at night; *Plakaten, Ordonnantiën en Andere Wetten, Uitgevaardigd in Suriname*, ii: 1190 (no. 935), 1230 (no. 968). For lack of hats, shoes and stockings as marks of enslavement, see DuPlessis, *The Material Atlantic*, 131.

[18] See Stewart R. King, *Blue Coat or Powdered Wig: Free People of Color in Pre-revolutionary Saint Domingue* (Athens: University of Georgia Press, 2001); John Garrigus, *Before Haiti: Race and Citizenship in French Saint-Domingue* (New York: Palgrave Macmillan, 2006).

[19] The fact that 'no substantial community of free people of colour existed in British America in the eighteenth century', as Trevor Burnard has shown (and contrasts to Saint-Domingue, 'where free coloureds made up nearly half of the free population ..., and where they were both wealthy and politically assertive'), likely explains the lack of such enactments in British colonies; see Burnard, *Planters, Merchants, and Slaves*, 153–154, 172–173.

pseudoscientific Enlightenment racism, by the well-developed metropolitan discourse about *luxe*, and by the competition offered by free people of colour in the French West Indies.[20] An initial sumptuary ordinance seems to have been promulgated in Martinique, but it is an apparently similar 1779 ruling in Saint-Domingue that has survived.[21]

The long peroration that began the *réglement* disclosed the issues at stake. Denouncing the 'extreme *luxe* in wearing apparel and adornments in which free people of colour, unsophisticated and freed people of both genders, indulge', it announced that such *luxe*, which 'astonished' officials and the general public, had to be restrained. The text went on to outline a view of the principles that should inform free people of colour's deportment, including but not limited to the sartorial: 'simplicity', 'propriety', 'respect, the essential adjunct of their status', and 'modesty, which many of them seem to have forgotten'; it also chastised merchants for violating 'the superior interest of *moeurs*' ('morality' but also 'habits' or 'customs') by pursuing mercenary self-interest, apparently by selling free people of colour inappropriate apparel rather than goods 'for use in moderation'. By way of conclusion, the directive defined free people of colour's 'excess or near-excess': dressing so as to resemble whites; flaunting 'magnificent and costly finery'; and 'arrogance that can accompany such dress and scandal that always does'. Leaving the racial inflection aside, the complaints differed little in substance from those directed against New Englanders 'of meane condition' a century earlier – striking evidence of how widely sociocultural change, unsettling to those in power, motivated sumptuary legislation.

The regulation mandated three remedies, listed in an order that wittingly or not underlined the preoccupations concerning comportment and racial ordering that animated at least officialdom's – and, in the act's telling, all whites' – apprehensions about the sartorial habits of free people of colour. The first enjoined all *gens de couleur* to accord 'the

[20] For the laws, see Louis-Élie Moreau de Saint-Méry, *Loix et Constitutions des Colonies Françoises de l'Amérique Sous le Vent*, 6 vols. (Paris: Chez l'Auteur et al., 1784–90), vols. iv and v; for the broader context of discrimination, Garrigus, *Before Haiti*. In the eighteenth century, *luxe* meant 'excessive sumptuousness [*somptuosité excessive*] in dress, furnishings, food, etc.' – not coincidentally the targets of sumptuary laws. See *Dictionnaires d'autrefois*: http://artflsrv02.uchicago.edu/cgi-bin/dicos/pubdico1look.pl?strippedhw=luxe [last accessed 6 January 2018].

[21] A 1778 letter advises the *Procureur-Général* (Attorney-General) of the *Conseil Supérieur* of Cap François, Saint-Domingue, to petition the *Administrateurs* of the colony (royal officials as distinct from the colonials on the *Conseils Supérieurs*) for an ordinance 'to repress the *luxe* that prevails among slaves [*Negres*] and free mulattos of both genders' like the one passed in Martinique (Moreau de Saint-Méry, *Loix et Constitutions*, v: 823), of which no copy appears to exist. The 1779 Saint-Domingue act, which does not mention slaves, was indeed issued by the *Administrateurs*.

greatest respect ... to each and every white person', threatening severe punishment including enslavement for violations. The next forbade free people of colour to 'feign in their garments, coiffures [at the time signifying both headgear and hairstyling], attire, or finery a reprehensible assimilation' of their mode of dressing to that of whites, then commanded them 'to maintain the signs that have served until today to denote the distinctive character of their attire and coiffures'. The order closed by prohibiting free people of colour from wearing 'externally visible objects of *luxe* incompatible with the plainness of their status and origins'.[22]

The act was at once sweeping, focused and vague. Borrowing a common observation about West Indian free colonist dress—that it was extravagant and ostentatious, tailored from luxurious fabrics and covered with showy ornamentation—the law criminalised such apparel when chosen by *gens de couleur*, while implicitly valorising it as part of white Antillean identity.[23] So while the regulation trumpeted precepts of moral dressing and associated them with general propriety, it applied them discriminatorily to racialised groups within the free population, in violation of articles 57 and 59 of the so-called 'Code Noir' of 1685 by which all free settlers were to enjoy the same rights and privileges.[24] By so doing, the 1779 ordinance instituted race as the governing sumptuary criterion, rather than wealth and traditional rank (as in New England), status (as in South Carolina and Surinam), or gender and occupation (as in many other sumptuary acts).[25] The decree also left the operable definition and quotidian application of the rules of dress and decorum wholly up to whites: with no statutory specification of what constituted permitted and forbidden attire, white perceptions would determine what was excess and what simplicity, what was decency and what immodesty, just as they would decide what conduct by free people of colour embodied respect and what arrogance. *Gens de couleur* were responsible for maintaining a proper distance from whites, but whites got to interpret – and reinterpret when and as often as they pleased – that distance's expanse and when and how free people of colour trespassed its borders.

---

[22] Moreau de Saint-Méry, *Loix et Constitutions*, v: 855–856.

[23] For examples and more discussion of the trope, see DuPlessis, *The Material Atlantic*, 164–165. At least with whites, the charge was not always misplaced: in 1762 the Superior Council of Port-au-Prince, Saint-Domingue, had to order attorneys and bailiffs to wear in court only black rather than the 'indecent' and undignified brightly coloured clothing they favoured; Moreau de Saint-Méry, *Loix et Constitutions*, iv: 508–509.

[24] *Édit du Roi, Touchant la Police des Isles de l'Amérique Françoise* (Paris: n.p., 1687). The articles never mention race or colour, only '*affranchis*' and '*personnes nées libres*'.

[25] Besides many of the essays in this collection, see, for example, a 1786 'Proclamation of good government' (*Bando de buen govierno*) by the incoming Spanish governor of Louisiana that included a provision directed solely at the hair and headgear styles of women of colour. See Charles Gayarré, *History of Louisiana. The Spanish Domination* (New York: Redfield, 1854), 178–179.

Judging by contemporary ordinances about uniforms for separate grenadier companies for *gens de couleur* and whites, officialdom intended sartorial differences between the two groups to be subtle but visible: for example, yellow cuffs (*paremens*) and epaulets for free men of colour, white for whites; white and yellow feathers in free coloured drummers' hats, white in whites'.[26] Both the subtlety and the visibility were the point. Marks of distinction, after all, are prized precisely because they are at once fine and likely to be noticed. Even more, the sumptuary law was exquisitely calculated to keep free people of colour off balance, subject to white whims and thus perpetually vulnerable to challenge whenever in public. In contrast to other sumptuary ordinances, the 1779 law's lack of any exceptions sharply narrowed the sartorial space that *gens de couleur* occupied, while the coercive power granted to whites was measurably increased by its inclusiveness: no item of the dress of free people of colour, just as no group of such people, was exempt from surveillance. Any and all aspects of their wardrobes were liable, the law announced, to fall under strictures of a *luxe* illicit because found on the bodies of *gens de couleur*, who thereby illegitimately bridged an undefined – but definable to and by whites – racial divide.

From all evidence, the sumptuary laws enacted against slaves and free people of colour had little influence on dress practices. All the fabrics deemed acceptable for slave clothing in South Carolina's ordinance were either already being worn by slaves, or were never found on their bodies.[27] Yet whatever that measure's sartorial intention, its main effect was to remind whites about the material signs of subordination, the tangible renderings of the social order of slavery. For their part, Saint-Domingue probate inventories indicate that free people of colour dressed the same as whites of their wealth level, occupation or gender; if anything, their outfits were more restrained, like those worn by the free mulatto planter and his wife depicted by Antonio Brunias in 1780 (Figure 13.1).[28] There, too, vestiary issues seem to have been of secondary concern to officials. Rather, the 1779 act was mainly notable for articulating a white vision of sartorially performed distinctive racial behaviour and for adding to the growing arsenal that increased white legal authority in the face of the economic and at least perceived cultural power of *gens de couleur*. The dress display of free people of colour apparently annoyed white Caribbean settlers because it indicated that their own hegemony was

---

[26] Moreau de Saint-Méry, *Loix et Constitutions*, v: 860–862. All wore blue woollen coats with stiff collar, white buttons and crosswise pocket, lined with off-white linen, along with white linen waistcoat and breeches.

[27] DuPlessis, *The Material Atlantic*, 138. Negro cloth was far and away the predominant textile in which the South Carolina enslaved were dressed, ozenbrig linen a distant second.

[28] Ibid., 190–194.

Figure 13.1 *Planter and his Wife, with a Servant,* by Agostino Brunias, c. 1780. Yale Center for British Art, Paul Mellon Collection, New Haven, Connecticut, B1981.25.81.

The well-to-do *gens de couleur* couple in the foreground of this West Indian scene dress soberly but well in fine fabrics, fashionable shoes and hats, and adornments befitting their position. The woman who accompanies them wears a domestic servant's version of the hegemonic slave costume.

insecure. Restrictions on *gens de couleur* attire were a synecdoche for restrictions on the group's position within the broader colonial social ecology in which *luxe* was permissible self-presentation if exhibited by whites, but a scandalous arrogance if displayed by free people of colour.

A 1785 enactment in the Dutch Caribbean island colony of St. Eustatius is instructive about the racial motives and stigmatising intent of late eighteenth century Antillean measures. It also represents something of a *reductio ad absurdum* of colonial sumptuary laws. After railing about the 'increasing insolence and licentiousness' of free people of colour, and the 'bad treatment' that they meted out to whites, all free people of colour were ordered – 'men as well as women' – to wear a red ribbon on the breast 'as a token of their freedom', while slaves were firmly forbidden to wear 'such a distinguished red ribbon of freedom'.[29] That a scrap of trim, or its absence, would represent both race and status was testimony at once to the perceived power and to the substantive triviality of sumptuary law.

'Plain Apparell': Codifying Normative Dress

Though conventional sumptuary laws were few in number in the British, Dutch and French New World, a plethora of regulations formal and informal, official and customary, powerfully shaped and in some instances closely determined how denizens of these colonies, and some of their aboriginal neighbours, dressed themselves. The most far-reaching and most successful rules governing attire issued from within small, homogeneous religious communities, constrained only their members (but all of them), were essentially unwritten, and rested solely on the groups' own internal coercive procedures.

Most comprehensive were dress regulations among the Amish and Mennonites, closely related Anabaptist sects that immigrated to rural Pennsylvania starting in the late seventeenth century.[30] Virtual non-state

---

[29] Jacob Adriaan Schiltkamp and Jacobus Thomas de Smidt (eds.), *West Indisch Plakaatboek: Publikaties en Andere Wetten Betrekking hebbende op St. Maarten St. Eustatius Saba, 1648/1681–1816* (Amsterdam: S. Emmering, 1979), 327 (no. 69). A similar act passed on St. Maarten in 1808 specified that men had to wear the ribbon on the left breast, women on the right, 'in such a way that everyone in public can see it'. Ibid., 210–211 (doc. 245).

[30] See Donald B. Kraybill, Karen Johnson-Weiner and Steven Nolt, *The Amish* (Baltimore: Johns Hopkins University Press, 2013), 33–34, 103–105, 125–130; Donald B. Kraybill, *The Riddle of Amish Culture*, rev. ed. (Baltimore: Johns Hopkins University Press, 2001), 45–46, 54–70, 112–115, 303–305; Melvin Gingerich, *Mennonite Attire Through Four Centuries* (Breinigsville, PA: Pennsylvania German Society, 1970). The complex and intertwined history of the two groups, formed by mutual excommunication in the late seventeenth century and frequent cooperation ever since, is well told in John Hostetler, *Amish Society*, 4th ed. (Baltimore: Johns Hopkins University Press, 1993).

sumptuary laws, the rules were at once more sweeping and more specific than any others in the colonies, covering nearly all aspects of clothing, head- and foot-gear and hairstyles. Central to each community's *Ordnung*, an orally transmitted code of conduct that governed daily life,[31] dictates about proper dress were considered essential to maintaining separation from 'worldliness', those material goods, styles of deportment, and individually determined attitudes that to Amish and Mennonites represented the immoral antithesis of plainness, modesty and adherence to communal norms that they valued. Not considered scripturally based, nor typically justified by reference to Biblical passages, dress rules changed over time, if slowly, and varied – if slightly – among the individual autonomous congregations; they also differentiated by gender, age, marital and baptismal status and context (e.g. whether garb was worn in public or private, or whether the wearer was in a position of authority).

As Donald Kraybill has pointed out, every *Ordnung* was both 'proscriptive' and 'prescriptive'. On the one hand, all forbade revealing apparel, rich materials and bodily ornamentation (jewellery, makeup, tattoos), and they rejected many recent styles and articles that emerged during the eighteenth century, such as long hair, moustaches, bright colours (notably yellow) and (among Amish) printed and patterned textiles.[32] On the other, *Ordnungen* ordained distinctive hair arrangements (parted in the middle among women, combed with bangs for men), solid colours, particular types of hats and caps, uncut beards, and in general an aura of simplicity and practicality. While dressing more sparely by excluding items suggestive of luxury, ornateness, newfangledness or worldly styles, eighteenth-century Amish and Mennonites were otherwise garbed much like their rural neighbours; over time, moreover, many sect members incorporated things like buttons on shirts and newer fabrics. Thus an *Ordnung* was not so much a blanket rejection of fashion or of sartorial change as a refusal to adopt quickly fashions created externally to the community that might blur, if not wholly efface, the boundaries between the sect and the surrounding society.

The Anabaptist sumptuary codes proved remarkably successful (and continue to function well today) not just because they are rooted in, nourish, and represent the groups' proud separatist and pietistic identities; they both unify the sects and visibly and legibly set them apart from other religions. The rules also work because they are comprehensive, consistent and widely understood. While unyielding in their

---

[31] *Ordnung* is best translated as 'code of discipline'. Still unwritten, *Ordnungen* remain widely understood and followed in the flourishing sectarian communities.

[32] Mennonites allowed patterns, checks and plaids in some garments.

requirements for certain items (such as women's caps and aprons, men's hats and beards) and styles (coverage of most of the body, single colours) that symbolise core values of simplicity and humility – and denote as well their sectarian identity – they are adapted to the specific needs of particular subgroups and open to innovations that do not threaten the core values.

Dress stipulations among Quakers (the Society of Friends), the sect of the Pennsylvania colony's founder William Penn, likewise emphasised simplicity and criticised excess.[33] An admonition issued following a 1698 Philadelphia-area Yearly Meeting, for instance, commended 'plain apparell' that excluded 'gaudy or flowered stuffs or silks', pleats and multi-hued coat linings, 'over Long Scarfs' on women and elaborate hair arrangements.[34] Later Meetings narrowed and more explicitly gendered their sumptuary concern by offering 'tender advice' to 'younger women' not to display 'pride and superfluity' by parting their hair, or by donning caps 'pinched' around the face, 'pleated and leaded sleeves', attire that was 'bare backt & brested', 'gay stomachers' and hoop petticoats.[35]

In contrast to Amish and Mennonites, however, eighteenth-century Friends did not translate 'plainness' into a distinctive costume intended to exhibit separatism or a sartorial opposition to worldliness.[36] No *Ordnung*-like regulations pertained across meetings, and while congregations might counsel Quakers as to what constituted inappropriate garb, the definition of proper plainness was left to the individual.[37] As a result, Friends' dress might legitimately incorporate the rich fabrics evident in numerous inventories and portraits such as Charles Willson Peale's 1772 likeness of Hannah Lambert Cadwalader, wife of a prominent Philadelphia physician (Figure 13.2). Again, Quaker plainness might be manifest in the undyed, barely tailored clothes and uncured leather shoes worn by the

---

[33] Amelia Gummere, *The Quaker: A Study in Costume* (Philadelphia: Ferris & Leach, 1901). For restatement and elaboration, see Deborah Kraak, 'Variations on Quaker Dress in Eighteenth-Century Philadelphia', *Costume* 34/1 (2000): 51–63.

[34] Friends Historical Library, Swarthmore College, Swarthmore, PA, USA, Darby Monthly Meeting, Miscellaneous Papers, Box 1, Advices 1698–1776 and undated, 21 [July] 1698. A Yearly Meeting is a regional organization of monthly meetings, the local congregations to which individual members belong, that makes decisions on matters of general import. All quotations are *sic*.

[35] Ibid., 1714 and 1739.

[36] I follow Robert Ross's definition: 'costume' is 'dress which is donned in order to demonstrate, unambiguously, a specific identity'. See Robert Ross, *Clothing: A Global History* (Cambridge: Polity Press, 2008), 6. As shown below, a costume can be imposed as well as chosen.

[37] For background, see David Shi, 'Early American Simplicity: The Quaker Ethic', in Daniel Doherty and Amitai Etzioni, eds., *Voluntary Simplicity: Responding to Consumer Culture* (Lanham, MD: Rowman & Littlefield, 2003), 101–110.

Figure 13.2 *Portrait of Hannah Lambert Cadwalader* (1712–1788), by Charles Willson Peale, c. 1771. Philadelphia Museum of Art, purchased for the Cadwalader Collection with funds contributed by the Mabel Pew Myrin Trust and the gift of an anonymous donor, 1983-90-2.

Mrs Cadwalader's expensive but muted silk dress, plain silk cap, simple linen cuffs and demure shawl encapsulate perfectly the Quaker elite's desire that their attire combine simplicity and style without ostentation or ornament.

antislavery activist and itinerant preacher John Woolman (1720–1772), depicted in Figure 13.3.[38] Yet because Woolman's attire did – as he intended – excite a great deal of comment, it actually ran counter to the dominant Quaker sartorial ideal, which was to avoid bringing notice to one's garb by either ostentation or inordinate simplicity, for both extremes meant undue attention was being paid to external matters rather than one's inner light. More typically, Deborah Kraak has shown, Friends in colonial North America apparelled in 'the conventional dress of the day, shorn of its excesses'.[39] More than Amish and Mennonites, Quakers accepted reigning fashions; and, like formal sumptuary laws, their dress rules emphasised not overall attire and style but details and selective omissions: for example, both Cadwalader and Woolman eschewed ornamentation on their bodies and their garments alike.

Religiously sanctioned dress rules did not necessarily gain traction, however. Bishops in late seventeenth-century New France learned this when seeking to outlaw styles that to them egregiously and sinfully defied a venerable European postulate that dress should cover virtually the entire body, and which to boot combined this 'nakedness' with '*luxe*' to beget 'immodesty'.[40] Between 1682 and 1697 the bishops repeatedly inveighed against 'the *luxe* and vanity of girls and women' who wore 'indecent' clothing – notably arms, shoulders, throats and heads 'scandalously naked' or at best covered with 'transparent linen' – not to mention curled hair, 'costly and dazzling fabrics ... much above their station or means' and profusions of ribbons and laces. Denying access to sacraments, repeated clerical admonitions, vain appeals to the colony's governor to take action: nothing yielded any results, Bishop Jean de Saint-Vallier ruefully acknowledged; little wonder that none of his eighteenth-century successors nor any secular official saw fit to resume his crusade.[41] As in the Caribbean, so in New France probate inventories

---

[38] See Geoffrey Plank, 'The First Person in Antislavery Literature: John Woolman, His Clothes and His Journal', *Slavery & Abolition* 30/1 (2009): 67–91. Though best known for his abolitionism, Woolman sought much broader reforms tending to simplicity and humility, intending his dress 'to teach by example'. Ibid., 70. See also John Woolman, *The Journal of John Woolman. With an introduction by John G. Whittier* (Boston: J. R. Osgood, 1872), 179–183, 269–270; Michael Meranze, 'Materializing Conscience. Embodiment, Speech, and the Experience of Sympathetic Identification', *Early American Literature* 37/1 (2002): 71–88; Shi, 'Early American Simplicity', 113–132.

[39] Kraak, 'Variations on 'Plainness', 52.

[40] For more on that postulate, see DuPlessis, *The Material Atlantic*, 30–32.

[41] For the bishops' memoranda, ordinances and pleas, see Henri Têtu and Charles-Octave Gagnon (eds.), *Mandements, Lettres Pastorales et Circulaires des Évêques de Québec*, 9 vols. (Quebec: A. Côté et Cie., 1887–98), i: 106–108, 172–173, 185–186, 268–270 and 365–366.

John Woolman

Figure 13.3 *John Woolman*, by anonymous artist. Courtesy of the Friends Historical Library, Swarthmore College, Swarthmore, Pennsylvania.

Woolman's costume eschewed dyed fabrics and 'changeable modes of dress', which he deemed prideful as well as dependent on oppressive slave labour; at the same time, he worried that his style of dress 'savored of an affected singularity' opposed to true humility.

attest that the complaints reflected the anxieties of those who voiced them rather than any sartorial reality.[42] Singling out one segment of the population rather than encompassing the whole community, imperious rather than consensual, wholly negative with no hint of flexibility, the bishops' declarations were little more than echoes of a position not only passé in the metropole from which colonists took their fashion cues but disregarded in colonists' own sartorial performances. The failure of the

[42] For New France dress, see DuPlessis, *The Material Atlantic*, 215–220.

Quebec proposals likewise parallels the fate of the New England laws that in many regards they resembled.

Besides faith-based directives, a broad range of clothing rules policed the right to dress in early modern European empires. Though not devised as sumptuary regulations, legislated provisioning codes for indentured servants and slaves had the largest effect on the dress of the largest number of people in British, Dutch and French American colonies, notably in the greater Caribbean zone that included the northern coast of South America and lowcountry South Carolina as well as the Antilles. Justified variously by the need to preserve public order, promote propriety and protect property, these regulations established minimum rather than maximum clothing rations for those in bondage. Nevertheless, they became de facto sartorial standards for the legally subordinate and the unfree, the normative costume of temporary and permanent subservience.

Masters were expected to supply indentured servants 'the attire necessary for dressing according to the custom of the country', and in the late seventeenth century several British Caribbean colonies – perhaps to attract such migrants at a time when the supply was diminishing – enacted laws to enforce the expectation.[43] The acts also articulated what that custom entailed in garments to be distributed annually. Likely because of metropolitan assumptions about suitable dress, the apparel was to be sufficient to ensure total corporeal coverage. Men were to receive three or four pairs of white ozenbrig or blue linen breeches, canvas or leather ('English') shoes and linen or cotton stockings, along with the same number of blue or white shirts, two jackets (a woollen coat was substituted in Jamaica), up to four hats or caps and, in Jamaica, neckcloths. Jamaica also specified female servants' dress: four each of calico hoods, close-fitting caps ('coiffes'), blue or white ozenbrig chemises ('smocks') and

---

[43] David W. Galenson, 'The Rise and Fall of Indentured Servitude in the Americas: An Economic Analysis', *Journal of Economic History* 44/1 (1984): 1–26, at 8. The quotation is from Moreau de Saint-Méry, *Loix et Constitutions*, i: 638 (1700). As a 1703 Barbados law acknowledged, once 'the Act ascertaining such custom' lapsed, 'many Masters ... dealt with them according to their laws and pleasures' – that is, outfitted servants badly if at all; *Acts Passed in the Island of Barbados From 1643, to 1762, Inclusive* (London: Richard Hall, 1764), 157. North and South Carolina laws called for 'competent' clothing; see Nicholas Trott, *The Laws of the Province of South-Carolina* (Charles-Town: Lewis Timothy, 1736), reprinted in John D. Cushing (ed.), *The Colony Laws of North America* (Wilmington, DE: M. Glazier, 1977–1978), xv: 315; *A Collection of all the Public Acts of Assembly of the Province of North-Carolina: Now in Force and Use* (Newbern: James Davis, 1751), reprinted in Cushing (ed.), *The Colony Laws of North America*, xiii: 161. See also Abbot Emerson Smith, *White Servitude and Convict Labor in America 1607–1776* (Chapel Hill: University of North Carolina Press, 1947), 237; Burnard, *Planters, Merchants, and Slaves*, 34–35, 71–75.

petticoats, ozenbrig or cotton stockings and shoes, and a woollen jacket ('gound' or 'westcoate').[44]

One contemporary noted that masters granted indentured servants 'noe more [apparel] then the lawes of the island [Jamaica] forces 'em to'.[45] His observation seems accurate. In the few surviving runaway advertisements from the period, none of the fugitives was noted as well dressed, even though it is likely that such listings would have mentioned striking attire to facilitate recognition, and a 1735 visitor to Jamaica similarly portrayed indentured servant dress as plain and comprising the same few items cited in the ordinances.[46] Thus the legislatively sanctioned costume of social subordination among white settlers also – perhaps unintentionally but certainly effectively – defined the upper bounds of indentured servant attire.[47]

The enslaved comprised far and away the greatest number of men and women included in statutory apparel provisioning.[48] Though most plantation colonies decreed that slaves be granted 'sufficient' clothing, only the leading Antillean sugar islands described what that term signified: two linen suits (jacket-like chemises – essentially tunics extending below the waist – and breeches or skirts) in French possessions, 'Jackets and Drawers [short trousers]' for men, 'Jackets and Petticoats or Frocks

---

[44] *Acts Passed in the Island of Barbados*, 157 (the text added that the outfit defined therein 'shall be taken and held to be the custom of the Country for the future allowance'); John Taylor, *Jamaica in 1687. The Taylor Manuscript at the National Library of Jamaica*, ed. David Buisseret (Kingston: University of the West Indies Press, 2008), 287–288; Smith, *White Servitude and Convict Labor*, 237. At least one of the most items was to be distributed quarterly.

[45] Taylor, *Jamaica in 1687*, 267 sic (quotation); see also Edward Long, *The History of Jamaica*, 3 vols. (London: T. Lowndes, 1774), ii: 291.

[46] *Weekly Jamaica Courant*, 30 July 1718, 5 August 1718, 11 February 1719, ? 1721, 20 June 1722, 22 March 1726, ? 1730, 24 June 1730; Charles Leslie, *A New and Exact Account of Jamaica* (Edinburgh: A. Kincaid, 1739), 35–36. In all colonies, the laws fell short of requiring the number of garments that Richard Ligon, a one-time Barbadian sugar planter, recommended in the 1650s; see Hilary Beckles, *White Servitude and Black Slavery in Barbados, 1627–1715* (Knoxville: University of Tennessee Press, 1989), 97.

[47] For a 1758 Virginia court decision that ordered a master to clothe a neglected servant in a barebones version of the costume outlined here, see Smith, *White Servitude and Convict Labor*, 246.

[48] For more detailed discussion of the topics of this and the next paragraph, see DuPlessis, *The Material Atlantic*, 130–135. For examples of early nineteenth-century legislation, see John Lunan, *An Abstract of the Laws of Jamaics Relating to Slaves* (Jamaica: Office of the Saint Jago de la Vega Gazette, 1819), 106 (1816); J. Th. de Smidt, T. van der Lee and H.J.M. van Dapperen (eds.), *Plakaatboek Guyana (Guyana Ordinance Book), 1670–1816* (The Hague: Huygens Institute for the History of the Netherlands, 2014), 19 October 1778, [Art. 13]; 1 October 1784, [Art.] 18; 2 October 1810; http://resources.huygens .knaw.nl/retroboeken/guyana/#page=0&accessor=search_in_text&view=homePane [last accessed 6 January 2018].

[one-piece gowns]' for women in British.[49] These allotments lacked shoes, stockings, headgear and coats, never mind any sort of ornamentation or accessories. Even where statute required garments to be given out, moreover, slaves were just as likely to receive only lengths of cloth, and the French Code Noir explicitly permitted masters to substitute four ells of linen for the two suits. Elsewhere, slave dress could be more minimal. According to John Gabriel Stedman, a soldier in and writer on late eighteenth-century Surinam, in that Dutch colony 'the slaves are kept nearly naked', by which he meant clothed only below the waist with a loincloth or skirt.[50] And when enslaved men and women did get the full provision mandated by law – and much testimony indicates that many did not – the quantity was insufficient not only to keep recipients clothed for an entire year, as more than one observer lamented, but also to afford the type of bodily coverage considered a *sine qua non* for free settlers – and even for indentured servants.

The laws did create – or at least formalised – a model costume (the female iteration of which can be seen on the woman on the extreme left of Figure 13.1), remarkably similar over time and space. As contemporary texts, images, and inventories demonstrate, this costume discernibly differentiated slaves from all free people, including indentured servants, whose clothing provision – 'pore' though it was judged at the time – included a much greater variety of types of garments, as well as many more of them.[51] A degree of 'nakedness' (more accurately, incomplete corporeal concealment) that would have been deemed scandalous for the free was accepted, indeed enjoined, for the enslaved.[52] For all that, however, the acts did not prevent some notable self-dressing initiatives by slaves who used earnings from selling crops grown on provision grounds, craft goods such as pottery or small wooden implements that

---

[49] *Édit du Roi, Touchant la Police des Isles de l'Amérique Françoise*, Art. XXV; *Laws of Jamaica* 1716, 227 (modelled on an earlier Barbados act). The French requirement was reiterated in 1784 using slightly different terms; Moreau de Saint-Méry, *Loix et Constitutions*, vi: 658.

[50] John Gabriel Stedman, *Narrative, Of a Five Years' Expedition; Against the Revolted Negroes of Surinam ...*, 2 vols. (London: J. Johnson & J. Edwards, 1796), ii: 273; cf. i: 15, 19; ii: 62, 280–282. Stedman's was not a solitary testimony; see DuPlessis, *The Material Atlantic*, 133–135, and de Smidt, van der Lee and van Dapperen (eds.), *Plakaatboek Guyana*, 2 October 1810; http://resources.huygens.knaw.nl/retroboeken/guyana/#page =0&accessor=search_in_text&view=homePane [last accessed 6 January 2018], where the authorities denounce planters for leaving 'many slaves ... naked and unprovided for ...'.

[51] Quotation from Taylor, *Jamaica in 1687*, 267.

[52] The deeply racist John Taylor justified the disparity: slaves 'deserve noe better [than 'only ... an arsclout or linen peticoat'], since they differ only from bruite beast only by their shape and speach'. Ibid., 268.

they had fashioned, or dry goods furnished by their masters.[53] From all depictions, verbal and visual, such garb also obeyed sumptuary rules – if de facto ones internal to slave communities – that dictated colours and materials, garments and styles, accessories and adornments. As such, they delineated an identifiable slave fancy-dress sartorial profile, which often involved items like shoes, stockings and hats that transgressed the usual attire boundaries between slave and free that provisioning-rule costumes obeyed.

Even non-settlers did not lie beyond the reach of sumptuary regulations: the Native inhabitants of the Americas came to dress at the intersection of indigenous and settler codes.[54] Pre-contact rules in the aboriginal New World were wide-ranging. Tattooing, for instance, was typically limited to men and among them often to those who were going to war, had achieved notable feats, and/or held positions of authority, though in some places high-status Amerindian women were also corporeally decorated. Distinctive hairstyles characterised groups by gender, age, marital status and other criteria. Particular garment colours and decorations were allotted by rank and office, and singular forms of otherwise similar garments characterised members of certain bands, tribes and nations.

Many of these norms of sartorial conduct persisted into the colonial era. But contact with settlers introduced novel materials, goods and fashions along with unfamiliar attiring codes. In contrast to Native dress conventions, in which adequate corporeal covering included not just (or not even) apparel but a wide range of accoutrements worn over as well as directly on the physical body, colonists' rules defined even partial absence of garments as 'nakedness' evincing a 'savagery' to be eradicated.[55] Some Indians encountered new items and ideas as slaves, being garbed like others of their status according to the formal regulations and informal practices outlined above. Free Natives were likewise affected. Intercultural voyagers and emissaries were ceremonially, sometimes elaborately and

[53] DuPlessis, *The Material Atlantic*, 151–159.
[54] The next three paragraphs draw on Ibid., 24–27, 48–50, 87–120 and Plates 1, 5, 6.
[55] So hegemonic was the equation of partial undress with nakedness and savagery that contemporaries deployed it to condemn all types of apparelling that offended them. See, e.g. the comments by the Anglican circuit rider Charles Woodmason on the settlers to whom he preached in the Carolina borderlands in 1768: the men and women who wore no footwear, headgear, or jackets struck him as 'so rude in their Manners as the Common Savages, and hardly a degree removed from them. Their Dresses almost as loose [and] as Naked as the Indians, and differing in Nothing save Complexion'. Charles Woodmason, *The Carolina Backcountry on the Eve of the Revolution. The Journal and Other Writings of Charles Woodmason, Anglican Itinerant*, ed. Richard J. Hooker (Chapel Hill: University of North Carolina Press, 1953), 56.

usually differentially reclothed (at least for public occasions or the painting of portraits) to demonstrate the 'civilising' behavioural potential of sumptuary conventions as well as their ability to project honour and rank as Europeans understood them. Missionaries often enforced new costumes, and some Indian converts took on religiously determined dress of their own volition, in both instances impelled by the time-honoured sumptuary purpose of sartorially expressing identification with a desired model.

Equally rule-driven were the gifts of clothing repeatedly offered Natives by colonial officials pursuing strategic objectives. Top headmen like the Mohawk sachem and important British ally 'King Hendrick' (Hendrick Peters Theyanoguin, 1692–1755) received complete suits (coat, jacket, breeches) typically of scarlet or royal blue woollen cloth, dazzling white ruffled linen shirts, satin waistcoats, hats decorated with lace or gold braid, European-style shoes and stockings, neckcloths, garters, buckles, silk handkerchiefs, decorative ribbons and gleaming buttons (Figure 13.4).[56] Men of lower but still significant rank got coats and breechclouts instead of suits, plain shirts, unadorned hats, boots without stockings; ordinary warriors had to be content with simple breechclouts, shirts, hats and boots. These were hardly outfits that Indians wore very much – perhaps only in the presence of the officials who had bestowed them. But along with imported garments, fabrics and styles acquired in other ways, the gifts acquainted Native communities with new means of expressing the social order, thereby contributing to the emergence of unwritten syncretic indigenous dress codes.

Colonial Sumptuary Projects: Status, Race and Sartorial Sorting

Sumptuary regulations appeared in the French, Dutch and British Americas from the early days of settlement to the end of the colonial era, but as elsewhere they were not monolithic. While all policed dress in pursuit of other objectives, those objectives varied over time and space, as did the contents of the measures that embodied them, the authorities that ordained them, the populations they targeted and their effectiveness. In their unctuous moralism, their obsession with details and dazzle, and particularly their growing anxiety to make clothing conform to social

---

[56] For Theyanoguin, see Eric Hinderaker, *The Two Hendricks: Unraveling a Mohawk Mystery* (Cambridge, MA: Harvard University Press, 2010); Timothy J. Shannon, 'Dressing for Success on the Mohawk Frontier: Hendrick, William Johnson, and the Indian Fashion', *William and Mary Quarterly*, 3rd ser. 53/1 (1996): 13–42.

Figure 13.4 *The Brave Old Hendrick the Great Sachem or Chief of the Mohawk Indians*, by anonymous artist, 1740? Courtesy of the John Carter Brown Library at Brown University.

Signalling its subject's intermediary status between Native and colonial cultures, Hendrick Peters Theyanoguin's portrait features a tomahawk-style hatchet in his right hand, wampum belt in his left hand and facial tattoos suitable for a Mohawk leader, together with costly apparel that recognises and rewards his role as an important British ally.

condition, the ordinances issued in New England (and urged in New France) represented the last gasp of European-style statist enactments. Belated as well as futile, unsurprisingly they lacked direct descendants.

The failure of those and many of the other regulations that emerged elsewhere in colonial North America and the Caribbean did not discredit the sumptuary project. The conviction that dress revealed and helped constitute ways of thinking and behaving as measured by a standard meaningful to those who promulgated the rules was as widely disseminated as it was firmly held. To ban wearing specific vestments, fabrics or styles was to repress dispositions and demeanour deemed wrong for ethical, religious, communitarian, economic and/or social reasons, just as to mandate other materials, attire and modes was to promote attitudes and comportment conforming to the desired norm. Among sectarian Protestants, such self-consciousness about dress and what it should and should not express enabled the creation of highly characteristic fashions. But the sects' engagement with and exploitation of clothing's denotations did not lead them to embrace novel precepts and conduct such as strategic sartorial choice, personal self-expression, or ceaselessly voguish innovation, as early modern Europeans purportedly did.[57] Rather than prompting a discourse – much less a practice – of the individualistic modern self, sumptuary regulation among Amish, Mennonites and Quakers reflected and reinforced group conformity and uniformity.

In colonies with substantial and growing numbers of slaves and free people of colour, leaders likewise found sumptuary rules appealing for their perceived capacity to correct presumptively problematic behaviour that attire exposed. Yet the deportment that such regulations sought to promote involved not social cohesion rooted in shared values and expressed in similar costume but social segregation based on status and racial discrimination and materialised in sartorial repression. Though as indicated in Chapter 10 by Francisco Bethencourt and Chapter 12 by Rebecca Earle in this volume, comparable measures had a venerable history in Spanish and Portuguese colonies,[58] South Carolina's law forbidding slaves to wear expensive fabrics was unprecedented in the non-Iberian Americas; that it was not more widely copied indicates both the hegemony of the standard provisioning outfit and the efficacy of the quotidian violence inflicted on the enslaved.[59]

---

[57] Martha Howell, *Commerce before Capitalism in Europe, 1300–1600* (New York: Cambridge University Press, 2010), 258–260.

[58] See also DuPlessis, *The Material Atlantic*, 155–156, 193, 207.

[59] For the violence, often extreme, to which slaves were routinely subjected, and its effectiveness, see Burnard, *Planters, Merchants, and Slaves.*

While sharing the sumptuary belief about the disclosive nature of dress and the attendant confidence in the disciplining potential of apparel restrictions, post-1760 Caribbean ordinances directed against free people of colour added a new twist (though again one also found in Iberian America). Whereas earlier North American statutes associated appropriate or improper comportment as sartorially performed with either social status (notably gender, occupation and wealth) or legal status (free and unfree), the late eighteenth-century Antillean acts yoked them to race. In the new formulation, intolerable conduct as displayed in dress was part of an inadmissible denial of profound and irreconcil- able differences between two races. In particular, while during the earlier eighteenth century *luxe* had been reinterpreted as a permissible – even desirable – component of consumption rather than morally dangerous and economically harmful prodigality,[60] colonial elites sought to con- fine its deployment to whites, to make it a marker of white privilege rather than of common human behaviour. Thus despite abundant con- temporary commentary disparaging Caribbean whites for their preten- tiously lavish dress and mindless adherence to unsuitable metropolitan fashions, no enactments ever sought to place any restrictions on them. In sharp contrast stood statutes criminalising the *luxe* of *gens de couleur* that, the ordinances acknowledged, took exactly the same vestimentary form as white *luxe*.

That, in fact, was the rub. To the colonial authorities, the issue was not that free people of colour were trying to assume a white identity but that they were taking on a signal of whiteness by appropriating white sartorial behaviour. The authorities were mistaken: probate inventories show that free people of colour deployed dress not to identify *with* whites but to identify *as* planters or merchants, overseers or artisans, affluent or less well-off members of the free colonial community. That is, they attired according to long-established codes of social sorting rather than in violation of a novel racial order. Whites saw it differently: now that *luxe* had been moralised and made respectable it could serve (along with reserved names, professions, titles and much else) as an emblem of innate racial dissimilarity, indeed of racial superiority. Hence whites viewed *luxe* among *gens de couleur* as a form of disrespect because it did not affirm the colonial social hierarchy that they were labouring to redraw along parameters of race and instantiate most visibly in distinctive dress exclusions. Like sectarian North American Christians, white West

---

[60] See Maxine Berg and Elizabeth Eger (eds.), *Luxury in the Eighteenth Century: Debates, Desires and Delectable Goods* (Basingstoke: Palgrave Macmillan, 2003); DuPlessis, *The Material Atlantic*, 155–156.

Indians reflected on the meanings of dress, but unlike the faith-based communities white Antilleans embraced an individual right to dress – for themselves. Racialised others, no matter what their wealth, occupation or legal status, had only a right to *be* dressed, and as we have seen whites also intended to define the substance of that right.

Sumptuary regulations of every stripe survived longer in the colonies of France, Holland and Britain than in the metropoles. Their persistence was not – apart from the early and soon abandoned New England efforts – rooted in a wish to sustain some version of a European-model social structure or customary dress.[61] Rather, they remained in favour because many settlers continued to believe that rules incorporating controls on dress could, by virtue of the correspondence thought to obtain between attire and attitude, serve new objectives in the new colonial societies.[62] In fact, some did – as long as they pertained to costumes in sharply delimited homogeneous groups that enforced the strictures themselves instead of relying on state power. Less formal codes, manifested in undertakings such as provisioning subordinates, gifting allies and demarcating converts, also had noticeable if weaker results. Yet supply shortcomings that often required dress recipients to self-attire, together with the continued vitality of prior existing codes and practices among indigenous people, the enslaved and the indentured, meant that their actual apparel was a hybrid of the imposed and the chosen. The resulting syncretic fashions expressed, more than any sumptuary code, the sartorial novelty of the colonial Americas.

---

[61] Mercantilist concerns to protect and/or develop national textile industries by forbidding the wearing of apparel made of foreign fabrics are, along with hopes of maintaining the established social hierarchy, often cited as motivating early modern sumptuary law; see Daniel Roche, *The Culture of Clothing. Dress and Fashion in the 'Ancien Régime'* (Cambridge: Cambridge University Press, 1994), esp. 28, 39–40, 49–50. In 1733 the French crown explicitly forbade the import of foreign cottons into its American colonies, affirming a prohibition that in metropolitan France dated back to 1686 (Moreau de Saint-Méry, *Loix et Constitutions*, iii: 360–361; cf. Ibid., ii: 560, Art. XII), but the decree was entirely ignored, and no other similar law was promulgated in the other colonies under consideration here.

[62] Though mainly directed toward political rather than social goals (the repeal of Coercive Acts), the boycott of imported British fabrics by the Continental Association of rebellious mainland North American British colonies starting on 1 December 1774 had a quasi-sumptuary aspect (as did renewed calls for exclusion of British textiles after the Revolution), for non-importation sought also to direct consumption toward woollens and linens of colonial manufacture, lauded as 'patriotic' and 'republican', and away from 'extravagant' textiles such as silks, while also discouraging 'frivolous' sartorial display. See Michael Zakim, *Ready-made Democracy: A History of Men's Dress in the American Republic, 1760–1860* (Chicago: University of Chicago Press, 2003), 11–31; Lawrence A. Peskin, *Manufacturing Revolution. The Intellectual Origins of Early American Industry* (Baltimore: Johns Hopkins University Press, 2003), 47–48.

Part IV

Early Modern World Empires

14 'Grandeur and Show': Clothing, Commerce and the Capital in Early Modern Russia

Matthew P. Romaniello

An Englishwoman, Elizabeth Justice, arrived in St Petersburg in 1734 to take up her new post as a governess to a British family residing in the city. She was notably impressed by Russia's capital and its society. Upon returning to Britain years later, she remarked upon the striking quality of the clothing in the city. 'The Cloaths of the Nobility', she wrote, 'both Gentlemen and Ladies, were very rich. Several of the Ladies were in Velvet; and most of 'em had Pearls of a large Size on the Robing and Facing of their Gowns. Others had plain Paduasay trim'd with *Point de Span*; The Gentlemen in general had Velvet, imbroidered with Gold and Silver; in which Work the Russians are famous; as also for Grandeur and Show'.[1]

Justice lived in St Petersburg only three decades after the city's foundation by Tsar Peter Alekseevich (the Great, r. 1676–1725). During Peter's reign, new laws required Russian nobles and townspeople to adopt 'Western' dress and habits. Previous studies of Peter's clothing regulations have positioned his actions within the context of the broader technical and scientific exchanges the tsar facilitated. These works have made important contributions. Historian Lindsey Hughes discussed the new laws as part of the ongoing Westernisation of the court, and, more recently, historians Paul Keenan and Christine Ruane analysed the changing styles of Russian fashions, and the fashion industry, in the eighteenth century.[2] Russian scholars have done valuable work viewing

[1] A version of this article was presented to the Medieval and Renaissance Study Group at Brigham Young University and the Early Modern Forum at University of Hawai'i. I thank the participants in those discussions for their comments. I also thank the anonymous referees for their comments. Elizabeth Justice, *A Voyage to Russia: Describing the Laws, Manners, and Customs of the Great Empire, as Governed at this Present by that Excellent Princess the Czarina*, 2nd ed. (London: G. Smith, 1746), 16–17.

[2] Lindsey Hughes, *Russia in the Age of Peter the Great* (New Haven: Yale University Press, 1998), 280–288, 447–461, and her earlier 'From Caftans into Corsets: The Sartorial Transformation of Women during the Reign of Peter the Great', in Peter I. Barta (ed.), *Gender and Sexuality in Russian Civilisation* (London: Routledge, 2001), 17–32; Paul Keenan, 'The Function of Fashion: Women and Clothing at the Russian Court (1700–1762)', in Wendy Rosslyn and Alessandra Tosi (eds.), *Women in Russian Culture and*

the sartorial transformation as a cultural shift, though their interest has focused on the material or fashion more than on the legal regulations.[3]

There can be no doubt that there was a visible transformation of society as it assumed the new style, but situating the clothing laws as a part of a broader cultural transformation is a challenge. Was the intention of the Petrine government to foster a new society, or simply to achieve a more practical goal?[4] Peter himself was personally indifferent to fashion, as John Bell, a Scottish doctor in his service, documented. According to Bell's recollection, when the tsar visited France on his second embassy to Western Europe in 1717, 'an Admiral was ordered to attend & shew him every thing that was curious about Paris. It seems the Admiral had a taste for dress, & put on a new suite every day, till his Wardrobe was exhausted and putting on a coat he had worn before, the Czar told him he was glad to see his Taylor had at last fitted him'.[5] If the style of the court was not the primary justification for the clothing regulations, then other options must be considered. As argued by Maria Giuseppina Muzzarelli in Chapter 6 of this volume for medieval Italy, there was an underlying financial benefit for the state, raised through short-term fines for failing to adopt Western clothing. The clothing fines were only one of a new array of taxes implemented by the state in an effort to raise as much money as possible.[6] Any analysis of Petrine policy must focus upon the state's fiscal exigencies, because the tsar 'was carrying on at an immense expence in forming an Army & Navy

Society, 1700–1825 (London: Palgrave Macmillan, 2007), 125–143; Christine Ruane, *The Empire's New Clothes: A History of the Russian Fashion Industry, 1700–1917* (New Haven: Yale University Press, 2009), 1–16.

[3] This includes E. Iu. Moiseenko (ed.), *Kostium v Rossii pervoi chetverti XVIII veka* (Leningrad: Ermitazh, 1984); and R. M. Kirsanova, *Russkii kostium i byt XVIII-XIX vekov* (Moscow: Slovo, 2002), 9–51. The exception is the study by V. Sedov, 'Reforma sluzhilogo plat'ia pri Fedore Alekseeviche', in Iu. N. Bespiatykh (ed.), *Trudy Vserossooskoi nauchnoi konferentsii 'Kogda Rossiia molodaia muzhala s genium Petra', posviashchennoi 300-letnemu iubileiu otechestvennogo flota* (Pereslavl-Zalesskii: Pereslavl-Zalesskii istoriko-arkhitekturnyi i khudozhestvennyi muzei-zapovednik, 1992), 77–84, which focuses on local changes in the 1680s.

[4] For a view of Petrine 'Westernisation' as a cultural break, see: James Cracraft, *The Petrine Revolution in Russian Culture* (Cambridge, MA: Belknap Press, 2004) or Hughes, *Russia in the Age of Peter the Great*. On Petrine policy as an evolution from the seventeenth century, see: Paul Bushkovitch, *Peter the Great: The Struggle for Power, 1671–1725* (Cambridge: Cambridge University Press, 2001); and Chester Dunning and Norman S. Smith, 'Moving beyond Absolutism: Was Early Modern Russia a Fiscal-military State?', *Russian History* 33/1 (2006): 19–43.

[5] The National Library of Scotland, Edinburgh (NLS), Carmichael and Gordon Papers, MS 189, John Bell, 'Sundry Anecdotes of Peter the first', ff. 10–29, here f. 29.

[6] For another example, see E. V. Anisimov, 'Remarks on the Fiscal Policy of the Russian Absolutism during the First Quarter of the Eighteenth Century: The Hearth Tax and the Introduction of the Soul (Poll) Tax', *Soviet Studies in History* 28/1 (1989): 10–32.

and the most unpopular of all, that of Build New Cities and Towns, as that of St. Petersburg and Crownstadt, the expense of which cannot easily be estimat'd'.[7]

This article begins with a consideration of Russian traditional clothing of the seventeenth century in the context of the period's social and economic reforms.[8] Peter the Great would build upon these earlier policies to finance his overhaul of the Russian military system, but found his government still in dire need of new funds. Therefore, the ongoing economic pressures required more radical changes to generate the necessary revenue. When Peter the Great passed his famous 1701 law requiring Russian urban society to adopt Western dress, it had little influence over his court, which had already adopted the new fashions. Rather, the clothing laws of the eighteenth century targeted the general urban population, merchants and other townspeople, to accept the new style or pay fines. This article will suggest Peter's efforts were designed to generate revenue as well as to foster 'Western' culture. This is not intended to challenge earlier studies of fashion or society, but to add a new dimension to these works. The society that Elizabeth Justice observed reflected the recent enactments, but the visual transformation of Russia was just another type of 'show' enacted by a state desperate for new revenue.

Traditional Styles

Peter the Great's 'Westernisation' program has long been presented as a break with earlier Russian traditions and customs. Both Western visitors to Russia in the sixteenth and seventeenth centuries and modern scholars have depicted Russia as resistant to outside influence, fostering the notion of Russian 'backwardness'. One of the origins of this idea was a religious prohibition on foreign customs. In fact, shortly after Tsar Ivan IV Vasil'evich (r. 1533–1584) established Russia's direct trade connection with Western Europe through the northern port of Arkhangel'sk, the Russian Orthodox Church announced its opposition to the non-Orthodox West. In 1551, the Church hierarchy issued the *Stoglav* (One-Hundred Chapters), a lengthy document intended to standardise Orthodox rituals within Russia's borders. The *Stoglav* also included a comprehensive ban on all foreign habits, declaring that the

---

[7] NLS, Bell, 'Sundry Anecdotes', ff. 2r–v.

[8] For a discussion of the economic policies, see: Jarmo T. Kotilaine, 'Mercantilism in pre-Petrine Russia', in Jarmo Kotilaine and Marshall Poe (eds.), *Modernizing Muscovy: Reform and Social Change in Seventeenth-century Russia* (London: Routledge Curzon, 2004), 143–174.

'evil customs' of other countries and faiths defiled Russia with their 'lawlessness'.[9] The Russian Orthodox Church's objections did not prevent Russian acceptance of foreign customs, but knowledge of the religious condemnation frequently appeared in Western merchants' explanations of why the Russian market was resistant to imported goods.

While Russian Orthodoxy may have encouraged resistance to foreign customs, upholding this notion as a blanket condemnation of the West is more problematic. A religious objection to foreign goods and habits was not a state ban. In 1628, when Tsar Mikhail Fedorovich (r. 1613–1645) issued a decree re-establishing the charter of the English Russia Company, the list of goods imported by the foreign merchants was extensive. It included 'all manner of Merchandize, as cloth, damask, sattins, traffityes, those that are good, such as have bin formerly brought the damask and traffityes to be weighty and good and their cloth to be fast and good measure'.[10] While Russian clothing in the seventeenth century was cut in a traditional style, much of the material itself was not produced in Russia, at least for those who could afford imported cloth.

Western visitors to Moscow viewed the luxurious court with admiration. Adam Olearius, secretary to the Duke of Holstein's ambassador to Persia in the 1630s, provided a detailed account of the Russian capital as the embassy travelled through the tsar's lands. On his visit to the court in 1634, Olearius wrote 'The Great Duke sate in his Chair, clad in a long Coat, embroider'd with Perls, and beset with all sorts of precious Stones. He had above his Cap, which was of Martins-skins, a Crown of Gold, beset with great Diamonds, and in his right hand a Scepter of the same metal, and no less rich, and so weighty, that he was forc'd to relieve one hand with the other'.[11] While other monarchs would be equally well appointed, Russian courtiers were no less adorned. There were 'two Bojares, and two Chancellors, or Secretaries of State, very richly clad, having Coats of stript Satin, embroidered with very great Perls and other precious stones, and great Golden Chains which made a Crosse upon their breasts. The Bojares had Caps, after the fashion of calotts, beset with Perls, having in the midst a cluster of Diamonds and precious stones. The other two had their Caps of black-fox fur, according to the ordinary fashion'.[12]

---

[9] This resolution is ch. 39 of the *Stoglav*, see: E. B. Emchenko (ed.), *Stolgav: issledovaniie i tekst* (Moscow: Indarik, 2000), 302.

[10] The National Archives, Kew, London (hereafter TNA), State Papers: Russia, SP 91/3, part 2, 'Decree from Czar Michael Restoring Privileges to the Company', 12 June 1628, ff. 186r.-193r., here 187v.

[11] Adam Olearius, *The Voyages & Travels of the Ambassadors from the Duke of Holstein, to the Great Duke of Muscovy, and the King of Persia*, trans. John Davies (London: Thomas Dring and John Starkey, 1662), 17.

[12] Ibid., 20.

What impressed Olearius the most, however, was the tsar's willingness to provide luxurious clothing to other visitors to the court. A group of Tatar supplicants arrived in Moscow wearing 'Their Cassocks, [which] were of a very coarse red Cloath; but at their return from audience, they were in Damask Coats, some red, some yellow, which the great Duke had bestow'd on them by way of present. There hardly passes a year, but these Gentlemen, as well as the other Tartars their Neighbours, send such an Embassy to Moscou; not so much for any businesse they have, as to get some Furs, Martins skins, and silk Vestments'.[13]

Other Western visitors observed the importance of the kaftan as the primary piece of Russian clothing. Jan Janszoon Struys, a merchant in Moscow in the 1660s, included an extensive description of the Russian wardrobe in his account of the city. He wrote that 'the ordinary Habit of Citizens, is first an upper Coat of dark green, red, brown or violet-colour'd Silk, open before and on the sides, and garnished with loops, having behind great Capes, almost like old fashioned-Cloaks in the Low-Countreys; Under that they wear another coat of Say or Silk, with a high and stiff Collar'. The outer kaftans protected the even more valuable fabric of the inner clothes: 'Under this they wear yet another Coat which nevertheless is not very close, for they affect looseness as well in their Habits as in their life. Their shirts they tuft with Silk on the back, as also the Necks, which the Gentry adorn with Pearls, Gold, Silver, or Precious stones'. Finally, in a comment echoed by others, Struys mentioned that men's and women's styles did not differ greatly: 'The Habit of Women is not so much different from that of their Men, as they differ from each other, agreeable to the Quality of the Person. They wear generally Caps turned with Sables or other Furs but greater than the Mens, set with Pearls and Rubies upon the Crown, under which they let their Hair hang in its full length, these are those of higher Rank and Quality; those of meaner Condition have them only turned with red Fox'.[14]

The multi-layered kaftans remained the traditional style of Russian clothing, but throughout the seventeenth century more Western clothing entered the market. Historian Richard Hellie reached this conclusion in his study of the Russian economy: while kaftans and hats were sold in great quantity, there are numerous transactions of imported clothing in 'Western' styles, including belts, blouses, pants, leggings, scarves, shoes,

---

[13] Ibid., 21.

[14] John Struys, *The Perilous and Most Unhappy Voyages of John Struys through Italy, Greece, Lifeland, Moscovia, Tartary, Media, Persia, East-India, Japan, and Other Places in Europe, Africa and Asia*, trans. John Morrison (London: Samuel Smith, 1683), 140–141.

stockings and even wigs by the end of the century.[15] He argued that while the Petrine era accelerated the change to Western clothing, it 'had quietly been having its small impact over the centuries anyway'.[16] Furthermore, Hellie's evidence and conclusion contradicts those scholars who suggest Western clothing had no role in Russian society before Peter the Great, an idea that reinforces a Petrine 'Westernisation' narrative, but does not allow for more open exchanges with Europe in the seventeenth century.[17] Considering the important role both English and Dutch merchants held in the seventeenth century in terms of importing fabric, it is not surprising to discover clothing was included among those imports.

Despite the earlier objections of the Russian Orthodox Church to foreign habits, there is no evidence that the state had any interest in restricting imported clothing or fabric until the last quarter of the seventeenth century. The *Ulozhenie of 1649*, the new law code promulgated by Tsar Aleksei Mikhailovich, imposed regulations on many aspects of the economy, including tobacco and alcohol sales, establishing a new toll system and transportation fees, and outlining seal fees for a wide variety of commercial transactions. However, it offered no restriction on clothing sales or styles, and offered no prohibition against any imported product except tobacco.[18] The *Torgovyi ustav* (Commercial Code) of 1653 added some clarifications to the toll system, adding specific details for merchants arriving in Arkhangel'sk from Western Europe or in Astrakhan from Iran or India, but only mandated visits to the customs officers, without prohibiting specific items from import or export.[19]

This situation would change only in 1667, following the disruptions to the economy created by revolts in 1648 and 1649, as well as the so-called 'copper riots' of the early 1660s inspired by the devaluation of the currency. The state attempted to address these challenges with a *Novotorgovyi ustav* (New Commercial Code) in 1667, which focused on controlling foreign trade for the state's benefit on a level never before attempted. It banned the export of specie from Russia, established higher tariffs on imported goods, and physically restricted all foreign merchants

---

[15] Richard Hellie, *The Economy and Material Culture of Russia, 1600–1725* (Chicago: University of Chicago Press, 1999), 346–386.

[16] Ibid., 386.

[17] A recent example of this argument is Alexander Maxwell, *Patriots Against Fashion: Clothing and Nationalism in Europe's Age of Revolutions* (London: Palgrave Macmillan, 2014), 59–62.

[18] On the *Ulozhenie* and tobacco regulation, see: Matthew P. Romaniello, 'Through the Filter of Tobacco: The Limits of Global Trade in the Early Modern World', *Comparative Studies of Society and History* 49/4 (2007): 914–937, here 918–921.

[19] *Gramot i dogovorov khraniashchikhsia v gosudarstvennoi kollegii inostrannykh del* (Moscow, 1828), #158, 25 October 1653, 490–493.

inside the kingdom. Foreign merchants could conduct business only in the border cities of Arkhangel'sk, Novgorod, Pskov, Smolensk and Putivl' for the West, and Astrakhan for all of Asia, severely curtailing their presence in the Muscovite market. The English and Dutch were limited to the north, the Swedes to the west and Indians and Iranians to the far south.[20]

Possibly the first sumptuary law in Russia targeted foreign merchants as another mechanism to increase revenue in 1660, though we no longer have the documentation relating to this new law.[21] The first extant decree was promulgated in August 1675, which declared that Russian 'administrators and officials, the Muscovite gentry, and other residents of Moscow' could not wear the 'clothing, kaftans, or hats' of 'foreigners and Germans' and vice versa.[22] Those who appeared in public were subjected to a new fine. It is also possible, though not expressly stated, that this law shared an intention with the new regulations on restricting the export of specie from the country. Wealthy Russians wore kaftans finished in gold thread, gems or pearls. Preventing the sale of kaftans to foreigners eliminated a potential loophole not first envisioned in the Commercial Code. In 1680, a new law reiterated this initial restriction to maintain the distinctions between Russians and foreigners, which suggests the first attempt at implementation was not a success.[23] Furthermore, historian P. V. Sedov uncovered other regulations that reinforced this restriction in specific localities, including the trade centre of Kazan, demonstrating the commitment of the state to enforcing its new ban.[24] Russia's first sumptuary laws may not have been successfully implemented, but it was not through lack of effort.

There was an exception to these early clothing restrictions. In 1681, a Moscow decree restricted the number of horses that boyars and minor nobles could employ to pull their carriages in the city.[25] Of all of the

---

[20] *Polnoe sobranie zakonov Rossiiskoi Imperii*, Series 1, 45 vols. (St. Petersburg, 1862–1928), hereafter PSZ,i, #408, 22 April 1667, 651–665. For a discussion of its implementation, see E. V. Chistiakova, 'Novotorgovnyi ustav 1667 goda', *Arkheograficheskii ezhegodnik za 1957 god* (Moscow, 1958), 102–126; Rudolph Matthee, *The Politics of Trade in Safavid Iran: Silk for Silver, 1600–1730* (Cambridge: Cambridge University Press, 1999), 192–197; and J. T. Kotilaine, *Russia's Foreign Trade and Economic Expansion in the Seventeenth Century: Windows on the World* (Leiden: Brill, 2005), 220–225.

[21] Sedov, 'Reforma sluzhilogo plat'ia', 78.

[22] *PSZ* I, #607, 6 August 1675, 1007–1008.

[23] Hughes, *Russia in the Age of Peter the Great*, 280.

[24] Sedov, 'Reforma sluzhilogo plat'ia', 80–81. A 1697 decree by Peter the Great's government appears to belong with these earlier restrictions, as it specifically forbade elite urban residents in the Siberian town of Iakutsk to wear 'expensive clothing'. *PSZ* III, 28 October 1697, 402–404.

[25] *PSZ* II, #902, 28 December 1681, 367.

sumptuary laws that the Russian government passed, this one seemed to most resemble the laws on 'conspicuous consumption' that were more common in Western Europe.[26] However, this law also was unique. Unlike the early clothing restrictions, it was not followed by other laws designed to reinforce its implementation.

Most of the early sumptuary laws fit within a broader set of mercantilist restrictions on the export of specie. In practice, these laws also attempted to maintain a visible separation between Russians and Western visitors, a policy that could be considered 'anti-Westernising'. Though determining the motivation for these laws is difficult, it is possible that the sumptuary laws were instituted on moral grounds, considering the Russian Orthodox Church's traditional condemnation of the West. If so, these sumptuary laws are not unlike those in the West of the same era, where the laws reflected a 'combination of social, economic, and moral regulation'.[27] By comparison, the eighteenth-century laws do not fit so easily within this formulation, as they originated in the economic needs of the state rather than in other motivations.

Petrine Style

Few clothing laws were promulgated in the seventeenth century, but the government produced a comparative flurry of such laws at the beginning of the eighteenth century. Tsar Peter Alekseevich passed a sweeping set of reforms after 1698 that included regulating clothing styles. However, as Western dress had already arrived in Russia, and was common among the tsar's inner circle before the regulations were passed, the new clothing laws confirmed a change in dress more than it imposed a new system. In fact, the Petrine reforms seemed to target townspeople beyond the court circle as a potential source of revenue for failing to adopt 'new' clothing more than they enforced a particular habit at court.

Peter the Great was among those in Russia who wore Western clothes before the clothing regulations. His household accounts indicate he purchased Western garb before his Grand Embassy departed for the West in 1696. It is unfortunately not clear what specific pieces of clothing this might have included, as they were listed under the broad category of 'German clothes' (*nemetskie kaftany*).[28] His wearing Western clothing was

---

[26] Alan Hunt, *Governance of the Consuming Passions: A History of Sumptuary Law* (New York: St. Martin's Press, 1996), 70–71.

[27] Ibid., 7.

[28] *Sbornik vypisok iz arkhivnykh bumag o Petre velikom* (Moscow: Universitetskaia Tipografia, 1872), vol. 1, 20 September 1691, 120–121.

not a surprise either. Many of Peter's close confidants and advisors in his youth were West Europeans, so adopting, or at least experimenting with, their style of dress could be the result of these associations.[29]

Visitors to the Russian capital at Moscow observed the Westernisation of the court by the 1690s. Johann Georg Korb, a secretary in the Austrian delegation to Peter the Great's capital, recorded his court and its habits in the period before the new clothing laws were passed. For example, when Peter returned to Moscow from his Grand Embassy to Western Europe on 5 September 1698, he greeted his subjects with a razor in hand to commence shaving the beards of his subjects. According to Korb:

> Those who, according to the fashion of that country, would cast themselves upon the ground to worship majesty, he lifted up graciously from their groveling posture, and embraced with a kiss, such as is only due among private friends. If the razor, that plied promiscuously among the beards of those present, can be forgiven the injury it did, the Muscovites may truly reckon that day among the happiest of their lives.[30]

Historians have frequently depicted the clean-shaven face as one of the most visible 'Western' reforms of the era, as a man's beard was a traditional element of Russian Orthodox belief. However, Peter managed to implement this change seven years before it became law.[31] Another Western element of the Petrine era was the inclusion of women in new court entertainments, but this was an accomplished feat by 1698.[32] These are indications that legislation was not necessary to facilitate the change in court culture.

There was a clear change implemented in 1700, when a new decree instructed all ranks of urban men to wear short 'Hungarian' kaftans. The law listed all groups by their social rank, from the elite boyars to 'all residents, men in service, and traders in Moscow or in other cities'.[33] It was possibly just an instruction to wear shorter kaftans, as there had been a push in the court to cut the long coats to more reasonable lengths before this law.[34] However, some Russian kaftans were encrusted with jewels and precious metals. Therefore, cutting clothes shorter freed some

[29] Hughes, *Russia in the Age of Peter the Great*, 357–363, 417–432; Maria di Salvo, 'The "Italian" Nemetskaia Sloboda', in Simon Dixon (ed.), *Personality and Place in Russian Culture* (London: UCL School of Slavonic and East European Studies, 2010), 96–109.

[30] Johann-Georg Korb, *Diary of an Austrian Secretary of Legation at the Court of Czar Peter the Great*, trans. Count MacDonell, 2 vols. (London: Bradbury and Evans, 1863), i: 155.

[31] *PSZ* IV, #2015, 16 January 1705, 282–283.

[32] For example, as described in the entry for 22 July 1698. Korb, *Diary of an Austrian Secretary*, 134–135.

[33] *PSZ* IV, #1741, 4 January 1700, 1.

[34] Hughes, *Russia in the Age of Peter the Great*, 282–283.

wealth to return to circulation rather than remaining for display. In any case, the decree was superseded by a much broader law the following year.

In 1701, the Petrine government promulgated its new law requiring urban residents to wear Western dress, specifying 'German, Saxon, or French'. As with the previous year's restriction, all ranks were specified in the law, with the clergy exempted. It was a sweeping declaration. All residents of Moscow and other towns were 'to wear German clothes, hats, and footwear, and to ride in German saddles; and women should wear such clothes as well'. It also specified that residents should no longer wear 'Russian or Ukrainian [*Cherkasskii*]' clothing.[35] Another law followed the next year which further clarified that on Sundays and holidays, Moscow's residents should wear 'French clothing'.[36] The need for the second law suggests that traditional clothing had continued to be worn to church, which the state now eliminated as a possibility.

While the laws reinforced changes the court had already adopted, almost immediately Western visitors linked the new laws to the change at all social levels, including the court. Cornelis de Bruijn was a Dutch merchant who arrived in Moscow in 1702. He was sufficiently well known as an artist that he received a commission to paint the portraits of Peter the Great's nieces, likely through his connection to the Dutch resident in the capital. In his portraits, Bruijn painted the princesses 'after the German mode, in which they commonly appear in public; but the heads, which were left to my choice, I dressed in the antique stile'.[37] Bruijn preferred Russian traditional dress, and he feared that, although Peter's reforms had not yet affected the peasantry, they 'may in time blot out the remembrance of the ancient dress of the country' (Figure 14.1).[38]

Bruijn reflected the state of knowledge about the changes in his writing, introducing small errors that conflated the timeline of the recent events:

Time has wrought great changes in this Empire, and especially since the Czar's return from his travels. He immediately altered the fashion of dress, as well with regard to the men as to the women, and particularly with regard to those who had dependence on the Court, or enjoyed any office there, not excepting one soul, not even children; and the Russian merchants and others dress so as not to be distinguished from the people of our country. The same year an order was published, forbidding all Russians to appear out of doors, without a coat of the Polish fashion, or being dressed after our manner. The servants to strangers

---

[35] *PSZ* IV, #1887, 1701, 182.
[36] *PSZ* IV, #1898, 28 February 1701, 189.
[37] Cornelius Le Bruyn, *Travels into Muscovy, Persia, and part of the East-Indies*, 2 vols. (London: A. Bettisworth and C. Hitch, 1737), i: 31.
[38] Ibid., i: 46.

Figure 14.1 'Demoiselle Russienne', from Cornelius Le Bruyn, *Travels into Muscovy, Persia, and Part of the East-Indies* (London: A. Bettisworth and C. Hitch, 1737). Courtesy Department of Special Collections, Stanford University Libraries.

were the first that were compelled to this, for if they did not comply, they were sure to be taken from behind hedges, and pay a fine before they had their liberty again.[39]

---

[39] Ibid.

The tsar returned from Europe in 1698, but the law requiring Western dress did not arrive until 1701. There was a gap in the timeline created by earlier expectations that the court would adopt the new style, which Peter imposed through his personal style, and the broader change to the city itself, which was imposed by the law. Bruijn also mentioned an important part of the new laws, which were the financial penalties on anyone not wearing Western-styled clothing after 1701. With the court already adopting Western clothes, it was merchants, servants and other urban residents who would have been forced to pay these fines. It was a financial trap, as those who could not afford new clothes paid fines, further delaying the opportunity to purchase appropriate clothing, which in turn generated additional fines. This was coupled with the difficulty of supply, as few tailors or seamstresses in Moscow were prepared to execute the new styles, requiring the state to hire foreign specialists to produce Western fashions.[40] Though there is no account of how much revenue was raised from the law, it must have been a steady source of funds for a few years following its promulgation.

The practice of arresting servants until they paid a fine became law on 22 December 1704. The government passed a law that echoed the 1701 decree, with the requirement to adopt Saxon or French clothing, but the broad category of all residents of Moscow gained new details, including peasants living in or visiting cities, who had not been named explicitly in the earlier decree.[41] Within two weeks of this law, the decree requiring all men to shave was promulgated, with those preferring to keep their traditional beards to pay a fine, which was set at one hundred rubles for the elites and sixty rubles for merchants and other townspeople.[42] The average carpenter's salary in Russia at the beginning of the century was approximately ten rubles per year, placing these fines well beyond the reach of the working classes.[43] Peter's court had adopted clean-shaven faces in 1698 upon his return from Western Europe, so it is likely that the court itself would not have been affected by the new fines. However, the rates imposed on either group under this law was set beyond the reach of any except the wealthiest, which is likely to have encouraged immediate adoption of the new habit.

Some of the Western visitors to Russia believed that the beard law was harder to implement than the change of clothing styles, which could

---

[40] Ruane's study of the fashion industry begins with the lack of skilled workers. See Ruane, *Empire's New Clothes*, 19–22.

[41] *PSZ* IV, #1999, 22 December 1704, 272–273.

[42] *PSZ* IV, #2015, 16 January 1705, 282–283.

[43] Boris N. Mironov, 'Wages and Prices in Imperial Russia, 1703–1913', *The Russian Review* 69/1 (2010): 56–58.

explain the extraordinary fines. Charles Whitworth, the English envoy to Moscow, mentioned this situation in one of his first dispatches to the Foreign Secretary in March 1705, shortly after the introduction of the new law. He wrote that:

His Majesty has also made a thorough change in the dress of his Country; In all this great City, & see no one of consideration appear otherwise than in German cloaths, one of the hardest tasks was the persuading them to lay aside their long beards; most of the chief nobility lost theirs in the Czars presence, where there was no room to dispute his orders. The common people however were not so easily bought to follow the new fashion, till a Tax was laid at the City gates, on every one, who went in or out with a beard, and this was to be paid as often as they passed, by which means they have at least been brought to conform.[44]

Whitworth's remarks explain the necessity of passing laws after the court had already adopted the custom. While Peter could control the habits and style of his court, his influence over the capital at large was limited. Only punitive laws regulating habits had the effect he desired, in addition to potentially serving as a short-term revenue supply to his government.

Revenue however does not explain all of the changes. By 1702, Peter was having discussions about new Western-style uniforms for his military with Tikhon Nikitch Streshnev, who ran several military offices. In their correspondence, Streshnev mentions uniforms from Holland, Paris and Venice that had been sent to Moscow for consideration, but Peter preferred the French or Hungarian styles, rejecting the Venetian and Dutch options.[45] The laws requiring standardised, Western uniforms would not be passed for decades, but, as with the changes to court dress or the requirement to shave, Peter's personal actions preceded formal legislation.[46]

The few refinements to the existing clothing laws in the decade after 1701 indicated that the government was satisfied with the state of affairs. In 1706, a brief decree was issued declaring that Siberia was not part of the region for implementation of the current laws, which only conforms to the general principle that Siberia was governed as a separate kingdom from European Russia.[47] This was a sensible decision. The size of Siberia

---

[44] The British Library, Blenheim Papers, vol. XLIX, Add. MS 61149, 'Charles Whitworth to Secretary Harley', 14 March 1705, ff. 37–42, here 42r.

[45] *Pis'ma i bumagi imperatora Petra Velikago* (St. Petersburg: Gosudarstvenniia tipografiia, 1887), II: Peter to Streshnev, #454, 10 September 1702, 85; Streshnev's response, 14 September 1702, 399–401; and Peter to Streshnev, #478, 30 November 1702, 115.

[46] On the uniform changes, see L. E. Shepelev, *Tituly, mundiry, ordena v Rossiiskoi imperii* (Leningrad: Nauka, 1991), 12–26.

[47] *PSZ* IV, #2132, [December] 1706, 362–363. On governing Siberia, see Erika Monahan, *The Merchants of Siberia: Trade in Early Modern Eurasia* (Ithaca: Cornell University Press, 2016), 112–117 and 132–141.

and its distance from Moscow made both enforcement of the new laws and providing sufficient supply of the new style difficult. In 1707, a law was passed that addressed maintaining the quality of the new German clothes, requiring that a master craftsman be responsible for those worn in the capital.[48]

Some foreigners living in Russia commented on the success of the reforms. John Perry, an Englishman in service to tsar from 1698 to 1712, recorded the sartorial transformation in great detail. Similar to Bruijn's earlier account, Perry believed that the entire change started with the tsar's decrees: 'The Czar therefore resolving to have this Habit changed, first gave Orders, that all his Boyars and People whatsoever, that came near his Court, and that were in his Pay, should, upon Penalty of falling under his Displeasure, according to their several Abilities, equip themselves with handsome Cloaths made after the English Fashion, and to appear with Gold and Silver Trimming, those that could afford it'.[49] After that, however, Perry added some further details about the tsar's ability to enforce the new style. The tsar 'commanded, that a Pattern of Cloaths of the English Fashion should be hung up at all the Gates of the City of Mosco, and that Publications should be made, that all Persons (excepting the common Peasants who brought Goods and Provisions into the City) should make their Cloaths according to the said Patterns'.[50] Finally, Perry specifically mentioned the fines for failing to conform to the new style: 'that whosoever should disobey the said Orders, and should be found passing any of the Gates of the City in their long Habits, should either pay 2 Grevens (which is 20 Pence) or be obliged to kneel down at the Gates of the City, and to have their Coats cut off just even with the Ground'.[51] For some Russians, the loss of the cloth covered with precious metals could be greater than the fines, therefore excising material was a considerable penalty. While others noted ongoing resistance to the new style, Perry suggested that it was rapidly accepted, though not because of the fines. Instead, Perry believed it was a personal choice, as 'the Russ Ladies soon reconciled themselves to the English Dress, which they found rendred them more agreeable'.[52]

Perry's belief in the widespread adoption of the change may have been accurate, but that did not mean the court had abandoned 'traditional'

---

[48] *PSZ* IV, #2175, 17 December 1707, 397.
[49] John Perry, *The State of Russia under the Present Czar* (London: Benjamin Tooke, 1716), 197.
[50] Ibid., 197–198.
[51] Ibid., 198.
[52] Ibid., 199–200.

fashion entirely. Kaftans became more of an amusement than a daily choice, becoming an option for a costume party in the 1710s. This was the case by 1712, when Charles Whitworth wrote to the Foreign Secretary in London with a description of a recent wedding reception held in the new capital in St Petersburg. Whitworth, at least, was not impressed by the change: 'The Czar had appointed a wedding to be kept after the old fashion, He himself, the Czarienne, the Princesses, the Ladys with the nobility and foreign ministers were all invited, and even to the footsmen, were oblidged to come in the old dresses, which are very extraordinary and inconvenient'.[53] Moreover, the Western contingent of the court was no longer equipped for traditional Russian clothing, resulting in the tsar providing 'habits to the forreigners, and the nobility had those which they or their ancestors had wore about thirty years ago'.[54] In Whitworth's opinion, the evening only demonstrated the limits of Peter's success in endorsing the new style, because the tsar 'took a particular delight in exposing the old methods of the country' but 'it was very plain that severall others acted their part with regret, and wished themselves in their former condition'.[55]

Whitworth's suggestion of the court's resistance to the new style was echoed by other foreign visitors. Friedrich Christian Weber, the Hanoverian envoy to the court from 1712 to 1719, observed the continuing tension between Western style and Russian traditions. At a court function early in his residence, he observed 'All the Beauties of Petersbourg appeared at the Entertainment, they were already at that time in the French Dress, but it seemed to sit very uneasy upon them, particularly the Hoop-Petticoats, and their black Teeth were a sufficient Proof, that they had not yet weaned themselves from that Notion so fast riveted in the Minds of the old Russians, that white Teeth only became Blackmoors and Monkeys'.[56] One habit the court had not discarded was their appreciation for luxurious fabrics. In fact, Weber was initially denied entrance to his first audience for not being appropriately attired for the court, not because of the style of his clothing, but because of their simplicity. The palace guards informed him that his garments needed to be 'trimmed all over with Gold and Silver' to be allowed entrance.[57] Even when Russia's ongoing military expenses led to a ban on the use of gold

---

[53] TNA, SP 91/7, 'Charles Whitworth to Secretary St. John', 8 June 1712, ff. 275r–281v, here 279r–v.
[54] Ibid.
[55] Ibid.
[56] Friedrich Christian Weber, *The Present State of Russia*, 2 vols. (London: W. Taylor, 1723), i: 27.
[57] Ibid., i: 4.

and silver on clothing in 1717, the court only turned toward increasingly expensive silk.[58] The 'grandeur and show' that Elizabeth Justice remarked upon a decade later was ingrained within the court long before her arrival.

However, criticism from court officials did not guarantee widespread acceptance among the public. While we do not have any estimates of the amount of revenue raised through fines from those who opted to wear their old clothing, numerous petitions have survived from the public that provide a glimpse of the objections to the clothing laws. The historians N. B. Golikova and Lindsey Hughes have discussed the protests that flooded the government during Peter's reign.[59] Unsurprisingly, a sizeable percentage arrived from clergymen, who complained the new clothes and clean-shaven faces were heretical actions. By far fewer petitions arrived from the lower ranks of society, though some did, indicating that objections were not only held by the clergy. As early as 1700, before the laws' promulgation, a peasant woman protested against the new 'German dress'.[60] After the 1701 law, a typical petition might decry men shaving their beards, wearing European clothing or smoking tobacco, all of which destroyed the true Christian faith.[61]

There is no doubt that the policies adopted by Peter's government generated protests. Nonetheless, the new style was adopted in Russia's cities, particularly in Moscow and St Petersburg. In a study of a 1719 household inventory of Anna Dorotea von Ronimert, a Russian lieutenant colonel's daughter, historian Carol B. Stevens details Ronimert's surprisingly extensive wardrobe. It featured 'two or three quite elegant outfits', in Stevens's words, including 'a floor-length green damask dress, with a matching underskirt decorated with gilt braid along the seams and on the sleeves' and 'a blue taffeta gown with silver trim and buttons'. Notably, there was not a kaftan to be found among Ronimert's possessions. While a lieutenant colonel's daughter was not among the poor, neither was she among the wealthy. Steven's estimate is that 'a significant percentage of Anna Dorotea's day-to-day expenditures went into her attire'.[62] Though complaints against the clothing laws arrived from

---

[58] Ibid., i: 193.
[59] N. B. Golikova, *Politicheskie protsessy pri Petre I: po materialam preobrazhenskogo prikaza* (Moscow: Izdatel'stvo Moskovskogo Universiteta, 1957); Hughes, *Russia in the Age of Peter the Great*, esp. 447–461.
[60] Hughes, *Russia in the Age of Peter the Great*, 451.
[61] Ibid., 283.
[62] Carol B. Stevens, 'A Woman in Possession: Household Goods and Social Status of a Single Woman in Early St. Petersburg', *Russian History* 42/1 (2015): 136–148, here 140–141.

all levels of society, within twenty years of the first legal change it was obvious that urban Russian style had become Western.

Conclusion

In the 1720s, a new round of laws reinforced the existing separation of urban and rural style. In 1722, a law forbade peasants from wearing foreign clothes, followed by another law in 1725 which fined all merchants who sold German clothes to peasants.[63] Immediately after the 'peasant' laws, a new law was passed fining any merchants who sold any residents of Siberia Western clothing.[64] This law reiterated the terms of the original 1706 decree, but indicated that it had not been successfully implemented. However, it was clear that the law now divided the Russian Empire into separate spheres of clothing. European Russia's townspeople were legally required to wear Western clothing, while the peasantry and all of the residents of Siberia were required to wear traditional Russian garments. Merchants or other subjects who defied the law would be fined.

The eighteenth-century Russian clothing laws were unlike those implemented in other parts of Europe or the American colonies. Within the city there was no legal or social hierarchy reinforced through these laws, as they applied equally to all urban residents, from the nobility to their servants as well as the middling ranks.[65] This is not to imply that elites and servants wore the same quality or style of clothing, only that there was no law that specified this difference within the urban population. It is possible that as the eighteenth century progressed, there was a trend toward limiting the extravagance of the elites. The ban on gold and silver for any fabrics began in 1717, but was reinforced with new laws in 1740 and 1742.[66] The later laws suggest a turn toward the sorts of 'conspicuous consumption' issues that had been raised elsewhere in Europe, as the new regulations avoided style but instead concerned the quality and luxury of particular fabrics. Alan Hunt argued that, at their core, sumptuary laws 'became a regular feature of the governance of social order ... with the rise of mercantile capitalism'.[67] While merchants were not targeted in the later laws, the controlling of the excess of the elite was an issue. At the same time, restricting the use of gold and silver was the recurring theme of Russian sumptuary laws, suggesting the state's

---

[63] *PSZ* VI, #3994, 7 May 1722, 671; *PSZ* VII, #4245, 14 June 1725, 77.

[64] *PSZ* VII, #4256, 28 June 1725, 86–87.

[65] Hunt, *Governance of the Consuming Passions*, 118–119.

[66] *PSZ* XI, #8301, 1740, 320; *PSZ* XI, #8680, 11 December 1742, 732–734.

[67] Hunt, *Governance of the Consuming Passions*, 147.

ongoing need for specie drove all of the legislation, more than the habits of select groups.

A more apt comparison might be found in the Ottoman Empire, which had its own increase in clothing regulations in the eighteenth century. Donald Quartaert argued that one motivation for these new laws was a need to regulate society in an era of upheaval, serving as a tool to '(re)concentrate political power around the person of the sultan'.[68] This idea seems as applicable to Russia under Peter the Great as it does to the Ottoman Empire under Selim III. Russia's clothing laws did function as a tool of the state, creating new taxes to fund the ongoing administrative and military overhaul. Equally, it remade the image of a Russian townsperson to more closely resemble Peter's inner court circle, creating a fixed distinction between town and country that later laws reified. As an opportunity to demonstrate political control from the centre, it was one of the more visible statements of the Petrine era.

Elizabeth Justice's suggestion that the new style of the court was as much for its 'grandeur' as its 'show' seems quite observant. By the end of Peter's reign, the law created a Western-dressed society at all levels in Russia's cities. The tsar's new capital at St Petersburg was visibly different from any other part of his empire. It was a sign of Russia's new Western orientation and a break from its past. Forcing his peasantry to keep traditional dress only reinforced the lesson for his population. To be an urban resident in the Russian Empire was to be a Western one, which no peasant could hope to emulate.

[68] Donald Quataert, 'Clothing Laws, State, and Society in the Ottoman Empire, 1720–1829', *International Journal of Middle East Studies* 29/3 (1997): 403–425, here 411.

15 Women, Minorities and the Changing Politics of Dress in the Ottoman Empire, 1650–1830

Madeline C. Zilfi

Vestimentary coding in the early modern Middle East had already had a long, tortuous history before the Ottoman dynasty succeeded to the Mediterranean domains of countless empires and statelets. The clothing practices in use when the Ottoman dynasty came to power at the turn of the fourteenth century reflected the exigencies of past and present and the interplay of environment, economy, coercion and volition. The vestimentary legacies inherited by the Ottomans in Anatolia and the Balkans in the fourteenth century and the Arab lands in the sixteenth offered an intricate patchwork of cloths and coverings. Most men and women understood the clothing on their backs and heads to be communally 'theirs': attire in some way linked to their religion, ethnicity and locale. Social stratum and vocation altered communal and regional patterns, but seldom enough to obscure those cardinal identifications of the early modern Middle East. For the most part, especially outside major cities, what the Ottomans found, they left in place, although the colour green would be regarded as reserved for Muslims, especially for descendants of the Prophet Muhammad, and head coverings would be expected of urban women of all faiths.

Diversity and Conformity

The genesis of a community's adherence to distinctive colours or cuts had been forgotten, even by the early modern era. Once a community became associated with particular usages, conservative conformity most often prevailed. Clothing styles were not static, but when changes occurred, they were usually slight and accretional rather than dramatic. Ottoman upper- and middling-class women's garments of the late seventeenth century through the early nineteenth century had left behind many of the indoor and outdoor styles of the sixteenth and early seventeenth centuries.[1] However, sumptuary decrees of the later period, commonly invoking the antiquity and timelessness of the Ottoman dispensation, engaged in wilful absentmindedness, claiming that prevailing modes, whatever they might be, had been in place 'since bygone days' (*ez kadim, kadimden*). State and community authorities (of the latter, especially religious authorities) were evenly matched in their desire to stake out boundaries between dominant and subordinate populations. Among other rationales, minority exemplars took pains to rein in their flocks lest they strayed to Islam. For their part, Muslims were keen to demonstrate the appealing specialness of the conquerors' faith. In the Islamic East, to a considerable extent, clothing styles mimicked habitation patterns. They were more often products of local custom, economics and communal self-definition than external coercion and ghettoising. Living alongside one's own folk was the common way, which offered communal cohesion, support networks and safety in numbers. Still, in Istanbul and other cities, most neighbourhoods were confessionally and ethnically mixed, some more than others. Clothing indicated who belonged to the confessional community and who did not.

As a rule, the Ottoman Empire did not impose a comprehensive directory of sartorial dos and don'ts on its non-Muslim subjects, though in general non-Muslims' clothing was mandated to be differentiated from that of Muslims in terms of restricted colours and access to status goods.[2] In any case, the full weight of imperially imposed sartorial constraints fell mainly on cities and townships, most especially Istanbul, as the imperial capital and domicile of the dynasty. As a consequence of the confessional and economic diversity of the urban population, social standing and government imperatives to maintain order registered most forcefully on the regulatory mind. In rural areas where Muslims were a small minority or absent entirely, imperial sartorial laws were all but non-existent.[3] Christians and Jews could expect to be ordered and sorted according to

---

[1] Jennifer M. Scarce, *Women's Costume of the Near and Middle East* (London: Routledge, 2003), 45–66; Nureddin Sevin, *On Üç Asırlık Türk Kıyafet Tarihine bir Bakış* (Istanbul: Başbakanlık Kültür Müsteşarlığı Kültür Yayınları, 1973), 75, 84, 96.

[2] Below, p. 408, regarding *ghiyar*.

[3] Although some regulations were promulgated in all the cities of the Empire, most grew out of specific circumstances in Istanbul, one of the largest cities in Europe and by far the most diverse. Provincial studies have revealed the limits of regulatory interest outside the capital. For example, Kemal Çiçek, 'Living Together: Muslim-Christian Relations in Eighteenth-Century Cyprus as Reflected by the Sharī'a Court Records', *Islam and Christian-Muslim Relations* 4/1 (1993): 36–64, notes that Muslims and non-Muslims wore essentially the same costume, with the exception of the Muslim-reserved white turban. Presumably the green turban, signifying descent from the Prophet Muhammad, was also restricted.

the protocols of their own communal authorities. For example, Greek Orthodox attire was broadly recognisable across the Empire, but it also answered to local custom. Orthodox attire in the Aegean varied from one island to another as well as from the clothing norms of co-religionists elsewhere in the Ottoman Mediterranean. Although particular bonnet styles distinct from those of Christians and Muslims were associated with the Jews of the Empire, sectarian differences within the overall Jewish population made for differentiated attire. Elements of Sephardic garb were distinct from Romaniote and Ashkenazi Jewish garb until the later centuries, at which point their clothing, like the sects themselves, became more blended.[4]

In all populations of the Empire throughout most of its history, headgear was the most important emblem of identity, readily drawing the observer's eye as it announced sectarian, regional and socio-economic differences.[5] Small wonder that a change of head covering could signal a fundamental change in life. 'Taking the turban' was synonymous with conversion to Islam.[6] The sine qua non of conversion was the pronouncement of the formula of faith (Arabic: *shahada*). However, the daily, concrete evidence of conversion for males, the public figures par excellence, was visual, via the donning of the turban. Women's conversion was less a matter of sartorial change than of physical space, which was apt to be somewhat more constrained and gender segregated than under their natal faiths.[7]

The attire of male and female Muslim subjects reflected a high degree of gendered uniformity across urban space. Still, regional variations among Muslims were almost as commonplace as among non-Muslims, especially in international entrepôts like Istanbul, Damascus, Cairo and Salonika. New Muslim settlers and transient merchant colonies in the seventeenth and eighteenth centuries brought Tatar, Caucasian,

---

[4] Minna Rozen, 'Metropolis and Necropolis: The Cultivation of Social Status among the Jews of Istanbul in the 17th and 18th Centuries', in Vera Costantini and Markus Koller (eds.), *Living in the Ottoman Ecumenical Community: Essays in Honour of Suraiya Faroqhi* (Leiden: Brill, 2008), 88–114.

[5] Cf. Gabriella Schubert, *Kleidung als Zeichen: Kopfbedeckung im Donau-Balkan-Raum* (Berlin: Harrassowitz, 1993).

[6] In Reconquista Spain, the removal of the turban symbolised conversion from Islam to Christianity; Maria Judith Feliciano, 'Assimilation or Segregation? Sumptuary Legislation against Moriscos' (unpublished paper delivered at the Annual Meeting of the Middle East Studies Association, 2000).

[7] Many Christian and Jewish communities, especially before the nineteenth century, were at least as conservative as Muslim counterparts regarding women's public visibility, gender mixing, bodily coverage, youthful age at marriage and the like. Many such practices pre-dated the advent of Islam, though their Islamic endorsement over the centuries no doubt reinforced their currency.

African, Iranian and Central Asian fashion to the already diverse urban mix. Those who decided to make their lives in Ottoman lands eventually adopted local garb, while transients kept to their own. Regardless, the constant influx of new people into the cities influenced local styles, with Tatar and Caucasian (Circassian, Abaza) styles frequently becoming popular with both men and women.[8]

European clothing would be more in evidence due to the lopsided trade with Europe in the eighteenth century, Europe's incontestable ascendancy in the nineteenth and the ever-increasing number of self-assured Europeans on eastern Mediterranean streets beginning in the later eighteenth century. Until the eighteenth century, though, Ottoman rulers conceived of their Empire as a world at their command. They struggled to secure their power even as it was ebbing away under European economic pressures and, by the turn of the nineteenth century, outright invasion.[9] On the homefront itself, clothing and 'the world of goods' were the cutting edge of the struggle against the new realities. Cloth and fashion unleashed consumerist tastes, with textiles the opening salvo in industrial Europe's global dominance.[10] Guarding the social structure against even the appearance of disruption was a perennial Ottoman preoccupation. The ideal was always elusive, and now increasingly so. The problem was all the more critical in these later centuries, when the appearance of control – over the subject population if not against foreign armies on the battlefield – was increasingly what remained of nostalgic memory. Latter-day sultans were unable to deliver stunning victories as their ancestors had done even into the mid-seventeenth century. Nonetheless, they could still lay claim to Islamic legitimacy, as upholders of Islamic law and of the shari'ah-informed social order set in place by those ancestors.

Powers of Dress

When the Ottomans became a world power in the early sixteenth century, the regime settled into a high imperialism of theatrical royal remoteness

---

[8] Joseph von Hammer-Purgstall, *Geschichte des Osmanischen Reiches*, 10 vols. (Pest: C. A. Hartleben, 1827–1835), vii: 54–55; Sevin, *On Üç Asırlık*, 102.

[9] Napoleon's invasion of Egypt in 1798, although short-lived, was preceded by Russia's annexation of the Crimea in 1783, and followed by the French conquest of Algeria in 1830, the British invasion of Egypt in 1882 and numerous European proxy wars in the decades before and after those events.

[10] Halil İnalcık with Donald Quataert (eds.), *An Economic and Social History of the Ottoman Empire, 1300–1914* (Cambridge: Cambridge University Press, 1994), 354–359; Edhem Eldem, *French Trade in Istanbul in the Eighteenth Century* (Leiden: Brill, 1999).

and strict elite–commoner differentiation. The Muslim patriciate, the so-called *askeri* stratum of male lay and religious officials, was distinguished in law by its exemption from taxation. On the streets and at court their elevated station was signalled both by the quality of their garments and by distinct turban styles specific to each man's official vocation and rank therein (Figure 15.1). Ottoman books of protocol (*teşrifat*) spelled out which variety of turban belonged on which official heads and what quality of fur pelt might appear on whose gowns. The stately quilted and pleated turbans (*kallavi kavuk, mücevveze*) that towered over ceremonial assemblies were reserved for vizierial heads, and sable, ermine, lynx, and black fox linings and plackets were meant for the robes of the highest religious and lay officeholders.[11] Appearance was to correlate with power. Thus in the eighteenth and early nineteenth centuries, unentitled Muslims as well as non-Muslims – 'the likes of servants, tradesmen, and people of the bazaar' of whatever faith – were regularly denounced, with at least some success, for donning the attire of their betters.[12] As the British traveller Aaron Hill (d. 1750) remarked, '[t]hose look great among the Turks [Ottomans] who really are so'.[13] Ottoman regulators would have been gratified to know that they had made their point.

The lower one's position on the socio-economic ladder, the more likely that the workaday attire of men in the same labouring vocations would be indistinguishable across the religious confessions.[14] Indeed, the line between *askeri* and commoner (*reaya*), which obtained regardless of religion, was as consistently drawn as that between Muslims and

---

[11] Mehmed Es'ad Efendi, *Osmanlı İmparatorluğu'nda Teşrifat* (Istanbul: Okur Kitaplığı, 2013), passim, regarding official protocol and garb required on ceremonial occasions; Ali Seydi Bey, *Teşrifat ve Teşkilatımız*, ed. Niyazi Ahmet Banoğlu (Istanbul: Tercüman Yayınları, n.d.), 69–89; Markus Koller, 'The Istanbul Fur Market in the Eighteenth Century', in Costantini and Koller, *Living in the Ottoman Ecumenical Community*, 115–129.

[12] Mehmed Hâkim, 'Tarih-i Hâkim', Istanbul, Topkapı Sarayı Ktp. (hereafter TKS), B (Bağdat) #231, 290a-291; B#233, 184a, 192a-193a.

[13] Aaron Hill, *A Full and Just Account of the Present State of the Ottoman Empire in All Its Branches* ... (London: G. Parker, 1733), ch.12. Although the designation 'Turk' is commonly used in referring to Ottomans, especially Muslim Ottomans, 'Ottoman' is the correct term for the ruling dynasty and ruling class as well as for Muslims of the Empire generally. The dynasty and imperial ruling circles from at least the early sixteenth century were of mixed ethnicity, with Bosnians, Serbs, Greeks, Albanians, Circassians and Georgians arguably more likely than ethnic Turks to occupy the highest administrative and palace posts. The sultans themselves had ceased marrying ethnic Turks by the early sixteenth century; thereafter, all Ottoman rulers were the sons of non-Muslim, non-Turkish, slave concubines. The language of the dynasty and of the administration was Ottoman Turkish.

[14] Donald Quataert, 'Clothing Laws, State and Society in the Ottoman Empire, 1720–1829', *International Journal of Middle East Studies* 29/3 (1997): 415–419, 425.

Figure 15.1 Mehmed Arif Pasha, 'Ottoman Bureaucratic Officials', in *Les Anciens Costumes de l'Empire Ottoman* (Paris: Lemercier, 1863), vol. 1. Image in public domain.

non-Muslims of middling and higher economic status. All commoner subjects in the city and its environs had cause to fear harsh punishment if they imitated the dress of *askeri* grandees, just as men and women could expect punishment, usually in the form of fines or thrashing, if they wore attire associated with another faith. Capital punishment was inflicted on males who chanced an *askeri* transgression in periods of heightened surveillance, such as between the mid-eighteenth and the early nineteenth centuries.[15] As more than one of Selim III's sumptuary decrees to his officers concluded: 'If anyone behaves contrary [to the decree], for sure let them be executed ... whomever I myself see, I'll kill, and you [police] will not have an excuse [for yourselves]'.[16] Osman III (1754–1757) and

---

[15] Hâkim, 'Hâkim Tarihi', Bağdat #233, 33b, for a case in 1173 Anno Hijri (hereafter as AH)/1760 CE. The victim, a non-Muslim translator (whether Christian or Jewish is unclear), was also suspected of passing information to European representatives. His sartorial infractions were thus only one of the charges against him. Decrees of Osman III (1754–1757) and Selim III (1789–1807) were particularly vehement regarding the imposition of capital punishment on sartorial offenders, with Osman also especially vicious regarding women.

[16] Enver Ziya Karal. *Selim III'ün Hat-tı Hümayunları* (Ankara: Türk Tarih Kurumu Basımevi, 1946), 101–102.

Selim's own father, Mustafa III (1757–1774), had been no less infuriated, calling for sartorial offenders 'to be dispatched into the abyss' without recourse of any kind.[17]

The privileges of the *askeri* class were reserved for Muslims, except for certain exempted individuals and categories. Among these were the Greek Orthodox Patriarch, other Christian ecclesiasts and high rabbinical authorities. Other non-Muslims – notably physicians – were also invested with the marks of official status by the Sultan or his chief deputy, the Grand Vizier.[18] So it was that non-Muslim medical practitioners (*tabib, cerrah*) like the Jewish physician Mosi ben Nesim in 1695 and the Orthodox Christian Stavraki in 1755, were not to be 'harassed or molested' for alleged transgressions against Muslim prerogatives. The men's petitions to the throne indicated that they had in fact been harassed by the populace. The two were confirmed in their right to ride horseback and wear such Muslim garb as yellow leather boots and sable fur.[19] Sovereign prerogative could thus make or break not only administrative rules of status but also even the shari'ah-prescribed sumptuary distinction between Muslim and non-Muslim.

Gendered Limits

Meanwhile, urban women's outdoor clothing across the confessions tended toward uniformity in cut, weight and drabness, including face and head coverings. In public space, Muslim, Christian and Jewish women were all obliged to 'de-sex' their female selves with similarly lacklustre, full-body coverings. Confessional differences in outerwear were nonetheless to be signified by differentiating hues in stout fabrics – usually dark blue or black for Christian and Jewish women, and dark green or red for Muslims.[20] Standard female outer garments of the eighteenth century into the mid-nineteenth were variations of the *ferace*, a neck-to-ankle coat or mantle (Figure 15.2). Modifications to it, whether in the form of decorative buttons, cape-like collars, pastel hues, or form- or face-revealing fabrics, were strictly forbidden. A typical remonstrance, issued in the fall of 1759, repeated the prohibition on 'Muslim and non-Muslim women—both Christians and Jews—dressed in outsized head dressings

---

[17] Hâkim, 'Hâkim Tarihi', Bağdat #231, 270a.
[18] On the *askeri* category in Ottoman usage, see İnalcık and Quataert, *An Economic and Social History*, 15–16.
[19] Ahmed Refik, *Hicrî On İkinci Asırda İstanbul Hayatı (1100–1200)* (Istanbul: Devlet Matbaası, 1930), 20, 84; Ahmet Kal'a et al. (eds.), *İstanbul Külliyâtı I: İstanbul Ahkâm Defterleri, İstanbul Esnaf Tarihi I* (Istanbul: İstanbul Araştırmaları Merkezi, 1997), 94.
[20] Hâkim, 'Hâkim Tarihi', Bağdat #233, 10b (Safer 1173 AH/ October 1759).

Figure 15.2 'Ottoman Woman in Outdoor Coat (*Ferace*)', from Octavian Dalvimart, *The Costume of Turkey* (London: William Miller, 1804). Image in public domain.

with their faces half-veiled and immodest' (Figure 15.3).[21] Another, from 1807, dictated that women's coats should not have collars 'larger than an *arşın*', that is twenty-eight inches.[22] Such targets were common fodder in social regulation.

Virtually every sumptuary ordinance of these decades justified the need for reissuance with a declamation against readily observable urban wrongdoers. On several fronts, however, the regulatory state was fighting an unwinnable battle. Women's 'large' and 'long' collars, which

[21] Hâkim, 'Hâkim Tarihi', Bağdat #233, 10b (Safer 1173 AH/ October 1759).
[22] Suha Umur, 'Kadınlara Buyruklar', *Tarih ve Toplum* 10/58 (1988): 13–15.

Femme Juive

Figure 15.3 'Femme Juive', showing a Jewish woman wearing a black entari and a white kuşak round her head and shoulders. From *Costumes turcs* (1790), vol. 2, fol. 31. Trustees of the British Museum 1974,0617,0.12.2.31.

met with repeated condemnation in Istanbul in the eighteenth century
on interlocked economic and religious-moral grounds, in fact grew to
nearly floor-length capes by the nineteenth. The periodic deployment
of scissor-wielding officers to seize female offenders and cut off such
proofs of shari'ah-defying immodesty and budget-busting immoder-
ation was harsh but usually short-lived. The police were apparently no
match for middling- and upper-class women's fashion assertions in this
vein. Veiling, too, was a telling case in point. Face-revealing veils were
taboo by law and could result in public humiliations, including on-the-
spot beatings by the authorities or punishment by women's own families. Family retribution was almost certain since the misbehaviour of
female dependents could spell fines or banishment for entire families.[23]
On this bodily battlefront as well, though, women were pushing against
the rule – as complaints in the eighteenth and nineteenth centuries
about transparent and loose veils attest.[24] Despite periodic respites from
intense surveillance and, increasingly as of the nineteenth century, the
relative freedom of European-frequented locales like the Pera and Galata
neighbourhoods, unveiling had no permanent success until the Young
Turk era around World War I and, finally, the secular Turkish Republic.

A royal decree from the turn of the nineteenth century, at the height
of regulatory zeal, was one of dozens that addressed the preoccupations
of the eighteenth and early nineteenth centuries. The tone of the decree
was the usual one of angry indignation, urging the Grand Vizier to put a
stop to what the Sultan himself – in this case Selim III (r. 1789–1807) –
had discovered on one of his incognito prowls: 'My Vizier, I have heard
and seen womenfolk going about in the markets and bazaars in light-
coloured coats (*ferace*) and behaving shamelessly. Hereafter you are to
serve warning that they are not to wear light-coloured coats or out-sized
collars, and that all must behave with purity and modesty. You must also
forcibly prohibit and prevent tailors from making such garb'.[25] Decrees

---

[23] Suha Umur. 'Kadınlara Buyruklar', 15, specifies in a decree from 1734 (1147 AH)
that husbands were to be expelled from the city, presumably with their families, or else
imprisoned for women's public misdeeds. Similar threats continued to be made and
acted on through the mid-nineteenth century; see Osman Nuri Ergin, *Mecelle-i Umur-i
Belediye*, 5 vols. (Istanbul: Matbaa-i Osmaniye, 1338/1922), i: 897.

[24] Ergin, *Mecelle*, 1:896; Küçük Çelebizade İsmail Asım, *Tarih-i Asım*. Vol. 6 of Raşid,
Tarih-i Raşid (Istanbul: Matbaa-i Âmire, 1282/1865), 375–376; M. Münir Aktepe (ed.),
Şem'dânî-zâde Fındıklılı Süleyman Efendi Tārihi, Mür'i't-Tevârih, 3 vols. (Istanbul: Edebiyat
Fakültesi Matbaası, 1976–81), i: 26, for the eighteenth and early nineteenth centuries.
Cf. Istanbul, *Ceride-i Havadis*, Ramadan 7, 1257/October 23 1857 and Şaban 12, 1258/
September 18 1258, for similar government actions at Istanbul during the *Tanzimat*
reform era.

[25] Necdet Sakaoğlu, 'Osmanlı Giyim Kuşamı ve "Elbise-i Osmaniyye"', *Tarih ve Toplum*
8/47(1987): 38. Indeed, tailors who acted on requisitions for such clothing orders

from early in the reign of Mahmud II (r. 1808–1839), the man who would later effect a clothing revolution for men,[26] drew a vivid picture of what was at stake when women went wrong. According to one such decree issued in 1811, women who dared to wear 'unaccustomed shapes' in coats or head covers, even if coverage was complete and colours and fabrics appropriate, were faulted, not just for the 'too-much-ness' of their dress but because disobedient women were the measure of society's moral disfigurement. Women as a group were 'the cause of depravity and disorder'. And, inasmuch as 'all women are snares of the devil', they endanger the entire believing community.[27] When they transgressed, they were defying the shari'ah itself: women who went about too much in public 'countenanced vice and debauchery in defiance of the shari'ah'.[28]

In the period encompassing the reigns of Mahmud I (1730–1754), Osman III (1754–1757), Mustafa III (1757–1774), Abdulhamid I (1774–1789), Selim III (1789–1807), Mustafa IV (1807–1808) and Mahmud II (1808–1839), the shari'ah was occasionally invoked regarding male consumption – for 'behaving contrary to the shari'ah and proper usage'. The few such references were tied to the shar'iah principle of necessary external distinctions between Muslims and non-Muslims and inserted without embellishment, almost as afterthoughts. For the most part they were buried under stern remonstrances tying men not to divine dispensation but to the will of the sovereign as voiced in his various orders (*emr*, *ferman*). Offending males were seldom called out generically but rather by vocation, confession or social status. An avalanche of decrees in these decades cite them for disobeying 'the imperial command', 'the noble/royal order', 'this noble rescript and ferman', or 'this prohibition and imperial order'.[29] Unlike women, who were invariably pinioned by strict gender norms, male wrongdoers were more often classed, segmented and stratified, and as such held up to the worldly limits of their social identity.

were to be physically punished, even to the point of being hanged and displayed at their shop doors; Ahmed Refik, *Hicrî On Üçüncü Asırda İstanbul Hayatı (1200–1255)* (Istanbul: Devlet Matbaası, 1932), 4; Ahmed Cevdet. *Tarih-i Cevdet*. 12 vols. (Istanbul: Matbaa-i Osmaniye, 1309/1891), i: 50–51.

26 Quataert, 'Clothing Laws', passim.
27 Umur, 'Kadınlara Buyruklar', 15, 'fesada sebeb', 'tamam-ün-nisâ habâil-üş-şeytan', from a decree of Mahmud II in 1811 (1226 AH). A contemporaneous complaint by the Greek Orthodox priest Mikha'il Burayk (fl.1782), angered by the dress and behaviour of Christian women in Damascus, echoes the state's view: 'Truly we say there is no harm or evil that is not caused by women'; Dana Sajdi, *The Barber of Damascus: Nouveau Literacy in the Eighteenth-Century Ottoman Levant* (Stanford: Stanford University Press, 2013), 16.
28 Umur, 'Kadınlara Buyruklar', 15; Ergin, *Mecelle*, i: 895. Similarly, Hâkim, ' Hâkim Tarihi', B#231, 234b
29 Hâkim, 'Hâkim Tarihi', B#231, 353a; B#233, 184a, 192a–193a.

The pronouncement of women as fully under shari'ah governance was contrastingly frequent and unambiguous: 'women were not to act contrary to the noble shari'ah ... they were not to defy Almighty God's decree'. Indeed, some of these shari'ah-infused ordinances regarding women took misogyny to its logical conclusion, exhorting women to remain confined to their houses except out of 'shari'ah-ordained necessity'. Here was a usefully vague intimidation affording street-level enforcers and conservative family heads wide latitude.[30] Women's clothing assertions thus epitomised the triple jeopardy of social impropriety, economic profligacy and irreligion. The conflation of woman with womankind, and woman/womankind with the integrity of the Islamic community rendered female misdeeds a collective danger, a matter of communal sin and contagious moral disorder.[31] Public space was expressly Islamicised, by the built environment and the visual sovereignty of ceremony, consumption and protocol, but regulatory discourse put forward a rendering that was essentially masculine as well.

Despite the feverish measures directed at women's behaviour in public space, the state did not unleash its police on the domestic household. The authorities as a rule did not inquire into what women chose to wear under their outdoor robes, nor did they intrude upon domestic space to uncover sumptuary wrongdoing. Breaking down doors on suspicion of prostitution was another matter. Men and women could indulge their sumptuary tastes and comforts among their intimates in the privacy of their homes or otherwise in the company of Qur'an-specified intimates. Public space – the streets and marketplace and, by extension, retail shops – constituted the quotidian imperial domain. Apart from Islamic monuments themselves, these constituted the showcase of Ottoman sovereignty and its socially grounded Islamic legitimacy. Istanbul since its establishment as the capital in 1453 was the centre of that urban conceit and the epicentre of the sumptuary regime. As a clothing ordinance of 1814 put it, albeit in a bit of wishful thinking, 'the people of the exalted capital are divided into numerous classes (sunuf, s., sınıf) and every class has its own attire. They are to go about in those garments, respect the usages of proper etiquette and all are to know the limits of their station

---

[30] Istanbul, İstanbul Müftülüğü, 2/184, 150a; Hâkim, 'Hâkim Tarihi', B#231, 234b, 290a-b. Also Madeline C. Zilfi, *Women and Slavery in the Late Ottoman Empire* (Cambridge: Cambridge University Press, 2010), 55–56, on the scriptural and legal-historical basis of the prescription.

[31] Madeline C. Zilfi, 'Muslim Women in the Early Modern Era', in Suraiya N. Faroqhi (ed.), *The Cambridge History of Turkey*, vol. 3, *The Later Ottoman Empire, 1603-1839* (Cambridge: Cambridge University Press, 2006), 226.

(*hadd*)'.[32] Of course, many people were *not* abiding by the bounds of their station, no matter how often the various sultans commanded it and even killed to make it come to pass.

The two distinguishing features of Ottoman clothing law from the sixteenth century through the first quarter of the nineteenth were its endurance and its relentless targeting of women. The Ottoman regime for most of its history sought to ensure that clothing functioned as the chief marker of social location and relationships to power. Sumptuary laws restricting such things as horseback riding in cities and the height of houses relative to those of Muslim neighbours were occasional annoyances for Christians and Jews who had the means to afford those accoutrements of wealth. In any case, non-elite Muslims were often forbidden to appear on horseback in the cities as well.[33] While sartorial dictates regarding non-Muslim male dress were demeaning in their denial of free choice and insistence on an appearance of inferiority or abasement relative to Muslims, none of these substantially interfered with men's physical mobility or their access to worship. Nor did they interfere with the freedom of Christians and Jews to make a living, even, in the case of some, to amass enviable wealth derived from government-granted privileges and concessions – wealth that in many cases could surpass that of most Muslims.

Laws affecting women did limit women's freedoms. Even into the last decades of the Ottoman era, social controls remained fixed on the governance of women. The too-common historiographical and popular view that non-Muslims, especially Christians, were the 'second-class citizens' of the Ottoman Empire has long since needed decentring in the story of Ottoman social and political organisation and the symbolics of power. There is no comparison between the debilitating strictures imposed on women by the state, family and faith and those on men, regardless of how much the Ottoman master narrative for the eighteenth and nineteenth centuries privileges ethnic categories, the rise of nationalism and (male-directed) struggles to combat autocracy. The *Tanzimat*, the period of modernising reforms inaugurated in 1839, gave male subjects irrespective of religion some of the entitlements of rights-based citizenship. Indeed, religious egalitarianism – its exclusive maleness understood – became the new watchword of imperial politics, mainly as an optimistic

---

[32] Refik, *Hicrî On Üçüncü Asırda İstanbul Hayatı (1200–1255)*, 13–14.
[33] Reşat Ekrem Koçu, *Osmanlı Tarihinde Yasaklar* (Istanbul: Şaka Matbaası, 1950), 33; Ahmet Kal'a et al. (eds.), *İstanbul Külliyatı: İstanbul'da Esnaf Tarihi* (Istanbul: İstanbul Araştırmaları Merkezi, 1997), i: 94, regarding an order of 1755 renewing the right of a non-Muslim physician to ride horseback in the city.

counterweight to growing ethnic separatism in the period.[34] In 1829, a decade before the promulgation of the *Tanzimat*, the then Sultan, Mahmud II, had put an end to clothing restrictions on non-Muslim men. The restrictions and the regulatory rhetoric regarding women, however, remained in place. In the new discourse of rights that would culminate in the First and Second Ottoman Constitutions of 1876 and 1908, women were a civic nonentity. Autocratic sultans and ministers made way for so-called 'modernisers', 'reformers' and even 'constitutionalists', with little impact on women's place in society. Indeed, the congratulatory termin-ology for the distinctiveness of the reform era and its exemplars does not accord with the continuities in the treatment of women. Muslim women remained dependent upon the authority of male relatives in keeping with Ottoman interpretations of shari'ah law, specifically interpretations regarding the male-bestowed shari'ah 'protections' that constrained women's autonomy and defined, for most women, the female sphere. Husbands or brothers succeeded fathers and grandfathers as women's guardians and executives. Even sons or nephews sometimes stood in as guardians regardless of a woman's age.

Ottoman history offers numerous examples of exceptions to the rule of male privilege and primacy.[35] Certainly individual families followed their own nonconforming paths when it came to gender relations. However, social expectation and the letter of the law, both primed by tendentious readings of Qur'anic and shari'ah enjoinments,[36] ensured that most women, for most of their lives, were legal minors. The sump-tuary regulations that reined in women's mobility and choices prior to the nineteenth century persisted into the twentieth. They lasted almost a century after Christian and Jewish men escaped the prohibitions that had denied them snow-white turbans and other 'colours of rule'. Christian and Jewish males joined their Muslim male countrymen in the elected

---

[34] Roderic H. Davison, *Reform in the Ottoman Empire* (Princeton: Princeton University Press, 1963), 3–81.

[35] The rather bleak picture drawn here can be counterbalanced to some extent by the important scholarship that underscores regional and class variations and offers numerous examples of differences between prescription and practical reality. Among the most revealing studies are those that examine religious court records, noting women's frequent use of the courts (somewhere between 20 and 30 per cent of cases in Ottoman Istanbul and Anatolia) to press for rights of alimony, child support, inheritance and civil damages as well as court appearances connected to their roles as testators, child guardians, legatees and owners of commercial properties. See for example studies by Ronald Jennings, Suraiya Faroqhi, Leslie Peirce, Abraham Marcus, Iris Agmon, Judith Tucker, Kemal Çiçek, Yvonne Seng and Rossitsa Gradeva, among others.

[36] Barbara Stowasser, *Women in the Qur'an, Traditions, and Interpretation* (Oxford: Oxford University Press, 1994), and Asma Barlas, *'Believing Women' in Islam: Unreading Patriarchal Interpretations of the Qur'an* (Austin: University of Texas Press, 2002),

parliaments of 1877 and 1908. In fact, Mahmud II's clothing reforms had completely abolished the classical *askeri* wardrobe, relegating it to museums and costume books.[37] Ottoman Christians and Jews took their seats in parliament wearing essentially the same garb as Muslims. Turbans had been abolished in favour of the fez, and brocaded caftans had made way for black frock coats and trousers for all but men of religion.[38] For men of religion, robes and, in the case of the ulema, turbans became their unique uniform. In the public mind, the association of turbans with Islam was so deeply felt that to many pious Muslims, scandalised by the new bans, Sultan Mahmud II would forever be the 'infidel Sultan'.[39] In fact, the turban was only Islamic to the extent that centuries of usage had inscribed it as such.[40] The political and social intentions behind these measures and their moment are the subject of the discussion that follows.

Gendering Divine Law?

Ottoman clothing regulations appear in abundance in imperial decrees, chronicles, advice literature and judicial registers. They offer critical perspectives on the linkages between clothing rules and the universe of Ottoman imperial politics in a troubled age. They also provide a framework for understanding how and why women and for so long the religious minorities were central to regulatory anxieties. In these regards, it is important to bear in mind that social regulations with regard to clothing and other sumptuary matters were imperial issuances. That is, they were the product of lay ruling authorities, basically emanations of the Sultan's will, not holy law, shari'ah, per se. To be sure, social regulations were premised on shari'ah principles as historically interpreted by Sunni Islamic theorists and as followed by the Sunni Ottoman Empire. However, the form that social regulations took in imperial issuances was as a man-made legal product, a function of different rulers' responses to historical contexts.

regarding the historical path of women's rights and roles in Islamic exegesis in pre-Ottoman centuries.

[37] Wendy M. K. Shaw, *Possessors and Possessed: Museums, Archaeology, and the Visualization of History in the Late Ottoman Empire* (Berkeley: University of California Press, 2003), 99–103.

[38] Quataert, 'Clothing Laws', 403–425.

[39] J.H.A. Ubicini, *Letters on Turkey: An Account of the Religious, Political, Social, and Commercial Condition of the Ottoman Empire*, 2 vols. (1856; Reprint, New York: Arno Press, 1973), i: 8–9; Recai G. Okandan, *Âmme Hukukumuzun Ana Hatları* (Istanbul: İstanbul Üniversitesi, 1957), 63.

[40] A century later, when the Turkish Republic abolished the fez, secularists would face the same charges of sinfulness and apostasy, on the same contention that the exterior mirrored the inner will.

Two key shari'ah premises of Ottoman social regulations were the exigent necessity of 'modesty' in women, and visible distinction (*ghiyar*)[41] between Muslims and non-Muslims. *Ghiyar* was historically interpreted to mean not only difference, but also inferiorising difference. Thus, clothing should make plain to wearers and observers that though Christianity and Judaism possessed divine truth and their adherents were free to gather and worship, to have churches, temples, clergies, monasteries, seminaries, rabbinical schools, communal laws and leadership, and even certain tax exemptions for their principal leaders and properties, both faiths were judged to be flawed and thus inferior to Islam. Just how disadvantaged or abased non-Muslims were obliged to look had varied from regime to regime over the centuries once clothing distinctions became Islamic practice in the early medieval era. Clothing rules clearly varied under the Ottomans, often from ruler to ruler, with those of the late eighteenth and early nineteenth centuries most fiercely single-minded. Classical Islamic thought on the subject had varied in any case. Some early jurists and later Ottoman counterparts adopted an extreme position, walking a fine line indeed between honouring the Islamic precepts that entitled 'People of the Book' to the free exercise of their faith, and disadvantaging Christians and Jews so severely as to encourage their conversion.[42] A similarly diverse body of opinion had also arisen from shari'ah and Qur'anic principles regarding 'modesty' and 'purity' in women. Comparable unevenness marked the attitudes and policies that historically oversaw the management of female behaviour. In the regulating of both non-Muslims and women, there was ample scope for political and economic contingencies, and individual rulers' inclinations, to ramp up or ease social strictures.

Ottoman clothing regulations in one form or another trace back to the fifteenth and sixteenth centuries. Never constituting a fixed code, the edicts of different sultans, under different pressures or with sartorially inflected notions of piety, nonetheless dwelt on four imperatives: that there be clear clothing distinctions between Muslims and non-Muslims in public space; that those distinctions be hierarchical and so make the superiority of Islam immediately legible on the streets and in the marketplace; that distinctions between *askeri* and commoner (*reaya*) be clear and visible, including the exclusive right of *askeri* officialdom to certain

[41] P. Bearman et al. (eds.), *Encyclopaedia of Islam*, 2nd ed. (Leiden: Brill, 1954–2005), s.v. 'Ghiyar', by M. Perlmann.
[42] *Encyclopaedia of Islam*, 2nd ed., s.v. 'Dhimma', by Claude Cahen. On the Kadizadelis, a seventeenth-century Ottoman school of thought in this vein, see Marc David Baer, *Honored by the Glory of Islam: Conversion and Conquest in Ottoman Europe* (New York: Oxford University Press, 2008).

coveted clothing stuffs; and that women's appearance in public space be practically spectral, covered up from head to toe and on the streets by sufferance. Despite those bottom-line consistencies, the overriding reality of the regulatory regime from the end of the seventeenth century was its need for reinforcing repetition. Imperial edicts drummed away at the same challenges and infractions, thus, as in other European lands, underscoring the practical porousness of sumptuary regulation.

Certainly the reissuing of virtually the same prohibitions – almost annually by the later eighteenth century and the first decades of the nineteenth – suggests that Ottoman subjects found fault with the prohibitions, did not perfectly understand them, disbelieved in their seriousness, thought the authorities incompetent, were committed to expressing their sartorial selves, rejected the notion of Ottoman Muslim superiority, or, specifically in the case of Christians, hoped for diplomatic or other intervention on their behalf. There was also the question of legislative vagueness – how large was a 'too-large' collar, and how thin were 'thin' veils? Since squirrel and rabbit fur were permitted to the masses, did that include a robe entirely of fur or did the permission extend only to bits and pieces? While the cognitive substance of key terms was deliberately vague, their negative charge was unambiguous. For one or a variety of reasons, many Ottoman subjects persisted in defying the law or – to hedge our bets regarding their degree of agency in such 'defiance' – for one reason or another running afoul of the law.[43] The repetitiveness of the issuances also points to a certain connivance on the part of the policing authorities, who may for a fee have looked the other way when confronted with individuals wearing the wrong kind of fur or headgear. Of course, whether policing authorities strictly enforced the law or let transgressions slide, sumptuary regulation was in many respects monetised. More often than not enforcement of the law boosted someone's income, either as fines levied or bribes offered.[44] Fines were a typical punishment, with or without strokes to the backside or the feet (bastinado). Also, the choice and severity of non-lethal punishments were often at the discretion of street-level enforcers. Wrongdoers could hope that a bribe would lead

[43] Zilfi, *Women and Slavery*, 59; Madeline C. Zilfi, 'Whose Laws? Gendering the Ottoman Sumptuary Regime', in Suraiya N. Faroqhi and Christoph K. Neumann (eds.), *Ottoman Costumes: From Textiles to Identity* (Istanbul: Eren, 2004), 125–141.

[44] [François] Baron de Tott, *Memoirs of Baron de Tott*. 2 vols. in 4 pts. (London, 1785; reprint New York: Arno Press, 1973), i: xxxiv, regarding the imperial *Bostancı* Corps' role in such exactions. Abraham Marcus, *The Middle East on the Eve of Modernity: Aleppo in the Eighteenth Century* (New York: Columbia University Press, 1989), 115, notes similar practices on the part of authorities in Aleppo. Cf. Bernard Heyberger, *Les Chrétiens du Proche Orient au temps de la Réforme catholique* (Rome: École Française de Rome, 1994), 52.

to a reduced fine or symbolic beating rather than banishment from the city or, in the case of tailors and other tradesmen who made or sold such goods, confiscation of unauthorised goods or boarding up of their shops.

Selim III is known for his military reforms and openness to change. He did not, however, extend his vision to social reform, certainly not with regard to women, although his military agenda meant enhanced mobility for several thousand Muslim males recruited for his new army (*Nizam-i Cedid*).[45] But Selim had no interest in revamping the social order. Like his father Mustafa III and mentor-uncle Abdülhamid I, Selim held fast to regulatory remedies. The statutes of their day set the pattern for consumer-targeted legislation that explicitly referenced trade imbalances. The various decrees, all of them studies in futility given the unavoidable foreign sources of the period's prestige goods, singled out the costly 'varieties of fur, flowered caftans and gowns, and cashmere and other Indian goods' that 'the likes of servants, merchants and tradesmen' were buying and wearing in trespass of grandee prerogative. Such imports were thus damaging the economy, all the more so because domestic cloths were said to be available from Istanbul, Bursa, Syria and other Ottoman territories.[46] The conflation of domestic social challenges with Europe-induced economic woes is unsurprising given the new climate of Ottoman decline. In such matters, unlike decrees aimed at women, invocations of shari'ah rectitude and principles were negligible or unmentioned. Regulations directed at male clothing transgressions sidestepped the moralising that suffused regulations regarding women. Male sumptuary transgressions were conceived as damages to the state, the fisc, local tradesmen and law and order generally. Apart from occasional allusions to the confessional differentiation principle (*ghiyar*), religion-informed morality was not held to be at risk. Men's wrongdoing destabilised worldly, not heavenly, dispensations. Their offences, unlike those of women, did not fundamentally compromise or taint the Islamic community in the eyes of God.

While the triggers of Selim's and his contemporaries' anxieties were women in non-standard garb and non-elite men ('servants, merchants, and tradesmen'), especially non-Muslim men, who affected elite and/or expensive garb, the sultans were alert to their officers' failings. Selim's incognito forays around the city could be a brutal teaching moment for police as well as law breakers.[47] In the decree quoted earlier, Selim made

[45] Stanford J. Shaw, *Between Old and New: The Ottoman Empire under Selim III, 1789–1807* (Cambridge, MA: Harvard University Press, 1971).
[46] Ahmed Rasım, *Resimli ve Haritalı Osmanlı Tarihi*, 4 vols. in 2 (Istanbul: İkbal Kütüphanesi, 1326–1330/1908–1912), iii: 1035.
[47] I employ 'police' as a term of convenience for the several military units whose peacetime responsibilities included law enforcement.

clear his displeasure with lax enforcement: 'My Vizier... while it is necessary that you take the time to watch out for these things, that you cut off collars and expel from the city these shameless ones, why are you not attending to it?'[48] In another issuance, he was equally direct: 'If I hear that you have issued pardons and been soft, you won't be able to have an answer [for me]'.[49] The sultans and the ruling elites were not ready to admit that the world-class Empire and command economy that had upheld the old social structure were practically dead letters. The global economy and Europe's imperial reach had seen to that. The command economy had never been fully operational in any case, as sumptuary decrees from the Ottomans' sixteenth-century heyday attest, but it had worked enough to nourish the myth.

It is not surprising that the frenetic outpouring of social legislation in the late eighteenth and early nineteenth centuries coincided with the onslaught of multiple perils. Perhaps the social laws of the period deserve the label of 'panic legislation'.[50] They were undoubtedly a reaction to the disastrous foreign wars after the 1760s and growing popular dissent of various kinds, including as of the late eighteenth century, open rebellion in the Balkan provinces. However, panic and crisis tell only part of the story. They can account for the expanded volume of legislation, and for the enfolding of status transgressions with state budgets. The resort to scapegoating, homing in on women and the religious minorities, is also not surprising; for both there was a richly stigmatising discourse of otherness ready to hand.

The Ottoman regime had long practice in the art of deflection. In these times, deflection away from military disasters was a constructive strategy. Not only was the Empire losing territories but also thousands of Muslim refugees, fleeing massacre and what would in the present day come to be known as ethnic cleansing, were pouring into an ever-shrinking Empire after the mid-1770s. The tens of thousands of soldiers and seamen who had perished in defence of the Empire – for the Ottomans were continually on the defensive after 1683 – also had to be explained to an incredulous, frightened public. The turn to sumptuary issues provided not all the answers, but some, by pinpointing a visible, proximate cause of degeneracy, one that had a chance of remediation or at least of satisfying retribution. For those kinds of dilemmas at least, the regime could assume an appearance of mastery. Repetition may also have been for

[48] Sakaoğlu, 'Osmanlı Giyim', 38.
[49] Karal, *Selim III'ün Hat-tı Hümayunları*, 101.
[50] Alan Hunt, *Governance of the Consuming Passion: A History of Sumptuary Law* (New York: St Martin's Press, 1996); Alan Hunt, *Governing Morals: A Social History of Moral Regulation* (Cambridge: Cambridge University Press, 1999).

repetition's sake, to keep the public's attention turned toward the possible, away from foreign quarrels that showcased the regime's incap-
acities. And since regulations, in fact, increasingly addressed economic
grievances – the state's trade balances, and real households struggling
with rising prices and consumerism – they answered a felt need of much
of the urban population.

Social legislation performed other, arguably more important, work, as
well. It buttressed the ruler's claim to legitimacy as the Sultan laboured
to maintain social order and keep social peace by calling the population back to its proper roles and relationships. Even more, social legislation was a constitutive call to arms to the Muslim population. The
visual reassurance it promoted reminded Muslims of who they were.
The time-honoured marks of Islam's superiority meant every Muslim's
superiority, every Muslim's special rights, which the sultans endeavoured
to reinforce in their barrage of pronouncements. Certainly elements of
the ruling class were key instigators behind sumptuary regulations, tirelessly guarding their privileges and exceptionalism against the claims
of the lower orders.[51] Clearly such initiatives can be attributed to the
Ottoman ruling elites and their relationship to social regulation. The
princes and princesses of the dynasty and their palace servitors were
obvious devotees of ruling class privileges and distinctions. Along with
the dynasty, various viziers of the seventeenth and eighteenth centuries,
as chief ministers of the realm and the apex of the social pyramid, were as
famous as their sovereigns for idiosyncratic measures regarding clothing
enjoinments and prohibitions.[52] Ordinary Muslims did not directly make
law. Nonetheless, they were dialogically invested in clothing rules and
the social architecture that the rules represented. The rules signalled an
intersection of shared values, the political primacy of material goods and
the enactment of hierarchy in practice. Whatever their wealth or vocation, most ordinary Muslims saw themselves reflected in the sartorial
signs of Muslims' superiority relative to the Christians and Jews in their

---

[51] Fernand Braudel, *Capitalism and Material Life, 1400–1800* (New York: Harper & Row,
1973), 226.

[52] When the monumental *mücevveze* turban style was losing favour with officials entitled
to wear it, the Grand Vizier of the time, Kalaylıkoz Ahmed (d. 1715), insisted on its
use, including a personally designed, much-embellished version for himself. At the
same time, he imposed draconian sumptuary penalties on Christians, Jews, women and
non-entitled Muslims. Hammer-Purgstall, *Geschichte*, vii: 55, 107–108; İsmail Hami
Danişmend, *İzahlı Osmanlı Tarihi Kronolojisi*. 2nd rev. ed., 6 vols. (Istanbul: Türkiye
Yayınevi, 1971–1972), v: 51–52. Monumental turban styles were reserved for ceremonial use, but since Ottoman rulership was awash in ceremony, the financial outlay for
ceremonial garb was immense. Such turbans required prodigious amounts of expensive
cloth to fabricate, and most were further adorned with precious gems, rare feathers
or gold.

midst. Statutes that forbade Christians and Jews from wearing (or at least from displaying in public) the styles and quality of dress of Muslim elites levelled down all non-Muslims, regardless of how wealthy. On the streets at least, Christian and Jewish subjects had, or should have had, the appearance of subservience.

In the eighteenth and early nineteenth centuries, clothing restrictions were in fact a response to the complaints and discomfort of ordinary Muslims as much as of jealous patricians. Urban Muslims daily witnessed Christians and Jews – some of them Ottoman subjects, others members of the ever-increasing European diplomatic and commercial missions – flouting the law. Europeans associated with the various embassies carried extraterritoriality and thus exemption from local laws. Since the embassies were able to extend their protections, including exemption from local laws and taxes, to Ottoman subjects in their employ,[53] exceptions to Ottoman clothing strictures were everywhere. Such visible exceptions, and the conspicuous fashions they paraded, prompted other Ottoman subjects, Muslim and non-Muslim, to question the crumbling sartorial regime.[54] The dynastic regime for its part could not unequivocally sanction the disintegration of the structure undergirding its own position. The sultans continued their harangues: in order to reassert a measure of control and thereby offer up evidence of Islamic rulership; in order to mollify the lower orders and the pious, who rallied to the prescriptive regime; in order to absolve the regime of its own responsibilities in bringing about economic dependency and an inept and politicised military; and to turn attention away from the ruling cadres' own luxuriant, import-dependent life styles.

Conclusion

Sumptuary regulations, especially with their invocation of shari'ah order and obedience, were a proactive defence given the acute pressures and challenges of the eighteenth and early nineteenth centuries. It is in this period of intensified social regulation that Selim III and Mahmud II were pursuing Western-style military and educational reforms. The need to draw on Western expertise in order to advance the reforms clashed with the worldview of many Ottomans, who blamed the West for the Empire's perilous condition and chafed at their sultans' turn to Christian

---

[53] Maurits H. van den Boogert, *The Capitulations and the Ottoman Legal System: Qadis, Consuls and Beraths in the 18th Century* (Leiden: Brill, 2005).

[54] Matthew Elliot, 'Dress Codes in the Ottoman Empire: The Case of the Franks', in Faroqhi and Neumann, *Ottoman Costumes*, 103–123.

Europeans for aid and advice. Selim and Mahmud and their new systems were castigated as un-Islamic by conservative domestic opponents,[55] most vehemently by opponents who could mobilise pious and institutional interests. Sultan Selim in 1808 was in fact assassinated by a coalition mobilised in the name of religious and economic grievances.[56] Selim's successor Mahmud, among other overtures to conservative sentiment,[57] ramped up controls on women. His ordinances were especially dogmatic in binding women to purported shari'ah norms and conflating women's upright behaviour with Islamic morality and Islamic communal integrity.

The jettisoning of men's clothing strictures in 1829 was an unanticipated first step toward the modernising, and occasionally liberalising, reforms that would shape domestic politics thenceforward. The Ottoman Empire was hardly alone in leaving women out of the new social compact. However, the Ottoman regime's agenda in this regard was consciously constructive rather than just reflexively exclusionary. Mahmud's clothing reforms sundered the sumptuary pairing of women and non-Muslims, and the reformist leadership forged ahead with institutional changes. In doing so, the regime encouraged the support of native non-Muslim men, not incidentally placating the European powers while simultaneously, through the prescribed timelessness of women's role and aspect, paying homage to tradition and continuity. Freeze-framing women in the clothing 'of time immemorial' and continuing the rhetorical assault on women's personhood and individuality provided a counter-discourse to offset the West-tainted rhetoric of reform. Change was not congenial to social cohesion, much less to moral unity within the majority, Muslim, population. The archaicising fusion of women with Islamic culture,[58] and the symbolic rendering of 'authentic' Islamic

---

[55] The puritanical Wahhabi movement in Arabia was also challenging the Ottoman Empire on religious grounds, adding to the dynasty's anxieties about its claims to Islamic legitimacy.

[56] Mahmud came within a hair's breadth of the same fate at the hands of the same rebels. Caroline Finkel, *Osman's Dream: The Story of the Ottoman Empire, 1300–1923* (New York: Basic Books, 2005), 413–428.

[57] Mahmud cultivated members of the ulema with promotions and emoluments and undertook building and restoration projects for religious institutions; Madeline C. Zilfi, 'Elite Circulation in the Ottoman Empire: Great Mollas of the Eighteenth Century', *Journal of the Economic and Social History of the Orient* 26/3 (1983): 318–364.

[58] Leila Ahmed, *Women and Gender in Islam* (New Haven: Yale University Press, 1992), sees European colonialism as the sine qua non for the 'discourse of the veil' and the cultural construction of Muslim women in the modern era. However, Ottoman responses to the many challenges to the Empire in the eighteenth century, topping off centuries of religiously justified patriarchist practice, ensured that the fusion of women and Islam was well underway before the colonial era. In the late nineteenth century, European

culture as the covering and sequestration of women, eased some of the tension between the normative domain of the regulatory regime and the reality of troubling economic dynamics and non-Muslim-skewed social differentiation.

colonial occupiers' condemnation of veiling, and through it, Islam, in Algeria, Egypt and elsewhere in the Mediterranean added resonant East-versus-West dimensions to the Islamic world's embattled defence of religion and culture.

16 Wearing the Hat of Loyalty: Imperial Power and Dress Reform in Ming Dynasty China

Bu Yun Chen

Introduction: Sartorial Knowledge and Imperial Power

In early 1368, soon after Zhu Yuanzhang conquered the Mongol Yuan dynasty (1271–1368) and proclaimed himself emperor of the new Ming dynasty (1368–1644), he called for the return to correct rituals including proper forms of dress and adornment:

At the beginning, when Yuan Shizu rose from the north and conquered the world, he changed the customs of the middle kingdom to barbarian customs [*husu*]. Scholars and commoners all braided their hair and left a tuft on their foreheads, and wore the wide-brim hat. Their clothes included the *kuzhe* [a riding suit composed of a separate jacket and trousers] with narrow-fitting sleeves, and braided waists and pleats. Women wore short robes with tight-fitting sleeves and skirts. They no longer wore the traditional dress of the middle kingdom ... His majesty detested it for a long time. And so, he ordered that dress be restored to the Tang style: all scholars and commoners tie their hair into topknots, officials wear black gauze caps, round-collared robes, belts, and black boots; scholars and commoners wear turbans, varicoloured round-collared robes, avoiding yellow, and black ... Hence, the barbarian customs that lasted over one hundred years will be replaced by the traditions of the middle kingdom.[1]

The founding emperor's disdain for Mongol Yuan dress, decried as 'barbarian custom' (*husu*), and his urgency in restoring Han Chinese attire betrayed a deep anxiety about the power of clothes. Forms of adornment, such as dress and hairstyle, were essential bearers of identity, social belonging and ritual. But these functions of adornment were exactly what made clothes and hair dangerous. Clothes could be removed and replaced, hair could be cut and changed, and consequently, identities

---

[1] Yao Guangxiao (1335–1418), Xia Yuanji (1366–1430) et al., Ming Taizu shilu [Veritable Records of Emperor Taizu], in *Ming shilu* [Veritable Records of the Ming Dynasty] (Nan'gang: Zhongyang yanjiu yuan lishi yuyan yanjiu suo, 1962), vol. 5, 525 (*juan* 30.10a). For a recent study on Zhu Yuanzhang's reforms, see Zhang Jia, 'Cong zheng guanshang: Hongwu shiqi de fushi gaige' [Restoring Chinese Costume: The Reform of the Clothing System during the Reign of Hongwu], *Journal of Chinese Studies* 58 (2014): 113–158.

turned upside down and inside out. Like dynasty-founding rulers before and after him, Zhu Yuanzhang recognised that conformity in dress was a necessary marker of a loyal subject, and regulation of dress was central to the establishment of his rule. In keeping with this tradition, the Ming founder viewed the promulgation of a new dress code as fundamental to the consolidation of his rule as the compilation of a comprehensive legal code. Whereas the dynastic legal code served to discipline subjects, dress and adornment were envisaged as the means by which to form a loyal subject. Both projects were key to the institution of a new and stable political and social order under the new ruling house.

Over the following couple of years, dress regulations were devised and elaborated for the palace, officials, eunuchs, scholars, craftsmen and commoners based on the sartorial codes of the Tang and Song dynasties.[2] The distinctions intrinsic to these codes – between ruler and subject, official and commoner, merchant and gentry, male and female – were constructs rooted in and perpetuated by a Confucian worldview that idealised traditional agrarian society. The strict regulation of dress, equipage and housing served to place these subjects within the social hierarchy, to make material their identities for both subject and spectator. Indeed, the fashioning of loyal subjects depended on a strict classification and, accordingly, a clear definition of privileges.[3]

Underpinning this sumptuary regime was an understanding of dress as investiture or 'deep-making', whereby the putting on of garments sanctioned by the emperor and bestowed upon the subject constituted a person as an empress, or an official, or a servant of the court. As Ann Rosalind Jones and Peter Stallybrass have argued in the context of Renaissance Europe, 'investiture was … the means by which a person was given a form, a shape, a social function, a "depth"'.[4] Clothes, equipage and housing constituted the corporate symbolism of the court and the authorised display of such possessions conveyed the loyalties of a subject and the patronage of the court. The dynastic dress code was designed in a similar way to the early modern institution of livery, to mark bodies

---

[2] For the influence of Tang dynasty regulations on Ming official dress code, see Li Yi, 'Tangdai dui Mingdai guanyuan changfu yingxiang' [On the Influence of the Tang Dynasty to the Official Daily Dress in the Ming Dynasty], *Zhejiang fangzhi fuzhuang zhiye jishu xueyuan xuebao* 1 (2013): 54–58.

[3] Yuan Zujie has argued that Ming sumptuary laws constituted an exercise of state power through regulation *by* clothing, not regulation *of* clothing. This distinction emphasises the use of clothing as 'a tool of state control over society'. Yuan Zujie, 'Dressing for Power: Rite, Costume, and State Authority in Ming Dynasty China', *Frontiers of History in China* 2/2 (2007): 181–212.

[4] Ann Rosalind Jones and Peter Stallybrass, *Renaissance Clothing and the Materials of Memory* (Cambridge: Cambridge University Press, 2001), 2.

so as to bind them to political and social institutions. This power, vested in the emperor, to mark subordinates was communicated through the codification of dress and the promulgation of sumptuary edicts. Dress was, in other words, a site of power.

Yet archaeological evidence from the tombs of Ming princes show that Mongol styles of dress persisted well into the sixteenth century, thus revealing both the limits of Zhu Yuanzhang's sartorial code and suggesting, more seriously, the failure of his efforts to eradicate the legacy of the MongolYuan.[5] Much of the scholarship on the Ming sumptuary regime has focused attention instead on the ineffectiveness of the court's regulation of dress, especially during the final century of the dynasty when the laws were most openly flouted.[6] These scholars emphasise that a new lord and master, in the guise of wealthy urban elites, gradually displaced the imperial court as the so-called 'consumption-regulating device'.[7] Such an approach to the dynasty's sumptuary legislation regards imperial power and ritual as standing in fundamental opposition to commerce, with the latter as the constant victor. This position further views dress not only as a site of power, but also as a site of contestation between competing systems of value.

In a shift away from thinking about the Ming dynasty regulatory project as evidence of the dazzling commercialised economy's triumph over imperial power, I argue that the court's sumptuary order constituted one among multiple systems of value that invested meaning in dress. The Ming dress code, as envisioned by the emperor and his bureaucrats and codified in texts, expressed a pointed interest in maintaining distinctions both within the official bureaucracy and between the official and

---

[5] David M. Robinson, 'The Ming Court and the Legacy of the Yuan Mongols', in David Robinson (ed.), *Culture, Courtiers, and Competition: The Ming Court (1368–1644)* (Cambridge, MA: Harvard University Press, 2008), 365–421. On the legacy of Zhu Yuanzhang in Chinese historiography, see Sarah Schneewind (ed.), *Long Live the Emperor! Uses of the Ming Founder Across Six Centuries of East Asian History* (Minneapolis: Society for Ming Studies, 2008).

[6] See, for example, Craig Clunas, *Superfluous Things: Material Culture and Social Status in Early Modern China* (Honolulu: University of Hawai'i Press, 1991); Timothy Brook, *The Confusions of Pleasure: Commerce and Culture in Ming China* (Berkeley: University of California Press, 1998); Sophie Volpp, 'The Gift of a Python Robe: The Circulation of Objects in 'Jin Ping Mei', *Harvard Journal of Asiatic Studies* 65/1 (2005): 133–158; Sarah Dauncey, 'Illusions of Grandeur: Perceptions of Status and Wealth in Late-Ming Female Clothing and Ornamentation', *East Asian History* 25–26 (2003): 43–68.

[7] This turn of phrase is taken from Arjun Appadurai's oft-cited characterisation of sumptuary regulations as an 'intermediate consumption-regulating device, suited to societies devoted to stable status displays in exploding commodity contexts, such as India, China, and Europe in the premodern period'. Arjun Appadurai (ed.), *The Social Life of Things: Commodities in Cultural Perspective* (New York: Cambridge University Press, 1986), 25.

non-official realms. This concern with policing boundaries remained at the forefront of the most significant dress reform since the dynasty's founding, which targeted official attire once again. Promulgated by the Jiajing emperor (r. 1522–1567) during the seventh year of his reign, the new edicts sought to rein in the sartorial misconduct of his officials by standardising their casual dress. I survey the Jiajing emperor's 1528 reforms, to show that while the court's regulation of dress was, above all, motivated by concerns about dynastic power and legitimacy, sartorial behaviour across the empire was governed by plural regimes of value. At stake in these texts were the external trappings of imperial authority, not the consuming passions of the greater empire.

The Ming Dress Code

In 1367, a year before Zhu Yuanzhang ascended the throne as the Hongwu emperor, he charged his senior chief councillor and a committee of scholars with the task of composing a set of guidelines for his subjects. The *Great Ming Commandment* (*Da Ming ling*) was completed in early 1368 and went into effect just eighteen days after he declared the founding of the Ming. Consisting of 145 articles, the *Commandment* was intended to bring order to the realm through the institution of norms for both state and society.[8] The second-longest document of the *Commandment* was Article 51, which detailed the proper forms of dress, headwear, residences, furnishings, utensils and carriages – the first act of Ming sumptuary regulation.

Following the customary statement that, 'The clothing colors, hats, belts, houses, and saddles of the officials and commoners all have gradations', Article 51 proceeded to list a total of fourteen separate provisions outlining the types of dress, caps, parasols, burial plots and even bed curtains suitable for persons of each rank. The use of gold-embroidered decoration was the leading indication of rank, and one which commoners were strictly prohibited from employing as orna-mentation on fabrics for dress furnishings. The gold embroidered five-clawed dragon (*long*) was reserved for the emperor, while officials were allowed to use select patterns depending on their rank. Civil officials who had completed their service and retired from court were 'subject to the same regulations as those still in service', and all were to 'follow the style appropriate to their rank'. This stipulation makes clear that the distinction between the official and non-official spheres, as well

---

[8] Edward L. Farmer, 'The Great Ming Commandment (Ta Ming Ling): An Inquiry into Early-Ming Social Legislation', *Asia Major*, 3rd Series, 6/1 (1993): 181–199.

as distinctions between official ranks, was the chief concern of these restrictions. Military officials, on the other hand, were not bound by the regulations put forth in the *Commandment*.[9] The liberty granted to the military may suggest the relative power wielded by those in service during the early years of the dynasty. Imperial bestowals were also safe from regulations. Such displays of favour belonged to a set of privileges that the emperor could grant according to his discretion. The emperor's right to dress (or not) his subjects, asserted through these fourteen provisions, was the premise from which all sumptuary laws followed.

The Hongwu emperor's early proclamations on dress situated him within a longstanding practice of founding emperors, who sought to order society through the regulation of appearances. In so doing, he – and those before him – laid claim to a system of fixed social and political hierarchies based on a self-sufficient agrarian economy idealised in the Confucian canonical texts, especially in the *Rituals of Zhou (Zhouli)*, edited during the first few centuries of the Han dynasty (206 BCE–221 CE).[10] The *Rituals of Zhou*, which first proposed a ceremonial dress code for the emperor, served as the model for the sumptuary laws of the successive dynasties, and all subsequent sumptuary regulations followed it in the assumption that the categories of rulers and subjects are absolute. Dress and accoutrements are then assigned to these categories. In other words, the sumptuary project asserted the symbolic and ritual significance of clothing – its role in creating and reinforcing individual and collective identities.

Adherence to the sumptuary laws was enforced by the *Great Ming Code (Da Ming lu)*, the final version of which was completed in 1397.[11] The punishment for violating regulations governing dress, houses and carriages varied according to rank. Officials were subject to one hundred lashes with a heavy stick and termination of office, whereas in the case of commoners, the heads of household were punished by fifty lashes with a light stick. If apprehended for wearing or displaying the

---

[9] Article 51 of the Great Ming Code, as translated in Edward L. Farmer, *Zhu Yuanzhang and Early Ming Legislation: The Reordering of Chinese Society Following the Era of Mongol Rule* (Leiden: Brill, 1995), 171–174.

[10] Schäfer and Kuhn have shown that annual production quotas for state-owned workshops were drawn from *Zhouli* precedents for sumptuary laws. Dagmar Schäfer and Dieter Kuhn, *Weaving and Economic Pattern in Ming Times (1368–1644): The Production of Silk Weaves in the State-Owned Workshops* (Heidelberg: Ed. Forum, 2002), 53–56.

[11] See Article 194 of the Great Ming Code, 'Violating Sumptuary Regulations on Clothing and Houses'. Liu Weiqian (1521–1565) et al., *Da Ming Lu* [Great Ming Code] (Yangzhou: Jiangsu Guangling guji keyin she, 1989), vol. 5, 29 (*juan* 12.13).

forbidden dragon or phoenix motif, both officials and commoners were to be disciplined by one hundred lashes with a heavy stick and penal servitude for three years. In all of these cases, artisans were not only penalised, but also suffered more severe punishments.

It took the Hongwu emperor nearly his entire reign to develop and institute dress codes for the emperor, the imperial family, officials and their wives, eunuchs, the military, scholars and commoners. Sumptuary regulations for the dynasty were compiled in a number of texts, including the *Treatise on Dress and Carriages* (*Yufu zhi*) of the official dynastic history (*Ming shu*) and the *Collected Statures of the Ming* (*Da Ming huidian*). Similar to the sumptuary codes of preceding dynasties, and in keeping with the tradition established by the *Rituals of Zhou*, the dress regulations outlined in both the *Treatise on Dress and Carriages* and the *Collected Statues of the Ming* were organised according to the social and political hierarchy. Beginning with the emperor and extending to Buddhist and Daoist clergy, the category of person (for example, prince or palace musician) is identified first, followed by the types of clothes assigned to their status. Changes to the regulations are noted under each immutable category and structured chronologically.

Civil and military officials were assigned five categories of dress (*guanfu*) organised according to the occasion on which they were to be worn: court dress (*chaofu*), sacrificial ceremony dress (*jifu*), audience dress (*gongfu*), everyday dress (*changfu*) and casual or leisure dress (*yanfu*). Since everyday dress (*changfu*) was worn most often when handling official affairs, it became a frequent object of regulation during the reigns of successive Ming emperors. The fabrication, colour and accessories of all five forms of an official's dress depended on their ranking in the bureaucracy.

Ranks were further differentiated by the patterns embroidered or woven on the badges worn on the front and back of the robe (Table 16.1). The emperor reserved the right to bestow robes with the *mang* (four-clawed dragon), the 'fighting bull' (*douniu*, dragon-like, with two large curved horns and a fish-like tail), and the 'flying fish' (*feiyi*, dragon's head, carp's body and two horns) on those whom he favoured. Court dress (*chaofu*) and audience dress (*gongfu*) were the first to be outlined by the Hongwu emperor at the beginning of his reign, while the guidelines for everyday dress (*changfu*) followed a few years later in 1373. Additional changes were made to vestments of officials until 1393, when the Hongwu emperor decreed standards for all five categories. Succeeding Ming emperors issued further regulations to reinforce the sumptuary order, such as the 1447 edict that made the production for

Table 16.1 *Rank Badges for Civil and Military Officials*

Rank	Civil (Hongwu 26, 1393)	Civil (Jiajing 16, 1536)
First	Crane or golden pheasant	Crane
Second		Golden pheasant
Third	Peacock or wild goose	Peacock
Fourth		Wild goose
Fifth	Silver pheasant	Silver pheasant
Sixth	Egret or mandarin duck	Egret
Seventh		Mandarin duck
Eighth	Oriole or quail or paradise flycatcher	Oriole
Ninth		Quail
Unclassified officials	Magpie or paradise flycatcher	Paradise flycatcher

unauthorised persons of prohibited patterns of the *mang, feiyi* and *douniu* a capital offence for artisans.[12] The repeated attempts to curb manufacture of *mang* robes for private use suggest that the Ming court struggled to control the production, and in turn the circulation, of these coveted symbols of imperial power.[13]

Regulations governing the dress of commoners, including farmers, merchants and servants, generally circumscribed the fabrication of their garments, headpieces, shoes and accessories. For example, in 1381 the Hongwu emperor decreed that farmers were permitted to wear plain weave silk, silk tabby and plain silk gauze, except for those households whose members were engaged in commercial activities.[14] Most of these ordinances, however, were issued under the Hongwu emperor. For the remainder of the dynasty, commoners received comparatively little attention in sumptuary statutes.

---

[12] An edict issued to the Ministry of Works by the Zhengtong Emperor in 1447 declared, 'There are clothing regulations for both officials and commoners. Now some people have custom-made robes embroidered with the prohibited patterns of four-clawed dragon, five-clawed dragon, flying fish, and "Big Dipper bull". Put the artisans to death and send their families to frontier garrisons as soldiers. People who wear them are to be punished without pardon'. Shen Defu, *Wanli yehuo bian* [Unofficial Gleanings of the Wanli Era] (Beijing: Zhonghua shuju, 1980), *juan* 1, 21.

[13] Sophie Volpp has argued, for example, that the state's continuous concern with regulating the production of these robes suggests that they were available for purchase in the marketplace, 'even though its prestige depended on the fiction that it was manufactured exclusively under imperial auspices' (151). Volpp, 'The Gift of a Python Robe', 133–158.

[14] Zhang Tingyu (1672–1755) et al., *Ming shi* [Official History of the Ming] (Beijing: Zhonghua shuju, 1995), vol. 6, *juan* 67, 1649.

In contrast to late medieval and early modern Europe, in China the rise of merchant capital was less of a concern than the appropriation of imperial insignia by individuals without political rank. By far the majority of attention was paid to the emperor, princes, nobles and civil and military officials, whose roles within the political and social hierarchy were constituted through the rituals of dress. Colour, fabric, insignia and ornament all endowed the body with a specific political and social function within the imperial order. Such markings simultaneously identified officials as loyal members of the court and the supremacy of the court as a corporate body. Thus, when officials removed their vestments, their loyalty – at least the appearance of such loyalties – provoked concern. Following Hongwu, the next and final Ming ruler to issue significant reforms to the official dress code was the Jiajing emperor (r. 1522–1567). Anxiety about the dress of officials peaked in his reign as he manoeuvred to consolidate his authority over the empire on the heels of a ritual controversy that embroiled the court.

Jiajing's Reforms: Illustrating the Right to Dress

Like the Hongwu emperor, Jiajing's 1528 edicts invoked classic ritual texts as a guide to bring order and distinction again to the empire's sartorial landscape. Indeed, the dress reforms were enacted as part of the emperor's moral claim to the throne in the wake of the Great Rites Controversy. The controversy had been caused by his succession, following the death of the heirless Zhengde emperor (r. 1505–1521), and it generated deep concern about the performance of correct ritual and political legitimacy.[15] The Jiajing emperor (Zhu Hucong) was the nephew of the deceased emperor and had been selected to ascend to the throne by a group of ministers, but ritual dictated that only an adopted son of the previous ruler could rightfully claim succession. Posthumous adoption was proposed by the incumbent Grand Secretary Yang Tinghe (1459–1529), but the Jiajing emperor opted instead to have his father declared emperor posthumously (the Xian emperor). Although he prevailed in the end, such a breach of imperial ritual caused great instability in the political order. This, in turn, spurred the Jiajing emperor

---

[15] Chu has argued that in the Jiajing emperor's conversations with his lecturers, '"Loyalty and affection", that is, an official's loyalty to and affection for his emperor, were especially emphasised ... the emperor was fond of using the phrase "loyalty and affection" to praise officials whose deeds he appreciated' (227). Hung-Lam Chu, 'The Jiajing Emperor's Interaction with His Lecturers', in David Robinson (ed.), *Courtiers and Competition: The Ming Court (1368–1644)* (Cambridge, MA: Harvard University Asia Center, 2008), 186–230.

to action and in particular to the restoration of the rituals of rulership – including the patterning of social and political order through prescribing forms of dress.

The new measures, however, concerned only the emperor, royal princes and ranked officials. More specifically, the target of Jiajing's reform was casual or leisure attire (*yanfu*), specifically clothes worn when not engaged in official duties. Finding his own leisure clothes too common or vulgar (*su*) and lacking in elegance (*ya*) to befit his status as emperor, Jiajing called upon the Grand Secretary Zhang Zong (1476–1539) to investigate the regulations governing the casual dress of emperors in antiquity. Zhang, following orders, consulted the *Book of Rites* (*Lishu*) and discovered that aside from the formal court attire (*mianfu*), the *xuanduan* (literally 'dark solemn') was most widely worn in antiquity. Soon after, the Jiajing emperor resolved that the leisure attire of the emperor and officials should take the *xuanduan* as its model, and dispatched Zhang to draw up the edicts.[16]

By the end of 1528, three new statutes had been promulgated: 'Dress of the Casual Hat' (*yanbian guanfu*) for the emperor, 'Dress of Loyalty and Tranquility (*zhongjing guanfu*)' for ranked officials, and 'Dress of Preserving Harmony' (*baohe guanfu*) for royal princes.[17] For officials, the significance of the emperor's measure was couched in the familiar discourse on the dangers of dressing without distinctions. Grand Secretary Zhang Zong memorialised (i.e. petitioned) the emperor, stating that:

'There have never been clear regulations on the leisure dress of ranked officials, and followers of the outlandish compete in their eccentric dressing, thereby causing greater disorder. I beg that it be modelled on the ancient *xuanduan* and put in a separate statue to be disseminated throughout the empire, so that noble and base are distinguished.' The emperor then ordered the creation of the 'Illustrations of the Loyal and Tranquil Hat and Dress', to be promulgated by the Board of Rites, together with an imperial edict stating, 'The Ancestors learned from antiquity and established regulations, so that the court and sacrificial dress of ranked officials each had distinctions. But the ordinary people are more cautious toward that which is clear, negligent of that which is obscure. The ancient sage kings were attentive to this, and ordered the *xuanduan* as the leisure dress for officials. Recently clothing styles have been outlandish, with no distinction between superior and inferior, so that the people's proclivities are without restraints. Hence, we have consulted the regulations on the ancient *xuanduan*, and changed its name to the 'Loyal and Tranquil', alluding to 'Thinking of utmost loyalty when entering, thinking of amending one's faults when retiring'. We have made pictures to instruct on the styles and construction. Officials in the capital

---

[16] *Ming Shizong huangdi shilu* [Veritable Records of Emperor Shizhong] in *Ming shilu*, vol. 74, 1929 (*juan* 85, 9a).
[17] *Zhongjing guanfu* appears as 忠靜冠服 or 忠靖冠服 across the textual record.

above the seventh rank, members of the Hanlin Academy, the Imperial Academy, officials in the Messenger's Office above the eighth rank; in the provinces, Regional Supervisors, Senior Officials of each prefecture, chief officials of each sub-prefecture and county, and the education officials of Confucian schools are to wear it. Military officials of the rank of commissioner-in-chief or above may wear it. The others are prohibited from exceeding the regulations.[18]

Eccentric dressing (*qifu*) was not only outlandish (*guiyi*), it flouted the social decorum long established since antiquity. In reviving the *xuanduan*, the dress of antiquity, the Jiajing emperor was harking back to an idealised past when the boundary between ruler and official was dutifully observed.

To accompany each new guideline, the emperor commissioned illustrated albums (*tu*) that depicted and named the categories of prescribed robes, headdress, accessories and patterns. The 1528 sumptuary measure is significant for its novel use of the illustrated manual (*tu*), a format generally reserved for the communication of specialist knowledge.[19] The Jiajing emperor's appeal to antiquity in these sumptuary measures, however, was not merely a trend towards archaism. The use of drawings to illustrate correct dress and adornment as an instrument of statecraft paralleled other trends in the use of *tu* as a tool for communicating imperial power, such as the production of territorial maps and charts of the empire. By ordering the explanation of each item of dress through text and image, the Jiajing emperor entered into a tradition of exegesis – a practice that confirmed the authority and erudition of the author.[20] This interplay between the pronouncement of imperial

[18] *Ming shi*, vol. 6, *juan* 67, 1639. The translation provided in Craig Clunas's essay, 'Regulation of Consumption and the Institution of Correct Morality by the Ming State', in Chun-chieh Huang and Erik Zürcher (eds.), *Norms and the State in China* (Leiden: Brill, 1993), erroneously translates *yanju zhi fu* as the dress of 'officials living out of office' and the dress of officials 'living in retirement'. *Yanfu* refers to the everyday dress worn at home by the emperor, officials and appointed ladies of the court.

[19] See Francesca Bray et al., *Graphics and Text in the Production of Technical Knowledge in China: The Warp and the Weft* (Leiden: Brill, 2007). There exists another album of illustrations of Ming official dress, entitled 'Pictures of Court Costumes and Manners in the Ming Dynasty of China' (Ming gong guanfu yizhang tu]. Six volumes of the album have survived with colour and black and white illustrations. The dating of the album is uncertain, but the scholars who have worked on the artefact have argued that one of the volumes can be dated to the reign of the Yongle emperor (r. 1403–1424). See Li Zhitan, Chen Xiaosu and Kong Fanyun, 'Zhengui de Ming dai fushi ziliao: Ming gong guanfu yizhang tu zhengli yanjiu zhaji' *[Notes of Ming Gong Guan Fu Yi Zhang Tu: Pictures of Court Costumes and Manners in the Ming Dynasty of China]*, Yishu sheji yanjiu 1 (2014): 23–28.

[20] Bray has argued that, '*Tu* were considered to contribute to a full understanding of all the classics, but were particularly important as exegetical devices for those which discussed rank and ritual, namely the *Zhouli* (Zhou rituals) and the *Liji* (Record of rituals). Here images helped recreate the embodied understanding and emotions imparted through the

authority on the one hand, and a demonstration of expertise on the other, was consistent with the aims of the Jiajing emperor to establish his right to rule – and his right to dress – during the Great Rites Controversy.

To ensure that all ranking officials were in conformity with the new regulations, the 'dress of loyalty and tranquillity' was instituted near and far, from the capital down to the county. For all officials, the *xuanduan* was to be made in dark green. Officials of third rank and above were granted the cloud pattern, while those ranking fourth and below were to wear plain robes (Figure 16.1).[21] For the emperor, the *xuanduan* conformed to colour – black (*xuan*). His robe would be bordered with a green trim and feature 143 dragon designs, including one large dragon medallion on the front (Figure 16.2).[22] The *xuanduan* of the royal princes, who were incorporated into Jiajing's reform only after reports that they had appropriated the 'dress of loyalty and tranquillity', were a simplification of the emperor's robe. Cut from green silk, it was adorned with a green trim and two rank badges with the dragon design.

Such designs suggest that neither accuracy nor frugality was a priority for the Jiajing emperor. What mattered was the propagation of his rights as emperor through the practice of inscription – imprinting bodies not only so as to make visible the wearer's place in the social and political hierarchy, but also to make material his authority. By targeting leisure attire (*yanfu*), clothing worn in one's private residence, Jiajing asserted his right to govern both public and private life. Such an intrusion into the non-official realm of his officials was an effort to rein in those who dressed as individuals rather than as representatives of the court. As in the institution of livery, the power to fix and mark subordinates through clothes served to affirm the emperor's position as master of the imperium. In other words, the *xuanduan* was the emperor's attempt to fashion – in the root sense of the term – 'loyal and tranquil' subjects. In court and at home, their corporate identity as office-holding subjects, defined by their shared loyalties to the emperor-as-institution, was established materially.

Archaeological and textual evidence suggests that the Jiajing emperor's initiative was a success. The 1966 excavation of the tomb of the sixteenth-century official Wang Xijue (1534–1610) yielded one 'hat of loyalty and tranquillity', a near-exact replication of the surviving illustration (Figure 16.3). In compliance with the 1528 regulations, Wang Xijue's square-shaped hat features two prominent peaks in the back, and

---

correct practice of liturgies and the manipulation of ritual paraphernalia'. *Graphics and Text*, 38.

[21] *Ming shi*, vol. 6, *juan* 67, 1639.

[22] *Ming shi*, vol. 6, *juan* 66, 1621.

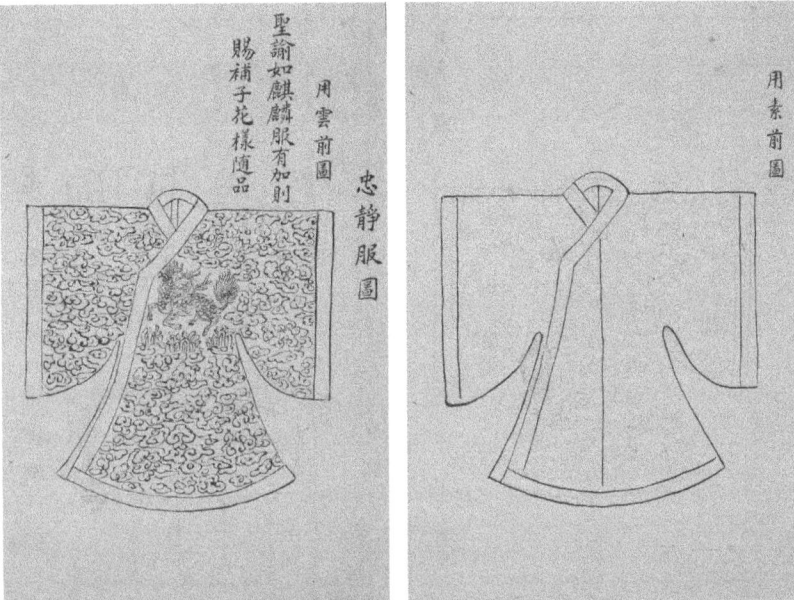

Figure 16.1 Illustrations of the robes of 'Loyalty and Tranquillity'. Left: cloud-patterned robe of officials of the third rank and above. Right: plain robe of officials of the fourth rank and below. After Li Dongyang (1447–1516) and Shen Shixing (1535–1614), *Da Ming huidian* [Collected Statues of the Ming Dynasty] (Beijing: Neifu kanben, 1587), vol. 24, *juan* 61, 215b–216a. National Library of China – Harvard-Yenching Library Chinese Rare Book Digitization Project, Harvard University.

the ridges and sides are edged in gold thread.[23] Although made from black velvet rather than the prescribed black gauze, the existence of such an object in the tomb of a Wanli-era (1572–1620) official implies that the Jiajing emperor's blueprint for leisurewear was successfully implemented. The hat became so popular that in 1574, the second year of the Wanli emperor's reign, the government banned all non-officials, such as candidates holding the provincial-level degree (*juren*), students of the Imperial Academy (*jiansheng*), Confucian scholars (*shengru*), and commoners and servants, from wearing it.[24] Consistent with the aims of

[23] *Ming shi*, vol. vi, *juan* 67, 1639.
[24] Li Dongyang (1447–1516) and Shen Shixing (1535–1614) et al., *Da Ming Hui Dian* [Collected Statues of the Ming Dynasty] (Taipei: Dongnan shubaoshe, 1963), ii: 1071 (*juan* 61, 317a). In contrast to the *Collected Statues*, the *Treatise on Carriages and Dress*

Figure 16.2 Illustration of the emperor's *xuanduan*. After *Da Ming huidian* [Collected Statues of the Ming Dynasty], vol. 24, *juan* 60, 28b–29a. National Library of China – Harvard-Yenching Library Chinese Rare Book Digitization Project, Harvard University.

Jiajing's reforms, the 1574 sumptuary measure sought to reinforce the division between the official and non-official realms.

Vernacular sources suggest that these regulations were quite successful. In the late sixteenth-century novel *Plum in the Golden Vase* (Jin Ping Mei), Ximen Qing – an upwardly mobile merchant – is described wearing the 'hat of loyalty and tranquillity' on four separate occasions.[25] On two of these occasions, Ximen's hat is described, letting the reader know that he had one made from white velvet and another from white satin. Ximen's extensive wardrobe brimmed with garments and accessories prohibited by Ming sumptuary protocol, which included the fine damask, satin and woollen robes he paired with

only lists the provincial-level degree-holders, students of the Academy, and Confucian scholars as the culprits. See *Ming shi*, vol. 6, *juan* 67, 1649.

[25] Xiaoxiaosheng (pseud.), *Jin Ping Mei ci hua [Plum in the Golden Vase]* (Hong Kong: Xianggang wenhai chubanshe, 1963), see vol. i, ch. 46, 506; vol. ii, ch. 61, 618; vol. ii, ch. 67, 810; vol. ii, ch. 69, 849. On the deviant consumption practices of the women of Ximen's household, see Dauncey, 'Illusions of Grandeur: Perceptions of Status and Wealth in Late-Ming Female Clothing and Ornamentation', 43–68.

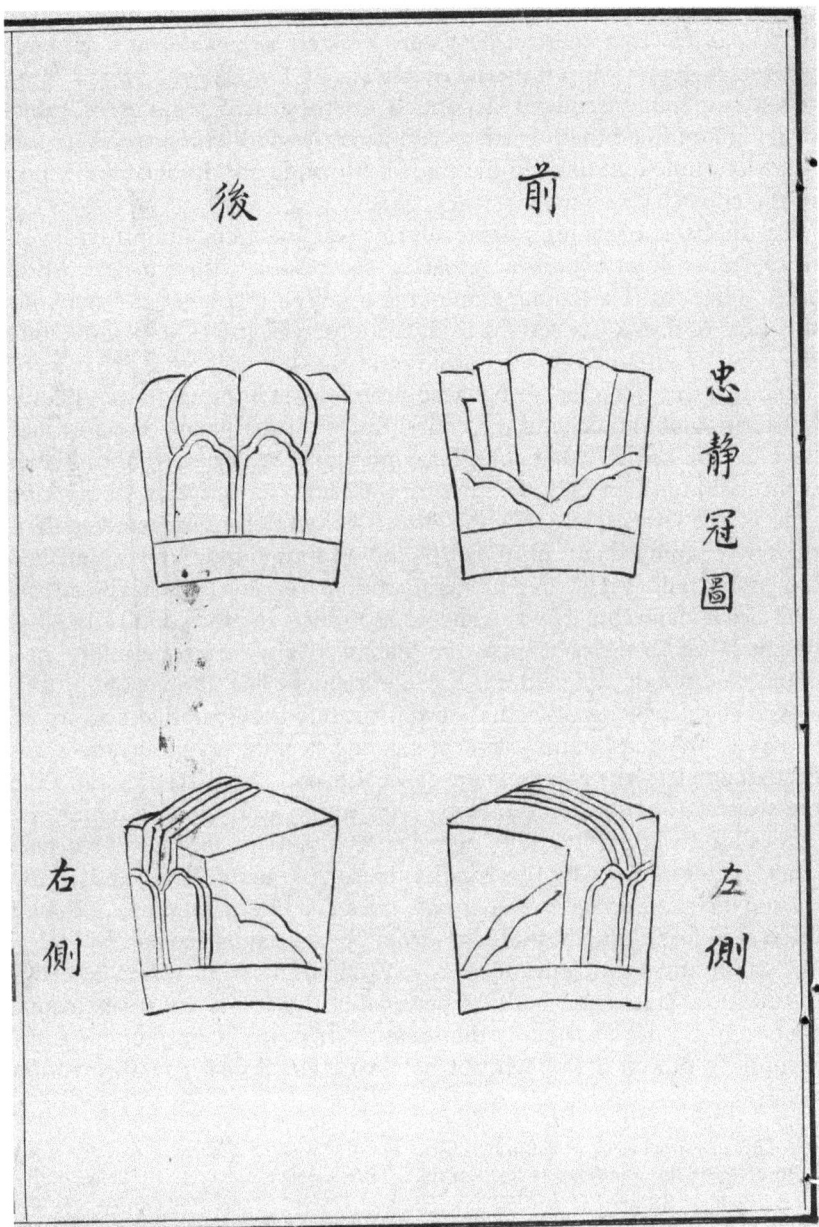

Figure 16.3 'Hats of Loyalty and Tranquillity'. After *Da Ming huidian* [Collected Statues of the Ming Dynasty], vol. 24, *juan* 61, 215a. National Library of China – Harvard-Yenching Library Chinese Rare Book Digitization Project, Harvard University.

his 'hats of loyalty and tranquillity'.[26] Ximen Qing's illicit consumption demonstrates that mercantile values existed alongside, and perhaps even in dialogue with, imperial dictates. The fluidity with which Ming robes and hats circulated depended on these two regimes of value, which guaranteed their worth as commodities with exchange value and as possessions that derived their power through a symbolic connection to the court.

At the heart of Jiajing's dress reforms was the recognition that investiture constituted a person, situating the person within a network of social relations. The Jiajing emperor recognised that since the symbolic function of dress was central to dynastic power, it was imperative that the court maintained its lead position in the sartorial game. That is, by creating a new set of covetable accoutrements of imperial power, he was bolstering the authority of the court. But what the Jiajing emperor may have overlooked was that sumptuary measures are beset by an inherent contradiction. Through the prescription and proscription of specific objects, the laws plainly reify the objects as symbols of rank and status – thereby opening them up to usurpation and imitation. What connected the provincial-level degree-holders, students of the Imperial Academy and Confucian scholars was a shared aspiration to office, indicating that by the Wanli emperor's reign, the 'hat of loyalty and tranquillity' had come to embody officialdom. For commoners like Ximen Qing, who lacked the privileges of formal power but had the means to acquire an expanding range of status-conferring goods, keeping up appearances was fundamental to their expression of wealth and social distinction. Like the wearing of robes embroidered with imperial insignia, donning the 'hat of loyalty and tranquillity' signalled access to the throne.[27] This, perhaps, accounts for why the Wanli emperor's court did not update the laws to include new types of luxury textiles, but did maintain a continued interest in forbidding non-officials from appropriating the hat.[28]

Owning and wearing the 'hat of loyalty and tranquillity' was to lay claim to the social status and political power that inhered in court vestments. Imitation did not necessarily diminish court power. Conspicuous competition to put on the raiment of state-sanctioned power reaffirmed the

[26] As Sophie Volpp has observed in her discussion of Ximen Qing's acquisition of a *mang* robe (which she translates as 'python robe'), his 'deviant consumption' signalled his 'volatile social aspirations' and his connections to persons of rank. Volpp, 'The Gift of a Python Robe', 158.

[27] Volpp makes a similar argument about the *mang* robe. Volpp, 'The Gift of a Python Robe', 157.

[28] Clunas, 'Regulation of Consumption and the Institution of Correct Morality by the Ming State', 44.

emperor's place at the centre of the empire.[29] More dangerous was the removal and replacement of official vestments with those of another master. To borrow from Jones and Stallybrass, 'Livery ends at the moment when one wears their own clothes'.[30] The lasting popularity of the 'hat of loyalty and tranquillity' was evidence of the court's hegemonial power – power that had to be visible in the appearance of the emperor and his court and exercised through the right to make and mark his subjects.

Coda: The Silver Century

The Wanli emperor's 1574 statute was the final piece of sumptuary legislation promulgated by the court. What transpired in the following century has been the main focus of scholarship on the function of sumptuary laws in China. As Craig Clunas has observed, Ming sumptuary laws were neither updated nor reinforced at a period when they were being most openly flouted.[31] Indeed, the late Ming world abounded with sumptuous delights. Among the goods to be found in the southern city of Nanjing, as illustrated in the scroll painting by an anonymous court painter, 'Prosperity of the Southern Capital', were furs and leathers from the northwest, Beijing-style boots, seafood from Fujian and Guangdong provinces, and even miscellaneous goods from the eastern and western seas. Situated on the lower Yangzi river, Nanjing was made prosperous by an expanding internal commercial network that traded everyday consumables, regional products and luxury goods across the empire.

With prosperity came innovation in production, which in turn spurred consumer desires. In a collection of anecdotes about Nanjing, the local literatus Zhou Hui (fl. late sixteenth century) recorded one of the new luxuries to hit the market: 'In the past twenty years, gilt thread wrapped around a core of silver, gold leaf lined in silver have appeared'. He went on to criticise the changes wrought by these extraordinary advances in gold work, lamenting that, 'the craftsmen have become more ingenious by the day, the prices cheaper by the day, and human relationships increasingly superficial. How regrettable!'[32] Anticipating Marx's theory of alienation, Zhou's concern stemmed

---

[29] See Norbert Elias's discussions of the court of Louis XIV. *The Civilising Process, Vol. I: The History of Manners* (Oxford: Basil Blackwell, 1978); *The Civilising Process, Vol. II: State Formation and Civilization* (Oxford: Basil Blackwell, 1982); and *The Court Society* (Oxford: Basil Blackwell, 1983).

[30] Jones and Stallybrass, eds. *Renaissance Clothing and the Materials of Memory*, 277.

[31] Clunas, *Superfluous Things: Material Culture and Social Status in Early Modern China*, 151–152. See also Brook, *The Confusions of Pleasure: Commerce and Culture in Ming China.*

[32] Zhou Hui (fl. sixteenth century), *Jinling suoshi* [Trivia about Nanjing] (Beijing: Wenxue guji kan xingshe, 1955), vol. 1, 259 (*juan* 4, 547).

from an anxiety about how the fetishisation of things was leading to an erosion of human relationships. Having lived through China's 'silver century' (1550–1650), Zhou belonged to a generation of Confucian officials who witnessed material wealth corrode traditional social norms. The marketplace was responsible for catalysing a desire for material comforts that liberated men and women from the rigid hierarchies and distinctions prescribed by Confucian norms – a world turned upside down by the 'lord of silver'.[33]

By the seventeenth century, consumption was a common discursive object of moralising officials living on the periphery of court power. Nowhere was the anxiety about things more evident than in their outcries against sartorial transgressions. Late Ming literati frequently bemoaned the speed with which garments changed. Gu Qiyuan (1565–1628), Zhou Hui's contemporary, observed that women's dress in Nanjing changed every two to three years, in contrast to thirty years ago when styles changed only once in a ten-year span.[34] He found the new variations in officials' and scholars' headdresses even more distressing, as there were 'differences from day to day and something new every month'.[35] One of the loudest critics was the scholar Shen Defu (1578–1642), who having obtained only the provincial-level degree was himself forbidden to don the 'hat of loyalty and tranquillity'. In his magnum opus *Unofficial Gleanings of the Wanli Era (Wanli yehua bian)*, Shen observed that there were 'three groups of people in the world who, ignoring distinctions, overstep the bounds of appropriate dress'. The first consisted of sons of nobles who dressed in the fourth rank, despite belonging only to the eighth. They were followed by eunuchs who paraded the streets of the capital wearing robes with the *mang* four-clawed dragon and the fighting bull insignia. The final culprits were women, in particular the wives of elites, who flaunted their coronets decorated with pearls and embroidered robes, some even with the designs of *qilin*, flying fish and seated *mang*, in front of senior officials. What greatly distressed Shen was that no one dared or, perhaps, cared to reproach them.[36]

The market was not solely to blame for the effacement of sartorial propriety. From Shen Defu's perspective, the fault lay with the emperor.

[33] See Brook, *The Confusions of Pleasure: Commerce and Culture in Ming China*.
[34] Gu Qiyuan (1565–1628), *Kezuo zhuiyu* [Superfluous chats from the guest's seat] (Beijing: Zhonghua shu ju, 1991), vol. 3, 235 (*juan* 9). Cited in Wu Jen-shu, 'Mingdai pingmin fushi de liuxing fengshang yu shidafu fanying' [Popular styles of clothing among the common people of the Ming, and the reaction of the gentry], *Xinshixue* 10/3 (September 1999), 74.
[35] Gu Qiyuan, *Kezuo zhuiyu*, vol. 1, 19 (*juan* 1).
[36] Shen Defu, *Wanli yehuo bian, juan* 5, 147–148.

As Shen saw it, the emperor's repeated bestowals of robes embroidered with the dragon, *mang*, 'flying fish' and 'fighting bull' upon his Grand Secretaries constituted a failure to regulate the possession of imperial insignia-adorned robes.[37] Transgressions of the dress code were a result of the emperor's negligence. Shen cited edicts that explicitly targeted the illicit manufacture of such insignia, suggesting that it was the court's exclusive right to production that had to be protected.[38] Following the reign of the Zhengde emperor (r. 1505–1521), the Ming court no longer attempted to regulate production through sumptuary legislation.

The critiques of Shen and his contemporaries have served as evidence of the state's failure to regulate consumption and, more significantly, the displacement of state power by local power. For Clunas, the government's lack of interest in updating the sumptuary laws to incorporate new goods points to the tacit recognition that the laws were no longer enforceable. Commercialisation is viewed as what finally wrested away the emperor's right to dress his subjects. The opposition between commercialisation (and the rise of self-fashioning among Ming urban elites) and effective sumptuary rule, however, does not account for why elites unrelentingly usurped symbols of court power. The late Ming world may have been turned upside down by material prosperity and social upheaval, but so long as imperial insignia continued to confer prestige on the wearer, the authority of the Ming ruling house remained intact. That is, the absence of enforcement does not mean the act of prescription was any less powerful. An expanding market for luxury goods made the trappings of imperial power available to a wider audience, but it did not erode their appeal.

To view the Ming court as standing in opposition to commerce on the one hand, and dress-as-deep-making as incompatible with dress-as-self-fashioning on the other hand, is to ignore the full complexity of the Ming sumptuary regime. This paper has only addressed one side of this system by showing how dress was instrumental in creating and maintaining Ming subjects. In particular, the Jiajing emperor's campaign highlights the relationship between the project of sumptuary regulation and political

[37] Ibid., *juan* 1, 20–21.
[38] In her research on craft production in the Ming, Schäfer has made a similar argument: 'During the Ming period, emperors and scholars had full confidence in their rights to silk and their knowledge about it. They felt in line with a cultural tradition when they used the symbols and styles of clothing of their predecessors as a symbol for social status and political power. The Ming rulers relied on their hegemonial power and rights when they exerted pressure on artisanal production in their Southern provinces'. Dagmar Schäfer, 'Silken Strands: Making Technology Work in China', in Dagmar Schäfer (ed.), *Cultures of Knowledge: Technology in Chinese History* (Leiden: Brill, 2011), 50.

power and legitimacy. Ming sumptuary legislation served to reinforce the rule of the dynastic house through defining and circumscribing the range of symbols, but more importantly it was the articulation of hegemonic power through a claim on ritual knowledge and production that made such laws meaningful.

17 Regulating Excess: The Cultural Politics of Consumption in Tokugawa Japan

Katsuya Hirano

'Townspeople are living a precarious life.'
Nishikawa Joken, *Chōnin Bukuro* [Lessons for Townspeople], 1719

In 1705, the Tokugawa shogunate stripped Tatsugoro Yodoya – one of the wealthiest merchants in the city of Osaka in western Japan – of all his assets, including his 171 estates, all his gold and silver, as well as his ships, mines and artworks, and banished him from the Kyoto-Osaka region. His crime was his violation of the existing sumptuary laws. In early modern Japan, asset forfeiture was called *Kessho* (闕所), and this legal action was taken against those who flaunted excessive luxuries and exorbitant spending beyond their station in society. Tatsugoro, the fifth head of the Yodoya (淀屋) merchant house, was said to possess assets worth over 20 *oku ryō* in *koban* (approximately 2 trillion US$ in today's currency) acquired through silk trading, shipping, money lending and estate business.[1] Legend has it that his loan to leading samurai was one hundred thousand *ryō* in gold (2 billion US$).[2] His conspicuous consumption and opulent lifestyle were also legendary: contemporaries gossiped that Tatsugoro spent 4 *oku ryō* in *koban* in less than two years – just for leisure and entertainment. His residence sprawled over 350,000 square feet, with extraordinarily lavish features. One room, for example, had a glass ceiling that revealed goldfish swimming over guests' heads.[3]

Widely circulated accounts, including stories written by popular writers such as Monzaemon Chikamatsu and Dansui Hōjō, characterised the demise of the gilded merchant's life as representative of what the 'arrogant merchants' faced when they transgressed their stations in early

---

[1] Masaaki Ueda (ed.), *Nihon Jinmei Daijiten* (Tokyo: Kodansha, 2001), 381. The *koban* was an oval gold coin used during the Tokugawa period. It was considered equal to one *ryō*, a unit of weight originally from China, the *tael*, which came into use during the Kamakura period (1192–1333). The *koban* was a central part of Tokugawa coinage.
[2] Osamu Wakita, *Kinsei Osaka no Machi to Hito* (Tokyo: Yoshikawa Kobunkan, 2015), 200.
[3] Masaki Ueda, *Nihon Jinmei Daijiten*, 381.

435

eighteenth-century Edo society through excessive consumption and conspicuous display of wealth.[4] Contemporaries and many historians have
accepted this straightforward interpretation. An eminent historian of early
modern Japan, Osamu Wakita, however, recently called it into question.
Tatsugoro's case involved five other people: an employee of the merchant
house and four customers. Tatsugoro suffered a severe financial penalty,
but his unfortunate associates were condemned to death and their heads
put to the gibbet. According to Wakita, with the single exception of the
Yodoya case, the death penalty was never applied to violators of sumptuary laws during the Tokugawa period. The common punishments were
either asset forfeiture or banishment. Wakita also argues that forgery of
legal and financial documents, which was a crime punishable by death
during the period, must have been central in the case of the five other
offenders.[5] Tatsugoro himself may have been innocent of forgery – but
simply too ostentatious to ignore.

While the story behind Yodoya's eclipse may be more complicated than
previously understood, the case clearly reflects an important and larger
trend in En'pō (1673–1681) and Genroku (1681–1709) politics: namely,
the emergence of notably uncompromising governmental policies regulating people's consumer behaviour in response to their increasingly
visible wealth. The shogunate began to implement tighter and more elaborate sumptuary regulations to consolidate status hierarchies and curb
the townspeople's conspicuous display of consumer power.[6]

Indeed, the En'po period witnessed the rising tide of people's conspicuous consumption.[7] Innovative and elaborate designs of everyday
wear reached their peak and 'fashion contests' (*ishō kurabe*, 衣装競べ
or *date kurabe*, 伊達くらべ) held by wealthy townspeople, with many
spectators of different social status, were in full swing. Sometime in
the late 1670s, Okachi Ishikawa, the wife of the wealthy Edo merchant
Rokubei Ishikawa, made a trip to Kyoto for a fashion contest organised
to determine the most fashionable lady in the realm. Okachi left Kyoto
victorious over Kiku Nanbaya, the wife of a Kyoto business tycoon,
Jūemon Nanbaya.[8] In 1681, with rumours of her luxurious lifestyle

---

[4] Monzaemon Chikamatsu wrote *Yodogoi Shusse no Takinobori* (1709) based on Tatsugoro,
and Dansui Hōjō included Tatsugoro's story in *Nihon Shin Eitaigura* (1717).

[5] Osamu Wakita, *Kinsei Osaka no Machi to Hito*, 198–200.

[6] Noritaka Doi, 'Shashi Kinrei to Ken'yakurei', in *Nihon Rekishi* vol. 526 (Tokyo:
Nihonrekishi sha, 1992), 62.

[7] For the term 'conspicuous consumption', I draw on Thorstein Veblen's formulation in
'Conspicuous Consumption', in Juliet B. Schor and Douglas B. Holt (eds.), *The Consumer
Society*, eds. (New York: New Press, 2000), 187–204. Veblen's original work is *The Theory
of Leisure Class* (New York: Macmillan, 1899).

[8] Noritaka Doi, 'Shashi Kinrei to Ken'yakurei', 63.

widely circulated, Okachi attracted the scrutiny of the fifth shogun, Tsunayoshi Tokugawa. According to an official record, the shogun's procession was on the way to the Ken'eiji temple when the sweet perfume of burning incense made from rare eaglewood (*kyara kōboku*, 伽羅香木) caught their attention. The shogun had his retainers trace its source to Okachi's residence, where they found the lady with eight maids fanning the incense toward her while she sat against a golden folding screen.[9] Offended by this profligate sight, Tsunayoshi ordered the city magistrate to confiscate Ishikawa's property and banish the couple from Edo for the crime of arrogance and this extravagance.[10]

A year after the incident, the shogunate began issuing a series of ordinances designed to control consumption of luxurious garments and other items. In 1682, based on an ordinance that banned luxurious garments, officers began more frequently to inspect the clothing of passers-by and arrested those who were too expensively dressed.[11] The same ordinance also retracted the law that had permitted merchants to wear swords. In the same year, the shogunate took control over prices for luxurious garments, such as richly embroidered or elaborately tie-dyed kimonos. In 1683, townspeople were forbidden to use 'golden foil, golden embroidery and *sō kanoko* [cloth entirely dappled], all very expensive but popular techniques for making upscale costumes for women's *kosode*'.[12] Housemaids working for samurai and townspeople were also ordered to wear only cotton clothes made without bright colours or of elaborate patterns. In 1689, merchants were banned from selling garments that cost more than two hundred silver coins and had glossy textures. In 1718, the Edo city magistrate issued an edict that warned townspeople against wearing luxurious undergarments.[13] Twenty-seven years later, the government made it a law that townspeople who violated these dress codes would be subject to arrest and confiscation of their garments.[14]

---

[9] Toda Mosui, *Gotōdaiki* (Tokyo: Heibonsha, 1998), 9–20. See a slightly different account in Eiko Ikegami, *Bonds of Civility: Aesthetic Networks and the Political Origins of Japanese Culture* (Cambridge: Cambridge University Press, 2005), 273–274.

[10] Toda Mosui, *Gotōdaiki*.

[11] Osamu Wakita, *Kinsei Osaka no Machi to Hito*, 196.

[12] Ikegami, *Bonds of Civility*, 274. The *kosode*, often referred to as *kimono* in modern times, was a T-shaped robe for both women and men. It was used as both an undergarment and an overgarment.

[13] Well-to-do townspeople customarily wore *kosode* over several layers of undergarments whose hems or collars showed through as an accent. Often townspeople deliberately wore luxurious undergarments to flout the sumptuary codes. I address this subject below.

[14] Osamu Wakita, *Kinsei Osaka no Machi to Hito*, 197–198.

While the Yodoya case was certainly in keeping with these late
seventeenth-century legal developments, the Yodoyas' dramatic downfall stood out as the best-known cautionary tale to many merchants and
townspeople who had enjoyed unprecedented prosperity in Tokugawa
Japan. The story continued to be told through popular tales and puppet
theatres as a vivid reminder of townspeople's potentially precarious lives
and of the perilous consequences of transgression in their social and cultural conduct.[15] Joken Nishikawa (1648–1724), a Nagasaki townsman
and renowned scholar of international studies and astronomy, summed
up the general sentiment in his 1719 mediation on the hazardous position in which townspeople found themselves as a result of their rapid
rise within social, economic and cultural spheres. In *Chōnin Bukuro*
(Lessons for Townspeople), Nishikawa openly admitted the increasing
economic prosperity of townspeople and its potentially subversive
implications for the status structure, but he remained adamant in
reminding his readers (presumably both his fellow townspeople and
samurai rulers) that townspeople must live within the bounds of their
given stations in society:

There are five statuses in the human world: emperor, regional lords, their
followers with official ranks, those without them, and the people ... Among
the people, there are four kinds: low-ranking samurai, peasants, artisan, and
merchants ... When these four kinds of people do not exist, the principle of five
statuses shall cease to exist. This is why there is no place in the world which does
not require four kinds of people ... Among these four, artisans and merchants
are called *chōnin* (townspeople). Although *chōnin* are located at the bottom of
the order, since our society witnessed the shift from a barter economy to a monetary economy in recent years, the wealth has fallen into the hands of *chōnin*.
Nowadays, *chōnin* are more frequently called to the nobles' presence. It looks as
though they stand above farmers in the status order ... But *chōnin* should not
seek to surpass those above them, they should not envy the power of those above
them, and they should observe simplicity and frugality. Above all, they should
accept what is given to them with gratitude, as in the saying 'as long as cattle flock
together, they shall live happily forever'.[16]

Within a century, however, Tokugawa society would roundly disregard
Nishikawa's caution. Prosperous men and women in towns and villages
frequently flouted codes of behaviour and appearance prescribed in
sumptuary regulations. The regulations lost their efficacy, and the government found itself constantly – and vainly – battling excessive consumption and fashion.

[15] Ibid., 200.
[16] Joken Nishikawa, 'Chōnin Bukuro', in *Nihon shisō taikei shinsōban: gei no shisō, michi no
shisō*, vol. 5 *Kinsei chōnin shisō*, ed. Yukijiko Nakamura (Tokyo: Iwanami, 1996), 95.

Tokugawa Political Economy and the Problem of Excess

During the century-long Warring States Period or Sengoku Period (late fifteenth to late sixteenth centuries), warlords such as Nobunaga Oda (1534–1582) and Hideyoshi Toyotomi (1536–1598) never implemented sumptuary laws that restricted ordinary people's fashion and consumption. Such laws applied only to their warrior retainers, since clothing and armour were considered the most palpable symbols of power, status and wealth among the warriors.[17] The warlords relished shiny, stylish armour and brilliantly coloured clothing to display their pre-eminence and flatter their egos. It was under the Tokugawa shogunate – which identified the consolidation and preservation of social order as its primary political goal – that ordinary people's everyday lives first drew official scrutiny. There are many ways to explain why and how sumptuary regulation came to constitute an essential part of the Tokugawa shogunate's approach to the governance of society.[18] Most historians would agree, however, that economic policies under the Tokugawa regime reflected the official view that consumer or behavioural 'excesses', including those relating to fashion and life-style embodying such excesses, were disruptive and even detrimental to political order and social harmony.[19] To understand how such an official view came about, we need to turn our discussion to the organisational principle of Tokugawa society, the economic idea that underlined the principle and the crisis of Tokugawa finances.

Tokugawa society was built on the notion that every individual was born with a predetermined status (*mibun*, 身分) and a particular occupation (*shokubun*, 職分) that corresponded to the matrix of hereditary social relations. From womb to tomb, individuals carried supposedly unalterable

---

[17] Jin-han Park, 'Kinseizenki ni okeru ken'yakurei no zengokutekitenkai to sono tokuchō', in *Shirin* 86 (Kyoto: Kyoto University Press, 2003), 143.

[18] Susan Hanley does not give serious consideration to sumptuary laws, based on the fact that the decrees were rarely enforced strictly after the eighteenth century. The chapter here calls into question her assumption by looking into the process by which popular fashion and other cultural innovations constantly negotiated both visible and invisible limits set up by the official discourse and decrees on frugality and simplicity. Furthermore, the occasional enforcement of the law might have engendered pressure, uncertainty and fear among the townspeople and this socio-psychological dimension might have played a decisive role in shaping and setting limits on the contour of popular cultural innovations. Due to the limited space, this interesting psychological dimension of cultural politics is beyond the scope of my discussion here. See Susan B. Hanley, 'Tokugawa Society: Material Culture, Standard of Living, and Life-styles' in J. W. Hall et al. (eds.), *The Cambridge History of Japan*, 6 vols. (Cambridge: Cambridge University Press, 1991), iv: 660–705.

[19] The discussion of political economy in this section draws heavily on my previous work. See Katsuya Hirano, *The Politics of Dialogic Imagination: Power and Popular Culture in Early Modern Japan* (Chicago: University of Chicago Press, 2013), ch. 1.

markers or 'social tattoos', reflected in their speech, appearance and habitation, that signified their permanent belonging to a given group and social function.[20] The government's founders codified this highly rigid social system to consolidate the hierarchical arrangement of power and facilitate material production and distribution. Peasants and artisans were allotted manual work. Merchants served a distributive function, while the ruling samurai status groups held bureaucratic responsibility for monitoring and regulating the mechanisms of production and distribution. In practice, of course, these functions were not always observed with strict consistency; functions of commerce and material production were more frequently merged in the same person, especially from the eighteenth century onward. But the classificatory scheme set up by the founders of Tokugawa Japan to organise people into different status categories and to require them to perform assigned productive functions constituted an essential part of a system of rule designed to lubricate the social hierarchy's interdependent relations.

This highly stratified set of social relations rested on a particular vision of wealth. First, the shogunate considered the accumulation of wealth a 'zero-sum game', because 'wealth could only be redistributed, not created'.[21] Second, wealth could consequently grow only through coercive means like taxation or self-discipline, such as hard work and thrift. And lastly, given the view of wealth as limited and scarce, resources had to be redistributed not on egalitarian grounds, but in line with the hierarchical arrangement of authority. Sorai Ogyū (1666–1728), a Confucian scholar to the fifth shogun Tsunayoshi Tokugawa and influential political theorist, expounded this restrictive economic view:

The amount of goods to be produced is generally limited. How much rice can be produced in the entire land of Japan? How much millet can be produced? How much lumber can be made available? Every good in this world has a limited quantity. Those of fine quality in particular are few, while coarse goods are many. Therefore, it would be perfectly logical to establish institutions whereby one has people of venerable status use the fine goods (from clothing, to food, to housing) and those of base status the poor goods, because the number of the former by nature is small, while that of the latter is large: that is, the fewer people use the fewer things and the more numerous people use the more numerous things. All the things available in this country will be used to the full extent by all the people to satisfy their respective needs.[22]

---

[20] 'Social tattoo' is a phrase used by Herman Ooms in 'Forms and Norms in Edo arts and Society', in Robert T. Singer (ed.), *Edo: Art in Japan 1615–1868* (New Haven: Yale University Press, 1998), 26.

[21] Ibid., 29.

[22] Sorai Ogyu, *Seidan* (Tokyo: Iwanami Shoten, 1987), 102.

Based on these principles, the Tokugawa authorities regarded excessive consumption by people of lower status as a type of idleness – and a clear indication of anarchy and governmental failure, as well as a direct cause of social conflict. Sorai summarised this view in the same treatise: 'If our institutions [of wealth distribution] fail, a vast number of lowly people will start acquiring fine goods, which will result in a dramatic increase in the price of commodities … Because it brings confusion to the order of high and low, it will open up a path to conflicts from which all kinds of vices will be born. Without institutional [arrangement and authority] the world becomes sumptuous as it is people's natural sentiment to relish extravagance.'[23]

For the Tokugawa state and its advisers, sumptuary regulations were the most logical way to maintain an equilibrium of production and consumption. Authorities regularly issued edicts to curtail waste and excess by urging people to exercise 'self-discipline in all matters of consumption' and to keep production levels high by maximising labour available through cooperation within the community.[24] All sumptuary laws implemented in villages during the Tokugawa period were based on the premise that peasants must produce as much as possible while consuming as little as possible. A Tokugawa injunction of 1642 stipulated that 'peasants should use as food the miscellaneous grains and should not eat much rice', wear straw capes and hats instead of cotton rain capes or umbrellas, and refrain from using 'leather-soled sandals, and combs (*kazarikushi*, 飾り櫛) and bodkins (*kōgai*, 笄) with metal ornamentation or of tortoise shell'.[25] They were allowed only small houses, without floor mats, paper-covered sliding doors or verandas. In some rural areas, silk, pongee (*kenchū* or a flat-woven silk textile), bleached cotton summer kimonos, bleached cotton towels, striped materials, tunics, trousers, sash materials, wooden clogs, mirrors, nail scissors, capes, incense, drums, blankets, lacquered chopsticks, swords, bows and arrows, spears and books were all prohibited.[26] The prohibition of swords, bows and arrows, spears and books reflected the ruling class's view that possessing these weapons and the acquisition of literacy would inspire insubordination among peasants or interfere with their agricultural production.[27] Even wedding and New Year's banquets were regulated in rural areas, limiting

---

[23] Ibid., 103.

[24] Herman Ooms, *Tokugawa Ideology: Early Constructs, 1570–1689* (Princeton: Princeton University Press, 1989), 145.

[25] Cited in Donald H. Shively, 'Sumptuary Regulation and Status in Early Tokugawa', *Harvard Journal of Asiatic Studies* 25 (1964–1965): 154.

[26] Ibid., 155

[27] Park, 'Kinseizenki ni okeru ken'yakurei no zengokutekitenkai to sono tokuchō', 149.

the celebrations to 'one soup, one viand, and one hors d'oeuvre, and to be concluded before dark'. The shogunate renewed these austere regulations across the centuries, in 1667, 1788 and 1842.[28]

Townspeople were permitted a much higher level of luxury than ordinary farmers or peasants, yet they were not allowed to wear wool capes and elaborate silk kimonos or to have an ostentatious appearance. Regulations also banned wearing long swords or large short swords. Their household articles could not have gold lacquer decoration, and their houses were limited to two-storey structures without gold or silver leaf trim. They were warned against conspicuous display at weddings, funerals and memorial services. Entertainments by and for townspeople, such as kabuki and puppet theatres (ningyō jōruri, 人形浄瑠璃), were held to the same standards of simplicity: no fine costumes and adornments were permitted.

As discussed so far, the particular understanding of wealth brought sumptuary regulation to the foreground in economic policy under the Tokugawa regime. What also contributed to the Tokugawa regime's increasing dependency on sumptuary regulation was its financial crisis.[29] The lords, whether the Shogun or daimyo, depended on taxation of land in terms of rice as their fiscal base. Since rice worked as the universal standard of tax and wealth during the Tokugawa period, the lords 'derived the bulk of their income – in many cases up to 80 per cent and more – from their land tax, calculated as a certain proportion (usually 40–50 per cent, but sometimes as much as 70 per cent) of the estimated annual production of any given piece of land'.[30] Accordingly, the Edo and domainal administrations lacked the system that allowed for the lords to fully benefit from the fruits of commercial activities that were increasing throughout the period under consideration. They had no effective means to access the magnitude of the flow of income generated from trade, commerce and commercial crops and then levy tax on it, unlike in a capitalist society where the concept of 'capital' and 'profit' constitutes the most basic logic and logistics of taxation.[31] This particular arrangement of the Tokugawa economy and its fiscal policies allowed for the merchants, entrepreneurial farmers and artisans

[28] Shively, 'Sumptuary Regulation', 154.
[29] Harold Bolitho offers a concise account of the financial crisis of many domains as well as the Tokugawa bakufu (Japanese military government) in the eighteenth century, in 'The Han' in The Cambridge History of Japan iv: 213–225.
[30] Ibid., 213.
[31] Needless to say, had the Tokugawa bakufu established a bureaucratic machinery designed specifically to impose tax on income, it would have needed to abolish the system of land tax in rice and certainly implied its own demise.

to accumulate wealth while making the ruling samurai class extremely vulnerable to ever-increasing expenditure to support their costly rituals (i.e. alternate attendance) and lifestyles (i.e. maintaining an elegant mansion in Edo), which were major drains on their finances. What was worse for the ruling samurai was that many domainal governments and samurai of high status turned to the help of moneylenders to temporarily alleviate their financial predicaments. By the end of the seventeenth century, every domain had gone into debt. 'Budget deficits and chronic debts', Bolitho writes, 'were as much a part of *han* (domainal) life as they are of our own'.[32]

The financial crisis of the ruling class, originating from declining income from taxation, growing expenditure on opulent lifestyles and swelling debts to merchants, could not be highlighted as it would have upset the axes of the hierarchical arrangement of power – that is, the symbolic status order and uneven distribution of material resources reflecting that order. Therefore, the shogunate and other domainal lords worked hard to contain the common people's unproductive expenditure while ensuring steady agricultural production through the enforcement of austerity and frugality.[33]

By promoting frugality, simplicity and communal loyalty as the foundational virtues for commoners, and enforcing these duties of everyday conduct through decrees and punishments, the Tokugawa authorities intended to purge the waste represented by pleasure and play – including spectacles, fashion, street trends and popular art and literature – which in their view had 'no end beyond themselves'.[34] They hoped that commoners would abide by the ideas that consumption was acceptable only if it took place within the limits of justifiable utilitarian ends – that there was a need for consuming no more than the volume necessary for subsistence without upsetting maximum productivity – and that transgressing these limits meant a serious deviation from and disruption to the moral imperatives of social harmony.

At the dawn of the eighteenth century, exactly when the Tokugawa shogunate dissolved the Yodoya house for excessive consumption, the shogunate faced the possibility of losing its power to rule, as large groups

---

[32] Bolitho, 'The Han', 223. Alternate attendance was a Tokugawa shogunate policy that required each domainal lord to spend a year in the shogun's capital of Edo every other year. The daimyo, furthermore, were also obliged to keep their wives and most of their children in permanent residence in Edo, where they served in effect as hostages.

[33] For the term 'unproductive expenditure', I draw on George Bataille's formulation in 'The Notion of Expenditure', in George Bataille, *Visions of Excess: Selected Writings, 1927–1939* (Minneapolis: University of Minnesota Press, 1985), 118.

[34] Ibid.

of vagrants began to flout the moral duties of frugality and productivity. Town lifestyle filled with excitement, and novelty prompted peasants, who suffered growing misery from famines and heavy taxes, to flee their villages and migrate to more commercially and culturally vibrant towns. Large vagrant populations consisting of beggars, peddlers, unlicenced prostitutes and street entertainers gathered in the major castle towns, especially Edo. In 1692 the official number of vagrants in Edo was 5,366; that number had grown to 13,266 by 1837.[35] The total population of Edo reached over one million by 1750, and as 60 per cent of this figure consisted of common people, the increase in the vagrant population indicated that approximately one out of fifty or sixty commoners was identified as a vagrant by the early nineteenth century. Beginning in the 1780s, the number of vagabonds coming to Edo increased dramatically due to the devastating Tenmei famine.[36] Sadanobu Matsudaira (1758–1829), senior counsellor to the shogun at the time, embarked on an aggressive policy of repatriating vagrant peasants to their native lands under a law entitled *Order for the Return of Unregistered and Wild Beggars to Their Former Native Places*. He created Edo's Stockade of Labour, a workhouse where vagrants and criminals were classified as one and the same – a common threat to social stability – and instigated a programme of 'rehabilitation' to mould them into fully functional workers. All inmates at the workhouse received payment for their labours and were required to 'deposit one-third of their wages in their individual savings accounts maintained at the accounting office', so that they would learn – according to the shogunate – to value the rewards of labour and understand the importance of saving and financial independence.[37] The workhouse also obliged every inmate to attend thrice-monthly lectures by eminent Confucian scholars from the Mind Studies School (*shingaku*, 心学) which saw all social reality as the consequence of the state of one's mind and thus placed the primacy on the morality of diligence and proper conduct. The shogunate viewed this combination of work, discipline and moral training as an effective strategy for limiting idle bodies and resuscitating productive social relations in Tokugawa's de facto capital. As time

---

[35] Yoshifumi Uramoto, *Edo, Tokyo no Hisabetsuburaku no rekishi: Danzaemon to hisabetsu Minshū* (Tokyo: Akashi shoten, 2003), 119–125.

[36] The Great Tenmei Famine lasted from 1782 to 1788. Due to a poor harvest and a series of natural disasters rice prices rose drastically; the resulting famine led to a population decline of more than 920,000 people across Tokugawa Japan. See Kanji Ishii, *Nihon Keizaishi* (Tokyo: University of Tokyo Press, 1991), 77.

[37] Fore more detailed accounts on the workhouse, see Takashi Kato's excellent essay 'Governing Edo', in James L. McClain, John M. Merriman, and Ugawa Kaoru (eds.), *Edo and Paris: Urban Life and the State in the Early Modern Era* (Ithaca: Cornell University Press, 1994), 60–61.

would tell, however, Sadanobu's policy proved to be a signal failure. It succeeded neither in halting the flow of displaced peasants into Edo, nor in containing the allure of pleasure and play that Edo's consumer culture exuded and disseminated. The resulting official anxieties were conveyed in an order issued at the time of a major ideological and political campaign in 1799, soon after the Kansei Reform of 1787–1793; it was repeated under similar circumstances in 1839, just before the Tenpō Reform of 1841–1843:[38]

Under the pretext of holding annual fairs and festivals, some people in villages perform plays imitating kabuki and make a profit. In addition there are villagers who invite itinerant traders, who bring in goods [comic fiction and *ukiyo-e*] that are wasteful of both time and thrift and are detrimental to the morality of village life. Others who invite outcasts [itinerant entertainers], spreading through lascivious mirth and levity the undesirable influences of pleasure and play, must also be punished. This sort of transgression naturally encourages peasants to cease their cultivation and to create more wasteland, and eventually leads them to impoverishment. As a result, peasants are forced out of their villages and migrate to cities. Urban performances such as kabuki and *jōruri* must therefore be strictly prohibited in villages.[39]

This order simultaneously confirmed the Tokugawa rulers' most basic ideological proposition – that morality and productivity together formed the basis of social unity and revealed officials' fear of the challenge to the established order posed by new, proliferating forms of urban culture structured around consumption. Characterising urban popular culture as intrinsically immoral, due to its propensity for favouring pleasure and play over the venerable virtues of thrift and hard work, the edict was aimed at containing the 'vice' of the culture of excess – conspicuous consumption and its putatively corrosive effect on productive activities.

Buyō Inshi, most likely a retired samurai in Edo or a samurai turned Confucian scholar, noted in the second decade of the nineteenth century the uncontainable vigour of Edo popular culture, even as he condemned its harmful effect on Tokugawa society's moral economy:

There are no limits to the popularity and prosperity of countless spectacles such as puppet shows, acrobatic shows, magic shows, impressions, storytelling, etc. They all use fine costumes for their performances. In recent years, large-scale spectacles that cost one or two thousand pieces of gold for their elaborate settings

---

[38] Both reforms were intended to resolve the *bakufu*'s financial crises by imposing thrift and frugality on townspeople and samurai retainers. People's consumer behaviour became the primary target. Prohibited luxuries included certain kinds of sushi and tofu as well as expensive crafts and clothing.

[39] Shinzō Takayanagi and Ryōsuke Ishii (eds.), *Ofuregaki Tenpō Shūsei* (Tokyo: Iwanami Shoten, 1958) ii: 439.

and performances have appeared. They amaze and dazzle the spectators and rob them of a lot of money for their vulgar performances. With their titillating effects on the public, they weaken the way of loyalty and filial piety, being a complete adversary to the old customs of promoting good and chastising evil. It is hard to estimate exactly how many people – more than tens of thousands of people at least – are making their livings in this business. Are they not the true idlers, in that they evade taxes and social responsibilities and lead their lives according to selfish desires? Are they not the true idlers, in that they spread wasteful expend-iture, the confusions of high/low distinctions and sins of libidinal indulgence? There are no limits to their prosperity. They must be stopped.[40]

The prosperity and new way of life that townspeople exalted threatened the Tokugawa government's hard-won and fundamentally unstable social hierarchy by erasing distinctions in everyday interactions between ruling status groups and the commoners. In the same treatise, Buyō admitted:

Samurai's pouches are light, and samurai themselves lack vigour. The towns-people are stalwart and full of vigour, and their pouches are heavy. For every ryō a samurai spends, a townsman spends two or three. Therefore he glows with importance wherever he goes, and all are attracted to him. All kind of idlers, such as performers of *waka* [Japanese poetry], linked verse, and *haikai* tea masters, flower arrangers, and players of the *koto* [a string instrument] or the *shamisen*, shun samurai and adore townspeople. Neither high nor low can make a living anymore unless they hold hands with townspeople.[41]

The shogunate's repeated attempts to sustain productivity and reclaim social control through the discourse and policies of moral and economic discipline proved futile. Indeed, villagers and townspeople alike often ridiculed the ineffectiveness of sumptuary laws, derisively calling them 'three days laws' (*mikka hatto* 三日法度), because the laws appeared absurdly irrelevant to rapidly changing realities and were so often disregarded. Buyō observed:

Townspeople have no expenses for public duties: their public duty is to be extravagant. Those who used to be banned from wearing even silk pongee today wear only silk crepe and never touch cotton. Cotton is worn by those who should not be wearing it, while those who should not wear silk crepe use it everyday. Townspeople even use foreign textiles such as striped sateen and Dutch imports. They frequently wear felted or worsted wool, velvet, and striped sateen. I am told that the use of felted wool even for spear scabbards was once restricted to province-holding daimyo. Later, it was allowed to lesser daimyo, and subse-quently to those holding fiefs of over three thousand koku. Today townspeople

[40] Buyō Inshi, *Seijikenbunroku* (Tokyo: Iwanami Shoten, 1994), 355–356.
[41] Ibid. The translation is taken from Mark Teeuwen and Kate Wildman Nakai, eds. and trans., *Lust, Commerce, and Corruption* (New York: Columbia University Press, 2014), 281.

use it for their *haori*, for bedding, and even for the thongs of their *geta*. This shows how radically customs have changed.[42]

Then Buyō probed the wider implications for the polity of the increasingly conspicuous presence of townspeople's material affluence:

Even though townspeople and city idlers are said to be filthy and inferior, they are so only in name. They are in reality the winners of our time, for they enjoy the fruits of unprecedented prosperity and continue to influence every aspect of our social life with their culture of debauchery ... It is increasingly common for samurai to choose to become townspeople, willingly renouncing their status and opting to live among these lowly people. Even peasants, violating our sacred law, leave their home villages for larger cities to live like townspeople ... The entire world has fallen into the hands of the townspeople. From samurai to peasants, everyone imitates their lifestyles, manners and appearance. Who could have anticipated such a dramatic dissolution of our sacrosanct moral order at the time of the Tokugawa system's founding?[43]

Buyo's language of crisis leads us to a key conclusion about the shogunate's continuous dependence on sumptuary regulations that were in large measure ineffective: these regulations were not merely intended to prevent the 'visual status reversals in which the merchants appeared to be living better than the samurai'.[44] Instead, they served the much more fundamental project of containing deep structural contradictions undermining the status-based social relations of production that the Tokugawa system had organised to support its hierarchical distribution of power and authority. The shogunate's perpetual efforts to regulate consumption were symptomatic of its complete failure to achieve the intended effects in the face of mounting socio-economic tensions between commoners and the governing classes.

The Archetype of the Sophisticated

Despite, or because of, sustained interventions from Tokugawa authorities, Edo urbanites' aesthetic sensibilities had taken on a distinctive form by the second half of the eighteenth century in the popular cultural archetype called *tsūjin* (通人). The concept of *tsū* evolved from *sui* (or *iki*; 粋): the essence of sophistication, a quality that had been valued in the Kyoto-Osaka area since the Genroku period (1688–1704).[45] Either

---

[42] Teeuwen and Nakai, *Lust, Commerce, and Corruption*, 268. *Geta* are traditional Japanese shoes.
[43] Buyō Inshi, *Seijikenbunroku*, 281–84.
[44] Ikegami, *Bonds of Civility*, 274.
[45] Cecilia Segawa Seigle, *Yoshiwara* (Honolulu: University of Hawai'i Press, 1993), 131.

a deed or a person might embody this essence of sophistication. *Tsū* directly opposes *yabo* (vulgar), and this common diacritical pairing reveals the essence of *tsūjin*. The *Lecture on Great Tsū* (*Daitsū hōwa*, 1779) defined *tsū* as follows: 'People used to call *iki* one's sensibility to understand another's mind by reflecting on one's own: that is, to know the other's pain through one's own. Or they referred to a person of that calibre as the person of *tsū*. Now we call it simply *tsū*'.[46] A decade later, the author of *A Thousand Stories* (*Hansenwa*, 1790) suggested that pleasure-quarter customers often misunderstood *tsū* as the demonstration of superficial cultural and material attributes, so they tended to dress up, enjoy a rich diet and immerse themselves in all kinds of fashionable art, music and poetry. They tried their best to pull off a handsome and well-to-do appearance in order to impress courtesans. But, the book continued, these behaviours came from their vanity and thus did not represent true *tsū*. This pretentiousness was the precise meaning of *yabo*. The author of the book concluded that such *yabo* behaviour inevitably led to self-destruction and was antithetical to people of true *tsū*, who were completely at ease with being themselves and did not put on any false airs (Figure 17.1).[47]

A comic fiction entitled *The Barbershop* (*Ukiyodoko*, 1813) depicts a scene where barbershop customers discuss a poor yet high-spirited old man, a barbershop regular, who lost his wife some years earlier and now lives a humble life alone. They praise him for his good nature and for having managed to bring up his son by himself. They conclude that he must be a true *tsūjin*, contrary to the word's ordinary meaning:

> Those guys admired as *tsū* are actually pretty ostentatious. If you don't believe, take a careful look at how messed up they are [in their personal lives]. On the other hand, those fellows regarded as *yabo* are actually pretty decent folks. They are never slighted by others, and even often extend their help to the poor and the downtrodden. I think this kind of fellow is a true *tsū*.[48]

The word *tsū* did not have a uniform definition and was open to many different meanings, embracing qualities like empathy, genuineness and decency, but all articulate an authentic attitude toward self and others. This sense of *tsū* brings us back to the concept of *sui* or *iki* – the essential quality of *tsūjin*. It referred not only to high aesthetic sensibility but also to moral sensitivity in lifestyle and demeanour. Although the term often implied men's thorough familiarity with the unstated rules and etiquette

---

[46] *Daitsū hōwa*, cited in Tatsuro Nakano, *Sui, Tsu, Iki* (Tokyo: Iyai shobo, 1985), 128.
[47] Tatsuro Nakano, *Sui, Tsu, Iki*, 130.
[48] Sanba Shikitei, *Ukiyodoko* (Tokyo: Tenbōsha, 1974), 58–59.

Figure 17.1 *Yabo and Tsū*, by Utagawa Kunisada I (Toyokuni III) (1786–1864), 1832. 37.2 x 51.6 cm. Museum of Fine Arts, Boston, William Sturgis Bigelow Collection 11.37809.3a-b. The print depicts the prototypes of *tsū* and *yabo*. The figure on the left represents *tsū*, as a knowledgeable and unpretentious connoisseur, whereas the figure on the right depicts *yabo* as an ostentatious big spender who lacks delicate sensibilities and sophisticated taste. The heads of the smaller figures bear the characters of 'good' and 'bad', the former referring to *tsū* and the latter *yabo*. The print represents a scene from a popular kabuki play, the *Grand Finale Dance Number Four Seasons*.

of Edo's pleasure quarter – not to mention an unassuming and courteous attitude toward courtesans – it was widely used, regardless of gender, to suggest an ideal persona, or more broadly a whole way of life, deemed refined and chic in both aesthetic and moral senses.

According to the theorist Shūzō Kuki (1888–1941), this aesthetic and moral idealism consisted of three behavioural attributes: erotic allure or 'coquetry', referred to as *bitai* (媚態), pride or honour, called *ikuji* (意気地), and resignation or acceptance, known as *akirame* (諦め).[49] These three elements balanced each other to create a disposition or personal

---

[49] Shūzō Kuki, *Iki no Kōzō* (Tokyo: Iwanamai, 1979), 21–26. The translations are taken from Shūzō Kuki, *The Structure of Detachment*, trans. Hiroshi Nara (Honolulu: University of Hawai'i Press, 2004), 19–21.

character inclined to shun aggressive pursuit of self-aggrandisement while exuding a charming, seductive aura in interactions with others.

While Kuki's theoretical formulation is germane to our discussion of *iki* and *tsu* in this chapter, I would like to stress that my approach to the aesthetic concepts differs radically from his in that it understands the much-praised quality of *iki/tsu* as an *historical* form, shaped by specific socio-economic policies and their underlying ideological system in early modern Japan.[50] Specifically, I see the aesthetic and moral form of *tsū* as a product of continuous negotiation between Tokugawa authorities aiming to regulate, or even purge, urbanites' 'excesses' and urbanites seeking to carve out spaces for asserting new tastes and sensibilities. Kuki, on the other hand, understood it as a timeless and fundamental structure of Japanese identity and the Japanese ethnicity's unique cultural being.[51] This chapter disavows Kuki's ethnic ontology.

One contentious site of this constant negotiation was fashion. Laws redirected contemporary trends at various moments in Tokugawa history from the late seventeenth century on. After the prohibition on expensive textile techniques significantly reduced the production of *sō kanoko* (tie-dye called *shibori*) and golden and silver embroidery, the fashion shifted to elegant and cleverly dyed designs. After 1683, Eiko Ikegami explains, 'artistic techniques for dyeing *kimono*, such as *yūzen* dyeing (hand-painting on silk fabric with starch resist), grew more sophisticated and refined'.[52] This quick response in the form of a new design trend during the Genroku era (1688–1704) did not simply imply submission to the shogunate's policy; rather, it was the result of the cumulative and innovative activities of fashion entrepreneurs and designers who produced several new trends in rapid succession in order to satisfy the increasingly refined taste of their customers within set political and ideological limits.[53]

This same period also saw continuous refinement of the lining of *haori* jackets, which became increasingly colourful inside, while the exterior remained dark and plain – a clever reversal that displayed the wearer's

---

[50] Kuki focused on the earlier concept of *iki* (*sui*), not *tsū*, as the main theme of his analysis. *Iki* and *tsū* were interchangeably used from the mid- to the late eighteenth century on, especially in Edo, and *tsū* was used more frequently during the period. For a critical assessment of Kuki's work, see Leslie Pincus, *Authenticating Culture in Imperial Japan* (Berkeley: University of California Press, 1996). Matsunosuke Nishiyama shares Kuki's ontological approach to Edo culture (cultural essentialist view), including the concept of *iki* and *tsū*, in his *Edo Culture* (Honolulu: University of Hawai'i Press, 1997). For a more nuanced history of the *tsū* concept, see Nakano, *Sui, Tsu, Iki*.

[51] Kuki, *The Structure of Detachment*, 14.

[52] Ikegami, *Bonds of Civility*, 275.

[53] Ibid.

taste in the form of concealment. A new trend of restrained, understated style increasingly became one of the definitive features of sophisticated urban fashion from the eighteenth century on. After the Kyōhō Reform (1716–1745) and the Kansei Reform (1787–1793), both of which were implemented to restore the government's and domainal lords' finances through frugality ordinances and tax increases, a simple, 'understated' (*jimi*, 地味) or 'astringent' (*shibumi*, 渋み) look, marked by extensive use of colours like black, grey, brown, indigo blue and pale yellow, came to be valued in fashion as an authentic expression of *tsū*, as opposed to overt display of flashy, bright colours such as red, pink and gold. Flashiness became a token of vulgar taste – *yabo*. Although this change inarguably signalled a dramatic reversal of aesthetic taste from the time of the Yodoya incident, Edo's taste for simplicity and understatement should not be taken as universal in eighteenth-century Japan. The Kyoto-Osaka area continued to embrace relatively gaudy, opulent taste in clothing, makeup and hairstyles as the epitome of elegance. Regional differences in aesthetic taste suggest that the metamorphosis of *tsū* style in Edo was due to the city's status as the Tokugawa administration's political centre, where government control was stricter and more immediately felt.[54]

For more than a century, the most popular fabric patterns in Edo and towns across Tokugawa Japan were partially dappled or dotted cotton (*kasuri*) textiles in brown, black or indigo with fine vertical pinstripes, usually white or pale yellow in colour.[55] For women, this type of pattern was used for a kimono's outer layer, worn over a bright, solid-coloured inner layer for a sharp contrast in colour and pattern (Figure 17.2). For men, the pinstriped textile was used for *haori, hakama* (wide-legged trousers) and *nagagi* (man's kimono) and commonly worn with a black, pale yellow or brown sash belt and black or indigo blue inner and outer clothes (Figure 17.3).

According to the *Guide for Contemporary Fashion* (*Tōsei Fūzoku Tsū*, 1773), a popular fashion handbook during the late eighteenth century, townspeople – both women and men – favoured dark-coloured garments with white or yellow vertical lines because they created the visual effect of a soft or blurry image when seen from a distance, while closer up the sharp and refined lines flattered wearers, making them seem taller and more slender.[56] The pattern's dual visual effect embodied both

---

[54] Ryūzō Saito, *Kinsei Nihon Sesōshi* (Tokyo: Hakubunkan, 1928), 795, 819–826.
[55] Kuki, *Iki no Kōzō*, 64–66. Saito, *Kinsei Nihon Sesōshi*, 795–797. As mentioned earlier, the Tokugawa government banned commoners from wearing silk garments and fully dappled patterns, because these expensive textiles were considered unsuitably luxurious.
[56] Kisanji Hōseido, *Tōsei Fūzoku Tsū*, in National Diet Library in Tokyo.

Figure 17.2 *Tatsumi Rokō* (an entertainer in Fukagawa, Edo), from the series *Renowned Six Beauties* by Kitagawa Utamaro I (early 1750s–1806), c. 1795–1796. 37.8 x 25 cm. Museum of Fine Arts, Boston, William S. and John T. Spaulding Collection, 21.5457.

resignation (a soft image suggesting a composed, non-assertive disposition) and pride (vertical lines representing strong character), two essential components of *tsū*, helping enhance the last attribute of the concept – erotic allure. The subdued, subtle representation of taste in this widespread and enduring fashion attested to the idealism of *tsūjin*.

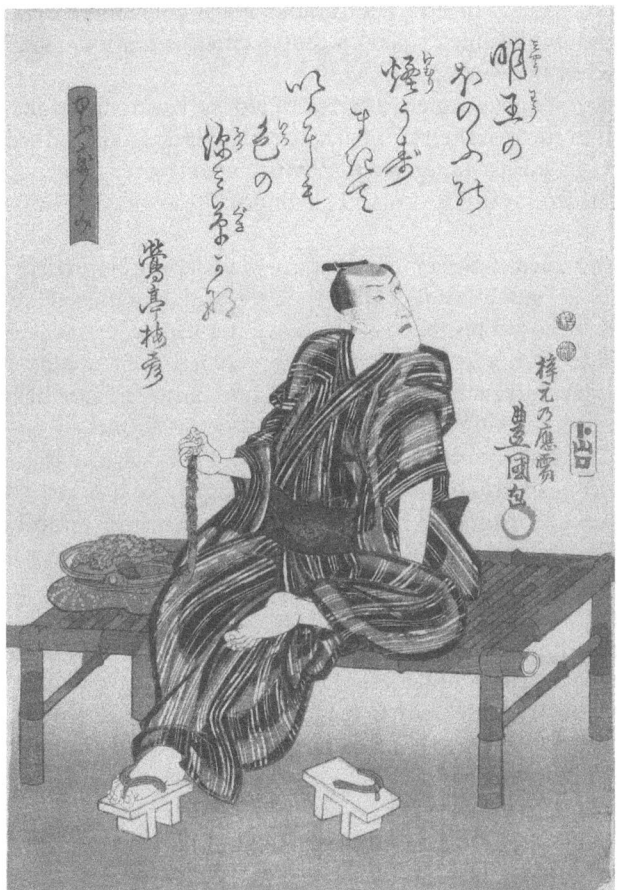

Figure 17.3 *Yū Suzumi* (actor Ichikawa Danjuro VIII depicted off-stage enjoying the coolness of evening), by Utagawa Kunisada I (Toyokuni III) (1786–1865), 1848. Victoria and Albert Museum, London, E.6489-1886.

The appreciation of simplicity and understatement also extended to women's makeup. Women in Edo, including courtesans in the pleasure quarter, preferred light cosmetics over the heavy makeup favoured in Kyoto during the pre-Genroku and Genroku periods. They applied a very thin layer of white powder to their faces, whereas women in Kyoto preferred to wear different layers of makeup emphasising light pink eyeliner under the eyes and accentuating the bridge of the nose with distinct white liner.[57] In Edo, a natural look was considered desirable and sophisticated, while thick makeup that seemed intentionally alluring or erotic branded the wearer as *yabo*.[58]

The Tokugawa government also restricted the use of luxurious personal items, such as tortoiseshell combs; hair ornaments decorated with pearls, gold, silver, or coral; paper scented with expensive eaglewood; tobacco cases crafted from pure silver; and small pouches woven of imported silk (Figure 17.4).

The authorities however never succeeded in keeping their watchful eyes on these small items. Townspeople widely ignored sumptuary regulations imposed on the less obtrusive luxurious crafts, as they were easier to hide than garments, and many fancied their quality materials and extremely intricate and refined designs and craftsmanship, especially those of carvings.[59] In fact, townspeople found in every small daily item an opportunity to pamper themselves with material refinement and its aesthetic pleasure. The Edo magistrate was forced to issue and reiterate an ordinance in 1820: 'Commoners are forbidden to use combs, hair ornaments, and other daily necessities made of gold, silver, and tortoiseshell'.[60] But the strident order was made entirely in vain.

Relatively well-to-do townspeople led the fashion trends, but people belonging to the lower classes, such as carpenters, scaffold constructors, shopkeepers, peddlers and firefighters also actively participated in the culture of *tsū*. One clue to their engagement in Edo's emerging culture of consumption can be found in the culture of *tenugui* (hand towels). A lightweight cotton hand towel was a practical item for workers and manual labourers and was inseparable from their daily lives. Towels were very affordable and thus never subject to sumptuary regulation, yet a hand towel could add a stylish flair to working clothes and testify to a worker's identity and pride. The base colour was always either white or pale yellow, printed with a wide variety of fashionable patterns in indigo blue. Carpenters, craftsmen, peddlers and firefighters enjoyed the practical and aesthetic accent of hand towels by draping them on their shoulders or around their necks like neckerchiefs, hanging them at their waists, or wearing them on their heads like bandanas (Figure 17.5).[61] For them, *tsū* never meant expensive and luxurious ornaments favoured

[57] Saito, *Kinsei Nihon Sesōshi*, 824.
[58] Ibid., 808.
[59] Ibid., 804–807.
[60] Ibid., 805.
[61] Ibid., 801.

Figure 17.4 'Town geisha', by Utagawa Kunisada I (Toyokuni III) (1786–1864). Victoria and Albert Museum, London, E8635.1886. The geisha appears to be adjusting her makeup with a paper scented with eaglewood that she is holding in her right hand, while replacing the remaining tissues in her kimono front with her left hand. Her elaborate hair ornaments made of tortoiseshell catch beholders' eyes more than her garments. And the makeup is simple and understated.

by upper-class townspeople, but an aesthetic to be found in the practical beauty of everyday items.

Both men and women of the lower class relied on used clothing shops to catch up with fashion trends. In 1723, there were over 1,200 stores

Figure 17.5 'Kabuki actors Onoe Kikugorô III as a carpenter and Arashi Koroku IV as his daughter Osono', by Gugadō Ashiyuki (active about 1814–1835), 1826. Museum of Fine Arts, Boston, William Sturgis Bigelow Collection, 11.35012.

selling second-hand kimono, belts and ornamental items, and that number grew to nearly 2,000 at the end of the eighteenth century. An historian estimates that close to 90 per cent of clothing worn by townspeople was second-hand.[62] Shopkeepers, peddlers and workers naturally tended to wear more practical garments made of cotton with simple

[62] Eisuke Ishikawa, *Ōedo Risaikuru Jijō* (Tokyo: Kodansha, 1997), 141–142, 319–320.

patterns for their daily work, but they dressed up with used yet fashionable items for outings, special events and ceremonial occasions.[63]

Lower-class townspeople also developed their own sphere of indulgence unrelated to practical needs: the culture of tattoo called *horimono* (文身).[64] Tattooing was originally practiced as a way of marking criminals in the early Tokugawa period, but beginning around the mid-eighteenth century, townspeople of the lower class began to get arm tattoos as a fashion statement. Tattooing of the entire body started around the end of the eighteenth century, and culminated in the first half of the nineteenth century. The most popular motifs were dragons, tigers and warriors, likely borrowed from the best-selling novel *The Water Margin* (*Suikoden*, 水滸伝) and the novel's visual adaptation in woodblock prints by the artists Kuniyoshi Utagawa and Toyokuni Utagawa III (Figure 17.6).[65] This seemingly masculine culture of tattoo was not limited to men. Women, especially prostitutes and teahouse girls, secretly and at times openly participated in the culture of body art. Extraordinarily beautiful tattoos cost a fortune and were widely believed to have supernatural power. People viewed them with reverence and fear. The trend of tattooing reached its zenith in the 1830s, becoming so prevalent that even samurai of reputable status went under the needle. In 1841, the Tokugawa government decided to intervene by imposing sumptuary regulations on tattoos as part of the larger political and ideological campaign to crack down on townspeople's consumer behaviour. The next two years saw the strictest sumptuary enforcement of the Tokugawa era. Yet, again, this reform did not last for a long time, as it proved itself to be utterly ineffective in reversing the course of historical transformations. Tattooing continued to be a popular practice among the working-class people until Japan's first modern regime, the Meiji government (1868–1911), embarked on an aggressive and total reshaping of popular customs (*fūzoku kairyō*, 風俗改良), including tattooing, as part of the programme of promoting modern civilisation and enlightenment in the 1870s and 1880s (Figure 17.6).[66]

---

[63] Saito., *Kinsei Nihon Sesōshi*, 816–819.

[64] Yoshimi Yamamoto, *Irezumi to Nihonjin* (Tokyo: Heibonsha, 2016).

[65] *The Water Margin* is a well-known novel written by Shi Nai'an. It is set in the Song Dynasty of China and tells the story of how a band of 108 outlaws forms an autonomous community at Mt. Liang and then gains amnesty from the government. The group eventually goes on working together to punish corrupt and evil officials and rescue the country. Edo writers like Bakin Kyokutei translated and adapted the story from 1807 to 1811 for Japanese readers and successfully popularised it.

[66] On the *fūzoku kairyō* movement, see Hirano, *The Politics of Dialogic Imagination*, ch. 5.

Figure 17.6 *Suikoden Mitate* ('Popular kabuki actors imitating the figures in *The Water Margin*'), by Utagawa Kunisada I (Toyokuni III) (1786–1864), 1858. 36.3 x 48.9 cm. Museum of Fine Arts, Boston, William Sturgis Bigelow Collection, 11.15472, 1.15475 and 11.42432.

Conclusion: Why Control Consumption?

The cultural politics of sumptuary regulation in early modern Japan offers an intriguing case for reflecting on why rulers in pre-modern societies were keenly concerned with ordinary people's consumer behaviour, and why they considered its regulation a central task for effective governance. Tokugawa rulers found it necessary to control consumption because they believed that society could produce only a limited amount of wealth. Furthermore, with the emergence of a vibrant commercial economy and the resultant acceleration of consumption in urban areas around the end of the seventeenth century, they felt more compelled to curb townspeople's patent consumption while defending the agrarian fundamentalism, a nominal yet foundational premise, upon which Tokugawa Japan was constructed. The palpable tensions between the agrarian mode of production and a commercial economy spurred by commodity exchange led Tokugawa rulers to frame consumption more aggressively as a wasteful loss that depleted limited resources. They believed that people's immoderate consumption threatened to disrupt the polity's order and stability. Unlike capitalist societies that view vigorous consumption as a necessary impetus for ensuring the endless cycle of expanding production, economic growth and wealth accumulation, Tokugawa rulers who held the zero-sum economic view considered the imposition of austerity and frugality on ordinary people as the most logical, if not necessarily effective, approach to maintaining the equilibrium between production and consumption. This economic view was further reinforced by the ruling samurai's growing financial crisis resulting from their increasing dependency on merchant capital. As the *bakufu* and many domains experienced a steady decline in tax revenue and accumulated considerable debts to wealthy merchants, the contrast between their predicaments and the prosperity of common people came to pose a serious problem for sustaining social order. The people's consumer behaviour became the primary target of government scrutiny and regulation.

The Tokugawa authorities' centuries-long intervention was also a response to the symbolic implications of consumption. Townspeople's cumulative consumer power seriously violated the ideological axiom of Tokugawa society, where appearance reflected reality and clothes indexed the inflexible social hierarchy. The cultural expression of consumption – in particular, clothing and fashion – made conspicuous not only townspeople's growing economic power, but also their playful decoupling of the body from the Tokugawa principle of stasis or fixed being. When townspeople detached themselves from the requirements of the social hierarchy the Tokugawa had carefully constructed over generations, these modish urbanites became metaphorical vagrants in Edo, capable of dangerously unleashing new, divergent meanings and ways of life. Townspeople's innovative responses to governmental regulations in design, aesthetics and fashion pronounced their ability to imagine and seek opportunities for self-making outside the putatively rigid socioeconomic and ideological paradigms of early modern Japan. In short, from the middle of the Tokugawa period, appearances no longer corresponded to the reality of the social hierarchy. The way people looked on the streets of Edo stopped signifying formal reality and replaced being with becoming, status with self-making. Indeed, appearances became the new reality. In this regard, Tokugawa Japan would have found much commonality with a similar phenomenon in Europe's later Middle Ages, which Ulinka Rublack and Giorgio Riello describe, where 'commerce and social dynamism had made clothing an unreliable signifier of social status which threatened hierarchies'.[67]

The aesthetic value of *tsū*, in particular, endowed the body with divergent meanings that flouted or countered the normative configuration of the body both as a marker of social status and as the vehicle of material

---

[67] See Ulinka Rublack and Giorgio Riello's introduction to this volume.

production. In this sense, the Tokugawa government's regulatory failures in Edo demonstrated that fashion and the aesthetic taste attached to it were not a matter of a superficial exteriority covering over an 'authentic' self hidden in the interior folds of spirituality. Rather, *tsū* and its material manifestations were a nodal point of social relations wherein political, economic and cultural forces all converged and intersected with one another in such a way that they revealed, even magnified, the fissures, frictions and dissonances of Tokugawa society. Fashion provided the townspeople with a field of innovation and self-making while, for the Tokugawa authorities, it represented societal chaos prompted by the visible rise of townspeople in both economic and cultural domains. Their ascent was truly disquieting to the authorities precisely because it made salient the disintegration of the period's socio-economic arrangement and the diversification of social identities – both of which meant the loss of the ruling class's grip on power. The futile yet repeated attempts to regulate consumption were nothing but the salient symptom of the legitimacy 'crisis' engendered by the mounting contradictions that the Tokugawa authorities could not contain or resolve.

18   Sumptuary Laws in Precolonial West Africa: The Examples of Benin and Dahomey

Toby Green

West African history prior to 1800 is in general little studied in the Western academy. Where precolonial African history is studied in detail, this tends to relate to the trans-Atlantic slave trade. Ever since the 1780s, the history of Africa in Western discourse either has been dismissed as non-existent, or has been associated more or less exclusively with the realities of slavery. The dearth of historians specialising in topics such as art, music or poetry in West African and indeed Atlantic history, or who consider changes in religious lives and practice that formed a crucial lens through which all these historical changes were experienced, is apparent.

Little or almost nothing has been written directly on sumptuary laws in West Africa in the precolonial period. However there is a vast array of material on the matter in a range of primary and printed sources in languages as different as Arabic, Dutch, English, French and Portuguese. To propose a full analysis in the space available here would be impossible, given the range of materials and the number and complexity of the different kingdoms in the region. As a result, in this chapter I consider two of the more famous kingdoms in West Africa, Dahomey and Benin. While Benin – located to the East of Lagos in what is now Nigeria – flourished from the mid-fifteenth century onwards, and remained a powerful kingdom into the late eigthteenth century, Dahomey's power rose through its direct access to the trans-Atlantic slave trade from the 1720s onwards and remained the major kingdom in what is now the Republic of Benin until the imposition of formal French colonial rule in the late nineteenth century (Map 18.1).

The inclusion of this chapter in this volume addresses a number of purposes. From the perspective of those interested in the history of West Africa, the analysis of sumptuary laws supports the development of historical discourse beyond the field of the study of slavery. But secondly it adds an important strand to the understanding of the process of political change on the continent. The regulation of consumption was a key strand

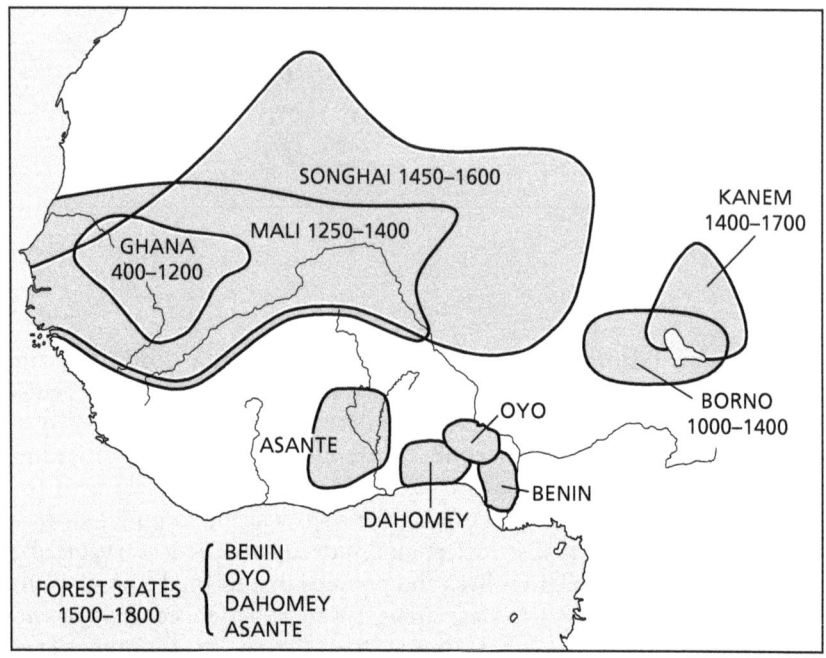

Map 18.1 Map of West Africa

in the armoury of increasing political power which was an important feature of many West African societies at this time. Understanding the nexus between consumption, display and power may therefore offer a useful perspective in understanding the concentration of political power which characterised many parts of the region during the era of the trade in enslaved persons. It helps in understanding the rise and establishment of the state in modern African history through a different lens.

With regard to the broader discussion of sumptuary laws undertaken in this volume, this chapter also offers an important perspective through the differences which emerge between the situation in West Africa and that studied in the other case studies in this volume. The regulation of expense, which is a key feature of sumptuary laws, can be seen in a different context in the case of West Africa. It was not through specific control of personal outlays on clothing that the kings of Benin and Dahomey exercised control over what was worn and displayed, but through other avenues: prohibitions, control over trade and the development of a legal framework which enshrined this power. Thus these case studies provide an interesting way of stretching the concept of the sumptuary law, and understanding more broadly how global patterns of consumption varied from one world region to another.

These case studies can therefore put the rise of mass consumption in European nations during the same period into an interesting perspective. Where the hold of the European nobility over consumption power waned in the seventeenth and the eighteenth centuries with the rise of the bourgeoisie, in both Benin and Dahomey monarchs retained great power over rights of consumption and display through strict control over imports, and the creation of special administrative posts which regulated this trade. The use of particular imported cloths and jewels, and the consumption of certain foods, remained limited to the royal elite, and this reinforced strict class divisions in each of these kingdoms. The large-scale import of goods from Asia and Europe into West Africa thus did not contribute to the democratisation of consumption, but rather cemented divisions in society which were manifested (in part) through differential access to the new goods.

Benin: Sumptuary Laws in a West African Forest Kingdom

Benin was one of the most enduring and important of precolonial West African kingdoms. Situated to the east of Lagos in what is now southern Nigeria, it was a state that had a long history prior to the arrival of Portuguese ships in the late 1480s. After being founded probably in around 1200 CE, it grew rapidly, with strong connections to the heart of Yoruba culture at Ile-Ife. Connections between Edo (the Bini name for the capital of Benin) and Ile-Ife remained close throughout the history of Benin. Towards the end of the thirteenth century, Oba Oguola is said to have sent to Ile-Ife for a master bronze caster to teach the craft to the Edo people, and exchange with Ile-Ife enhanced the craft in Edo as the centuries passed. Moreover, as the historians Peter Roese and Dmitri Bondarenko have shown, Edo rituals reveal the close links to the Yoruba, since the heads of deceased Obas were sent to Ile-Ife for burial right up to the time of the British conquest.[1]

By the 1450s, a series of changes began to affect Benin. To the north of Benin, in Oyo and Nupe, dynasties became consolidated and developed new relationships with the Edo people of Benin. In Benin, Oba Ewuare (enthroned c. 1440) responded by strengthening town chiefs against palace factions in a bid for unity. Administrative changes consolidated

---

[1] Peter M. Roese and Dmitri M. Bondarenko, *A Popular History of Benin: The Rise and Fall of a Mighty Forest Kingdom* (Frankfurt-am-Main: Peter Lang, 2003), 61–63.

the kingdom, with the establishment of three associations of palace chiefs and royal festivals designed to protect and renew the kingdom. Ewuare also expanded the urban structures of Edo, improving the road system. These developments were facilitated by growing military power.[2]

Thus in the decades prior to the Portuguese arrival in the 1480s, Benin had expanded territorially as well as consolidating as a state. A key facet of this was that, as A.F.C. Ryder noted, Oba Ewuare's power was strengthened by his reputation as both a magician and warrior.[3] The belief that the dynasty was supernaturally gifted fed military success, which in turn nurtured this belief. This aspect of Benin would play a key part in the kingdom's early relationship with European powers, since it rapidly became clear that the Edo showed no signs of converting to Christianity.

The next fifty years saw the evolution of the trading connections which characterised the first two centuries of Benin's relations with European traders. The initial focus of trade in the 1490s was in Benin pepper, which served as a popular substitute for Indian spices and was marketed by Portuguese traders through their strong networks in the city of Antwerp in Flanders. But when spices from India came onto the market following Vasco da Gama's voyage to Calicut at the end of the fifteenth century, the focus began to shift to the trade in enslaved persons.[4] Traders from the Portuguese island of São Tomé were trading captives from Benin by 1510, often to sell them further along the West African coast in Elmina for gold, which was then shipped to Europe (Map 18.1).

Nevertheless the slave trade in Benin was at this time very different from that in other parts of Atlantic Africa such as Kongo and Senegambia. The Obas of Benin were unwilling to sell men from the kingdom, who were vital for warfare and were in any case seen as 'slaves of the king'. As early as 1516, according to Ryder, the Oba of Benin had established separate markets for male and female slaves; restrictions on the sale of male slaves developed by 1530 into a total embargo on the Atlantic slave trade that persisted more or less until 1700.[5] By the end of the 1530s, both Portuguese missionaries and traders had concluded that the profits to be found here were not what they had hoped or required.[6] Benin therefore

---

[2] Ibid., 80–86; A.F.C. Ryder, *Benin and the Europeans 1485–1897* (Harlow: Longmans, Green & Co., 1969), 8.

[3] Ibid., 12.

[4] Ibid., 38–40 on the early pepper trade and the impact of the Indian spice trade, and shift towards the slave trade.

[5] Ibid., 45.

[6] On the disappointment of missionaries in 1539, see António Brásio (ed.), *Monumenta Misonária Africana: África Ocidental*, 15 vols. (Lisbon: Agência Geral do Ultramar,

offers a striking example of a West African kingdom which strongly resisted the demands of European slave traders and instead traded with the wider world through local cloth production.

In this context of a powerful, autonomous West African kingdom, it is noteworthy that the place of laws regulating consumption and production was described very early by European observers of the kingdom. Moreover, as the art historian Kathleen Bickford Berzock points out, these laws were vital in controlling two of the major mediums used for manifestations of royal power: brass and coral.[7] In the case of brass, this was one of the most important imports brought by the Portuguese during the sixteenth century, when large quantities of manillas (arm rings) made of the metal were imported and melted down; much of this molten metal was then reused by brass-casters in forging the famous Benin bronzes, many of which can be observed today in the British Museum.[8] However access to this brass was controlled by the Oba, and was strictly limited to the castes of brass casters (*Igun Eronmwon*) who formed the highest-ranking court guild in Edo. As the volumes of the metal available increased, so too did the prestige of the guild, and the attempts to control the use of the metal by the Obas, as all royal artists belonged to hereditary guilds within the Iwebo palace society.[9]

The case of coral was also important, for it was a key marker of nobility in Benin, and remained so for many centuries. The Dutch sailor Willem Bosman noted in a book published in 1705 how in Benin, nobility was designated by 'a String of Coral [which] … they are obliged to wear continually about their Necks'.[10] Another Dutch traveller, Nyendael, visiting in 1702, described how two nobles who had lost or broken chains of coral had been killed for the offence.[11] One 1786 description of the Royal Council of Benin described how the 'Council consisted of sixty

1952–88 – hereafter MMA), ii: 79–80; on the economic problems with the trading post at Benin, see ibid., i: 52.

[7] Kathleen Bickford Berzock, *Benin: Royal Arts of a West African Kingdom* (New Haven and London: Yale University Press, 2008), 5.

[8] For the manilla trade in 1517, see Robert Garfield, *A History of São Tomé Island, 1470–1655: The Key to Guinea* (San Francisco: Mellen Research University Press, 1992), 46; and for the early 1520s see Ryder, *Benin and the Europeans*, 53, 303.

[9] Berzock, *Benin*, 5. The best recent discussion of the brass casting is Gregor M. Metzig, 'Corals, Brass and Firearms: Material Commodities in Cultural Interactions between Edo and Portuguese in Benin', in Harriet Rudolph and Gregor M. Metzig (eds.), *Entangled Objects and Hybrid Practices? The Material Culture of Transcultural Diplomacy* (Göttingen: European History Yearbook 107, 2016), 29–54.

[10] Willem Bosman, *A New and Accurate Description of the Coast of Guinea, Divided into the Gold, Slave, and the Ivory Coasts* (London: Frank Cass & Co, [1705] 1969), 436.

[11] H. Ling Roth, *Great Benin: Its Customs, Art and Horrors* (London: Routledge & Kegan Paul, [1903] 1968), 95.

"big men", who wore round the neck, on the wrists and on the ankles their double strings of coral'.[12] The importance of this coral as a token of nobility, and the hierarchy within the kingdom, was expressed through the fact that 'the King keeps these Corals in his own Possession; and the Counterfeiting or having any of them in Possession without his Grant, is punished with Death'.[13] Thus it is clear that there was strict royal regulation of access to these necklaces, as who could wear them was a core sign of political power and social prestige.

The place of coral within the manifestation of royal power had long been important in Benin. The archaeologist Akinwumi Ogundiran suggests that it was related to the longstanding interest in Benin and also in Yoruba kingdoms in the firing of glass beads of many different colours as insignias of power, dating he suggests to at 1000 CE or earlier.[14] And long before Bosman was writing, in around 1604, the German traveller Andreas Ulsheimer gave a vivid description of the place of corals in affirming royal power in Benin. At the annual royal festivities at Edo, which Ulsheimer witnessed, the Oba appeared 'riding out into the town on a horse decorated with red scarlet and draped with red corals. He sits side-saddle on it … imposingly dressed after their fashion in red scarlet cloth [ododo] and draped not only with fine red corals but also with other strange things'.[15]

In Benin, it was crucial that royal power was both a temporal and a religious experience. In the fifteenth century, before the arrival of the Portuguese, the Obas had renewed religious shrines as part of the kingdom's expansion, and this strengthened the kingdom in the face of external influences from the Atlantic. The adoption of coral as a symbol of royal power was merely an adaption of existing frameworks. Royal power however was accentuated through the control the Obas were able to exert over the import of coral, which – alongside the increasing number of bronze plaques that lined the palace walls – were manifestations of the history and power of the kingdom. Through control of who could and could not display the tokens of nobility and refashion history through the bronze plaques, the Obaship gained in power.

The evolution of these laws of consumption and display in the kingdom in the sixteenth and seventeenth centuries is therefore important. They

---

[12] Ibid., 93.

[13] Bosman, *A New and Accurate Description*, 437.

[14] Akinwumi Ogundiran, 'Of Small Things Remembered: Beads, Cowries, and Cultural Translations of the Atlantic Experience in Yorubaland', *International Journal of African Historical Studies* 35/2–3 (2002): 433–434.

[15] Adam Jones, ed. and trans., *German Sources for West African History 1599–1669* (Wiesbaden: Franz Steiner Verla GMBH, 1983), 38.

may well have grown out of very old laws regulating access to the Oba, and the relationship between the Oba and his subjects. Early outside observers noted that there were strict taboos over the death of Obas and the ability of subjects of the kingdom to interact with them. An (in)famous story recounted in around 1550 by a Portuguese pilot who knew the coast well held that when the Oba died, his subjects accompanied the body into the grave, and were then covered with a large rock, where they died one by one and accompanied the Oba into the life to come.[16] Meanwhile, in Benin's relationship with the religious centre of Yorubaland at Ife there were also important laws of separation observed: the Benin ambassador to Ife never saw the king (Oni), just some silk curtains which he sat behind, and when the ambassador took his leave a foot would appear from behind the curtains in symbol of acknowledging departure.[17]

In these accounts of taboos and prescriptions, the relationships of the king of Benin to the nobility is very important. The king controlled trade in coral and then distributed it to his nobility, who would wear it in council meetings as a symbol of their authority. Consumption, too, was constrained, and not only in Benin, but also in other kingdoms along the West African coast. One visitor in 1604 described how in the Gold Coast kingdom of Fetu, once the king had drunk, the nobles took the drinking vessel from him and finished off the contents.[18] Perhaps most importantly, the sight of the king itself was a privilege and a rarity; the Oba would allow himself to be seen by the general population just once a year, when he entered in the manner described above by Ulsheimer, but for the rest of the year, as two Capuchin missionaries described in around 1651, he kept himself secluded in his palace, just as the Oni of Ife kept his distance from the ambassadors of the Oba as seen above.[19]

Distance, secrecy and representation through visual bronze reproductions and the power of royal apparel were thus integral to the performance of majesty in Benin in the sixteenth and seventeenth centuries. Shoring up this semi-divine power required the redistribution of some of the trappings of power among the nobility and control of this trade grew with the Atlantic dimension, so as to regulate access to vital materials such as bronze and coral accordingly. The Dutch geographer Olfert Dapper, who compiled reports from travellers around 1670, wrote that even clothing was circumscribed, as no one was allowed to go clothed

---

[16] Brasio (ed.), Monumenta Misonária Africana, iv: 619–620.
[17] *Asia de João de Barros: Primeira Década* (Lisbon: Agência Geral das Colónias, 1945), 90.
[18] Jones, *German Sources*, 30.
[19] Mateo de Anguiano, *Misiones Capuchinas en África* (Madrid: Consejo Superior de Investigaciones Científicas, 1957), ii: 34.

in the court without royal approval, and there were many members of the Benin nobility 'who go stark naked, without any sign of shame, only with a Chain of fine Coral or Jasper around their Necks'.[20] Three royal officials acted as intermediaries between the Oba and the people, and anyone wanting to apply to the Oba had to go through them.[21]

The mention of nudity here is significant, for in tandem with other sources it suggests that there was strict regulation of dress by the Oba (as the laws relating to coral would suggest). A striking passage in Mary Kingsley's *Travels in West Africa* (1897) is noteworthy here. Writing of the secret societies among Yoruba peoples (to whom Benin was related, as noted here through Ife), she writes that 'among some of [them], the boy has to remain under the rule of the presiding elders of the [secret] society, painted white, and wearing only a bit of grass cloth, if he wears anything' until his initiation is complete.[22] While this account of Kingsley's is significantly later, the rules regarding dress and secret societies were clearly strict, and nudity certainly represents these nobles' subordination to the Oba (their elder) and his control over their attire. In many Yoruba societies, nobility was also shown through the wearing of *agbadas* (flowing robes worn by men), to which again access was strictly controlled, revealing the importance of the regulation of consumption then at work in this part of West Africa.

Written evidence on Benin for the precolonial period is somewhat patchy, but the overall picture is unambiguous. Royal power was maintained through a combination of the growth of state power – expanding military and administrative apparatus, control over trade – and the manifestation of this power. The ways in which royal power was performed before the population annually at the royal festivals required strict laws to regulate access to the core insignia of the nobility in terms of coral and clothing. The growth of an autochthonous history as narrated through the bronze plaques at the palace also required increased brass imports and control over their distribution. While these were not sumptuary laws in terms of regulating what could be spent by whom, the social impact of this strict regulation was rather similar. Control over consumption and distribution of prestige goods was a core element of Obaship in Benin, as the kingdom evolved from the late fifteenth to the eighteenth centuries.

<hr>

[20] John Ogilby, ed. and trans., *Olfert Dapper: Africa, Being an Accurate Description of ...* (London: Tho. Johnson, 1670), 472.
[21] Bosman, *A New and Accurate Description*, 464; Roth, *Great Benin*, 92.
[22] Mary Kingsley, *Travels in West Africa: Congo Français, Corisco, and Cameroons* (London: Penguin, [1897] 2015), 538.

Dahomey: The Performance of Power in the Eighteenth Century

One of the most powerful states in West Africa in the eighteenth and nineteenth centuries was Dahomey, located in what is now the Republic of Benin. Dahomey was a relatively new polity, supplanting the nearby kingdoms of Allada and Hueda in the 1720s; thereafter it became a major participant in the trans-Atlantic trade in enslaved persons, through its port at Ouidah. However, though having supplanted Allada, Dahomey borrowed idioms of political power through cults of the royal ancestors, and indeed its kings claimed to be heirs to the Allada monarchy.[23]

During the seventeenth century, the most powerful kingdom in the region had been that of Allada, a kingdom of Ajá people who had also borrowed many Yoruba traditions. Allada was a major trading partner of the Europeans, selling cloth, ivory and enslaved Africans to Dutch, French and Portuguese traders. Atlantic trade in Allada was underway by the 1580s, and there was a close connection to the Portuguese settlement on the island of São Tomé in the Gulf of Guinea. By the 1660s, however, Allada was weakening as the growth of trade saw the king of Hueda (Whydah) becoming more powerful. The king of Allada sent embassies to Spain in 1658 and France in 1670, but to no avail. In the early 1680s European traders moved their forts to Hueda: the Dutch in 1682, the English in 1683 and the Brandenburgers in 1684. Dahomey, meanwhile, was still a small kingdom, having been founded between 1620 and 1650. But when the Europeans signed a six-clause convention with Whydah in 1704, recognising it as an international neutral port, and Whydah's internal strength then began to weaken, Agaja, king of Dahomey seized his chance; under his leadership, Dahomey conquered Allada in 1724 and Whydah in 1727, becoming at once the most powerful kingdom in the region.[24]

Once in the political ascendancy, Dahomey maintained extensive political connections to its neighbours, as of course did many other West African kingdoms in this era. From 1730 until the early nineteenth century, it was a tributary of the Yoruba kingdom of Oyo (located in what is now southern Nigeria), and indeed borrowed several administrative structures from Oyo, including the royal slaves known as *Ilari*. In the context of this chapter, it is also significant that Dahomey had

---

[23] Robin Law, *The Kingdom of Allada* (Leiden: CNWS, 1997), 65–66, 82.
[24] On the origins of Dahomey and the early history of Allada, see ibid., and also I.A. Akinjogbin, *Dahomey and its Neighbours: 1708–1818* (Cambridge: Cambridge University Press, 1967), 22.

strong connections with Benin, and indeed in 1799 sent ambassadors to the Oba at Edo to see if he would cooperate in a joint attack on the Dutch at the fortress of Elmina on the Gold Coast.[25] The official charged with dealing with the Europeans, the *Yovogan*, wore necklaces of coral, which also suggests strong connections to Benin as already seen.[26] These interconnections formed part of what the historian I.A. Akinjogbin described as the 'Yoruba-Ajà commonwealth' – peoples with a shared history dating back to the fourteenth century – and thus the reciprocal cultural, economic and political influence were an important part of life in the region throughout the precolonial period.[27]

In this context, it is not surprising to see a shared approach towards the authority of the king and the construction of a separate and semi-mythic figure in the person of the king in Dahomey, much as had already emerged in Benin even before Dahomey arose as a kingdom in the seventeenth century. Indeed, these characteristics were also apparent in Dahomey's immediate predecessor, Hueda, in the late seventeenth century. Bosman described how 'no Man is permitted to see [the King of Hueda] eat',[28] while one visitor from the Brandenburg Chartered Company, in 1793, described a similar situation of awe before the monarch as had pertained in Benin:

[The King] receives his dignitaries ... sitting on the throne. At a distance of 20 paces from this throne they throw themselves down, kiss the ground and clap their hands, continuing to do so until a sign is given from the throne for them to approach. Thereupon they creep up to the steps of the throne on all fours and remain in a kneeling position there during the [audience].[29]

This pattern of prostration before the monarch was, as the historian Robin Law points out, also shared by the successor state of Dahomey, and conveys well the sense of awe and separation cultivated by monarchs along this part of the West African coast by the later seventeenth and into the eighteenth century. Moreover, just as in Benin, annual royal festivities saw the enactment of this semi-mystical power by the king, which was attended by representatives of the European chartered companies with trading posts at the port of Ouidah.

[25] Arquivo Histórico Ultramarino, Lisbon (hereafter AHU), Conselho Ultramarino (hereafter CU), Bahia, Caixa 213, Doc. 12, fol. 2r.

[26] Clado Ribeiro de Lessa (ed.), *Viagem de África em o Reino de Dahomé, escrito pelo Padre Vicente Ferreira Pires no ano de 1800 e até agora Inédito* (São Paulo: Companhia Editora Nacional, 1957), 31.

[27] Akinjogbin, *Dahomey and its Neighbours*, 11–17.

[28] Bosman, *A New And Accurate Description*, 363.

[29] Adam Jones, ed. and trans., *Brandenburg Sources for West African History, 1680–1700* (Stuttgart: Franz Steiner Verlag Wiesbaden GMBH, 1985), 195.

A good description of these annual festivities was given by the English trader Robert Norris, in a book published in 1789. Norris described how, on the last day of the annual customs, 'a large stage is erected near one of the palace gates, adorned with flags and umbrellas, and surrounded with a fence of thorns, to keep off the rabble; on this are piled heaps of silesias, checks, callicoes, and a variety of other European and Indian goods; a great many fine cotton cloths that are manufactured in the *Eyo* [Oyo] country; and a prodigious quantity of cowries'; significantly, it was for the king to disburse the cloths to his nobility and to the ship captains, while the cowries (the major form of money used in Dahomey) were thrown to the crowd.[30]

In other words, the use and display of those luxury imported goods was regulated by the king, and it was in this that the display and performance of power lay; cowrie money itself was useful, and was accessible to all, but it could not supplant the true manifestation of nobility, which lay in access to these luxury imported goods. This description also suggests strict regulation of the wearing of particular cloths (in this case those from Oyo). This was something also implied elsewhere by Norris, when he described a standard dress among commoners in Dahomey, where 'country dress ... consists of a pair of wide drawers, and a piece of cloth about three yards long, and two broad, worn loosely around the body'.[31]

As in Benin, one of the methods by which the King of Dahomey retained control over these manifestations of power was through absolute authority over imports into the kingdom. As noted above, the *Yovogan* was charged with managing all European trade there, charging taxes and regulating the import of key goods – contraband gold, Brazilian tobacco, cowries (used as currency in the kingdom) and cloth – in exchange for enslaved persons. A sense of the control that the King exercised over this trade was given by the Brazilian priest, Vicente Pires, who described how in 1797 any ship beached at the bar beside the Brazilian fort of Ajudá at Ouidah was seized and all its goods held to be the property of the King of Dahomey. No one other than the king was permitted to build a house with more than one storey (such an area existed at his palace at Abomey), and if they did he usually seized it for himself.[32]

By this time, a complex administration had been developed by the kingdom of Dahomey. There were regulated markets in different towns on different days of the week, and a series of officials to deal with

---

[30] Robert Norris, *Memoirs of the Reign of Bossa Ahádee, King of Dahomy an Inland Country of Guiney* ... (London: Frank Cass & Co., [1789] 1968), 125.
[31] Ibid., ix.
[32] Lessa, *Viagem de África*, 27 and 35.

international trade, agriculture and national affairs. The laws of the kingdom made it clear that regulated dress and access to luxury goods were the prerogative of the king: the precise regulation of clothing is also shown through the fact that only senior heads of lineages were allowed to wear fine hats, while no one could trade tobacco, rum or enslaved persons without royal permission, and the king inherited from all his vassals.[33] Moreover, by the mid-eighteenth century under King Tegbesu, if any subject of the kingdom was convicted of a crime, all of his property was forfeited to the king;[34] with legal enslavement on the increase owing to the pressures of Atlantic trade and the incentives offered by merchants in captives, this was another legal avenue to ensure control over the access to and ownership of goods that could be used to manifest nobility and wealth.

One of the implications to emerge from these accounts of the control of trade and the distribution of luxury goods is that clothing was a key marker of nobility, and jealously guarded by the crown. Umbrellas, too, were seen as a sign of status, and could be used only by favoured dignitaries and wives of the king.[35] That access to fine clothing was seen as a prerequisite of nobility in the kingdom is made apparent by the embassies sent by the king of Dahomey around the turn of the nineteenth century to Salvador da Bahia and Lisbon. The costs of these embassies were paid for by the Portuguese crown, and the bills that were kept make it clear that clothing was the principal expense for the ambassadors from Dahomey. In the case of the 1795/6 embassy, the major costs listed included fine cloths, capes, hats, jackets, coats and shoes, itemised for both the king's son and for the official ambassador.[36] In the case of the 1805 embassy, there were again fine silk cloths given as gifts to the royal party.[37] In other words, access to luxury imported cloths and the ability to wear them was a defining feature of nobility and prestige in Dahomey by the late eighteenth century; the nobility sought to gain access to these whenever they could, and the King ensured that this access was regulated through control of trade at the port of Ouidah and through strict inheritance laws.[38]

---

[33] Ibid., 98–115.
[34] Norris, *Memoirs of the Reign of Bossa Ahádee*, 10.
[35] Ibid., 108.
[36] AHU, CU, São Tomé, Caixa 27, doc. 45ª.
[37] AHU, CU, São Tomé, Caixa 39A, doc. 1.
[38] In general, on the embassies of Dahomey in Brazil and Portugal, see: Ana Lucia Araujo, 'Dahomey, Portugal, and Bahia: King Adandozan and the Atlantic Slave Trade', *Slavery and Abolition* 33/1 (2012): 1–19; Joice de Souza Santos, 'As Embaixadas dos Reinos da Costa Africana Como Mediadores Culturais: Missões Diplomáticas em Salvador, Rio de Janiero e Lisboa (1750–1823)' (Unpublished MA thesis, Rio de Janeiro: Pontificia

As we have seen, the development of these laws relating to imports and inheritance was not something that happened in Dahomey in isolation. It was a characteristic shared with Benin, with which Dahomey had diplomatic connections. It was the best method for kings to shore up their hold on power and their ability to distribute the apparel of power to their trusted followers, thereby consolidating their rule in an era of widespread political instability in West Africa. The growth of political unrest and the repeated overthrow of the *Alafins* of Oyo in the later eighteenth century meant that access to and control of the display of wealth and influence was vital to kingship in West Africa. Thus, regulation over display and clothing did not decline in this period of history, in contrast to the situation in Europe where consumption was becoming democratised; if anything, such regulations became more rigidly enforced.

That this was a common political and structural change in this part of West Africa is shown by the description made by the Danish traveller Paul Erdmann Isert of the king of Great Popo in 1789.[39] This was the neighbouring kingdom to the west of Dahomey, also a major trader in captives for the Atlantic trade, where some traders were wealthy enough by this time to have built three-storey houses, and to educate their children in Europe.[40] According to Isert, on meeting the King of Great Popo, they were all offered brandy, but 'the king did not drink, since he must never partake of anything in public'.[41]

As we have seen, such rituals of taboo and separation were shared in common in kingdoms between Benin in the east and Dahomey and Great Popo in the west. These were taboos which had religious origins in the connection between royalty and the religious cults originating from Ife, and interconnecting with the Aja and Fon religious practices which were found in Dahomey. The rise of Atlantic trade provoked intense political competition, and made access to and retention of political power a very difficult task. In this circumstance, the semi-mystic power of the kings which had been safeguarded through strict regulation began slowly to be transformed, and to incorporate strict regulations requiring consumption which ensures the continued 'splendid isolation' of the king

---

Universidad Católica do Rio de Janeiro, 2012); and Luis Nicolau Parés, 'Cartas do Daomé: Uma Introdução', *Afro-Asia* 47 (2013): 295–395.

[39] The best recent study of Great Popo is Silke Strickrodt, *Afro-European Trade in the Atlantic World: The Western Slave Coast, c. 1550–1885* (Martlesham: Boydell & Brewer / James Currey, 2015).

[40] Selena Axelrod Winsnes, ed. and trans., *Letters on West Africa and the Slave Trade: Paul Erdmann Isert's Journey to Guinea and the Caribbean Islands in Columbia (1788)* (Oxford: Oxford University Press for the British Academy, 1992), 90–91.

[41] Ibid., 99.

and nobility. What was thereby enshrined was the accentuated distance between the king and nobility on the one hand, and the commoners on the other. These laws thereby enabled this growing distance, and the accentuation of political power that accompanied the growth of Atlantic trade between the sixteenth and eighteenth centuries; their impact was very similar to the sumptuary laws that had existed in other parts of the world theretofore.

Conclusion: Power and Majesty in West African History

The 2015 exhibition on the precolonial Kingdom of Kongo at the Metropolitan Museum of Art in New York was subtitled, 'Power and Majesty'. This chapter has shown how these features, and the way in which they were manifested, are important aspects of understanding changes in state power in the West African kingdoms of Benin and Dahomey. These case studies offer important starting points for beginning to think through how regulations regarding clothing, display and consumption changed in West Africa from the sixteenth to the nineteenth century, and also how this contrasts with the situation in other world regions. These kingdoms were connected to one another culturally and commercially, and as we have seen the regulation of consumption became if anything more strict in this period, in contrast to the situation in Europe.

Study of the ways in which these laws changed from the sixteenth to the nineteenth centuries offers an important new perspective on the changes to the West African state and the manifestation of kingship in this vital historical period, going beyond the stranglehold which the study of slavery so often has over the historical discussion of Africa. However it is also significant to try to consider in this chapter just how wide-reaching this framework was in the region, since building a general conclusion from just these two case studies could present a danger of over-generalisation. To bring the discussion to a conclusion, it may therefore be helpful to consider in brief evidence from different regions of West Africa, in order to consider how widespread this pattern actually was, and how useful the region is as a comparator to the other case studies examined in this book.

In this context, some examples from the oral literatures of the broader region of West Africa are quite revealing. The oral literatures from what is now the republic of Mali provide several pieces of evidence relating to the general importance of analogues to sumptuary laws during the precolonial period. Several decades ago the French anthropologist Christine Seydou compiled a fascinating book, derived from the Fula praise-singer Tinguidji, a Mâbo or praise-singer to the nobility from Massina. Massina became an important Islamic kingdom in what is now central Mali in the nineteenth century, and the tale of Silâmaka and Poullôri was, says Seydou, a *noddol* or call to the Fula chief of Massina to reinvigorate the historical consciousness of his predecessors.

The significance for this discussion is that one part of Tinguidji's recital makes clear the importance of the regulation of consumption in Fula culture by the late eighteenth and early nineteenth centuries:

A real Fula from the West	*Pullo gorgal piir duu*
Does not eat before his sister	*nyaamtaa yeeso banndum-debbo nyaamtaa*
Does not eat before his wife!	*yeeso deekum!*
People say that whoever sees the mouthful	*'Be mbi ' i nedd'o si yii lonnge*
that you take will lose all respect for you.	*maad'a fuu hafete!*[42]

In this case, the act of consumption is closely connected to rituals of purity and the gendered division of activity and life, which has been well studied by many anthropologists in the tradition of Mary Douglas.[43] However there is also the implication here that there was also a class hierarchy when it came to consumption: it was not just women who did not see a 'real' Fula eating; anyone might lose the respect they had for a person if they observed the act of consumption. Class and gender hierarchies were clearly represented in the question of practice related to consumption in this region by 1800.

A similar regulation of consumption at this time is also clear from oral literatures found in the Gambia region. The Federation of Kaabu was a large state that prospered from the sixteenth to the nineteenth centuries in the region of what is now Guinea-Bissau, southern Senegal (the Casamance), and the south bank of the Gambia River.[44] A highly hierarchised society evolved here, and one of the oral narratives describes a well in the Badora region, on the borderlands of Casamance and north-eastern Guinea-Bissau. This well was called Njampeng Njai, and according to one account recorded in the 1960s, 'It was surrounded by pawpaw trees and by silk cotton trees with smoothish earth. / The women

---

[42] Christiane Seydou (ed.), *Silâmaka et Poullôri: Récit Épique Peul Raconté Par Tinguidji* (Paris: Armand Colin, 1972), 82–85.

[43] Mary Douglas, *Purity and Danger: An Analysis of the Concepts of Pollution and Taboo* (London: Routledge, [1966] 1989).

[44] For general literature on Kaabu, see: Carlos Lopes, *Kaabunké: Espaço, Poder, Território e Poder na Guiné-Bissau,. Gâmbia e Casamance Pre-Coloniais* (Lisbon: Comissão Nacional para as Comemorações dos Descobrimentos Portugueses, 1999); and Toby Green,

of the princely house used to draw water from it. / Poor women did not draw water from it'.[45]

These two examples both come from the latter part of the precolonial period, from the late eighteenth or early nineteenth centuries. It is therefore important to note the process of change from the earlier times documented by these oral literatures in the region. Here one oral account of the first emperor of the empire of Mali, Sunjata Keita (fl. c. 1235–55) is very important. The Sunjata epic is the centrepiece of oral literatures of the region of what the historian Boubacar Barry called 'Greater Senegambia', and many different versions exist.[46] In that of Lansine Diabaté from Kela, recorded and published by Jan Jansen, Esger Duintjer and Boubacar Traore, a rather different view of patterns of eating and consumption is recorded:

Just then	*O tuma,*
at Manko Farako Mangankèn's home	*Manko Farakɔ Mangankèn*
when Sogolòn Kejùgu had given birth,	*Sogolon Kejugu jigilen*
when the old woman had been sent	*musokɔrɔnin dɛ bilalen k'o ka waa*
to announce the child's arrival...	*denko fɔla...*
At that time, the king's breakfast	*o tuma yan, mansakɛ ka daraka*
was taken in the company of the whole population.	*bɛɛbe, jamabɛɛ be ajɛ ka damun.*[47]

Thus where in the Fula narrative the 'real' Fula eats unobserved, in the narrative about the origins of Mali, the king of Mali was observed by the whole population. Read together, these oral sources suggest a shift in the regulation of consumption and power in the heartland of the old Mali empire, which resonates strongly with the case studies we have looked at on Benin and Dahomey. Whereas in the distant past there had been fewer barriers between the king and the commoners, and they might watch him eat, the passage of time saw more divisions grow up between different social groups, and in time power came to be displayed in part through separation and the guarding of these taboos by elites.

As we have seen in this chapter, a core contributory factor in this change was the rise of a greater preponderance of imported cloths and

---

'Architects of Knowledge, Builders of Power: Constructing the Kaabu 'Empire', 16th-17th centuries', *Journal of Mande Studies* 11 (2009): 91–112.

[45] National Centre for Arts and Culture, Research and Documentation Division, Fajara, The Gambia, Transcribed Cassette 23A, page 3.

[46] See Boubacar Barry, *Senegambia and the Atlantic Slave Trade*, trans. Armah A. Kwei (Cambridge: Cambridge University Press, 1998).

[47] Jan Jansen, Esger Duintjer and Boubacar Tamboura, eds. and trans., *L'Épopée de Sunjata, d'après Lansine Diabate de Kela* (Leiden: Research School CNWS, 1995), 85.

greater variety of foodstuffs, which accompanied the expansion of trade to and from West Africa from the fourteenth to the nineteenth centuries. The examples discussed here have shown that this process was accompanied not so much by a democratisation of consumption as by the establishment of more universal regulation of consumption in many different societies. In this case therefore, what may be preserved is not necessarily the distinct details of the audience that the Mansa of Mali had when he ate breakfast, but rather the sense of the growing regulation which attended the consumption patterns of the elite over a long period of time.

An important idea of how this process may have taken place in West Africa is provided by the Song of Bagauda, a Hausa homily transcribed and translated by the scholar Mervyn Hiskett. In what is now Northern Nigeria, Hausa peoples controlled important kingdoms, especially the city of Kano, which was a major terminus for the trans-Saharan trade to Tripoli from the fifteenth century onwards. The 'Song of Bagauda' described well the rule of the Kano king Babba Zaki, from c. 1747–1771, stating that 'it was he who introduced remoteness into kingship/Setting body-guards to rebuke the people. /One could not see him – the Great One – except through an intermediary'.[48] Importantly, these changes were also connected to the growing power of Kano, since 'It was his sovereignty that has set the standard for Kano. /It was in his time that horses were amassed'.[49]

By the middle of the eighteenth century, therefore, perhaps the most important kingdom of the Sahel was developing the sort of separation between kings and people that is suggested too in the Fula narrative from Massina to the east, and which we have seen also in the examples from Benin and Dahomey considered in more detail in this chapter. The growth of trade and state power which emerged in the eighteenth century, with expanded cavalry, and the importing of large numbers of firearms and other trade goods which bolstered state authority, was leading in many different West African kingdoms to a concentration of power. This was manifested in a growing separation between ruling elites and populations, and this separation was embodied through the regulation of consumption which made real and apparent this separation. The rise in trade and consumer goods therefore produced divisions in society that would lead to great political tensions by the nineteenth century.

The trajectory of sumptuary laws in West African societies is therefore somewhat different to the case of many European societies, where

[48] Mervyn Hiskett, 'The "Song of Bagauda": A Hausa King List and Homily in Verse: II', *SOAS Bulletin* 28/1 (1965): 118.
[49] Ibid.

increased trade led to a democratisation of consumption patterns as the rising bourgeoisie lobbied for similar rights to the aristocracy. In West Africa, consumption and deportment were strictly regulated, though there were no precise laws over who could spend money on what. In this regulation, the question of class was fundamental. The absence of a strong and independent bourgeoisie in Benin and Dahomey – other than those court officials who worked for the kings – meant that there was not the same pressure to relax sumptuary laws as was the case in European countries. Where a 'middle class' could lobby for the end to such differentials of display, this was not the case in West Africa, which meant that the divide between the aristocracies and the commoners (who were always potentially enslaveable) grew quickly.

The result was a crisis of power in the nineteenth century, where revolutionary movements swept many areas, from Senegambia in the west to the Niger Bend and northern Nigeria. These movements, grounded in deep-seated class antagonisms, led to the overthrow of the traditional aristocracies in many of these areas. While access to trade goods and political capital had grown, the control of these and their distribution among the nobility had enabled the growth of a ruling elite class and steady encroachment on the rights of peoples in many kingdoms, as the examples of Benin and Dahomey have shown in detail in this chapter. In many parts of West Africa, the movements that arose in the nineteenth century dispensed with these ruling elites, and the inevitable struggles which followed in their turn paved the way for the swift rise of formal colonialism.

Select Bibliography

Akinjogbin, I. A., *Dahomey and its Neighbours: 1708–1818* (Cambridge: Cambridge University Press, 1967).

Aktepe, M. Münir, *Şem'dânî-zâde Fındıklılı Süleyman Efendi Tärihi, Mür'i't-Tevârih*. 3 vols. (Istanbul, 1976–81).

Anderson, Ruth Matilda, *The Golilla: A Spanish Collar of the 17th Century* (New York: Hispanic Society of America, 1969).

Araujo, Ana Lucia, 'Dahomey, Portugal, and Bahia: King Adandozan and the Atlantic Slave Trade', *Slavery and Abolition* 33/1 (2012): 1–19.

Ares Queija, Berta, 'Mestizos en hábito de indios: ¿estrategias transgresoras o identidades difusas?', in Rui Manuel Loureiro and Serge Gruzinski (eds.) *Passar as fronteiras. Il coloquio internacional sobre mediadores culturais, séculos XV a XVIII* (Lagos: Centro de Estudios Gil Eanes, 1999), 133–146.

Baldwin, F. E., *Sumptuary Legislation and Personal Regulation in England* (Baltimore: Johns Hopkins University, 1926).

Bass, Laura R. and Amanda Wunder, 'The Veiled Ladies of the Early Modern Spanish World: Seduction and Scandal in Seville, Madrid, and Lima', *Hispanic Review* 77/1 (2009): 97–144.

Bastien, Pascal, ' "Aux tresors dissipez l'on cognoist le malfaict": Social Hierarchy and Transgressions of French Sumptuary Laws, 1543–1606', *Renaissance & Reformation/Renaissance et Reforme* 23/4 (1999): 23–43.

Bataille, George, *Visions of Excess: Selected Writings, 1927–1939* (Minneapolis: University of Minnesota Press, 1985).

Baumgarten, Linda, *What Clothes Reveal: The Language of Clothing in Colonial and Federal America: The Colonial Williamsburg Collection* (New Haven: Yale University Press, 2002).

Baur, Veronika, *Kleiderordnungen in Bayern vom 14. bis zum 19. Jahrhundert* (Munich: Wölfle, 1975).

Belfanti, Carlo Marco, 'Was Fashion a European Invention?', *Journal of Global History* 3/3 (2008): 419–443.

Berchtold, Jacques and Michel Porret (eds.), *Etre riche au siècle de Voltaire: actes du colloque de Genève (18–19 juin 1994)* (Geneva: Droz, 1996).

Berg, Maxine and Helen Clifford (eds.), *Consumers and Luxury. Consumer Culture in Europe 1650–1850* (Manchester: Manchester University Press, 1999).

Berg, Maxine and Elizabeth Eger (eds.), *Luxury in the Eighteenth Century: Debates, Desires and Delectable Goods* (Basingstoke and New York: Palgrave, 2003).

Bernis, Carmen, *Indumentaria española en tiempos de Carlos V* (Madrid: Instituto Diego Velázquez del Consejo Superior de Investigaciones Científicas, 1962). *Trajes y modas en la España de los Reyes Católicos*, 2 vols. (Madrid: Instituto Diego Velázquez del Consejo Superior de Investigaciones Científicas, 1978–79).

Berry, Christopher J., *The Idea of Luxury: A Conceptual and Historical Investigation* (Cambridge: Cambridge University Press, 1994).

Bhabha, Homi, 'Of Mimicry and Man: The Ambivalence of Colonial Discourse', *October* 28 (1984): 125–133.

Bickford Berzock, Kathleen, *Benin: Royal Arts of a West African Kingdom* (New Haven and London: Yale University Press, 2008).

Bistort, Giulio, Il magistrato alle pompe nella repubblica di Venezia: studio storico, *Miscellanea di Storia Veneta*, series 3, vol. 5 (Venice: R. Deputazione Veneta di Storia Patria, 1912).

Blanc, Odile, *Parades et Parures. L'invention du corps de mode à la fin du Moyen Âge* (Paris: Éditions Gallimard, 1997).

Blondé, Bruno, Jeroen Puttevils and Isis Sturtewagen, 'Silks and the "Golden Age" of Antwerp', in Bruno Blondé and Jeroen Puttevils (eds.), *Antwerp and the Renaissance* (Turnhout: Brepols Publishers, in press).

Bolitho, Harold, 'The Han', in J. W. Hall, Marius Jansen, Madoka Kanai, and Denis Teitchett (eds.), *The Cambridge History of Japan*, vol. 4 (Cambridge: Cambridge University Press, 1991).

Bonardi, Antonio, *Il lusso d'altri tempi in Padova. Studio storico con documenti inediti* (Padova: R. Deputazione Veneta di Storia Patria, 1910).

Brewer, John, and Roy Porter (eds.), *Consumption and the World of Goods* (London and New York: Routledge, 1993).

Bridgeman, Jane, ' "Pagare le Pompe": Why Quattrocento Sumptuary Laws did not Work', in Letizia Panizza (ed.), *Women in Italian Renaissance Culture and Society* (Oxford: European Humanities Research Centre, 2000), 209–226.

Bulst, Neithard, 'La legislazione suntuaria in Francia (secoli XIII–XVIII)', in Maria Giuseppina Muzzarelli and Antonella Campanini (eds.), *Disciplinare il lusso. La legislazione suntuaria in Italia e in Europa tra Medioevo ed età moderna* (Rome: Carocci, 2003), 121–136.
'Zum Problem städtischer und territorialer Kleider-, Aufwands- und Luxusgesetzgebung in Deutschland (13. bis Mitte des 16. Jahrhundert)', in André Gouron and Albert Rigaudière (eds.), *Renaissance du pouvoir législatif et genèse de l'Etat* (Montpellier: Socapress, 1988), 29–57.

Bushkovitch, Paul, *Peter the Great: The Struggle for Power, 1671–1725* (Cambridge: Cambridge University Press, 2001).

Buylaert, Frederik, Wim De Clercq and Jan Dumolyn, 'Sumptuary Legislation, Material Culture and the Semiotics of "Vivre Noblemen" in the County of Flanders (14th–16th Centuries)', *Social History* 36/4 (2011): 393–417.

Calvi, Giulia, 'Leggi suntuarie e la storia sociale', in Maria Giuseppina Muzzarelli and Antonella Campanini (eds.), *Disciplinare il lusso. La legislazione suntuaria in Italia e in Europa tra Medioevo ed età moderna* (Rome: Carocci, 2003), 213–230.

Chaturvedula, Nandini, 'In the Precipice of Ruin: Consumption, Sumptuary Laws, and Decadence in Early Modern Portuguese India', *Journal of World History* 26/2 (2015): 355–384.

Chijs, J. A. van der, *Nederlandsch-Indisch Plakaatboek*, 17 vols. (Batavia: Landsdrukkerij, 1885–1900).

Clunas, Craig, *Superfluous Things: Material Culture and Social Status in Early Modern China* (Cambridge: Polity, 1991).

Coetzee, Liza-Mari, 'Clothing, Gender and Social Identity at the Cape of Good Hope, 1652–1795' (Unpublished MA thesis, University of Johannesburg, 2014).

Colomer, José Luis and Amalia Descalzo (eds.), *Spanish Fashion at the Courts of Early Modern Europe*, 2 vols. (Madrid: Centro de Estudios Europa Hispánica, 2014).

Cracraft, James, *The Petrine Revolution in Russian Culture* (Cambridge, MA: Belknap Press, 2004).

Crespo, Hugo Miguel, 'Trajar as aparências, vestir para ser: o testemunho da pragmatica de 1609', in Gonçalo Vasconcelos e Sousa (ed.), *O luxo na região do Porto no tempo de Filipe II de Portugal (1610)* (Porto: Universidade Católica Editora, 2012), 93–148.

Currie, Elizabeth, *Fashion and Masculinity in Renaissance Florence* (London: Bloomsbury, 2017).

Dal Prà, Laura and Paolo Peri (eds.), *Dalla testa ai piedi. Costume e moda in età gotica* (Trento: Provincia Autonoma di Trento, 2006).

Dauncey, Sarah, 'Illusions of Grandeur: Perceptions of Status and Wealth in Late-Ming Female Clothing and Ornamentation', *East Asian History* 25/26 (2003): 43–68.

De Clercq, Wim, Jan Dumolyn, and Jelle Haemers, ' "Vivre Noblement": Material Culture and Elite Identity in Late Medieval Flanders', *Journal of Interdisciplinary History* 38/1 (2007): 1–31.

De Laet, Veerle, *Brussel Binnenskamers. Kunst- en luxebezit in het spanningsveld tussen hof en stad, 1600–1735* (Amsterdam: Amsterdam University Press, 2011).

Dean, Carolyn and Dana Leibsohn, 'Hybridity and its Discontents: Considering Visual Culture in Colonial Spanish America', *Colonial Latin American Review* 12/1 (2003): 5–35.

Deceulaer, Harald, *Pluriforme patronen en een verschillende snit. sociaal-economische, institutionele en culturele transformaties in de kledingsector in Antwerpen, Brussel en Gent, 1585–1800* (Amsterdam: Stichting Beheer, 2001).

Deusen, Nancy E. van, 'Seeing *Indios* in Sixteenth-Century Castile', *William and Mary Quarterly* 69/2 (2012): 205–234.

Dias, Luís Fernando de Carvalho, *Luxo e pragmáticas no pensamento económico do século XVI* (Coimbra: Coimbra Editora, 1958).

Donati, Claudio, *L'idea di nobiltà in Italia. Secoli XIV-XVIII* (Rome and Bari: Editori Laterza: 1988).

DuPlessis, Robert S., *The Material Atlantic: Clothing, Commerce, and Colonization in the Atlantic World, 1650–1800* (Cambridge: Cambridge University Press, 2016).

Earle, Rebecca, 'Luxury, Clothing and Race in Colonial Spanish America', in Maxine Berg and Elizabeth Eger (eds.), *Luxury in the Eighteenth Century: Debates, Desires and Delectable Goods* (London: Palgrave, 2003), 219–227.

'The Pleasures of Taxonomy: Casta Painting, Classification, and Colonialism', *William and Mary Quarterly* 73/3 (2016): 427–466.

'"Two Pairs of Pink Satin Shoes!!"': Clothing, Race and Identity in the Americas, 17th-19th Centuries', *History Workshop Journal* 52 (2001): 175–195.

Eisenbart, Lieselotte Constanze, *Kleiderordnungen der deutschen Städte zwischen 1350 und 1700: Ein Beitrag zur Kulturgeschichte des deutschen Bürgertums* (Gö ttingen: Musterschmidt, 1962).

Elliot, Matthew, 'Dress Codes in the Ottoman Empire: The Case of the Franks', in Suraiya N. Faroqhi and Christoph K. Neumann (eds.), *Ottoman Costumes: From Textiles to Identity* (Istanbul: EREN, 2014), 103–123.

Ergin, Osman Nuri, *Mecelle-i Umur-i Belediye*. 5 vols. (Istanbul, 1338 AH/ 1922 CE).

Farmer, Edward L., *Zhu Yuanzhang and Early Ming Legislation: The Reordering of Chinese Society Following the Era of Mongol Rule* (Leiden: Brill, 1995).

Ferriol, Charles de, *Recueil de cent estampes représentant differentes nations du Levant, tirées sur des tableaux peints d'après nature en 1707 et 1708* (Paris, 1714).

Frick, Carole Collier, *Dressing Renaissance Florence: Families, Fortunes and Fine Clothing* (Baltimore: Johns Hopkins University Press, 2004).

Gaastra, Femme, *The Dutch East India Company: Expansion and Decline* (Zutpen: Walburg Pers, 2003).

García Marsilla, Juan Vicente, 'Ordenando el lujo: Ideología y normativa suntuaria en las ciudades valencianas (siglos XIV y XV)', in Sophie Brouquet and Juan V. García Marsilla (eds.), *Mercados del lujo, mercados del arte: El gusto de las élites mediterráneas en los siglos XIV y XV* (València: Universitat de València, 2015), 561–591.

Garrigus, John, *Before Haiti: Race and Citizenship in French Saint-Domingue* (New York: Palgrave Macmillan, 2006).

Gingerich, Melvin, *Mennonite Attire through Four Centuries* (Breinigsville, PA: Pennsylvania German Society, 1970).

González Arce, José Damián, *Apariencia y poder. La legislación suntuaria castellana en los siglos XIII y XV* (Jaén: Universidad de Jaén, 1998).

Grieco, Allen J., 'From the Cookbook to the Table: A Florentine Table and Italian Recipes of the Fourteenth and Fifteenth Centuries', in Carole Lambert (ed.), *Du manuscrit à la table: Essais sur la cuisine au Moyen Âge et répertoire des manuscrits médiévaux contenant des recettes culinaires (Etudes Médiévales)* (Montréal: Presses de l'Université de Montréal, 1992), 29–38.

Gschwend, Annemarie Jordan and K. J. P. Lowe (eds.), *The Global City on the Streets of Renaissance Lisbon* (London: Paul Holberton, 2015).

Guarino, Gabriel, *Representing the King's Splendour: Communication and Reception of Symbolic Forms of Power in Viceregal Naples* (Manchester: Manchester University Press, 2010).

"Spanish Fashions and Sumptuary Legislation in Habsburg Italy", in Amalia Descalzo and José Luis Colomer (eds.), *Spanish Fashion at the Courts of Early Modern Europe* (Madrid: Centro de Estudios Europa Hispánica, 2014), 233–250.

Hampl-Kallbrunner, Gertraud, *Beiträge zur Geschichte der Kleiderordnungen mit besonderer Berücksichtigung Österreichs* (Wien: H. Geyer, 1962).

Harte, Negley B., 'State Control of Dress and Social Change in Pre-industrial England', in Donald C. Coleman and A. H. John (eds.), *Trade, Government and Economy in Pre-Industrial England: Essays Presented to F. J. Fisher* (London: Weidenfeld and Nicolson, 1976), 132–165.

Hayward, Maria, *Rich Apparel: Clothing and the Law in Henry VIII's England* (Aldershot: Ashgate, 2009).

Heller, Sarah-Grace, 'Anxiety, Hierarchy, and Appearance in Thirteenth-Century Sumptuary Laws and the Romance of the Rose', *French Historical Studies* 27/2 (2004): 311–348.

Hellie, Richard, *The Economy and Material Culture of Russia, 1600–1725* (Chicago: University of Chicago Press, 1999).

Hinderaker, Eric, *The Two Hendricks: Unraveling a Mohawk Mystery* (Cambridge, MA: Harvard University Press, 2010).

Hirano, Katsuya, *The Politics of Dialogic Imagination: Power and Popular Culture in Early Modern Japan* (Chicago: University of Chicago Press, 2013).

Hooper, Wilfred, 'The Tudor Sumptuary Law', *English Historical Review* 30/119 (1915): 433–449.

Howell, Martha C., *Commerce Before Capitalism in Europe, 1300–1600* (Cambridge: Cambridge University Press, 2010).

Hughes, Diane Owen, 'Regulating Women's Fashion', in Christiane Klapisch-Zuber (ed.), *A History of Women in the West. Vol. 2. Silences of the Middle Ages* (gen. ed. Georges Duby and Michelle Perrot) (Cambridge, MA, and London: The Belknap Press of Harvard University Press, 1992), 136–158.

Hughes, Lindsey, 'From Caftans into Corsets: The Sartorial Transformation of Women during the Reign of Peter the Great', in Peter I. Barta (ed.), *Gender and Sexuality in Russian Civilisation* (London: Routledge, 2001), 17–32.

Russia in the Age of Peter the Great (New Haven: Yale University Press, 1998).

Hunt, Alan, *Governance of the Consuming Passions: A History of Sumptuary Law* (Basingstoke: Macmillan, 1996).

Ikegami, Eiko, *Bonds of Civility: Aesthetic Networks and Political Origins of Japanese Culture* (Cambridge: Cambridge University Press, 2005).

Inshi, Buyō, Mark Teeuwen and Kate Wildman Nakai (eds. and trans.), *Lust, Commerce, and Corruption* (New York: Columbia University Press, 2014).

Irigoyen-García, Javier, *'Moors Dresses as Moors': Clothing, Social Distinction, and Ethnicity in Early Modern Iberia* (Toronto: University of Toronto Press, 2017).

J. C., 'The Sumptuary Laws of Scotland', *Journal of Jurisprudence* 35 (1891): 290–297.

Jaritz, Gerhard, 'Social Grouping and the Languages of Dress in the Late Middle Ages', *Medieval History Journal* 3/2 (2000): 235–259.

Jones, Adam (ed. and trans.), *German Sources for West African History 1599–1669* (Wiesbaden: Franz Steiner Verlag GMBH, 1983).

Jordan, Anne-Marie, 'Portuguese Royal Collections after 1521: The Choice between Flanders and Italy', in K. J. Lowe (ed.), *Cultural Links between Portugal and Italy in the Renaissance* (Oxford: Oxford University Press, 2000), 265–293.

'The Development of Catherine of Austria's Collection in the Queen's Household: Its Character and Cost' (Unpublished PhD thesis, Brown University, 1994).

Kapossy, Béla, 'Introduction. From Republicanism to Welfare Liberalism', *Schweizerische Zeitschrift für Geschichte* 50 (2000): 275–303.

Iselin contra Rousseau. Sociable Patriotism and the History of Mankind (Basel: Schwabe, 2006).

Karl, Barbara, *Embroidered Histories. Indian Textiles for the Portuguese Market during the Sixteenth and Seventeenth Centuries* (Vienna: Böhlau Verlag, 2016).

Karras, Ruth Mazo, *Common Women: Prostitution and Sexuality in Medieval England* (Oxford: Oxford University Press, 1996).

Kato, Takashi, 'Governing Edo', in James L. McClain, John M. Merriman and Ugawa Kaoru (eds.), *Edo and Paris: Urban Life and the State in the Early Modern Era* (Ithaca: Cornel University Press, 1994), 41–67.

Keenan, Paul, 'The Function of Fashion: Women and Clothing at the Russian Court (1700–1762)', in Wendy Rosslyn and Alessandra Tosi (eds.), *Women in Russian Culture and Society, 1700–1825* (London: Palgrave Macmillan, 2007), 125–143.

Kehoe, Marsely L., 'Dutch Batavia: Exposing the Hierarchy of the Dutch Colonial City', *Journal of Historians of Netherlandish Art* 7/1 (2015). doi: 10.5092/jhna.2015.7.1.3 Available at https://jhna.org/articles/dutch-batavia-exposing-hierarchy-dutch-colonial-city/.

Kirsanova, R. M., *Russkii kostium i byt XVIII-XIX vekov* (Moscow: Slovo, 2002).

Kirshner, Julius. 'Li emergenti bisogni matrimoniali in Renaissance Florence', in William J. Connell (ed.), *Society and Individual in Renaissance Florence* (Berkeley, Los Angeles, London: University of California Press, 2002), 79–109.

Konetzke, Richard (ed.), *Colección de documentos para la historia de la formación social de Hispanoamérica, 1493–1810*, 3 vols. (Madrid: Consejo Superior de Investigaciones Científicas, 1962).

König, Benno, *Luxusverbote im Fürstbistum Münster* (Frankfurt-am-Main: Klostermann, 1999)

Kovesi, Catherine. 'What is Luxury? The Rebirth of a Concept in the Early Modern World', *Luxury: History, Culture, Consumption* 2/1 (2015): 25–40.

Kovesi Killerby, Catherine, '"Heralds of a Well-Instructed Mind": Nicolosa Sanuti's Defence of Women and their Clothes', *Renaissance Studies* 13/3 (1999): 255–282.

  'Practical Problems in the Enforcement of Italian Sumptuary Law, 1200–1500', in Trevor Dean and Kate J. P. Lowe (eds.), *Crime, Society and the Law in Renaissance Italy* (New York: Cambridge University Press, 1994), 99–120.

  Sumptuary Legislation in Italy, 1200–1500 (Oxford: The Clarendon Press, 2001).

Kraak, Deborah, "Variations on Quaker Dress in Eighteenth-Century Philadelphia," *Costume* 34/1 (2000): 51–63.

Kraybill, Donald B., *The Riddle of Amish Culture*, rev. ed. (Baltimore: Johns Hopkins University Press, 2001).

Lara, Silvia Hunold, 'Customs and Costumes: Carlos Julião and the Image of Black Slaves in Late Eighteenth-Century Brazil', *Slavery and Abolition* 23/2 (2002): 125–146.

  'Sedas, panos e balangandãs: o traje de senhoras e escravas nas cidades do Rio de Janeiro e Salvador (século XVIII)', in Maria Beatriz Nizza da Silva (ed.), *Brazil: colonização e escravidão* (Rio de Janeiro: Nova Fronteira, 2000), 177–191.

'The Signs of Color: Women's Dress and Racial Relations in Salvador and Rio de Janeiro, ca. 1750–1815', *Colonial Latin American Review* 6/2 (1997): 205–224.

Levi-Pisetzky, Rosita, *Storia del costume in Italia. Vol. 3. Il Cinquecento. Il Seicento* (Milan: Istituto Editoriale Italiano. and Fondazione Giovanni Treccani degli Alfieri per la Storia di Milano, 1964–69).

Lewis, Laura, *Hall of Mirrors: Power, Witchcraft, and Caste in Colonial Mexico* (Durham: Duke University Press, 2003).

Li Dongyang (1447–1516) and Shen Shixing (1535–1614) et al., *Da Ming Hui Dian* [Collected Statues of the Ming Dynasty] (Taipei: Dongnan shubaoshe, 1963).

Li Zhitan, Chen Xiaosu and Kong Fanyun, 'Zhengui de Ming dai fushi ziliao: Ming gong guanfu yizhang tu zhengli yanjiu zhaji' [Notes of *Ming Gong Guan Fu Yi Zhang Tu:* Pictures of Court Costumes and Manners in the Ming Dynasty of China], *Yishu sheji yanjiu* 1 (2014): 23–28.

Liu Weiqian (1521–1565) et al., *Da Ming Lu* [Great Ming Code] (Yangzhou: Jiangsu Guangling guji keyin she, 1989).

Marques, A. H. de Oliveira, 'A pragmática de 1340', *Revista da Faculdade de Letras de Lisboa* XXII, 2nd series, 2 (1956): 130–154.

'Dress', in *Daily Life in Portugal in the Late Middle Ages*, trans. S. S. Wyatt with drawings by Victor André (Madison, WI: The University of Wisconsin Press, 1971), 39–96.

Marshall, Rosalind K., 'Conscience and Costume in Seventeenth-Century Scotland', *Costume* 6 (1972): 32–35.

Costume in Scottish Portraits, 1560–1830 (Edinburgh: Scottish National Portrait Gallery, 1986).

Martínez Bermejo, Saúl, 'Beyond Luxury: Sumptuary Legislation in 17th-Century Castile', in Günther Lottes, Eero Medijainen, and Jón Vidar Sigurdsson (eds.), *Making, Using and Resisting the Law in European History* (Pisa: PLUS-Pisa University Press, 2008), 93–108.

Medick, Hans, 'Une Culture de la considération. Les vêtements et leur couleur à Laichingen entre 1750 et 1820', *Annales. Histoire, Sciences Sociales* 50 (1995): 753–774.

Weben und Überleben in Laichingen 1650–1900. Lokalgeschichte als Allgemeine Geschichte (Göttingen: Vandenhoeck, 1996).

Ming shilu [Veritable Records of the Ming Dynasty], 133 vols. (Nan'gang: Zhongyang yanjiu yuan lishi yuyan yanjiu suo, 1962).

Moiseenko, E. Iu. (ed.), *Kostium v Rossii pervoi chetverti XVIII veka* (Leningrad: Ermitazh, 1984).

Molà, Luca, 'Leggi suntuarie in Veneto', in Maria Giuseppina Muzzarelli and Antonella Campanini (eds.), *Disciplinare il Lusso. La legislazione suntuaria in Italia e in Europa tra Medioevo ed età moderna* (Rome: Carocci, 2003), 47–57.

The Silk Industry of Renaissance Venice (Baltimore and London: Johns Hopkins University Press, 2000).

Molina, Álvaro and Jesusa Vega, *Vestir la identidad, construir la apariencia: La cuestión del traje en la España del siglo XVIII* (Madrid: Ayuntamiento de Madrid, Área de Gobierno de las Artes, 2004).

Molmenti, Pompeo, *La storia di Venezia nella vita privata dalle origini alla caduta della Repubblica*, 3 vols. (Trieste: Edizioni Lint, 1880).

Münkler, Herfried, 'Die Idee der Tugend. Ein politischer Leitbegriff im vorrevolutionären Europa', *Archiv für Kulturgeschichte* 73 (1991): 379–403.

Muzzarelli, Maria Giuseppina, '"Contra formam statutorum": regole, controlli e provvedimenti sanzionatori in materia suntuaria. Il caso di Bologna', in Didier Lett (ed.), *Statuts, écritures et pratiques sociales dans les sociétés de la Méditerranée occidentale à la fin du Moyen Âge (XIIe-XVe siècle). Les statuts vus de l'extérieur: les références à la norme dans les sources de la pratique* (Rome: École Française de Rome, forthcoming 2018).

'Il corpo spogliato. Multe, scomuniche e strategemmi per il rispetto delle leggi suntuarie', *Micrologus* 15 (2007): 399–423.

'Le leggi suntuarie', in Carlo Marco Belfanti and Fabio Giusberti (eds.), *Storia d'Italia. Annali 19: La moda* (Turin: Einaudi, 2003), 185–220.

'Reconciling the Privilege of a Few with the Common Good: Sumptuary Laws in Medieval and Early Modern Europe', *Journal of Medieval and Early Modern Studies* 39/3 (2009): 597–617.

'"Vesti bollate": The Italian Fashion Gazette of the Fourteenth and Fifteenth Centuries (Shapes, Colours, Decorations)', in Catherine Kovesi (ed.), *Luxury and the Ethics of Greed in Early Modern Italy* (Turnhout: Brepols, forthcoming 2018).

Muzzarelli, Maria Giuseppina (ed.), *La legislazione suntuaria. Secoli XIII-XVI. Emilia-Romagna; Umbria* (Rome: Ministero per i beni e le attività culturali. Direzione generale degli archivi, 2002).

(ed.), *Belle vesti, dure leggi: 'In hoc libro continentur et descripte sunt omnes eet singules vestes'* (Bologna: Costa editore, 2003).

Muzzarelli, Maria Giuseppina and Antonella Campanini (eds.), *Disciplinare il lusso: la legislazione suntuaria in Italia e in Europa tra Medioevo ed età moderna* (Rome: Carocci, 2003).

Nakano, Tatsuro, *Sui, Tsu, Iki* (Tokyo: Iyai shobo, 1985).

Nenadic, Stana, *Lairds and Luxury: The Highland Gentry in Eighteenth-Century Scotland* (Edinburgh: John Donald, 2007).

Newett, Mary Margaret, 'The Sumptuary Laws of Venice in the Fourteenth and Fifteenth Centuries', in T. F. Tout and James Tait (eds.), *Historical Essays by Members of the Owens College, Manchester* (London: Longmans Green, 1902), 245–277.

Newton, Stella Mary, *The Dress of the Venetians, 1495–1525* (Aldershot: Scolar Press, 1988).

Nico Ottaviani, Maria Grazia (ed.), *La legislazione suntuaria. Secoli XIII-XVI. Umbria* (Rome: Ministero per i beni e le attività culturali. Direzione generale degli archivi, 2005).

Nierstrasz, Chris, *In the Shadow of the Company: The Dutch East India Company and its Servants in the Period of its Decline (1740–1796)* (Leiden: Brill, 2012).

Ogilvie, Sheilagh, Küpker, Markus and Maegraith, Janine, "Die lokale Regulierung des Konsums im frühneuzeitlichen Württemberg", in Sigrid Hirbodian, Sheilagh Ogilvie and R. Joanna Regnath (eds.), *Revolution des Fleißes, Revolution des Konsums? Leben und Wirtschaften im ländlichen Württemberg von 1650–1800* (Ostfildern: Thorbecke, 2015), 55–74.

Ooms, Herman, 'Forms and Norms in Edo Arts and Society', in Robert T. Singer (ed.), *Edo: Art in Japan 1615–1868* (New Haven: Yale University Press, 1998), 23–46.

Orfali, Moisés, 'Del lujo y de las leyes suntuarias: Ordenanzas sobre la vestimenta femenina en su contexto social y halájico', in Yolanda Moreno Koch (ed.), *La mujer judía*, (Córdoba: Ediciones El Almendro, 2007), 161–179.

Pallach, Ulrich-Christian, *Materielle Kultur und Mentalitäten im 18. Jahrhundert* (München: Oldenbourg, 1987).

Plank, Geoffrey, 'The First Person in Antislavery Literature: John Woolman, his Clothes and his Journal', *Slavery & Abolition* 30/1 (2009): 67–91.

Prinz, Michael (ed.), *Der lange Weg in den Überfluss. Anfänge und Entwicklung der Konsumgesellschaft seit der Vormoderne* (Paderborn: Schöningh, 2003).

Quataert, Donald, 'Clothing Laws, State, and Society in the Ottoman Empire, 1720–1829', *International Journal of Middle East Studies* 29/3 (1997): 403–425.

Radeff, Anne, *Du café dans le chaudron. Economie globale d'Ancien Régime* (Lausanne: Société d'histoire de la Suisse romande, 1996).

Rainey, Ronald, 'Dressing Down the Dressed Up: Reproving Feminine Attire in Renaissance Florence', in John Monfasani and Ronald G. Musto (eds.), *Renaissance Society and Culture: Essays in Honor of Eugene F. Rice, Jr.* (New York: Italica Press, 1991), 217–237.

Rappaport, Joanne, *The Disappearing Mestizo. Configuring Difference in the Colonial New Kingdom of Granada* (Durham: Duke University Press, 2014).

Refik, Ahmet, *Hicrî On İkinci Asırda İstanbul Hayatı (1100–1200 [1688–1786])* (Istanbul, 1930).

Hicrî On Üçüncü Asırda İstanbul Hayatı (1200–1255 [1786–1840]) (Istanbul, 1932).

On Altıncı Asırda İstanbul Hayatı (1553–1591) (Istanbul, 1935).

Reinke-Williams, Tim, 'Women's Clothes and Female Honour in Early Modern London', *Continuity and Change* 26/1 (2011): 69–88.

Reith, Reinhold and Torsten Meyer (eds.), *Luxus und Konsum. Eine historische Annäherung* (Münster: Waxmann, 2003).

Riello, Giorgio, *Cotton: The Fabric that Made the Modern World* (Cambridge: Cambridge University Press, 2013).

Riisøy, Anne Irene, *Sexuality, Law and Legal Practice and the Reformation in Norway* (Leiden: Brill, 2009).

Robinson, David M. (ed.), *Culture, Courtiers, and Competition: The Ming Court (1368–1644)* (Cambridge, MA: Harvard University Press, 2008).

Roche, Daniel, *The Culture of Clothing: Dress and Fashion in the "Ancien Régime"* (Cambridge: Cambridge University Press, [or. French ed. 1991] 1994).

Rodrigues, Ana Maria, 'The Treasures and Foundations of Isabel, Elisenda and Leonor. The Art Patronage of Four Iberian Queens in the Fourteenth Century', in Therese Martin (ed.), *Reassessing the Role of Women as 'Makers' of Medieval Art and Architecture* (Leiden: Brill, 2012), 903–936.

Roese, Peter M. and Dmitri M. Bondarenko, *A Popular History of Benin: The Rise and Fall of a Mighty Forest Kingdom* (Frankfurt-am-Main: Peter Lang, 2003).

Ross, Robert, *Clothing. A Global History: Or, the Imperialists' New Clothes* (Cambridge: Polity, 2008).

'Sumptuary Laws in Europe, the Netherlands and the Dutch Colonies', in Nigel Worden (ed.), *Contingent Lives: Social Identity and Material Culture in the VOC World* (Rondebosch: University of Cape Town, 2007), 382–391.

Ruane, Christine, *The Empire's New Clothes: A History of the Russian Fashion Industry, 1700–1917* (New Haven: Yale University Press, 2009).

Rublack, Ulinka, *Dressing Up: Cultural Identity in Early Modern Germany* (Oxford: Oxford University Press, 2010).

Rublack, Ulinka and Hayward, Maria (eds.), *The First Book of Fashion: The Book of Clothes of Matthäus and Veit Konrad Schwarz* (London: Bloomsbury, 2015).

Runefelt, Leif, *Att hasta mot undergången: anspråk, flyktighet, förställning i debatten om konsumtion i Sverige 1730–1830* (Lund: Nordic Academic Press, 2015).

Ryder, A. F. C., *Benin and the Europeans 1485–1897* (Harlow: Longmans, Green & Co., 1969).

Saito, Ryūzō, *Kinsei Nihon Sesōshi* (Tokyo: Hakubunkan, 1928).

Sakaoğlu, Necdet, 'Osmanlı Giyim Kuşamı ve 'Elbise-i Osmaniyye', *Tarih ve Toplum* 8/47 (1987): 36–41.

Schäfer, Dagmar and Dieter Kuhn, *Weaving and Economic Pattern in Ming Times (1368–1644): The Production of Silk Weaves in the State-Owned Workshops* (Heidelberg: Ed. Forum, 2002).

Schäfer, Dagmar, 'Silken Strands: Making Technology Work in China', in Dagmar Schäfer (ed.) *Cultures of Knowledge: Technology in Chinese History* (Leiden: Brill, 2011), 45–73.

Sedov, V., 'Reforma sluzhilogo plat'ia pri Fedore Alekseeviche', in Iu. N. Bespiatykh (ed.), *Trudy Vserossooskoi nauchnoi konferentsii "Kogda Rossiia molodaia muzhala s genium Petra", posviashchennoi 300-letnemu iubileiu otechestvennogo flota* (Pereslavl-Zalesskii: Pereslavl Zalesskii istoriko-arkhitekturnyi i khudozhestvennyi muzei-zapovednik, 1992), 77–84.

Seigle, Cecilia Segawa, *Yoshiwara* (Honolulu: University of Hawai'i Press, 1993).

Sempere y Guariños, Juan, *Historia del luxo y de las leyes suntuarias de España* (Madrid, 1788; reprinted València: Institució Alfons el Magnànim, 2000).

Sevin, Nureddin, *On Üç Asırlık Türk Kıyafet Tarihine bir Bakış* (Istanbul, 1973).

Shannon, Timothy J., 'Dressing for Success on the Mohawk Frontier: Hendrick, William Johnson, and the Indian Fashion', *William and Mary Quarterly*, 3rd ser. 53/1 (1996): 13–42.

Shaw, F. J., 'Sumptuary Legislation in Scotland', *The Juridical Review* 24 (1979): 81–115.

Shen Defu, *Wanli yehuo bian* [Unofficial Gleanings of the Wanli Era] (Beijing: Zhonghua shuju, 1980).

Shi, David E., 'Early American Simplicity: The Quaker Ethic', in Daniel Doherty and Amitai Etzioni (eds.), *Voluntary Simplicity: Responding to Consumer Culture* (Lanham, MD: Rowman & Littlefield, 2003), 101–124.

Shively, Donald H., 'Sumptuary Regulation and Status in Early Tokugawa', *Harvard Journal of Asiatic Studies* 25 (1964–65): 132–164.

Shūzō, Kuki, *The Structure of Detachment*, trans. Hiroshi Nara (Honolulu: University of Hawai'i Press, 2004).

Silva, Maria Beatriz Nizza da, 'Trajo', in *Vida privada e quotidiano no Brasil na época de D. Maria I e D. João VI*, 2nd ed. (Lisbon: Estampa, 2004).

Silva, Nuno Vassalo and Helmut Trnek (eds.), *Exotica. Os descobrimentos portugueses e as câmaras de maravilhas do Renascimento* (Lisbon: Museu Calouste Gulbenkian, 2001).

Smith, Woodruff D., *Consumption and the Making of Respectability, 1600–1800* (London: Routledge, 2002).

Stevens, Carol B., 'A Woman in Possession: Household Goods and Social Status of a Single Woman in Early St. Petersburg', *Russian History* 42 (2015): 136–148.

Sturtewagen, Isis, 'All Together Respectably Dressed' (unpublished PhD thesis, University of Antwerp, 2016). Available at https://repository.uantwerpen.be/docman/irua/2cb264/11226.pdf

Taylor, Jean Gelman, 'Meditations on a Portrait from Seventeenth-Century Batavia', *Journal of Southeast Asian Studies* 37/1 (2006): 23–41.

The Social World of Batavia: Europeans and Eurasians in Colonial Indonesia. 2nd ed. (Madison: University of Wisconsin Press, 2009).

Tröhler, Daniel, 'Kommerz und Patriotismus. Pestalozzis Weg vom politischen zum christlichen Republikanismus (1764–1780)', *Schweizerische Zeitschrift für Geschichte* 50 (2000): 325–352.

Twinam, Ann, *Purchasing Whiteness: Pardos, Mulattos, and the Quest for Social Mobility in the Spanish Indies* (Stanford: Stanford University Press, 2015).

Umur, Suha, 'Kadınlara Buyruklar', *Tarih ve Toplum* 10/58 (1988): 13–15.

Uramoto, Yoshifumi, *Edo, Tokyo no Hisabetsuburaku no rekishi: Danzaemon to hisabetsu Minshū* (Tokyo: Akashi Shoten, 2003).

Van Uytven, Raymond, 'Showing off One's Rank in the Middle Ages', in Wim Blockmans and Antheun Janse (eds.), *Showing Status, Representation of Social Positions in the Late Middle Ages* (Turnhout: Brepols, 1999), 19–34.

Veblen, Thorstein, *The Theory of the Leisure Class* (New York: Macmillan, 1899).

Verga, Ettore, 'Le leggi suntuarie e la decadenza dell'industria in Milano, 1565–1750', *Archivio Storico Lombardo* 27 (1900): 49–116.

'Le leggi suntuarie milanesi: gli statuti del 1396 e del 1498', *Archivio Storico Lombardo* 25 (1898): 5–79.

Vincent, John Martin, *Costume and Conduct in the Laws of Basel, Bern, and Zurich, 1370–1800* (Baltimore: Johns Hopkins Press, 1935).

Vincent, Susan, *Dressing the Elite. Clothes in Early Modern England* (Oxford: Berg, 2003).

Volpp, Sophie, 'The Gift of a Python Robe: The Circulation of Objects in "Jin Ping Mei"', *Harvard Journal of Asiatic Studies* 65/1 (2005): 133–158.

Vries, Jan de, 'Luxury in the Dutch Golden Age in Theory and Practice', in Maxine Berg and Elizabeth Eger (eds.), *Luxury in the Eighteenth Century. Debates, Desires and Delectable Goods* (Basingstoke: Palgrave, 2003), 41–56.

Wakita, Osamu, *Kinsei Osaka no Machi to Hito* (Tokyo: Yoshikawa Kōbunkan, 2015).

Walker, Corinne, 'Images du luxe à Genève. Douze années de répression par la Chambre de la Réformation (1646–1658)', *Revue du Vieux Genève* 17 (1987): 21–26.

'Les lois somptuaires ou le rêve d'un ordre social. Evolution et enjeux de la politique somptuaire à Genève (XVIe-XVIIIe siècles)', *Equinoxe* 11 (1994): 111–129.

Walker, Tamara, *Exquisite Slaves: Race, Clothing and Status in Colonial Lima* (Cambridge: Cambridge University Press, 2017).

Weber, Matthias, *Die Reichspolizeiordnungen von 1530, 1548 und 1577. Historische Einführung und Edition* (Frankfurt-am-Main: Klostermann, 2002).

Welch, Evelyn (ed.), *Fashioning the Early Modern: Dress, Textiles and Innovation in Europe, 1500–1800* (Oxford: Oxford University Press, 2017).

Wu Jen-shu, 'Mingdai pingmin fushi de liuxing fengshang yu shidafu fanying' [Popular styles of clothing among the common people of the Ming, and the reaction of the gentry], *Xinshixue* 10/3 (1999): 55–109.

Wunder, Amanda, 'Women's Fashions and Politics in Seventeenth-Century Spain: The Rise and Fall of the *Guardainfante*', *Renaissance Quarterly* 68/1 (2015): 133–186.

'Innovation and Tradition at the Court of Philip IV of Spain (1621–1665): The Invention of the *Golilla* and the *Guardainfante*', in Evelyn Welch (ed.), *Fashioning the Early Modern: Dress, Textiles, and Innovation in Europe, 1500–1800* (Oxford: Oxford University Press, 2017), 111–133.

Yuan Zujie, 'Dressing for Power: Rite, Costume, and State Authority in Ming Dynasty China', *Frontiers of History in China* 2/2 (2007): 181–212.

Zakim, Michael, *Ready-made Democracy: A History of Men's Dress in the American Republic, 1760–1860* (Chicago: University of Chicago Press, 2003).

Zander-Seidel, Jutta, *Textiler Hausrat: Kleidung und Haustextilien in Nürnberg von 1500–1650* (Munich: Deutscher Kunstverlag, 1990).

Zander-Seidel, Jutta (ed.), *In Mode: Kleider und Bilder aus Renaissance und Frühbarock* (Nürnberg: Germanisches Nationalmuseum, 2015).

Zandvliet, Kees (ed.), *The Dutch Encounter with Asia, 1600–1950* (Zwolle: Waanders, 2002).

Zhang Jia, 'Cong zheng guanshang: Hongwu shiqi de fushi gaige' [Restoring Chinese Costume: The Reform of the Clothing System during the Reign of Hongwu], *Journal of Chinese Studies* 58 (2014): 113–158.

Zhang Tingyu et al., *Ming shi* [Official History of the Ming] (Beijing: Zhonghua shuju, 1995).

Zilfi, Madeline C., 'Whose Laws? Gendering the Ottoman Sumptuary Regime', in Suraiya N. Faroqhi and Christoph K. Neumann (eds.), *Ottoman Costumes: From Textiles to Identity* (Istanbul: EREN, 2014), 125–141.

Women and Slavery in the Late Ottoman Empire: The Design of Difference (Cambridge: Cambridge University Press, 2010).

Zurbuchen, Simone, 'Patriotismus und Nation: Der schweizerische Republikanismus des 18. Jahrhunderts', in Michael Böhler and Etienne Hoffman (eds.), *Republikanische Tugend. Ausbildung eines Schweizer Nationalbewusstseins und Erziehung eines neuen Bürgers*, (Geneva: Slatkine, 2000), 151–181.

Index

Lightning Source UK Ltd.
Milton Keynes UK
UKHW030719060722
405454UK00009B/603